Wetlands Regulation

A Complete Guide to Federal and California Programs

Paul D. Cylinder, Kenneth M. Bogdan,
Ellyn Miller Davis, and Albert I. Herson

Solano Press Books
Point Arena, California

Wetlands Regulation

A Complete Guide to Federal and California Programs

Copyright © 1995 by Paul D. Cylinder,
Kenneth M. Bogdan, Ellyn Miller Davis,
and Albert I. Herson.

Second printing, 1995

Solano Press Books
Post Office Box 773
Point Arena, California 95468
Phone (707) 884-4508
Fax (707) 884-4109

Cover design by Judy Hicks, Berkeley, California
Cover photograph by Louisa Squires
Book design by Canterbury Press, Berkeley, California
Index by Paul Kish, Mendocino, California
Printed by Braun-Brumfield, Inc., Ann Arbor, Michigan

ISBN 0-923956-20-4

Trees are one of nature's renewable resources.
To preserve this invaluable resource for future
generations, Solano Press Books makes annual
contributions to the *American Forests Global
ReLeaf Program. American Forests* is the nation's
oldest nonprofit citizens' conservation organization.

✪ Printed on partially recycled paper

NOTICE

This book is designed to assist you in understanding
wetland regulations. It is necessarily general in nature
and does not discuss all exceptions and variations to
general rules. Also, it may not reflect the latest changes
in the law. It is not intended as legal advice and should
not be relied on to address legal problems. You should
always consult an attorney for advice regarding your
specific factual situation.

Preface

California's rapid growth and development pressures have collided with efforts to protect its wetlands. Those wishing to protect or develop these valuable and dwindling resources can become lost in the maze of federal, state, and local laws and regulations. The authors have attempted to unravel the intricacies of the regulatory programs that control activities in wetlands and have provided advice, drawn from extensive experience, on how to most effectively and efficiently navigate the regulatory process. The authors have written this book for–

- ▶ Land use planners
- ▶ Project managers with agencies that prepare environmental compliance documents
- ▶ Developers
- ▶ Landowners
- ▶ Regulatory agency personnel
- ▶ Elected officials
- ▶ Environmental consultants
- ▶ Members of environmental organizations
- ▶ Lawyers
- ▶ Water suppliers
- ▶ Growers and others involved in agriculture
- ▶ Mine operators
- ▶ Foresters
- ▶ Ranchers
- ▶ Environmentally concerned citizens

The authors believe that readers will find this book and its extensive appendices to be a valuable and trusted reference on wetland regulation and the environmental permitting process. Both federal and state regulatory schemes are presented, with examples from California to highlight key issues. Thorough treatments are provided of wetland regulation under Section 404 of the Clean Water Act, Section 10 of the Rivers and Harbors Act, Sections 1600-1607 of the California Fish and Game Code, and the California Coastal Act, along with introductions to other federal and California laws related to wetland regulation. Readers will find information and advice on–

- ▶ Wetland ecology
- ▶ Wetlands identification
- ▶ Federal, state, and regional wetland regulatory programs
- ▶ Best approaches to the permit process and permitting agencies
- ▶ Mitigation planning and implementation
- ▶ Watershed planning
- ▶ Mitigation banking

The authors hope that the advice they provide in this practical guide will be applied to projects and programs involving wetlands in California and elsewhere.

About the Authors

All of the authors are employed at Jones & Stokes Associates, an environmental planning and natural resource science firm with offices in Sacramento, California; Bellevue, Washington; and Phoenix, Arizona.

Paul D. Cylinder is a trained botanist and plant ecologist with experience in wetland delineation, biological resources impact assessment, mitigation planning, rare plant surveying, habitat management planning, and ecological research. He has conducted wetland delineations, vegetation surveys, and rare plant surveys throughout California and prepared reports pursuant to Section 404 of the Clean Water Act, National Environmental Policy Act, California Environmental Quality Act, California Fish and Game Code Sections 1600-1607, California Coastal Act, federal and California Endangered Species Acts, and local regulations. Dr. Cylinder teaches courses on wetland regulation and endangered species issues through the University of California, Davis, Extension and other educational forums.

Before joining Jones & Stokes Associates, Dr. Cylinder was a lecturer in plant ecology at the University of California, Berkeley. He is currently chairman of the Wetlands Conservation Committee of the California Native Plant Society. Dr. Cylinder received a Ph.D. in botany from the University of California, Berkeley, in 1987 and a B.A. in biological sciences from the University of Chicago in 1980.

Kenneth M. Bogdan is an environmental planner and attorney with more than five years of experience managing projects for Jones & Stokes Associates. He specializes in analyzing issues regarding compliance with environmental laws and regulations, including Section 404 of the Clean Water Act, the state and federal

Endangered Species Acts, CEQA, and NEPA. He is a speaker at workshops on wetland issues, endangered species issues, CEQA, and NEPA.

Mr. Bogdan formerly worked for the U.S. Department of Interior Solicitor's Office. He is a member of the California State Bar and is currently legal advisor to the 10,000-member California Native Plant Society. He received a J.D., with an emphasis in environmental and land use issues, from the University of California, Davis, School of Law in 1989 and a B.S. in environmental management from Rutgers University in 1986.

Ellyn Miller Davis is a restoration ecologist with Jones & Stokes Associates in Sacramento, California. She is experienced in preparing mitigation and monitoring plans for wetland and riparian habitats and sensitive plant populations. She has extensive experience with wetland regulatory issues involving Sections 404 and 401 of the Clean Water Act and Sections 1600-1607 of California Fish and Game Code and has prepared mitigation plans in compliance with Section 7 of the federal Endangered Species Act. Ms. Davis has lectured on wetland regulatory policy issues for University of California Extension and has conducted and managed field assessments of general biological, botanical, and wetland resources. She has completed wetland and rare plant surveys throughout California and prepared biological assessments for environmental documentation required under CEQA and NEPA. Ms. Davis has provided agency liaison between clients and regulatory agencies and has assisted numerous clients with the preparation of permit applications and habitat mitigation plans for submittal to the U.S. Army Corps of Engineers and the California Department of Fish and Game.

Ms. Davis received an M.E.M. in resource ecology from Duke University in 1986 and a B.S. in botany from the University of California, Davis, in 1984.

Albert I. Herson, AICP, is an environmental planner and attorney with 17 years of experience in environmental planning and law. Mr. Herson, senior vice president at Jones & Stokes Associates, has served as principal-in-charge or project manager for more than 100 environmental impact and planning studies. Mr. Herson specializes in assisting clients with complying with wetland and endangered species regulations, NEPA, and CEQA.

Mr. Herson regularly teaches courses on wetland regulation, CEQA, and NEPA for University of California Extension and other educational forums. He is author of "Wetlands Regulation,"

Chapter 69 in Matthew Bender and Company's treatise on California Environmental Law and Land Use Practice. He is also coauthor of Solano Press books on CEQA and NEPA compliance.

Mr. Herson formerly served as an environmental attorney in private practice and as a regional planner for the Southern California Association of Governments. He has published extensively on CEQA and NEPA compliance, lectured extensively on environmental law topics, and served as an expert witness on CEQA matters. Past president of the 5,000-member California chapter of the American Planning Association and on the editorial board of the *California Environmental Law Reporter,* Mr. Herson is also a member of the Executive Committee of the State Bar of California's Environmental Law section. He received a J.D. from the McGeorge School of Law, Sacramento, California, in 1984 and an M.A. in urban planning from the University of California, Los Angeles, in 1976.

Acknowledgments

The authors would like to thank several individuals without whom this book could not have been produced in the clear, useful style that was achieved. Victoria Axiaq and Cynthia Casanova provided proofreading, editing, and rewriting to improve the style and clarity of all chapters. Faye Ong also provided editing assistance. Fern Weston, through both word processing skill and patience, produced the drafts of the book under a tight schedule, meeting the demands of authors and publisher. The contributions of Christy Anderson, who coordinated graphics production, bring the pages of this document to life by displaying complex ideas in understandable figures and charts. Sheri Brown produced original line drawings for several figures. We greatly appreciate the diligence of Erik Spiess, our legal research assistant, in assembling the appendices that provide wetland laws and regulations in their original text. We thank Timothy Messick for writing several stories explaining some of his experiences with wetland regulations.

The authors would also like to thank the following reviewers of an earlier draft of the book for their thoughtful comments: James Monroe, U.S. Army Corps of Engineers; Paul Jones, U.S. Environmental Protection Agency; Matt Mitchell of the state of California Resources Agency; and Madeline Glickfeld, a regulatory specialist.

Chapters at a Glance

Contents

Chapter 7 Epilogue   139

List of Tables

List of Figures

Vernal pools in southern Sacramento County. Pools in the foreground are disturbed by construction vehicles.

1

Introduction

Wetlands are highly productive, complex ecosystems. Once considered of little or no use, wetlands have now taken center stage in the political arena as their many values and rapid rate of loss have been recognized. Wetlands protection is a challenge nationally and especially in California, which has lost a greater proportion of its original wetlands than has any other state (Dahl 1990). The continued decline of wetlands throughout the country has encouraged federal, state, and local governments to regulate the activities that threaten these soggy habitats.

This book provides a practical guide to wetland regulation in California. It is intended to be used as a desktop reference manual for anyone seeking to understand wetland regulation. Extensive appendices contain the text of federal and state laws, key regulations, and regulatory guidance.

What Are Wetlands?

Wetlands are areas of land which, either permanently or seasonally, are wet and support specially adapted vegetation. To regulate activities in wetlands, federal and state agencies have developed specific definitions and methods for identifying wetland boundaries. Identification methods, which vary among the agencies, focus on hydrologic, soil, and vegetative parameters, and for sites to be identified as wetlands they must have specific indicators of wetland conditions for each of these three parameters. Changes in identification methods have been controversial because they have resulted in increases and decreases in the size of areas

Wetlands are areas of land which, either permanently or seasonally, are wet and support specially adapted vegetation.

1

considered subject to jurisdiction. An explanation of the basic ecological concepts underlying what constitutes a wetland is provided in chapter 2. Not all wetlands are easily recognizable, especially those that are bone-dry during California's long summer droughts. The authors also explain in chapter 2 what has happened to California's wetlands in the past 150 years.

The methods by which federal and California agencies identify wetlands for regulatory purposes are presented in chapter 3. Other water bodies and water-associated habitats, extending beyond wetlands and also regulated by various agencies, are described. The authors present recommendations on how to most efficiently conduct wetland identification and mapping efforts to satisfy several regulatory agencies simultaneously.

What Is the Value of Wetlands?

Many of the functions that wetlands perform are valuable to people.

Wetlands affect our lives and livelihoods in many ways, some obvious and some not so obvious. Many of the functions that wetlands perform are valuable to people. For example, wetlands can provide flood protection, taking the peak off floods by slowing flows and storing water. Wetlands are often the site of recharge for ground water that serves as the source of public water supplies. Toxics and pollutants are transformed or removed by wetlands as water passes through them, and water quality is improved. Wetlands can protect stream banks and shorelines from erosion. Wetlands are valuable for food production because they provide food, spawning, and nursery areas for many commercial fish and shellfish.

Recreation, open space, and aesthetic values are provided by wetlands. Boating, swimming, fishing, hunting, hiking, photography, bird and other wildlife observation, and scientific study are all activities that take place in or are dependent on wetlands and from which people benefit.

How Are Wetlands Regulated?

Corps = U.S. Army Corps of Engineers

DFG = Department of Fish and Game

CCC = California Coastal Commission

SWRCB = State Water Resources Control Board

In California, the regulation of wetlands is complex and often confusing. The U.S. Army Corps of Engineers (Corps), through the authority of Section 404 of the Clean Water Act, is the major agency involved in wetland regulation. State and local agencies also regulate activities in wetlands. California Department of Fish and Game (DFG), California Coastal Commission (CCC), State Lands Commission, California State Water Resources Control Board (SWRCB), and many regional and local agencies are also involved in wetland regulation. In some cases, state or local agencies may

Table 1-1. Agencies That Regulate Activities in Wetlands

Agency	Regulation	Authority
U.S. Army Corps of Engineers	Clean Water Act, Section 404	Regulates placement of dredged or fill material into waters of the United States
	Rivers and Harbors Act of 1899 Section 10	Regulate work in navigable waters of the United States
U.S. Environmental Protection Agency	Clean Water Act	Enforcement of regulations, may veto Corps permit
	CEQA, NEPA	Commenting authority
U.S. Fish and Wildlife Service	Fish and Wildlife Coordination Act	Reviews/comments on federal actions that affect wetlands and other waters, including 404 permit applications
	Endangered Species Act	Corps must consult with USFWS if endangered species on site
	CEQA, NEPA	Commenting authority
National Marine Fisheries Service	Fish and Wildlife Coordination Act	Reviews/comments on federal actions that affect coastal waters, including Section 404 permit applications
	Endangered Species Act	Corps must consult with NMFS if endangered marine species on site
	CEQA, NEPA	Commenting authority
California Department of Fish and Game	California Fish and Game Code Sections 1600-1607	Regulates activities resulting in alternation of streams and lakes
	CEQA, NEPA	Commenting authority
Regional Water Quality Control Boards	Clean Water Act, Section 401	Issues water quality certification; certification required for Section 404 permits
	Clean Water Act, Section 402	Regulates discharge of waste into waters of the United States
	CEQA, NEPA	Commenting authority
California Coastal Commission	Coastal Act of 1976	Issues all coastal development permits
	Coastal Zone Management Act of 1972	Issues notice that work is consistent with state coastal management plan
	CEQA, NEPA	Commenting authority
San Francisco Bay Conservation and Development Commission	McAteer-Petris Act of 1965	Regulates work within the bay, certain creeks and a shoreline band 100 feet inland from line of highest tidal action
State Lands Commission	Public Trust Doctrine	May preclude the use of submerged lands and tidelands if this use is inconsistent with public trust

Great egrets feeding in seasonal freshwater marsh, Sacramento County.

regulate wetlands where the federal government does not exert jurisdiction. In some parts of the state, such as the coastal zone, wetlands are regulated more strictly. State and federal permitting processes can be long and difficult for the regulated, the regulator, and the environmentally concerned public.

The regulation of wetlands by the federal government is detailed in chapter 4 with a focus on Section 404 of the Clean Water Act and the permit process. Important cases highlighting judicial interpretations of Section 404 clarify when the federal government can regulate privately owned wetlands.

The numerous California laws that regulate activities in wetlands and the agencies that enforce these laws are presented in chapter 5. The combination of state and federal regulation often results in a complex web of interacting laws and exertion of jurisdiction by numerous regulatory agencies over the same wetland sites. The authors have worked with federal and California wetland laws in a wide range of activities, including–

- ▶ Field identification
- ▶ Permitting
- ▶ Mitigation planning and implementation
- ▶ Local and regional conservation planning

They have worked on projects affecting wetlands throughout California with regulated landowners and permit applicants, both public and private; with the regulating agencies; and with conservation organizations whose mission is to protect and restore wetlands. From this experience, the authors offer observations and recommendations for all sides of the wetland regulatory and conservation issues. At the end of chapter 5, the authors propose an integrated approach to wetland permitting for effectively navigating through the regulatory process.

Can Wetland Losses Be Mitigated?

The mitigation of impacts on wetlands can be a complicated affair that requires good scientific information, careful planning, close coordination among all concerned, and effective mitigation design and implementation. Traditional methods of creating, restoring, or enhancing wetlands on project sites can be successful if mitigation is properly planned and implemented. Chapter 6 describes the wetland mitigation process, addresses key issues, and provides important recommendations. A framework for effective and efficient mitigation planning and implementation is also provided.

What Is the Future of Wetland Regulation?

The future of wetland regulation will likely involve breaking away from project-specific wetland planning and impact mitigation. Advanced planning on a regional or watershed basis is one concept that is gaining favor. Advanced identification of resources and designation of important wetland conservation areas allows a context for assessing the relative impacts of individual projects within the planning area. Advanced planning can be used by project proponents to locate their projects more effectively and by regulatory agencies to streamline the permitting process.

Mitigation banking, the use of predesignated sites where active establishment of wetland habitat is conducted as mitigation for wetland impacts elsewhere, is a new tool that can be used in the mitigation of wetland impacts. Mitigation banks can be incorporated into regional wetland conservation plans. Federal and state policies behind advanced wetland and watershed planning and the concepts, policies, and benefits of mitigation banking are described in chapter 6.

Present and future policy challenges surrounding wetland regulation and conservation planning that face federal, state, and local agencies, landowners, project proponents, and environmentally concerned citizens are summarized in chapter 7.

Vernal pools in early spring, Monterey County.

2

Wetland Ecology

Wetlands are characterized by unique physical, chemical, and biological features, including distinctive hydrology, soils, and vegetation. Once abundant, wetland habitat in California has shrunk to a fraction of its historical extent. This chapter explains the unique features of wetlands and describes the various types of wetland habitats, wetland extent, and rate of loss in California. This chapter also presents some examples of human activities that can greatly change or destroy wetlands.

Wetland Hydrology and Soils

Wetland ecosystems often develop in a transitional zone between upland and deep water habitats (*see* Figure 2-1). Sites that support wetlands are frequently flooded or ponded or have permanently or seasonally saturated soils. Unlike the well drained soils of upland habitats, which may become saturated for short intervals, wetland soils are poorly drained and remain waterlogged for long periods. Water levels in wetlands, characterized by daily, seasonal, or yearly fluctuations, are generally more shallow than in deep water habitats such as ponds, lakes, and bays.

Knowing how these wet conditions develop is key to understanding wetlands. The water in wetlands derives from direct precipitation, overland flow, rising groundwater, or some combination of these processes. Ponding of water in wetlands may result from direct precipitation or from groundwater rising above the surface, while flooding may be due to headwater or backwater flooding of rivers and streams or tidal action. Soil saturation may

Unlike the well drained soils of upland habitats, which may become saturated for short intervals, wetland soils are poorly drained and remain waterlogged for long periods.

The water in wetlands derives from direct precipitation, overland flow, rising groundwater, or some combination of these processes.

Figure 2-1. Wetlands Cross-Section. Wetlands are transitional habitats between uplands and deep water habitats.

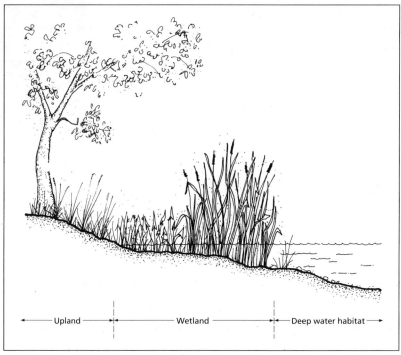

Water is lost from wetlands through evaporation, surface or subsurface flow, percolation into the groundwater, or tidal action.

result from a high water table or from the aftermath of ponding and flooding. Water is lost from wetlands through evaporation, surface or subsurface flow, percolation into the groundwater, or tidal action. All these processes by which water reaches and leaves a site are known as wetland 'hydrology'.

Soils that are saturated for long periods undergo chemical and physical changes which set them apart from the well drained uplands soils. The most immediate effect of soil saturation is a rapid loss of oxygen. The solid materials making up soils typically have many pores which are filled with air. Oxygen diffuses through these pores rapidly, keeping the soil well oxygenated, and plant roots and soil microorganisms consume this oxygen.

When soils become saturated, the pores fill with water. Plant roots and soil microorganisms rapidly consume the available oxygen, and, because oxygen moves through water very slowly, the soil is soon depleted. This oxygenless state is referred to as an 'anaerobic' condition. Anaerobic conditions prevail in wetland soils, and soils with water-induced anaerobic conditions are referred to as 'hydric' soils.

In hydric soils, the anaerobic conditions significantly reduce microbial activity and thus reduce the decomposition of dead plant material. Many wetland soils, such as peats and mucks, have a very high organic material content as a result of the dead plant material that has accumulated over centuries or millennia. In the absence of oxygen, other soil changes take place. Nutrients important to plants and microorganisms, such as nitrogen, iron, manganese, and sulfur, are converted to unusable forms. The altered metals and chemicals become more mobile and leach from the soil, sometimes reaching toxic levels (Mitsch and Gosselink 1993). These chemical changes also result in physical changes, most noticeably in soil color. Wetland soils composed of minerals are typically dark gray or black in contrast to the bright red, brown, and yellow mineral soils of upland habitats. The dark-colored soil of some wetlands (especially seasonal wetlands) are mottled in the upper part with patches of bright-colored material where iron and manganese ions become concentrated and oxidized (Vepraskas 1992).

Wetland Plants

Plants that grow in wetlands have adapted to the anaerobic soil conditions of saturated soils. To survive, these plants have evolved ways to supply their roots with oxygen. Many wetland plants, for example, have a shallow root system. In waterlogged soils, more oxygen is present near the soil surface where it can enter the soil from the atmosphere. A plant with a shallow root system can take advantage of this thin surface layer of oxygenated soil (*see* Figure 2-2). Other wetland plants have hollow stems through which oxygen can be transported from the shoots to the roots. Wetland plants also have developed unique physiological mechanisms to cope with anaerobic soil conditions, such as temporarily shutting down their metabolism, developing alternative chemical pathways, and storing chemical intermediates for later use (Mitsch and Gosselink 1993).

Plants that have adapted to wetland conditions are known as 'hydrophytes', or water plants. Some hydrophytes, called 'obligates', specifically require wetland conditions for survival and reproduction. Examples of wetland obligates include cattail, tule, water plantain, pondweed, and arrowhead. Other hydrophytes are tolerant of wetland conditions but can also survive in nonwetland upland habitats. Because they can live under a variety of conditions, these plants are known as 'facultative' species. Examples of facultative plants common to California include valley oak, Italian ryegrass, prickly

Figure 2-2. Wetland Plant Adaptations. A shallow root system is a common adaptation seen in wetland plants. The shallow roots take advantage of the thin oxygenated surface layer of soil.

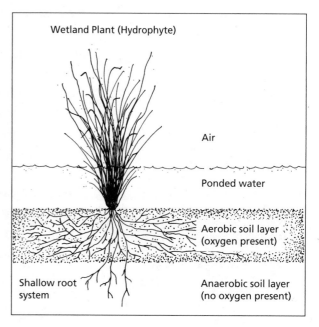

Wetland Plant (Hydrophyte)

Air

Ponded water

Aerobic soil layer (oxygen present)

Anaerobic soil layer (no oxygen present)

Shallow root system

Table 2-1. Wetland Plant Indicator Categories*

Classification	Symbol	Definition
Obligate wetland	OBL	Occur almost always (estimated probability >99%) under natural conditions in wetlands
Facultative wetland	FACW	Usually occur in wetlands (estimated probability 67-99%), but occasionally found in nonwetlands
Facultative	FAC	Equally likely to occur in wetlands or nonwetlands (estimated probability 34-66%)
Facultative upland	FACU	Usually found in nonwetlands (estimated probability 67-99%), but occasionally found in wetlands (estimated probability 1-33%)
Upland	UPL	Occur almost always (estimated probability >99%) under natural conditions in nonwetlands

* From Reed 1988.

lettuce, creeping wildrye, and Mediterranean barley. Examples of plants characteristic of California's upland habitats are coast live oak, wild oats, manzanita, creosote bush, and ponderosa pine. Upland plants will not survive in soils that are frequently saturated or inundated for a long period.

The U.S. Fish and Wildlife Service has developed a classification system for hydrophytic plants (Reed 1988) (*see* Table 2-1). Under this system, plant species are separated into 'indicator categories' based on the probability that individuals of the species will be found in wetland rather than upland habitat.

The Variety of California Wetlands

California supports a wide variety of wetland habitats, which are usually defined by the types of plants and animals they support. These vary, depending on the hydrologic regime, substrate, water source, and water quality of the site.

Water may reach a wetland from many sources—including direct rainfall, surface runoff, rising groundwater, percolation,

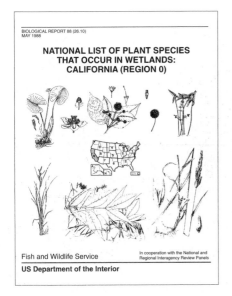

BIOLOGICAL REPORT 88 (26.10)
MAY 1988

NATIONAL LIST OF PLANT SPECIES THAT OCCUR IN WETLANDS: CALIFORNIA (REGION 0)

Fish and Wildlife Service

In cooperation with the National and Regional Interagency Review Panels

US Department of the Interior

tidal flooding, overbank flooding, and backwater flooding. The water may be fresh, brackish, salty, or hypersaline. It may also be high or low in nutrients and acidic, neutral, or alkaline.

The hydrologic regime, or pattern of occurrence of water in the wetland, may vary in its frequency, duration, depth, scouring action, and seasonal timing. For example, tidal marshes are inundated twice daily, but desert playa wetlands may only pond during years of high rainfall. The freshwater marshes of the Sacramento-San Joaquin Delta are flooded or saturated year round, while vernal pools in the surrounding Central Valley may only hold water for several weeks. Wet alpine meadows obtain just enough water to saturate the soil, while tule marshes may be inundated to depths of six feet.

The substrates on which a wetland develops include cobbles, gravels, sand, fine silts, dense clays, organic material, and combinations of these. Substrates may vary in thickness from several inches to tens of feet, and can vary greatly in nutrient content, acidity, and chemical composition.

Water source, water quality, hydrologic regime, and substrate properties are not independent factors, but rather each factor usually affects all the others. Different combinations result in different types of wetlands. For example, riparian forests grow along river banks and are dominated by trees, such as willows and cottonwoods. Usually their source of water is from overbank or backwater flooding, and the water is fresh with neutral acidity. Seasonal flooding takes place in late winter and early spring and can last for a few weeks to a month or more (*see* Figure 2-3). The site may flood annually or less frequently, perhaps 50 of every 100 years. Strong scouring can occur, and the summertime water table generally lies within 20 feet of the surface. Typically the substrate is deep sand or gravel, highly enriched with nutrients carried in with the flood water.

Tidal salt marsh, dominated by low, perennial plants such as salt grass, pickleweed, and cord grass, is another example of a wetland habitat. Tidal flooding from the ocean is its primary source of water, which is saltiest during the summer, with neutral to basic acidity. Twice daily flooding, varying in duration from one to several hours depending on elevation, characterizes the hydrologic regime (*see* Figure 2-3). Monthly variations in the level of highest and lowest tides correlate with the phases of the moon. The soil, with its typical substrate of fine silts or clay, is saturated at all times, and tidal scouring can be strong.

The hydrologic regime, or pattern of occurrence of water in the wetland, may vary in its frequency, duration, depth, scouring action, and seasonal timing.

Water source, water quality, hydrologic regime, and substrate properties are not independent factors, but rather each factor usually affects all the others. Different combinations result in different types of wetlands.

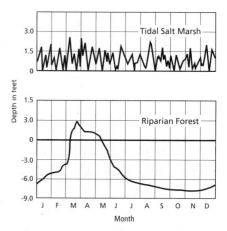

Figure 2-3. Typical Annual Hydrologic Cycles for Tidal Salt Marsh and Riparian Forest. Schematic only, not from actual data.

Coastal salt marsh at Tomales Bay in Marin County.

Vernal pools, dominated by small annual plants such as meadowfoams, popcorn flowers, goldfields, and downingias, is an example of a uniquely Californian wetland. Vernal pools are depressions filled by winter rains. Warm spring temperatures bring colorful wildflower displays and slow evaporation of the pools. By summer the pools are completely dry and the flowers gone. Most plants and invertebrate animals of the vernal pools wait out the dry summer and fall as dormant seeds and eggs. Vernal pool soils are shallow and underlaid by an impervious layer of dense clay, cemented hardpan, or bedrock that allows the pool to hold water while upland habitats do not.

Wetlands can be classified in a variety of ways. They are seasonal or perennial, also called permanent, depending on the duration of ununundation or saturation. Vernal pools, alkali seeps, and seasonal freshwater marsh are examples of seasonal wetlands, while tidal salt marsh, bogs, and perennial freshwater marsh are examples of perennial wetlands.

Whether their dominant vegetation is woody or herbaceous, sometimes called emergent, is another way wetlands can be classified. Riparian forest and riparian scrub are examples of woody wetland habitat, while freshwater marsh, tidal salt marsh, and vernal pools are examples of herbaceous wetland habitat.

In California, two commonly used wetlands classifications are the Holland system (Holland 1986) and the Cowardin system (Cowardin *et al.* 1979). Holland (*see* Table 2-2) is part of a larger classification system that is based on the type and relative dominance of plant species present. The Cowardin system (*see* Table 2-3), which classifies both wetland and deep water habitats, is based hierarchically on the large-scale ecosystem, hydrology, vegetative cover, and substrate. Moyle and Ellison (1991) have developed a classification system for California's inland waters that focuses on fish habitat but also includes many fishless wetland habitats.

Loss of Wetlands in California

Human activities have greatly reduced the historical extent of wetlands in the United States. Dahl (1990) estimates that over the last 200 years 53 percent of wetlands in the 48 contiguous states have been lost. And California, with an estimated 91 percent of its presettlement wetlands lost, tops the list. Of the many factors

Dahl (1990) estimates that over the last 200 years 53 percent of wetlands in the 48 contiguous states have been lost. And California, with an estimated 91 percent of its presettlement wetlands lost, tops the list.

Table 2-2. Wetland and Riparian Habitats in California

Bogs and Fens
Sphagnum bog
Darlingtonia bog
Fen

Marshes and Swamps
Northern coastal salt marsh
Southern coastal salt marsh
Coastal brackish marsh
Cismontane alkali marsh
Transmontane alkali marsh
Coastal and valley freshwater marsh
Transmontane freshwater marsh
Montane freshwater marsh
Vernal marsh
Freshwater swamp
Ledum swamp

Riparian Forests
North coast black cottonwood
  riparian forest
North coast alluvial redwood forest
Red alder riparian forest
Central coast cottonwood-
  sycamore riparian forest
Central coast live oak riparian forest
Central coast arroyo willow
  riparian forest
Southern coast live oak riparian forest
Southern arroyo willow riparian forest
Southern cottonwood-willow
  riparian forest
Great Valley cottonwood
  riparian forest
Great Valley mixed riparian forest
Great Valley valley oak riparian forest
White alder riparian forest
Aspen riparian forest
Montane black cottonwood
  riparian forest
Modoc-Great Basin cottonwood-
  willow riparian forest
Mojave riparian forest
Sonoran cottonwood-willow
  riparian forest
Mesquite bosque

Riparian Woodlands
Sycamore alluvial woodland
Desert dry wash woodland
Desert fan palm oasis woodland
Southern sycamore-alder
  riparian woodland

Riparian Scrubs
North coast riparian scrub
Woodwardia thicket
Central coast riparian scrub
Mule fat scrub
Southern willow scrub
Great Valley willow scrub
Great Valley mesquite scrub
Buttonbush scrub
Elderberry savanna
Montane riparian scrub
Modoc-Great Basin riparian scrub
Mojave desert wash scrub
Tamarisk scrub
Arrowweed scrub

Vernal Pools
Northern hardpan vernal pool
Northern claypan vernal pool
Northern basalt flow vernal pool
Northern volcanic mudflow
  vernal pool
Southern interior basalt flow
  vernal pool
San Diego mesa hardpan vernal pool
San Diego mesa claypan vernal pool

Wet Meadows and Seeps
Wet montane meadow
Wet subalpine and alpine meadow
Alkali meadow
Alkali seep
Freshwater seep
Alkali playa community

Source: Holland 1986.

Table 2-3. Classification of Wetlands and Deepwater Habitats Used by U.S. Fish and Wildlife Service (from Cowardin *et al.* 1979)

System	Subsystem	Class
Marine	Subtidal	Rock bottom
		Unconsolidated bottom
		Aquatic bed
		Reef
		Open water
	Intertidal	Aquatic bed
		Reef
		Rocky shore
		Unconsolidated shore
	Subtidal	Estuarine
		Rock bottom
		Unconsolidated bottom
		Aquatic bed
		Reef
		Open water
	Intertidal	Aquatic bed
		Reef
		Streambed
		Rocky shore
		Unconsolidated shore
		Emergent
		Scrub-shrub
		Forested
Riverine	Tidal	Rock
		Unconsolidated bottom
		Streambed
		Aquatic bed
		Rocky shore
		Unconsolidated shore
		Emergent
		Open water
	Lower perennial	Rock
		Unconsolidated bottom
		Streambed
		Aquatic bed
		Rocky shore
		Unconsolidated shore
		Emergent
		Open water
	Upper perennial	Rock
		Unconsolidated bottom

System	Subsystem	Class
	Upper perennial (cont.)	Streambed
		Aquatic bed
		Rocky shore
		Unconsolidated shore
		Emergent
		Open water
	Intermittent	Rock
		Unconsolidated bottom
		Streambed
		Aquatic bed
		Rocky shore
		Unconsolidated shore
		Emergent
		Open water
	Unknown perennial	Rock
		Unconsolidated bottom
		Streambed
		Aquatic bed
		Rocky shore
		Unconsolidated shore
		Emergent
		Open water
Lacustrine	Limnetic	Rock bottom
		Unconsolidated bottom
		Aquatic bed
		Open water
	Littoral	Rock bottom
		Unconsolidated bottom
		Aquatic bed
		Rocky shore
		Unconsolidated shore
		Emergent
		Open water
Palustrine		Rock bottom
		Unconsolidated bottom
		Aquatic bed
		Rocky shore
		Unconsolidated shore
		Moss-lichen
		Emergent
		Scrub-shrub
		Forested
		Open water

Riparian forest, Santa Clara County.

Note: Classes are further divided into subclasses based on substrate or plant and animal cover. Modifiers, which describe hydrologic regimes, water chemistry, soils, and disturbances, also may be added to the classification of sites.

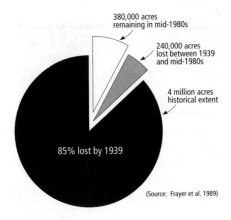

380,000 acres remaining in mid-1980s

240,000 acres lost between 1939 and mid-1980s

4 million acres historical extent

85% lost by 1939

(Source: Frayer et al. 1989)

Figure 2-4. Loss of Wetlands in California's Central Valley.

Only 379,000 acres, representing 9 percent of the original Central Valley wetland acreage, remained by the mid-1980s.

contributing to the loss of California's wetlands, the most important has been their conversion to agricultural land, flood control projects, water diversions, and urban development.

In the 1850s, California's Central Valley contained about four million acres of wetlands associated with riparian areas and grassland. More than 60 percent of the waterfowl migrating along the Pacific Flyway once stopped in the Central Valley wetlands, and the Delta (Frayer *et al.* 1989). The grasslands of the Central Valley were dotted with seasonal wetlands, including vernal pools, while jungle-like riparian forests covered the natural river levees along the Sacramento, Feather, American, Cosumnes, Mokelumne, Merced, San Joaquin, Kings, Kaweah, and Kern Rivers, and many smaller streams. In 1848 to 1850, an estimated 775,000 acres of riparian forest existed in the Central Valley, with some major riparian corridors as much as ten miles wide (Smith 1977).

Overflow areas along the Sacramento River, especially the Butte and Yolo Basins, supported wide areas of tule and cattail freshwater marsh. These seasonal and perennial wetlands were major wintering grounds for ducks and geese of the Pacific Flyway. In 1860, the Sacramento-San Joaquin Delta supported approximately 350,000 acres of freshwater marsh cut by rivers and sloughs (San Francisco Estuary Project 1991). Enormous flocks of ducks and geese descended on the Delta marshes in winter, and tule elk were once abundant there and in the surrounding perennial grasslands (McCullough 1971).

The southern San Joaquin Valley is a drainageless basin where the Kern, Kaweah, and Kings Rivers once fed huge tule marshes and lakes. Tulare Lake was the largest of these great shallow inland lakes. Early observers reported large numbers of swans, geese, and ducks between October and April, along with wintering sandhill cranes and breeding white pelicans (Jones & Stokes Associates 1987), while beaver, mink, and river otter were abundant in Tulare Lake and its feeder streams (Preston 1981).

By 1939, less than 15 percent of the Central Valley wetlands remained, the rest lost mainly to agricultural conversion (*see* Figure 2-4). Between 1939 and the mid-1980s, Central Valley wetlands disappeared at an average rate of 5,200 acres per year. Only 379,000 acres, representing 9 percent of the original Central Valley wetland acreage, remained by the mid-1980s (Frayer *et al.* 1989). By 1930, 97 percent of the original Sacramento-San Joaquin Delta wetlands had been leveed, drained, and converted to agricultural use (San Francisco Estuary Project 1991). Habitat loss in the

Central Valley has substantially reduced populations of many wildlife species, including waterfowl and other water birds, a variety of threatened and endangered bird species (bald eagle, greater sandhill crane, yellow-billed cuckoo, and Swainson's hawk), large mammals (tule elk, pronghorn antelope, and mule deer), and many other species of wildlife.

Before 1850, San Francisco Bay supported about 200,000 acres of tidal marsh (San Francisco Estuary Project 1991). Bay salt marshes and mudflats supported huge flocks of shorebirds that fed on the invertebrate life generated by this tremendously productive biological system. Today, about 25,500 acres of undiked tidal marsh, 48,500 acres of diked wetlands, and 36,600 acres of salt ponds remain in the San Francisco Bay (San Francisco Estuary Project 1991). The reported 200,000 wintering shorebirds and 75,000 wintering waterfowl on salt ponds in south San Francisco Bay are but a fraction of the number this area once supported (Cohen 1991). Suisun Bay, at the juncture of salt water and freshwater zones, is still the largest brackish marsh in California.

Remaining salt marsh habitat in coastal southern California is estimated at about 16,800 acres, or between 10 and 25 percent of its historic extent (Ferren 1990). The loss of salt marsh in San Diego Bay between 1919 and 1970 is estimated to have been 85 percent, from approximately 2,400 acres to 350 acres (Mudie 1970 in Macdonald 1988). In 1973, Humboldt Bay in northern coastal California was estimated to support less than 9 percent, or about 600 acres, of an original 6,800 acres of salt marsh (Macdonald 1988).

Remaining salt marsh habitat in coastal southern California is estimated at about 16,800 acres, or between 10 and 25 percent of its historic extent.

California's remaining wetlands still support tremendous numbers of waterfowl, especially in the Central Valley, San Francisco Bay Area, and Modoc Plateau. The Central Valley provides habitat for up to 20 percent of all wintering ducks in the United States (Central Valley Habitat Joint Venture Report 1990), and California's coastal salt marsh and mudflats are still highly productive communities supporting large numbers of shore birds.

Activities Affecting Wetlands

Conversion to agricultural land, urban development, flood control projects, and water diversions are the general causes of most wetland losses.

Activities that directly destroy or greatly change the hydrology, soil, vegetation, or wildlife of wetlands include–

- ▶ Pumping water or excavating ditches, which can cause them to drain
- ▶ Filling, which can severely disrupt or eliminate wetland hydrology by raising bottom elevation
- ▶ Excavating so that the resulting water level is too deep, which can change wetland hydrology to an open water system
- ▶ Construction and management of dams, diversions, and levees, which can change the type of wetland or destroy it altogether due to changes in the frequency, timing, or duration of inundation
- ▶ Plowing too deeply or ripping through the claypan or hardpan in seasonal wetlands, such as vernal pools, which can cause them to drain
- ▶ Mowing, plowing, burning, or otherwise removing plants and vegetation, which can degrade or destroy the function of wetlands as wildlife habitat
- ▶ Grazing, which can remove much of the vegetation and thus their function as wildlife habitat

Activities in locations away from wetlands may also destroy or greatly change hydrology, soils, vegetation, or wildlife. These indirect impacts, which typically manifest more slowly, include–

- ▶ Sediments deposited in the wetland from upslope erosion, which can change bottom contours and affect hydrology
- ▶ Erosion of the wetland substratum due to changes in hydrology (increased input of high energy water, for example), which can change the bottom contours
- ▶ Flooding due to dam impoundment or increased streamflows, which can drown vegetation
- ▶ Reductions in the size of a watershed, which can reduce the amount of water that flows to the wetland
- ▶ Shading from structures such as bridges, which can result in the loss of wildlife habitat and vegetative cover
- ▶ Introduction of nonnative plant and animal species, which can outcompete or consume native species
- ▶ Contamination by pesticides, herbicides, fertilizers, heavy metals, oils, or other chemicals in runoff from mining sites, agricultural land, urban development, industrial waste, and oil drilling sites, which can poison plants and animals, make the soil infertile, cause overgrowth of plants, destroy the invertebrate food base, or result in bioaccumulation of toxic materials in the food chain

Riparian forest and cattail marsh, Sacramento County.

3

Determining Jurisdictional Limits of Wetlands and Other Waters

A complex array of state and federal regulatory guidelines directs how the jurisdictional boundaries of wetlands are defined and identified. Activities within wetlands and other waters throughout the United States are regulated under Section 404 of the Clean Water Act. State laws governing wetlands and other waters in California include provisions within the California Fish and Game Code and the California Coastal Act. Full discussions of the federal and state regulatory authority over wetlands can be found in chapters 4 and 5.

This chapter addresses the means by which the jurisdictional boundaries are defined by the various regulatory agencies and presents a practical approach for integrating the identification of wetland resources. To ensure compliance with all the applicable federal and state regulations, an integrated approach to identifying wetlands is necessary.

Clean Water Act, Section 404 Waters of the United States

'Waters of the United States' is the broadest category of regulated water bodies and includes wetlands along with nonwetland habitats, such as streams, rivers, lakes, ponds, bays, and oceans. Section 404 of the Clean Water Act (CWA) regulates activities that result in the discharge of dredged or fill material into waters of the United States (*see* chapter 4 for a full discussion of the Section 404 regulatory program). Waters of the United States are defined in the Code of Federal Regulation as follows–

'Waters of the United States' is the broadest category of regulated water bodies and includes wetlands along with nonwetland habitats, such as streams, rivers, lakes, ponds, bays, and oceans.

CWA = Clean Water Act

(1) All waters which are currently used, or were used in the past, or may be susceptible to use in interstate or foreign commerce, including all waters which are subject to the ebb and flow of the tide;

(2) All interstate waters including interstate wetlands;

(3) All other waters such as intrastate lakes, rivers, streams (including intermittent streams), mudflats, sandflats, wetlands, sloughs, prairie potholes, wet meadows, playa lakes, or natural ponds, the use, degradation or destruction of which could affect interstate or foreign commerce including any such waters:

    (i) Which are or could be used by interstate or foreign travelers for recreational or other purposes; or

    (ii) From which fish or shellfish are or could be taken and sold in interstate or foreign commerce; or

    (iii) Which are used or could be used for industrial purpose by industries in interstate commerce;

(4) All impoundments of waters otherwise defined as waters of the United States under the definition;

(5) Tributaries of waters identified in paragraphs (1) though (4) of this section;

(6) The territorial seas;

(7) Wetlands adjacent to waters (other than waters that are themselves wetlands) identified in paragraphs (1) through (6) of this section. (33 CFR 328.3[a]; 40 CFR 230.3[s])

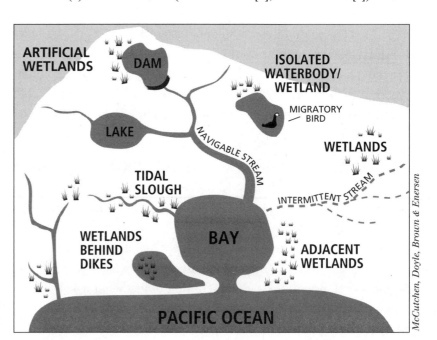

Figure 3-1. Waters of the United States (Section 404 of the Clean Water Act). From a flyer printed by the San Francisco Corps office.

Wetlands are just one type of these waters of the United States. Essentially all natural bodies of water in California are included under the definition of waters of the United States–

- ▶ The ocean
- ▶ Bays
- ▶ Rivers
- ▶ Perennial streams
- ▶ Intermittent streams
- ▶ Ephemeral swales
- ▶ Desert arroyos
- ▶ Lakes
- ▶ Ponds
- ▶ Seasonal ponds
- ▶ Desert playas
- ▶ Vernal pools
- ▶ Wetlands

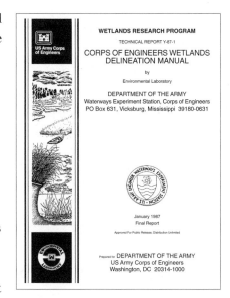

Many artificial or disturbed water bodies also fall under this definition, including–

- ▶ Reservoirs
- ▶ Farm or stock ponds fed by direct rainfall or impoundment of a stream (not by pumped water)
- ▶ Artificial wetlands that receive water without artificial controls (such as pumps, valves, or gates)
- ▶ Farmed wetlands

However, some bodies of water are excluded from Section 404 regulation–

- ▶ Irrigation ditches
- ▶ Drainage ditches excavated in uplands
- ▶ Temporary sediment basins on construction sites
- ▶ Reflecting pools
- ▶ Wastewater systems, including treatment ponds and lagoons
- ▶ Ponds and wetlands created as part of an ongoing mining operation (unless created as mitigation for past impacts)

As waters of the United States, wetlands are regulated under the Clean Water Act. Under federal regulations, wetlands are identified as follows–

> The term 'wetlands' means those areas that are inundated or saturated by surface or ground water at a frequency and duration sufficient to support, and that under normal circumstances do support, a prevalence of vegetation typically adapted for life in saturated soil conditions. Wetlands generally include swamps, marshes, bogs, and similar areas. (33 CFR 328.3[b]; 40 CFR 230.3[t])

The U.S. Army Corps of Engineers used this regulatory definition to develop a field method for determining wetland jurisdictional boundaries. The Corps is the main regulatory authority designated to permit activities involving the discharge

As waters of the United States, wetlands are regulated under the Clean Water Act.

Figure 3-2. Data Form—Routine Wetland Determination (1987 Corps Wetlands Delineation Manual).

DATA FORM
ROUTINE WETLAND DETERMINATION
(1987 COE Wetlands Delineation Manual)

Project/Site: _____ Date: _____
Applicant/Owner: _____ County: _____
Investigator: _____ State: _____

Do Normal Circumstances exist on the site?   Yes   No   Community ID: _____
Is the site significantly disturbed (Atypical Situation)?   Yes   No   Transect ID: _____
Is the area a potential Problem Area?   Yes   No   Plot ID: _____
        (If needed, explain on reverse.)

VEGETATION

Dominant Plant Species	Stratum	Indicator	Dominant Plant Species	Stratum	Indicator
1. _____	_____	_____	9. _____	_____	_____
2. _____	_____	_____	10. _____	_____	_____
3. _____	_____	_____	11. _____	_____	_____
4. _____	_____	_____	12. _____	_____	_____
5. _____	_____	_____	13. _____	_____	_____
6. _____	_____	_____	14. _____	_____	_____
7. _____	_____	_____	15. _____	_____	_____
8. _____	_____	_____	16. _____	_____	_____

Percent of Dominant Species that are OBL, FACW or FAC
(excluding FAC–)

Remarks:

HYDROLOGY

__ Recorded Data (Describe in Remarks):
____ Stream, Lake, or Tide Gauge
____ Aerial Photographs
____ Other
__ No Recorded Data Available

Field Observations:

Depth of Surface Water: _____ (in.)

Depth to Free Water in Pit: _____ (in.)

Depth to Saturated Soil: _____ (in.)

Remarks:

Wetland Hydrology Indicators
Primary Indicators:
____ Inundated
____ Saturated in Upper 12 Inches
____ Water Marks
____ Drift Lines
____ Sediment Deposits
____ Drainage Patterns in Wetlands
Secondary Indicators (2 or more required):
____ Oxidized Root Channels in Upper 12 Inches
____ Water-Stained Leaves
____ Local Soil Survey Data
____ FAC-Neutral Test
____ Other (Explain in Remarks)

of dredged or fill material into waters of the United States (*see* detailed discussion in chapter 4).

The Wetland Delineation Method Used by the Corps

In 1987, the Corps Waterways Experiment Station in Vicksburg, Mississippi, published a manual to be used by staff to identify and delineate wetland boundaries for the purpose of Section 404 regulation (Corps 1987). The techniques described in the manual are presently (as of October 1994) the Corps' officially recognized method for delineating wetlands.

To determine whether a site is a wetland, the manual uses a three-parameter test. The three parameters are vegetation, soils, and hydrology. If a site supports positive indicators of hydrophytic

SOILS

Map Unit Name
(Series and Phase): _____ Drainage Class: _____
Field Observations
Taxonomy (Subgroup): _____ Confirm Mapped Type?   Yes   No

Profile Description

Depth (inches)	Horizon	Matrix Color (Munsell Moist)	Mottle Colors (Munsell Moist)	Mottle Abundance/Contrast	Texture, Concretions Structure etc.
_____	_____	_____	_____	_____	_____
_____	_____	_____	_____	_____	_____
_____	_____	_____	_____	_____	_____
_____	_____	_____	_____	_____	_____
_____	_____	_____	_____	_____	_____
_____	_____	_____	_____	_____	_____

Hydric Soil Indicators:

____ Histosol
____ Histic Epipedon
____ Sulfidic Odor
____ Aquic Moisture Regime
____ Reducing Conditions
____ Gleyed or Low-Chroma Colors

____ Concretions
____ High Organic Content in Surface Layer in Sandy Soils
____ Organic Streaking in Sandy Soils
____ Listed on Local Hydric Soils List
____ Listed on National Hydric Soils List
____ Other (Explain in Remarks)

Remarks:

WETLAND DETERMINATION

Hydrophytic Vegetation Present?   Yes   No   (Circle)   (Circle)
Wetland Hydrology Present?   Yes   No
Hydric Soils Present?   Yes   No   Is this Sampling Point Within a Wetland?   Yes   No

Remarks:

Approved by HQUSACE 3/92

vegetation, hydric soils, and wetland hydrology, the Corps considers the wetland to be within its jurisdiction. Except in disturbed or nonnormal circumstances, positive indicators for all three of these parameters must be present for a site to qualify. The boundary between wetland and nonwetland habitat is defined as the location where positive indicators of one of the three parameters are no longer present. At its upper elevational boundary, a wetland gives way to upland habitat. A lower elevational boundary, where it exists, marks where the wetland gives way to open water habitat in which wetland vegetation cannot survive. (*See* chapter 2 for a discussion of wetland ecology and positive indicators of wetlands.)

Because wetlands are the focus of much regulatory attention, all other forms of waters of the United States are often referred to

If a site supports positive indicators of hydrophytic vegetation, hydric soils, and wetland hydrology, the Corps considers the wetland to be within its jurisdiction.

Not All Jurisdictional Wetlands Are Obvious

A local water resources agency along the central California coast wanted to build a regulating reservoir to store diverted river water for irrigation of agricultural land. District engineers found what they thought was a perfect site in a low-lying, fallow agricultural field. However, the fallow field was adjacent to a slough that supported salt marsh and, it turned out, the field historically had been salt marsh.

Because wetland hydrology was still present and wetland plants were invading the fallow field, the Corps classified the site as a 'farmed wetland' and determined that the construction of levees to create the reservoir would require placing fill in the farmed wetland. The water agency tried to convince the Corps that its proposed reservoir would create open water and freshwater marsh habitat as mitigation for impacts on jurisdictional wetlands. The Corps replied that, because it was out-of-kind, creating open water and freshwater marsh habitat was not an appropriate mitigation, a conclusion based on the prediction that the farmed wetland would revert to salt marsh habitat if farming were to cease.

In the end, the district redesigned its project so that the regulating reservoir would not be necessary to meet the project's purpose. Not all jurisdictional wetlands are obvious. Secure expert help early in the planning process so that you can choose your project site carefully.

as 'other waters of the United States' or simply 'other waters'. Mapping waters of the United States into two categories—wetlands and other waters—is widely practiced in jurisdictional delineation.

The Corps is also responsible for identifying wetlands or verifying wetland delineations on nonagricultural land. The Natural Resources Conservation Service (NRCS) bears this responsibility for agricultural lands (59 FR 12, January 19, 1994); but, since NRCS has not implemented its authority in all areas, in some California counties the Corps continues to take responsibility for wetland delineation on agricultural lands. The nine counties of the San Francisco Bay have been exempted from the Corps-NRCS agreement and all determinations on agricultural lands are still Corps responsibility. These nine counties are—

NRCS = Natural Resources Conservation Service

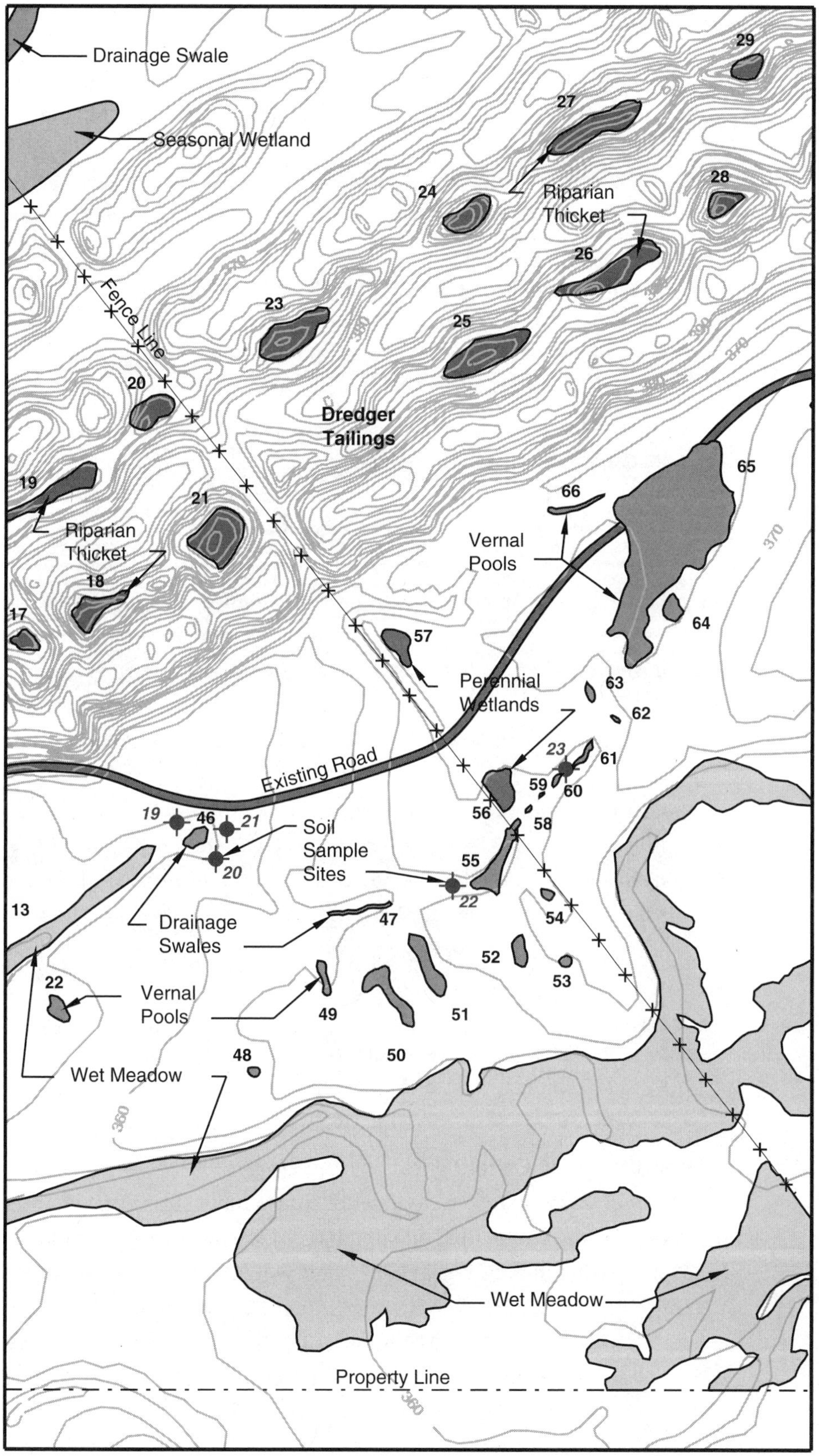
Drainage Swale
Seasonal Wetland
29
27
28
24
Riparian Thicket
26
Fence Line
23
25
20
Dredger Tailings
19
21
Riparian Thicket
18
17
65
66
Vernal Pools
64
57
Perennial Wetlands
63
62
Existing Road
23
61
59
60
56
19
46
21
Soil Sample Sites
58
20
55
22
13
Drainage Swales
47
54
52
53
22
Vernal Pools
49
51
48
50
Wet Meadow
Wet Meadow
Property Line
360
370

Figure 3-3. Example of a Wetland Delineation.

Delineate Wetlands Accurately

During the late 1980s, a development company in Sacramento County proposed a large residential and commercial project. Knowing that wetlands would be a central issue in the environmental process, the company hired a consultant to delineate the wetlands on the property and asked the Corps to verify the delineations well before an Environmental Impact Statement was prepared. The developers hired the same consultant to prepare a mitigation plan for incorporation into the project description.

Although wise to incorporate wetlands into their plans early in the process, the consultants who prepared the EIS found discrepancies between wetlands mapped for the wetland delineation and those mapped for the mitigation plan. The wetland map in the mitigation plan was far more detailed and precise than the verified wetland delineation map. Impact acreages based on the 'official' (Corps-verified) delineation could not be reconciled with the more accurate (but unofficial) map in the mitigation plan. As a result, the developers and their attorneys, the consultants, and agency staff all expended additional time and money trying to resolve discrepancies between the maps.

Be sure that delineations of wetlands are sufficiently accurate to support the subsequent assessment of impact and mitigation planning. On a large project site, the Corps may verify a delineation without visiting every wetland. Small wetlands, like vernal pools, should be individually numbered and measured on delineation maps.

EIS = Environmental Impact Statement

▶ Marin   ▶ Alameda   ▶ Solano

▶ Sonoma   ▶ San Francisco   ▶ Santa Clara

▶ Napa   ▶ San Mateo   ▶ Contra Costa

Boundaries of Other Waters of the United States

Although some waters of the United States have adjacent wetlands, many do not. In the absence of adjacent wetlands, the boundaries of waters for the territorial seas, tidal waters, and nontidal waters are defined in the Code of Federal Regulation as follows–

(a) Territorial Seas. The limit of jurisdiction in the territorial seas is measured from the baseline (the line on the shore reached by ordinary low tides) in a seaward direction a distance of three nautical miles.

(b) Tidal Waters of the United States. The landward limits of jurisdiction in tidal waters:

    (1) Extends to the high tide line (encompasses spring high tides and other high tides that occur with periodic frequency), or

    (2) When adjacent nontidal waters of the United States are present, the jurisdiction extends to the limits identified in paragraph (c) of this section.

(c) Nontidal Waters of the United States. The limits of jurisdiction in nontidal waters:

    (1) In the absence of adjacent wetlands, the jurisdiction extends to the ordinary high water mark (*see* definition below), or

    (2) When adjacent wetlands are present, the jurisdiction extends beyond the ordinary high water mark to the limit of the adjacent wetlands.

    (3) When the water of the United States consists only of wetlands the jurisdiction extends to the limit of the wetland. (33 CFR 328.4)

Tidal areas in California include coastal areas, river mouths, deltas, and bays. Nontidal waters of the United States include

Figure 3-4. Scope of Corps Regulatory Jurisdiction. From a flyer printed by the San Francisco Corps office.

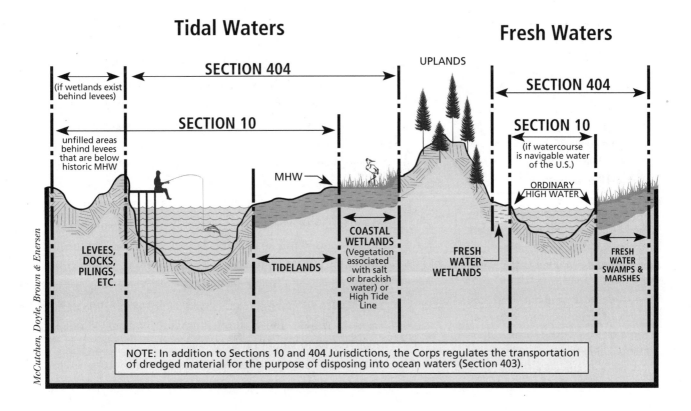

Tidal Waters

Fresh Waters

NOTE: In addition to Sections 10 and 404 Jurisdictions, the Corps regulates the transportation of dredged material for the purpose of disposing into ocean waters (Section 403).

McCutchen, Doyle, Brown & Enersen

rivers, streams, lakes, and ponds. Corps jurisdiction in nontidal waters is measured to the ordinary high water mark, defined in the federal regulations as follows–

> The term 'ordinary high water mark' means that line on the shore established by the fluctuations of water and indicated by physical characteristics such as [a] clear, natural line impressed on the bank, shelving, changes in the character of soil, destruction of terrestrial vegetation, the presence of litter and debris, or other appropriate means that consider the characteristics of the surrounding areas. (33 CFR 328.3[e])

Special Aquatic Sites

Particular kinds of waters of the United States receive special attention by the Corps and U.S. Environmental Protection Agency (EPA) under the CWA. These waters, referred to as 'special aquatic sites', are geographic areas that possess unique ecological characteristics of productivity, habitat, wildlife protection, or other important ecological values. These areas are generally recognized as significantly influencing or positively contributing to the overall environmental health or vitality of the entire ecosystem of a region. Special aquatic sites adversely affected by a project are subject to greater scrutiny than other waters in the determination of appropriate mitigation measures. The six types of special aquatic sites are–

▶ Wetlands
▶ Sanctuaries and refuges. Federal, state, or locally designated sites managed for the purpose of fish and wildlife resources
▶ Mud flats. Periodically inundated and exposed unvegetated areas such as tidal coastal areas and the edges of inland lakes, ponds, and rivers
▶ Vegetated shallows. Permanently inundated sites with rooted, submerged vegetation
▶ Coral reefs. Calcium- or silica-based deposits produced by invertebrates that establish reefs in warm ocean waters (coral reefs are found in Florida and Hawaii, but not in California)
▶ Riffle and pool complexes. High quality fish and wildlife habitat on steep gradient portions of rivers or streams where a rapid current flowing over a coarse substrate results in turbulence (riffles) and a slower moving current in deeper areas results in smooth flow (pools)

Special aquatic sites are given particular attention in the analysis of project alternatives prepared pursuant to EPA's CWA

EPA = Environmental Protection Agency

Conduct Preliminary Surveys Before Committing to Wetland Delineation Methods

The Corps needed a wetland delineation at a military installation on San Francisco Bay. The regulatory section of the Corps decided that the site would likely support extensive wetlands. Based on this assumption, the Corps chose to survey the site using the comprehensive method of wetland delineation. Unlike the routine method, 'comprehensive determinations' involve the collection of detailed vegetation, soils, and hydrological data and require significantly more time and expense.

The survey resulted in the identification of only eight jurisdictional wetlands, totalling about 11 acres on a site of approximately 700 acres. The task could have been accomplished using the routine method at less cost with the same result.

Section 404(b)(1) guidelines. (*See* chapter 4 for a discussion of these guidelines pertaining to special aquatic sites.)

Rivers and Harbors Act, Section 10: Navigable Waters

Under Section 10 of the Rivers and Harbors Act of 1899, the construction of structures in, over, or under; excavation of material from; or deposition of material into 'navigable waters' are regulated by the Corps. (*See* chapter 4 for a full discussion of regulations under Section 10 of the Rivers and Harbors Act.) Navigable waters are defined in the federal regulations as follows—

> Navigable waters of the United States are those waters that are subject to the ebb and flow of the tide and/or are presently used, or have been used in the past, or may be susceptible for use to transport interstate or foreign commerce. A determination of navigability, once made, applies laterally over the entire surface of the water body, and is not extinguished by later actions or events which impede or destroy navigable capacity. (33 CFR 329.4)

Soil pit in riparian habitat, Santa Cruz County.

In tidal areas the limit of navigable waters is the mean high tide line and in nontidal areas the ordinary high water mark. Navigable waters typically have the same boundaries as, or lie within the boundaries of, waters of the United States. Larger streams, rivers, lakes, bays, and oceans are navigable waters that may represent all or a part of waters of the United States. Wetlands are typically not part of navigable waters. In some cases—such as where coastal salt marsh or tidal freshwater marsh lies below the mean high water line—wetlands may exist within navigable waters. In addition to the navigable waters described above, historically navigable waters are also subject to federal regulation under Section 10 of the Rivers and Harbors Act. Historically navigable waters are those areas that are no longer navigable as a result of artificial modifications, such as levees, dikes, and dams. To identify sites that were historically below mean high tide or the ordinary high water mark, and hence historically navigable, the Corps uses records such as geological survey maps and other topographic maps that were prepared in the late 1800s after California achieved statehood.

Navigable waters typically have the same boundaries as, or lie within the boundaries of, waters of the United States.

To identify sites that were historically navigable, the Corps uses records such as geological survey maps and other topographic maps that were prepared in the late 1800s after California achieved statehood.

California Fish and Game Code: Bed, Bank, and Channel of Streams and Lakes

Under Sections 1600-1607 of the California Fish and Game Code, the California Department of Fish and Game regulates activities that would alter the flow, bed, channel, or bank of streams and lakes. (*See* chapter 5 for a full discussion of California Fish and Game Code Sections 1600-1607.) The limits of DFG jurisdiction are defined in the code as the–

> . . . bed, channel or bank of any river, stream or lake designated by the department [DFG] in which there is at any time an existing fish or wildlife resource or from which these resources derive benefit. . . . (Section 1601)

This broad definition gives DFG great flexibility in deciding what constitutes a river, stream, or lake. Streams are defined in the California Code of Regulations as follows–

> A stream is a body of water that flows at least periodically or intermittently through a bed or channel having banks and supports fish or other aquatic life. This includes watercourses having a surface or subsurface flow that supports or has supported riparian vegetation. (14 CCR 1.72)

DFG defines streams under the jurisdiction of Sections 1600-1607 as follows–

1. The term stream can include intermittent and ephemeral streams, rivers, creeks, dry washes, sloughs, blue-line streams (United States Geological Survey maps [USGS]), and watercourses with subsurface flows. Canals, aqueducts, irrigation ditches, and other means of water conveyance can also be considered streams if they support aquatic life, riparian vegetation, or stream-dependent terrestrial wildlife.

2. Biological components of a stream may include aquatic and riparian vegetation, all aquatic animals including fish, amphibians, reptiles, invertebrates, and terrestrial species which derive benefits from the stream system.

3. As a physical system, a stream not only includes water (at least on an intermittent or ephemeral basis), but also a bed or channel, a bank and/or levee, instream features such as logs or snags, and various flood plains depending on the return frequency of flood event being considered (that is, 10, 50, or 100 years, etc.).

4. The lateral extent of a stream can be measured in several ways depending on a particular situation and the type of fish or wildlife resource at risk. The following criteria are presented in order from the most inclusive to the least inclusive:

   A. The flood plain of a stream can be the broadest measurement of a stream's lateral extent depending on the return frequency of the flood event used. For most flood control purposes, the 100-year event is the standard measurement, and maps of the 100-year flood plain exist for many streams. However, because it may include significant amounts of upland or urban habitat, in many cases the 100-year flood plain may not be appropriate.

B. The outer edge of riparian vegetation is generally used as the line of demarcation between riparian and upland habitats and is therefore a reasonable and identifiable boundary for the lateral extent of a stream. In most cases, the use of this criterion should result in protecting the fish and wildlife resources at risk.

C. Most streams have a natural bank which confines flows to the bed or channel except during flooding. In some instances, particularly on smaller streams or dry washes with little or no riparian habitat, the bank should be used to mark the lateral extent of a stream.

D. A levee or other artificial stream bank could also be used to mark the lateral extent of a stream. However, in many instances, there can be extensive areas of valuable riparian habitat located behind a levee. (DFG 1992)

Saturated soils in freshwater marsh habitat, Riverside County. Water quickly filled this unlined soil pit, indicating that the water table is at the surface and that the soil is saturated to the surface.

In practice, DFG usually marks its jurisdictional limit at the top of the stream or lake bank or at the outer edge of the riparian vegetation, whichever is wider. As a resource agency, because its emphasis is on fish and wildlife habitat, DFG includes within its jurisdiction riparian vegetation associated with streams and lakes. Riparian habitats flooded for long duration at a frequency greater than 50 out of every 100 years would come under Corps Section 404 jurisdiction as wetlands. However, some riparian habitats may flood on average only one year out of five or ten years.

DFG usually marks its jurisdictional limit at the top of the stream or lake bank or at the outer edge of the riparian vegetation, whichever is wider.

Since riparian habitats do not always support wetland hydrology or hydric soils, federal Section 404 wetland boundaries sometimes include only portions of the riparian habitat adjacent to a river, stream, or lake. Therefore, jurisdictional boundaries under Sections 1600-1607 may encompass an area greater than under Section 404. The situation is often reversed for isolated wetlands such as vernal pools which the Corps regulates under Section 404, but which are not subject to Section 1600-1607 regulation by DFG.

California Coastal Act: Wetlands, Other Water Bodies, and Other Water-Associated Habitats

In California's coastal zone, wetlands are regulated under California Coastal Act (CCA) and the federal Coastal Zone Management

CCA = California Coastal Act

Act (CZMA) and fall within the jurisdiction of the California Coastal Commission. (*See* chapter 5 for a detailed description of the CCA.) Under the CCA, wetlands are defined as follows–

> 'Wetland' means lands within the coastal zone which may be covered periodically or permanently with shallow water and include saltwater marshes, freshwater marshes, open or closed brackish water marshes, swamps, mudflats, and fens. (Ca. Pub. Res. Code Section 30121)

Under the California Code of Regulations, which guides the California Coastal Commission (CCC), wetlands are defined as follows–

> Wetlands shall be defined as land where the water table is at, near, or above the land surface long enough to promote the formation of hydric soils or to support the growth of hydrophytes, and shall also include types of wetlands where vegetation is lacking and soil is poorly developed or absent as a result of frequent and drastic fluctuations of surface water levels, wave action, water flow, turbidity or high concentrations of salts or other substances in the substrate. Such wetlands can be recognized by the presence of surface water or saturated substrate at some time during each year and their location within, or adjacent to, vegetated wetland or deepwater habitats. (14 CCR 13577[b])

This definition is similar to the Corps' definition of wetlands, but also encompasses mudflat and salt panne habitats as wetlands. The Corps regulates mudflats and salt pannes as other waters of the United States because they do not contain vegetation. In practice, under the Coastal Act definition, boundaries identified for vegetated wetlands should be the same as those identified for the Corps' jurisdictional wetlands. The main difference between Corps and CCC jurisdictional boundaries is that CCC's jurisdictional area not only includes the wetland, but an additional 100-foot-wide buffer, measured from the upland edge of the wetland (14 CCR 13577).

Other water bodies and water-associated habitats that CCC regulates in the coastal zone are–

▶ Riparian habitats. Associations of plant species that grow next to freshwater streams, lakes, and other systems, plus a 100-foot-wide upland buffer measured from the landward edge of the riparian habitat

▶ Streams. Mapped on U.S. Geological Survey 7.5-minute quadrangle series or identified in a local coastal program, plus a 100-foot-wide buffer measured from the top of the bank

▶ Estuaries. Typically semi-enclosed, coastal water bodies receiving open or intermittent exchange with the ocean and fresh water from land, plus a 300-foot-wide buffer measured landward from the mean high tide line

▶ Tidelands. Lands between mean high tide and mean low tide

▶ Submerged lands that lie below mean low tide

▶ Public trust lands. Subject to Common Law Public Trust (a sovereign public property right held by the state for the benefit of the people) for commerce, navigation, fisheries, recreation, and other public purposes

▶ Beaches. The sandy beach, plus a 300-foot-wide buffer measured landward from the inland extent of the beach

These habitats and buffer zone widths are defined in the California Code of Regulations (14 CCR 13577) and in CCC's statewide interpretive guidelines (California Coastal Commission 1981). CCC usually relies on DFG to make or verify boundary determinations for habitats under its jurisdiction. Before it will act on permits, CCC recommends that project proponents provide a Corps-verified delineation of Section 404 jurisdictional wetlands and other waters of the United States and a DFG-verified delineation of CCC jurisdictional wetlands, riparian, and other habitats.

Integrated Method for Identifying Wetland Resources

Identification of wetlands at project sites should use an integrated method that addresses all potential regulatory boundaries and identifies other regulated water bodies and wetland-associated habitats. The mapping effort should identify as separate units—

▶ Section 404 jurisdictional wetlands

▶ Other special aquatic sites listed in the Section 404 (b)(1) guidelines

▶ Other Section 404 waters of the United States

▶ Section 10 navigable waters

▶ Section 10 historically navigable waters

▶ Sections 1600-1607 riparian habitat

Where only portions, if any, of the riparian habitat are regulated by Section 404, the simultaneous identification of Corps and DFG jurisdiction is recommended. Sites such as these are common in California. Often, the wetlands under Corps jurisdiction are mapped, but

Coastal salt marsh at San Pablo Bay in Marin County.

identification of nonwetland riparian habitats subject to DFG regulatory authority is overlooked. Later, when determining DFG jurisdiction under Section 1600-1607, a separate mapping effort must be conducted to identify riparian habitats. Delineating federal and state jurisdictional boundaries in a single effort is the most expeditious approach.

If a project site lies within the coastal zone, the mapping effort should identify the boundaries of habitats under CCC jurisdiction that may or may not overlap with Corps and DFG jurisdictional areas and the CCC buffer zones associated with these habitats. In addition to CCC jurisdictional wetlands, other water bodies and wetland-associated habitats in the coastal zone that should be mapped are—

- ▶ Streams
- ▶ Estuaries
- ▶ Tidelands
- ▶ Submerged lands
- ▶ Public trust lands
- ▶ Beaches

The use of an integrated approach to identifying federal and state jurisdictional boundaries will streamline the analysis of environmental effects, permit processing, and mitigation planning. Local agencies may have wetland policies or ordinances to be considered, and site maps should incorporate appropriate boundaries. Where jurisdictions overlap, a single impact analysis and mitigation plan can resolve the needs of all regulatory agencies involved. (*See* chapter 6 for a discussion of mitigation planning.) Mapping all jurisdictional boundaries simultaneously allows project planners to see the extent of regulatory constraints and opportunities for use of the site.

Although the Corps recognizes wetlands as a single jurisdictional entity, many types of wetlands exist (*see* chapter 2). Maps should identify each wetland by habitat type. The ability to determine the type and extent of wetland habitats that could be affected by a project provides invaluable information for site planning, permit processing, and mitigation planning.

Debris piles in a floodplain that previously supported riparian forest, Santa Cruz County. Remnant riparian forest can be seen in background.

4

Federal Wetlands Regulation

The federal government currently attempts to address the protection and use of wetlands through a number of detailed programs and statutes. Although its approach to wetlands regulation has many components, the primary statute regulating wetlands activities is the Federal Water Pollution Control Act, 33 USC 1251-1387, commonly known as the CWA. Although the CWA does not use the term 'wetlands', Section 404 of the CWA (*see* Appendix A for full text of Section 404) requires that private, state, and federal entities (other than the Corps) obtain a permit from the Corps before depositing dredged or fill materials into waters of the United States which include wetlands. (*See* chapter 3 for definitions of 'waters of the United States' and 'wetlands'.)

Although the CWA does not use the term 'wetlands', Section 404 of the CWA requires that private, state, and federal entities (other than the Corps) obtain a permit from the Corps before depositing dredged or fill materials into waters of the United States which include wetlands.

This chapter, which reviews the history of federal regulatory authority leading up to the CWA and the roles of the Corps and EPA in regulating wetlands activities, discusses the jurisdictional limits, permit requirements and the individual permit review process, and enforcement authorities under Section 404.

The Corps' issuance of a permit pursuant to Section 404 is a federal action that requires the Corps to comply with other federal laws and regulations involving detailed analysis of project activities beyond the project's effects on wetlands. This chapter reviews these and other federal laws and regulations, including provisions of the CWA, pertaining to the management of wetlands activities. The chapter concludes with a presentation of the Fifth Amendment 'takings' issue as it relates to the regulatory authority of the CWA over private property.

The Corps' issuance of a permit pursuant to Section 404 is a federal action that requires the Corps to comply with other federal laws and regulations involving detailed analysis of project activities beyond the project's effects on wetlands.

History of Federal Wetlands Regulation

The federal government's concern for wetlands began in the nineteenth century with attempts to diminish rather than protect wetlands. Historically, the attitude toward wetland areas, at that time more commonly referred to as 'swamps', was that they were nuisance areas to be eliminated if possible. Through the U.S. Department of Agriculture, the federal government provided many incentives for converting these wetlands to agriculture, and federal policies encouraged states to drain and fill areas considered 'swamp and overflow lands unsuited for agriculture' (*see* Swamp Lands Act of 1849, 1850, and 1860).

Early Federal Wetlands Protection

Not until the 1960s did the federal government, through the Corps, first promulgate regulations that could protect wetlands. The Corps' authority over wetlands activities gradually developed into the present permit system that has become both complex and controversial.

Originally created by Congress to erect and maintain frontier forts and other defense facilities (Act of March 16, 1802), the Corps did not have the authority to regulate activities within waterways until Congress authorized the Corps, in the Act of May 10, 1824, to undertake river and harbor improvements promoting navigation.

The extension of Corps jurisdiction into areas considered 'waters of the United States' began in the 1960s with new interpretations of the Rivers and Harbors Act of 1899.

The extension of Corps jurisdiction into areas considered 'waters of the United States' began in the 1960s with new interpretations of the Rivers and Harbors Act of 1899 (33 USC 401-413) (*see* Appendix B for the full text of this Act). The Rivers and Harbors Act generally authorizes the Corps to protect commerce in navigable streams and waterways, with three sections addressing permit authority—

> ► Section 9 requires a permit from the Corps for the construction of a dike or dam in navigable waters of the United States.

> ► Section 10 requires a permit from the Corps for any obstruction to 'the navigable capacity of any waters of the United States' (including the placement of piers or the activities of dredging, filling, and other construction activities).

> ► Section 13 requires a permit from the Corps for the discharge of 'any refuse matter of any kind' into any navigable water of the United States.

Before the CWA was enacted in 1972, questions arose as to whether the Corps, under the authority of the Rivers and Harbors Act, could deny issuance of permits on the basis of the public interest in wildlife resources, and whether, under Section 13 of the Rivers and Harbors Act, the Corps could prosecute dischargers of pollution (such as industrial waste) for unpermitted discharges into United States navigable waters.

In 1968–as a result of the Fish and Wildlife Coordination Act's (16 USC 662) direction that federal agencies involved in the alteration of a water body consult with the U.S. Fish and Wildlife Service (USFWS) for assistance in the conservation of wildlife resources–the Corps adopted regulations to include a public interest review standard for issuance of permits under the Rivers and Harbors Act. The courts upheld the Corps' public interest review standard when they upheld Corps denial of a Section 10 permit because of fish and wildlife concerns (*Zabel v. Tabb*, 430 F.2d 199 [5th Cir. 1970]; *cert. denied*, 401 U.S. 910 [1972]).

USFWS = U.S. Fish and Wildlife Service

In 1970, the National Environmental Policy Act (NEPA) expanded the scope of the Corps' analysis of the environmental effects of its permit actions. Finally in 1972, after many years of contention about the proper scope of Corps authority to review project effects, Congress passed the CWA. Over time, this act has resolved questions about Corps jurisdiction over wetlands and has proven to be the leading regulatory authority of the federal government to oversee activities in wetlands.

NEPA = National Environmental Policy Act

Rivers and Harbors Act of 1899

Corps jurisdiction under the Rivers and Harbors Act of 1899 (33 USC 401-413) is limited to those activities affecting the navigable waters of the United States. According to the Corps' current regulations implementing the Rivers and Harbors Act, navigable waters of the United States are defined as those waters subject to the ebb and flow of the tide shoreward to the mean high water mark and/or those that are presently used, have been used in the past, or may be susceptible to use to transport interstate or foreign commerce (33 CFR 329.4). (*See* chapter 3 for a detailed discussion of the boundaries of the Corps' jurisdiction under the Rivers and Harbors Act).

Intermittent stream in spring, Sonoma County.

To a great extent the regulatory authority of the Corps under the Rivers and Harbors Act of 1899 has been superseded by the CWA. The jurisdiction of the Corps under the CWA overlaps and extends beyond the geographic scope of its jurisdiction under the Rivers and Harbors Act; therefore, when discussing Corps regulatory authority over wetlands, the Rivers and Harbors Act of 1899 will generally be of little consequence. Corps permit authority under the Rivers and Harbors Act of 1899, however, is not subject to EPA oversight or any other restrictions specific to the CWA, and, in some cases–such as with certain exemptions under the CWA–the Rivers and Harbors Act alone will apply to wetland activities.

Clean Water Act

The Clean Water Act is primarily intended to authorize the EPA to regulate water quality through the restriction of pollution discharges.

The CWA is primarily intended to authorize the EPA to regulate water quality through the restriction of pollution discharges. Sections 301 and 402 of the CWA prohibit the discharge of all pollution unless permitted under the National Pollution Discharge Elimination System, by EPA, or by a state with a federally approved control program (33 USC 1311, 1342). The authority of EPA under the CWA to regulate all 'pollution' activities affecting the waters of the United States is modified by Section 404. The Corps in Section 404 retains the principal authority to regulate discharges of dredged or fill material into waters of the United States (33 USC 1344). Under the CWA, however, EPA has a specific oversight role over the Corps' authority.

The Corps in Section 404 retains the principal authority to regulate discharges of dredged or fill material into waters of the United States (33 USC 1344).

Because the CWA authorizes only the EPA to prosecute dischargers of pollution, the Corps does not have the authority to prosecute polluters under the Rivers and Harbors Act of 1899. The Corps does have the authority under the CWA or Rivers and Harbors Act to regulate activities involving obstructions to navigable waters of the United States and, under the CWA, discharges of dredged or fill material into waters of the United States. The following section presents the framework of Section 404 and the extension of the Corps' CWA jurisdiction to wetlands.

Section 404 of the Clean Water Act

This section describes the general provisions of Section 404 and the development of the jurisdictional boundaries that make up those definitions. (*See* chapter 3 for definitions of 'waters of the United States' and 'wetlands' as regulated by the CWA.)

Section 404 Program

Section 404 (Appendix A) specifically delegates certain authorities to the Corps and EPA, which include–

> ▶ Section 404(a), authorizing the Corps to issue permits, after notice and opportunity for comment, for the discharge of dredged or fill material into waters of the United States at specified disposal sites.

▶ Section 404(b), requiring that the Corps issue permits under Section 404 in compliance with guidelines developed by EPA (commonly known as EPA's 'Section 404(b)(1) Guidelines', requiring that the Corps issue a permit only in the absence of practicable alternatives to the proposed discharge that would have less adverse impacts on the aquatic ecosystem).

▶ Section 404(c), authorizing the EPA to veto a Corps decision to issue a permit allowing for the discharge of dredged or fill material if that discharge "will have an unacceptable adverse effect on municipal water supplies, shellfish beds and fishery areas, wildlife, or recreational areas."

Although Section 404 of the CWA gives the Corps direct authority over proposed discharges of dredged or fill material into waters of the United States, EPA plays a significant role in developing regulations with which the Corps must comply and in reviewing the issuance of the permit by the Corps. Beyond the 404(b)(1) process and 404(c) veto authority, EPA has promulgated regulations governing implementation of Section 404 that parallel Corps regulations.

The following is a discussion of the jurisdictional boundaries of Section 404, consistent with Corps and EPA regulations, as it relates to the terms 'waters of the United States' and 'disposal of dredged or fill material' and how various parts of Section 404 pertain to the Corps' permit process.

Jurisdictional Limits of Waters of the United States

In general, federal regulatory authority over the states and private property is derived from the interstate commerce clause of the U.S. Constitution. In addition to traditional navigable waters, 'waters of the United States' is currently defined to include all 'other waters', such as intrastate lakes, rivers, streams (including intermittent streams), mudflats, sandflats, wetlands, sloughs, prairie potholes, wet meadows, playa lakes, or natural ponds, and wetlands adjacent to any waters of the United States (other than waters that are themselves wetlands) *the use [or] degradation of which could affect interstate or foreign commerce* (33 CFR 328.3, 40 CFR 230.3[s]). (*See* chapter 3 for regulatory definitions of wetlands and other waters, and see Appendix C for Corps regulations.)

Freshwater marsh in winter, Sacramento County. Recreational use of wetlands can adversely affect wildlife but is also important to the development of public appreciation for wetlands.

Historically, federal regulatory authority over waterways was restricted to navigable waters (those that might carry foreign or interstate commerce) and not necessarily wetlands. Because the CWA does not use the word 'wetlands', to understand how Corps jurisdiction applies, it is necessary to understand how the term 'navigable waters' (originally used in Section 404[a] of the CWA) is related to 'waters of the United States' (as used in regulatory and judicial interpretations of the CWA), and how it is related to interstate and foreign commerce.

Development of Definition of 'Waters of the United States' through the Courts. Corps jurisdiction under the Rivers and Harbors Act of 1899 is limited to navigable waters of the United States (those waters subject to the ebb and flow of the tide and/or those that have been or could be used to transport interstate or foreign commerce). Therefore, the initial Section 404 regulations issued after 1972, governing the jurisdiction of the Corps, interpreted the CWA's directive to remain within the jurisdictional limits of the Rivers and Harbors Act.

NRDC = National Resources Defense Council

In 1975, the Natural Resources Defense Council (NRDC) challenged the Corps' limitation of Section 404 jurisdiction in federal court. Agreeing with the NRDC, the district court ordered the Corps to revise its regulations to reflect the full regulatory mandate of the CWA. In an attempt to regulate the discharge of pollutants on small, nonnavigable tributaries, the court stated that Congress, through the CWA, had asserted overall federal jurisdiction over the 'waters of the United States'.

Although the language of the CWA indicated that this term was to be equated with 'navigable waters of the United States', the court held that the mandate of the CWA was to greatly expand the federal jurisdiction to the maximum extent permissible under the commerce clause

Although the language of the CWA indicated that this term was to be equated with 'navigable waters of the United States' (*see* definition in chapter 3), the court held that the mandate of the CWA was to greatly expand the federal jurisdiction to the maximum extent permissible under the commerce clause (*National Resources Defense Council [NRDC] v. Callaway*, 392 F. Supp. 685 [D.D.C. 1975]). In 1975, Corps regulations were revised to be consistent with this decision.

Another court decision in the 1970s interpreting the extent of the CWA's authority affected Corps jurisdiction over the placement of dredged or fill material into waters of the United States. In *United States v. Holland*, 373 F. Supp. 665 (M.D. Fla. 1974), decided prior to *NRDC v. Callaway*, the court concluded that the CWA extended federal jurisdiction to all waters that might affect commerce, without regard to traditional navigability. The court held that tidelands are considered 'waters of the United States' and should be regulated under the CWA (including Section 404 as regulated by the Corps), even though the discharge activity in question was beyond the mean high water mark and therefore beyond traditional navigable waters. According to the Corps' current regulations implementing the CWA, wetlands are an integral part of the definition of waters of the United States (33 CFR 328.3). The CWA's jurisdiction is directly related to whether the area in question falls within the definition of a wetland. (*See* chapter 3 for the federal definition of wetlands.)

Flood control channel, Fresno County. Channelized waterways typically support little or no wetland habitat because the banks are too steep and maintenance is often conducted to remove vegetation.

Relation to Interstate Commerce. As for the relation of its jurisdiction over wetlands to interstate commerce, Corps regulations state that wetlands are considered waters of the United States when their use, degradation, or destruction could affect interstate or foreign commerce.

Although the Corps, when making a jurisdictional determination, does not consistently consider the link of wetlands to interstate or foreign commerce, courts have upheld at least the times where Corps jurisdiction could be linked directly to interstate commerce. In *Avoyelles Sportsmen's League, Inc. v. Marsh*, 715 F.2d 897 (5th Cir. 1983), the court upheld the Corps' assertion that because the forested land in question (on which certain land clearing and discharge activities were planned) was subject to the average annual flood in a river basin it is considered waters of the United States and is regulated under Section 404 of the CWA. The court held that vegetation "typically adapted for life in saturated soils" is not limited to species surviving their entire life cycle in saturated soils. Therefore, even though the forested land did not resemble typical wetland traits it could still be proven to be waters of the United States.

The Supreme Court has also definitively addressed the question of the limits of Corps jurisdictional boundaries. In *United States v. Riverside Bayview Homes*, 474 U.S. 121 (1985), the Supreme Court upheld the Corps' interpretation that waters of the United States include adjacent wetlands. According to its regulations, the Corps considers low-lying, marshy land next to a navigable water to be an adjacent wetland and therefore a water of the United States. Its determination for the area in question was based on the vegetation, saturated soils, and hydrologic connection to adjacent navigable waters of the marshy land, even though the land was not subject to flooding by adjacent navigable waters.

The Supreme Court held that Corps regulations clearly state that "saturation by either surface or ground water is sufficient to bring an area within the category of wetlands, provided that the saturation is sufficient to and does support wetland vegetation" and that this regulation is consistent with the Congressional intent of the CWA, demonstrating the "evident breadth of concern for protection of water quality and aquatic ecosystems."

Following the Supreme Court's approval of the Corps' broad assertion of federal jurisdiction in *Riverside Bayview*, lower courts have approved the extension of the Corps' CWA jurisdiction over isolated wetlands and water bodies if a functional link between the wetlands and interstate commerce exists (that is, if there is evidence that the activity affecting the wetland would affect interstate commerce). Waters of the United States under the Corps' CWA jurisdiction have been interpreted to include–

Following the Supreme Court's approval of the Corps' broad assertion of federal jurisdiction in Riverside Bayview, *lower courts have approved the extension of the Corps' CWA jurisdiction over isolated wetlands if there is evidence that the activity would affect interstate commerce.*

- ▶ Usually dry arroyos with only occasional surface flows (in *Quiviera Mining Company v. United States Environmental Protection Agency*, 765 F.2d 126 [10th Cir. 1985])

- ▶ An isolated lake (in *Utah v. Marsh*, 740 F.2d 799 [10th Cir. 1984])

- ▶ An isolated wetland (in *National Wildlife Federation v. Laubscher* [*Pond 12*,], 662 F. Supp. 548 [S.D. Tex. 1987])

- ▶ Wetlands adjacent to a recreational lake used by interstate travelers (in *United States v. Byrd*, 609 F.2d 1204 [7th Cir. 1979]; *Bailey v. U.S.*, 647 F. Supp. 44 [D. Idaho 1986])

- ▶ Private lands flooded by releases from a federal dam (in *Swanson v. United States*, 789 F.2d 1368 [9th Cir. 1986])

- ▶ A mangrove forest (in *United States v. Rivera Torres*, 656 F. Supp. 251 [D.P.R. 1987])

- ▶ Hardwood bottomland (in *United States v. Larkins*, 852 F.2d 189 [6th Cir. 1988])

- ▶ Wetlands connected to waters of the U.S. by artificial ditches (in *United States v. Hobbs*, 32 ERC 2091 [E.D. Va. 1990])

- ▶ An artificially created wetland (in *United States v. Ciampitti*, 583 F. Supp. 483 [D. N.J. 1984]; *United States v. Akers*, 651 F. Supp. 320 [E.D. Cal. 1987]; *Leslie Salt Co. v. United States*, 896 F.2d 354 [9th Cir. 1990]; *cert. denied*, 498 U.S. 1126 [1991]; *see below*)

Isolated Wetlands. As a general rule, the Corps, in the spirit of *NRDC v. Callaway and Riverside Bayview Homes*, extends its jurisdiction over wetlands beyond 'adjacent wetlands' and regulates the discharge of dredged or fill material into wetlands that do not have a link to other waters of the United States. These isolated wetlands are considered waters of the United States because the use, degradation, or destruction of these wetlands could affect interstate or foreign commerce. The rule, as generally applied, would allow the Corps to assert jurisdiction over isolated wetlands that goes beyond traditional notions of 'commerce' and even extends to areas that have the potential to be used as habitat for migratory birds (the rationale being that migratory birds are considered interstate foreign commerce because of links to recreation and other industries, and therefore if an activity is in a wetland that could be habitat to a migratory bird the activity could affect interstate or foreign commerce). In effect, this rule would allow the Corps to regulate any wetland that meets the Corps' delineation criteria.

Whether this policy will be the formal Corps practice when making jurisdictional determinations remains to be seen. As evidenced in the sidebar discussion of isolated wetlands, although the most recent court case seems to side with the Corps, the circuit courts have not yet given clear guidance on whether the potential for habitat of migratory birds is a sufficient link to the commerce clause.

Prior Converted Cropland and Farmed Wetlands. Another question about the definition of wetlands centers on its application to areas that have been under agricultural production. Specifically, the issue concerns the precise meaning of 'normal circumstances' as it applies to disturbed wetlands (ones that have been farmed). In August 1993, the Corps issued a final regulation clarifying that 'prior converted cropland' is not subject to Section 404 jurisdiction (58 FR 45008). Prior converted cropland is generally defined–consistent with the Soil Conservation Service 'Swampbuster' program–as wetlands that before December 23, 1985, were cropped and manipulated to remove excess water such that inundation lasts no more than 14 consecutive days during the growing season. Essentially, prior converted croplands have been effectively drained or filled and no longer exhibit wetland characteristics. In contrast, farmed wetlands might

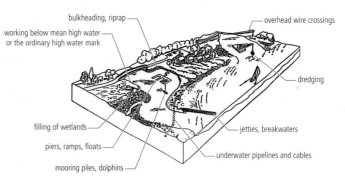

Figure 4-1. Diagram of examples of activities requiring a Corps permit under Section 404 of the CWA and Section 10 of the River and Harbors Act. From a flyer printed by the San Francisco Corps office.

Essentially, prior converted croplands have been effectively drained or filled and no longer exhibit wetland characteristics. In contrast, farmed wetlands might revert to full wetland function with cessation of farming activities.

Regulation of Isolated Wetlands and the Migratory Bird Test

The issue of regulating isolated wetlands began in 1985 when the Corps issued a memorandum listing several factors which connected a wetland to interstate commerce, thereby bringing it under the jurisdiction of the CWA. In this memorandum the Corps asserted jurisdiction over those isolated wetlands "which are or *could be used as* habitat by migratory birds that cross state lines" and therefore could be linked to interstate commerce [emphasis added]. This criterion became known as the 'migratory bird' test.

In 1989, the memorandum was challenged as a violation of the federal Administrative Procedures Act (APA) because no notice and opportunity to comment on this 'agency rule' had been provided to the public. In *Tabb Lakes v. United States*, 10 F.3d 796 (4th Cir. 1989) the circuit court agreed, holding that the memorandum was agency rulemaking, which needed to go through proper APA procedures. The court found that this memorandum did not qualify as an "interpretative rule or general policy statement as under the recognized exception to the requirements of [the APA]." The Corps, therefore, was found to lack jurisdiction in applying the migratory bird test to require a Section 404 permit.

Neither the Corps nor the EPA, which has the ultimate authority to determine the extent of CWA jurisdiction, has gone through the notice and comment procedures required by the APA concerning the migratory bird issue. Although the Fourth Circuit ruling is only applicable to Corps decisions in that particular geographic region of the southeast, in practice some districts of the Corps are avoiding the issue altogether. Whether wetlands that *could* be used by migratory birds would be enough of a link to interstate commerce to assert CWA jurisdiction is not clear. In practice, these districts assert jurisdiction

revert to full wetland function with cessation of farming activities (Corps Regulatory Guidance Letter 90-7). (*See also* Appendix H.)

Discharge of Dredged or Fill Material

Section 404 of the CWA prohibits the discharge of dredged or fill material into the waters of the United States, including wetlands, without a permit from the Corps. The following section presents only when there is a positive link to isolated wetlands which *are, in fact,* used by migratory birds that cross state lines.

Some consider the 1990 ruling in the *Leslie Salt* case to have resolved this issue. In *Leslie Salt Co. v. United States,* 896 F.2d 354 (9th Cir. 1990); *cert. denied,* 498 U.S. 1126 (1991), the court held that "the Commerce Clause and thus the CWA is broad enough to extend the Corps' jurisdiction to local waters which potentially provide habitat to migratory birds and endangered species." The California landowner petitioned the Supreme Court to decide whether the Corps had jurisdiction over isolated, nonnavigable bodies of water on its property. The landowner had argued that "once the [CWA] was held to authorize regulation of non-navigable isolated sites, it is very difficult to hold agencies to any strict line distinguishing between land and water." However, in February 1991, the Supreme Court declined to consider the landowner's appeal and let the Ninth Circuit decision stand.

This issue again came into play with an Illinois developer in *Hoffman Homes, Inc. v. Administrator, United States Environmental Protection Agency,* 961 F.2d 1310 (7th Cir. 1992), *rehearing granted and opinion vacated,* 975 F.2d 1554 (1992). The Seventh Circuit reached the opposite conclusion to the Leslie Salt case, holding that neither the CWA nor the Commerce Clause authorizes regulation of isolated wetlands. Later in 1992, without explanation, the Seventh Circuit set aside the *Hoffman Homes* opinion. To further confuse the issue, in 1993 the Seventh Circuit held that EPA was authorized to issue regulations giving it authority over isolated wetlands based on their potential effect on interstate commerce; the court, however, ruled that EPA had improperly imposed a $50,000 administrative penalty on a developer under the facts of the case *Hoffman Homes, Inc. v. Administrator, United States Environmental Protection Agency,* 999 F.2d 256 (7th Cir. 1993).

the definition of 'discharge of dredged or fill material' and examples of what is considered a 'discharge' activity subject to regulation under Section 404.

Clean Water Act Definition. In general, the CWA prohibits the discharge of any pollutant without a permit. Implicit in its definition of 'pollutant' is dredged and fill material regulated by Section 404 (33

Section 404 regulates the placement of materials into waters of the United States, including wetlands.

The Corps has interpreted the term 'discharge' broadly to include the secondary effects that may involve only very small discharges of material.

USC 1362). 'Discharge' of a pollutant is defined as the addition of any pollutant to waters of the United States from any point source (33 USC 1362).

Section 404 regulates the placement of materials into waters of the United States, including wetlands. The discharge of 'dredged material' typically means adding into waters of the United States materials that were removed from waters of the United States. The discharge of 'fill material' typically means adding into waters of the United States materials (such as concrete, dirt, rock, pilings, or side cast material) that are for the purpose or have the effect of either replacing an aquatic area with dry land or raising the elevation of an aquatic area.

The Corps has interpreted the term 'discharge' broadly to include not only the direct placement of materials into wetlands, but also the secondary effects from what is typically considered a dredging or removal activity that may involve only very small discharges of dredged or fill material. In August 1993, the Corps clarified its position regarding 'discharges' as part of the settlement agreement to a case brought by an environmental group (*North Carolina Wildlife Federation v. Tulloch* [E.D.N.C. 1992, Civil No. C90-713-CIV-5-BO. 58 Federal Register 45008, August 25, 1993; 33 C.F.R. Sec. 323.2(d)(1)]).

The August 1993 regulation, known as the 'excavation rule', clarifies that incidental redeposition of material (such as soil and rock) associated with mechanized land clearing, ditching, channelization, and other excavation activities which destroy or degrade wetlands or other waters of the United States are considered discharges of dredged or fill material and are therefore subject to Section 404 regulation. Excluded from regulation are discharges that have only minimal environmental effects. However, the burden is on the proposed discharger to prove that the effects of the discharge will be minimal. Certain activities are not considered discharge activities, including certain types of land clearing. An activity that involves only the cutting or removal of vegetation above the ground, where the root system is not substantially disturbed or where no mechanized pushing, dragging, or similar activities that redeposit excavated materials are involved, is not considered a discharge of dredged or fill material. (33 CFR 323.2[d][2].) A discharge by a wheeled or tracked vehicle while cutting

Urban encroachment and channelization of a stream, Santa Clara County.

vegetation off above ground may, however, be sufficient to be considered a discharge activity regulated by Section 404.

As part of the *Tulloch* settlement agreement, the Corps also clarified that the placement of pilings to construct structures in waters of the United States is subject to Section 404 regulation when that placement has the effect of a discharge of fill material (58 FR 45008, August 25, 1993; 33 CFR 323.3[c]). Examples include projects where the placement of pilings are so close that sedimentation rates increase or the bottom of the water body is effectively replaced. Applying this standard, linear projects constructed on pilings–such as bridges, piers, and power line towers–generally will not have the physical effect of fill material and will not be regulated under Section 404. This determination is, however, made by the Corps and EPA, on a case-by-case basis.

Examples of Regulated Activities. In addition to the common types of discharges, the following are some examples of activities that the courts have upheld as constituting a 'discharge of pollutants' (and therefore a 'discharge of dredged or fill material')–

- ▶ Redeposit of spoil dredged by boat propellers (in *United States v. M.C.C. of Florida, Inc.*, 772 F.2d 1501 [11th Cir. 1985]; *vacated on other grounds*, 481 U.S. 1034 [1987]; *on remand*, 848 F.2d 1133 [11th Cir. 1988]; *on rehearing*, 863 F.2d 802 [11th Cir. 1988])
- ▶ Land leveling either with earth and vegetative debris or by mechanized activities (in *Avoyelles Sportsmen's League, Inc.*)
- ▶ Removal of vegetation (in *U.S. v. Huebner*, 752 F.2d 1235 [7th Cir. 1985])
- ▶ Nonestablished farming activities (in *U.S. v. Larkins*, 657 F. Supp. 76 [W.D. Ky. 1987]; *Huebner*; *Avoyelles Sportsmen's League, Inc.*)
- ▶ Filling in and grading or changing the bottom elevations of a body of water (in *U.S. v. Zanger*, 91 Daily Journal D.A.R. 8445 [N.D. Ca. 1991])

Exemptions

Certain activities are specifically exempt from Section 404 permit requirements.

Exemptions under Section 404(f). The only outright exemptions to the Corp permit requirements contained in Section 404 for discharges are listed in Section 404(f). The following activities are exempted from regulation under Section 404–

The only outright exemptions to the Corps permit requirements contained in Section 404 for discharges are listed in Section 404(f).

- ▶ Normal farming, ranching, and forestry activities, such as plowing, minor draining, and harvesting
- ▶ Constructing and maintaining stock ponds or irrigation ditches, or maintaining drainage ditches
- ▶ Constructing or maintaining farm, forest, or mining roads
- ▶ Maintaining or reconstructing structures that are currently serviceable
- ▶ Constructing temporary sedimentation basins on uplands
- ▶ Activities regulated by an approved best management practices program authorized by Section 208(b)(4) of the CWA

A 'recapture' of regulatory authority from these exemptions is provided in Section 404(f)(2). The recapture provision states that the exemptions under Section 404(f) do not apply if the activity would violate toxic effluent standards or constitute a new use impairing the flow, circulation, or reach of waters. Although the Corps initially determines whether the activities fall under Section 404(f), EPA has ultimate administrative authority over the interpretation. The change in use of agricultural lands has been frequently used by the Corps to invoke the recapture clause for the normal farming activities exemption.

Exempted normal silviculture, farming, and ranching activities have been narrowly construed by the courts to allow exemptions from the Section 404 permitting process only when they are part of 'ongoing, normal operations' (in *Bayou Marcus Livestock v. United States Environmental Protection Agency* [N.D. Fla. 1989], *Larkins, Avoyelles, Huebner,* and *Akers*). Activities cannot be related to preparing the property for new uses separate from ongoing silviculture or agriculture operations (in *United States v. Johnson,* 891 F.2d 287 [4th Cir. 1989]). Therefore, the exemption does not apply to converting wetlands to new farmland or grazed land to farmland but does cover conventional rotation of fields, which may leave an area lying fallow for a season. (*See* Appendix I.)

Wildlife viewing in riparian forest, Sacramento County.

Exemptions under Section 404(r). Section 404(r) of the CWA exempts a narrow class of federal activities from Section 404 permit requirements. The activities under this exemption must be part of a specific, congressionally authorized, federal construction project. Furthermore, before authorization and funding, the federal agency must submit to Congress an environmental impact statement, prepared pursuant to NEPA, that includes consideration of the EPA's Section 404(b)(1) Guidelines.

Department of the Army Permit Requirements

In California, the Corps' permit process under the CWA currently applies to all activities that are regulated by Section 404. This process could change, however, if California were to assume the authority for administering a portion or all of the Section 404 program. (*See* chapter 5 for a discussion of California wetland regulations and the potential for state assumption of the Section 404 program.) Under Section 404(g), qualified states may apply to EPA to assume administration of the Section 404 program, except for navigable waters.

Two types of permits, individual and general permits, are issued by the Corps that allow for the deposit of dredged or fill material into waters of the United States, including wetlands. These permits are generally referred to as '404', 'wetlands', or 'fill' permits. However, the official title of a Corps-issued permit under Section 404 of the CWA and Section 10 of the Rivers and Harbors Act of 1899 is a 'Department of the Army' or 'DA' permit.

DA = Department of the Army

Individual permits required by the Corps for specific activities may be issued only after an individual application is submitted and the formal review process is complete (*see* Figure 4-2). The minimum time necessary for the Corps to process an individual permit is 60 days; however, processing a complicated individual permit (one involving a complex project, public controversy, or significant environmental impacts) may take two years or more.

General permits are prior-authorized permits (in certain circumstances notification requirements must be met) for specified categories of activities on a state, regional, or national basis. General permits are issued to cover those activities with minimal impacts on aquatic resources and require minimal time, if any, for Corps review. Nationwide permits are a type of general permit (*see* Figure 4-3). As described below, activities authorized under either an individual or general permit require compliance with Corp Section 404 regulations, EPA Section 404(b)(1) Guidelines, NEPA, the federal Endangered Species Act, Section 106 of the National Historic Preservation Act, Section 401 of the CWA, and the Coastal Zone Management Act. Actions authorized under a general permit, however, are presumed to have completed NEPA review and 404(b)(1) compliance when the general permit was issued.

General permits are prior-authorized permits (in certain circumstances notification requirements must be met) for specified categories of activities on a state, regional, or national basis.

Nationwide permits are a type of general permit.

Although Corps permit procedures are specified under both Corps and EPA Section 404 regulations (33 CFR 323, 40 CFR 230) (*see* Appendices C and D), the nuances of the permit process are sometimes subjective and dependent on the particular Corps district

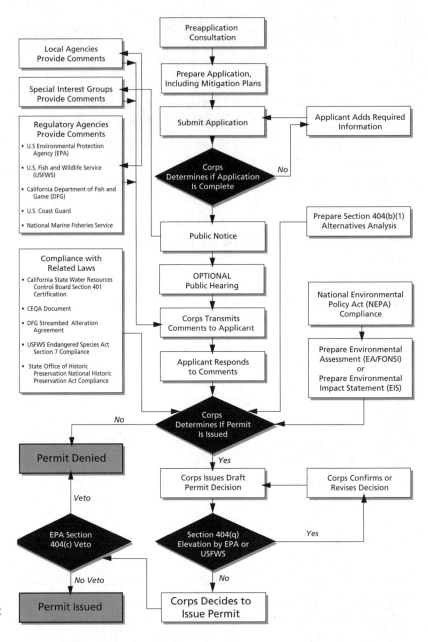

Figure 4-2. Section 404 Individual Permit Process Flow Chart.

and Corps permit manager. California is divided into three Corps districts: Los Angeles, San Francisco, and Sacramento, each administered by a District Engineer (*see* Figure 4-4). The district with permit authority is determined by the location of the activity in relation to district boundaries. If the activity is on the boundary between two districts or occurs over a large area falling within two different districts, both districts should be notified to determine which will have authority (only one district will retain permit authority over the project).

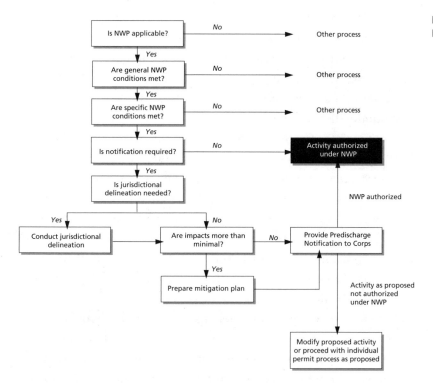

Figure 4-3. Approach to the Nationwide Permit Process.

Jurisdictional Determination

If wetlands may be affected by a proposed activity, the first step in the permitting process is to determine the boundaries of jurisdictional waters of the United States, including wetlands, on the project site. A project proponent must obtain a permit from the Corps only if the proposed activity would involve the deposit of dredged or fill material *into wetlands or other waters of the United States*; therefore, it is best for the project proponent to obtain a verified jurisdictional determination from the Corps before filing an application for a permit. Also, depending on the activity, amount of fill, and the location and acreage of wetlands affected, the project proponent may be able to modify the design to avoid either the requirements of Section 404 completely, or qualify for a general permit.

Although the Corps is ultimately responsible for the wetlands determination, due to Corps staffing and funding limitations the project proponent typically performs the preliminary delineation to determine the Section 404 jurisdictional boundaries. Data forms and a map should be submitted to the Corps with a request for verification. The regulatory staff of the Corps typically performs a field review. After any required adjustments are incorporated into the delineation, the Corps supplies the project proponent with a verification letter confirming the jurisdictional boundaries on the project site.

Figure 4-4. Corps Districts in California.

Preapplication Meeting

The regulatory branch of the Corps may be contacted at any time to answer questions about Corps jurisdiction over a project site or proposed activity (*see* Appendix O for addresses and telephone numbers of the Corps offices in California). Although not required, a preapplication meeting with the Corps, EPA, and USFWS (and, as appropriate, the National Marine Fisheries Service [NMFS], California Department of Fish and Game, other relevant state resource agencies, and local and regional agencies with authority over land use at the project location) is encouraged to allow the attending resource agencies to contribute information that may expedite the permit process. At this meeting the project proponent may be informed of modifications or mitigation features that may be required to be incorporated into the project design as part of the Corps' formal application process.

Before scheduling this meeting, a project proponent should have an accurate wetland delineation and be fairly certain that a permit may be required. At least ten days prior to the meeting, the proponent should provide a summary of the project to the Corps, EPA, USFWS, and other appropriate resource agencies. The project proponent is required to attend the preapplication meeting to present (not sell) the proposed project and to receive any response the attending agencies might have regarding technical or procedural problems with the proposed project. After the meeting, the project proponent should be better informed about the requirements for an individual permit and the project's potential environmental effects.

Definition of Discharge Activity Area

Any activity that adversely affects wetlands or other waters of the United States and involves placement, no matter how small the amount, of dredged or fill material into jurisdictional areas is considered a discharge, and the Corps will require a permit under Section 404 before commencement of that activity. For actions with minor effects on wetlands, a general permit (for example, nationwide permits) may have already been issued by the Corps authorizing the activity.

The EPA Section 404(b)(1) Guidelines (Appendix D) and the Corps' and EPA's Memorandum of Agreement (MOA) (Appendix G) on wetlands mitigation require that a project proponent, when entering the market for a suitable project site, should assess alternative available sites to determine on which site the project could be completed with the least amount of adverse impacts on

NMFS = National Marine Fisheries Service

Any activity that adversely affects wetlands or other waters of the United States and involves placement of dredged or fill material into jurisdictional areas is considered a discharge, and the Corps will require a Section 404 permit before commencement of that activity.

MOA = Memorandum of Agreement

wetlands and other waters of the United States. In practice, the analysis of alternative sites is usually conducted after a project site has been chosen and rarely at the time of market entry, putting the project proponent at risk of the Corps denying the permit. The Section 404(b)(1) Guidelines and the Corps' and EPA's MOA require that projects should avoid or minimize negative effects on wetlands. According to the MOA, the proper sequence of mitigation priority in project design is to–

▶ First, avoid adverse effects on wetlands

▶ Second, if avoiding adverse effects is not practicable, minimize effects on wetlands to the extent practicable

▶ Third, compensate for those impacts on wetlands that are unavoidable

If the discharge activities cannot avoid the jurisdictional areas, the project proponent should, according to EPA Section 404(b)(1) Guidelines and the MOA on wetlands mitigation, strive to minimize disturbance to 'special aquatic sites' (*see* description in chapter 3), and amount of acreage affected within the jurisdictional boundaries. The type of discharge activity and the number of acres involved could allow the project to be authorized under a general permit, such as a nationwide permit with a reduced permitting process (*see* discussion below under 'general permits'). Also, reduction in the amount of jurisdictional acreage affected will reduce the amount of mitigation required by the Corps.

Tidal mudflat habitat at San Francisco Bay, Santa Clara County. Mudflats are waters of the United States, but, because they are not vegetated, mudflats are not considered wetlands under the Corps definition. Mudflats are special aquatic sites designated in EPA's Section 404(b)(1) Guidelines.

Individual Permit Application

After consulting with the Corps and reviewing the regulations, the project proponent should know whether the proposed activity is subject to a Corps individual permit, general permit, or no permit requirements (*see* Figures 4-2 and 4-3). Individual permits require submission of an individual application and compliance with the Corps' formal review process. This process provides opportunities for public notice and comment; requires preparation of an alternatives analysis as required by EPA Section 404(b)(1) Guidelines and NEPA; and requires compliance with NEPA's environmental review process. The Corps' decision to issue an individual permit is based on an evaluation of probable impacts of the proposed activity, analyzed according to section 404(b)(1) Guidelines, and the effect the proposed activity will have on the public interest.

Individual permits may be issued before or, in certain circumstances, after a discharge occurs. Permits issued after the unpermitted discharge has occurred, called 'after-the-fact' permits,

Permits issued after the unpermitted discharge has occurred, called 'after-the-fact' permits, may allow the fill to remain with implementation of conditions issued by the Corps.

may allow the fill to remain with implementation of conditions issued by the Corps. However, if the Corps determines through the individual permit process that a permit should not be issued, it can require that the unpermitted fill be removed. Performing fill activities prior to application to the Corps is not encouraged and can lead to both civil and criminal penalties (*see* discussion on enforcement below).

The Corps permit requirement applies to all private, state, and federal entities other than the Corps. Although it does not literally issue permits to itself (that is, the regulatory branch does not review an application submitted by the engineering branch), the Corps is required to comply with the same laws that apply to applicants for Corps permits.

The application for a permit to discharge dredged or fill material into waters of the United States, including wetlands, must include–

- ▶ Location, purpose of, and need for the proposed project (all reasonably related activities should be included in the same permit application)
- ▶ Purpose of the activities involving the discharge of dredged or fill material and the type and quantity of material to be discharged
- ▶ Drawings, sketches, or plans sufficient for public notice (usually all submittals must be 8½" by 11" with a 1" border; detailed engineering drawings are typically not required)
- ▶ Schedule of project activities
- ▶ Names and addresses of owners of all adjoining property
- ▶ Locations and dimensions of adjacent structures
- ▶ Authorizations required by other federal, interstate, state, or local agencies for the work (including all approvals or denials already received)
- ▶ Additional specific information for activities involving the construction of structures for certain improvements, such as compliance with dam safety criteria

When wetland impacts are expected, the Corps typically requires mitigation; therefore, permit applications will often include a proposed mitigation plan for agency review.

When wetland impacts are expected, the Corps typically requires mitigation; therefore, permit applications will often include a proposed mitigation plan for agency review. The application should contain sufficient information to demonstrate compliance with the EPA 404(b)(1) Guidelines, although at the start of the permit process this also is not required. Application fees, assessed only if the permit is granted, are $10 for non-commercial projects and $100 for commercial projects (as of January 1, 1994). Requirements for an individual permit application are specified by regulation (33 CFR 325), but the application form itself may vary somewhat among districts. Therefore, obtaining an application from the local Corps district is advisable.

Public Notice/Hearings. Corps regulations require that, within 15 days of receiving the permit application, the district must either notify the applicant of any additional information necessary to make the application complete or prepare and distribute a public notice. The Corps may issue a public notice even if all the information (for example, the mitigation plan or alternatives analysis) is not submitted with the application. In practice, the Corps does not usually meet the 15-day deadline for issuing a public notice.

The public notice contains the information submitted in the permit application. Typically, the public notice contains sufficient relevant information about the project necessary to facilitate comments on the issuance of a permit. Further details may be obtained from the Corps district's project manager or project proponent's contact listed on the public notice.

The public notice is sent to the district's mailing list for all notices (including EPA, USFWS, NMFS, and other interested federal and state agencies), those listed as owners of adjoining property, and any others requesting notice. After issuing a public notice, the Corps must allow a minimum of 15 to a maximum of 30 days for comment. If the circumstances justify extension, the Corps can grant another 30 days. This often is granted if the review agencies request extension and justify the request. When responding to a public notice, the comment should always identify the subject activity by stating the application and file number.

The comment may include a request for a public hearing. The Corps may decide internally, or based on a written request, that a public hearing is necessary. Although formal guidelines do not say when to hold a public hearing, and the presence of a request does not require that one be held, the Corps will usually grant requests for hearings with sufficient demonstration of general public interest from responses to the public notice. At least 30 days prior to the hearing, the Corps will issue a notice of the time, place, and date and any additional information available pertaining to the permit application. Hearings are informal and nonadversarial. The presiding officer may ask questions, although cross-examination is

Wet montane meadow dominated by corn lily in the Sierra Nevada, Placer County.

not permitted. Where possible, the Corps' public hearings can be combined with other required public hearings, such as for compliance with CEQA. Statements made at the hearing are transcribed and become part of the administrative record.

The Corps must consider all comments submitted in response to the public notice and at the public hearing. The Corps transmits the comment letters and comments submitted at the public hearing to the project applicant, who is then given an opportunity to respond.

Substantive Standards for the Corps' Decision. The substantive requirements for the decision by the Corps to issue a permit under Section 404 of the CWA are found in EPA's Section 404(b)(1) Guidelines and the Corps' public interest review regulations. Issuance of conditions or denial of the permit is governed by these standards, and compliance with NEPA may also affect the conditions listed in the permit.

ROD = Record of Decision

The Corps' analysis under EPA guidelines is usually performed simultaneously with its public review process, with an applicant typically supplying much of the information necessary for the Corps to document its findings. The district must prepare a statement of findings, or, when an environmental impact statement is prepared, a record of decision (ROD) on whether to issue or deny the permit. The findings or ROD must include a statement of facts, an analysis indicating conformity with EPA Section 404(b)(1) Guidelines, an environmental assessment or EIS (as required by NEPA), and the views of the district about how the project will affect the public interest.

EPA Section 404(b)(1) Guidelines. Section 404(b) of the CWA directs that permits comply with EPA Section 404(b)(1) Guidelines (Appendix D). These guidelines require that the Corps issue a permit only in the absence of 'practicable' alternatives to the proposed discharge which would have a less adverse impact on the aquatic ecosystem. Nonconformance with EPA's Section 404(b)(1) Guidelines is grounds for permit denial.

Nonconformance with the EPA's Section 404(b)(1) Guidelines is grounds for permit denial.

Compliance with the Section 404(b)(1) guidelines is qualitative and involves excercise of the Corps' judgement in applying the guidelines to a permit application. The guidelines direct that when the proposed activity is not water-dependent, there is a presumption that less damaging practicable upland alternatives exist. The 404(b)(1) section guidelines consider wetlands to be 'special aquatic sites'. (*See* chapter 3 for a discussion of special aquatic sites.) The guidelines apply an additional burden: the presumption that the project is not the least-damaging practicable alternative when special aquatic sites, such as wetlands, are affected. (40 CFR 230.10(a).)

Practicable alternatives are a function of cost, technical, and logistical factors including availability to the project proponent at the time of market entry. If it is otherwise a practicable alternative, an area not presently owned by the applicant that could be reasonably obtained, utilized, expanded, or managed in order to fulfill the basic purpose of the proposed action may be considered an alternative. The applicant bears the burden to demonstrate that no practicable alternatives that will meet the project purpose exist. The selection of alternatives that should be analyzed to select the least damaging practicable alternative is based on the effectiveness of an alternative in meeting the purpose of the project. The Corps does not allow the applicant to define the purpose so narrowly as to eliminate any other alternative. Typically, the applicant must extensively justify the project's purpose and need as well as the selection of the proposed project location as compared to offsite and onsite alternatives. If cost is a factor in defining practicable alternatives, the applicant is required to provide justification of financial commitments and expenditures.

The applicant bears the burden to demonstrate that no practicable alternatives that will meet the project purpose exist.

The following are guidelines from court decisions with regard to practicable alternatives–

► A letter from a realtor claiming that the site was the only one suitable for a project to build two houses and a tennis court is not a sufficient basis to conclude that no alternatives were available (in *Hough v. Marsh*, 557 F. Supp. 74 [D. Mass. 1982]).

► The fact that other sites would offer a less attractive marketing package to purchasers was sufficient to conclude that feasible alternatives were not available (in *National Audubon Society v. Hartz Mountain Development*, 14 EnvH. L. Rep. [Envtl. L. Inst.] 20724 [D. N.J. 1983]).

► The Corp guidelines impose a duty on the Corps to take the permit applicant's objectives into account when considering whether practicable alternatives exist for the proposed project (in *Louisiana Wildlife Federation, Inc. v. York*, 761 F.2d 1044 [5th Cir. 1985]).

► The fact that the project (a log storage and export facility) was water-dependent allowed the preclusion of alternatives because they were too costly or logistically infeasible (in *Friends of the Earth v. Hintz*, 800 F.2d 822 [9th Cir. 1986]).

▶ The Federal Power Act does not preempt the application of the CWA with respect to assessing alternatives to the licensing of a hydroelectric power project. The court stated that Section 404 transmits a "crisp and unwavering message: all significant discharges, whether or not exempt from the permit requirement, must be subjected to Section 404(b)(1) scrutiny." (in *Monongahela Power Company v. Marsh,* 809 F.2d 41 [D.C. Cir. 1987]; *cert. denied,* 484 U. S. 816 [1987]).

▶ The significant additional cost of an alternative may not by itself eliminate it from consideration as a practicable alternative (in *Friends of the Earth v. Hall,* 693 F.Supp. 904 [W.D. Wash. 1988]).

▶ Availability of an alternative is not determined at the time of application, but is determined at least by the time the applicant begins the site-selection process (*see Sweeden's Swamp* case example below).

Beyond proving that the alternative selected is the least environmentally damaging practicable alternative, the Section 404(b)(1) Guidelines further restrict permitting of discharge activities that violate water quality or toxic effluent standards, jeopardize the continued existence of a species listed under the Federal Endangered Species Act, or violate marine sanctuary protections (40 CFR 230.10 (b)). EPA Section 404(b)(1) Guidelines also require certain findings regarding the immediate physical impacts caused by the fill activity. The guidelines prohibit discharges that will "cause or contribute to significant degradation of the waters of the United States." Corps findings should include information about the effect of the fill on the water bottom, water flow and circulation, turbidity, the aquatic ecosystem and organisms, contamination of the water, and downstream resources (40 CFR 230.10 (c)). The Corps is required to deny the issuance of a permit if the findings show that the proposed discharge, even with mitigation, would result in 'significant degradation'.

The project must be implemented in a way that minimizes adverse impacts. EPA Section 404(b)(1) Guidelines state that "no discharge shall be permitted unless appropriate and practicable steps have been taken to minimize potential adverse impacts of the discharge on the aquatic ecosystem." The guidelines set forth standards to minimize various kinds of impacts. These rules apply to the mitigation plan, which should not only include methods to mitigate effects of the discharge, but also methods to compensate

Section 404(b)(1) Guidelines further restrict permitting of discharge activities that violate water quality or toxic effluent standards, jeopardize the continued existence of a species listed under the Federal Endangered Species Act, or violate marine sanctuary protections.

for impacts on wetlands for which no other mitigation is available (40 CFR 230.10 (d)). *See* Corps Regulatory Guidance Letter 93-2 on guidance on flexibility of the 404(b)(1) Guidelines and mitigation banking.

Corps regulations authorize the imposition of permit conditions to mitigate for discharge impacts on wetlands. The NEPA process requires that the Corps, when issuing a permit, disclose and evaluate the effects of the permit decision and alternatives on the environment. This process may also involve the imposition of other conditions that, when applied to the project, would ensure that environmental impacts are mitigated to a less-than-significant level. The Corps typically relies on the opinions of the USFWS and the California Department of Fish and Game to assess the adequacy of the proposed mitigation.

Compliance with NEPA. NEPA, which applies to the Corps' permit decision, requires the Corps to analyze a broad array of environmental effects from the project. Corps procedure is to prepare an environmental assessment (EA) on the potential environmental consequences of the proposed permit decision. Based on the EA, the Corps either issues a finding of no significant impact (FONSI) or an environmental impact statement (EIS). Unless the EA concludes that the action will have a significant effect on the human environment, the Corps prepares a FONSI.

EA = Environmental Assessment

FONSI = Finding of No Significant Impact

EIS = Environmental Impact Statement

In practice, most Corps permit decisions are based on an EA/FONSI and not an EIS. Typically an EIS is prepared for large projects with major environmental issues. Some projects may have major environmental issues at the beginning of the permit process but still avoid the NEPA requirement for preparation of an EIS. This is because other environmental analyses are prepared concurrently to comply with other laws–such as an environmental impact report (EIR) under the California Environmental Quality Act (CEQA)– which alter the project design to below a level of significance and incorporate measures to mitigate environmental impacts prior to the Corps' permit decision.

CEQA = California Environmental Quality Act

The scope of the Corps' NEPA analysis is typically limited to those portions of the project within the 'area of [the Corp's permit decision's] potential effect' (that is, those portions of the project within the jurisdictional boundaries of the Corps, and not upland portions of the project, unless those portions are directly related to the Corps' discretionary authority). However, the Corps, through the NEPA process, may address the impacts of upland portions of the permitted activity when addressing secondary and cumulative effects of the proposed project (33 CFR 325). In a case involving the issuance of a permit by the Corps for the discharge of fill material in 11 acres of wetlands for a golf course in Nevada, the Ninth Circuit federal court upheld the Corps' restriction of its NEPA analysis to only the environmental effects of the golf course and not to the associated resort hotel. The court found that the golf course and resort were not 'joined' which would have required the Corps to issue a permit for the golf course incorporating the resort hotel into the 'major federal action' (*Sylvester v. U.S. Army Corps of Engineers*, 871 F.2d 817 [9th Cir. 1989]).

Public Interest Review. The Corps' decision to issue a permit is based on an evaluation of the probable impacts of the proposed project and its 'intended use on the public interest'. The Corps' determination of effect on the public interest is based on the balance of the benefits reasonably expected to accrue from the project against the reasonably foreseeable detriments of the proposed project. Factors considered in the public interest review include conservation, economics, aesthetics, environmental quality, historic values, fish and wildlife values, flood control, land use, navigation, recreation, water supply and quality, energy needs, safety, food production, and the general public and private need and welfare (33 CFR 320.4). Subject to the restrictions of EPA Section 404(b)(1) Guidelines, the Corps will grant a permit unless issuing the permit is determined to be contrary to the public interest.

Factors considered in the public interest review include conservation, economics, aesthetics, environmental quality, historic values, fish and wildlife values, flood control, land use, navigation, recreation, water supply and quality, energy needs, safety, food production, and the general public and private need and welfare.

The public interest review includes a presumption against discharge into 'important' wetlands. A permit allowing such a discharge cannot be granted unless the District Engineer determines that the benefits of the discharge outweigh the damage to the wetlands resource.

EPA, USFWS, and NMFS Review of Proposed Permit. Section 404(q) of the CWA provides for the Corps to enter into an MOA with appropriate federal agencies to "minimize, to the maximum extent practicable, duplication, needless paperwork and delays in the issuance of permits" under Section 404. The Corps has signed MOAs with EPA, the U.S. Department of Interior (for USFWS review), and the U.S. Department of Commerce (for NMFS review) to establish policies and procedures to implement Section 404(q). The MOAs define the process for EPA, USFWS, and NMFS in elevating disputes over both specific permit application decisions and general policy matters. The elevation process is a type of balance to ensure higher level agency review for local agency disputes.

The MOAs establish a threshold for the elevation process for those permit decisions involving discharges that will have "a substantial and unacceptable impact on aquatic resources of national importance [ARNIs]." The agencies must state during the public comment period (in response to the public notice) that they believe the project may result in a substantial impact on ARNIs. Absent this statement, the agencies have no right to request 404(q) review. However, if the Corps has received notification from the agencies, the district's findings or ROD act as notice to EPA, USFWS, and NMFS that, absent their objection, the Corps intends to issue the permit. According to the MOAs, the Corps transmits a draft permit decision with proposed special conditions to address the agencies' concern and draft EA for the agencies to review. The agencies must then indicate if they wish to continue the elevation process. The higher level agency offices review local agency disputes and decide whether the district's decision should reach the Corps' Assistant Secretary of the Army for Civil Works in Washington, D.C. The Corps, however, retains the ultimate authority to issue the permit and can reject the arguments of other agencies.

This elevation process may not 'eliminate delays' in every case. Although the MOAs link the permit elevation process to potential impacts on aquatic resources of national importance, ARNIs are not defined in the MOAs or in any of the relevant federal regulations. Because these agencies have not defined what is considered an ARNI, the elevation permit process remains uncertain and could subject individual applications to longer delays while the agencies determine whether the aquatic resource to be affected by the permitted activity is considered an ARNI on a case-by-case basis.

EPA Permit Review Authority. Separate from EPA's involvement in the Corps' proposed permit decision under the Section 404(q) MOA, the CWA Section 404(c) grants EPA the power to 'veto' a permit issued by the Corps if EPA determines that the discharge would have unacceptable adverse impacts on water supplies or fishing, wildlife, or recreation areas. The EPA must give public notice and opportunity for public hearing prior to its veto decision. The final determinations on Corps permits issued under Section 404 are made by EPA's administrator. EPA has no authority to review the Corps' decision to issue a permit pursuant to the Rivers and Harbors Act of 1899.

EPA has vetoed a permit issued under Section 404 only on rare occasions. These include–

Cement-lined flood control channel. Cement lining of channels improves flow for flood control purposes but provides no substrate on which wetland plants can root. In addition, riparian habitats are deprived of water by the cement side walls.

ARNI = Aquatic Resources of National Importance

Aquatic Resources of National Importance and the Churchill Downs Case

A developer applied to the Corps for discharge activities associated with the Churchill Downs residential housing project southeast of Sacramento. The permit application requested authorization to discharge fill material into approximately 17 acres of jurisdictional waters consisting of vernal pools and seasonal wetlands. In November 1992, the Corps notified EPA of its intent to issue a permit. As a condition of issuance, the Corps required a mitigation plan which preserved dense complexes of vernal pools and seasonal wetlands on the site and creation of similar wetlands as compensation offsite.

On December 10, 1992, EPA (pursuant to their MOA with the Corps) requested elevation of the Corps' (Sacramento District) decision to issue a permit for the Churchill Downs project. EPA's elevation request was based on its finding that "the completed and proposed discharges of dredged or fill material into vernal pools and seasonal wetlands associated with the project would result in substantial and unacceptable adverse effects to aquatic resources of national importance at the site." EPA argued that "Vernal pools and seasonal swales are widely recognized as high quality habitat providing unique aquatic functions and values including wildlife habitat for numerous species as migrating waterfowl and shorebirds in the Pacific flyway, and endangered species habitat." EPA, stating that "vernal pools in the Central Valley of California have suffered historical losses of ninety to ninety-five percent, with corresponding impacts to associated aquatic values and functions," argued that all the vernal pools on the project site should be preserved.

On January 11, 1993, the Assistant Secretary of the Army Corps of Engineers for Civil Works (ASACW) rejected EPA's request for elevation of the permit action for the Churchill Downs project. The Corps recommended that some of the vernal pools at the project site, which were indeed ARNIs, be preserved, but that impacts on the others, which were not, could be mitigated by creating new vernal pools offsite. According to the Corps, the vernal pools at the project site vary in size and depth, with fairy shrimp (species listed as threatened and endangered under the federal Endangered Species Act) present in some of

ASACW = Assistant Secretary of the Army Corps of Engineers for Civil Works

the larger pools. Generally, the number of plant species increases as the size of the vernal pool increases, causing larger vernal pools to be richer in flora than smaller, more shallow pools, which warrants their preservation as ARNIs.

On February 9, 1993, the Sacramento District of the Corps notified the USFWS of its intent to issue the permit (because of delays in finalizing the USFWS/Corps Section 404[q] MOA, the notification process was bifurcated between EPA and USFWS). On March 15, 1993, the USFWS requested higher level review of the Corps' permit action pursuant to its MOA, contending that the value and function of the vernal pools to be preserved were essentially the same as those to be removed. Arguing that the rationale for designating only some of the vernal pools as ARNIs was unclear, the USFWS requested that the Corps gather further baseline data from the onsite wetlands to support its permit decision and that the Corps also establish clear and detailed success criteria for the proposed mitigation of the vernal pools and seasonal wetlands to be filled.

On April 14, 1993, the ASACW rendered a decision that, "Based on our evaluation we have concluded that the majority of vernal pools on the Churchill Downs site qualify as ARNIs, including the approximately five acres [of vernal pools proposed to be removed] adjacent to the on-site preserve in the northwest portion of the project area." The Washington, D.C. Corps went on to say ". . . our field visit and additional discussions with vernal pool experts led us to conclude that there is no ecological difference between the areas that we originally designated ARNIs and the five acres that remain in question. In future §404(q) MOA elevation requests, a Washington-level representative of this office will conduct an on-site meeting with appropriate parties."

The ASACW concluded that "sufficient questions remain concerning the restoration and creation of vernal pools to warrant additional evaluation before a final determination on the impacts to filling the additional five acres of ARNI vernal pools can be made…[and] further evaluation of the practicability of avoiding the five acres is also required." The ASACW gave the Sacramento District Corps further guidance and stipulated that "all compensatory mitigation for impacts to ARNI vernal pools at the Churchill Downs site will be completed and monitored for a minimum of two years before filling of the ARNI pools can occur."

EPA Veto Actions and
What Is a Practicable Alternative

In the *Sweeden's Swamp* (also known as the Attleboro Mall) case, a developer proposed the construction of a shopping mall in the Attleboro, Massachusetts area. After surveying several sites (including a site with only one acre of wetlands), the developer purchased the 49-acre red maple Sweeden's Swamp, determined by the EPA, USFWS, and the Corps to have high wildlife habitat values. The developer's permit application to the Corps for filling 32 acres of the swamp included measures to mitigate for the loss of wetlands by converting nine acres of uplands into marsh and creating another 36 acres of wetlands at a gravel pit offsite.

The EPA objected to the issuance of a permit under Section 404. The Corps first indicated that the permit would be denied because another site (with only one acre of wetlands and previously surveyed by the developer) was available. When a competing developer purchased the alternative site, the Corps reversed its decision and issued the permit claiming that, because the alternative site was lost and the suggested replacement mitiga-

tion was acceptable, no other site could be environmentally preferable.

Pursuant to its authority under Section 404(c), EPA vetoed the issuance of the permit because, even if successful, the proposed mitigation would not eliminate the adverse effects on wildlife. Given the experimental state of wetland creation, EPA would not allow mitigation measures based on artificially created wetlands to substitute for analysis of available alternative sites.

Because the loss could be avoided by using an available alternative site, the EPA considered the wetlands loss 'unacceptable'. The other site was still available to the applicant, according to the EPA, because the determination of availability for the Section 404(b)(1) alternatives analysis is not limited to the time of permit application but includes the developer's entire site-selection process, beginning with the project proponent's entry into the market. This has become known as the 'market entry test.'

The veto followed a court's rejection of a challenge by the

developer that EPA did not have independent authority to disagree with the Corps' findings. The applicant tried unsuccessfully to persuade a court in a district outside the Massachusetts circuit to stop the initiation of the EPA 404(c) proceedings (*Newport Galleria Group v. Deland*, 618 F. Supp. 1179 [D. D.C. 1985]). The developer contested EPA's veto on the grounds that the EPA had taken too long to make a permit decision, but the court rejected that argument in *Bersani v. Deland*, 640 F. Supp. 716 (D. Mass. 1986).

Finally, the developer challenged the reasonableness of the agency's decision. The court affirmed the EPA's independent authority to disagree with the Corps and to apply its own independent interpretation of 'practicable alternatives'. The court declared the EPA's finding (the existence of a practicable, less damaging alternative for the mall) to be reasonable and specifically upheld the 'market entry' test for the availability of practicable alternatives. *Bersani v. United States Environmental Protection Agency*, 674 F. Supp. 405 (N.D. N.Y. 1987); *affirmed*, 850 F.2d

36 (2d Cir. 1988); *cert. denied,* 489 U.S. 1089 (1989).

In the case of *James City County, Virginia,* the Corps issued a permit to allow the placement of fill to construct a dam for a proposed reservoir in Virginia. The Corps had determined that no environmentally preferable, practicable alternatives were identified to meet the project purpose of supplying the local community with water. The EPA vetoed the permit under Section 404(c), claiming that the presumption that the project would have an unacceptable adverse effect because less environmentally damaging, practicable alternatives were available was not rebutted. The EPA determined that the Corps did not have sufficient information to conclude that no alternatives were available and that an alternative, such as a yet-to-be designed regional water source, was practicable.

The county proposing the reservoir challenged the EPA veto decision. Agreeing with the county that EPA improperly presumed that available alternatives existed without proof to the contrary, the district court stated that this presumption applies only when the project is not water-dependent. The court found that the reservoir, to fulfill its basic purpose of impounding a stream, must be located in wetlands and was therefore water-dependent. The court, declaring that the presumption that practicable alternatives exist should not be applied, found instead that alternatives cited by EPA were not practicable even if its presumption was proper. Because EPA did not demonstrate the existence of available alternatives, the court held that EPA did not meet its statutory duty of showing that the discharge would have an unacceptable adverse impact.

The court sent the issue back to EPA to determine whether environmental considerations alone (and not the availability of practicable alternatives) would warrant a veto of the Corps' permit. EPA reissued its veto decision on the basis of unacceptable adverse effects to the environment. Reviewing the district court's ruling that the EPA veto was not justified, the circuit court stated that the "veto based solely on environmental harms was proper," because EPA was only required to assess issues of water quality and not to incorporate the county's need for water when evaluating the project's unacceptable adverse effects.

The circuit court also reversed the district court's decision not to defer to EPA's determination that the environmental effects of the project were severe enough to warrant a permit veto. While the district court held that EPA did not accurately account for any mitigation implemented as part of the project, the circuit court stated that the record "supports EPA's conclusion that the project [even with incorporation of mitigation measures] nevertheless would cause significant harm." In upholding EPA's veto decision, the circuit court stated that "EPA based its veto decision on several factors, including harm to existing fish and wildlife species, damage to the ecosystem, destruction of wetlands, and inadequate mitigation. Its findings are supported by the administrative record, are not arbitrary and capricious, and, for that matter, are supported by substantial evidence" *James City County, Va., v. United States Environmental Protection Agency,* 758 F.Supp. 348 (E.D. Va. 1990), 12 F.3d 1330 (4th Cir. 1994).

- ▶ A recreational facility at North Miami Landfill, 46 FR 10203 (1981)

- ▶ A warehouse and storage yard in Mobile Bay, Alabama, 49 FR 29142 (1984)

- ▶ An impoundment to manage water levels for waterfowl in Jehosee Island, South Carolina, 50 FR 20291 (1985)

- ▶ Flood control and reclamation of land in southern Louisiana, 50 FR 47268 (1985)

- ▶ Agricultural conversion in Dade County, Florida, 53 FR 30093 (1988)

- ▶ A warehouse and office facility in New Jersey (*see Russo Development Corporation v. Thomas,* 735 F. Supp. 631 [D. N.J. 1989])

- ▶ Big River reservoir in Rhode Island, 56 FR 10666 (1990)

- ▶ A recreational lake in Georgia (*see City of Alma v. United States,* 744 F.Supp. 1546 [S.D. Ga. 1990])

- ▶ A dam for water supply project in Two Forks Dam, Colorado, 56 FR 76 (1991)

In most of these instances, EPA used Section 404(c) to enforce its interpretation of Section 404(b)(1) Guidelines. However, as discussed in the case of *James City County, Virginia,* EPA may base its veto decision solely on the fact that the project would cause adverse environmental effects. Although its 404(c) veto authority is rarely invoked, EPA's threat to veto the Corps' permit has led to EPA sometimes playing a major role in the permit process before the Corps has even issued a permit (such as in the case where EPA has used the Section 404(c) threat to cause an applicant to withdraw a permit application).

General Permits, including Nationwide Permits

Section 404(e) of the CWA authorizes the Corps to issue general permits on a state, regional, or nationwide basis. The general permits issued by the Corps on a national level are called nationwide permits (NWPs). Both NWPs and other general permits are designed to apply to categories of discharge activities that are similar in nature and will cause only minimal adverse environmental effects. All permits authorized under Section 404(e) must be reviewed by the Corps every five years. Technically, NWPs and general permits are prior-issued by rule; therefore, if the proposed project fits the conditions of the general permit, the permit has already been issued. However, compliance with the specific conditions of a particular NWP or general permit as well as Corps

Both NWPs and other general permits are designed to apply to categories of discharge activities that are similar in nature and will cause only minimal adverse environmental effects.

NWP = Nationwide permit

review may be necessary to satisfy Section 404 of the CWA prior to implementing the project activity.

Corps regulations set forth that certain activities are authorized on a nationwide basis and do not require a detailed individual permit review process. Thirty-six NWPs cover activities such as placement of navigational aids, fish and wildlife harvesting devices, outfall structures, survey activities, bank stabilization activities, and small hydropower projects (*see* Table 4-1). NWPs are most widely used for backfill/bedding for utility lines, minor road crossings, and discharges into less than ten acres of wetlands and other waters located above the headwaters (where the mean annual flow is less than 5 cfs) or into isolated wetlands and other waters (not part of a surface tributary system).

Commonly used in California, NWPs are an important part of the environmental authorizations necessary for certain development activities. Applicants should carefully review a proposed activity to determine whether an NWP is applicable, or whether the project can be modified to allow application of an NWP, because project authorization for an NWP is typically much less costly and time-consuming than for an individual permit (*see* Figure 4-3).

Applicants should carefully review a proposed activity to determine whether an NWP is applicable because project authorization for an NWP is typically much less costly and time-consuming than for an individual permit

Regulations authorizing NWPs give the Corps the authority to modify, suspend, or revoke NWPs for specific activities, and the district may even apply its own conditions (33 CFR 330.1(d)). Besides the discretionary authority to review any NWPs for public interest, the district can impose special conditions beyond those associated with a particular NWP or require an individual permit if the fill activity would have more than a minimal adverse impact on the aquatic ecosystem, even if all standard NWP conditions are met. Also, certain NWPs require predischarge notification (PDN) to the Corps of information regarding delineation of wetlands and compliance with other conditions.

PDN = Predischarge Notification

Two or more different NWPs can be combined, or 'stacked', to authorize a single complete project. However, an NWP and an individual permit cannot be used for separate components of the same project. The two can be used only if the activity authorized under the NWP has independent utility and can function or meet its purpose independently of the larger project.

All NWPs are subject to certain general conditions (*see* Appendix J), while some have conditions specifically applicable to that particular discharge activity. Beyond the Corps' public interest review of activity under all NWPs, as well as compliance

Table 4-1. Nationwide Permits
(Effective January 21, 1992)

Permit Number	Permit Title	Require Notification	Require Notification in Certain Circumstances*
1.	Aids to Navigation		
2.	Structures in Artificial Canals		
3.	Maintenance		
4.	Fish and Wildlife Harvesting Activities		
5.	Scientific Measurement Devices		X
6.	Survey Activities		
7.	Outfall Structures	X	
8.	Oil and Gas Structures		
9.	Structures in Fleeting and Anchorage Areas		
10.	Mooring Buoys		
11.	Temporary Recreational Structures		
12.	Utility Line Bedding and Backfill		
13.	Bank Stabilization		X
14.	Road Crossings		X
15.	Fills at U.S. Coast Guard Approved Bridges		
16.	Return Water from Upland Contained Disposal Areas		
17.	Hydropower Projects	X	
18.	Minor Discharges (25 cubic yards)		X
19.	Minor Dredging (25 cubic yards)		
20.	Oil and Gas Cleanup		
21.	Surface Mining Activities (Coal)	X	
22.	Removal of Vessels		
23.	Categorical Exclusions		
24.	State Administered Section 404 Programs		
25.	Structural Discharges		
26.	Headwaters and Isolated Waters		X
27.	Wetland Restoration Activities		
28.	Modification of Existing Marinas		
29.	Reserved		
30.	Reserved		
31.	Reserved		
32.	Completed Enforcement Actions		
33.	Temporary Construction and Access	X	
34.	Cranberry Production Activities	X	
35.	Maintenance Dredging of Existing Basins		
36.	Boat Ramps		
37.	Emergency Watershed Protection	X	
38.	Cleanup of Hazardous and Toxic Waste	X	
39.	Reserved		
40.	Farm Buildings		

---

* The following nationwide permits require notification only in certain circumstances. The specific reasons are listed below—

5. Small weirs and flumes that involve 10-25 cubic yards of fill require notification.

13. Bank stabilization requires notification to the district engineer when the activity exceeds 500 feet in total length or exceeds an average of one cubic foot per linear foot of shoreline.

14. Road crossings activities under this nationwide permit require notification only if the project involves a discharge of dredged or fill material into a special aquatic site.

18. Minor discharges activities under this nationwide permit require notification only if the discharge exceeds ten cubic yards or the discharge is in a special aquatic site.

26. Headwaters and isolated waters discharges under this nationwide permit require notification only if the area of wetland disturbance exceeds one acre.

Indirect Impacts on Wetlands and Corps Authority

An irrigation district sought to build a dam and reservoir on a tributary to the South Platte River in Colorado. The Corps determined that the deposit of fill material associated with construction of the dam did not meet the conditions required for a nationwide permit because the increased use of water facilitated by the reservoir would deplete the streamflow and adversely affect the critical habitat of the whooping crane, an endangered species. While the fill itself would not affect the whooping crane, the dam facility the Corps would have to permit as necessary for dam operations would affect the species.

The circuit court upheld the Corps' denial of the use of an NWP, finding that the CWA and Corps regulations "authorize the Corps to consider downstream effects of changes in water quantity in determining whether a proposed discharge qualified for a NWP." The court stated that the fact that the reduction in water does not result from direct federal action does not lessen the Corps' duty. The Corps was "required to consider all effects, direct and indirect, of the discharge for which authorization was sought" *Riverside Irrigation District v. Andrews,* 758 F.2d 508 (10th Cir. 1985) (*see* also *Lotz Realty Company, Inc. v. United States,* 757 F. Supp. 692 [E.D. Va. 1990]).

with other environmental regulations required for all permits issued under Section 404 (*see* discussion below), the activity will not be able to operate under an NWP and will require an individual permit if the activity affects–

- ▶ Navigation, erosion, siltation, or aquatic life more than minimally
- ▶ Species listed as endangered or designated critical habitat (to the point where the activity would jeopardize the continued existence of the listed species)
- ▶ Properties eligible for listing on or listed on the National Register of Historic Places
- ▶ Tribal properties
- ▶ Designated wild and scenic rivers

The PDN process is a required condition for 11 NWPs (*see* Table 4-1). The proponent must notify the Corps of the intent to perform fill activities authorized under the particular NWP and

California Refuses to Certify the Corps NWP Program

Section 401 of the CWA authorizes states to determine whether activities permitted by the federal government meet state water quality standards, with states therefore retaining the right to certify consistency of NWPs with state water quality standards. States may choose to certify NWPs generally or retain jurisdiction to review them individually. If the state has not certified the NWP, the Corps district must ensure that the state has received the appropriate information; however, water quality certification may still be approved under the NWP and not by authority of an individual permit.

In 1992, the Corps issued a regulatory guidance letter notifying its districts that any state-imposed conditions for certification of a nationwide permit for state water quality standards that would change the permit substantially should be considered a denial of certification.

California has not provided state certification for certain NWPs that were reissued in 1992 (*see* 33 CFR 330, as noticed in 56 FR 59110, 59117). Therefore, these NWPs are not considered 'in effect' in California unless they have been individually certified by the SWRCB. The SWRCB denied certification of 12 categories of NWPs, including the most commonly used NWP 26, and certified the other 24. The applicant must seek state certification for each individual activity to be authorized under these 'uncertified' NWPs.

must submit a wetlands delineation before beginning the activity. The applicant should also include information about compliance with the federal Endangered Species Act and the National Historic Preservation Act. The Corps may also require that the same type of information be submitted for the alternative selection process for the project and the environmental effects of the fill activity as required under the individual permit process.

Through the PDN process, the applicant transmits the required project information to USFWS, NMFS, California State Water Resources Control Board (SWRCB), and EPA, and notifies the Corps that these processes are complete. The Corps then notifies these agencies, who have five days to contact the Corps

SWRCB = California State Water Resources Control Board

as to whether they will have substantive comments. The Corps has 30 days to review the intended activity, and may, within its discretionary review of the project under the PDN process, impose conditions regarding mitigation. If the Corps does not respond within 30 days, the activity may proceed (although it is recommended that the Corps be contacted before engaging in the activity even if it has not responded in the 30-day period).

To avoid potential delays and reduce legal uncertainty about Section 404 authority over a project, the Corps should be advised of *any* nationwide permit activity, whether or not a formal PDN process is required. Typically the Corps will notify a project proponent to verify that the NWP is appropriate.

The most commonly used NWP in California is for the authorization of discharges affecting less than ten acres of isolated wetlands and other waters or those wetlands and other waters located above the headwaters (NWP 26). Wetlands are considered 'above the headwaters' when they are upstream of a watercourse where the average annual flow is less than five cubic feet per second. 'Isolated waters' are those nontidal waters of the United States that are not part of or adjacent to a surface tributary system to interstate or navigable waters of the United States.

The most commonly used NWP in California is for the authorization of discharges affecting less than ten acres of isolated wetlands and other waters or those wetlands and other waters located above the headwaters (NWP 26).

PDN is required under NWP 26 if the activity will affect more than one acre. For the activity to fall under NWP 26, the activity's total jurisdictional area *affected* cannot be more than ten acres. Compensation and replacement acreage from the project's mitigation plan do not offset the total amount of jurisdictional waters affected. Sometimes the project's fill activity will be within an area of less than ten acres, but the project will affect a larger amount of jurisdictional waters (for example, through secondary effects), and therefore NWP 26 will not apply. Also, the entire project's fill activities are aggregated for the purpose of meeting the conditions of NWP 26.

State and regional general permits are typically issued by specific Corps districts authorizing particular activities. These permits are subject to notice and comment and are usually conditioned with certain requirements, like those imposed on NWPs (for example, predischarge notification). Some districts of the Corps intend to use a general permit to authorize certain activities within California, because those activities are subject to sufficient state regulatory authority (for example, discharges associated with suction dredging, because these discharges are already regulated by DFG under its permit authority).

Bridge over seasonal wetland, Sacramento County. Bridge crossings remove wetland habitat directly by placement of fill for pilings and indirectly by shading habitat under the bridge.

Federal Laws Related to Issuance of a Corps Permit

Permit decisions of the Corps under Section 404 of the CWA, for both individual and general permits, require compliance with other federal laws. This section discusses those laws. Federal laws, other than the CWA and the Rivers and Harbors Act of 1899, that either contain specific provisions—or, as a secondary purpose, provide for wetlands protection—are discussed in a separate section.

Prior to submitting a permit application to the Corps, applicants should prepare a strategy for compliance with all environmental regulations necessary for the Corps to process a DA permit, as well as for all other regulations necessary for wetland activities. The applicant's goal should be to integrate all permit conditions into a single project description and process to avoid duplicative, successive environmental reviews. In most cases, the environmental laws with which the Corps must comply will not impede the Corps from eventually issuing a permit. However, these federal laws may make mitigation for project effects more difficult and will certainly delay the permit review process. Furthermore, if compliance with these other laws involves especially sensitive resources, the Corps may not allow the project to proceed under a nationwide permit, or may require, in the case of an individual permit, the applicant to assist the Corps in preparing of an EIS, rather than the typical EA/FONSI.

National Environmental Policy Act. Whenever any federal agency proposes to undertake an action or grant a permit, NEPA requires the agency to assess the effects of its action on the human environment (42 USC 4332; 40 CFR 1501). This includes assessing the significance of the effects of a proposed project based on society as a whole, affected interests, the affected region, and the locality in which the impact would occur. The assessment includes a project's effects on a particular resource and possible mitigation measures available to reduce that significance.

Some form of NEPA compliance, through preparation of an EA leading to either a FONSI or an EIS, is required by the Corps for all individual permits. NEPA review was performed as part of the administrative rule-making process prior to issuance of NWP's and, by definition, NWPs and other general permits typically do not have any adverse effects on the human environment (because if they did, an individual permit would be required). Where a project must be approved by more than one agency, the lead agency responsible for conducting the environmental review should be identified. The federal agency with the greatest discretionary authority over the project is typically designated the lead agency. For the purposes of preparing the NEPA document, if the project is proposed by another federal agency or if the private or state project requires other federal agency discretionary review, the Corps may not be the lead agency.

When the Corps requires an individual permit for the project proposed, the strategy for compliance with NEPA is to first determine if actions by other federal agencies are necessary. In practice, the Corps does not assume the role of lead agency for permit actions unless no other federal agencies are involved. Even when it is the lead agency, the Corps typically seeks to avoid preparing an EIS. To facilitate the Corps' NEPA review, a project proponent should first complete all the environmental reviews required by other laws (such as CEQA), and then furnish the Corps with all relevant information regarding the environmental effects of the project. However, if the project will require proparation of an EIS, the project proponent may want to combine NEPA's environmental review with others (prepare an EIR/EIS).

Desert ephemeral drainage, Kern County. Desert ephemeral drainages usually do not support wetlands, but are often determined to be waters of the United States by the Corps.

Endangered Species Act. The federal Endangered Species Act requires that all federal agencies ensure that their actions do not jeopardize the continued existence of listed species or adversely modify the species' critical habitat (16 USC 1536). Therefore, the federal Endangered Species Act becomes an issue for activities disturbing wetlands only when the property contains a federally listed threatened or endangered species that may be adversely affected by a permit decision. In that event, the Corps must initiate consultation with USFWS (or NMFS) pursuant to Section 7 of the federal Endangered Species Act (16 USC 1536; 40 CFR 402).

The Corps is required to provide to USFWS all available information regarding the potential effect of the permit action on the listed species. This procedure may require the Corps to prepare a biological assessment of the effect of the permit action (but not necessarily the effect of the entire project) on the listed species. If formal consultation is required, USFWS or NMFS will issue a biological opinion stating whether the permit action is likely to jeopardize the continued existence of the listed species.

The biological opinion's reasonable and prudent alternatives (RPAs) intended to minimize the effects on the listed species become special conditions to the Corps permit. However, if the

RPA = Reasonable and prudent alternative

biological opinion concludes that jeopardy would occur and there are no RPAs, the Corps is required, under the Section 404(b)(1) Guidelines, to deny the permit.

The strategy for compliance with the federal Endangered Species Act is to assist the Corps in the initial phases of consultation with USFWS. The project proponent should request a list from USFWS of the species protected under the federal Endangered Species Act that may occur in the project area. If required, appropriate surveys should be conducted early in the project planning phase to allow for sufficient time for consultation between the Corps and USFWS. When possible, the project proponent should design a project to avoid any potential effect on a listed species.

National Historic Preservation Act. Section 106 of the National Historic Preservation Act requires a federal agency to review all actions which may affect a property listed on the National Register of Historic Places, or which may affect a property eligible for listing. The Corps has regulations to guide the review of permit decisions and specific procedures for initial review of permit applications, public notice, site investigations, eligibility determinations, assessing effects, consultation with the State Historic Preservation Officer (SHPO) and Advisory Council on Historic Preservation (ACHP), and decision making. The permit decision must reflect consideration of the effects of the project's fill activities on historic properties and should incorporate conditions to avoid or reduce those effects.

SHPO = State Historic Preservation Officer

ACHP = Advisory Council on Historic Preservation

The project proponent should check the National Register of Historic Places for resources occurring in the project area and should survey the project site for those properties eligible for future listing. This process should begin as early as possible to avoid delays when coordinating between the Corps' cultural resource staff, SHPO, and ACHP. When feasible, the project should be designed to avoid any potential affect on a property listed or eligible for listing.

Section 401 of the Clean Water Act. Section 401 of the CWA and EPA Section 404(b)(1) Guidelines require that the discharge of dredged or fill material into waters of the United States does not violate state water quality standards. Neither individual permits nor NWPs will be issued under Section 404 until the state has been notified and the applicant has obtained a certification of state water quality standards. Typically, the individual permit applicant sends the relevant information to the Regional Water Quality Control Board, under the SWRCB's jurisdiction, for a certification that the discharge activity does not violate state water quality standards.

Neither individual permits nor NWPs will be issued under Section 404 until the state has been notified and the applicant has obtained a certification of state water quality standards.

Whether the fill activity complies with state water quality standards is considered by SWRCB and regional boards to be a discretionary act that requires compliance with CEQA. In practice, SWRCB and regional boards will not assume lead agency authority under CEQA and will delay action on the permit until compliance with CEQA is complete.

Coastal Zone Management Act. Section 404 requires the Corps to obtain proof of certification that the proposed project is consistent with the federal Coastal Zone Management Act of 1972. The CZMA creates a broad program based on land development controls within coastal zones, incorporating state involvement through the development of programs for comprehensive state management. Under the California Coastal Act, California has promulgated a state management program that encourages local agencies to develop local coastal programs (LCPs). For projects affecting wetlands in the coastal zone, permit applicants must certify to the Corps that the proposed activity complies with (and will be conducted in a manner consistent with) CZMA, the California Coastal Act, and the LCP. Absent such certification, a waiver must be provided.

LCP = Local Coastal Program

After determining whether the site falls within the designated coastal zone, the project proponent should design the project to be compatible with the California Coastal Act and the LCP. The project proponent should obtain necessary approvals under the CZMA when applying to the Corps for a permit.

Violations and Enforcement

The following section, which discusses the avenues for challenging Corps decisions under Section 404 of the CWA, presents the enforcement functions of the Corps and the EPA and discusses the liabilities and criminal and civil penalties that may be involved for Section 404 violations.

Judicial Review

Federal courts have jurisdiction to review many Corps and EPA administrative actions under the CWA. However, the Act does not provide for judicial review of certain decisions affecting wetlands, such as the method for determining the extent of jurisdictional wetlands on a proposed site. These decisions must be challenged through other federal laws, such as the Administrative Procedures Act (*see* the case of *Tabb Lakes*) or federal questions of constitutional authority (*see Hoffman Homes*).

The Corps' decision to grant or deny a permit under Section 404 of the CWA is subject to review by the federal courts.

EPA's decision to veto a permit under Section 404(c) is also subject to judicial review.

The Corps' decision to grant or deny a permit under Section 404 of the CWA is subject to review by the federal courts. An applicant can challenge the permit denial, but cannot challenge the Corps' permit conditions except by refusing to accept the entire permit. Other interested parties may challenge the Corps' decision to issue a permit, as long as they meet federal requirements for standing. Corps and EPA regulations are subject to judicial review under the CWA as to whether they are consistent with the Act, and EPA's decision to veto a permit under Section 404(c) is also subject to judicial review.

Courts lack jurisdiction to review the Corps' negative response to a request for a determination about the application of a nationwide permit to a particular property. The response is not considered by the courts to be an order or license. Even if it were an order, under the Administrative Procedures Act it is not considered a final action with binding legal effect. (In *Avella v. United States Army Corps of Engineers*, 916 F.2d 721[11th Cir. 1990]; *Mulberry Hills Development Corporation v. U.S.*, 32 Env't. Rep. Cas. [BNA] 1195 [D.C. Md. 1989].)

Under the 'arbitrary and capricious' standard to review a decision by the Corps or EPA, federal courts give deference to the administrative agency–provided that the administrative record is complete and that the agency had a rational basis for its decision. The court must defer to the administrative agency–or be overturned on appeal–even if the court does not agree with the agency decision.

The remedy available to a party challenging Corps and EPA decision errors is typically limited to the court entering a declaration of errors by Corps or EPA, reversal of the agency's decision, and remand of the decision back to the agency for revision in light of the court's findings. The court is not permitted to substitute itself and undertake the agency action.

Since the CWA contains no statute of limitations for filing challenges to Corps and EPA actions under Section 404 or NEPA, the general six-year statute of limitations for civil actions against the government of the United States applies.

Corps and EPA Enforcement Authority

Section 404 of the CWA can be enforced through administrative orders and penalties, civil judicial enforcement by the government or interested citizens, and criminal prosecutions. EPA and the Corps share administrative enforcement authority under Section

404. Under a 1989 MOA between the Corps and EPA (*see* Appendix G), the Corps will conduct the initial investigations for enforcement cases. The Corps or EPA may issue administrative orders requiring compliance with permit conditions, and may issue cease-and-desist orders against unpermitted discharges of dredged or fill material.

Courts will not review Corps or EPA compliance orders under the CWA until the federal government brings an enforcement proceeding (in *Southern Pines Associates v. United States*, 31 ERC 2020 [4th Cir. 1990]; *Hoffman Group, Inc. v. United States Environmental Protection Agency*, 902 F.2d 567 [7th Cir. 1990]; *Mulberry Hills Development Corporation*; *McGown v. United States*, 747 F. Supp. 539 [E.D. Mo. 1990]).

Liability. CWA obligations apply to a 'person', which is defined as 'an individual, corporation, partnership, association, state, municipality, commission, or political subdivision of a state, or any interstate body', for administrative and civil enforcement (33 USC 1362). For criminal enforcement, the term 'person' also includes 'any responsible corporate officer' (33 USC 1319).

In general, the test for liability under the CWA extends to anyone who performed, exercised control over, or had responsibility for the unpermitted discharge activity (in *United States v. Board of Trustees of Florida Keys Community College*, 531 F.Supp. 267 [S.D. Fla. 1981]). This includes the owner of the property, contractors who perform the physical work, and even design engineers. Although subsequent landowners are not liable for the penalties for an unpermitted discharge activity which took place on the land prior to ownership, illegal discharges are considered to be "continuing violations" and may still require removal or mitigation.

In general, the test for liability under the CWA extends to anyone who performed, exercised control over, or had responsibility for the unpermitted discharge activity.

Civil and Criminal Actions. Under Section 309 of the CWA, both the Corps and EPA have independent enforcement authority. Although administrative orders are not independently enforceable against a violator, the Corps will refer the violation of the administrative order to the United States Department of Justice for either civil or criminal judicial enforcement. For cases determined to be appropriate, the Corps and EPA may recommend criminal or civil actions to obtain penalties for violations, compliance with the orders and directives issued, and other relief as appropriate. The federal government is not required to elect between pursuing an administrative remedy or filing a judicial enforcement action.

The Corps and EPA assess administrative penalties for violations of Section 404 under two classes. Class I violations are for

A Landowner Goes to Jail for Filling a Wetland

The United States brought action against a landowner in Pennsylvania under the CWA, alleging that fill had been discharged into wetlands without a permit pursuant to Section 404. The wetlands site is adjacent to an unnamed tributary to the Pennsylvania Canal which flows into the Delaware River. The landowner had cleared old tires and other refuse and then filled and leveled part of the property to build a garage. Between April 1987 and November 1987, the Corps repeatedly warned the landowner, both orally and by issuance of a cease-and-desist letter, not to continue filling the site until a permit was obtained. Each time the Corps biologist visited the site, however, he noted that substantial additional filling had taken place.

In December 1987, the Corps issued an administrative directive instructing the defendant landowner to cease and desist the filling activity and to remove the fill within 45 days, or to cease and desist filling and apply for an 'after the fact' permit within ten days. The landowner did not apply for a permit and continued to fill the site through 1988 (EPA actually videotaped the landowner filling wetlands after the cease-and-desist order was issued). In August 1988, the federal district court issued a temporary restraining order. After the landowner continued to fill the site, using a bulldozer to level the fill, the court issued a preliminary restraining order and a contempt of court order against the defendant landowner.

Also implicated in the unpermitted discharges of fill material at the site were a demolition, excavation, and hauling company and a demolition and metal and concrete recycling company that saved over $142,800 and $30,262, respectively, by

less serious unpermitted activities and for EPA carry a maximum of $10,000 per violation, with a total maximum of $25,000. Class II violations are for more serious unpermitted activities and, under EPA authority, carry a maximum of $10,000 per day for each day during which the violation continues, with a total maximum of $125,000. The penalty authority of the Corps does not distinguish between classes. Although the Corps has less formal penalty proceedings for Class I violations, both classes are subject to penalties of up to $25,000 per day. Both class violations under Corps and EPA authority allow for notice and opportunity for hearing.

disposing of the fill at the landowner's site rather than at a permitted landfill.

Finding the defendants strictly liable for the unpermitted discharges, the court issued a permanent injunction against further filling of the wetlands site without first obtaining a permit under Section 404. The court also issued a Corps-submitted restoration order for the site, to be implemented by the defendants. (*United States v. Pozsgai*, 31 Env't Rep. Czs. [BNA] 1230 [E.D. Pa. 1990].)

In the related criminal prosecution, the defendant landowner was convicted of 40 counts of illegal discharge of pollutants under the CWA and was sentenced to three years in jail, fined $202,000, and ordered to restore the wetlands in which the violations occurred. The Supreme Court refused to review the conviction and sentence (*cert. denied*, 498 U.S. 812 [1990]).

The landowner also challenged the constitutional reach of the CWA's imposition of civil sanctions for filling wetlands. The defendant argued that the wetland's only connection to interstate commerce was a nearby canal used to transport coal in the nineteenth century. The Supreme Court again refused to hear his appeal and allowed the third circuit ruling that in this case the CWA's jurisdiction was properly applied. (*Pozsgai v. United States*, cert. denied, 114 S. Ct. 1052 [1994].)

As of the Supreme Court's latest denial of the appeal, the landowner had served approximately two years of his three-year sentence and was paying off his civil penalty in installments. He is still seeking an after-the-fact permit (as well as applying for a new wetlands delineation for the site) and permission to use NWP 26 for his discharge activities.

Under the federal court system, through prosecution by the United States Department of Justice, the typical remedy is an injunction to require a party either to stop further unpermitted discharge activities or to remove and restore the unpermitted fill. Courts may award civil penalties of up to $25,000 per day per violation. The CWA does not provide a statute of limitations for civil actions. However, courts typically apply a five-year statute of limitations, which begins when the government *learns of the violation*, not on the date when the violation occurred. Criminal enforcement for violations of Section 404 are rarely pursued and

The CWA does not provide a statute of limitations for civil actions. However, courts typically apply a five-year statute of limitations, which begins when the government learns of the violation, not on the date when the violation occurred.

usually apply to those unpermitted discharges that involve significant environmental harm, abusive conduct, continued illegal conduct after notice, and other serious knowing and willful violations. Negligent violations carry misdemeanor sanctions, including penalties of $2,500 to $25,000 per day and imprisonment of up to one year. Knowing violations carry felony sanctions, including penalties of $5,000 to $50,000 per day and imprisonment of up to three years. A knowing violation that places another person in danger of death or injury carries a maximum fine of $250,000 and 15 years' imprisonment, and corporations can be fined up to $1,000,000.

Suits by Citizens

Under Section 505 of the CWA, any person having an interest that is adversely affected can bring a civil action against any person, including the United States, for violation of the CWA or against the EPA or Corps for failure to perform nondiscretionary duties under the CWA.

Under Section 505 of the CWA, any person having an interest that is or may be adversely affected can bring a civil action against any person, including the United States, for violation of the CWA, including Section 404, or against the EPA or Corps for failure to perform nondiscretionary duties under the CWA. Citizens must first notify the violator and the state and federal governments of intent to sue. This must be done at least 60 days prior to filing suit and cannot proceed if either the federal or state government is prosecuting the violation.

Citizens may intervene in a case where the federal or state government has brought proceedings to prosecute a violation of Section 404. If the citizen proceeds with a suit, a copy of the complaint must be furnished to the government, and the government must be given 45 days to review a consent decree. The federal government may use its authority to intervene in the citizen suit or to present *amicus* (advice to the court) briefs to address matters affecting the government's authority. Plaintiffs who prevail in citizen suits may be awarded their costs, including attorney's fees.

Other Federal Regulatory Authority Protecting Wetlands

While the previous section described those laws with which the Corps is required to comply when issuing a permit under Section 404, federal laws other than the Rivers and Harbors Act of 1899 and Section 404 of the CWA specifically or indirectly provide wetlands protection. A project proponent should prepare a strategy for compliance with all environmental regulations that may be necessary for activities occurring in wetlands before submitting a permit application to the Corps. These other federal laws should not prevent project implementation. However, compliance may make

finalizing the project description, including mitigation requirements, more difficult and may delay the date the project can
begin. Even if the Corps does not require an EIS prior to issuing
a permit, preparation of an EIS may be required by the permit
review process of another federal agency.

To avoid successive environmental reviews, the applicant
should prepare a project description integrating all regulatory requirements with the Corps' permit conditions. If high value wetlands are present, the project proponent should also investigate
wetlands preservation programs applying to the project site to
determine whether the proposed activities would be allowable
or whether entering the site into these programs may be more
advantageous than implementing the project.

Clean Water Act Sections 301 and 402

The CWA, which provides sweeping revision of earlier water
pollution control laws, calls for restoring and maintaining the
chemical, physical, and biological integrity of the nation's waters.
Its principal goal is to address the problems of water pollution
through the National Pollution Discharge Elimination System
(NPDES). Section 301 prohibits the discharge of any pollutant
without a permit, and Section 402 sets up the permit program
administered by the EPA.

**NPDES = National Pollution
Discharge Elimination System**

Although a project may not involve the deposit of dredged or
fill material into waters of the United States, the Section 301/402
provisions of the CWA may still apply and regulate aspects of a
project—such as wastewater discharges during construction—that
could provide some protection for wetlands. By generally regulating water pollution, the CWA provisions, beyond Section 404,
have the effect of regulating activities that may affect wetlands.

National Environmental Policy Act

NEPA and its implementing regulations direct federal agencies to
assess the effects of their actions on the 'human environment.'
NEPA's directive is considered to be the basic national charter for
environmental protection. NEPA analysis includes assessing the
significance of the effects of a proposed project on a particular
resource and mitigation measures available to reduce that significance. Federal agencies are also required to consider the
cumulative effects of the planned action and other reasonably
foreseeable projects.

While NEPA does not specifically require their protection,
wetlands are mentioned as a resource to be evaluated when

Fill activity in riparian scrub habitat, Riverside County.

determining whether a project will have a significant effect on the human environment. In instances where a Corps permit is not required for activities adversely affecting wetlands (that is, no discharge of dredged or fill material is involved), NEPA will require an assessment of the project's effect on wetlands. NEPA does not provide for uniform wetland protection, but does require the federal agency to evaluate a project's effects on wetlands—including its effects on wildlife and plant species of concern located in wetlands—and, where appropriate, recommend mitigation to reduce these impacts to less-than-significant levels. When reviewing NEPA documents, USFWS and EPA typically value wetlands, indicating that mitigation should be provided when they are affected adversely. Also, the NEPA process has its own public interest review criteria that allow the public to review and comment on the method of analysis and the conclusions made in the environmental documentation, including assessment of impacts on wetlands.

Endangered Species Act

The purpose of the federal Endangered Species Act is "to provide a means whereby the ecosystems upon which endangered species and threatened species depend may be conserved." (16 USC 1531) The Act establishes an official listing process for plants and animals considered to be in danger of extinction, requires development of specific plans of action for the recovery of listed species, restricts activities perceived to harm or kill listed species or affect critical habitat, and requires federal agencies to ensure that the agencies' actions do not jeopardize the continued existence of listed species (16 USC 1532, 1536).

A wetland, although a sensitive resource, is not subject to listing under the Endangered Species Act. However, because wetlands can provide habitat for species of threatened or endangered plants and wildlife, certain wetlands are protected. The Endangered Species Act may, therefore, prohibit projects from adversely affecting wetlands considered habitat for listed species, without consultation with or permission from USFWS or NMFS.

Fish and Wildlife Coordination Act

The Fish and Wildlife Coordination Act requires that all federal agencies consult with USFWS, NMFS, and the state's wildlife agency

(DFG) for activities that affect, control, or modify waters of any stream or other bodies of water. Under the authority of the Fish and Wildlife Coordination Act, USFWS and NMFS review applications for permits issued under Section 404 and provide comments to the Corps about the environmental impacts of the proposed project.

Considerable overlap exists between the environmental review contained in the NEPA and Endangered Species Act processes and the Fish and Wildlife Coordination Act process. Through the Fish and Wildlife Coordination Act, USFWS and NMFS have an expanded responsibility for project review that includes concerns about general plant and wildlife species that may not be addressed by NEPA and the Endangered Species Act. In particular, this expanded responsibility may include a project's secondary effects on wetlands.

Food Security Act of 1985

The Food Security Act of 1985 contains a provision for penalizing agricultural producers who plant commodities on wetlands that have been drained, filled, or otherwise altered. Commonly known as 'Swampbuster', this provision, which is administered by the U.S. Department of Agriculture through SCS, removes the producer's eligibility for all government price and income support programs for violation of the Act. Rather than having their federal subsidies completely withheld, farmers who inadvertently drain wetlands may be fined $750-$10,000 and the landowner, to qualify to pay the fine, must restore the converted wetland.

The Food Security Act of 1985 contains a provision for penalizing agricultural producers who plant commodities on wetlands that have been drained, filled, or otherwise altered.

As amended by the 1990 Farm Act, the Food Security Act of 1985 authorizes a voluntary program for farmers to reduce water pollution from agricultural practices. Those reducing pesticide, fertilizer, and other pollutant drainage may get federal cost-sharing assistance. The Act created a Conservation Reserve Program that pays landowners to take highly erodible land out of crop production and to plant vegetation that controls soil erosion and helps wildlife, including vegetation typical of certain types of wetland areas. The Act also created the Wetlands Reserve Program which seeks out farmed and converted wetlands critical for migratory bird and other wildlife habitat for wetland conservation easements. The areas within the wetland conservation easement plan, which must be approved by both SCS and USFWS, carry specific use prohibitions and allowances intended to further restore and protect the wetlands. According to SCS, California farmers submitted 78,500 acres for application to the Wetlands Reserve Program in 1992.

Executive Orders

Executive Order 11990: Protection of Wetlands (1977) is an overall wetlands policy for all agencies managing federal lands, sponsoring federal projects, or providing federal funds to state or local projects. Executive Order 11990 requires federal agencies to follow avoidance/mitigation/preservation procedures with public input, before proposing new construction in wetlands. When federal lands are proposed for lease or sale to nonfederal parties, Executive Order 11990 requires that restrictions be placed in the lease or conveyance to protect and enhance the wetlands on the property.

Although it does not apply to federal discretionary authority for nonfederal projects (other than funding) on nonfederal land, Executive Order 11990 has the effect of restricting the sale of federal lands with wetlands. Also, its restrictions apply to wetlands on property within military installations proposed for closure and on land taken over through the federal bail-out program for failed mortgage companies.

Executive Order 11988: Flood Plain Management (1977) is a flood hazard policy for federal agencies. Executive Order 11988 requires that all federal agencies take action to reduce the risk of flood loss, to restore and preserve the natural and beneficial values served by flood plains, and to minimize the impact of floods on human safety, health, and welfare. An agency's action must reflect consideration of alternatives to avoid adverse impacts in flood plains. Where location in a flood plain is unavoidable, the federal agency must modify the action to minimize the effects of a project. Because many wetlands are located in flood plains, Executive Order 11988 has the secondary effect of protecting wetlands.

The Takings Issue

The Fifth Amendment to the U.S. Constitution prohibits the government from 'taking' private property without just compensation.

The Fifth Amendment to the U.S. Constitution prohibits the government from 'taking' private property without just compensation. Courts have recognized that governmental regulation of land use may sometimes be so restrictive that, by eliminating the economic use of the property, the action constitutes a taking. As a defense to imposition of permit requirements under Section 404 of the CWA, landowners may assert that a regulatory taking has occurred; however, this assertion has not been demonstrated to be a valid defense to violations of Section 404 of the CWA or to permit conditions imposed by the Corps. Takings claims are more appropriate for project applicants who have been denied a permit. Although much judicial activity has involved alleged takings under all government activities, including Section 404, the takings defense is not likely to constitute a substantial restraint on substantial implementation of Section 404.

Typically, if a link exists between the federal government's assertion of jurisdiction and the regulated activity, and if some economically viable use of the land remains, a taking is not considered to have occurred. Therefore, government requirements for a permit or strict permit conditions must be directly related to the reasons for regulating the activity and requiring a permit in the first place. This issue is exemplified by a Supreme Court decision in which the court rejected the government's attempt to require public access to a privately owned marina-style residential community in Hawaii. After securing appropriate local approvals, the developer constructed a private marina on a pond adjacent to navigable waters and excavated a channel to connect the pond to the navigable waters. The Corps claimed that the development changed the character of the land from private property to property that must be opened to the public; but the court held that the Corps exceeded the bounds of ordinary regulation, and therefore such a requirement may be imposed only by paying compensation under the Fifth Amendment (*Kaiser Aetna v. United States*, 444 U.S. 164 [1979]).

The forum to decide takings claims for permit denial is in the U.S. Court of Federal Claims (formerly the Court of Claims). Takings claims seeking monetary compensation in excess of $10,000 are initially heard in the claims court (as opposed to other CWA issues that are brought in federal district courts), and appeals from the claims court are heard in the Federal Circuit Court of Appeals. The claims court will hear takings claims only after final permit denial, after denial has been appealed through the regulatory process.

In August 1993 the Government Accounting Office (GAO) issued a report summarizing the status of 28 takings claims under Section 404 as of May 31, 1993 (*see* U.S. General Accounting Office, "CWA: Takings Claims Under the Section 404 Program," GAO/RCED-93-176FS). Of the 28 claims, 14 were still pending, one had been settled, and 13 had been decided by the claims court. Of the 13 cases that had been decided, ten were decided in favor of the government. Two cases currently pending in the claims court address whether the federal government, after refusing to issue a permit to fill wetlands, is required to pay for the loss of property value (*see* 'Landowners' Claim Corps' Permit Denial Is Taking of Private Property').

GAO = Government Accounting Office

Landowners Claim Corps' Permit Denial Is Taking of Private Property

A landowner in a Florida case, who had purchased thousands of acres of mangrove wetlands in coastal Florida in 1964, received permits from the Corps under Section 10 of the Rivers and Harbors Act of 1899 to develop two of its five tracts (prior to enactment of the CWA). In 1976, the landowner applied for permits from the Corps under Section 404 to fill the remaining tracts, approximately one-third of the landowner's total planned lots. The Corps denied the permits, and the landowner claimed a regulatory taking.

The court of claims rejected the landowner's argument. The court ruled that the landowner failed to show that the denial left the landowner with "no economically viable use of its land." Because the denial was for only one-third of the proposed development, and even on that one-third some areas could be developed without a permit, the court rejected the argument that the property was denied its most profitable use. The court also rejected the allegation that the earlier Section 10 permits created a reasonable expectation of subsequent approvals. *Deltona Corp. v. United States* 657 F.2d 1184 (Ct. Cl. 1981); *cert. denied*, 455 U.S. 1017 (1982).

In another Florida case, a large-scale miner of limestone in 1972 purchased a tract of 1,560 acres for the sole purpose of mining limestone. The Corps denied a permit under Section 404 that would have enabled the landowner to mine 98 acres of the tract. Rather than appeal the denial, the landowner claimed a regulatory taking.

Although the claims court agreed with the landowner that a taking existed and awarded more than $1 million (*Florida Rock Industries, Inc. v. United States*, 8 Cl. Ct. 160 [1985]), the Federal Circuit Court of Appeals overturned the decision because the denial of the permit only precluded mining and did not foreclose other economically viable uses, such as sale of the property. The court ruled that a valid defense to this type of takings claim was that the property's fair market value had increased (even if the reason for the increase was that speculators would be willing to buy the property in the hope that future regulatory policies might change). The case was remanded back to the claims court to determine the taking questions in light of fair market values. *Florida Rock Industries, Inc. v. United States*, 791 F.2d 893 (Fed. Cir. 1986); *cert. denied*, 479 U.S. 1053 (1987).

The claims court, in deciding the question of the fair market value of the property after application of the regulation, accepted the landowner's valuation that the highest and best use of the property was only "future recreational/water management" (open space). The court rejected the government's argument (and ignored the direction of the circuit court) that the land had a much higher investment value because speculators may not fully comprehend the regulatory restrictions placed on the property. Comparing the value of the property before regulation (when mining was a permitted use) to its value after regulation (when open space was the best use), the court stated that the value of the property was reduced by 95 percent as a result of the Corps' permit denial under Section 404. The court found that the Corps' denial constituted a taking and awarded the plaintiff more than $1 million. *Florida Rock Industries, Inc. v. United States*, 21 Cl. Ct. 161 (1990); see also companion case, *Loveladies Harbor, Inc. v. United States*, 21 Cl. Ct. 153 (1990), in which the claims court awarded more than $2.6 million to a developer who was denied a Section 404 permit to develop 11.5 acres of wetlands.

For the second time, the Federal Circuit Court of Appeals reversed the claims court's calculation of the valuation of the property before and after imposition of the regulation. The circuit court directed the claims court to determine the fair market value of the land based on the speculative market in the project area (west of Miami). If the court finds that land has decreased in value, the claims court is required to find whether that reduction should be considered a 'noncompensable diminution' in value or a taking of some portion of value. Within this finding, the claims court is required to assess the compensating benefits from the regulatory environment to the property and others similarly situated, whether the benefits are widely shared by society while the costs are borne by few, and whether alternative activities permitted are economically realistic. *Florida Rock Industries, Inc. v. United States*, ___ F.3d ___, No. 91-5156 (Fed. Cir. March 10, 1994).

Although recent court decisions have favored landowners who claim a regulatory taking, landowners still must prove that property values diminish when a land use regulation is imposed which cannot be justified by the legal necessity to protect important natural resources.

Created wetland with water control structure, Yolo County.

5

California Wetlands Regulation

In addition to federal laws and regulations, California provides another layer of regulation and review of actions to protect wetlands. In particular regions of California–along the coastal zone, San Francisco Bay, and the Lake Tahoe basin–even more regulatory layers are added. Finally, cities and counties throughout California are attempting to protect wetlands through general plan policies, ordinances, and by other methods.

This chapter summarizes California's recently adopted wetlands conservation policy, and then discusses state laws protecting wetlands, including the California Fish and Game Code Sections 1600-1607, the California Coastal Act, and the California Environmental Quality Act. Important regional programs describe yet another layer of review and regulation, pointing to the need for permit applicants to undertake an integrated approach if all the permitting requirements of all the agencies involved are to be satisfied.

The multiplicity of federal, state, and local regulatory requirements often makes it difficult for wetlands permit applicants to successfully navigate the permit maze and for environmentally concerned citizens to seek the protection and enhancement of wetlands. The integrated permitting approach offered at this chapter's conclusion represents the authors' recommended approach to increase the probability of success in the permitting process.

Permit applicants and environmental activists alike continue to be challenged in the 1990s by overlapping and inconsistent regulatory programs, agencies pursuing narrow statutory missions, and agency staff with inadequate budgets and excessive workloads.

The multiplicity of federal, state, and local regulatory requirements often makes it difficult for wetlands permit applicants to successfully navigate the permit maze and for environmentally concerned citizens to seek the protection and enhancement of wetlands.

The result is often much expense and delay, with little achieved in terms of either wetlands permitting or wetlands protection.

More fundamental reforms in federal and state wetlands policy will be needed to improve the efficiency of wetlands permitting and the effectiveness of wetlands protection in California. The 1993 Clinton and Wilson administration wetlands policies recognize the need for such reforms, and the reality that the state's most valuable wetlands cannot be protected using a permit-by-permit regulatory approach. Observations on the effectiveness of these policy changes, and additional changes that may be needed, are included in the Epilogue to this book.

1993 California Wetlands Conservation Policy

Until recently, California lacked a comprehensive approach to wetlands regulation and protection. On August 23, 1993, the Governor attempted to remedy this situation by issuing an executive order on wetlands creating a California State Wetlands Conservation Policy. An interagency wetlands task force, jointly headed by the state Resources Agency and the California Environmental Protection Agency (Cal-EPA), is responsible for implementing the new policy. The California State Wetlands Conservation Policy has three goals—

Cal-EPA = California Environmental Protection Agency

▶ To ensure no overall net loss and a long-term net gain in wetlands acreage and values in a manner that fosters creativity, stewardship, and respect for private property

▶ To reduce the procedural complexity of state and federal wetlands conservation program administration

▶ To encourage partnerships that make restoration, landowner incentives, and cooperative planning the primary focus of wetlands conservation

California is implementing three regional projects to serve as pilot programs to test the new wetlands policy—

▶ The Central Valley project which includes support for the Central Valley Habitat Joint Venture and other existing programs that will initiate a cooperative planning process for conservation of wetlands in a defined area of the Valley, develop pilot wetlands mitigation banks, and initiate a flood management/wetlands habitat program in the Yolo Bypass

▶ The San Francisco Bay Area project which includes development of a comprehensive regional wetlands plan and assumption by the state of some Section 404 permitting responsibilities

Assumption of Wetland Permitting Authority by the State of Maryland

In 1989, the state of Maryland passed the Maryland Nontidal Wetlands Protection Act. This program went beyond the restrictions of Section 404 of the CWA to regulate various types of activities occurring in wetland areas, including activities that occur in designated buffer zones outside the wetland area.

In 1991, the Corps issued a nontidal wetlands general permit to the State of Maryland. This general permit delegates to the Maryland Department of Natural Resources, under the Maryland Nontidal Wetlands Protection Act regulatory program, the authority to regulate and issue permits for activities involving the discharge of dredged or fill material into wetlands where the project affects fewer than five acres of nontidal wetlands.

In Maryland, the applicant would submit a permit application for activities affecting less than five acres in nontidal waters to Maryland's Department of Natural Resources which forwards copies to the Corps and other interested resource agencies. The Corps has 45 days to determine if the application meets the general permit requirements. If the project qualifies, a permit from Maryland without a separate permit from the Corps will fulfill the requirements of Section 404 of the CWA.

▶ The Southern California project which includes creation of a Southern California Wetlands Joint Venture to coordinate regional wetlands conservation activities

The Governor's 1993 wetlands policy included several regulatory reforms. The state will—

▶ Assume Section 404 permit authority on an incremental basis. A San Francisco Bay Area pilot program will allow the state to gain practical experience with Section 404 administration. On a statewide basis, the state will develop consistent standards and guidelines necessary to assume Section 404, including wetland definitions and mitigation standards

▶ Encourage regulatory flexibility and promote wetlands creation and restoration. The California State Water Resources Control Board is to develop a 'balanced' policy on federal nationwide permits

The state has proposed other nonregulatory measures, whereby the state will be—

- ▶ Using existing data and new satellite imagery to create a statewide wetlands inventory, which is not to be used for regulatory purposes
- ▶ Identifying regional and statewide goals, starting with the San Fransisco Bay Area, for conserving, restoring, and enhancing wetlands, and encouraging the maintenance of economic uses of restored or enhanced wetlands through voluntary landowner participation
- ▶ Encouraging local and regional agencies to integrate wetlands conservation into their planning processes through techniques such as watershed planning, advanced wetlands identification, and flood plain management
- ▶ Supporting a variety of state and federal funding programs to voluntarily acquire, restore, enhance, and manage wetlands (the state is to publish a landowners' assistance guide detailing available incentive programs)
- ▶ Authorizing the California Department of Fish and Game and other agencies to develop new guidelines for mitigation banking that recognize regional concerns and planning needs and contain flexible mitigation ratios

California Fish and Game Code Sections 1600-1607

DFG has jurisdictional authority over wetland resources associated with rivers, streams, and lakes under California Fish and Game Code Sections 1600-1607. These code sections are included as Appendix P. A map of DFG Regions and addresses of regional offices are provided in Appendix T.

DFG has the authority to regulate work that will substantially divert, obstruct, or change the natural flow of a river, stream, or lake; substantially change the bed, channel, or bank of a river, stream, or lake; or use material from a streambed.

DFG has the authority to regulate work that will substantially divert, obstruct, or change the natural flow of a river, stream, or lake; substantially change the bed, channel, or bank of a river, stream, or lake; or use material from a streambed. Activities of state and local agencies and public utilities that are project proponents are regulated by DFG under Section 1601 of the code, and activities of private individuals that are project proponents are regulated under Section 1603. DFG enters into a streambed alteration agreement with a project proponent and can impose conditions on the agreement to ensure no net loss of wetland values or acreage. The streambed or lakebed alteration agreement is not a permit, but rather a mutual agreement between DFG and the project proponent.

Because DFG includes under its jurisdiction streamside habitats that under the federal definition may not qualify as

California Department of Fish and Game May Regulate Where the Corps Does Not

In 1989, a nationwide discount retailer proposed construction of a new store at a 20-acre site in the foothills of the central Sierra Nevada. The site supported an intermittent stream with large oak trees on the banks and approximately half an acre of Corps jurisdictional wetland (wet meadow). The project proponent planned to remove all the trees, fill the wetland, and move the stream channel. A county-prepared negative declaration under CEQA did not require the project proponent to provide for mitigation. The Corps verified that the wetlands could be filled under a nationwide general permit and that no mitigation would be required.

Although it appeared that mitigation for habitat removal was not required, at this point the California Department of Fish and Game, choosing to exert its jurisdiction over the intermittent stream under Section 1603 of the California Fish and Game Code, required a streambed alteration agreement. The discount store, as a condition of this agreement, had to prepare and implement a mitigation and monitoring plan for impacts on the stream and the oak riparian habitat. The store in fact was built, with new trees planted on the banks of the realigned stream channel, and monitoring is conducted annually.

wetlands on a particular project site, DFG jurisdiction may be broader than the jurisdiction of the Corps. Riparian forests in California often lie outside the plain of ordinary high water regulated under Section 404 of the Clean Water Act, and often do not have all three parameters (wetland hydrology, hydrophytic vegetation, and hydric soils) sufficiently present to be regulated as a wetland. However, riparian forests are frequently within DFG regulatory jurisdiction under Sections 1600-1607.

The type of activities DFG regulates under Sections 1600-1607 authority include rechanneling and diverting streams, stabilizing banks, implementing flood control projects, crossings of rivers or streams (including bridges and culverted crossings), diverting water, damming streams, mining gravel, and logging operations.

A project proponent must submit a notification for streambed alteration to DFG before construction. The package should contain a formal application form (FG 2023 'Notification of Removal of Materials and/or Alteration of Lake, River, or Streambed Bottom

The type of activities DFG regulates under Sections 1600-1607 authority include rechanneling and diverting streams, stabilizing banks, implementing flood control projects, crossings of rivers or streams (including bridges and culverted crossings), diverting water, damming streams, mining gravel, and logging operations.

or Margin'), and include: the project location; assessor's parcel number; property owner's name and address; construction period; type and quantity of material to be removed, displaced, or added; construction methods proposed; impacts to vegetation, fish, and wildlife resources; and proposed mitigation measures. (*See* Appendix S for a sample application.)

The notification requires an application fee for streambed alteration agreements, with a specific fee schedule based on the cost of the project. This fee schedule is provided in Appendix R. The project proponent should also include copies of the California Environmental Quality Act compliance document and other available environmental documents in the notification package. If the proposed work is in a designated wild and scenic river, a written determination of consistency with the California Wild and Scenic Rivers Act from the Secretary for Resources must be included with the notification. The notification should be submitted to the headquarters of the DFG region in which the project will occur.

Private timber harvest plans submitted under the provisions of the California Public Resources Code Section 4581 may be used to fulfill the notification requirement of Section 1603.

After receiving notification of streambed alteration, DFG assigns the agreement process to the local game warden. The game warden has 30 days to review the notification and provide recommendations, if any, on the existence of fish and wildlife resources and propose measures to protect these resources. During the 30-day review period, the game warden often makes a request that a site survey be conducted to evaluate the possible effects of the proposed project on natural resources.

DFG may add reasonable conditions to the approval, but Sections 1600-1607 provide that disputed conditions can be resolved by arbitration in the event an agreement cannot be reached.

DFG may add reasonable conditions to the approval, but Sections 1600-1607 provide that disputed conditions can be resolved by arbitration in the event an agreement cannot be reached. Within 14 days following receipt of DFG's recommendations, the project proponent must accept the conditions of the agreement in writing. If the conditions are unacceptable, the project proponent may request a meeting to discuss the issues in question. Within seven days DFG must meet with the project proponent to develop mutually acceptable proposals. If agreement cannot be reached, the project proponent and DFG may request that a panel of arbitrators be established.

Within seven days, an arbitration panel consisting of one DFG representative, one representative of the project proponent, and one mutually agreed-upon person must meet to address unresolved issues. The panel has legal authority to make binding decisions regarding impacts on fish and wildlife resources, and the panel has 14 days to reach a mutually acceptable agreement.

For public agencies that propose ongoing or routine work in areas subject to DFG jurisdiction for the maintenance and operation of water supply, drainage, flood control, or waste treatment facilities, only one initial notification and agreement is required. A Memorandum of Understanding (MOU) between the public agency and DFG can cover recurring operation and maintenance activities, but additional agreements may be needed if the work substantially changes or if conditions affecting fish and wildlife resources substantially change and would be affected adversely by the proposed operation.

MOU = Memorandum of Understanding

California Coastal Act

The California Coastal Commission has jurisdiction over wetlands in the coastal zone under both state legislation (California Coastal Act of 1976, Public Resources Code Sections 30000 *et seq.*) and federal legislation (Coastal Zone Management Act, 16 USC 1451 *et seq.*). The coastal zone generally extends 1,000 yards inland from the mean high tide line, except in certain significant areas where it extends inland to the closest of either the first major ridgeline parallel to the sea or five miles from the mean high tide line.

The California Coastal Commission has jurisdiction over wetlands in the coastal zone under both state and federal legislation.

The federal Coastal Zone Management Act requires federal permit applicants to obtain a certification that activities proposed within the coastal zone are consistent with state coastal zone management programs. Of particular importance is the requirement that applicants for Corps Section 404 permits obtain a Coastal Commission determination of consistency with the California coastal zone management program (see 33 CFR 325.2[b][2][ii]).

Also, the Coastal Act establishes state planning and permit requirements. Each city or county within the coastal zone must prepare a local coastal program for Coastal Commission certification. Coastal development permits are issued by the Coastal Commission until LCPs are certified, and by local governments after certification. Coastal development permits issued by local governments are subject to appeal to the Coastal Commission.

Coastal development permits issued by the Coastal Commission before LCP certification must comply with wetlands policies and other policies established by the California Coastal Act and with the Coastal Commission's statewide interpretive guidelines for wetlands. In general, these policies allow wetlands to be filled

Urban encroachment and channelization of a stream, Riverside County. This stream was channelized and surrounded by urban development. Even if wetland vegetation reestablishes in the stream channel, there is no buffer area to separate the development from the stream. Human activity, trash, dogs, cats, night lighting, noise, and other disturbances resulting from the development will adversely affect any wildlife that may try to use the stream.

only for water-dependent activities when no feasible upland alternatives exist, and they require wetland impacts to be avoided or minimized. The Coastal Commission in 1993 issued detailed "procedural guidance for the review of wetlands progress in California's coastal zone." Applicants seeking commission permits involving wetlands should carefully review this guidance. Coastal development permits issued by local governments following LCP certification must conform to wetland policies and other policies in the certified LCP. Developments between the nearest public road and the sea or shoreline of any water body must also comply with the California Coastal Act's public access and recreation policies.

State Coastal Conservancy

The State Coastal Conservancy, which is not a regulatory agency, was created by the California Coastal Act of 1976 to preserve and restore coastal resources. The Coastal Conservancy is authorized to acquire fee title and easements on land located in the coastal zone and to award grants to local agencies for coastal restoration projects (Government Code Sections 31000 *et seq.*).

State Lands Commission

The State Lands Commission manages submerged lands, tidelands, and swamp and overflowed lands owned by the state.

The State Lands Commission manages submerged lands, tidelands, and swamp and overflowed lands owned by the state. Submerged lands are permanently covered by tidal waters. Tidelands are subject to the ebb and flow of tides and lie between the ordinary high and low water mark of tidal water bodies. Swamp and overflowed lands are landward of the ordinary high water mark, but are subject to periodic overflow and flooding and require levees or drainage.

Although the state has sold much of these lands, once conveyed, submerged lands and tidelands are still subject to the public trust even if filled. Under the doctrine of public trust, the state may preclude uses inconsistent with the purposes of the public trust, which include commerce, navigation, fisheries, and recreation.

If project proponents need to use submerged lands and tidelands still owned by the state, State Lands Commission permits or land use leases with conditions to protect the purposes of the public trust may be required.

California Environmental Quality Act

CEQA (Pub. Res. Code Sec. 21000 *et seq.*) is an environmental law that covers a broad range of resources, including wetlands. CEQA applies to projects proposed to be carried out or requiring approval by state and local public agencies. It requires these agencies to disclose a project's significant environmental effects and provide mitigation whenever feasible. DFG, the State Lands Commission, the CCC, and other agencies with jurisdiction over wetlands must be notified when CEQA documents for a project are to be prepared. Significant effects on the environment identified in Appendix G of the State CEQA Guidelines (Office of Planning and Research 1992) that may pertain to wetlands are actions that would–

CEQA requires state and local agencies to disclose a project's significant environmental effects and provide mitigation for these impacts whenever feasible.

▶ Substantially affect a rare or endangered species of animal or plant or the habitat of the species

▶ Interfere substantially with the movement of any resident or migratory fish or wildlife species

▶ Substantially diminish habitat for fish, wildlife, or plants

These conditions for significant effects would apply to wetlands where species in the project area are wholly or substantially dependent on wetland habitat.

DFG will comment on CEQA documents where wetlands resources are identified and significant impacts on wetlands may occur. DFG usually considers impacts on wetlands to be significant, and DFG policy holds that no net loss of wetland functions or values should result. Typically DFG recommends to the CEQA lead agency that adverse effects on wetland habitats be fully mitigated and that, as the first priority, the mitigation include the avoidance of wetland resources. DFG also considers impacts on riparian habitats to be significant and recommends their full mitigation.

DFG considers impacts on riparian habitats to be significant and recommends their full mitigation.

A mitigated negative declaration or environmental impact report prepared under CEQA that DFG has found adequate in its treatment of wetland resources can usually be used to satisfy DFG requirements for Sections 1600-1607 agreements.

California Regional Programs

Tahoe Regional Planning Agency

The Tahoe Regional Planning Agency (TRPA) was created by an interstate compact between California and Nevada. In California, TRPA's jurisdiction consists of the Lake Tahoe Basin portions of Placer and El Dorado Counties. The regional plan and regulations of TRPA set forth many land use and environmental controls that can protect wetlands. TRPA grants development permits only for those projects consistent with its regional plan and regulations, and projects are reviewed to ensure that the established environmental carrying capacity thresholds are not exceeded.

TRPA = Tahoe Regional Planning Agency

San Francisco Bay Conservation and Development Commission

The San Francisco Bay Conservation and Development Commission (BCDC), created in 1965 by the McAteer-Petris Act (Government Code Sections 66600 *et seq.*), has jurisdiction over all areas of San Francisco Bay subject to tidal action, including a shoreline band extending 100 feet inland. BCDC also has jurisdiction over saltponds, managed wetlands, certain other waterways, and the primary management area of Suisun Marsh.

BCDC has authority to grant development permits for projects within its San Francisco Bay jurisdiction involving filling, excavation, or substantial change in use. BCDC evaluates permit applications for consistency with policies in the McAteer-Petris Act and the San Francisco Bay Plan. In general, these policies authorize fill or excavation of wetlands only for water-dependent projects where no feasible upland alternatives exist, and only if wetlands impacts are mitigated. BCDC issues four types of permits: major permits, administrative permits, emergency permits, and regionwide permits.

Suisun Marsh development permits are issued by BCDC for the primary management area and by Solano County for the secondary management area. Permit applications are evaluated for consistency with policies in the Suisun Marsh Preservation Act of 1977 (Public Resource Code Sections 29000 *et seq.*) and the Suisun Marsh Protection Plan.

Also, for areas within its jurisdiction BCDC, rather than the Coastal Commission, issues federal consistency determinations under the Coastal Zone Management Act.

Delta Protection Commission

The Delta Protection Commission was created by the Delta Protection Act of 1992 (Public Resource Code Sections 29700 *et seq.*). Jurisdiction extends to the Sacramento-San Joaquin Delta, as defined by the California Water Code Section 12220.

Although it is not a regulatory agency, the Delta Protection Commission is required to develop a comprehensive long-term regional plan for the Delta. A draft of this plan was released in July 1994. Local governments are then required to amend their general plans to be consistent with the Delta Protection Act and the regional plan. The Act's policies call for preservation and protection of riparian and wetlands habitat within the Delta.

Regional Water Quality Control Board Basin Plans

Each of California's nine RWQCBs (*see* Appendix U for map and address) must prepare and periodically update basin plans pursuant to the Porter-Cologne Act. Each basin plan sets forth water quality standards for surface water and groundwater, as well as actions to control nonpoint and point sources of pollution to achieve and maintain these standards.

Basin plans offer an opportunity to achieve wetlands protection based on water quality objectives. Another opportunity for wetland protection is RWQCB Section 401 certification of Section 404 permits. However, the interests of each RWQCB in regulating wetlands vary greatly. The San Francisco Bay Area RWQCB has been the most ambitious RWQCB in attempting to regulate wetlands.

In 1987, the San Francisco RWQCB adopted amendments to its basin plan authorizing the board to regulate discharges of earthen fill into wetlands directly. However, these rules were invalidated judicially (*State Water Resources Control Board v. Office of Administrative Law* 12 Cal.App.4th 697 [1993]), and thus are not being implemented.

Local Wetland Regulation

Cities and counties often use their planning and land use control authorities to protect or regulate wetlands. Local wetlands regulation programs vary widely throughout the state. Local governments also protect wetlands indirectly through CEQA, which

Each of California's RWQCB basin plans sets forth water quality standards for surface water and groundwater, as well as actions to control nonpoint and point sources of pollution to achieve and maintain these standards.

Local Agencies Protect Wetlands

Counties and other local agencies are becoming more involved in wetland protection and sometimes provide protection for wetlands not offered by the Corps or other agencies.

In 1989, a small development company planned to develop a 50-acre parcel in southern Sacramento County into nine large lots. A wetland delineation identified 16 vernal pools and a seasonal swale, totalling 1.2 acres. To spare himself from Corps regulation under Section 404, the developer designed the project to avoid placing fill in any of the wetlands. Because the pools would be scattered across several private lots, the county was concerned about the long-term protection of the vernal pools. The county required that building restrictions be put on the deeds of each lot that supported vernal pools before approving the tentative map, with restriction areas including vernal pools and their watersheds. These building restriction areas were recorded on the final plat, and the project was approved by the county.

requires local governments, whenever feasible, to mitigate significant wetland impacts of projects they carry out or approve.

Local government tools that can be used to regulate and protect wetlands include general plans, specific plans, zoning, special use permits, subdivision maps, and development agreements. In addition, local governments are essential participants in regional attempts to protect wetlands through, for example, establishment of mitigation banks.

Integrated Approach to Wetlands Permitting in California

This section is addressed to landowners and permit applicants desiring to successfully navigate through the California wetlands regulatory maze; however the standards presented can also be used by regulatory agencies and environmentally concerned citizens to evaluate proposed projects. By using the following process landowners and permit applicants can increase their chances of success in obtaining necessary permits where projects may affect wetland resources.

- ▶ Hire knowledgeable experts
- ▶ Address wetlands concerns early in project planning
- ▶ Prepare a comprehensive inventory of all regulatory requirements
- ▶ Develop a permitting strategy plan
- ▶ Commit to facilitate the regulatory process proactively

Hire Knowledgeable Experts

Landowners and permit applicants should retain competent wetlands scientists and regulatory specialists as part of their project team. Wetlands scientists should be skilled in the complete range of wetlands services, including delineation, impact analysis, and mitigation planning. Regulatory specialists (such as environmental planners or attorneys) should have in-depth knowledge of and experience with all pertinent federal, state, regional, and local regulatory programs, and permitting experience with all the relevant agencies. Experts that have established good professional relationships with agency staff assigned to the project will be especially helpful in facilitating the permit process.

Address Wetlands Concerns Early in Project Planning

When planning a project, landowners and applicants should consult with experts to identify wetlands as early as possible. All Corps jurisdictional wetlands should be mapped to an appropriate scale for analysis of impacts, and all additional bodies of water and

Avoid Impact on Wetlands Where Possible

A regional water quality control board required a city in central coastal California to upgrade its wastewater treatment facility to full secondary treatment to achieve and maintain full compliance with state and federal water quality regulations. The facility is adjacent to a lagoon which supports marsh habitat. To comply with RWQCB requirements, the city proposed that new clarifier tanks be added to the system in a linear configuration.

As initially designed, the project required the removal of approximately one acre of wetlands and other waters under the jurisdiction of the California Coastal Commission and the Corps. To avoid wetland impacts and regulatory delays, the city's consultant suggested that the project be redesigned. By placing the tanks in an L-shaped configuration rather than in the standard linear array, city engineers avoided all impacts on wetlands, and no permits or mitigation for wetland impacts were required.

water-associated habitats that may be regulated by federal, state, or local agencies should be identified and mapped. When feasible, the project should be designed to avoid or minimize impacts on wetlands and avoid triggering wetlands regulatory requirements.

If a project cannot be feasibly designed to avoid impacts on wetlands, the alternatives analysis principals established by the Section 404(b)(1) Guidelines (*see* chapter 4 for discussion of these guidelines) should be applied early in the project planning process. Project purposes should be clearly defined, the non-availability of upland sites to achieve these purposes should be documented, and mitigation sequencing should be followed.

Prepare Inventory of Regulatory Requirements

Landowners and applicants should always consider nonregulatory approaches (*see* chapter 6) to achieve their objectives. When these are not appropriate, landowners and permit applicants should prepare a comprehensive inventory of relevant federal, state, and local wetlands regulatory requirements. The following major requirements are usually applicable–

Federal

▶ Section 404 permit

▶ NEPA environmental document (environmental assessment or environmental impact statement)

State, Regional, or Local

- ▶ Section 401 water quality certification
- ▶ Section 1600-1607 agreement
- ▶ Local or regional land use entitlements
- ▶ CEQA environmental document (an initial study or environmental impact report)

Develop a Permit Strategy Plan

For each regulatory requirement, the applicant should detail permitting steps and schedule, and then a coordinated permitting plan should be developed. Agencies with the strictest requirements or the most control over the permit process (usually the Corps) should receive special attention. Meeting the requirements of these agencies will likely meet most or all the requirements of other agencies concerned with wetlands.

Survey a Project Site for Wetlands Before Acquisition and Project Planning

A residential development was planned for a site in the central Sierra Nevada foothills. The project was designed to include 65 one-acre lots on a 77-acre site. After the project was designed, the site was found to support 24 acres of waters of the United States, including 12.5 acres of wetlands.

The developer redesigned the project to reduce the impacts on waters of the United States by increasing the size of the lots and reducing their number to 40. The redesigned project included wetland restoration to compensate for 4.5 acres of waters that would be filled. Because wetlands preserved on the site would be subdivided among numerous future property owners, the Corps and U.S. Fish and Wildlife Service were skeptical that these wetlands could be effectively protected and managed after the project was completed. As the project's size diminished and the cost of wetland mitigation increased, the project proponent eventually abandoned the idea of residential development.

The developer should have conducted wetland surveys before purchasing an interest in the site and before planning the use of the property. Under prevailing regulatory policies, the proposed residential development was not a feasible use for a site that is more than 30% jurisdictional waters.

Placer County 1994 General Plan
Wetlands Goals and Policies

California local governments are increasingly taking advantage of the general plan process to develop wetlands protection programs. For example, Placer County's 1994 General Plan sets forth the following goals and policies for wetlands and riparian areas.

Goal

The general plan's stated goal is to protect wetland communities and related riparian areas throughout Placer County as valuable resources.

Policies

The general plan includes the following policies:

1. The County shall support the "no net loss" policy for wetland areas regulated by the U.S. Army Corps of Engineers, the U.S. Fish and Wildlife Service, and the California Department of Fish and Game. Coordination with these agencies at all levels of project review shall continue to ensure that appropriate mitigation measures and the concerns of these agencies are adequately addressed.

2. The County shall require new development to mitigate wetland loss in both regulated and non-regulated wetlands to achieve "no net loss" through any combination of the following, in descending order of desirability: (1) avoidance, (2) where avoidance is not possible, minimization of impacts on the resource; or (3) compensation, including use of a mitigation banking program that provides the opportunity to mitigate impacts to rare, threatened, and endangered species and/or the habitat which supports these species in wetland and riparian areas.

3. The County shall discourage direct runoff of pollutants and siltation into wetland areas from outfalls serving nearby urban development. Development shall be designed in such a manner that pollutants and siltation will not significantly adversely affect the value or function of wetlands.

4. The County shall strive to identify and conserve remaining upland habitat areas adjacent to wetlands and riparian areas that are critical to the survival and nesting of wetland and riparian species.

5. The County shall require development that may affect a wetland to employ avoidance, minimization, and/or compensatory mitigation techniques. In evaluating the level of compensation to be required with respect to any given project, (a) on-site mitigation shall be preferred to off-site, and in-kind mitigation shall be preferred to out-of-kind mitigation; (b) functional replacement ratios may vary to the extent necessary to incorporate a margin of safety reflecting the expected degree of success associated with the mitigation plan; and (c) acreage replacement ratios may vary depending on the relative functions and values of those wetlands being lost and those being supplied, including compensation for temporal losses. The County shall continue to implement and refine criteria for determining when an alteration to a wetland is considered a less-than-significant impact under CEQA.

Ideally, a CEQA or NEPA environmental document should serve as the umbrella for demonstrating compliance with wetlands regulatory requirements. Timing of the preparation of the CEQA or NEPA document should be closely integrated with the timing of the wetland permit processes.

Some applicants obtain local land use entitlements and complete CEQA compliance before initiating the Section 404 process, a strategy which provides certainty about local approval before further investment in the Section 404 process. However, if the Section 404(b)(1) analysis produces new information about project impacts or alternatives, additional time and expense may be required because this information could trigger the need for a subsequent CEQA document.

CEQA and NEPA environmental documents may be prepared before regulatory agencies issue permits. To avoid delay and duplication of effort, landowners and permit applicants should normally integrate the CEQA and NEPA processes with permitting for wetlands.

Facilitate the Process

Since federal, state, and local wetlands regulatory agencies have considerable workloads and are generally understaffed, landowners and applicants should work proactively to obtain timely permit approvals. To facilitate the process, landowners and permit applicants should contact agencies early in the process to ensure that application packages are complete, schedule frequent progress meetings, arrange for multiple agency coordination meetings, and conduct or fund special technical studies needed to support permit decisions.

Naturally establishing cottonwoods on the banks of an artificial oxbow, Yolo County.

6

Wetland Resource Planning and Mitigation

Successful wetland mitigation requires effective advance planning and an integrated, cooperative approach to mitigation design and implementation. Traditional regulatory methods of managing wetlands are giving way to new techniques, such as watershed planning and mitigation banking, that can be achieved through public and private partnerships. This chapter describes how to proceed effectively using traditional mitigation methods; the state of wetland and watershed planning in the 1990s; and the concepts, policies, and benefits of mitigation banking. Recent laws, policies, and guidelines governing wetland resource planning and mitigation are also explained.

Wetland Mitigation Planning and Implementation

The planning methods described below can apply to both large- and small-scale mitigation projects. The relative level of effort directed toward planning for small projects can be modified to reflect the reduced expectations of the mitigation plan.

Because Section 404 of the Clean Water Act restricts the placement of dredged or fill material within waters of the United States, including wetlands, unless permitted by the U.S. Army Corps of Engineers, the regulatory guidelines require a permit applicant to justify project-related impacts on waters of the United States and to provide mitigation to avoid, minimize, or compensate for unavoidable impacts. Compensatory mitigation is a fundamental component of the federal wetland regulatory program under Section 404.

Because Section 404 of the Clean Water Act restricts the placement of dredged or fill material within waters of the United States unless permitted by the U.S. Army Corps of Engineers, the regulatory guidelines require a permit applicant to avoid, minimize, or compensate for unavoidable impacts.

The goal of compensatory mitigation is to prevent any net loss of acreage, function, or value.

The goal of compensatory mitigation is to prevent any net loss of acreage, function, or value. Wetland functions are the natural physical, chemical, and biological processes and attributes of the wetland ecosystem, and wetland values are those functions that people consider desirable, useful, or important. A wetland may have many functions, only some of which are considered valuable, such as wildlife habitat, flood storage, water quality improvement, and groundwater recharge. The functions and values provided by a wetland vary by the type, location, and quality of each individual wetland.

Three methods for compensatory wetland mitigation are generally recognized: enhancement, restoration, and creation.

▶ Wetland enhancement is achieved by increasing the functions and values of existing wetlands at a mitigation site, and by improving the functions and values of degraded wetlands.

▶ Wetland restoration involves re-establishing wetlands where they once existed but were lost due to disturbance of one or more of the physical or biological components.

▶ Wetland creation is the development of new wetlands where they have not historically occurred.

Successful mitigation planning relies on several key concepts–

▶ Working with whole ecosystems rather than individual components ensures that the developed wetland system is self-sustaining

▶ Integrating wetland habitat into the entire landscape provides a network of wetlands and uplands supporting many species that constitute a functioning biological community

▶ Using a holistic, multidisciplinary approach to evaluate all aspects of the ecosystem when developing and implementing a plan ensures the most viable result, based on the principle that whole ecosystems are greater than the sum of their parts

The San Francisco and Los Angeles Corps districts have published detailed mitigation and monitoring guidelines (U.S. Army Corps of Engineers, San Francisco District 1991; U.S. Army Corps of Engineers, Los Angeles District Regulatory Branch 1993). These guidelines should be followed for projects planned within the districts. The Sacramento Corps District is in the process of preparing mitigation and monitoring guidelines, as of mid-1994.

Establishing Mitigation Objectives

A mitigation project may have many, potentially conflicting goals. Therefore, goals must be well defined and prioritized before designing a plan for mitigation or restoration.

Regulatory Objectives. When defining the goals of a mitigation plan, the most influential considerations are the kinds of impacts to be mitigated and the extent of mitigation mandated by regulatory requirements. Identifying and addressing all mitigation requirements at once is the most efficient way to mitigate project-related impacts. Planning for all project-related impacts is more cost-effective, practical, and valuable than addressing each measure separately. In California, wetland mitigation requirements must be identified for both the federal Section 404 process and the

Figure 6-1. Recommended restoration project process (applies to small or large sites)

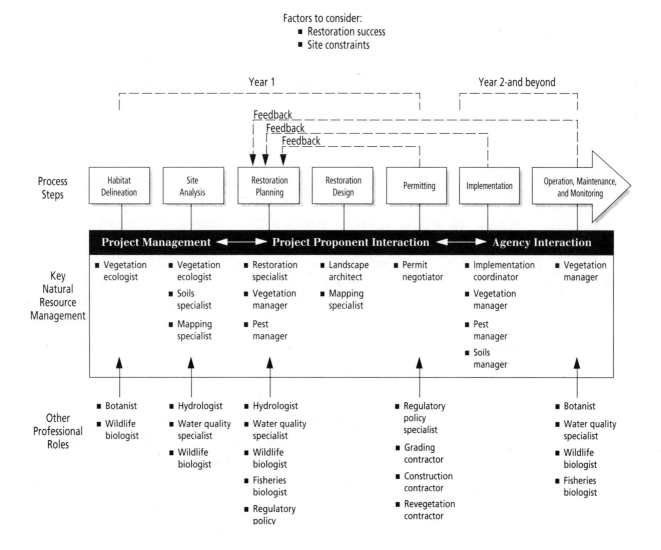

California Department of Fish and Game's streambed alteration agreement process (Sections 1600-1607 of the California Fish and Game Code). Both sets of regulations can influence mitigation goals, and fulfilling the regulatory requirements of one will not necessarily satisfy the other. In addition, to compensate for wetland losses, conditions for compliance with the National Environmental Protection Act and the California Environmental Quality Act may identify even more requirements.

In some cases, indirect and cumulative impacts must be considered. Under CEQA and NEPA, indirect and cumulative impacts on wetlands could be identified as significant; and under these acts direct, indirect, and cumulative impacts on wetland resources may need to be mitigated.

Familiarity with the policies of regulatory agencies is essential to the smooth progression of a mitigation project, because differences between regulatory requirements and the goals of a project proponent must be resolved. Section 404 guidelines require a proponent to show that the project maximizes wetland avoidance and minimizes impacts on resources. Compensatory mitigation can then be proposed for unavoidable impacts.

Typically, regulatory agencies prefer onsite rather than off-site mitigation, which may conflict with project proponents who prefer to maximize the amount of onsite development. Regional limitations can also dictate the need for onsite mitigation. Some wildlife species, for example, may have specific site requirements that limit the feasibility of offsite mitigation.

The type of wetland impact must be in balance with the compensatory habitat proposed, and the project proponent and regulatory agencies must agree about what constitutes 'in-kind' versus 'out-of-kind' mitigation. Resource agencies generally recommend in-kind mitigation because it involves compensating for habitat loss with habitat of equal value to what was affected. However, certain types of wetlands with relatively low values are sometimes mitigated out-of-kind by creating higher value wetlands. Out-of-kind mitigation may be the only option for wetlands that cannot be effectively replicated, such as seeps and some types of vernal pools.

The project proponent and the regulatory agencies must agree on the ratio of mitigation area to impact area. One-for-one replacement may be satisfactory for low-value wetlands, but high value wetlands may require higher ratios due to the uncertainty of retaining full values on an acre-for-acre basis in created wetlands. In addition, regulatory agencies usually request higher

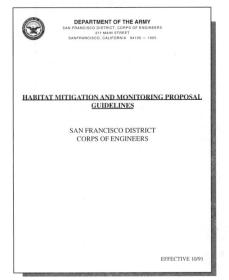

DEPARTMENT OF THE ARMY
SAN FRANCISCO DISTRICT, CORPS OF ENGINEERS
211 MAIN STREET
SAN FRANCISCO, CALIFORNIA 94105 — 1905

HABITAT MITIGATION AND MONITORING PROPOSAL GUIDELINES

SAN FRANCISCO DISTRICT
CORPS OF ENGINEERS

EFFECTIVE 10/91

Habitat Mitigation and Monitoring Proposal Guidelines
San Francisco District Corps of Engineers
Effective October 1991

SUGGESTED TABLE OF CONTENTS

ratios of mitigation area to impact area because a temporary loss of functions and value occurs between the time of impact and the time the mitigation area is fully functioning.

Multipurpose Objectives. Because regulations generally focus on acreage and do not require that affected wetlands be assessed for function and value, little emphasis is placed on the anticipated function and value of mitigation wetlands. This becomes a problem when evaluating the success of a mitigation plan. To help define target functions and values for compensatory habitat, the function and value of the affected wetland should be documented before the impact occurs. Use of formal valuation techniques such as the habitat evaluation procedure (HEP) or wetland evaluation technique (WET) can facilitate the determination of wetland habitat values at both the impact and mitigation sites, with the replacement of wildlife habitat identified as part of the mitigation plan's goals.

Wetlands often have different functions and values and therefore different mitigation goals. Some examples of mitigation goals are–

HEP = Habitat Evaluation Procedure

WET = Wetland Evaluation Technique

► Enhance, create, or restore wildlife and fisheries habitat
► Protect water quality (for example, by sediment trapping, chemical detoxification, nutrient removal, and nutrient cycling)
► Provide flood protection (for example, by reducing discharge velocity or increasing storage capacity)
► Stabilize shorelines
► Facilitate groundwater recharge
► Maintain streamflow
► Protect socioeconomic values, such as recreation and aesthetics

When identifying the goals of a mitigation design, all pertinent functions and values should be considered.

In most urban areas, it may be important to integrate into the design goals for educational and recreational use as well as compensation for wetland habitat. However, since educational and recreational use of a wetland may reduce wildlife habitat value, the plan should clearly recognize the trade-off between achieving goals for habitat and public use.

The Section 404 process does not explicitly require mitigation for all the associated wetland functions and values. However, environmental review for CEQA and NEPA may require that these multipurpose objectives be addressed in response to the concerns

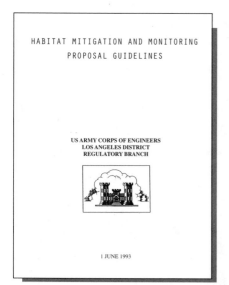

HABITAT MITIGATION AND MONITORING
PROPOSAL GUIDELINES

US ARMY CORPS OF ENGINEERS
LOS ANGELES DISTRICT
REGULATORY BRANCH

1 JUNE 1993

U.S. Army Corps of Engineers
Los Angeles District Regulatory Branch
Habitat Mitigation and Monitoring Proposal Guidelines

RECOMMENDED TABLE OF CONTENTS

SUMMARY

I. PROJECT DESCRIPTION
   A. Location of Project
   B. Brief Summary of Overall Project
   C. Responsible Parties
   D. Jurisdictional Areas to be Filled by Habitat Type
   E. Type(s), Functions, and Values of the Jurisdictional
      Areas to Be Directly and Indirectly Impacted

II. GOAL OF MITIGATION
   A. Type(s) of Habitat to Be Created/Enhanced
   B. Functions and Values of Habitat to Be Created/Enhanced
   C. Time Lapse
   D. Estimated Cost
   E. Special Aquatic Habitats

III. FINAL SUCCESS CRITERIA
   A. Target Functions and Values
   B. Target Hydrological Regime
   C. Target Jurisdictional Acreage to Be Created/Enhanced

IV. PROPOSED MITIGATION SITE
   A. Location and Size of Mitigation Area
   B. Ownership Status
   C. Existing Functions and Values of Mitigation Area
   D. Present and Proposed Uses of Mitigation Area
   E. Jurisdictional Delineation (if applicable)
   F. Present and Proposed Uses of All Adjacent Areas
   G. Zoning

V. IMPLEMENTATION PLAN
   A. Rationale for Expecting Implementation Success
   B. Responsible Parties
   C. Schedule
   D. Site Preparation
   E. Planting Plan
   F. Irrigation Plan
   G. As-Built Conditions

VI. MAINTENANCE DURING MONITORING PERIOD
   A. Maintenance Activities
   B. Responsible Parties
   C. Schedule

VII. MONITORING PLAN
   A. Performance Criteria
   B. Monitoring Methods
   C. Annual Reports
   D. Schedule

VIII. COMPLETION OF MITIGATION
   A. Notification of Completion
   B. Corps Confirmation

IX. CONTINGENCY MEASURES
   A. Initiating Procedures
   B. Alternative Locations for Contingency Mitigation
   C. Funding Mechanism
   D. Responsible Parties

APPENDIX A FORMAT INFORMATION
   A. Text Format Notes for Mitigation/Monitoring Proposals,
      as Built Reports, and Annual Reports
   B. List of Figures to Be Submitted
   C. Figure Format Notes
   D. Schedule

of a local agency's planning, public works, or parks department, or its mosquito and vector control district. For these reasons, it is important to build consensus with the local agencies, as well as the state and federal regulatory agencies, about the goals of the mitigation plan.

Since achieving all mitigation goals and objectives may not be feasible, priorities should be established. Because the project proponent is legally obligated to meet mitigation requirements as a condition of permit approval, replacement of wetland habitat acreage at a specified ratio, as required for Section 404 permit compliance, is often the highest priority of wetland mitigation projects.

Mitigation Site Analysis

After identifying and setting priorities for mitigation goals, and after consensus is reached on these goals between the project proponent and regulatory agencies, a site analysis should be conducted by a multidisciplinary team of environmental scientists.

Mitigation should be modelled after naturally occurring ecosystems. When selecting a mitigation site, initial evaluation should determine whether the mitigation will involve enhancing, restoring, or creating wetlands. Creative combination of these strategies may lead to the best plan.

Conducting a mitigation site analysis is for the purpose of evaluating the site's existing physical and biological conditions. Collected information about the topography, hydrology, structures, soils, vegetation, and wildlife will help define opportunities and constraints. In special circumstances, data on chemical features of soils or water may need to be gathered. More than one site should be evaluated to identify the one most suitable for compensatory mitigation, considering several criteria for selection–

▶ Existing wetland resources. The mitigation site may require a wetland delineation to determine if wetland resources are present and whether these wetlands will be avoided or enhanced.

▶ Upland resource values. Identify resources that should be preserved.

▶ Topography. Correct topographic gradients are critical to establishing wetland hydrology, a key element of successful wetland restoration and creation. Unless good topographic data for a site is available, hydrology cannot be accurately evaluated.

- ▶ Soils. Soils determine water percolation rates, provide the growing medium for plants, help identify historical uses of the site, and reveal the extent of groundwater fluctuation.

- ▶ Hydrology. Identify peak events, minimum water levels, water fluctuation, water quality, base flows, groundwater recharge, and past and future alterations to the site's hydrology.

- ▶ Site history. Past uses or management such as grazing, burning, irrigation, grading, compaction, and herbicide use can all affect site conditions. A one-time site analysis may not identify these important issues. Knowledge of the history of a site is important to understanding present site conditions and planning future uses.

- ▶ Land use issues. Identify land use constraints such as ownership, easements, planning and zoning designations, cultural resources, incompatible land uses, access to water rights, and the presence of hazardous materials.

- ▶ Size of property and adjacent land uses. The property size should be adequate to provide wetland compensation and sufficient upland buffer areas. Land uses on adjacent parcels that would influence mitigation plans should be identified.

Collecting tule plugs (underground stems) from freshwater marsh for transplanting to a marsh restoration site, Yolo County.

Opportunities and Constraints Evaluation

A comparison of the mitigation goals with the information obtained from the site analysis will determine possible opportunities and constraints. If conflicts between mitigation goals and the existing conditions and suitability of the site arise, the goals may have to be revised or alternative mitigation sites may have to be identified. To resolve these conflicts, a meeting between the project proponent and regulatory agencies may be necessary.

Design Approach

The mitigation design should preserve as much existing high value natural habitat as possible.

To maximize the possibility of successful mitigation, the design team should consist of individuals with diverse backgrounds—in disciplines such as wildlife biology, plant ecology, soil science, hydrology, and geotechnical engineering—to reflect the complex environmental conditions of the site.

Mitigation goals should always be kept in mind during the design process. Regulatory compliance—avoidance; type and extent; onsite or offsite; creation, enhancement, or restoration; in-kind or out-of-kind habitat mitigation—should be the key consideration influencing the design.

Conceptual Plan Development. Developing a constraints map can help identify sites with specific physical or biological constraints and opportunities for mitigation. A constraints map is produced by identifying areas of a site with high, moderate, or low physical or biological values.

When preparing a mitigation design, develop and evaluate several alternatives. Based on the site analysis, alternatives should focus on the goals of mitigation and address key issues and conflicts.

Select the alternative that best addresses the goals, is most sensitive to site conditions, and minimizes conflicts. The preferred design alternative can then be refined into a conceptual mitigation plan, which generally includes such elements as layout of the development, the extent of mitigation acreage, trailway alignments, and hydrologic connections. To avoid misunderstandings and possible future major revisions, the conceptual plan should be taken to the regulatory agencies for review and comments.

Figure 6-2. Design Process

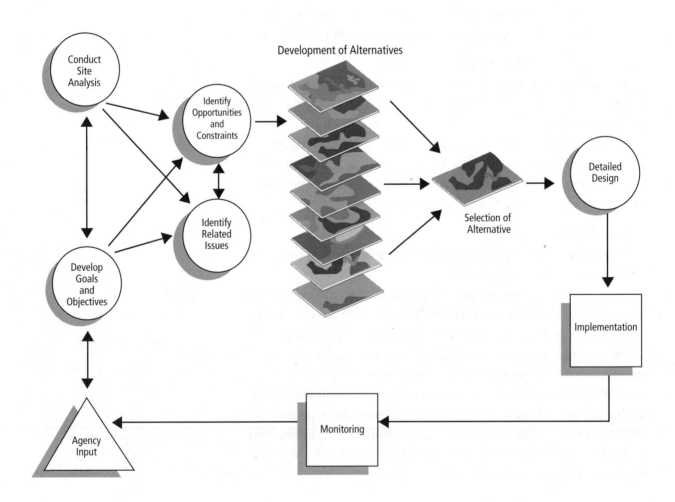

Detailed Design Development. A detailed mitigation design can be a refined version of the conceptual plan. Best illustrated on a topographic map of the site to ensure that the appropriate elevations can be developed, the detailed plan should specify trailway configurations, planting and buffer zones, and the location and extent of each mitigation feature. It should also identify the hydrologic regime and vegetative composition expected at the mitigation area. Discuss the detailed mitigation design with the regulatory agencies to help build consensus on key issues. Eventually specification packages can be developed that include detailed grading, planting, and irrigation plans.

A detailed mitigation plan should address multidisciplinary and multi-objective design elements. The site must meet the particular spatial and timing needs of target wildlife and must include adequate buffer areas to ensure that the site will provide adequate habitat, meet water quality objectives, and minimize disturbance caused by humans. The plan should also identify what portion of the site is the buffer area and how much of a buffer is needed to protect habitat.

A detailed design should identify the source of water, its quality, quantity, and management regime, and specify the timing of flow, inundation, and its long-term viability. If an artificial source of water is used, the plan should consider how long vegetation on the site can be sustained in the absence of the artificial water source. In most cases, Corps, EPA, USFWS, and DFG do not accept wetland mitigation using artificial water sources because of the risk that the water availability may not be permanent.

Usually too much emphasis is put on the revegetation aspects of the detailed plan. If the hydrology and other physical aspects are correct, target plant species are likely to establish naturally given a nearby source of propagules. However, revegetation considerations should include the location of plantings (depending on the hydrologic and soil needs of the species) and methods for planting versus allowing natural revegetation. The plan should also identify the type and recommended sources of planting material, allowing for some mortality over time while still permitting the anticipated vegetation objective to be achieved. The plan should identify the use of native, local plant material and specify the need to maintain extra stock for replacement planting.

Preparing willow cuttings for planting at a riparian habitat restoration site, Tehama County.

The plan should evaluate the type of grading necessary for the required wetland hydrology. Consult a soil scientist and an engineer to ensure that adequate elevations and suitable substrate are specified. Details of soil compacting, top dressing, sealing, ripping, or disking, as well as measures for weed control before and after construction should be part of the plan. In addition, it should include management techniques to monitor and control sediment loading and trash accumulation at the site.

Because the local acceptance of wetland mitigation projects can also depend on adequate mosquito control measures, work with the local mosquito abatement district to identify appropriate strategies for management.

Mitigation Construction

Attention to details of construction will help ensure that the mitigation plan is properly implemented. Construction drawings, with detailed grading plans developed in consultation with an engineer and a soil scientist, should address soil preparation in response to specific conditions—such as the need to import clay, rip through a subsurface hardpan, control for erosion, or provide top dressing to increase the soil's suitability for growing plants.

Figure 6-3. Cross Section of Planned Vegetation Zones for a Restoration Project

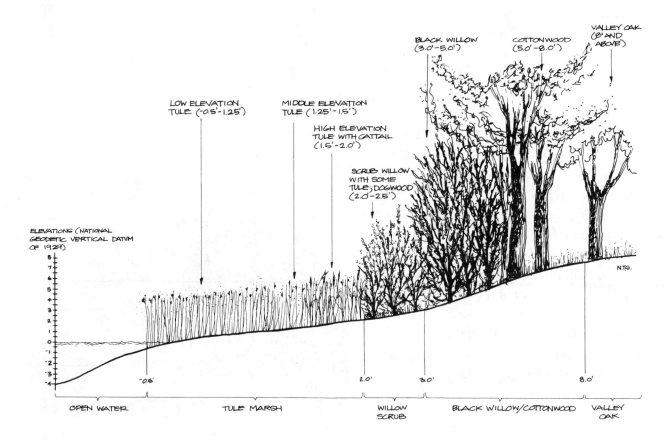

Mitigation plans and specifications should be clear and complete, with contracts specifying who is responsible for site preparation, construction, planting, maintenance, and monitoring.

A schedule of events should identify proper timing of implementation and specify how plantings and water management should be set up at appropriate times. The schedule should clearly define responsibilities for everyone involved. Because a continuous link between the construction and mitigation design teams is important, a member of the mitigation design team should supervise construction so that onsite troubleshooting can resolve any unanticipated problems that arise. Team members familiar with the goals of the mitigation plan can best resolve unexpected problems encountered during construction.

Maintenance of Mitigation Areas. Resource agencies generally require the project proponent to identify who will be responsible for a mitigation site's short- and long-term maintenance and management. Usually, a project proponent is responsible for maintenance and monitoring for the first five to ten years. Long-term ownership, habitat protection, and management can be assigned to public agencies, nonprofit organizations, or entities in the private

Figure 6-4. Examples of planting details for restoration plans

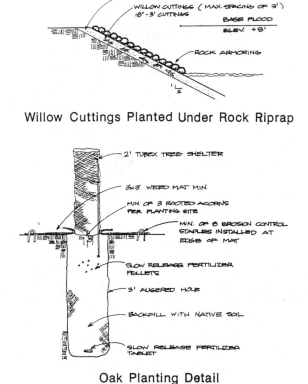

Willow Cuttings Planted Under Rock Riprap

Oak Planting Detail

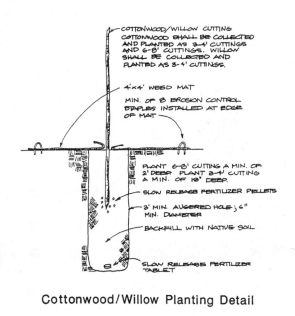

Cottonwood/Willow Planting Detail

sector. Deed restrictions must often be placed on mitigation sites to prevent changes in use should ownership change. Often the project proponent will establish a trust fund for long-term operation and management to ensure that the mitigation site will be preserved as wildlife habitat. The type of maintenance activity varies by project and can include water management, replacement planting, weed and pest management, sediment and trash removal, and mosquito management.

Monitoring and Performance Standards. Developed to measure the success of a mitigation project, performance standards for mitigation wetlands can be based on the conditions of the wetlands to be removed or can be established by evaluating the vegetative composition or hydrologic conditions of the target habitat. They can also be based on a variety of physical or biological conditions such as use by wildlife, depth and duration of ponding, and percentage of plant cover.

The purpose of monitoring is to evaluate the establishment of and changes in wetland functions at mitigation sites through time. Results are compared to the goals and performance standards of the mitigation plan to measure the project's relative success. Monitored data are most often used to determine if ample

Figure 6-5. Example of an annual monitoring schedule for a restoration site.

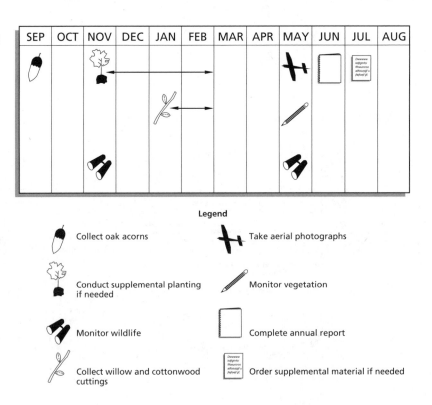

acreage and species composition has been established to satisfy regulatory requirements.

Naturally occurring wetlands on or near the mitigation site that support functions and values similar to the requirements for mitigation wetlands can be used during monitoring as examples of habitat that mitigation wetlands should eventually support. These naturally occurring 'control' wetlands must reflect the type and quality of habitat that the mitigation wetlands aim to achieve. Collecting data simultaneously from mitigation wetlands and naturally occurring controls allows annual or longer-term fluctuations in natural systems to be measured. For example, if a performance standard for hydrology is based on average annual rainfall and that rainfall is below normal, the standard may not be met. Comparing mitigation wetlands to naturally occurring wetlands nearby more accurately evaluates the performance of the mitigation site.

Performance standards should acknowledge variation over time. The first-year performance standard for vegetation, reflecting the immaturity of planted material, could be based on plant survivorship, while the final-year standard, anticipating more mature vegetation, could be based on the percentage of vegetative cover. Performance standards should reflect the minimum acceptable level of success that satisfies regulatory requirements.

Monitoring Methods. Developing a thorough and cost-effective monitoring program requires advance planning. Methods for monitoring mitigation should be scientifically acceptable and statistically valid, and should be accomplished within a relatively brief period. They should be specific to the project and document progress toward achieving the project's goals.

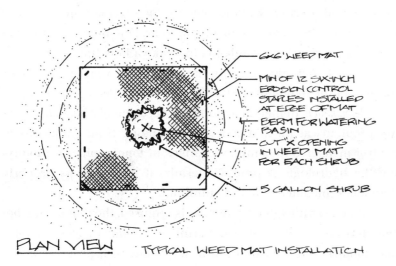

Figure 6-6. Typical weed mat installation for a restoration planting.

Identify permanent photographic stations to provide a visual record of the mitigation site before, during, and after construction, and for the duration of the monitoring.

Photographic documentation is an invaluable tool for evaluating the progress of restoration efforts. Identify permanent photographic stations to provide a visual record of the mitigation site before, during, and after construction, and for the duration of the monitoring. Examples of ecological parameters to be evaluated during monitoring include–

▶ Aerial extent of habitat, by type

▶ Planting survival (percentage of total plants installed or minimum number of surviving plants)

▶ Vegetative cover (relative and absolute cover of target species)

▶ Species richness (the number of different species that are present)

▶ Hydrology (depth, frequency, and duration of inundation)

▶ Wildlife use (by birds, mammals, amphibians, reptiles, fish, or invertebrates)

▶ Disturbance (natural and artificial impacts)

Even though natural ecosystems take many years to establish, mitigation monitoring is generally conducted for only a short period following initial construction of habitat. Therefore, monitoring should focus on critical components–such as hydrology and composition of plant species–recognizing that associated functions and values will develop gradually. All of the functions and values associated with some types of ecosystems may not be present at a site during the mitigation monitoring period.

Timing and Schedule for Mitigation Monitoring. Although mitigation monitoring is generally required for a five-to-ten-year period following implementation, for some types of habitats state and federal agencies are beginning to require longer periods. The timing depends on the type of wetland and the critical resources to be documented. Certain wildlife species, for example, may be present only for short periods during the year. For some systems–like high terrace riparian woodlands that take a long time to mature– it may be beneficial to monitor every other year for a longer period of time to obtain data on long-term trends.

Remediation. Remedial actions are occasionally needed to rectify problems at the mitigation site, ranging from simple weed control measures to complex changes in topography for modifying the hydrologic regime. Generally, if mitigation is properly planned, remedial actions are minimal.

When significant remediation is required, the monitoring period may have to be extended. Permit conditions typically require additional monitoring time in these instances. If progress is ob-

Be Careful When Many Jurisdictions Overlap and Land Use Requirements Conflict

A development company wanted to construct a resort and conference center in coastal Santa Cruz County. The development would affect a small stream that flowed into the ocean, portions of which were identified as jurisdictional wetlands by the California Coastal Commission and the Corps. The Coastal Commission also claimed jurisdiction over the streambed and adjacent riparian habitat, and the California Department of Fish and Game claimed jurisdiction over the stream and riparian habitat under Section 1603. The Corps, under a nationwide general permit, allowed fill of the wetlands and other waters. However, Santa Cruz County, with an approved program for local coastal land use in effect, prescribed to the developer the mitigation measures needed for a coastal consistency determination.

The county required that several, somewhat conflicting actions be taken within the narrow stream corridor: (1) regrading the streambed for erosion control, (2) restoring riparian habitat, and (3) constructing a trail for access to the beach. The developer agreed to take these actions.

Soon after the erosion control and trail construction were complete and just before riparian plantings were installed, a heavy winter storm created tremendous flows in the usually dry stream channel. New areas of streambed and bank eroded, and floodwater undermined and damaged the trail. The project was redesigned and reconstructed with less emphasis on riparian habitat restoration and more on erosion control. In the end, the development company met the requirements of the coastal consistency determination and the Section 1603 streambed alteration agreement.

Attempting to accomplish too many objectives at a single mitigation site that is too small to support them is a recipe for failure. Project proponents and regulatory agencies need to recognize that trade-offs may be necessary where objectives conflict.

served but performance standards are not met after the designated time period, a viable remediation measure could be a longer monitoring period to give the wetland habitat more time to become established.

Common Reasons for Mitigation Failure

Although the science of wetland creation, restoration, and enhancement is still evolving, many lessons have been learned.

Some common reasons for failure include unrealistic objectives, lack of data on soils or hydrology, inadequate planning and design detail, lack of project control during construction, a mitigation area of insufficient size, unforeseen events such as fire or flooding, lack of long-term management, and unrealistic success criteria or monitoring requirements.

Conclusion

Successful wetland mitigation is often difficult and expensive. Avoiding impacts on wetlands by prudent project planning is usually the most successful and cost-effective form of mitigation.

The process described here integrates numerous physical, regulatory, and design factors. To ensure the long-term viability of mitigation areas and to comply with regulations, good mitigation planning includes the evaluation of natural systems to integrate many factors into the design.

Establishing a list of priorities creates the baseline, but communication between the project proponents and regulatory agencies to build consensus throughout the goal-setting and design phases of the plan will alleviate unanticipated discrepancies between mitigation design and regulatory expectations. The extent of mitigation efforts should be dictated by the site's physical and biological conditions, using site constraints and opportunities to develop a realistic program with a high probability of success. For mitigation to succeed, construction parameters should be well planned and documented. Before beginning construction, carefully define the responsibilities of all participants, and during construction be sure that someone familiar with the mitigation goals is onsite to solve problems and ensure proper implementation. Finally, performance standards and monitoring methods should evaluate the progress of mitigation with cost-effective and scientifically sound and defensible techniques.

Before beginning construction, carefully define the responsibilities of all participants, and during construction be sure that someone familiar with the mitigation goals is onsite to solve problems and ensure proper implementation.

Advanced Wetland and Watershed Planning

The early 1990s have seen a new emphasis on advance planning and cooperative efforts for wetlands protection as an alternative to project-by-project permit battles and regulatory gridlock. Advance planning and cooperative efforts for wetlands protection offers several advantages over the traditional regulatory approach—

▶ The highest-value wetlands can be identified and protected
▶ Landowners have greater notice and opportunity to integrate wetlands early in their development plans

- ▶ Needs of landowners, environmental groups, and other stakeholders can be better met through a voluntary, cooperative process
- ▶ Regional programs can better achieve wetlands conservation than the project-by-project approach
- ▶ Wetlands protection can be more easily integrated with more comprehensive natural resource values, such as habitat management and water quality protection.

Channels cut for creation of backwater sloughs in the Sacramento-San Joaquin Delta, San Joaquin County

Federal and State Advance Planning and Cooperative Programs Policies

Federal. A key principle embodied in current federal wetlands policy is to encourage nonregulatory programs such as advance planning, research, and public/private cooperative efforts. The essence of this approach is that–

- ▶ Federal agencies will provide increased technical assistance and promote voluntary cooperative wetlands planning and restoration efforts.
- ▶ A revised Executive Order on wetlands which recognizes the importance of restoration will require federal agencies to take a comprehensive watershed approach to wetlands protection.
- ▶ Continued funding will be provided for the U.S. Department of Agriculture's Wetland Reserve Program, which helps farmers restore wetlands on their property.

Current federal wetlands policy also supports new Clean Water Act incentives for comprehensive state and local watershed planning. Advance planning for wetlands protection can take a variety of forms, but a regional, watershed-based approach offers the greatest opportunity for protecting the highest value wetlands, as well as for integrating wetlands protection with water quality protection and flood control. For example, pursuant to the National Estuaries program (Section 320 of the Clean Water Act), the U.S. Environmental Protection Agency prepared a 1993 Comprehensive Conservation and Management Plan for the San Francisco Bay and Delta with major wetlands protection features.

State. A key goal of current state policy is to make restoration, landowner incentives, and cooperative planning the primary focus of wetlands conservation–

A regional, watershed-based approach offers the greatest opportunity for protecting the highest value wetlands, as well as for integrating wetlands protection with water quality protection and flood control.

► Local and regional agencies are encouraged to integrate wetlands into their planning processes through techniques such as watershed planning

► A variety of voluntary wetlands protection programs are supported, and a landowner's assistance guide which inventories available programs is available

► Regional cooperative advance planning projects in the Central Valley, Bay Area, and Southern California are encouraged

Federal-Local Partnerships for Wetland Planning

EPA and the Corps have regulatory and nonregulatory programs to assist local, state, and federal agencies in wetland conservation planning. Regulations and policies promulgated under Section 404 of the Clean Water Act provide mechanisms for partnerships between local agencies and EPA and the Corps, the federal agencies that regulate activities in wetlands under Section 404. Advanced identification (ADID), general permits, and special area management plans (SAMPs) are three tools that can be used to plan for wetland conservation through federal-local partnerships in areas of rapid development.

ADIDs, general permits, and SAMPs are discussed below. However, it should be noted that less formal means of federal-local wetland planning partnerships can be conducted. EPA and the Corps can provide wetland conservation planning assistance without using the formal ADID or SAMP processes. In many cases, it may be more efficient and flexible to use an informal planning process that follows the concepts of ADIDs and SAMPs without entering into the official processes.

Advanced Identifications

Advanced identification is a method, in accordance with EPA's Section 404(b)(1) Guidelines, of identifying the suitability of wetland sites for the future disposal of dredged or fill material. Two types of sites are identified under the ADID process:

► Possible future disposal sites, including existing disposal sites and nonsensitive areas, and

► Areas generally unsuitable for disposal site specifications (for example, sites unsuitable for placement of dredged or fill material). (40 CFR 230.80.)

Classifying sites in either of these categories provides information that can be used to facilitate the process for individual or

ADID = Advanced identification

SAMP = Special area management plan

Advanced identification is a method, in accordance with EPA's Section 404(b)(1) Guidelines, of identifying the suitability of wetland sites for the future disposal of dredged or fill material.

general Section 404 permits. The identification of areas as 'possible future disposal sites' does not constitute a permit for the discharge of dredged or fill material into wetlands but serves as an indicator to potential developers that issuance of a permit is likely. Conversely, the designation of a site as generally unsuitable for disposal serves as a warning to developers that issuance of a permit is unlikely or that extensive conditions will likely accompany a permit.

The identification of areas as 'possible future disposal sites' does not constitute a permit for the discharge of dredged or fill material into wetlands but serves as an indicator to potential developers that issuance of a permit is likely.

Information provided in an ADID allows EPA and the Corps to focus their regulatory efforts to reduce wetland losses where resource values and scarcity are greatest and come into conflict with development pressures. The ADID–

▶ Enables more effective advanced planning;

▶ Increases public awareness of the importance and value of aquatic ecosystems; and

▶ Provides the regulated community with an indication of the likelihood of permit issuance (Sullivan and Richardson 1993).

Local agencies may request that EPA initiate an ADID in their area after consultation with the state.

EPA Region 9 has recently completed an ADID for the Verde River and its tributaries located northeast of Phoenix, Arizona. A detailed assessment of the functions and values of wetland resources of the Verde River was prepared (Sullivan and Richardson 1993). The Verde River was selected for an ADID based on three key factors–

▶ High wetland and riparian functions and values,

▶ A high probability of wetland loss or degradation without proper management and planning, and

▶ The opportunity to participate and work cooperatively in other comprehensive planning efforts (Sullivan and Richardson 1993).

An ADID can be made more effective as a wetland conservation and development planning tool if it is followed by Corps issuance of a general permit that streamlines regulatory requirements in nonsensitive sites. One disadvantage of an ADID is that it can be labor intensive and time consuming to complete, requiring a substantial amount of coordination among various agencies and interest groups.

General Permits

General permits are Section 404 permits issued by the Corps on a regional, statewide, or nationwide basis designed to apply to categories of discharge activities that are similar in nature and will cause only minimal adverse environmental effects. General permits serve to streamline the permitting process, avoiding the more complex and sometimes extended process of issuing individual permits. Special and general conditions are part of the general permit and must be met by the project proponent for the general permit to apply. Local agencies and the Corps can work in partnership to develop appropriate regional general permit conditions.

Regional general permits may be issued by the Corps where local ordinances, or a combination of state and local agency ordinances and regulations, provide protections for wetlands that achieve the objectives of the Section 404 permit program. The Corps must still verify that proposed actions are authorized under the general permit, but the local agency essentially can assume portions of the Corps' wetland regulatory responsibility for their area. For example, General Permit no. 16 was issued, effective August 1, 1994, by the Corps' Sacramento District for construction, modification, and repair work in wetlands and other waters in the Lake Tahoe region. The region covered by the general permit is the same as the jurisdictional boundaries for the Tahoe Regional Planning Agency. Discharges into wetlands and other waters are authorized if the activities meet the requirements of TRPA, state and local agencies, and the general permit.

General permits are reviewed by the Corps every five years and at that point may lapse or be reauthorized with or without modification.

Special Area Management Plans

Special area management plans were authorized under amendments to the 1980 Coastal Zone Management Act. The process is defined as—

> A comprehensive plan providing for natural resource protection and reasonable coastal-dependent economic growth containing a detailed and comprehensive statement of policies, standards, and criteria to guide public and private uses of lands and waters; and mechanisms for timely implementation in specific geographic areas within the coastal zone.

Although the SAMP process was originally intended to be applied to the coastal zone, Corps guidance issued in 1986 (and extended in 1992) for the use of SAMPs stated that the process of collaborative interagency planning within a geographic area of special sensitivity is just as applicable in noncoastal areas (Corps Regulatory Guidance Letter 86-10).

A successfully developed SAMP can–

▶ Reduce the problems associated with the traditional case-by-case review of wetland impacts and mitigation and individual permit applications

▶ Provide some predictability to the development process

▶ Address individual and cumulative impacts on wetlands in the context of broad ecosystem needs

One disadvantage of a SAMP is that it can be labor-intensive and time-consuming to develop, requiring a substantial amount of coordination among various agencies and interest groups.

According to Corps guidance, the advantages of a SAMP may outweigh the disadvantages if the following elements exist before a SAMP is proposed–

▶ The area is environmentally sensitive and under strong developmental pressure

▶ A sponsoring local agency ensures that the plan fully reflects local needs and interests

▶ Full public involvement is encouraged in the planning and development process

▶ All parties express a willingness at the outset to conclude the SAMP process with a definitive regulatory product. (Corps Regulatory Guidance Letter 86-10.)

According to Corps guidance, the ideal SAMP concludes with two products–

▶ Appropriate local/state approvals and a Corps general permit or abbreviated processing procedure for activities in specifically defined situations and

▶ A local/state restriction and/or an EPA Section 404(c) restriction (preferably both) for undesirable activities. (Corps Regulatory Guidance Letter 86-10.)

Under Section 404(c), EPA may veto Corps issuance of a discharge permit. A Section 404(c) restriction is an EPA action to prevent discharges before a permit application is even submitted. Although the Corps may still be requested to issue individual permits for activities that do not fall into either category above, individual permits should represent a small number of the total permit actions within the area covered by the SAMP.

An example of a SAMP considered successful is the Anchorage, Alaska SAMP enacted in 1982 (Salvesen 1990). Under this SAMP, wetlands were classified into four categories–

▶ Preservation. Sites where no development is allowed except in special cases

- ▶ Conservation. Sites where some development is allowed
- ▶ Developable. Sites where development is not hindered by wetlands present
- ▶ Special study. Sites with wetlands that require additional study before they can be classified into categories 1, 2, or 3

Under this SAMP, a general permit was issued by the Corps for sites designated as developable, while sites designated as preservation or conservation are permitted by the Corps on a project-by-project basis (Salvesen 1990). Since enactment of the Anchorage SAMP, most development has occurred in sites designated as developable (Salvesen 1990).

In California, the Corps' Sacramento District is presently involved in the development of one SAMP and regional general permit for a six-square-mile area around the City of Bridgeport in Mono County. The purpose of the Bridgeport SAMP is to–

- ▶ Provide guidance to landowners, developers, and agencies
- ▶ Protect wetland resources
- ▶ Allow for orderly community growth while preserving, protecting and, where possible, enhancing wetland functions and values (U.S. Army Corps of Engineers public notice no. 1993000607, November 1, 1993).

The Bridgeport SAMP is being developed in accordance with Corps regulatory guidance on SAMPs and the Mono County General Plan Update. A general wetlands map of the SAMP area has been prepared and accepted by the Corps for the area. The SAMP is expected to include three categories of wetlands–

- ▶ Wetlands of high values that are generally considered unsuitable for disposal of dredged or fill material
- ▶ Wetlands of low values with poor potential for enhancement (certain types of fill may be allowed in these wetlands, provided impacts are minimized and full mitigation conducted)
- ▶ Wetlands where additional evaluation is needed to determine whether to include them in category 1 or 2.

The SAMP will require a minimum of 1:1 compensation of functions and values for all wetlands lost in the area. The use of mitigation banks will be addressed in the SAMP. Anticipated signatory agencies to the final SAMP are the Corps, USFWS, Mono County Planning Department, and Lahontan Regional Water Quality Control Board. (Corps public notice no. 199300607, November 1, 1993.)

Comparison of ADIDs, General Permits, and SAMPs

Wetlands designated under ADIDs are nonregulatory. The approval process for SAMPs, however, end with Corps and EPA regulatory decisions designating sites where the streamlined general permit process applies and sites where discharges into wetlands are restricted. ADIDs provide land developers and local agencies with valuable information for land purchase and planning decisions. Although the practice is not encouraged, permit applications can still be filed and permits approved for fill in wetland sites designated under an ADID as 'unsuitable' for placement of fill material. Conversely, fill permits may still be denied for wetlands designated as 'non-sensitive' under an ADID.

ADIDs provide land developers and local agencies with valuable information for land purchase and planning decisions.

SAMPs provide much of the same wetland locational information as ADIDs, but with regulatory restrictions attached. SAMPs may designate wetland sites legally restricted from fill activities (Section 404[c] restrictions). In addition, the SAMP specifically designates wetland sites where general permits developed under the SAMP are applicable.

General permits may be issued without undergoing an ADID or SAMP process. However, completion of an ADID prior to the formulation of a general permit provides valuable information for establishing the local agency responsibilities and the scope and conditions of the general permit. By providing specific data on wetland extent, location, and value within a region, an ADID also lends credibility to the local wetland regulations established, activities approved under the general permit program, and the special and general conditions of the general permit.

Wetland Mitigation Banking

In wetland banking, to mitigate impacts on those wetland resources affected by independent projects, offsite wetland areas are enhanced, created, or restored. A mitigation banking program uses a credit system to enable the purchase of compensation credits, with each credit representing a unit of restored or created wetlands which can be withdrawn to offset impacts incurred at a development site. In most cases, wetlands are created at a mitigation bank site prior to the removal of wetlands at a project site. Recent regulatory guidance suggests that it may be appropriate to allow incremental distribution of credits corresponding to the appropriate stage of successful wetland establishment. In those circumstances variable mitigation ratios may be used to reflect wetland values at any given point in time.

A mitigation banking program uses a credit system to enable the purchase of compensation credits, with each credit representing a unit of restored or created wetlands which can be withdrawn to offset impacts incurred at a development site.

Usually based on an estimate of the functions and values of the habitat lost and the functions and values anticipated for habitat established at the mitigation site, mitigation ratios determine the number of acres to be replaced for each acre removed. For example, higher ratios would be required when a mitigation bank is not fully functioning at the time credits are withdrawn (Memorandum to the Field, August 23, 1993 [59 FR 5913, February 3, 1994]).

Under Section 404 of the Clean Water Act, the use of a wetland mitigation bank can satisfy compensatory mitigation as long as its use is consistent with the sequencing approach to mitigation outlined in the EPA/Corps MOA.

Under Section 404 of the Clean Water Act, the use of a wetland mitigation bank can satisfy compensatory mitigation as long as its use is consistent with the sequencing approach to mitigation outlined in the EPA/Corps MOA (see description of this MOA in chapter 4). Given the sequencing requirement, participation in a wetland mitigation bank is acceptable only when a project proponent can demonstrate that the project has avoided and minimized wetland impacts to the greatest extent practicable.

Critics suggest that the priority given to avoiding wetlands in the sequencing requirement has led to an abundance of isolated wetland fragments that have lost most of their functions and values because they are surrounded by urban development. (Shabman *et al.* 1993).

A project proponent can purchase compensatory wetland credits from a mitigation bank operator who has developed wetlands specifically for this purpose. The bank operator has primary financial liability and responsibility for land acquisition and wetland construction, monitoring, and management.

Benefits of Mitigation Banking

By using a wetland mitigation bank, regulatory agencies and a project sponsor can save the time otherwise necessary to develop and approve a suitable mitigation design. Regulatory agencies increase their efficiency by simultaneously monitoring and overseeing construction of individual wetland mitigation programs for a number of projects. The use of a mitigation bank can also expedite the permit review and approval process.

Because a wetland mitigation bank consists of wetlands created, restored, or enhanced to compensate for a future loss resulting from state or Section 404 program regulations, compensatory mitigation can be implemented and functioning prior to project-related impacts. Compensation in advance prevents losses of wetland habitat values during the time between impact and mitigation.

A mitigation bank can also consolidate small, dispersed resources into a large, contiguous wetland preserve that includes upland habitats. Large, well managed preservation areas have higher natural resource values than smaller, fragmented areas, especially if the small patches are surrounded by urban development.

Mitigation banks are structured to bring together technical expertise in wetland resources planning and restoration with the financial resources necessary to construct and manage sites as wetland habitat in perpetuity. They allow government agencies and private landowners various options for offsite mitigation. Regional planners can identify where high value wetland habitats already exist and can set priorities for the creation of mitigation banks within designated resource conservation areas. In addition, public or private entities can establish mitigation banks and sell credits to permit applicants for offsite mitigation.

Landowners and entrepreneurs who wish to expand the value of wildlife habitat on their property, and profit from the sale of mitigation credits, can capitalize on mitigation banking opportunities. Developers and public agencies who manage a number of projects can mitigate unavoidable wetland impacts at their own mitigation bank sites designed to meet their specific needs.

Soil test pit to determine suitability for vernal pool creation, Tehama County.

Federal Mitigation Banking Policies

The federal government has lent its support to wetland mitigation banking in recent years with its Proposal on Protection of U.S. Wetlands (White House Office of Environmental Policy, August 24, 1993); and the U.S. Army Corps of Engineers Institute for Water Resources is completing regulatory guidance on the use of mitigation banks in the Section 404 permit process. The federal guidance will work in concert with state laws when a permit is required under Section 404 of the Clean Water Act.

The Corps Role in Reviewing Mitigation Banking Proposals. The Corps is responsible for reviewing and approving mitigation banking proposals submitted in conjunction with a Section 404 permit application. In addition, development of a mitigation bank may require a Section 404 permit if a project calls for the discharge of dredged or fill material into waters of the United States.

Corps review of mitigation banking proposals is guided by the 1993 memorandum for the field and the 1990 EPA/Corps MOA on mitigation. In addition, the San Francisco and Los Angeles Corps districts have issued more detailed mitigation and monitoring guidelines (U.S. Army Corps of Engineers, San Francisco District 1991; U.S. Army Corps of Engineers, Los Angeles District Regulatory Branch 1993) that will likely be incorporated into mitigation

The Corps is responsible for reviewing and approving mitigation banking proposals submitted in conjunction with a Section 404 permit application.

banking programs in those districts. Although not specifically directed toward mitigation banking proposals, these district mitigation guidelines contain general planning guidance that should be considered when developing any mitigation project. Corps guidelines do not specify substantive criteria that must be met to establish a mitigation bank, but rather outline the types of information an applicant would need to submit to support a mitigation proposal, including–

▶ Project description

▶ Mitigation goals

▶ Final success criteria

▶ Proposed mitigation site

▶ Implementation plan

▶ Maintenance during monitoring period

▶ Monitoring plans

▶ Notification of completion of mitigation

▶ Contingency measures

The U.S. Environmental Protection Agency's Role in Mitigation Banking. EPA is responsible for oversight of the Section 404 permit program. On December 20, 1991, EPA Region 9 in San Francisco issued procedural guidance on the use of mitigation banks for wetlands and other aquatic habitats associated with development projects permitted under Section 404 (U.S. Environmental Protection Agency 1991). The Region 9 guidance incorporates and expands mitigation concepts first presented in the 1990 EPA/Corps MOA on mitigation under Section 404, which established a sequential approach to mitigation of wetlands and aquatic habitats: avoid impacts; minimize impacts; and, finally, compensate for unavoidable impacts after all practicable minimization has been achieved.

Region 9 guidance specifically defines mitigation banking as "the creation, restoration, or enhancement of wetland or other aquatic habitats and their functional values expressly for the purpose of providing compensatory mitigation in advance of proposed discharges . . . where mitigation cannot be achieved at the site of impact." The guidance supports the use of mitigation banking as compensatory mitigation for the impacts of any project when it has been determined that offsite mitigation is appropriate.

Generally, EPA will not approve the use of mitigation banking for compensatory mitigation when onsite mitigation is practicable or when a mitigation bank would not lower the adverse impacts of a project below the threshold of significant degradation defined by the Section 404(b)(1) guidelines.

The Role of the U.S. Fish and Wildlife Service in Mitigation Banking. The U.S. Fish and Wildlife Service is developing guidelines for mitigation banking, but has not yet (as of mid-1994) issued a final policy. However, the USFWS position on wetland mitigation is addressed in its national mitigation policy (46 FR 7644) and in a 1988 biological report on mitigation banking (U.S. Fish and Wildlife Service 1988).

USFWS mitigation goals focus on habitat values. The national mitigation policy identifies four categories of habitat based on value and relative abundance.

▶ Resource Category 1 wetlands include one-of-a-kind areas of high value with listed species or those providing irreplaceable habitat. Because the mitigation goal for Category 1 is no loss of existing habitat value, USFWS believes that mitigation banking is not appropriate for this category.

▶ Resource Category 2 wetlands include those whose habitat is of high value for evaluation species and is relatively scarce. The mitigation goal for Category 2 is no net loss of in-kind habitat value, which could be achieved through compensatory mitigation. However, the policy of USFWS, like that of the EPA, suggests that mitigation sequencing should be applied and that compensatory mitigation will be considered only after all feasible avoidance and minimization of impacts has occurred.

▶ Resource Category 3 wetlands are relatively abundant and have high to medium value for evaluation species. USFWS's goal is no net loss of habitat values and the minimization of in-kind habitat loss. Therefore, where unavoidable impacts to Category 3 habitats occur, compensatory mitigation of equivalent habitat values could be applicable.

▶ Resource Category 4 habitats have medium to low value for listed and candidate species, and the goal of USFWS is to minimize the loss of any habitat value. Category 4 wetlands provide the greatest flexibility for using mitigation banks, since this category may accept out-of-kind mitigation.

USFWS mitigation policy defines mitigation banking as "habitat protection or improvement actions taken expressly for the purpose of compensating for unavoidable losses from specific future development actions" (46 FR 7644). USFWS suggests that withdrawals from the bank to offset future unavoidable losses should be based on habitat value replacement and not on acreage or cost for land purchase and management.

California State Mitigation Banking Policies and Laws

California Department of Fish and Game Draft Guidelines for Wetland Mitigation Banking. In 1990, the California Department of Fish and Game drafted guidelines for the establishment and use of wetland mitigation banks, which include financial and project qualifications, accounting, administration, and general conditions for their use. Although never made final, the draft guidelines represent DFG's position on requirements for approval, implementation, and management of a successful wetland mitigation bank.

The Sacramento-San Joaquin Valley Wetlands Mitigation Banking Act of 1993. The Sacramento-San Joaquin Valley Wetlands Mitigation Bank Act of 1993 (Section 1775-1796 of the California Fish and Game Code) was enacted to provide an alternative for accomplishing offsite wetland mitigation in California's Central Valley. The law authorizes DFG to adopt regulations to qualify sites in the region as wetland mitigation banks. The law allows a Section 404 permit applicant to make payments to a bank operator for wetland credits, and authorizes DFG to credit wetlands created in the bank against wetlands lost in a nearby urban area.

The Sacramento-San Joaquin Valley Wetlands Mitigation Bank Act of 1993 allows a Section 404 permit applicant to make payments to a bank operator for wetland credits, and authorizes DFG to credit wetlands created in the bank against wetlands lost in a nearby urban area.

The goal of California's Central Valley program to promote wetland protection and encourage wetland habitat expansion in concert with other environmental regulatory programs includes—

▶ Improving cooperation between private, nonprofit, and public entities for the management and protection of wetlands

▶ Ensuring no net loss of wetlands

▶ Encouraging and maintaining a predictable, efficient, and timely regulatory framework for environmentally acceptable development

▶ Ensuring no loss of tax base

▶ Providing an alternative form for offsite compensatory mitigation under Section 404

In the Central Valley, compensatory mitigation at a mitigation bank approved by DFG is authorized only if the bank is located within the same urban area and not more than 40 miles from the impact site. Establishing a wetland mitigation bank constitutes a project for the purposes of CEQA. The siting of the bank must therefore comply with CEQA guidelines prior to construction.

The Sacramento-San Joaquin Valley Wetlands Mitigation Banking Act directs DFG to adopt standards and criteria for qualifying a mitigation bank, designating wetland credits, and evaluating operation and maintenance. The Act specifically authorizes DFG to (1) qualify bank sites, (2) credit wetlands in a bank for impacts within a qualifying urban area, and (3) provide for payments to the bank operator. The Act recognizes that large wetland preserves can provide environmentally preferable alternatives to small, isolated preserves surrounded by urban development.

The Act specifically authorizes the Department of Fish and Game to qualify bank sites, credit wetlands in a bank for impacts within a qualifying urban area, and provide for payments to the bank operator.

For a site to qualify as a mitigation bank under the Act, DFG will consider numerous factors, including–

▶ Availability of water to support created wetlands

▶ Feasibility of wetlands construction at the site

▶ Maintenance needs to sustain created wetlands

▶ Proximity to other significant wildlife habitats

▶ Proximity to urban areas that could interfere with long-term habitat values

▶ Site operator's financial, technical, and managerial credibility

▶ Quality and quantity of existing wetland resources at the mitigation bank site

After qualifying a site, but prior to construction, DFG will coordinate and sign a memorandum of understanding with the bank operator and other interested resource agencies. The MOU must provide that (1) the site be maintained as wetland habitat in perpetuity, (2) a trust fund or bond be established to fund long-term maintenance and administration of the site if the operator defaults, and (3) a breach of the MOU terms would result in replacement of the operator. DFG determines the number of acres and types of habitat available for credit against prospective wetland loss from development in the qualifying urban area.

DFG evaluates the relative habitat value of a bank once the site supports 20 acres of established wetlands or, if vernal pools are involved, once the successful creation of vernal pools on a site adds up to 20 acres or more. Units of restored or created wetlands are expressed as credits, and accumulated credits can be withdrawn to offset impacts incurred at a development site. Wetland creation at a qualified mitigation bank must be implemented and functioning in advance of assigning availability of credits.

Once DFG has determined the credits available, the bank operator must provide an accounting of the average cost of each wetland credit. Factors contributing to the unit cost include–

- ► Land cost
- ► Construction cost
- ► Taxes
- ► DFG costs
- ► Monitoring, reporting, and oversight costs
- ► Other costs associated with preservation in perpetuity

A permit applicant with offsite mitigation requirements under Section 404 who agrees to purchase credits from a designated mitigation bank must provide full payment at the time of purchase. After payment, the applicant has no further obligations with respect to the mitigation wetlands at the bank site.

Mitigation Banking Credit Systems

The exchange system used in a mitigation bank is mitigation credits, with a unit of credit measured as acreage, function, or value.

The exchange system used in a mitigation bank is mitigation credits, with a unit of credit measured as acreage, function, or value. Withdrawals should be based on the same unit as the one used for credit. Credit determination, a critical component of mitigation banking, is one of the most difficult issues to address. Wetland banking credits are used to measure the replacement acreage, function, and values available from a mitigation bank to compensate for impacts on wetland resources.

No specific regulatory procedure dictates when mitigation credits should be determined, but early credit determination, at the time the bank is approved, has the advantage of documenting the number and type of credits potentially available. Although actual certification will occur at the time credits are withdrawn, early documentation affords bank operators a basis for establishing their cost.

Using acreage as the primary unit of credit may be insufficient to represent those wetlands that are ecologically significant or have especially high function or value. Compared to acreage, functions and values are more difficult to identify, require technical expertise, and are prone to subjectivity (especially in the case of values). The advantage is that an assessment of function or value, if done appropriately, can better represent relative wetland quality and thus better compensate for specific types of impacts on wetlands.

Functional evaluation techniques that can be used to determine wetland credits include standard indices of species diversity as well as USFWS and Corps habitat and wetland evaluation techniques (HEP or WET), or a modified version of these techniques. They can be tailored to each individual system to consistently assess functions and values at a mitigation bank over time.

The value of a wetland at a mitigation bank is expected to improve as the habitat matures. Credit withdrawals early after construction of a mitigation bank are appropriately at a higher compensation ratio. As the mitigation bank wetlands mature, the compensation ratio can be lowered, and the availability of credits can be adjusted in response to periodic monitoring. This means that compensation ratios will decrease over time as the function and value of mitigation wetlands increase.

Once a specific wetland is withdrawn, if acreage is used as the unit of credit, additional values provided by that wetland over time cannot be withdrawn.

Financial Assurances and Contingency Plans for Mitigation Banks

Federal and state mitigation guidelines require a mechanism for maintenance and management of mitigation sites, and EPA Region 9 guidance specifies the need to provide a fund for remedial actions in all mitigation banking programs. Various methods provide financial assurance or contingency funding to ensure the success of mitigation. Optional methods include the use of bonds, trust funds, escrow accounts, or insurance (Environmental Law Institute 1993).

Financial assurances can fund maintenance and monitoring requirements until the mitigation bank reaches maturity and meets all performance standards, with all credits withdrawn. In certain circumstances, financial assurances can be set up to provide long-term maintenance funding in perpetuity.

Financial assurances can also fund remedial actions or contingency plans, offering regulatory agencies some guarantee of the bank's success. If a bank operator fails to rectify problems after credits have been withdrawn, the bank's permits could be revoked and the withdrawal of additional credits denied. If the operator defaults, the Corps could take legal measures to force compliance, including forfeiture of financial assurances.

The value of a mitigation bank is expected to improve as the habitat matures.

Wet montane meadow, montane riparian scrub, and aspen riparian forest at mid-elevation in the Sierra Nevada, Placer County.

7

Epilogue

In this book, we have shared our collective knowledge and experience about how wetlands are protected and regulated in California, describing in detail the scope of existing government programs and periodically suggesting how to successfully negotiate the permit maze.

Notwithstanding the good intentions of legislators and regulators seeking to protect wetlands, the existing system is not working well. Many of the problems are well known and were expressed in President Clinton's 1993 wetlands policy (*Protecting America's Wetlands: A Fair, Flexible, and Effective Approach*, August 24, 1993), which states, in part–

> [C]ontradictory policies from feuding federal agencies have blocked progress, creating uncertainty and confusion. (page 2)

> In addition to assailing the 1989 [Interagency Wetlands Delineation] Manual, critics of federal wetlands regulatory programs effectively characterized these programs as unfair, inflexible, inconsistent, and confusing. (page 3)

> Typically, decisions affecting wetlands are made on a project-by-project, permit-by-permit basis. This often precludes effective consideration of the cumulative effects of piecemeal wetlands loss and degradation. It also hampers the ability of state . . . and local governments to integrate wetlands conservation objectives into the planning, management, and regulatory tools they use to make decisions regarding development and other natural resource issues. This can often result in inconsistent and inefficient

Notwithstanding the good intentions of legislators and regulators seeking to protect wetlands, the existing system is not working well.

Freshwater seep in the Sierra Nevada, Placer County.

efforts among agencies at all levels of government, and frustration and confusion among the public. (page 7)

The 1993 federal and state wetlands policies seek to solve these and other pressing problems within the existing system of regulation by emphasizing advance planning and voluntary cooperation. These new policies represent a major shift in the government's historical approach to wetlands protection and regulation, shifts that will probably require years to be adopted by agency staffs and embraced by the private sector.

Whether the changes are sufficiently timely or far reaching remains to be seen. In the meantime, landowners, permit applicants, and environmentally concerned citizens seeking to modify or protect wetlands will need to rely on the existing, admittedly imperfect tools and systems catalogued in this book.

Appendices

Federal Materials

Appendix A

Section 404, Clean Water Act
33 USC 1344 (1994)

Title 33. Navigation and Navigable Waters

CHAPTER 26. WATER POLLUTION PREVENTION AND CONTROL PERMITS AND LICENSES

1344. Permits for dredged or fill material

(a) Discharge into navigable waters at specified disposal sites.

The Secretary may issue permits, after notice and opportunity for public hearings for the discharge of dredged or fill material into the navigable waters at specified disposal sites. Not later than the fifteenth day after the date an applicant submits all the information required to complete an application for a permit under this subsection, the Secretary shall publish the notice required by this subsection.

(b) Specification for disposal sites.

Subject to subsection (c) of this section, each such disposal site shall be specified for each such permit by the Secretary (1) through the application of guidelines developed by the Administrator, in conjunction with the Secretary, which guidelines shall be based upon criteria comparable to the criteria applicable to the territorial seas, the contiguous zone, and the ocean under section 403(c) [33 USCS | 1343(c)], and (2) in any case where such guidelines under clause (1) alone would prohibit the specification of a site, through the application additionally of the economic impact of the site on navigation and anchorage.

(c) Denial or restriction of use of defined areas as disposal sites.

The Administrator is authorized to prohibit the specification (including the withdrawal of specification) of any defined area as a disposal site, and he is authorized to deny or restrict the use of any defined area for specification (including the withdrawal of specification) as a disposal site, whenever he determines, after notice and opportunity for public hearings, that the discharge of such materials into such area will have an unacceptable adverse effect on municipal water supplies, shellfish beds and fishery areas (including spawning and breeding areas), wildlife, or recreational areas. Before making such determination, the Administrator shall consult with the Secretary. The Administrator shall set forth in writing and make public his findings and his reasons for making any determination under this subsection.

(d) "Secretary" defined.

The term "Secretary" as used in this section means the Secretary of the Army, acting through the Chief of Engineers.

(e) General permits on State, regional, or nationwide basis.

(1) In carrying out his functions relating to the discharge of dredged or fill material under this section, the Secretary may, after notice and opportunity for public hearing, issue general permits on a State, regional, or nationwide basis for any category of activities involving discharges of dredged or fill material if the Secretary determines that the activities in such category are similar in nature, will cause only minimal adverse environmental effects when performed separately, and will have only minimal cumulative adverse effect on the environment. Any general permit issued under this subsection shall (A) be based on the guidelines described in subsection (b)(1) of this section, and (B) set forth the requirements and standards which shall apply to any activity authorized by such general permit.

. (2) No general permit issued under this subsection shall be for a period of more than five years after the date of its issuance and such general permit may be revoked or modified by the Secretary if, after opportunity for public hearing, the Secretary determines that the activities authorized by such general permit have an adverse impact on the environment or such activities are more appropriately authorized by individual permits.

(f) Non-prohibited discharge of dredged or fill material.

(1) Except as provided in paragraph (2) of this subsection, the discharge of dredged or fill material–

(A) from normal farming, silviculture, and ranching activities such as plowing, seeding, cultivating, minor drainage, harvesting for the production of food, fiber, and forest products, or upland soil and water conservation practices;

(B) for the purpose of maintenance, including emergency reconstruction of recently damaged parts, of currently serviceable structures such as dikes, dams, levees, groins, riprap, breakwaters, causeways, and bridge abutments or approaches, and transportation structures;

(C) for the purpose of construction or maintenance of farm or stock ponds or irrigation ditches, or the maintenance of drainage ditches;

(D) for the purpose of construction of temporary sedimentation basins on a construction site which does not include placement of fill material into the navigable waters;

(E) for the purpose of construction or maintenance of farm roads or forest roads, or temporary roads for moving mining equipment, where such roads are constructed and maintained, in accordance with best management practices, to assure that flow and circulation patterns and chemical and biological characteristics of the navigable waters are not impaired, that the reach of the navigable waters is not reduced, and that any adverse effect on the aquatic environment will be otherwise minimized;

(F) resulting from any activity with respect to which a State has an approved program under section 208(b)(4) [33 USCS | 1288(b)(4)] which meets the requirements of subparagraphs (B) and (C) of such section, is not prohibited by or otherwise subject to regulation under this section or section 301(a) or 402 of this Act [33 USCS || 1311(a), 1342] (except for effluent standards or prohibitions under section 307 [33 USCS | 1317]).

(2) Any discharge of dredged or fill material into the navigable waters incidental to any activity having as its purpose bringing an area of the navigable waters into a use to which it was not previously subject, where the flow or circulation of navigable waters may be impaired or the reach of such waters be reduced, shall be required to have a permit under this section.

(g) State administration.

(1) The Governor of any State desiring to administer its own individual and general permit program for the discharge of dredged or fill material into the navigable waters (other than those waters which are presently used, or are susceptible to use in their natural condition or by reasonable improvement as a means to transport interstate or foreign commerce shoreward to their ordinary high water mark, including all waters which are subject to the ebb and flow of the tide shoreward to their mean high water mark, or mean higher high water mark on the west coast, including wetlands adjacent thereto) within its jurisdiction may submit to the Administrator a full and complete description of the program it proposes to establish and administer under State law or under an interstate compact. In addition, such State shall submit a statement from the attorney general (or the attorney for those State agencies which have independent legal counsel), or from the chief legal officer in the case of an interstate agency, that the laws of such State, or the interstate compact, as the case may be, provide adequate authority to carry out the described program.

(2) Not later than the tenth day after the date of the receipt of the program and statement submitted by any State under paragraph (1) of this subsection, the Administrator shall provide copies of such program and statement to the Secretary and the Secretary of the Interior, acting through the Director of the United States Fish and Wildlife Service.

(3) Not later than the ninetieth day after the date of the receipt by the Administrator of the program and statement submitted by any State, under paragraph (1) of this subsection, the Secretary and the Secretary of the Interior, acting through the Director of the United States Fish and Wildlife Service, shall submit any comments with respect to such program and statement to the Administrator in writing.

(h) Determination of State's authority to issue permits under State program approval; notification; transfers to State program.

(1) Not later than the one-hundred-twentieth day after the date of the receipt by the Administrator of a program and statement submitted by any State under paragraph (1) of this subsection, the Administrator shall determine, taking into account any comments submitted by the Secretary and the Secretary of the Interior, acting through the Director of the United States Fish and Wildlife Service, pursuant to subsection (g) of this section, whether such State has the following authority with respect to the issuance of permits pursuant to such program:

(A) To issue permits which–

(i) apply, and assure compliance with, any applicable requirements of this section, including, but not limited to, the guidelines established under subsection (b)(1) of this section, and sections 307 and 403 of this Act [33 USCS || 1317, 1343];

(ii) are for fixed terms not exceeding five years; and

(iii) can be terminated or modified for cause including, but not limited to, the following:

(I) violation of any condition of the permit;

(II) obtaining a permit by misrepresentation, or failure to disclose fully all relevant facts;

(III) change in any condition that requires either a temporary or permanent reduction or elimination of the permitted discharge.

(B) To issue permits which apply, and assure compliance with, all applicable requirements of section 308 of this Act [33 USCS | 1318], or to inspect, monitor, enter, and require reports to at least the same extent as required in section 308 of this Act [33 USCS | 1318].

(C) To assure that the public, and any other State the waters of which may be affected, receive notice of each application for a permit and to provide an opportunity for public hearing before a ruling on each such application.

(D) To assure that the Administrator receives notice of each application (including a copy thereof) for a permit.

(E) To assure that any State (other than the permitting State), whose waters may be affected by the issuance of a permit may submit written recommendations to the permitting State (and the Administrator) with respect to any permit application and, if any part of such written recommendations are not accepted by the permitting State, that the permitting State will notify such affected State (and the Administrator) in writing of its failure to so accept such recommendations together with its reasons for so doing.

(F) To assure that no permit will be issued if, in the judgment of the Secretary, after consultation with the Secretary of the department in which the Coast Guard is operating, anchorage and navigation of any of the navigable waters would be substantially impaired thereby.

(G) To abate violations of the permit or the permit program, including civil and criminal penalties and other ways and means of enforcement.

(H) To assure continued coordination with Federal and Federal-State water-related planning and review processes.

(2) If, with respect to a State program submitted under subsection (g)(1) of this section, the Administrator determines that such State–

(A) has the authority set forth in paragraph (1) of this subsection, the Administrator shall approve the program and so notify (i) such State and (ii) the Secretary, who upon subsequent notification from such State that it is administering such program, shall suspend the issuance of permits under subsections (a) and (e) of this section for activities with respect to which a permit may be issued pursuant to such State program; or

(B) does not have the authority set forth in paragraph (1) of this subsection, the Administrator shall so notify such State, which notification shall also describe the revisions or modifications necessary so that such State may resubmit such program for a determination by the Administrator under this subsection.

(3) If the Administrator fails to make a determination with respect to any program submitted by a State under subsection (g)(1) of this section within one-hundred-twenty days after the date of the receipt of such program, such program shall be deemed approved pursuant to paragraph (2)(A) of this subsection and the Administrator shall so notify such State and the Secretary who, upon subsequent notification from such State that it is administering such program, shall suspend the issuance of permits under subsection (a) and (e) of this section for activities with respect to which a permit may be issued by such State.

(4) After the Secretary receives notification from the Administrator under paragraph (2) or (3) of this subsection that a State permit program has been approved, the Secretary shall transfer any applications for permits pending before the Secretary for activities with respect to which a permit may be issued pursuant to such State program to such State for appropriate action.

(5) Upon notification from a State with a permit program approved under this subsection that such State intends to administer and enforce the terms and conditions of a general permit issued by the Secretary under subsection (e) of this section with respect to activities in such State to which such general permit applies, the Secretary shall suspend the administration and enforcement of such general permit with respect to such activities.

(i) Withdrawal of approval.

Whenever the Administrator determines after public hearing that a State is not administering a program approved under section (h)(2)(A) of this section, in accordance with this section, including, but not limited to, the guidelines established under subsection (b)(1) of this section, the Administrator shall so notify the State, and, if appropriate corrective action is not taken within a reasonable time, not to exceed ninety days after the date of the receipt of such notification, the Administrator shall (1) withdraw approval of such program until the Administrator determines such corrective action has been taken, and (2) notify the Secretary that the Secretary shall resume the program for the issuance of permits under subsections (a) and (e) of this section for activities with respect to which the State was issuing permits and that such authority of the Secretary shall continue in effect until such time as the Administrator makes the determination described in clause (1) of this subsection and such State again has an approved program.

(j) Copies of applications for State permits and proposed general permits to be transmitted to Administrator.

Each State which is administering a permit program pursuant to this section shall transmit to the Administrator (1) a copy of each permit application received by such State and provide notice to the Administrator of every action related to the consideration of such permit application, including each permit proposed to be issued by such State, and (2) a copy of each proposed general permit which such State intends to issue. Not later than the tenth day after the date of the receipt of such permit application or such proposed general permit, the Administrator shall provide copies of such permit application or such proposed general permit to the Secretary and the Secretary of the Interior, acting through the Director of the United States Fish and Wildlife Service. If the Administrator intends to provide written comments to such State with respect to such permit application or such proposed general permit, he shall so notify such State not later than the thirtieth day after the date of the receipt of such application or such proposed general permit and provide such written comments to such State, after consideration of any comments made in writing with respect to such application or such proposed general permit by the Secretary and the Secretary of the Interior, acting through the Director of the United States Fish and Wildlife Service, not later than the ninetieth day after the date of such receipt. If such State is so notified by the Administrator, it shall not issue the proposed permit until after the receipt of such comments from the Administrator, or after such ninetieth day, whichever first occurs.

Such State shall not issue such proposed permit after such ninetieth day if it has received such written comments in which the Administrator objects (A) to the issuance of such proposed permit and such proposed permit is one that has been submitted to the Administrator pursuant to subsection (h)(1)(E), or (B) to the issuance of such proposed permit as being outside the requirements of this section, including, but not limited to, the guidelines developed under subsection (b)(1) of this section unless it modifies such proposed permit in accordance with such comments. Whenever the Administrator objects to the issuance of a permit under the preceding sentence such written objection shall contain a statement of the reasons for such objection and the conditions which such permit would include if it were issued by the Administrator. In any case where the Administrator objects to the issuance of a permit, on request of the objection. If the State does not resubmit such permit revised to meet such objection within 30 days after completion of the hearing or, if no hearing is requested within 90 days after the date of such objection, the Secretary may issue the permit pursuant to subsection (a) or (e) of this section, as the case may be, for such source in accordance with the guidelines and requirements of this Act.

(k) Waiver.

In accordance with guidelines promulgated pursuant to subsection (i)(2) of section 304 of this Act [33 USCS | 1314(i)(2)], the Administrator is authorized to waive the requirements of subsection (j) of this section at the time of the approval of a program pursuant to subsection (h)(2)(A) of this section for any category (including any class, type, or size within such category) of discharge within the State submitting such program.

(l) Categories of discharges not subject to requirements.

The Administrator shall promulgate regulations establishing categories of discharges which he determines shall not be subject to the requirements of subsection (j) of this section in any State with a program approved pursuant to subsection (h)(2)(A) of this section. The Administrator may distinguish among classes, types, and sizes within any category of discharges.

(m) Comments on permit applications or proposed general permits by Secretary of the Interior acting through Director of United States Fish and Wildlife Service.

Not later than the ninetieth day after the date on which the Secretary notifies the Secretary of the Interior, acting through the Director of the United States Fish and Wildlife Service that (1) an application for a permit under subsection (a) of this section has been received by the Secretary, or (2) the Secretary proposes to issue a general permit under subsection (e) of this section, the Secretary of the Interior, acting through the Director of the United States Fish and Wildlife Service, shall submit any comments with respect to such application or such proposed general permit in writing to the Secretary.

(n) Enforcement authority not limited.

Nothing in this section shall be construed to limit the authority of the Administrator to take action pursuant to section 309 of this Act [33 USCS | 1319].

(o) Public availability of permits and permit applications.

A copy of each permit application and each permit issued under this section shall be available to the public. Such permit application or portion thereof, shall further be available on request for the purpose of reproduction.

(p) Compliance.

Compliance with a permit issued pursuant to this section, including any activity carried out pursuant to a general permit issued under this section, shall be deemed compliance, for purposes of sections 309 and 505 [33 USCS || 1319, 1365], with sections 301, 307 and 403 [33 USCS || 1311, 1317, 1343].

(q) Minimization of duplication, needless paperwork, and delays in issuance; agreements.

Not later than the one-hundred-eightieth day after the date of enactment of this subsection [enacted Dec. 27, 1977], the Secretary shall enter into agreements with the Administrator, the Secretaries of the Departments of Agriculture, Commerce, Interior, and Transportation, and the heads of other appropriate Federal agencies to minimize, to the maximum extent practicable, duplication, needless paperwork, and delays in the issuance of permits under this section. Such agreements shall be developed to assure that, to the maximum extent practicable, a decision with respect to an application for a permit under subsection (a) of this section will be made not later than the ninetieth day after the date the notice for such application is published under subsection (a) of this section.

(r) Federal projects specifically authorized by Congress.

The discharge of dredged or fill material as part of the construction of a Federal project specifically authorized by Congress, whether prior to or on or after the date of enactment of this subsection [enacted Dec. 27, 1977], is not prohibited by or otherwise subject to regulation under this section, or a State program approved under this section, or section 301(a) or 402 of the Act [33 USCS | 1311(a) or 1342] (except for effluent standards or prohibitions under section 307 [33 USCS | 1317]), if information on the effects of such discharge, including consideration of the guidelines developed under subsection (b)(1) of this section, is included in an environmental impact statement for such project pursuant to the National Environmental Policy Act of 1969 and such environmental impact statement has been submitted to Congress before the actual discharge of dredged or fill material in connection with the construction of such project and prior to either authorization of such project or an appropriation of funds for such construction.

(s) Violation of permits.

(1) Whenever on the basis of any information available to him the Secretary finds that any person is in violation of any condition or limitation set forth in a permit issued by the Secretary under this section, the Secretary shall issue an order requiring such person to comply with such condition or limitation, or the Secretary shall bring a civil action in accordance with paragraph (3) of this subsection.

(2) A copy of any order issued under this subsection shall be sent immediately by the Secretary to the State in which the violation occurs and other affected States. Any order issued under this subsection shall be by personal service and shall state with reasonable specificity the nature of the violation, specify a time for compliance, not to exceed thirty days, which the Secretary determines is reasonable, taking into account the seriousness of the violation and any good faith efforts to comply with applicable requirements. In any case in which an order under this subsection is issued to a corporation, a copy of such order shall be served on any appropriate corporate officers.

(3) The Secretary is authorized to commence a civil action for appropriate relief, including a permanent or temporary injunction for any violation for which he is authorized to issue a compliance order under paragraph (1) of this subsection. Any action under this paragraph may be brought in the district court of the United States for the district in which the defendant is located or resides or is doing business, and such court shall have jurisdiction to restrain such violation and to require compliance. Notice of the commencement of such acton [action] shall be given immediately to the appropriate State.

(4) Any person who violates any condition or limitation in a permit issued by the Secretary under this section, and any person who violates any order issued by the Secretary under paragraph (1) of this subsection, shall be subject to a civil penalty not to exceed "$ 25,000 per day for each violation". In determining the amount of a civil penalty the court shall consider the seriousness of the violation or violations, the economic benefit (if any) resulting from the violation, any history of such violations, any good-faith efforts to comply with the applicable requirements, the economic impact of the penalty on the violator, and such other matters as justice may require.

(5) [Redesignated]

(t) Navigable waters within State jurisdiction.

Nothing in this section shall preclude or deny the right of any State or interstate agency to control the discharge of dredged or fill material in any portion of the navigable waters within the jurisdiction of such State, including any activity of any Federal agency, and each such agency shall comply with such State or interstate requirements both substantive and procedural to control the discharge of dredged or fill material to the same extent that any person is subject to such requirements. This section shall not be construed as affecting or impairing the authority of the Secretary to maintain navigation.

Appendix B

Section 10, River and Harbors Act of 1899
33 USC 403 (1994)
Title 33. Navigation and Navigable Waters

403. Obstruction of navigable waters generally; wharves; piers, etc.; excavations and filling in

The creation of any obstruction not affirmatively authorized by Congress, to the navigable capacity of any of the waters of the United States is hereby prohibited; and it shall not be lawful to build or commence the building of any wharf, pier, dolphin, boom, weir, breakwater, bulkhead, jetty, or other structures in any port, roadstead, haven, harbor, canal, navigable river, or other water of the United States, outside established harbor lines, or where no harbor lines have been established, except on plans recommended by the Chief of Engineers and authorized by the Secretary of War [Secretary of the Army]; and it shall not be lawful to excavate or fill, or in any manner to alter or modify the course, location, condition, or capacity of, any port, roadstead, haven, harbor, canal, lake, harbor of refuge, or inclosure within the limits of any breakwater, or of the channel of any navigable water of the United States, unless the work has been recommended by the Chief of Engineers and authorized by the Secretary of War [Secretary of the Army] prior to beginning the same.

Appendix C

U.S. Army Corps of Engineers
33 CFR 320-330

PART 320
GENERAL REGULATORY POLICIES

*Authority: 33 U.S.C. 401 et seq.;
33 U.S.C. 1344; 33 U.S.C. 1413.*

*Source: 51 FR 41220, Nov. 13, 1986,
unless otherwise noted.*

§ 320.1   Purpose and scope.

(a) *Regulatory approach of the Corps of Engineers.*

(1) The U.S. Army Corps of Engineers has been involved in regulating certain activities in the nation's waters since 1890. Until 1968, the primary thrust of the Corps' regulatory program was the protection of navigation. As a result of several new laws and judicial decisions, the program has evolved to one involving the consideration of the full public interest by balancing the favorable impacts against the detrimental impacts. This is known as the "public interest review." The program is one which reflects the national concerns for both the protection and utilization of important resources.

(2) The Corps is a highly decentralized organization. Most of the authority for administering the regulatory program has been delegated to the thirty-six district engineers and eleven division engineers. If a district or division engineer makes a final decision on a permit application in accordance with the procedures and authorities contained in these regulations (33 CFR parts 320 through 330), there is no administrative appeal of that decision.

(3) The Corps seeks to avoid unnecessary regulatory controls. The general permit program described in 33 CFR parts 325 and 330 is the primary method of eliminating unnecessary federal control over activities which do not justify individual control or which are adequately regulated by another agency.

(4) The Corps is neither a proponent nor opponent of any permit proposal. However, the Corps believes that applicants are due a timely decision. Reducing unnecessary paperwork and delays is a continuing Corps goal.

(5) The Corps believes that state and federal regulatory programs should complement rather than duplicate one another. The Corps uses general permits, joint processing procedures, interagency review, co-

ordination, and authority transfers (where authorized by law) to reduce duplication.

(6) The Corps has authorized its district engineers to issue formal determinations concerning the applicability of the Clean Water Act or the Rivers and Harbors Act of 1899 to activities or tracts of land and the applicability of general permits or statutory exemptions to proposed activities. A determination pursuant to this authorization shall constitute a Corps final agency action. Nothing contained in this section is intended to affect any authority EPA has under the Clean Water Act.

(b) *Types of activities regulated.*

This part and the parts that follow (33 CFR parts 321 through 330) prescribe the statutory authorities, and general and special policies and procedures applicable to the review of applications for Department of the Army (DA) permits for controlling certain activities in waters of the United States or the oceans. This part identifies the various federal statutes which require that DA permits be issued before these activities can be lawfully undertaken; and related Federal laws and the general policies applicable to the review of those activities. Parts 321 through 324 and 330 address special policies and procedures applicable to the following specific classes of activities:

(1) Dams or dikes in navigable waters of the United States (part 321);

(2) Other structures or work including excavation, dredging, and/or disposal activities, in navigable waters of the United States (part 322);

(3) Activities that alter or modify the course, condition, location, or capacity of a navigable water of the United States (part 322);

(4) Construction of artificial islands, installations, and other devices on the outer continental shelf (part 322);

(5) Discharges of dredged or fill material into waters of the United States (part 323);

(6) Activities involving the transportation of dredged material for the purpose of disposal in ocean waters (part 324); and

(7) Nationwide general permits for certain categories of activities (part 330).

(c) *Forms of authorization.*

DA permits for the above described activities are issued under various forms of authorization. These include individual permits that are issued following a review of individual applications and general permits that authorize a category or categories of activities in specific geographical regions or nationwide. The term "general permit" as used in these regulations (33 CFR parts 320 through 330) refers to both those regional permits issued by district or division engineers on a regional basis and to nationwide permits which are issued by the Chief of Engineers through publication in the Federal Register and are applicable throughout the nation. The nationwide permits are found in 33 CFR part 330. If an activity is covered by a general permit, an application for a DA permit does not have to be made. In such cases, a person must only comply with the conditions contained in the general permit to satisfy requirements of law for a DA permit. In certain cases pre-notification may be required before initiating construction. (See 33 CFR 330.7)

(d) *General instructions.*

General policies for evaluating permit applications are found in this part. Special policies that relate to particular activities are found in parts 321 through 324. The procedures for processing individual permits and general permits are contained in 33 CFR part 325. The terms "navigable waters of the United States" and "waters of the United States" are used frequently throughout these regulations, and it is important from the outset that the reader understand the difference between the two. "Navigable waters of the United States" are defined in 33 CFR part 329. These are waters that are navigable in the traditional sense where permits are required for certain work or structures pursuant to Sections 9 and 10 of the Rivers and Harbors Act of 1899. "Waters of the United States" are defined in 33 CFR part 328. These waters include more than navigable waters of the United States and are the waters where permits are required for the discharge of dredged or fill material pursuant to section 404 of the Clean Water Act.

§ 320.2   Authorities to issue permits.

(a) Section 9 of the Rivers and Harbors Act, approved March 3, 1899 (33 U.S.C. 401) (hereinafter referred to as section 9), prohibits the construction of any dam or dike across any navigable water of the United States in the absence of Congressional consent and approval of the plans by the Chief of Engineers and the Secretary of the Army. Where the navigable portions of the waterbody lie wholly within the limits of a single state, the structure may be built under authority of the legislature of that state if the location and plans or any modification thereof are approved by the Chief of Engineers and by the Secretary of the Army. The instrument of authorization is designated a permit (See 33 CFR part 321.) Section 9 also pertains to bridges and causeways but the authority of the Secretary of the Army and Chief of Engineers with respect to bridges and causeways was transferred to the Secretary of Transportation under the Department of Transportation Act of October 15, 1966 (49 U.S.C. 1155g(6)(A)). A DA permit pursuant to section 404 of the Clean Water Act is required for the discharge of dredged or fill material into waters of the United States associated with bridges and causeways. (See 33 CFR part 323.)

(b) Section 10 of the Rivers and Harbors Act approved March 3, 1899, (33 U.S.C. 403) (hereinafter referred to as section 10), prohibits the unauthorized obstruction or alteration of any navigable water of the United States. The construction of any structure in or over any navigable water of the United States, the excavating from or depositing of material in such waters, or the accomplishment of any other work affecting the course, location, condition, or capacity of such waters is unlawful unless the work has been recommended by the Chief of Engineers and authorized by the Secretary of the Army. The instrument of authorization is designated a permit. The authority of the Secretary of the Army to prevent obstructions to navigation in navigable waters of the United States was extended to artificial islands, installations, and other devices located on the seabed, to the seaward limit of the outer continental shelf, by section 4(f) of the Outer Continental Shelf Lands Act of 1953 as amended (43 U.S.C. 1333(e)). (See 33 CFR part 322.)

(c) Section 11 of the Rivers and Harbors Act approved March 3, 1899, (33 U.S.C. 404), authorizes the Secretary of the Army to establish harbor lines channelward of which no piers, wharves, bulkheads, or other works may be extended or deposits made without approval of the Secretary of the Army. Effective May 27, 1970, permits for work shoreward of those lines must be obtained in accordance with section 10 and, if applicable, section 404 of the Clean Water Act (see § 320.4(o) of this part).

(d) Section 13 of the Rivers and Harbors Act approved March 3, 1899, (33 U.S.C. 407), provides that the Secretary of the Army, whenever the Chief of Engineers determines that anchorage and navigation will not be injured thereby, may permit the discharge of refuse into navigable waters. In the absence of a permit, such discharge of refuse is prohibited. While the prohibition of this section, known as the Refuse Act, is still in effect, the permit authority of the Secretary of the Army has been superseded by the permit authority provided the Administrator, Environmental Protection Agency (EPA), and the states under sections 402 and 405 of the Clean Water Act, (33 U.S.C. 1342 and 1345). (See 40 CFR parts 124 and 125.)

(e) Section 14 of the Rivers and Harbors Act approved March 3, 1899, (33 U.S.C. 408), provides that the Secretary of the Army, on the recommendation of the Chief of Engineers, may grant permission for the temporary occupation or use of any sea wall, bulkhead, jetty, dike, levee, wharf, pier, or other work built by the United States. This permission will be granted by an appropriate real estate instrument in accordance with existing real estate regulations.

(f) Section 404 of the Clean Water Act (33 U.S.C. 1344) (hereinafter referred to as section 404) authorizes the Secretary of the Army, acting through the Chief of Engineers, to issue permits, after notice and opportunity for public hearing, for the discharge of dredged or fill material into the waters of the United States at specified disposal sites. (See 33 CFR part 323.) The selection and use of disposal sites will be in accordance with guidelines developed by the Administrator of EPA in conjunction with the Secretary of the Army and published in 40 CFR part 230. If these guidelines prohibit the selection or use of a disposal site, the Chief of Engineers shall consider the economic impact on navigation and anchorage of such a prohibition in reaching his decision. Furthermore, the Administrator can deny, prohibit, restrict or withdraw the use of any defined area as a disposal site whenever he determines, after notice and opportunity for public hearing and after consultation with the Secretary of the Army, that the discharge of such materials into such areas will have an unacceptable adverse effect on municipal water supplies, shellfish beds and fishery areas, wildlife, or recreational areas. (See 40 CFR part 230).

(g) Section 103 of the Marine Protection, Research and Sanctuaries Act of 1972, as amended (33 U.S.C. 1413) (hereinafter referred to as section 103), authorizes the Secretary of the Army, acting through the Chief of Engineers, to issue permits, after notice and opportunity for public hearing, for the transportation of dredged material for the purpose of disposal in the ocean where it is determined that the disposal will not unreasonably degrade or endanger human health, welfare, or amenities, or the marine environment, ecological systems, or economic potentialities. The selection of disposal sites will be in accordance with criteria developed by the Administrator of the EPA in consultation with the Secretary of the Army and published in 40 CFR parts 220 through 229. However, similar to the EPA Administrator's limiting authority cited in paragraph (f) of this section, the Administrator can prevent the issuance of a permit under this authority if he finds that the disposal of the material will result in an unacceptable adverse impact on municipal water supplies, shellfish beds, wildlife, fisheries, or recreational areas. (See 33 CFR part 324).

§ 320.3 Related laws.

(a) Section 401 of the Clean Water Act (33 U.S.C. 1341) requires any applicant for a federal license or permit to conduct any activity that may result in a discharge of a pollutant into waters of the United States to obtain a certification from the State in which the discharge originates or would originate, or, if appropriate, from the interstate water pollution control agency having jurisdiction over the affected waters at the point where the discharge originates or would originate, that the discharge will comply with the applicable effluent limitations and water quality standards. A certification obtained for the construction of any facility must also pertain to the subsequent operation of the facility.

(b) Section 307(c) of the Coastal Zone Management Act of 1972, as amended (16 U.S.C. 1456(c)), requires federal agencies conducting activities, including development projects, directly affecting a state's coastal zone, to comply to the maximum extent practicable with an approved state coastal zone management program. Indian tribes doing work on federal lands will be treated as a federal agency for the purpose of the Coastal Zone Management Act. The Act also requires any non-federal applicant for a federal license or permit to conduct an activity affecting land or water uses in the state's coastal zone to furnish a certification that the proposed activity will comply with the state's coastal zone management program. Generally, no permit will be issued until the state has concurred with the non-federal applicant's certification. This provision becomes effective upon approval by the Secretary of Commerce of the state's coastal zone management program. (See 15 CFR part 930.)

(c) Section 302 of the Marine Protection, Research and Sanctuaries Act of 1972, as amended (16 U.S.C. 1432), authorizes the Secretary of Commerce, after consultation with other interested federal agencies and with the approval of the President, to designate as marine sanctuaries those areas of the ocean waters, of the Great Lakes and their connecting waters, or of other coastal waters which he determines necessary for the purpose of preserving or restoring such areas for their conservation, recreational, ecological, or aesthetic values. After designating such an area, the Secretary of Commerce shall issue regulations to control any activities within the area. Activities in the sanctuary authorized under other authorities are valid only if the Secretary of Commerce certifies that the activities are consistent with the purposes of Title III of the Act and can be carried out within the regulations for the sanctuary.

(d) The National Environmental Policy Act of 1969 (42 U.S.C. 4321-4347) declares the national policy to encourage a productive and enjoyable harmony between man and his environment. Section 102 of that Act directs that "to the fullest extent possible:

(1) The policies, regulations, and public laws of the United States shall be interpreted and administered in accordance with the policies set forth in this Act, and

(2) All agencies of the Federal Government shall * * * insure that presently unquantified environmental amenities and values may be given appropriate consideration in decision-making along with economic and technical considerations * * *". (See Appendix B of 33 CFR part 325.)

(e) The Fish and Wildlife Act of 1956 (16 U.S.C. 742a, *et seq.*), the Migratory Marine Game-Fish Act (16 U.S.C. 760c-760g), the Fish and Wildlife Coordination Act (16 U.S.C. 661-666c) and other acts express the will of Congress to protect the quality of the aquatic environment as it affects the conservation, improvement and enjoyment of fish and wildlife resources. Reorganization Plan No. 4 of 1970 transferred certain functions, including certain fish and wildlife-water resources coordination responsibilities, from the Secretary of the Interior to the Secretary of Commerce. Under the Fish and Wildlife Coordination Act and Reorganization Plan No. 4, any federal agency that proposes to control or modify any body of water must first consult with the United States Fish and Wildlife Service or the National Marine Fisheries Service, as appropriate, and with the head of the appropriate state agency exercising administration over the wildlife resources of the affected state.

(f) The Federal Power Act of 1920 (16 U.S.C. 791a *et seq.*), as amended, authorizes the Federal Energy Regulatory Agency (FERC) to issue licenses for the construction and the operation and maintenance of dams, water conduits, reservoirs, power houses, transmission lines, and other physical structures of a hydropower project. However, where such structures will affect the navigable capacity of any navigable water of the United States (as defined in 16 U.S.C. 796), the plans for the dam or other physical structures affecting navigation must be approved by the Chief of Engineers and the Secretary of the Army. In such cases, the interests of navigation should normally be protected by a DA recommendation to FERC for the inclusion of appropriate provisions in the FERC license rather than the issuance of a separate DA permit under 33 U.S.C. 401 *et seq.* As to any other activities in navigable waters not constituting construction and the operation and maintenance of physical structures licensed by FERC under the Federal Power Act of 1920, as amended, the provisions of 33 U.S.C. 401 *et seq.* remain fully applicable. In all cases involving the discharge of dredged or fill material into waters of the United States or the transportation of dredged material for the purpose of disposal in ocean waters, section 404 or section 103 will be applicable.

(g) The National Historic Preservation Act of 1966 (16 U.S.C. 470) created the Advisory Council on Historic Preservation to advise the President and Congress on matters involving historic preservation. In performing its function the Council is authorized to review and comment upon activities licensed by the Federal Government which will have an effect upon properties listed in the National Register of Historic Places, or eligible for such listing. The concern of Congress for the preservation of significant historical sites is also expressed in the Preservation of Historical and Archeological Data Act of 1974 (16 U.S.C. 469 *et seq.*), which amends the Act of June 27, 1960. By this Act, whenever a federal construction project or federally licensed project, activity, or program alters any terrain such that significant historical or archeological data is threatened, the Secretary of the Interior may take action necessary to recover and preserve the data prior to the commencement of the project.

(h) The Interstate Land Sales Full Disclosure Act (15 U.S.C. 1701 *et seq.*) prohibits any developer or agent from selling or leasing any lot in a subdivision (as defined in 15 U.S.C. 1701(3)) unless the purchaser is furnished in advance a printed property report containing information which the Secretary of Housing and Urban Development may, by rules or regulations, require for the protection of purchasers. In the event the lot in question is part of a project that requires DA authorization, the property report is required by Housing and Urban Development regulation to state whether or not a permit for the development has been applied for, issued, or denied by the Corps of Engineers under section 10 or section 404. The property report is also required to state whether or not any enforcement action has been taken as a consequence of non-application for or denial of such permit.

(i) The Endangered Species Act (16 U.S.C. 1531 *et seq.*) declares the intention of the Congress to conserve threatened and endangered species and the ecosystems on which those species depend. The Act requires that federal agencies, in consultation with the U.S. Fish and Wildlife Service and the National Marine Fisheries Service, use their authorities in furtherance of its purposes by carrying out programs for the conservation of endangered or threatened species, and by taking such action necessary to insure that any action authorized, funded, or carried out by the Agency is not likely to jeopardize the continued existence of such endangered or threatened species or result in the destruction or adverse modification of habitat of such species which is determined by the Secretary of the Interior or Commerce, as appropriate, to be critical. (See 50 CFR part 17 and 50 CFR part 402.)

(j) The Deepwater Port Act of 1974 (33 U.S.C. 1501 *et seq.*) prohibits the ownership, construction, or operation of a deepwater port beyond the territorial seas without a license issued by the Secretary of Transportation. The Secretary of Transportation may issue such a license to an applicant if he determines, among other things, that the construction and operation of the deepwater port is in the national interest and consistent with national security and other national policy goals and objectives. An application for a deepwater port license constitutes an application for all federal authorizations required for the ownership, construction, and operation of a deepwater port, including applications for section 10, section 404 and section 103 permits which may also be required pursuant to the authorities listed in § 320.2 and the policies specified in § 320.4 of this part.

(k) The Marine Mammal Protection Act of 1972 (16 U.S.C. 1361 *et seq.*) expresses the intent of Congress that marine mammals be protected and encouraged to develop in order to maintain the health and stability of the marine ecosystem. The Act imposes a perpetual moratorium on the harassment, hunting, capturing, or killing of marine mammals and on the importation of marine mammals and marine mammal products without a permit from either the Secretary of the Interior or the Secretary of Commerce, depending upon the species of marine mammal involved. Such permits may be issued only for purposes of scientific research and for public display if the purpose is consistent with the policies of the Act. The appropriate Secretary is also empowered in certain restricted circumstances to waive the requirements of the Act.

(l) Section 7(a) of the Wild and Scenic Rivers Act (16 U.S.C. 1278 *et seq.*) provides that no department or agency of the United States shall assist by loan, grant, license, or otherwise in the construction of any water resources project that would have a direct and adverse effect on the values for which such river was established, as determined by the Secretary charged with its administration.

(m) The Ocean Thermal Energy Conversion Act of 1980, (42 U.S.C. section 9101 *et seq.*) establishes a licensing regime administered by the Administrator of NOAA for the ownership, construction, location, and operation of ocean thermal energy conversion (OTEC) facilities and plantships. An application for an OTEC license filed with the Administrator constitutes an application for all federal authorizations required for ownership, construction, location, and operation of an OTEC facility or plantship, except for certain activities within the jurisdiction of the Coast Guard. This includes applications for section 10, section 404, section 103 and other DA authorizations which may be required.

(n) Section 402 of the Clean Water Act authorizes EPA to issue permits under procedures established to implement the National Pollutant Discharge Elimination System (NPDES) program. The administration of this program can be, and in most cases has been, delegated to individual states. Section 402(b)(6) states that no NPDES permit will be issued if the Chief of Engineers, acting for the Secretary of the Army and after consulting with the U.S. Coast Guard, determines that navigation and anchorage in any navigable water will be substantially impaired as a result of a proposed activity.

(o) The National Fishing Enhancement Act of 1984 (Pub. L. 98-623) provides for the development of a National Artificial Reef Plan to promote and facilitate responsible and effective efforts to establish artificial reefs. The Act establishes procedures to be followed by the Corps in issuing DA permits for artificial reefs. The Act also establishes the liability of the permittee and the United States. The Act further creates a civil penalty for violation of any provision of a permit issued for an artificial reef.

§ 320.4 General policies for evaluating permit applications.

The following policies shall be applicable to the review of all applications for DA permits. Additional policies specifically applicable to certain types of activities are identified in 33 CFR parts 321 through 324.

(a) *Public Interest Review.*

(1) The decision whether to issue a permit will be based on an evaluation of the probable impacts, including cumulative impacts, of the proposed activity and its intended use on the public interest. Evaluation of the probable impact which the proposed activity may have on the public interest requires a careful weighing of all those factors which become relevant in each particular case. The benefits which reasonably may be expected to accrue from the proposal must be balanced against its reasonably foreseeable detriments. The decision whether to authorize a proposal, and if so, the conditions under which it will be allowed to occur, are therefore determined by the outcome of this general balancing process. That decision should reflect the national concern for both protection and utilization of important resources. All factors which may be relevant to the proposal must be considered including the cumulative effects thereof: among those are conservation, economics, aesthetics, general environmental concerns, wetlands, historic properties, fish and wildlife values, flood hazards, floodplain values, land use, navigation, shore erosion and accretion, recreation, water supply and conservation, water quality, energy needs, safety, food and fiber production, mineral needs, considerations of property ownership and, in general, the needs and welfare of the people. For activities involving 404 discharges, a permit will be denied if the discharge that would be authorized by such permit would not comply with the Environmental Protection Agency's 404(b)(1) guidelines. Subject to the preceding sentence and any other applicable guidelines and criteria (see §§ 320.2 and 320.3), a permit will be granted unless the district engineer determines that it would be contrary to the public interest.

(2) The following general criteria will be considered in the evaluation of every application:

(i) The relative extent of the public and private need for the proposed structure or work:

(ii) Where there are unresolved conflicts as to resource use, the practicability of using reasonable alternative locations and methods to accomplish the objective of the proposed structure or work; and

(iii) The extent and permanence of the beneficial and/or detrimental effects which the proposed structure or work is likely to have on the public and private uses to which the area is suited.

(3) The specific weight of each factor is determined by its importance and relevance to the particular proposal. Accordingly, how important a factor is and how much consideration it deserves will vary with each proposal. A specific factor may be given great weight on one proposal, while it may not be present or as important on another. However, full consideration and appropriate weight will be given to all comments, including those of federal, state, and local agencies, and other experts on matters within their expertise.

(b) *Effect on wetlands.*

(1) Most wetlands constitute a productive and valuable public resource, the unnecessary alteration or destruction of which should be discouraged as contrary to the public interest. For projects to be undertaken or partially or entirely funded by a federal, state, or local agency, additional requirements on wetlands considerations are stated in Executive Order 11990, dated 24 May 1977.

(2) Wetlands considered to perform functions important to the public interest include:

(i) Wetlands which serve significant natural biological functions, including food chain production, general habitat and nesting, spawning, rearing and resting sites for aquatic or land species;

(ii) Wetlands set aside for study of the aquatic environment or as sanctuaries or refuges;

(iii) Wetlands the destruction or alteration of which would affect detrimentally natural drainage characteristics, sedimentation patterns, salinity distribution, flushing characteristics, current patterns, or other environmental characteristics;

(iv) Wetlands which are significant in shielding other areas from wave action, erosion, or storm damage. Such wetlands are often associated with barrier beaches, islands, reefs and bars;

(v) Wetlands which serve as valuable storage areas for storm and flood waters;

(vi) Wetlands which are ground water discharge areas that maintain minimum baseflows important to aquatic resources and those which are prime natural recharge areas;

(vii) Wetlands which serve significant water purification functions; and

(viii) Wetlands which are unique in nature or scarce in quantity to the region or local area.

(3) Although a particular alteration of a wetland may constitute a minor change, the cumulative effect of numerous piecemeal changes can result in a major impairment of wetland resources. Thus, the particular wetland site for which an application is made will be evaluated with the recognition that it may be part of a complete and interrelated wetland area. In addition, the district engineer may undertake, where appropriate, reviews of particular wetland areas in consultation with the Regional Director of the U. S. Fish and Wildlife Service, the Regional Director of the National Marine Fisheries Service of the National Oceanic and Atmospheric Administration, the Regional Administrator of the Environmental Protection Agency, the local representative of the Soil Conservation Service of the Department of Agriculture, and the head of the appropriate state agency to assess the cumulative effect of activities in such areas.

(4) No permit will be granted which involves the alteration of wetlands identified as important by paragraph (b)(2) of this section or because of provisions of paragraph (b)(3), of this section unless the district engineer concludes, on the basis of the analysis required in paragraph (a) of this section, that the benefits of the proposed alteration outweigh the damage to the wetlands resource. In evaluating whether a particular discharge activity should be permitted, the district engineer shall apply the section 404(b)(1) guidelines (40 CFR part 230.10(a) (1), (2), (3)).

(5) In addition to the policies expressed in this subpart, the Congressional policy expressed in the Estuary Protection Act, Pub. L. 90-454, and state regulatory laws or programs for classification and protection of wetlands will be considered.

(c) *Fish and wildlife.* In accordance with the Fish and Wildlife Coordination Act (paragraph 320.3(e) of this section) district engineers will consult with the Regional Director, U.S. Fish and Wildlife Service, the Regional Director, National Marine Fisheries Service, and the head of the agency responsible for fish and wildlife for the state in which work is to be performed, with a view to the conservation of wildlife resources by prevention of their direct and indirect loss and damage due to the activity proposed in a permit application. The Army will give full consideration to the views of those agencies on fish and wildlife matters in deciding on the issuance, denial, or conditioning of individual or general permits.

(d) *Water quality.* Applications for permits for activities which may adversely affect the quality of waters of the United States will be evaluated for compliance with applicable effluent limitations and water quality standards, during the construction and subsequent operation of the proposed activity. The evaluation should include the consideration of both point and non-point sources of pollution. It should be noted, however, that the Clean Water Act assigns responsibility for control of non-point sources of pollution to the states. Certification of compliance with applicable effluent limitations and water quality standards required under provisions of section 401 of the Clean Water Act will be considered conclusive with respect to water quality considerations unless the Regional Administrator, Environmental Protection Agency (EPA), advises of other water quality aspects to be taken into consideration.

(e) *Historic, cultural, scenic, and recreational values.* Applications for DA permits may involve areas which possess recognized historic, cultural, scenic, conservation, recreational or similar values. Full evaluation of the general public interest requires that due consideration be given to the effect which the proposed structure or activity may have on values such as those associated with wild and scenic rivers, historic properties and National Landmarks, National Rivers, National Wilderness Areas, National Seashores, National Recreation Areas, National Lakeshores, National Parks, National Monuments, estuarine and marine sanctuaries, archeological resources, including Indian religious or cultural sites, and such other areas as may be established under federal or state law for similar and related purposes. Recognition of those values is often reflected by state, regional, or local land use classifications, or by similar federal controls or policies. Action on permit applications should, insofar as possible, be consistent with, and avoid significant adverse effects on the values or purposes for which those classifications, controls, or policies were established.

(f) *Effects on limits of the territorial sea.* Structures or work affecting coastal waters may modify the coast line or base line from which the territorial sea is measured for purposes of the Submerged Lands Act and international law. Generally, the coast line or base line is the line of ordinary low water on the mainland; however, there are exceptions where there are islands or lowtide elevations offshore (the Submerged Lands Act, 43 U.S.C. 1301(a) and United States v. California, 381 U.S.C. 139 (1965), 382 U.S. 448 (1966)). Applications for structures or work affecting coastal waters will therefore be reviewed specifically to determine whether the coast line or base line might be altered. If it is determined that such a change might occur, coordination with the Attorney General and the Solicitor of the Department of the Interior is required before final action is taken. The district engineer will submit a description of the proposed work and a copy of the plans to the Solicitor, Department of the Interior, Washington, DC 20240, and request his comments concerning the effects of the proposed work on the outer continental rights of the United States. These comments will be included in the administrative record of the application. After completion of standard processing procedures, the record will be forwarded to the Chief of Engineers. The decision on the application will be made by the Secretary of the Army after coordination with the Attorney General.

(g) *Consideration of property ownership.* Authorization of work or structures by DA does not convey a property right, nor authorize any injury to property or invasion of other rights.

(1) An inherent aspect of property ownership is a right to reasonable private use. However, this right is subject to the rights and interests of the public in the navigable and other waters of the United States, including the federal navigation servitude and federal regulation for environmental protection.

(2) Because a landowner has the general right to protect property from erosion, applications to erect protective structures will usually receive favorable consideration. However, if the protective structure may cause damage to the property of others, adversely affect public health and safety, adversely impact floodplain or wetland values, or otherwise appears contrary to the public interest, the district engineer will so advise the applicant and inform him of possible alternative methods of protecting his property. Such advice will be given in terms of general guidance only so as not to compete with private engineering firms nor require undue use of government resources.

(3) A riparian landowner's general right of access to navigable waters of the United States is subject to the similar rights of access held by nearby riparian landowners and to the general public's right of navigation on the water surface. In the case of proposals which create undue interference with access to, or use of, navigable waters, the authorization will generally be denied.

(4) Where it is found that the work for which a permit is desired is in navigable waters of the United States (see 33 CFR part 329) and may interfere with an authorized federal project, the applicant should be apprised in writing of the fact and of the possibility that a federal project which may be constructed in the vicinity of the proposed work might necessitate its

removal or reconstruction. The applicant should also be informed that the United States will in no case be liable for any damage or injury to the structures or work authorized by Sections 9 or 10 of the Rivers and Harbors Act of 1899 or by section 404 of the Clean Water Act which may be caused by, or result from, future operations undertaken by the Government for the conservation or improvement of navigation or for other purposes, and no claims or right to compensation will accrue from any such damage.

(5) Proposed activities in the area of a federal project which exists or is under construction will be evaluated to insure that they are compatible with the purposes of the project.

(6) A DA permit does not convey any property rights, either in real estate or material, or any exclusive privileges. Furthermore, a DA permit does not authorize any injury to property or invasion of rights or any infringement of Federal, state or local laws or regulations. The applicant's signature on an application is an affirmation that the applicant possesses or will possess the requisite property interest to undertake the activity proposed in the application. The district engineer will not enter into disputes but will remind the applicant of the above. The dispute over property ownership will not be a factor in the Corps public interest decision.

(h) *Activities affecting coastal zones.* Applications for DA permits for activities affecting the coastal zones of those states having a coastal zone management program approved by the Secretary of Commerce will be evaluated with respect to compliance with that program. No permit will be issued to a non-federal applicant until certification has been provided that the proposed activity complies with the coastal zone management program and the appropriate state agency has concurred with the certification or has waived its right to do so. However, a permit may be issued to a non-federal applicant if the Secretary of Commerce, on his own initiative or upon appeal by the applicant, finds that the proposed activity is consistent with the objectives of the Coastal Zone Management Act of 1972 or is otherwise necessary in the interest of national security. Federal agency and Indian tribe applicants for DA permits are responsible for complying with the Coastal Zone Management Act's directives for assuring that their activities directly affecting the coastal zone are consistent, to the maximum extent practicable, with approved state coastal zone management programs.

(i) *Activities in marine sanctuaries.* Applications for DA authorization for activities in a marine sanctuary established by the Secretary of Commerce under authority of section 302 of the Marine Protection, Research and Sanctuaries Act of 1972, as amended, will be evaluated for impact on the marine sanctuary. No permit will be issued until the applicant provides a certification from the Secretary of Commerce that the proposed activity is consistent with the purposes of Title III of the Marine Protection, Research and Sanctuaries Act of 1972, as amended, and can be carried out within the regulations promulgated by the Secretary of Commerce to control activities within the marine sanctuary.

(j) *Other Federal, state, or local requirements.*

(1) Processing of an application for a DA permit normally will proceed concurrently with the processing of other required Federal, state, and/or local authorizations or certifications. Final action on the DA permit will normally not be delayed pending action by another Federal, state or local agency (See 33 CFR 325.2 (d)(4)). However, where the required Federal, state and/or local authorization and/or certification has been denied for activities which also require a Department of the Army permit before final action has been taken on the Army permit application, the district engineer will, after considering the likelihood of subsequent approval of the other authorization and/or certification and the time and effort remaining to complete processing the Army permit application, either immediately deny the Army permit without prejudice or continue processing the application to a conclusion. If the district engineer continues processing the application, he will conclude by either denying the permit as contrary to the public interest, or denying it without prejudice indicating that except for the other Federal, state or local denial the Army permit could, under appropriate conditions, be issued. Denial without prejudice means that there is no prejudice to the right of the applicant to reinstate processing of the Army permit application if subsequent approval is received from the appropriate Federal, state and/or local agency on a previously denied authorization and/or certification. Even if official certification and/or authorization is not required by state or federal law, but a state, regional, or local agency having jurisdiction or interest over the particular activity comments on the application, due consideration shall be given to those official views as a reflection of local factors of the public interest.

(2) The primary responsibility for determining zoning and land use matters rests with state, local and tribal governments. The district engineer will normally accept decisions by such governments on those matters unless there are significant issues of overriding national importance. Such issues would include but are not necessarily limited to national security, navigation, national economic development, water quality, preservation of special aquatic areas, including wetlands, with significant interstate importance, and national energy needs. Whether a factor has overriding importance will depend on the degree of impact in an individual case.

(3) A proposed activity may result in conflicting comments from several agencies within the same state. Where a state has not designated a single responsible coordinating agency, district engineers will ask the Governor to express his views or to designate one state agency to represent the official state position in the particular case.

(4) In the absence of overriding national factors of the public interest that may be revealed during the evaluation of the permit application, a permit will generally be issued following receipt of a favorable state determination provided the concerns, policies, goals, and requirements as expressed in 33 CFR parts 320-324, and the applicable statutes have been considered and followed: e.g., the National Environmental Policy Act; the Fish and Wildlife Coordination Act; the Historical and Archeological Preservation Act; the National Historic Preservation Act; the Endangered Species Act; the Coastal Zone Management Act; the Marine Protection, Research and Sanctuaries Act of 1972, as amended; the Clean Water Act, the Archeological Resources Act, and the American Indian Religious Freedom Act. Similarly, a permit will generally be issued for Federal and Federally-authorized activities; another federal agency's determination to proceed is entitled to substantial consideration in the Corps' public interest review.

(5) Where general permits to avoid duplication are not practical, district engineers shall develop joint procedures with those local, state, and other Federal agencies having ongoing permit programs for activities also regulated by the Department of the Army. In such cases, applications for DA permits may be processed jointly with the state or other federal applications to an independent conclusion and decision by the district engineer and the appropriate Federal or state agency. (See 33 CFR 325.2(e).)

(6) The district engineer shall develop operating procedures for establishing official communications with Indian Tribes within the district. The procedures shall provide for appointment of a tribal representative who will receive all pertinent public notices, and respond to such notices with the official tribal position on the proposed activity. This procedure shall apply only to those tribes which accept this option. Any adopted operating procedures shall be distributed by public notice to inform the tribes of this option.

(k) *Safety of impoundment structures.* To insure that all impoundment structures are designed for safety, non-Federal applicants may be required to demonstrate that the structures comply with established state dam safety criteria or have been designed by qualified persons and, in appropriate cases, that the design has been independently reviewed (and modified as the review would indicate) by similarly qualified persons.

(l) *Floodplain management.*

(1) Floodplains possess significant natural values and carry out numerous functions important to the public interest. These include:

(i) Water resources values (natural moderation of floods, water quality maintenance, and groundwater recharge);

(ii) Living resource values (fish, wildlife, and plant resources);

(iii) Cultural resource values (open space, natural beauty, scientific study, outdoor education, and recreation); and

(iv) Cultivated resource values (agriculture, aquaculture, and forestry).

(2) Although a particular alteration to a flood-plain may constitute a minor change, the cumulative impact of such changes may result in a significant degradation of floodplain values and functions and in increased potential for harm to upstream and downstream activities. In accordance with the requirements of Executive Order 11988, district engineers, as part of their public interest review, should avoid to the extent practicable, long and short term significant adverse impacts associated with the occupancy and modification of floodplains, as well as the direct and indirect support of floodplain development whenever there is a practicable alternative. For those activities which in the public interest must occur in or impact upon floodplains, the district engineer shall ensure, to the maximum extent practicable, that the impacts of potential flooding on human health, safety, and welfare are minimized, the risks of flood losses are minimized, and, whenever practicable the natural and beneficial values served by floodplains are restored and preserved.

(3) In accordance with Executive Order 11988, the district engineer should avoid authorizing floodplain developments whenever practicable alternatives exist outside the floodplain. If there are no such practicable alternatives, the district engineer shall consider, as a means of mitigation, alternatives within the floodplain which will lessen any significant adverse impact to the floodplain.

(m) *Water supply and conservation.* Water is an essential resource, basic to human survival, economic growth, and the natural environment. Water conservation requires the efficient use of water resources in all actions which involve the significant use of water or that significantly affect the availability of water for alternative uses including opportunities to reduce demand and improve efficiency in order to minimize new supply requirements. Actions affecting water quantities are subject to Congressional policy as stated in section 101(g) of the Clean Water Act which provides that the authority of states to allocate water quantities shall not be superseded, abrogated, or otherwise impaired.

(n) *Energy conservation and development.* Energy conservation and development are major national objectives. District engineers will give high priority to the processing of permit actions involving energy projects.

(o) *Navigation.*

(1) Section 11 of the Rivers and Harbors Act of 1899 authorized establishment of harbor lines shoreward of which no individual permits were required. Because harbor lines were established on the basis of navigation impacts only, the Corps of Engineers published a regulation on 27 May 1970 (33 CFR 209.150) which declared that permits would thereafter be required for activities shoreward of the harbor lines. Review of applications would be based on a full public interest evaluation and harbor lines would serve as guidance for assessing navigation impacts. Accordingly, activities constructed shore-ward of harbor lines prior to 27 May 1970 do not require specific authorization.

(2) The policy of considering harbor lines as guidance for assessing impacts on navigation continues.

(3) Protection of navigation in all navigable waters of the United States continues to be a primary concern of the federal government.

(4) District engineers should protect navigational and anchorage interests in connection with the NPDES program by recommending to EPA or to the state, if the program has been delegated, that a permit be denied unless appropriate conditions can be included to avoid any substantial impairment of navigation and anchorage.

(p) *Environmental benefits.* Some activities that require Department of the Army permits result in beneficial effects to the quality of the environment. The district engineer will weigh these benefits as well as environmental detriments along with other factors of the public interest.

(q) *Economics.* When private enterprise makes application for a permit, it will generally be assumed that appropriate economic evaluations have been completed, the proposal is economically viable, and is needed in the market place. However, the district engineer in appropriate cases, may make an independent review of the need for the project from the perspective of the overall public interest. The economic benefits of many projects are important to the local community and contribute to needed improvements in the local economic base, affecting such factors as employment, tax revenues, community cohesion, community services, and property values. Many projects also contribute to the National Economic Development (NED), (i.e., the increase in the net value of the national output of goods and services).

(r) *Mitigation.*{1}

(1) Mitigation is an important aspect of the review and balancing process on many Department of the Army permit applications. Consideration of mitigation will occur throughout the permit application review process and includes avoiding, minimizing, rectifying, reducing, or compensating for resource losses. Losses will be avoided to the extent practicable. Compensation may occur on-site or at an off-site location. Mitigation requirements generally fall into three categories.

{FN1} This is a general statement of mitigation policy which applies to all Corps of Engineers regulatory authorities covered by these regulations (33 CFR parts 320-330). It is not a substitute for the mitigation requirements necessary to ensure that a permit action under section 404 of the Clean Water Act complies with the section 404(b)(1) Guidelines. There is currently an interagency Working Group formed to develop guidance on implementing mitigation requirements of the Guidelines.

(i) Project modifications to minimize adverse project impacts should be discussed with the applicant at pre-application meetings and during application processing. As a result of these discussions and as the district engineer's evaluation proceeds, the district engineer may require minor project modifications. Minor project modifications are those that are considered feasible (cost, constructability, etc.) to the applicant and that, if adopted, will result in a project that generally meets the applicant's purpose and need. Such modifications can include reductions in scope and size; changes in construction methods, materials or timing; and operation and maintenance practices or other similar modifications that reflect a sensitivity to environmental quality within the context of the work proposed. For example, erosion control features could be required on a fill project to reduce sedimentation impacts or a pier could be reoriented to minimize navigational problems even though those projects may satisfy all legal requirements (paragraph (r)(1)(ii) of this section) and the public interest review test (paragraph (r)(1)(iii) of this section) without such modifications.

(ii) Further mitigation measures may be required to satisfy legal requirements. For Section 404 applications, mitigation shall be required to ensure that the project complies with the 404(b)(1) Guidelines. Some mitigation measures are enumerated at 40 CFR 230.70 through 40 CFR 230.77 (Subpart H of the 404(b)(1) Guidelines).

(iii) Mitigation measures in addition to those under paragraphs (r)(1) (i) and (ii) of this section may be required as a result of the public interest review process. (See 33 CFR 325.4(a).) Mitigation should be developed and incorporated within the public interest review process to the extent that the mitigation is found by the district engineer to be reasonable and justified. Only those measures required to ensure that the project is not contrary to the public interest may be required under this subparagraph.

(2) All compensatory mitigation will be for significant resource losses which are specifically identifiable, reasonably likely to occur, and of importance to the human or aquatic environment. Also, all mitigation will be directly related to the impacts of the proposal, appropriate to the scope and degree of those impacts, and reasonably enforceable. District engineers will require all forms of mitigation, including compensatory mitigation, only as provided in paragraphs (r)(1) (i) through (iii) of this section. Additional mitigation may be added at the applicants' request.

PART 321
PERMITS FOR DAMS AND DIKES IN NAVIGABLE WATERS OF THE UNITED STATES

Authority: 33 U.S.C. 401.

Source: 51 FR 41227, Nov. 13, 1986, unless otherwise noted.

§ 321.1   General.

This regulation prescribes, in addition to the general policies of 33 CFR part 320 and procedures of 33 CFR part 325, those special policies, practices, and procedures to be followed by the Corps of Engineers in connection with the review of applications for Department of the Army (DA) permits to authorize the construction of a dike or dam in a navigable water of the United States pursuant to section 9 of the Rivers and Harbors Act of 1899 (33 U.S.C. 401). See 33 CFR 320.2(a). Dams and dikes in navigable waters of the United States also require DA permits under section 404 of the Clean Water Act, as amended (33 U.S.C. 1344). Applicants for DA permits under this part should also refer to 33 CFR part 323 to satisfy the requirements of section 404.

§ 321.2   Definitions.

For the purpose of this regulation, the following terms are defined:

(a) The term *navigable waters of the United States* means those waters of the United States that are subject to the ebb and flow of the tide shoreward to the mean high water mark and/or are presently used, or have been used in the past, or may be susceptible to use to transport interstate or foreign commerce. See 33 CFR part 329 for a more complete definition of this term.

(b) The term *dike* or *dam* means, for the purposes of section 9, any impoundment structure that completely spans a navigable water of the United States and that may obstruct interstate waterborne commerce. The term does not include a weir. Weirs are regulated pursuant to section 10 of the Rivers and Harbors Act of 1899. (See 33 CFR part 322.)

§ 321.3   Special policies and procedures.

The following additional special policies and procedures shall be applicable to the evaluation of permit applications under this regulation:

(a) The Assistant Secretary of the Army (Civil Works) will decide whether DA authorization for a dam or dike in an interstate navigable water of the United States will be issued, since this authority has not been delegated to the Chief of Engineers. The conditions to be imposed in any instrument of authorization will be recommended by the district engineer when forwarding the report to the Assistant Secretary of the Army (Civil Works), through the Chief of Engineers.

(b) District engineers are authorized to decide whether DA authorization for a dam or dike in an intrastate navigable water of the United States will be issued (see 33 CFR 325.8).

(c) Processing a DA application under section 9 will not be completed until the approval of the United States Congress has been obtained if the navigable water of the United States is an interstate waterbody, or until the approval of the appropriate state legislature has been obtained if the navigable water of the United States is an intrastate waterbody (i.e., the navigable portion of the navigable water of the United States is solely within the boundaries of one state). The district engineer, upon receipt of such an application, will notify the applicant that the consent of Congress or the state legislature must be obtained before a permit can be issued.

PART 322

PERMITS FOR STRUCTURES OR WORK IN OR AFFECTING NAVIGABLE WATERS OF THE UNITED STATES

Authority: 33 U.S.C. 403.

Source: 51 FR 41228, Nov. 13, 1986, unless otherwise noted.

§ 322.1   General.

This regulation prescribes, in addition to the general policies of 33 CFR part 320 and procedures of 33 CFR part 325, those special policies, practices, and procedures to be followed by the Corps of Engineers in connection with the review of applications for Department of the Army (DA) permits to authorize certain structures or work in or affecting navigable waters of the United States pursuant to section 10 of the Rivers and Harbors Act of 1899 (33 U.S.C. 403) (hereinafter referred to as section 10). See 33 CFR 320.2(b). Certain structures or work in or affecting navigable waters of the United States are also regulated under other authorities of the DA. These include discharges of dredged or fill material into waters of the United States, including the territorial seas, pursuant to section 404 of the Clean Water Act (33 U.S.C. 1344; see 33 CFR part 323) and the transportation of dredged material by vessel for purposes of dumping in ocean waters, including the territorial seas, pursuant to section 103 of the Marine Protection, Research and Sanctuaries Act of 1972, as amended (33 U.S.C. 1413; see 33 CFR part 324). A DA permit will also be required under these additional authorities if they are applicable to structures or work in or affecting navigable waters of the United States. Applicants for DA permits under this part should refer to the other cited authorities and implementing regulations for these additional permit requirements to determine whether they also are applicable to their proposed activities.

§ 322.2   Definitions.

For the purpose of this regulation, the following terms are defined:

(a) The term *navigable waters of the United States* and all other terms relating to the geographic scope of jurisdiction are defined at 33 CFR part 329. Generally, they are those waters of the United States that are subject to the ebb and flow of the tide shoreward to the mean high water mark, and/or are presently used, or have been used in the past, or may be susceptible to use to transport interstate or foreign commerce.

(b) The term *structure* shall include, without limitation, any pier, boat dock, boat ramp, wharf, dolphin, weir, boom, breakwater, bulkhead, revetment, riprap, jetty, artificial island, artificial reef, permanent mooring structure, power transmission line, permanently moored floating vessel, piling, aid to navigation, or any other obstacle or obstruction.

(c) The term *work* shall include, without limitation, any dredging or disposal of dredged material, excavation, filling, or other modification of a navigable water of the United States.

(d) The term *letter of permission* means a type of individual permit issued in accordance with the abbreviated procedures of 33 CFR 325.2(e).

(e) The term *individual permit* means a DA authorization that is issued following a case-by-case evaluation of a specific structure or work in accordance with the procedures of this regulation and 33 CFR part 325, and a determination that the proposed structure or work is in the public interest pursuant to 33 CFR part 320.

(f) The term *general permit* means a DA authorization that is issued on a nationwide or regional basis for a category or categories of activities when:

(1) Those activities are substantially similar in nature and cause only minimal individual and cumulative environmental impacts; or

(2) The general permit would result in avoiding unnecessary duplication of the regulatory control exercised by another Federal, state, or local agency provided it has been determined that the environmental consequences of the action are individually and cumulatively minimal. (See 33 CFR 325.2(e) and 33 CFR part 330.)

(g) The term *artificial reef* means a structure which is constructed or placed in the navigable waters of the United States or in the waters overlying the outer continental shelf for the purpose of enhancing fishery resources and commercial and recreational fishing opportunities. The term does not include activities or structures such as wing deflectors, bank stabilization, grade stabilization structures, or low flow key ways, all of which may be useful to enhance fisheries resources.

§ 322.3   Activities requiring permits.

(a) *General.* DA permits are required under section 10 for structures and/or work in or affecting navigable waters of the United States except as otherwise provided in § 322.4 below. Certain activities specified in 33 CFR part 330 are permitted by that regulation ("nationwide general permits"). Other activities may be authorized by district or division engineers on a regional basis ("regional general permits"). If an activity is not exempted by section 322.4 of this part or authorized by a general permit, an individual section 10 permit will be required for the proposed activity. Structures or work are in navigable waters of the United States if they are within limits defined in 33 CFR part 329. Structures or work outside these limits are subject to the provisions of law cited in paragraph (a) of this section, if these structures or work affect the course, location, or condition of the waterbody in such a manner as to impact on its navigable capacity. For purposes of a section 10 permit, a tunnel or other structure or work under or over a navigable water of the United States is considered to have an impact on the navigable capacity of the waterbody.

(b) *Outer continental shelf.* DA permits are required for the construction of artificial islands, installations, and other devices on the seabed, to the seaward limit of the outer continental shelf, pursuant to section 4(f) of the Outer Continental Shelf Lands Act as amended. (See 33 CFR 320.2(b).)

(c) *Activities of Federal agencies.*

(1) Except as specifically provided in this paragraph, activities of the type described in paragraphs (a) and (b) of this section, done by or on behalf of any Federal agency are subject to the authorization procedures of these regulations. Work or structures in or affecting navigable waters of the United States that are part of the civil works activities of the Corps of Engineers, unless covered by a nationwide or regional general permit issued pursuant to these regulations, are subject to the procedures of separate regulations. Agreement for construction or engineering services performed for other agencies by the Corps of Engineers does not constitute authorization under this regulation. Division and district engineers will therefore advise Federal agencies accordingly, and cooperate to the fullest extent in expediting the processing of their applications.

(2) Congress has delegated to the Secretary of the Army in section 10 the duty to authorize or prohibit certain work or structures in navigable waters of the United States, upon recommendation of the Chief of Engineers. The general legislation by which Federal agencies are empowered to act generally is not considered to be sufficient authorization by Congress to satisfy the purposes of section 10. If an agency asserts that it has Congressional authorization meeting the test of section 10 or would otherwise be exempt from the provisions of section 10, the legislative history and/or provisions of the Act should clearly demonstrate that Congress was approving the exact location and plans from which Congress could have considered the effect on navigable waters of the United States or that Congress intended to exempt that agency from the requirements of section 10. Very often such legislation reserves final approval of plans or construction for the Chief of Engineers. In such cases evaluation and authorization under this regulation are limited by the intent of the statutory language involved.

(3) The policy provisions set out in 33 CFR 320.4(j) relating to state or local certifications and/or authorizations, do not apply to work or structures

undertaken by Federal agencies, except where compliance with non-Federal authorization is required by Federal law or Executive policy, e.g., section 313 and section 401 of the Clean Water Act.

§ 322.4   Activities not requiring permits.

(a) Activities that were commenced or completed shoreward of established Federal harbor lines before May 27, 1970 (see 33 CFR 320.4(o)) do not require section 10 permits; however, if those activities involve the discharge of dredged or fill material into waters of the United States after October 18, 1972, a section 404 permit is required. (See 33 CFR part 323.)

(b) Pursuant to section 154 of the Water Resource Development Act of 1976 (Pub. L. 94-587), Department of the Army permits are not required under section 10 to construct wharves and piers in any waterbody, located entirely within one state, that is a navigable water of the United States solely on the basis of its historical use to transport interstate commerce.

§ 322.5   Special policies.

The Secretary of the Army has delegated to the Chief of Engineers the authority to issue or deny section 10 permits. The following additional special policies and procedures shall also be applicable to the evaluation of permit applications under this regulation.

(a) *General.* DA permits are required for structures or work in or affecting navigable waters of the United States. However, certain structures or work specified in 33 CFR part 330 are permitted by that regulation. If a structure or work is not permitted by that regulation, an individual or regional section 10 permit will be required.

(b) *Artificial Reefs.*

(1) When considering an application for an artificial reef, as defined in 33 CFR 322.2(g), the district engineer will review the applicant's provisions for siting, constructing, monitoring, operating, maintaining, and managing the proposed artificial reef and shall determine if those provisions are consistent with the following standards:

(i) The enhancement of fishery resources to the maximum extent practicable; '

(ii) The facilitation of access and utilization by United States recreational and commercial fishermen;

(iii) The minimization of conflicts among competing uses of the navigable waters or waters overlying the outer continental shelf and of the resources in such waters;

(iv) The minimization of environmental risks and risks to personal health and property;

(v) Generally accepted principles of international law; and

(vi) the prevention of any unreasonable obstructions to navigation. If the district engineer decides that the applicant's provisions are not consistent with these standards, he shall deny the permit. If the district engineer decides that the provisions are consistent with these standards, and if he decides to issue the permit after the public interest review, he shall make the provisions part of the permit.

(2) In addition, the district engineer will consider the National Artificial Reef Plan developed pursuant to section 204 of the National Fishing Enhancement Act of 1984, and if he decides to issue the permit, will notify the Secretary of Commerce of any need to deviate from that plan.

(3) The district engineer will comply with all coordination provisions required by a written agreement between the DOD and the Federal agencies relative to artificial reefs. In addition, if the district engineer decides that further consultation beyond the normal public commenting process is required to evaluate fully the proposed artificial reef, he may initiate such consultation with any Federal agency, state or local government, or other interested party.

(4) The district engineer will issue a permit for the proposed artificial reef only if the applicant demonstrates, to the district engineer's satisfaction, that the title to the artificial reef construction material is unambiguous, that responsibility for maintenance of the reef is clearly established, and that he has the financial ability to assume liability for all damages that may arise with respect to the proposed artificial reef. A demonstration of financial responsibility might include evidence of insurance, sponsorship, or available assets.

(i) A person to whom a permit is issued in accordance with these regulations and any insurer of that person shall not be liable for damages caused by activities required to be undertaken under any terms and conditions of the permit, if the permittee is in compliance with such terms and conditions.

(ii) A person to whom a permit is issued in accordance with these regulations and any insurer of that person shall be liable, to the extent determined under applicable law, for damages to which paragraph (i) does not apply.

(iii) Any person who has transferred title to artificial reef construction materials to a person to whom a permit is issued in accordance with these regulations shall not be liable for damages arising from the use of such materials in an artificial reef, if such materials meet applicable requirements of the plan published under section 204 of the National Artificial Reef Plan, and are not otherwise defective at the time title is transferred.

(c) *Non-Federal dredging for navigation.*

(1) The benefits which an authorized Federal navigation project are intended to produce will often require similar and related operations by non-Federal agencies (e.g., dredging access channels to docks and berthing facilities or deepening such channels to correspond to the Federal project depth). These non-Federal activities will be considered by Corps of Engineers officials in planning the construction and maintenance of Federal navigation projects and, to the maximum practical extent, will be coordinated with interested Federal, state, regional and local agencies and the general public simultaneously with the associated Federal projects. Non-Federal activities which are not so coordinated will be individually evaluated in accordance with these regulations. In evaluating the public interest in connection with applications for permits for such coordinated operations, equal treatment will be accorded to the fullest extent possible to both Federal and non-Federal operations. Permits for non-Federal dredging operations will normally contain conditions requiring the permittee to comply with the same practices or requirements utilized in connection with related Federal dredging operations with respect to such matters as turbidity, water quality, containment of material, nature and location of approved spoil disposal areas (non-Federal use of Federal contained disposal areas will be in accordance with laws authorizing such areas and regulations governing their use), extent and period of dredging, and other factors relating to protection of environmental and ecological values.

(2) A permit for the dredging of a channel, slip, or other such project for navigation may also authorize the periodic maintenance dredging of the project. Authorization procedures and limitations for maintenance dredging shall be as prescribed in 33 CFR 325.6(e). The permit will require the permittee to give advance notice to the district engineer each time maintenance dredging is to be performed. Where the maintenance dredging involves the discharge of dredged material into waters of the United States or the transportation of dredged material for the purpose of dumping it in ocean waters, the procedures in 33 CFR parts 323 and 324 respectively shall also be followed.

(d) *Structures for small boats.*

(1) In the absence of overriding public interest, favorable consideration will generally be given to applications from riparian owners for permits for piers, boat docks, moorings, platforms and similar structures for small boats. Particular attention will be given to the location and general design of such structures to prevent possible obstructions to navigation with respect to both the public's use of the waterway and the neighboring proprietors' access to the waterway. Obstructions can result from both the existence of the structure, particularly in conjunction with other similar facilities in the immediate vicinity, and from its inability to withstand wave action or other forces which can be expected. District engineers will inform applicants of the hazards involved and encourage safety in location, design, and operation. District engineers will encourage cooperative or group use facilities in lieu of individual proprietary use facilities.

(2) Floating structures for small recreational boats or other recreational purposes in lakes con-

trolled by the Corps of Engineers under a resource manager are normally subject to permit authorities cited in § 322.3, of this section, when those waters are regarded as navigable waters of the United States. However, such structures will not be authorized under this regulation but will be regulated under applicable regulations of the Chief of Engineers published in 36 CFR 327.19 if the land surrounding those lakes is under complete Federal ownership. District engineers will delineate those portions of the navigable waters of the United States where this provision is applicable and post notices of this designation in the vicinity of the lake resource manager's office.

(e) *Aids to navigation.* The placing of fixed and floating aids to navigation in a navigable water of the United States is within the purview of Section 10 of the Rivers and Harbors Act of 1899. Furthermore, these aids are of particular interest to the U.S. Coast Guard because of its control of marking, lighting and standardization of such navigation aids. A Section 10 nationwide permit has been issued for such aids provided they are approved by, and installed in accordance with the requirements of the U.S. Coast Guard (33 CFR 330.5(a)(1)). Electrical service cables to such aids are not included in the nationwide permit (an individual or regional Section 10 permit will be required).

(f) *Outer continental shelf.* Artificial islands, installations, and other devices located on the seabed, to the seaward limit of the outer continental shelf, are subject to the standard permit procedures of this regulation. Where the islands, installations and other devices are to be constructed on lands which are under mineral lease from the Mineral Management Service, Department of the Interior, that agency, in cooperation with other federal agencies, fully evaluates the potential effect of the leasing program on the total environment. Accordingly, the decision whether to issue a permit on lands which are under mineral lease from the Department of the Interior will be limited to an evaluation of the impact of the proposed work on navigation and national security. The public notice will so identify the criteria.

(g) *Canals and other artificial waterways connected to navigable waters of the United States.* A canal or similar artificial waterway is subject to the regulatory authorities discussed in § 322.3, of this part, if it constitutes a navigable water of the United States, or if it is connected to navigable waters of the United States in a manner which affects their course, location, condition, or capacity, or if at some point in its construction or operation it results in an effect on the course, location, condition, or capacity of navigable waters of the United States. In all cases the connection to navigable waters of the United States requires a permit. Where the canal itself constitutes a navigable water of the United States, evaluation of the permit application and further exercise of regulatory authority will be in accordance with the standard procedures of these regulations. For all other canals,

the exercise of regulatory authority is restricted to those activities which affect the course, location, condition, or capacity of the navigable waters of the United States. The district engineer will consider, for applications for canal work, a proposed plan of the entire development and the location and description of anticipated docks, piers and other similar structures which will be placed in the canal.

(h) *Facilities at the borders of the United States.*

(1) The construction, operation, maintenance, or connection of facilities at the borders of the United States are subject to Executive control and must be authorized by the President, Secretary of State, or other delegated official.

(2) Applications for permits for the construction, operation, maintenance, or connection at the borders of the United States of facilities for the transmission of electric energy between the United States and a foreign country, or for the exportation or importation of natural gas to or from a foreign country, must be made to the Secretary of Energy. (Executive Order 10485, September 3, 1953, 16 U.S.C. 824(a)(e), 15 U.S.C. 717(b), as amended by Executive Order 12038, February 3, 1978, and 18 CFR parts 32 and 153).

(3) Applications for the landing or operation of submarine cables must be made to the Federal Communications Commission. (Executive Order 10530, May 10, 1954, 47 U.S.C. 34 to 39, and 47 CFR 1.766).

(4) The Secretary of State is to receive applications for permits for the construction, connection, operation, or maintenance, at the borders of the United States, of pipelines, conveyor belts, and similar facilities for the exportation or importation of petroleum products, coals, minerals, or other products to or from a foreign country; facilities for the exportation or importation of water or sewage to or from a foreign country; and monorails, aerial cable cars, aerial tramways, and similar facilities for the transportation of persons and/or things, to or from a foreign country. (Executive Order 11423, August 16, 1968).

(5) A DA permit under section 10 of the Rivers and Harbors Act of 1899 is also required for all of the above facilities which affect the navigable waters of the United States, but in each case in which a permit has been issued as provided above, the district engineer, in evaluating the general public interest, may consider the basic existence and operation of the facility to have been primarily examined and permitted as provided by the Executive Orders. Furthermore, in those cases where the construction, maintenance, or operation at the above facilities involves the discharge of dredged or fill material in waters of the United States or the transportation of dredged material for the purpose of dumping it into ocean waters, appropriate DA authorizations under section 404 of the Clean Water Act or under section 103 of the Marine Protection, Research and Sanctuaries Act of 1972, as amended, are also required. (See 33 CFR parts 323 and 324.)

(i) *Power transmission lines.*

(1) Permits under section 10 of the Rivers and Harbors Act of 1899 are required for power transmission lines crossing navigable waters of the United States unless those lines are part of a water power project subject to the regulatory authorities of the Department of Energy under the Federal Power Act of 1920. If an application is received for a permit for lines which are part of such a water power project, the applicant will be instructed to submit the application to the Department of Energy. If the lines are not part of such a water power project, the application will be processed in accordance with the procedures of these regulations.

(2) The following minimum clearances are required for aerial electric power transmission lines crossing navigable waters of the United States. These clearances are related to the clearances over the navigable channel provided by existing fixed bridges, or the clearances which would be required by the U.S. Coast Guard for new fixed bridges, in the vicinity of the proposed power line crossing. The clearances are based on the low point of the line under conditions which produce the greatest sag, taking into consideration temperature, load, wind, length or span, and type of supports as outlined in the National Electrical Safety Code.

Nominal system voltage, kV	Minimum additional clearance (feet) above clearance required for bridges
115 and below	20
138	22
161	24
230	26
350	30
500	35
700	42
750-765	45

(3) Clearances for communication lines, stream gaging cables, ferry cables, and other aerial crossings are usually required to be a minimum of ten feet above clearances required for bridges. Greater clearances will be required if the public interest so indicates.

(4) Corps of Engineer regulation ER 1110-2-4401 prescribes minimum vertical clearances for power and communication lines over Corps lake projects. In instances where both this regulation and ER 1110-2-4401 apply, the greater minimum clearance is required.

(j) *Seaplane operations.*

(1) Structures in navigable waters of the United States associated with seaplane operations require DA permits, but close coordination with the Federal Aviation Administration (FAA), Department of Transportation, is required on such applications.

(2) The FAA must be notified by an applicant whenever he proposes to establish or operate a seaplane base. The FAA will study the proposal and advise the applicant, district engineer, and other interested parties as to the effects of the proposal on the use of airspace. The district engineer will, therefore, refer any objections regarding the effect of the proposal on the use of airspace to the FAA, and give due consideration to its recommendations when evaluating the general public interest.

(3) If the seaplane base would serve air carriers licensed by the Department of Transportation, the applicant must receive an airport operating certificate from the FAA. That certificate reflects a determination and conditions relating to the installation, operation, and maintenance of adequate air navigation facilities and safety equipment. Accordingly, the district engineer may, in evaluating the general public interest, consider such matters to have been primarily evaluated by the FAA.

(4) For regulations pertaining to seaplane landings at Corps of Engineers projects, see 36 CFR 327.4.

(k) *Foreign trade zones.* The Foreign Trade Zones Act (48 Stat. 998-1003, 19 U.S.C. 81a to 81u, as amended) authorizes the establishment of foreign-trade zones in or adjacent to United States ports of entry under terms of a grant and regulations prescribed by the Foreign-Trade Zones Board. Pertinent regulations are published at Title 15 of the Code of Federal Regulations, part 400. The Secretary of the Army is a member of the Board, and construction of a zone is under the supervision of the district engineer. Laws governing the navigable waters of the United States remain applicable to foreign-trade zones, including the general requirements of these regulations. Evaluation by a district engineer of a permit application may give recognition to the consideration by the Board of the general economic effects of the zone on local and foreign commerce, general location of wharves and facilities, and other factors pertinent to construction, operation, and maintenance of the zone.

(l) *Shipping safety fairways and anchorage areas.* DA permits are required for structures located within shipping safety fairways and anchorage areas established by the U.S. Coast Guard.

(1) The Department of the Army will grant no permits for the erection of structures in areas designated as fairways, except that district engineers may permit temporary anchors and attendant cables or chains for floating or semisubmersible drilling rigs to be placed within a fairway provided the following conditions are met:

(i) The installation of anchors to stabilize semisubmersible drilling rigs within fairways must be temporary and shall be allowed to remain only 120 days. This period may be extended by the district engineer provided reasonable cause for such extension can be shown and the extension is otherwise justified.

(ii) Drilling rigs must be at least 500 feet from any fairway boundary or whatever distance necessary to insure that minimum clearance over an anchor line within a fairway will be 125 feet.

(iii) No anchor buoys or floats or related rigging will be allowed on the surface of the water or to a depth of 125 feet from the surface, within the fairway.

(iv) Drilling rigs may not be placed closer than 2 nautical miles of any other drilling rig situated along a fairway boundary, and not closer than 3 nautical miles to any drilling rig located on the opposite side of the fairway.

(v) The permittee must notify the district engineer, Bureau of Land Management, Mineral Management Service, U.S. Coast Guard, National Oceanic and Atmospheric Administration and the U.S. Navy Hydrographic Office of the approximate dates (commencement and completion) the anchors will be in place to insure maximum notification to mariners.

(vi) Navigation aids or danger markings must be installed as required by the U.S. Coast Guard.

(2) District engineers may grant permits for the erection of structures within an area designated as an anchorage area, but the number of structures will be limited by spacing, as follows: The center of a structure to be erected shall be not less than two (2) nautical miles from the center of any existing structure. In a drilling or production complex, associated structures shall be as close together as practicable having due consideration for the safety factors involved. A complex of associated structures, when connected by walkways, shall be considered one structure for the purpose of spacing. A vessel fixed in place by moorings and used in conjunction with the associated structures of a drilling or production complex, shall be considered an attendant vessel and its extent shall include its moorings. When a drilling or production complex includes an attendant vessel and the complex extends more than five hundred (500) yards from the center or the complex, a structure to be erected shall be not closer than two (2) nautical miles from the near outer limit of the complex. An underwater completion installation in and anchorage area shall be considered a structure and shall be marked with a lighted buoy as approved by the United States Coast Guard.

PART 323
PERMITS FOR DISCHARGES OF DREDGED OR FILL MATERIAL INTO WATERS OF THE UNITED STATES

Authority: 33 U.S.C. 1344.

Source: 51 FR 41232, Nov. 13, 1986, unless otherwise noted.

§ 323.1 General.

This regulation prescribes, in addition to the general policies of 33 CFR part 320 and procedures of 33 CFR part 325, those special policies, practices, and procedures to be followed by the Corps of Engineers in connection with the review of applications for DA permits to authorize the discharge of dredged or fill material into waters of the United States pursuant to section 404 of the Clean Water Act (CWA) (33 U.S.C. 1344) (hereinafter referred to as section 404). (See 33 CFR 320.2(g).) Certain discharges of dredged or fill material into waters of the United States are also regulated under other authorities of the Department of the Army. These include dams and dikes in navigable waters of the United States pursuant to section 9 of the Rivers and Harbors Act of 1899 (33 U.S.C. 401; see 33 CFR part 321) and certain structures or work in or affecting navigable waters of the United States pursuant to section 10 of the Rivers and Harbors Act of 1899 (33 U.S.C. 403; see 33 CFR part 322). A DA permit will also be required under these additional authorities if they are applicable to activities involving discharges of dredged or fill material into waters of the United States. Applicants for DA permits under this part should refer to the other cited authorities and implementing regulations for these additional permit requirements to determine whether they also are applicable to their proposed activities.

§ 323.2 Definitions.

For the purpose of this part, the following terms are defined:

(a) The term *waters of the United States* and all other terms relating to the geographic scope of jurisdiction are defined at 33 CFR part 328.

(b) The term *lake* means a standing body of open water that occurs in a natural depression fed by one or more streams from which a stream may flow, that occurs due to the widening or natural blockage or cutoff of a river or stream, or that occurs in an isolated natural depression that is not a part of a surface river or stream. The term also includes a standing body of open water created by artificially blocking or restricting the flow of a river, stream, or tidal area. As used in this regulation, the term does not include artificial lakes or ponds created by excavating and/or diking dry land to collect and retain water for such purposes as stock watering, irrigation, settling basins, cooling, or rice growing.

(c) The term *dredged material* means material that is excavated or dredged from waters of the United States.

(d)(1) Except as provided below in paragraph (d)(2), the term *discharge of dredged material* means any addition of dredged material into, including any redeposit of dredged material within, the waters of the United States. The term includes, but is not limited to, the following:

(i) the addition of dredged material to a specified discharge site located in waters of the United States;

(ii) the runoff or overflow from a contained land or water disposal area; and

(iii) any addition, including any redeposit, of dredged material, including excavated material, into waters of the United States which is incidental to any activity, including mechanized landclearing, ditching, channelization, or other excavation.

(2) The term *discharge of dredged material* does not include the following:

(i) discharges of pollutants into waters of the United States resulting from the onshore subsequent processing of dredged material that is extracted for any commercial use (other than fill). These discharges are subject to section 402 of the Clean Water Act even though the extraction and deposit of such material may require a permit from the Corps or applicable state Section 404 program.

(ii) activities that involve only the cutting or removing of vegetation above the ground (e.g., mowing, rotary cutting, and chainsawing) where the activity neither substantially disturbs the root system nor involves mechanized pushing, dragging, or other similar activities that redeposit excavated soil material.

(3) Section 404 authorization is not required for the following:

(i) any incidental addition, including redeposit, of dredged material associated with any activity that does not have or would not have the effect of destroying or degrading an area of waters of the United States as defined in paragraphs (d)(4) and (d)(5) of this section; however, this exception does not apply to any person preparing to undertake mechanized landclearing, ditching, channelization and other excavation activity in a water of the United States, which would result in a redeposit of dredged material, unless the person demonstrates to the satisfaction of the Corps, or EPA as appropriate, prior to commencing the activity involving the discharge, that the activity would not have the effect of destroying or degrading any area of waters of the United States, as defined in paragraphs (d)(4) and (d)(5) of this section. The person proposing to undertake mechanized landclearing, ditching, channelization or other excavation activity bears the burden of demonstrating that such activity would not destroy or degrade any area of waters of the United States.

(ii) incidental movement of dredged material occurring during normal dredging operations, defined as dredging for navigation in navigable waters of the United States, as that term is defined in part 329 of this chapter, with proper authorization from the Congress and/or the Corps pursuant to part 322 of this Chapter; however, this exception is not applicable to dredging activities in wetlands, as that term is defined at section 328.3 of this Chapter.

(iii) those discharges of dredged material associated with ditching, channelization or other excavation activities in waters of the United States, including wetlands, for which Section 404 authorization was not previously required, as determined by the Corps district in which the activity occurs or would occur, provided that prior to August 25, 1996, the excavation activity commenced or was under contract to commence work and that the activity will be completed no later than August 25, 1994. This provision does not apply to discharges associated with mechanized landclearing. For those excavation activities that occur on an ongoing basis (either continuously or periodically), e.g., mining operations, the Corps retains the authority to grant, on a case-by-case basis, an extension of this 12-month grandfather provision provided that the discharger has submitted to the Corps within the 12-month period an individual permit application seeking Section 404 authorization for such excavation activity. In no event can the grandfather period under this paragraph extend beyond August 25, 1993.

(iv) certain discharges, such as those associated with normal farming, silviculture, and ranching activities, are not prohibited by or otherwise subject to regulation under Section 404. See 33 CFR 323.4 for discharges that do not required permits.

(4) For purposes of this section, an activity associated with a discharge of dredged material destroys an area of waters of the United States if it alters the area in such a way that it would no longer be a water of the United States.

[Note: Unauthorized discharges into waters of the United States do not eliminate Clean Water Act jurisdiction, even where such unauthorized discharges have the effect of destroying waters of the United States.]

(5) For purposes of this section, an activity as-

sociated with a discharge of dredged material degrades an area of waters of the United States if it has more than a de minimis (i.e., inconsequential) effect on the area by causing an identifiable individual or cumulative adverse effect on any aquatic function.

(e) The term fill material means any material used for the primary purpose of replacing an aquatic area with dry land or of changing the bottom elevation of an waterbody. The term does not include any pollutant discharged into the water primarily to dispose of waste, as that activity is regulated under section 402 of the Clean Water Act. See § 323.3(c) concerning the regulation of the placement of pilings in waters of the United States.

(f) The term *discharge of fill material* means the addition of fill material into waters of the United States. The term generally includes, without limitation, the following activities: Placement of fill that is necessary for the construction of any structure in a water of the United States; the building of any structure or impoundment requiring rock, sand, dirt, or other material for its construction; site-development fills for recreational, industrial, commercial, residential, and other uses; causeways or road fills; dams and dikes; artificial islands; property protection and/or reclamation devices such as riprap, groins, seawalls, breakwaters, and revetments; beach nourishment; levees; fill for structures such as sewage treatment facilities, intake and outfall pipes associated with power plants and subaqueous utility lines; and artificial reefs. The term does not include plowing, cultivating, seeding and harvesting for the production of food, fiber, and forest products (See § 323.4 for the definition of these terms). See § 323.3(c) concerning the regulation of the placement of pilings in waters of the United States.

(g) The term *individual permit* means a Department of the Army authorization that is issued following a case-by-case evaluation of a specific project involving the proposed discharge(s) in accordance with the procedures of this part and 33 CFR part 325 and a determination that the proposed discharge is in the public interest pursuant to 33 CFR part 320.

(h) The term *general permit* means a Department of the Army authorization that is issued on a nationwide or regional basis for a category or categories of activities when:

(1) Those activities are substantially similar in nature and cause only minimal individual and cumulative environmental impacts; or

(2) The general permit would result in avoiding unnecessary duplication of regulatory control exercised by another Federal, state, or local agency provided it has been determined that the environmental consequences of the action are individually and cumulatively minimal. (See 33 CFR 325.2(e) and 33 CFR part 330.) [58 FR 45037, August 25, 1993]

§ 323.3   Discharges requiring permits.

(a) *General.* Except as provided in § 323.4 of this part, DA permits will be required for the discharge of dredged or fill material into waters of the United States. Certain discharges specified in 33 CFR part 330 are permitted by that regulation ("nationwide permits"). Other discharges may be authorized by district or division engineers on a regional basis ("regional permits"). If a discharge of dredged or fill material is not exempted by § 323.4 of this part or permitted by 33 CFR part 330, an individual or regional section 404 permit will be required for the discharge of dredged or fill material into waters of the United States.

(b) *Activities of Federal agencies.* Discharges of dredged or fill material into waters of the United States done by or on behalf of any Federal agency, other than the Corps of Engineers (see 33 CFR 209.145), are subject to the authorization procedures of these regulations. Agreement for construction or engineering services performed for other agencies by the Corps of Engineers does not constitute authorization under the regulations. Division and district engineers will therefore advise Federal agencies and instrumentalities accordingly and cooperate to the fullest extent in expediting the processing of their applications.

(c) *Pilings.*

(1) Placement of pilings in waters of the United States constitutes a discharge of fill material and requires a Section 404 permit when such placement has or would have the effect of a discharge of fill material. Examples of such activities that have the effect of a discharge of fill material include, but are not limited to, the following: Projects where the pilings are so closely spaced that sedimentation rates would be increased; projects in which the pilings themselves effectively would replace the bottom of a waterbody; projects involving the placement of pilings that would reduce the reach or impair the flow or circulation of waters of the United States; and projects involving the placement of pilings which would result in the adverse alteration or elimination of aquatic functions.

(2) Placement of pilings in waters of the United States that does not have or would not have the effect of a discharge of fill material shall not require a Section 404 permit. Placement of pilings for linear projects, such as bridges, elevated walkways, and powerline structures, generally does not have the effect of a discharge of fill material. Furthermore, placement of pilings in waters of the United States for piers, wharves, and an individual house on stilts generally does not have the effect of a discharge of fill material. All pilings, however, placed in the navigable waters of the United States, as that term is defined in part 329 of this chapter, require authorization under section 10 of the Rivers and Harbors Act of 1899 (see part 322 of this chapter). [58 FR 45037, August 25, 1993

§ 323.4 Discharges not requiring permits.

(a) *General.* Except as specified in paragraphs (b) and (c) of this section, any discharge of dredged or fill material that may result from any of the following activities is not prohibited by or otherwise subject to regulation under section 404:

(1)(i) Normal farming, silviculture and ranching activities such as plowing, seeding, cultivating, minor drainage, and harvesting for the production of food, fiber, and forest products, or upland soil and water conservation practices, as defined in paragraph (a)(1)(iii) of this section.

(ii) To fall under this exemption, the activities specified in paragraph (a)(1)(i) of this section must be part of an established (i.e., on-going) farming, silviculture, or ranching operation and must be in accordance with definitions in § 323.4(a)(1)(iii). Activities on areas lying fallow as part of a conventional rotational cycle are part of an established operation. Activities which bring an area into farming, silviculture, or ranching use are not part of an established operation. An operation ceases to be established when the area on which it was conducted has been converted to another use or has lain idle so long that modifications to the hydrological regime are necessary to resume operations. If an activity takes place outside the waters of the United States, or if it does not involve a discharge, it does not need a section 404 permit, whether or not it is part of an established farming, silviculture, or ranching operation.

(iii) (A) Cultivating means physical methods of soil treatment employed within established farming, ranching and silviculture lands on farm, ranch, or forest crops to aid and improve their growth, quality or yield.

(B) Harvesting means physical measures employed directly upon farm, forest, or ranch crops within established agricultural and silvicultural lands to bring about their removal from farm, forest, or ranch land, but does not include the construction of farm, forest, or ranch roads.

(C)(*1*) Minor Drainage means:

(*i*) The discharge of dredged or fill material incidental to connecting upland drainage facilities to waters of the United States, adequate to effect the removal of excess soil moisture from upland croplands. (Construction and maintenance of upland (dryland) facilities, such as ditching and tiling, incidental to the planting, cultivating, protecting, or harvesting of crops, involve no discharge of dredged or fill material into waters of the United States, and as such never require a section 404 permit.);

(*ii*) The discharge of dredged or fill material for the purpose of installing ditching or other such water control facilities incidental to planting, cultivating, protecting, or harvesting of rice, cranberries or other wetland crop species, where these activities and the discharge occur in waters of the United States which are in established use for such agricultural and silvicultural wetland crop production;

(*iii*) The discharge of dredged or fill material for the purpose of manipulating the water levels of, or regulating the flow or distribution of water within, existing impoundments which have been constructed in accordance with applicable requirements of CWA, and which are in established use for the production of rice, cranberries, or other wetland crop species. (The provisions of paragraphs (a)(1)(iii)(C)(*1*)(*ii*) and (*iii*) of this section apply to areas that are in established use exclusively for wetland crop production as well as areas in established use for conventional wetland/non-wetland crop rotation (e.g., the rotations of rice and soybeans) where such rotation results in the cyclical or intermittent temporary dewatering of such areas.)

(*iv*) The discharges of dredged or fill material incidental to the emergency removal of sandbars, gravel bars, or other similar blockages which are formed during flood flows or other events, where such blockages close or constrict previously existing drainageways and, if not promptly removed, would result in damage to or loss of existing crops or would impair or prevent the plowing, seeding, harvesting or cultivating of crops on land in established use for crop production. Such removal does not include enlarging or extending the dimensions of, or changing the bottom elevations of, the affected drainageway as it existed prior to the formation of the blockage. Removal must be accomplished within one year of discovery of such blockages in order to be eligible for exemption.

(*2*) Minor drainage in waters of the U.S. is limited to drainage within areas that are part of an established farming or silviculture operation. It does not include drainage associated with the immediate or gradual conversion of a wetland to a non-wetland (e.g., wetland species to upland species not typically adapted to life in saturated soil conditions), or conversion from one wetland use to another (for example, silviculture to farming). In addition, minor drainage does not include the construction of any canal, ditch, dike or other waterway or structure which drains or otherwise significantly modifies a stream, lake, swamp, bog or any other wetland or aquatic area constituting waters of the United States. Any discharge of dredged or fill material into the waters of the United States incidental to the construction of any such structure or waterway requires a permit.

(D) Plowing means all forms of primary tillage, including moldboard, chisel, or wide-blade plowing, discing, harrowing and similar physical means utilized on farm, forest or ranch land for the breaking up, cutting, turning over, or stirring of soil to prepare it for the planting of crops. The term does not include the redistribution of soil, rock, sand, or other surficial materials in a manner which changes any area of the waters of the United States to dry land. For example, the redistribution of surface materials by blading, grading, or other means to fill in wetland areas is not plowing. Rock crushing activities which result in the loss of natural drainage characteristics, the reduction of water storage and recharge capabilities, or the overburden of natural water filtration capacities do not constitute plowing. Plowing as described above will never involve a discharge of dredged or fill material.

(E) Seeding means the sowing of seed and placement of seedlings to produce farm, ranch, or forest crops and includes the placement of soil beds for seeds or seedlings on established farm and forest lands.

(2) Maintenance, including emergency reconstruction of recently damaged parts, of currently serviceable structures such as dikes, dams, levees, groins, riprap, breakwaters, causeways, bridge abutments or approaches, and transportation structures. Maintenance does not include any modification that changes the character, scope, or size of the original fill design. Emergency reconstruction must occur within a reasonable period of time after damage occurs in order to qualify for this exemption.

(3) Construction or maintenance of farm or stock ponds or irrigation ditches, or the maintenance (but not construction) of drainage ditches. Discharges associated with siphons, pumps, headgates, wingwalls, weirs, diversion structures, and such other facilities as are appurtenant and functionally related to irrigation ditches are included in this exemption.

(4) Construction of temporary sedimentation basins on a construction site which does not include placement of fill material into waters of the U.S. The term "construction site" refers to any site involving the erection of buildings, roads, and other discrete structures and the installation of support facilities necessary for construction and utilization of such structures. The term also includes any other land areas which involve land-disturbing excavation activities, including quarrying or other mining activities, where an increase in the runoff of sediment is controlled through the use of temporary sedimentation basins.

(5) Any activity with respect to which a state has an approved program under section 208(b)(4) of the CWA which meets the requirements of sections 208(b)(4) (B) and (C).

(6) Construction or maintenance of farm roads, forest roads, or temporary roads for moving mining equipment, where such roads are constructed and maintained in accordance with best management practices (BMPs) to assure that flow and circulation patterns and chemical and biological characteristics of waters of the United States are not impaired, that the reach of the waters of the United States is not reduced, and that any adverse effect on the aquatic environment will be otherwise minimized. These BMPs which must be applied to satisfy this provision shall include those detailed BMPs described in the state's approved program description pursuant to the requirements of 40 CFR 233.22(i), and shall also include the following baseline provisions:

(i) Permanent roads (for farming or forestry activities), temporary access roads (for mining, forestry, or farm purposes) and skid trails (for logging) in waters of the U.S. shall be held to the minimum feasible number, width, and total length consistent with the purpose of specific farming, silvicultural or mining operations, and local topographic and climatic conditions;

(ii) All roads, temporary or permanent, shall be located sufficiently far from streams or other water bodies (except for portions of such roads which must cross water bodies) to minimize discharges of dredged or fill material into waters of the U.S.;

(iii) The road fill shall be bridged, culverted, or otherwise designed to prevent the restriction of expected flood flows;

(iv) The fill shall be properly stabilized and maintained during and following construction to prevent erosion;

(v) Discharges of dredged or fill material into waters of the United States to construct a road fill shall be made in a manner that minimizes the encroachment of trucks, tractors, bulldozers, or other heavy equipment within waters of the United States (including adjacent wetlands) that lie outside the lateral boundaries of the fill itself;

(vi) In designing, constructing, and maintaining roads, vegetative disturbance in the waters of the U.S. shall be kept to a minimum;

(vii) The design, construction and maintenance of the road crossing shall not disrupt the migration or other movement of those species of aquatic life inhabiting the water body;

(viii) Borrow material shall be taken from upland sources whenever feasible;

(ix) The discharge shall not take, or jeopardize the continued existence of, a threatened or endangered species as defined under the Endangered Species Act, or adversely modify or destroy the critical habitat of such species;

(x) Discharges into breeding and nesting areas for migratory waterfowl, spawning areas, and wetlands shall be avoided if practical alternatives exist;

(xi) The discharge shall not be located in the proximity of a public water supply intake;

(xii) The discharge shall not occur in areas of concentrated shellfish production;

(xiii) The discharge shall not occur in a component of the National Wild and Scenic River System;

(xiv) The discharge of material shall consist of suitable material free from toxic pollutants in toxic amounts; and

(xv) All temporary fills shall be removed in their entirety and the area restored to its original elevation.

(b) If any discharge of dredged or fill material resulting from the activities listed in paragraphs (a) (1) through (6) of this section contains any toxic pollutant listed under section 307 of the CWA such discharge shall be subject to any applicable toxic effluent standard or prohibition, and shall require a Section 404 permit.

(c) Any discharge of dredged or fill material into waters of the United States incidental to any of the activities identified in paragraphs (a) (1) through (6) of this section must have a permit if it is part of an activity whose purpose is to convert an area of the waters of the United States into a use to which it was not previously subject, where the flow or circulation of waters of the United States nay be impaired or the reach of such waters reduced. Where the proposed discharge will result in significant discernible alterations to flow or circulation, the presumption is that flow or circulation may be impaired by such alteration. For example, a permit will be required for the conversion of a cypress swamp to some other use or the conversion of a wetland from silvicultural to agricultural use when there is a discharge of dredged or fill material into waters of the United States in conjunction with construction of dikes, drainage ditches or other works or structures used to effect such conversion. A conversion of a Section 404 wetland to a non-wetland is a change in use of an area of waters of the United States. A discharge which elevates the bottom of waters of the United States without converting it to dry land does not thereby reduce the reach of, but may alter the flow or circulation of, waters of the United States.

(d) Federal projects which qualify under the criteria contained in section 404(r) of the CWA are exempt from section 404 permit requirements, but may be subject to other state or Federal requirements.

§ 323.5   Program transfer to states.

§ 404(h) of the CWA allows the Administrator of the Environmental Protection Agency (EPA) to transfer administration of the section 404 permit program for discharges into certain waters of the United States to qualified states. (The program cannot be transferred for those waters which are presently used, or are susceptible to use in their natural condition or by reasonable improvement as a means to transport interstate or foreign commerce shoreward to their ordinary high water mark, including all waters which are subject to the ebb and flow of the tide shoreward to the high tide line, including wetlands adjacent thereto). See 40 CFR parts 233 and 124 for procedural regulations for transferring Section 404 programs to states. Once a state's 404 program is approved and in effect, the Corps of Engineers will suspend processing of section 404 applications in the applicable waters and will transfer pending applications to the state agency responsible for administering the program. District engineers will assist EPA and the states in any way practicable to effect transfer and will develop appropriate procedures to ensure orderly and expeditious transfer.

§ 323.6   Special policies and procedures.

(a) The Secretary of the Army has delegated to the Chief of Engineers the authority to issue or deny section 404 permits. The district engineer will review applications for permits for the discharge of dredged or fill material into waters of the United States in accordance with guidelines promulgated by the Administrator, EPA, under authority of section 404(b)(1) of the CWA. (see 40 CFR part 230.) Subject to consideration of any economic impact on navigation and anchorage pursuant to section 404(b)(2), a permit will be denied if the discharge that would be authorized by such a permit would not comply with the 404(b)(1) guidelines. If the district engineer determines that the proposed discharge would comply with the 404(b)(1) guidelines, he will grant the permit unless issuance would be contrary to the public interest.

(b) The Corps will not issue a permit where the regional administrator of EPA has notified the district engineer and applicant in writing pursuant to 40 CFR 231.3(a)(1) that he intends to issue a public notice of a proposed determination to prohibit or withdraw the specification, or to deny, restrict or withdraw the use for specification, of any defined area as a disposal site in accordance with section 404(c) of the Clean Water Act. However the Corps will continue to complete the administrative processing of the application while the section 404(c) procedures are underway including completion of final coordination with EPA under 33 CFR part 325.

PART 324 PERMITS FOR OCEAN DUMPING OF DREDGED MATERIAL

Authority: 33 U.S.C. 1413.

Source: 51 FR 41235, Nov. 13, 1986, unless otherwise noted.

§ 324.1 General.

This regulation prescribes in addition to the general policies of 33 CFR part 320 and procedures of 33 CFR part 325, those special policies, practices and procedures to be followed by the Corps of Engineers in connection with the review of applications for Department of the Army (DA) permits to authorize the transportation of dredged material by vessel or other vehicle for the purpose of dumping it in ocean waters at dumping sites designated under 40 CFR part 228 pursuant to section 103 of the Marine Protection, Research and Sanctuaries Act of 1972, as amended (33 U.S.C. 1413) (hereinafter referred to as section 103). See 33 CFR 320.2(h). Activities involving the transportation of dredged material for the purpose of dumping in the ocean waters also require DA permits under Section 10 of the Rivers and Harbors Act of 1899 (33 U.S.C. 403) for the dredging in navigable waters of the United States. Applicants for DA permits under this part should also refer to 33 CFR part 322 to satisfy the requirements of Section 10.

§ 324.2 Definitions.

For the purpose of this regulation, the following terms are defined:

(a) The term *ocean waters* means those waters of the open seas lying seaward of the base line from which the territorial sea is measured, as provided for in the Convention on the Territorial Sea and the Contiguous Zone (15 UST 1606: TIAS 5639).

(b) The term *dredged material* means any material excavated or dredged from navigable waters of the United States.

(c) The term *transport* or *transportation* refers to the conveyance and related handling of dredged material by a vessel or other vehicle.

§ 324.3 Activities requiring permits.

(a) *General.* DA permits are required for the transportation of dredged material for the purpose of dumping it in ocean waters.

(b) *Activities of Federal agencies.*

(1) The transportation of dredged material for the purpose of disposal in ocean waters done by or on behalf of any Federal agency other than the activities of the Corps of Engineers is subject to the procedures of this regulation. Agreement for construction or engineering services performed for other agencies by the Corps of Engineers does not constitute authorization under these regulations. Division and district engineers will therefore advise Federal agencies accordingly and cooperate to the fullest extent in the expeditious processing of their applications. The activities of the Corps of Engineers that involve the transportation of dredged material for disposal in ocean waters are regulated by 33 CFR 209.145.

(2) The policy provisions set out in 33 CFR 320.4(j) relating to state or local authorizations do not apply to work or structures undertaken by Federal agencies, except where compliance with non-Federal authorization is required by Federal law or Executive policy. Federal agencies are responsible for conformance with such laws and policies. (See EO 12088, October 18, 1978.) Federal agencies are not required to obtain and provide certification of compliance with effluent limitations and water quality standards from state or interstate water pollution control agencies in connection with activities involving the transport of dredged material for dumping into ocean waters beyond the territorial sea.

§ 324.4 Special procedures.

The Secretary of the Army has delegated to the Chief of Engineers the authority to issue or deny section 103 permits. The following additional procedures shall also be applicable under this regulation.

(a) *Public notice.* For all applications for section 103 permits, the district engineer will issue a public notice which shall contain the information specified in 33 CFR 325.3.

(b) *Evaluation.* Applications for permits for the transportation of dredged material for the purpose of dumping it in ocean waters will be evaluated to determine whether the proposed dumping will unreasonably degrade or endanger human health, welfare, amenities, or the marine environment, ecological systems or economic potentialities. District engineers will apply the criteria established by the Administrator of EPA pursuant to section 102 of the Marine Protection, Research and Sanctuaries Act of 1972 in making this evaluation. (See 40 CFR parts 220-229) Where ocean dumping is determined to be necessary, the district engineer will, to the extent feasible, specify disposal sites using the recommendations of the Administrator pursuant to section 102(c) of the Act.

(c) *EPA review.* When the Regional Administrator, EPA, in accordance with 40 CFR 225.2(b), advises the district engineer, in writing, that the proposed dumping will comply with the criteria, the district engineer will complete his evaluation of the application under this part and 33 CFR parts 320 and 325. If, however, the Regional Administrator advises the district engineer, in writing, that the proposed dumping does not comply with the criteria, the district engineer will proceed as follows:

(1) The district engineer will determine whether there is an economically feasible alternative method or site available other than the proposed ocean disposal site. If there are other feasible alternative methods or sites available, the district engineer will evaluate them in accordance with 33 CFR parts 320, 322, 323, and 325 and this part, as appropriate.

(2) If the district engineer determines that there is no economically feasible alternative method or site available, and the proposed project is otherwise found to be not contrary to the public interest, he will so advise the Regional Administrator setting forth his reasons for such determination. If the Regional Administrator has not removed his objection within 15 days, the district engineer will submit a report of his determination to the Chief of Engineers for further coordination with the Administrator, EPA, and decision. The report forwarding the case will contain the analysis of whether there are other economically feasible methods or sites available to dispose of the dredged material.

(d) *Chief of Engineers review.* The Chief of Engineers shall evaluate the permit application and make a decision to deny the permit or recommend its issuance. If the decision of the Chief of Engineers is that ocean dumping at the proposed disposal site is required because of the unavailability of economically feasible alternatives, he shall so certify and request that the Secretary of the Army seek a waiver from the Administrator, EPA, of the criteria or of the critical site designation in accordance with 40 CFR 225.4

PART 325 PROCESSING OF DEPARTMENT OF THE ARMY PERMITS

Authority: 33 U.S.C. 401 et seq.; 33 U.S.C. 1344; 33 U.S.C. 1413.

Source: 51 FR 41236, Nov. 13, 1986, unless otherwise noted.

§ 325.1 Applications for permits.

(a) *General.* The processing procedures of this part apply to any Department of the Army (DA) permit. Special procedures and additional information are contained in 33 CFR parts 320 through 324, 327 and part 330. This part is arranged in the basic timing sequence used by the Corps of Engineers in processing applications for DA permits.

(b) *Pre-application consultation for major applications.* The district staff element having responsibility for administering, processing, and enforcing federal laws and regulations relating to the Corps of Engineers regulatory program shall be available to advise potential applicants of studies or other information foreseeably required for later federal action. The district engineer will establish local procedures and policies including appropriate publicity programs which will allow potential applicants to contact the district engineer or the regulatory staff element to request pre-application consultation. Upon receipt of such request, the district engineer will assure the conduct of an orderly process which may involve other staff elements and affected agencies (Federal, state, or local) and the public. This early process should be brief but thorough so that the potential applicant may begin to assess the viability of some of the more obvious potential alternatives in the application. The district engineer will endeavor, at this stage, to provide the potential applicant with all helpful information necessary in pursuing the application, including factors which the Corps must consider in its permit decision making process. Whenever the district engineer becomes aware of planning for work which may require a DA permit and which may involve the preparation of an environmental document, he shall contact the principals involved to advise them of the requirement for the permit(s) and the attendant public interest review including the development of an environmental document. Whenever a potential applicant indicates the intent to submit an application for work which may require the preparation of an environmental document, a single point of contact shall be designated within the district's regulatory staff to effectively coordinate the regulatory process, including the National Environmental Policy Act (NEPA) procedures and all attendant reviews, meetings, hearings, and other actions, including the scoping process if appropriate, leading to a decision by the district engineer. Effort devoted to this process should be commensurate with the likelihood of a permit application actually being submitted to the Corps. The regulatory staff coordinator shall maintain an open relationship with each potential applicant or his consultants so as to assure that the potential applicant is fully aware of the substance (both quantitative and qualitative) of the data required by the district engineer for use in preparing an environmental assessment or an environmental impact statement (EIS) in accordance with 33 CFR part 230, Appendix B.

(c) *Application form.* Applicants for all individual DA permits must use the standard application form (ENG Form 4345, OMB Approval No. OMB 49-R0420). Local variations of the application form for purposes of facilitating coordination with federal, state and local agencies may be used. The appropriate form may be obtained from the district office having jurisdiction over the waters in which the activity is proposed to be located. Certain activities have been authorized by general permits and do not require submission of an application form but may require a separate notification.

(d) *Content of application.*

(1) The application must include a complete description of the proposed activity including necessary drawings, sketches, or plans sufficient for public notice (detailed engineering plans and specifications are not required); the location, purpose and need for the proposed activity; scheduling of the activity; the names and addresses of adjoining property owners; the location and dimensions of adjacent structures; and a list of authorizations required by other federal, interstate, state, or local agencies for the work, including all approvals received or denials already made. See § 325.3 for information required to be in public notices. District and division engineers are not authorized to develop additional information forms but may request specific information on a case-by-case basis. (See § 325.1(e)).

(2) All activities which the applicant plans to undertake which are reasonably related to the same project and for which a DA permit would be required should be included in the same permit application. District engineers should reject, as incomplete, any permit application which fails to comply with this requirement. For example, a permit application for a marina will include dredging required for access as well as any fill associated with construction of the marina.

(3) If the activity would involve dredging in navigable waters of the United States, the application must include a description of the type, composition and quantity of the material to be dredged, the method of dredging, and the site and plans for disposal of the dredged material.

(4) If the activity would include the discharge of dredged or fill material into the waters of the United States or the transportation of dredged material for the purpose of disposing of it in ocean waters the application must include the source of the material; the purpose of the discharge, a description of the type, composition and quantity of the material; the method of transportation and disposal of the material; and the location of the disposal site. Certification under section 401 of the Clean Water Act is required for such discharges into waters of the United States.

(5) If the activity would include the construction of a filled area or pile or float-supported platform the project description must include the use of, and specific structures to be erected on, the fill or platform.

(6) If the activity would involve the construction of an impoundment structure, the applicant may be required to demonstrate that the structure complies with established state dam safety criteria or that the structure has been designed by qualified persons and, in appropriate cases, independently reviewed (and modified as the review would indicate) by similarly qualified persons. No specific design criteria are to be prescribed nor is an independent detailed engineering review to be made by the district engineer.

(7) *Signature on application.* The application must be signed by the person who desires to undertake the proposed activity (i.e. the applicant) or by a duly authorized agent. When the applicant is represented by an agent, that information will be included in the space provided on the application or by a separate written statement. The signature of the applicant or the agent will be an affirmation that the applicant possesses or will possess the requisite property interest to undertake the activity proposed in the application, except where the lands are under the control of the Corps of Engineers, in which cases the district engineer will coordinate the transfer of the real estate and the permit action. An application may include the activity of more than one owner provided the character of the activity of each owner is similar and in the same general area and each owner submits a statement designating the same agent.

(8) If the activity would involve the construction or placement of an artificial reef, as defined in 33 CFR 322.2(g), in the navigable waters of the United States or in the waters overlying the outer continental shelf, the application must include provisions for siting, constructing, monitoring, and managing the artificial reef.

(9) *Complete application.* An application will be determined to be complete when sufficient information is received to issue a public notice (See 33 CFR 325.1(d) and 325.3(a).) The issuance of a public notice will not be delayed to obtain information necessary to evaluate an application.

(e) *Additional information.* In addition to the information indicated in paragraph (d) of this section, the applicant will be required to furnish only such additional information as the district engineer deems essential to make a public interest determination including, where applicable, a determination of compliance with the section 404(b)(1) guidelines or ocean dumping criteria. Such additional information may include environmental data and information on alternate methods and sites as may be necessary for the preparation of the required environmental documentation.

(f) *Fees.* Fees are required for permits under section 404 of the Clean Water Act, section 103 of the Marine Protection, Research and Sanctuaries Act of 1972, as amended, and sections 9 and 10 of the Rivers and Harbors Act of 1899. A fee of $100.00 will be charged when the planned or ultimate purpose of the project is commercial or industrial in nature and is in support of operations that charge for the production, distribution or sale of goods or services. A $10.00 fee will be charged for permit applications when the proposed work is non-commercial in nature and would provide personal benefits that have no connection with a commercial enterprise. The final decision as to the basis for a fee (commercial vs. non-commercial) shall be solely the responsibility of the district engineer. No fee will be charged if the applicant withdraws the application at any time prior to issuance of the permit or if the permit is denied. Collection of the fee will be deferred until the proposed activity has been determined to be not contrary to the public interest. Multiple fees are not to be charged if more than one law is applicable. Any modification significant enough to require publication of a public notice will also require a fee. No fee will be assessed when a permit is transferred from one property owner to another. No fees will be charged for time extensions, general permits or letters of permission. Agencies or instrumentalities of federal, state or local governments will not be required to pay any fee in connection with permits.

§ 325.2   Processing of applications.

(a) *Standard procedures.*

(1) When an application for a permit is received the district engineer shall immediately assign it a number for identification, acknowledge receipt thereof, and advise the applicant of the number as-

signed to it. He shall review the application for completeness, and if the application is incomplete, request from the applicant within 15 days of receipt of the application any additional information necessary for further processing.

(2) Within 15 days of receipt of an application the district engineer will either determine that the application is complete (see 33 CFR 325.1(d)(9) and issue a public notice as described in § 325.3 of this part, unless specifically exempted by other provisions of this regulation or that it is incomplete and notify the applicant of the information necessary for a complete application. The district engineer will issue a supplemental, revised, or corrected public notice if in his view there is a change in the application data that would affect the public's review of the proposal.

(3) The district engineer will consider all comments received in response to the public notice in his subsequent actions on the permit application. Receipt of the comments will be acknowledged, if appropriate, and they will be made a part of the administrative record of the application. Comments received as form letters or petitions may be acknowledged as a group to the person or organization responsible for the form letter or petition. If comments relate to matters within the special expertise of another federal agency, the district engineer may seek the advice of that agency. If the district engineer determines, based on comments received, that he must have the views of the applicant on a particular issue to make a public interest determination, the applicant will be given the opportunity to furnish his views on such issue to the district engineer (see § 325.2(d)(5)). At the earliest practicable time other substantive comments will be furnished to the applicant for his information and any views he may wish to offer. A summary of the comments, the actual letters or portions thereof, or representative comment letters may be furnished to the applicant. The applicant may voluntarily elect to contact objectors in an attempt to resolve objections but will not be required to do so. District engineers will ensure that all parties are informed that the Corps alone is responsible for reaching a decision on the merits of any application. The district engineer may also offer Corps regulatory staff to be present at meetings between applicants and objectors, where appropriate, to provide information on the process, to mediate differences, or to gather information to aid in the decision process. The district engineer should not delay processing of the application unless the applicant requests a reasonable delay, normally not to exceed 30 days, to provide additional information or comments.

(4) The district engineer will follow Appendix B of 33 CFR part 230 for environmental procedures and documentation required by the National Environmental Policy Act of 1969. A decision on a permit application will require either an environmental assessment or an environmental impact statement unless it is included within a categorical exclusion.

(5) The district engineer will also evaluate the application to determine the need for a public hearing pursuant to 33 CFR part 327.

(6) After all above actions have been completed, the district engineer will determine in accordance with the record and applicable regulations whether or not the permit should be issued. He shall prepare a statement of findings (SOF) or, where an EIS has been prepared, a record of decision (ROD), on all permit decisions. The SOF or ROD shall include the district engineer's views on the probable effect of the proposed work on the public interest including conformity with the guidelines published for the discharge of dredged or fill material into waters of the United States (40 CFR part 230) or with the criteria for dumping of dredged material in ocean waters (40 CFR parts 220 to 229), if applicable, and the conclusions of the district engineer. The SOF or ROD shall be dated, signed, and included in the record prior to final action on the application. Where the district engineer has delegated authority to sign permits for and in his behalf, he may similarly delegate the signing of the SOF or ROD. If a district engineer makes a decision on a permit application which is contrary to state or local decisions (33 CFR 320.4(j) (2) & (4)), the district engineer will include in the decision document the significant national issues and explain how they are overriding in importance. If a permit is warranted, the district engineer will determine the special conditions, if any, and duration which should be incorporated into the permit. In accordance with the authorities specified in § 325.8 of this part, the district engineer will take final action or forward the application with all pertinent comments, records, and studies, including the final EIS or environmental assessment, through channels to the official authorized to make the final decision. The report forwarding the application for decision will be in a format prescribed by the Chief of Engineers. District and division engineers will notify the applicant and interested federal and state agencies that the application has been forwarded to higher headquarters. The district or division engineer may, at his option, disclose his recommendation to the news media and other interested parties, with the caution that it is only a recommendation and not a final decision. Such disclosure is encouraged in permit cases which have become controversial and have been the subject of stories in the media or have generated strong public interest. In those cases where the application is forwarded for decision in the format prescribed by the Chief of Engineers, the report will serve as the SOF or ROD. District engineers will generally combine the SOF, environmental assessment, and findings of no significant impact (FONSI), 404(b)(1) guideline analysis, and/or the criteria for dumping of dredged material in ocean waters into a single document.

(7) If the final decision is to deny the permit, the applicant will be advised in writing of the reason(s) for denial. If the final decision is to issue the permit and a standard individual permit form will be used, the issuing official will forward the permit to the applicant for signature accepting the conditions of the permit. The permit is not valid until signed by the issuing official. Letters of permission require only the signature of the issuing official. Final action on the permit application is the signature on the letter notifying the applicant of the denial of the permit or signature of the issuing official on the authorizing document.

(8) The district engineer will publish monthly a list of permits issued or denied during the previous month. The list will identify each action by public notice number, name of applicant, and brief description of activity involved. It will also note that relevant environmental documents and the SOF's or ROD's are available upon written request and, where applicable, upon the payment of administrative fees. This list will be distributed to all persons who may have an interest in any of the public notices listed.

(9) Copies of permits will be furnished to other agencies in appropriate cases as follows:

(i) If the activity involves the construction of artificial islands, installations or other devices on the outer continental shelf, to the Director, Defense Mapping Agency, Hydrographic Center, Washington, DC 20390 Attention, Code NS12, and to the Charting and Geodetic Services, N/CG222, National Ocean Service NOAA, Rockville, Maryland 20852.

(ii) If the activity involves the construction of structures to enhance fish propagation (e.g., fishing reefs) along the coasts of the United States, to the Defense Mapping Agency, Hydrographic Center and National Ocean Service as in paragraph (a)(9)(i) of this section and to the Director, Office of Marine Recreational Fisheries, National Marine Fisheries Service, Washington, DC 20235.

(iii) If the activity involves the erection of an aerial transmission line, submerged cable, or submerged pipeline across a navigable water of the United States, to the Charting and Geodetic Services N/CG222, National Ocean Service NOAA, Rockville, Maryland 20852.

(iv) If the activity is listed in paragraphs (a)(9) (i), (ii), or (iii) of this section, or involves the transportation of dredged material for the purpose of dumping it in ocean waters, to the appropriate District Commander, U.S. Coast Guard.

(b) *Procedures for particular types of permit situations:*

(1) *Section 401 Water Quality Certification.* If the district engineer determines that water quality certification for the proposed activity is necessary under the provisions of section 401 of the Clean Water Act, he shall so notify the applicant and obtain from him or the certifying agency a copy of such certification.

(i) The public notice for such activity, which will contain a statement on certification requirements (see § 325.3(a)(8)), will serve as the notification to the Administrator of the Environmental Protection Agency (EPA) pursuant to section 401(a)(2) of the Clean Water Act. If EPA determines that the proposed discharge may affect the quality of the waters of any state other than the state in which the discharge will originate, it will so notify such other state, the district engineer, and the applicant. If such notice or a request for supplemental information is not received within 30 days of issuance of the public notice, the district engineer will assume EPA has made a negative determination with respect to section 401(a)(2). If EPA determines another state's waters may be affected, such state has 60 days from receipt of EPA's notice to determine if the proposed discharge will affect the quality of its waters so as to violate any water quality requirement in such state, to notify EPA and the district engineer in writing of its objection to permit issuance, and to request a public hearing. If such occurs, the district engineer will hold a public hearing in the objecting state. Except as stated below, the hearing will be conducted in accordance with 33 CFR part 327. The issues to be considered at the public hearing will be limited to water quality impacts. EPA will submit its evaluation and recommendations at the hearing with respect to the state's objection to permit issuance. Based upon the recommendations of the objecting state, EPA, and any additional evidence presented at the hearing, the district engineer will condition the permit, if issued, in such a manner as may be necessary to insure compliance with applicable water quality requirements. If the imposition of conditions cannot, in the district engineer's opinion, insure such compliance, he will deny the permit.

(ii) No permit will be granted until required certification has been obtained or has been waived. A waiver may be explicit, or will be deemed to occur if the certifying agency fails or refuses to act on a request for certification within sixty days after receipt of such a request unless the district engineer determines a shorter or longer period is reasonable for the state to act. In determining whether or not a waiver period has commenced or waiver has occurred, the district engineer will verify that the certifying agency has received a valid request for certification. If, however, special circumstances identified by the district engineer require that action on an application be taken within a more limited period of time, the district engineer shall determine a reasonable lesser period of time, advise the certifying agency of the need for action by a particular date, and that, if certification is not received by that date, it will be considered that the requirement for certification has been waived. Similarly, if it appears that circumstances may reasonably require a period of time longer than sixty days, the district engineer, based on information provided by the certifying agency, will determine a longer reasonable period of time, not to exceed one year, at which time a waiver will be deemed to occur.

(2) *Coastal Zone Management Consistency.* If the proposed activity is to be undertaken in a state operating under a coastal zone management program approved by the Secretary of Commerce pursuant to the Coastal Zone Management (CZM) Act (see 33 CFR 320.3(b)), the district engineer shall proceed as follows:

(i) If the applicant is a federal agency, and the application involves a federal activity in or affecting the coastal zone, the district engineer shall forward a copy of the public notice to the agency of the state responsible for reviewing the consistency of federal activities. The federal agency applicant shall be responsible for complying with the CZM Act's directive for ensuring that federal agency activities are undertaken in a manner which is consistent, to the maximum extent practicable, with approved CZM Programs. (See 15 CFR part 930.) If the state coastal zone agency objects to the proposed federal activity on the basis of its inconsistency with the state's approved CZM Program, the district engineer shall not make a final decision on the application until the disagreeing parties have had an opportunity to utilize the procedures specified by the CZM Act for resolving such disagreements.

(ii) If the applicant is not a federal agency and the application involves an activity affecting the coastal zone, the district engineer shall obtain from the applicant a certification that his proposed activity complies with and will be conducted in a manner that is consistent with the approved state CZM Program. Upon receipt of the certification, the district engineer will forward a copy of the public notice (which will include the applicant's certification statement) to the state coastal zone agency and request its concurrence or objection. If the state agency objects to the certification or issues a decision indicating that the proposed activity requires further review, the district engineer shall not issue the permit until the state concurs with the certification statement or the Secretary of Commerce determines that the proposed activity is consistent with the purposes of the CZM Act or is necessary in the interest of national security. If the state agency fails to concur or object to a certification statement within six months of the state agency's receipt of the certification statement, state agency concurrence with the certification statement shall be conclusively presumed. District engineers will seek agreements with state CZM

agencies that the agency's failure to provide comments during the public notice comment period will be considered as a concurrence with the certification or waiver of the right to concur or non-concur.

(iii) If the applicant is requesting a permit for work on Indian reservation lands which are in the coastal zone, the district engineer shall treat the application in the same manner as prescribed for a Federal applicant in paragraph (b)(2)(i) of this section. However, if the applicant is requesting a permit on non-trust Indian lands, and the state CZM agency has decided to assert jurisdiction over such lands, the district engineer shall treat the application in the same manner as prescribed for a non-Federal applicant in paragraph (b)(2)(ii) of this section.

(3) *Historic Properties.* If the proposed activity would involve any property listed or eligible for listing in the National Register of Historic Places, the district engineer will proceed in accordance with Corps National Historic Preservation Act implementing regulations.

(4) *Activities Associated with Federal Projects.* If the proposed activity would consist of the dredging of an access channel and/or berthing facility associated with an authorized federal navigation project, the activity will be included in the planning and coordination of the construction or maintenance of the federal project to the maximum extent feasible. Separate notice, hearing, and environmental documentation will not be required for activities so included and coordinated, and the public notice issued by the district engineer for these federal and associated non-federal activities will be the notice of intent to issue permits for those included non-federal dredging activities. The decision whether to issue or deny such a permit will be consistent with the decision on the federal project unless special considerations applicable to the proposed activity are identified. (See § 322.5(c).)

(5) *Endangered Species.* Applications will be reviewed for the potential impact on threatened or endangered species pursuant to section 7 of the Endangered Species Act as amended. The district engineer will include a statement in the public notice of his current knowledge of endangered species based on his initial review of the application (see 33 CFR 325.2(a)(2)). If the district engineer determines that the proposed activity would not affect listed species or their critical habitat, he will include a statement to this effect in the public notice. If he finds the proposed activity may affect an endangered or threatened species or their critical habitat, he will initiate formal consultation procedures with the U.S. Fish and Wildlife Service or National Marine Fisheries Service. Public notices forwarded to the U.S. Fish and Wildlife Service or National Marine Fisheries Service will serve as the request for information on whether any listed or proposed to be listed

endangered or threatened species may be present in the area which would be affected by the proposed activity, pursuant to section 7(c) of the Act. References, definitions, and consultation procedures are found in 50 CFR part 402.

(c) [Reserved]

(d) *Timing of processing of applications.* The district engineer will be guided by the following time limits for the indicated steps in the evaluation process:

(1) The public notice will be issued within 15 days of receipt of all information required to be submitted by the applicant in accordance with paragraph 325.1.(d) of this part.

(2) The comment period on the public notice should be for a reasonable period of time within which interested parties may express their views concerning the permit. The comment period should not be more than 30 days nor less than 15 days from the date of the notice. Before designating comment periods less than 30 days, the district engineer will consider:

(i) Whether the proposal is routine or non-controversial,

(ii) Mail time and need for comments from remote areas,

(iii) Comments from similar proposals, and

(iv) The need for a site visit. After considering the length of the original comment period, paragraphs (a)(2) (i) through (iv) of this section, and other pertinent factors, the district engineer may extend the comment period up to an additional 30 days if warranted.

(3) District engineers will decide on all applications not later than 60 days after receipt of a complete application, unless (i) precluded as a matter of law or procedures required by law (see below),

(ii) The case must be referred to higher authority (see § 325.8 of this part),

(iii) The comment period is extended,

(iv) A timely submittal of information or comments is not received from the applicant,

(v) The processing is suspended at the request of the applicant, or

(vi) Information needed by the district engineer for a decision on the application cannot reasonably be obtained within the 60-day period. Once the cause for preventing the decision from being made within the normal 60-day period has been satisfied or eliminated, the 60-day clock will start running again from where it was suspended. For example, if the comment period is extended by 30 days, the district engineer will, absent other restraints, decide on the application within 90 days of receipt of a complete application. Certain laws (e.g., the Clean Water Act, the CZM Act, the National Environmental Policy Act, the National Historic Preservation Act, the Preservation of Historical and Archeological Data Act, the Endangered Species Act, the Wild and Scenic Rivers Act, and the Marine Protection, Research

and Sanctuaries Act) require procedures such as state or other federal agency certifications, public hearings, environmental impact statements, consultation, special studies, and testing which may prevent district engineers from being able to decide certain applications within 60 days.

(4) Once the district engineer has sufficient information to make his public interest determination, he should decide the permit application even though other agencies which may have regulatory jurisdiction have not yet granted their authorizations, except where such authorizations are, by federal law, a prerequisite to making a decision on the DA permit application. Permits granted prior to other (non-prerequisite) authorizations by other agencies should, where appropriate, be conditioned in such manner as to give those other authorities an opportunity to undertake their review without the applicant biasing such review by making substantial resource commitments on the basis of the DA permit. In unusual cases the district engineer may decide that due to the nature or scope of a specific proposal, it would be prudent to defer taking final action until another agency has acted on its authorization. In such cases, he may advise the other agency of his position on the DA permit while deferring his final decision.

(5) The applicant will be given a reasonable time, not to exceed 30 days, to respond to requests of the district engineer. The district engineer may make such requests by certified letter and clearly inform the applicant that if he does not respond with the requested information or a justification why additional time is necessary, then his application will be considered withdrawn or a final decision will be made, whichever is appropriate. If additional time is requested, the district engineer will either grant the time, make a final decision, or consider the application as withdrawn.

(6) The time requirements in these regulations are in terms of calendar days rather than in terms of working days.

(e) *Alternative procedures.* Division and district engineers are authorized to use alternative procedures as follows:

(1) *Letters of permission.* Letters of permission are a type of permit issued through an abbreviated processing procedure which includes coordination with Federal and state fish and wildlife agencies, as required by the Fish and Wildlife Coordination Act, and a public interest evaluation, but without the publishing of an individual public notice. The letter of permission will not be used to authorize the transportation of dredged material for the purpose of dumping it in ocean waters. Letters of permission may be used:

(i) In those cases subject to section 10 of the Rivers and Harbors Act of 1899 when, in the opinion of the district engineer, the proposed work would be minor, would not have significant individual or cumulative impacts on environmental values, and should encounter no appreciable opposition.

(ii) In those cases subject to section 404 of the Clean Water Act after:

(A) The district engineer, through consultation with Federal and state fish and wildlife agencies, the Regional Administrator, Environmental Protection Agency, the state water quality certifying agency, and, if appropriate, the state Coastal Zone Management Agency, develops a list of categories of activities proposed for authorization under LOP procedures;

(B) The district engineer issues a public notice advertising the proposed list and the LOP procedures, requesting comments and offering an opportunity for public hearing; and

(C) A 401 certification has been issued or waived and, if appropriate, CZM consistency concurrence obtained or presumed either on a generic or individual basis.

(2) *Regional permits.* Regional permits are a type of general permit as defined in 33 CFR 322.2(f) and 33 CFR 323.2(n). They may be issued by a division or district engineer after compliance with the other procedures of this regulation. After a regional permit has been issued, individual activities falling within those categories that are authorized by such regional permits do not have to be further authorized by the procedures of this regulation. The issuing authority will determine and add appropriate conditions to protect the public interest. When the issuing authority determines on a case-by-case basis that the concerns for the aquatic environment so indicate, he may exercise discretionary authority to override the regional permit and require an individual application and review. A regional permit may be revoked by the issuing authority if it is determined that it is contrary to the public interest provided the procedures of § 325.7 of this part are followed. Following revocation, applications for future activities in areas covered by the regional permit shall be processed as applications for individual permits. No regional permit shall be issued for a period of more than five years.

(3) *Joint procedures.* Division and district engineers are authorized and encouraged to develop joint procedures with states and other Federal agencies with ongoing permit programs for activities also regulated by the Department of the Army. Such procedures may be substituted for the procedures in paragraphs (a)(1) through (a)(5) of this section provided that the substantive requirements of those sections are maintained. Division and district engineers are also encouraged to develop management techniques such as joint agency review meetings to expedite the decision-making process. However, in doing so, the applicant's rights to a full public interest review and independent decision by the district or division engineer must be strictly observed.

(4) *Emergency procedures.* Division engineers are authorized to approve special processing procedures in emergency situations. An "emergency" is a situation which would result in an unacceptable hazard to life, a significant loss of property, or an immediate, unforeseen, and significant economic hardship if corrective action requiring a permit is not undertaken within a time period less than the normal time needed to process the application under standard procedures. In emergency situations, the district engineer will explain the circumstances and recommend special procedures to the division engineer who will instruct the district engineer as to further processing of the application. Even in an emergency situation, reasonable efforts will be made to receive comments from interested Federal, state, and local agencies and the affected public. Also, notice of any special procedures authorized and their rationale is to be appropriately published as soon as practicable.

§ 325.3 Public notice.

(a) *General.* The public notice is the primary method of advising all interested parties of the proposed activity for which a permit is sought and of soliciting comments and information necessary to evaluate the probable impact on the public interest. The notice must, therefore, include sufficient information to give a clear understanding of the nature and magnitude of the activity to generate meaningful comment. The notice should include the following items of information:

(1) Applicable statutory authority or authorities;

(2) The name and address of the applicant;

(3) The name or title, address and telephone number of the Corps employee from whom additional information concerning the application may be obtained;

(4) The location of the proposed activity;

(5) A brief description of the proposed activity, its purpose and intended use, so as to provide sufficient information concerning the nature of the activity to generate meaningful comments, including a description of the type of structures, if any, to be erected on fills or pile or float-supported platforms, and a description of the type, composition, and quantity of materials to be discharged or disposed of in the ocean;

(6) A plan and elevation drawing showing the general and specific site location and character of all proposed activities, including the size relationship of the proposed structures to the size of the impacted waterway and depth of water in the area;

(7) If the proposed activity would occur in the territorial seas or ocean waters, a description of the activity's relationship to the baseline from which the territorial sea is measured;

(8) A list of other government authorizations obtained or requested by the applicant, including required certifications relative to water quality, coastal zone management, or marine sanctuaries;

(9) If appropriate, a statement that the activity is

a categorical exclusion for purposes of NEPA (see paragraph 7 of Appendix B to 33 CFR part 230);

(10) A statement of the district engineer's current knowledge on historic properties;

(11) A statement of the district engineer's current knowledge on endangered species (see § 325.2(b)(5));

(12) A statement(s) on evaluation factors (see § 325.3(c));

(13) Any other available information which may assist interested parties in evaluating the likely impact of the proposed activity, if any, on factors affecting the public interest;

(14) The comment period based on § 325.2(d)(2);

(15) A statement that any person may request, in writing, within the comment period specified in the notice, that a public hearing be held to consider the application. Requests for public hearings shall state, with particularity, the reasons for holding a public hearing;

(16) For non-federal applications in states with an approved CZM Plan, a statement on compliance with the approved Plan; and

(17) In addition, for section 103 (ocean dumping) activities:

(i) The specific location of the proposed disposal site and its physical boundaries;

(ii) A statement as to whether the proposed disposal site has been designated for use by the Administrator, EPA, pursuant to section 102(c) of the Act;

(iii) If the proposed disposal site has not been designated by the Administrator, EPA, a description of the characteristics of the proposed disposal site and an explanation as to why no previously designated disposal site is feasible;

(iv) A brief description of known dredged material discharges at the proposed disposal site;

(v) Existence and documented effects of other authorized disposals that have been made in the disposal area (e.g., heavy metal background reading and organic carbon content);

(vi) An estimate of the length of time during which disposal would continue at the proposed site; and

(vii) Information on the characteristics and composition of the dredged material.

(b) *Public notice for general permits.* District engineers will publish a public notice for all proposed regional general permits and for significant modifications to, or reissuance of, existing regional permits within their area of jurisdiction. Public notices for statewide regional permits may be issued jointly by the affected Corps districts. The notice will include all applicable information necessary to provide a clear understanding of the proposal. In addition, the notice will state the availability of information at the district office which reveals the Corps' provisional determination that the proposed activities comply with the requirements for issuance of general permits. District engineers will publish a public notice for nationwide permits in accordance with 33 CFR 330.4.

(c) *Evaluation factors.* A paragraph describing the various evaluation factors on which decisions are based shall be included in every public notice.

(1) Except as provided in paragraph (c)(3) of this section, the following will be included:

"The decision whether to issue a permit will be based on an evaluation of the probable impact including cumulative impacts of the proposed activity on the public interest. That decision will reflect the national concern for both protection and utilization of important resources. The benefit which reasonably may be expected to accrue from the proposal must be balanced against its reasonably foreseeable detriments. All factors which may be relevant to the proposal will be considered including the cumulative effects thereof; among those are conservation, economics, aesthetics, general environmental concerns, wetlands, historic properties, fish and wildlife values, flood hazards, floodplain values, land use, navigation, shoreline erosion and accretion, recreation, water supply and conservation, water quality, energy needs, safety, food and fiber production, mineral needs, considerations of property ownership and, in general, the needs and welfare of the people."

(2) If the activity would involve the discharge of dredged or fill material into the waters of the United States or the transportation of dredged material for the purpose of disposing of it in ocean waters, the public notice shall also indicate that the evaluation of the impact of the activity on the public interest will include application of the guidelines promulgated by the Administrator, EPA, (40 CFR part 230) or of the criteria established under authority of section 102(a) of the Marine Protection, Research and Sanctuaries Act of 1972, as amended (40 CFR parts 220 to 229), as appropriate. (See 33 CFR parts 323 and 324).

(3) In cases involving construction of artificial islands, installations and other devices on outer continental shelf lands which are under mineral lease from the Department of the Interior, the notice will contain the following statement: "The decision as to whether a permit will be issued will be based on an evaluation of the impact of the proposed work on navigation and national security."

(d) *Distribution of public notices.*

(1) Public notices will be distributed for posting in post offices or other appropriate public places in the vicinity of the site of the proposed work and will be sent to the applicant, to appropriate city and county officials, to adjoining property owners, to appropriate state agencies, to appropriate Indian Tribes or tribal representatives, to concerned Federal agencies, to local, regional and national shipping and other concerned business and conservation organizations, to appropriate River Basin

Commissions, to appropriate state and areawide clearing houses as prescribed by OMB Circular A-95, to local news media and to any other interested party. Copies of public notices will be sent to all parties who have specifically requested copies of public notices, to the U.S. Senators and Representatives for the area where the work is to be performed, the field representative of the Secretary of the Interior, the Regional Director of the Fish and Wildlife Service, the Regional Director of the National Park Service, the Regional Administrator of the Environmental Protection Agency (EPA), the Regional Director of the National Marine Fisheries Service of the National Oceanic and Atmospheric Administration (NOAA), the head of the state agency responsible for fish and wildlife resources, the State Historic Preservation Officer, and the District Commander, U.S. Coast Guard.

(2) In addition to the general distribution of public notices cited above, notices will be sent to other addressees in appropriate cases as follows:

(i) If the activity would involve structures or dredging along the shores of the seas or Great Lakes, to the Coastal Engineering Research Center, Washington, DC 20016.

(ii) If the activity would involve construction of fixed structures or artificial islands on the outer continental shelf or in the territorial seas, to the Assistant Secretary of Defense (Manpower, Installations, and Logistics (ASD(MI&L)), Washington, DC 20310; the Director, Defense Mapping Agency (Hydrographic Center) Washington, DC 20390, Attention, Code NS12; and the Charting and Geodetic Services, N/CG222, National Ocean Service NOAA, Rockville, Maryland 20852, and to affected military installations and activities.

(iii) If the activity involves the construction of structures to enhance fish propagation (e.g., fishing reefs) along the coasts of the United States, to the Director, Office of Marine Recreational Fisheries, National Marine Fisheries Service, Washington, DC 20235.

(iv) If the activity involves the construction of structures which may affect aircraft operations or for purposes associated with seaplane operations, to the Regional Director of the Federal Aviation Administration.

(v) If the activity would be in connection with a foreign-trade zone, to the Executive Secretary, Foreign-Trade Zones Board, Department of Commerce, Washington, DC 20230 and to the appropriate District Director of Customs as Resident Representative, Foreign-Trade Zones Board.

(3) It is presumed that all interested parties and agencies will wish to respond to public notices; therefore, a lack of response will be interpreted as meaning that there is no objection to the proposed project. A copy of the public notice with the list of the addresses to whom the notice was sent will be included in the record. If a question develops with respect to an activity for which another agency has responsibility and that other agency has not responded to the public notice, the district engineer may request its comments. Whenever a response to a public notice has been received from a member of Congress, either in behalf of a constituent or himself, the district engineer will inform the member of Congress of the final decision.

(4) District engineers will update public notice mailing lists at least once every two years.

§ 325.4   Conditioning of permits.

(a) District engineers will add special conditions to Department of the Army permits when such conditions are necessary to satisfy legal requirements or to otherwise satisfy the public interest requirement. Permit conditions will be directly related to the impacts of the proposal, appropriate to the scope and degree of those impacts, and reasonably enforceable.

(1) Legal requirements which may be satisfied by means of Corps permit conditions include compliance with the 404(b)(1) guidelines, the EPA ocean dumping criteria, the Endangered Species Act, and requirements imposed by conditions on state section 401 water quality certifications.

(2) Where appropriate, the district engineer may take into account the existence of controls imposed under other federal, state, or local programs which would achieve the objective of the desired condition, or the existence of an enforceable agreement between the applicant and another party concerned with the resource in question, in determining whether a proposal complies with the 404(b)(1) guidelines, ocean dumping criteria, and other applicable statutes, and is not contrary to the public interest. In such cases, the Department of the Army permit will be conditioned to state that material changes in, or a failure to implement and enforce such program or agreement, will be grounds for modifying, suspending, or revoking the permit.

(3) Such conditions may be accomplished on-site, or may be accomplished off-site for mitigation of significant losses which are specifically identifiable, reasonably likely to occur, and of importance to the human or aquatic environment.

(b) District engineers are authorized to add special conditions, exclusive of paragraph (a) of this section, at the applicant's request or to clarify the permit application.

(c) If the district engineer determines that special conditions are necessary to insure the proposal will not be contrary to the public interest, but those conditions would not be reasonably implementable or enforceable, he will deny the permit.

(d) *Bonds.* If the district engineer has reason to consider that the permittee might be prevented from completing work which is necessary to protect the public interest, he may require the permittee to post a bond of sufficient amount to indemnify the government against any loss as a result of corrective action it might take.

§ 325.5   Forms of permits.

(a) *General discussion.*

(1) DA permits under this regulation will be in the form of individual permits or general permits. The basic format shall be ENG Form 1721, DA Permit (Appendix A).

(2) The general conditions included in ENG Form 1721 are normally applicable to all permits; however, some conditions may not apply to certain permits and may be deleted by the issuing officer. Special conditions applicable to the specific activity will be included in the permit as necessary to protect the public interest in accordance with § 325.4 of this part.

(b) *Individual permits*–

(1) *Standard permits.* A standard permit is one which has been processed through the public interest review procedures, including public notice and receipt of comments, described throughout this part. The standard individual permit shall be issued using ENG Form 1721.

(2) *Letters of permission.* A letter of permission will be issued where procedures of § 325.2(e)(1) have been followed. It will be in letter form and will identify the permittee, the authorized work and location of the work, the statutory authority, any limitations on the work, a construction time limit and a requirement for a report of completed work. A copy of the relevant general conditions from ENG Form 1721 will be attached and will be incorporated by reference into the letter of permission.

(c) *General permits*–

(1) *Regional permits.* Regional permits are a type of general permit. They may be issued by a division or district engineer after compliance with the other procedures of this regulation. If the public interest so requires, the issuing authority may condition the regional permit to require a case-by-case reporting and acknowledgment system. However, no separate applications or other authorization documents will be required.

(2) *Nationwide permits.* Nationwide permits are a type of general permit and represent DA authorizations that have been issued by the regulation (33 CFR part 330) for certain specified activities nationwide. If certain conditions are met, the specified activities can take place without the need for an individual or regional permit.

(3) *Programmatic permits.* Programmatic permits are a type of general permit founded on an existing state, local or other Federal agency program and designed to avoid duplication with that program.

(d) *Section 9 permits.* Permits for structures in interstate navigable waters of the United States under section 9 of the Rivers and Harbors Act of 1899 will be drafted at DA level.

§ 325.6   Duration of permits.

(a) *General.* DA permits may authorize both the work and the resulting use. Permits continue in effect until they automatically expire or are modified, suspended, or revoked.

(b) *Structures.* Permits for the existence of a structure or other activity of a permanent nature are usually for an indefinite duration with no expiration date cited. However, where a temporary structure is authorized, or where restoration of a waterway is contemplated, the permit will be of limited duration with a definite expiration date.

(c) *Works.* Permits for construction work, discharge of dredged or fill material, or other activity and any construction period for a structure with a permit of indefinite duration under paragraph (b) of this section will specify time limits for completing the work or activity. The permit may also specify a date by which the work must be started, normally within one year from the date of issuance. The date will be established by the issuing official and will provide reasonable times based on the scope and nature of the work involved. Permits issued for the transport of dredged material for the purpose of disposing of it in ocean waters will specify a completion date for the disposal not to exceed three years from the date of permit issuance.

(d) *Extensions of time.* An authorization or construction period will automatically expire if the permittee fails to request and receive an extension of time. Extensions of time may be granted by the district engineer. The permittee must request the extension and explain the basis of the request, which will be granted unless the district engineer determines that an extension would be contrary to the public interest. Requests for extensions will be processed in accordance with the regular procedures of § 325.2 of this part, including issuance of a public notice, except that such processing is not required where the district engineer determines that there have been no significant changes in the attendant circumstances since the authorization was issued.

(e) *Maintenance dredging.* If the authorized work includes periodic maintenance dredging, an expiration date for the authorization of that maintenance dredging will be included in the permit. The expiration date, which in no event is to exceed ten years from the date of issuance of the permit, will be established by the issuing official after evaluation of the proposed method of dredging and disposal of the dredged material in accordance with the requirements of 33 CFR parts 320 to 325. In such cases, the district engineer shall require notification of the maintenance dredging prior to actual performance to insure continued compliance with the requirements of this regulation and 33 CFR parts 320 to 324. If the permittee desires to continue maintenance dredging beyond the expiration date, he must request a new permit. The permittee should be advised to apply for the new permit six months prior to the time he wishes to do the maintenance work.

§ 325.7   Modification, suspension, or revocation of permits.

(a) *General.* The district engineer may reevaluate the circumstances and conditions of any permit, including regional permits, either on his own motion, at the request of the permittee, or a third party, or as the result of periodic progress inspections, and initiate action to modify, suspend, or revoke a permit as may be made necessary by considerations of the public interest. In the case of regional permits, this reevaluation may cover individual activities, categories of activities, or geographic areas. Among the factors to be considered are the extent of the permittee's compliance with the terms and conditions of the permit; whether or not circumstances relating to the authorized activity have changed since the permit was issued or extended, and the continuing adequacy of or need for the permit conditions; any significant objections to the authorized activity which were not earlier considered; revisions to applicable statutory and/or regulatory authorities; and the extent to which modification, suspension, or other action would adversely affect plans, investments and actions the permittee has reasonably made or taken in reliance on the permit. Significant increases in scope of a permitted activity will be processed as new applications for permits in accordance with § 325.2 of this part, and not as modifications under this section.

(b) *Modification.* Upon request by the permittee or, as a result of reevaluation of the circumstances and conditions of a permit, the district engineer may determine that the public interest requires a modification of the terms or conditions of the permit. In such cases, the district engineer will hold informal consultations with the permittee to ascertain whether the terms and conditions can be modified by mutual agreement. If a mutual agreement is reached on modification of the terms and conditions of the permit, the district engineer will give the permittee written notice of the modification, which will then become effective on such date as the district engineer may establish. In the event a mutual agreement cannot be reached by the district engineer and the permittee, the district engineer will proceed in accordance with paragraph (c) of this section if immediate suspension is warranted. In cases where immediate suspension is not warranted but the district engineer determines that the permit should be modified, he will notify the permittee of the proposed modification and reasons therefor, and that he may request a meeting with the district engineer and/or a public hearing. The modification will become effective on the date set by the district engineer which shall be at least ten days after receipt of the notice by the permittee unless a hearing or meeting is requested within that period. If the permittee fails or refuses to comply with the modification, the district engineer will proceed in accordance with 33 CFR part 326. The district engineer shall consult with resource agencies before modifying any permit terms or conditions, that would result in greater impacts, for a project about which that agency expressed a significant interest in the term, condition, or feature being modified prior to permit issuance.

(c) *Suspension.* The district engineer may suspend a permit after preparing a written determination and finding that immediate suspension would be in the public interest. The district engineer will notify the permittee in writing by the most expeditious means available that the permit has been suspended with the reasons therefor, and order the permittee to stop those activities previously authorized by the suspended permit. The permittee will also be advised that following this suspension a decision will be made to either reinstate, modify, or revoke the permit, and that he may within 10 days of receipt of notice of the suspension, request a meeting with the district engineer and/or a public hearing to present information in this matter. If a hearing is requested, the procedures prescribed in 33 CFR part 327 will be followed. After the completion of the meeting or hearing (or within a reasonable period of time after issuance of the notice to the permittee that the permit has been suspended if no hearing or meeting is requested), the district engineer will take action to reinstate, modify, or revoke the permit.

(d) *Revocation.* Following completion of the suspension procedures in paragraph (c) of this section, if revocation of the permit is found to be in the public interest, the authority who made the decision on the original permit may revoke it. The permittee will be advised in writing of the final decision.

(e) *Regional permits.* The issuing official may, by following the procedures of this section, revoke regional permits for individual activities, categories of activities, or geographic areas. Where groups of permittees are involved, such as for categories of activities or geographic areas, the informal discussions provided in paragraph (b) of this section may be waived and any written notification nay be made through the general public notice procedures of this regulation. If a regional permit is revoked, any permittee may then apply for an individual permit which shall be processed in accordance with these regulations.

§ 325.8 Authority to issue or deny permits.

(a) *General.* Except as otherwise provided in this regulation, the Secretary of the Army, subject to such conditions as he or his authorized representative may from time to time impose, has authorized the Chief of Engineers and his authorized representatives to issue or deny permits for dams or dikes in intrastate waters of the United States pursuant to section 9 of the Rivers and Harbors Act of 1899; for construction or other work in or affecting navigable waters of the United States pursuant to section 10 of the Rivers and Harbors Act of 1899; for the discharge of dredged or fill material into waters of the United States pursuant to section 404 of the Clean Water Act; or for the transportation of dredged material for the purpose of disposing of it into ocean waters pursuant to section 103 of the Marine Protection, Research and Sanctuaries Act of 1972, as amended. The authority to issue or deny permits in interstate navigable waters of the United States pursuant to section 9 of the Rivers and Harbors Act of March 3, 1899 has not been delegated to the Chief of Engineers or his authorized representatives.

(b) *District engineer's authority.* District engineers are authorized to issue or deny permits in accordance with these regulations pursuant to sections 9 and 10 of the Rivers and Harbors Act of 1899; section 404 of the Clean Water Act; and section 103 of the Marine Protection, Research and Sanctuaries Act of 1972, as amended, in all cases not required to be referred to higher authority (see below). It is essential to the legality of a permit that it contain the name of the district engineer as the issuing officer. However, the permit need not be signed by the district engineer in person but may be signed for and in behalf of him by whomever he designates. In cases where permits are denied for reasons other than navigation or failure to obtain required local, state, or other federal approvals or certifications, the Statement of Findings must conclusively justify a denial decision. District engineers are authorized to deny permits without issuing a public notice or taking other procedural steps where required local, state, or other federal permits for the proposed activity have been denied or where he determines that the activity will clearly interfere with navigation except in all cases required to be referred to higher authority (see below). District engineers are also authorized to add, modify, or delete special conditions in permits in accordance with § 325.4 of this part, except for those conditions which may have been imposed by higher authority, and to modify, suspend and revoke permits according to the procedures of § 325.7 of this part. District engineers will refer the following applications to the division engineer for resolution:

(1) When a referral is required by a written agreement between the head of a Federal agency and the Secretary of the Army;

(2) When the recommended decision is contrary to the written position of the Governor of the state in which the work would be performed;

(3) When there is substantial doubt as to authority, law, regulations, or policies applicable to the proposed activity;

(4) When higher authority requests the application be forwarded for decision; or

(5) When the district engineer is precluded by law or procedures required by law from taking final action on the application (e.g. section 9 of the Rivers and Harbors Act of 1899, or territorial sea baseline changes).

(c) *Division engineer's authority.* Division engineers will review and evaluate all permit applications referred by district engineers. Division engineers may authorize the issuance or denial of permits pursuant to section 10 of the Rivers and Harbors Act of 1899; section 404 of the Clean Water Act; and section 103 of the Marine Protection, Research and Sanctuaries Act of 1972, as amended; and the inclusion of conditions in accordance with § 325.4 of this part in all cases not required to be referred to the Chief of Engineers. Division engineers will refer the following applications to the Chief of Engineers for resolution:

(1) When a referral is required by a written agreement between the head of a Federal agency and the Secretary of the Army;

(2) When there is substantial doubt as to authority, law, regulations, or policies applicable to the proposed activity;

(3) When higher authority requests the application be forwarded for decision; or

(4) When the division engineer is precluded by law or procedures required by law from taking final action on the application.

§ 325.9 Authority to determine jurisdiction.

District engineers are authorized to determine the area defined by the terms "navigable waters of the United States" and "waters of the United States" except:

(a) When a determination of navigability is made pursuant to 33 CFR 329.14 (division engineers have this authority); or

(b) When EPA makes a section 404 jurisdiction determination under its authority.

§ 325.10 Publicity.

The district engineer will establish and maintain a program to assure that potential applicants for permits are informed of the requirements of this regulation and of the steps required to obtain permits for activities in waters of the United States or ocean waters. Whenever the district engineer becomes aware of plans being developed by either private or public entities which might require permits for implementation, he should advise the potential applicant in writing of the statutory requirements and the provisions of this regulation. Whenever the district engineer is aware of changes in Corps of Engineers regulatory jurisdiction, he will issue appropriate public notices.

APPENDIX A TO PART 325—
PERMIT FORM AND SPECIAL CONDITIONS

A. Permit Form
DEPARTMENT OF THE ARMY PERMIT

Permittee _____

Permit No. _____

Issuing Office _____

Note. The term "you" and its derivatives, as used in this permit, means the permittee or any future transferee. The term "this office" refers to the appropriate district or division office of the Corps of Engineers having jurisdiction over the permitted activity or the appropriate official of that office acting under the authority of the commanding officer.

You are authorized to perform work in accordance with the terms and conditions specified below.

Project Description: (Describe the permitted activity and its intended use with references to any attached plans or drawings that are considered to be a part of the project description. Include a description of the types and quantities of dredged or fill materials to be discharged in jurisdictional waters.)

Project Location: (Where appropriate, provide the names of and the locations on the waters where the permitted activity and any off-site disposals will take place. Also, using name, distance, and direction, locate the permitted activity in reference to a nearby landmark such as a town or city.)

Permit Conditions:
General Conditions:

1. The time limit for completing the work authorized ends on _____. If you find that you need more time to complete the authorized activity, submit your request for a time extension to this office for consideration at least one month before the above date is reached.

2. You must maintain the activity authorized by this permit in good condition and in conformance with the terms and conditions of this permit. You are not relieved of this requirement if you abandon the permitted activity, although you may make a good faith transfer to a third party in compliance with General Condition 4 below. Should you wish to cease to maintain the authorized activity or should you desire to abandon it without a good faith transfer, you must obtain a modification of this permit from this office, which may require restoration of the area.

3. If you discover any previously unknown historic or archeological remains while accomplishing the activity authorized by this permit, you must immediately notify this office of what you have found. We will initiate the Federal and state coordination required to determine if the remains warrant a recovery effort or if the site is eligible for listing in the National Register of Historic Places.

4. If you sell the property associated with this permit, you must obtain the signature of the new owner in the space provided and forward a copy of the permit to this office to validate the transfer of this authorization.

5. If a conditioned water quality certification has been issued for your project, you must comply with the conditions specified in the certification as special conditions to this permit. For your convenience, a copy of the certification is attached if it contains such conditions.

6. You must allow representatives from this office to inspect the authorized activity at any time deemed necessary to ensure that it is being or has been accomplished in accordance with the terms and conditions of your permit.

Special Conditions: (Add special conditions as required in this space with reference to a continuation sheet if necessary.)

Further Information:

1. Congressional Authorities: You have been authorized to undertake the activity described above pursuant to:

( ) Section 10 of the Rivers and Harbors Act of 1899 (33 U.S.C. 403).

( ) Section 404 of the Clean Water Act (33 U.S.C. 1344).

( ) Section 103 of the Marine Protection, Research and Sanctuaries Act of 1972 (33 U.S.C. 1413).

2. Limits of this authorization.

a. This permit does not obviate the need to obtain other Federal, state, or local authorizations required by law.

b. This permit does not grant any property rights or exclusive privileges.

c. This permit does not authorize any injury to the property or rights of others.

d. This permit does not authorize interference with any existing or proposed Federal project.

3. Limits of Federal Liability. In issuing this permit, the Federal Government does not assume any liability for the following:

a. Damages to the permitted project or uses thereof as a result of other permitted or unpermitted activities or from natural causes.

b. Damages to the permitted project or uses thereof as a result of current or future activities undertaken by or on behalf of the United States in the public interest.

c. Damages to persons, property, or to other permitted or unpermitted activities or structures caused by the activity authorized by this permit.

d. Design or construction deficiencies associated with the permitted work.

e. Damage claims associated with any future modification, suspension, or revocation of this permit.

4. Reliance on Applicant's Data: The determination of this office that issuance of this permit is not contrary to the public interest was made in reliance on the information you provided.

5. Reevaluation of Permit Decision. This office may reevaluate its decision on this permit at any time the circumstances warrant. Circumstances that could require a reevaluation include, but are not limited to, the following:

a. You fail to comply with the terms and conditions of this permit.

b. The information provided by you in support of your permit application proves to have been false, incomplete, or inaccurate (See 4 above).

c. Significant new information surfaces which this office did not consider in reaching the original public interest decision.

Such a reevaluation may result in a determination that it is appropriate to use the suspension, modification, and revocation procedures contained in 33 CFR 325.7 or enforcement procedures such as those contained in 33 CFR 326.4 and 326.5. The referenced enforcement procedures provide for the issuance of an administrative order requiring you to comply with the terms and conditions of your permit and for the initiation of legal action where appropriate. You will be required to pay for any corrective measures ordered by this office, and if you fail to comply with such directive, this office may in certain situations (such as those specified in 33 CFR 209.170) accomplish the corrective measures by contract or otherwise and bill you for the cost.

6. Extensions. General condition 1 establishes a time limit for the completion of the activity authorized by this permit. Unless there are circumstances requiring either a prompt completion of the authorized activity or a reevaluation of the public interest decision, the Corps will normally give favorable consideration to a request for an extension of this time limit.

Your signature below, as permittee, indicates that you accept and agree to comply with the terms and conditions of this permit.

(Permittee)

(Date)

This permit becomes effective when the Federal official, designated to act for the Secretary of the Army, has signed below.

(District Engineer)

(Date)

When the structures or work authorized by this permit are still in existence at the time the property is transferred, the terms and conditions of this permit will continue to be binding on the new owner(s) of the property. To validate the transfer of this permit and the associated liabilities associated with compliance with its terms and conditions, have the transferee sign and date below.

(Transferee)

(Date)

B. Special Conditions.

No special conditions will be preprinted on the permit form. The following and other special conditions should be added, as appropriate, in the space provided after the general conditions or on a referenced continuation sheet:

1. Your use of the permitted activity must not interfere with the public's right to free navigation on all navigable waters of the United States.

2. You must have a copy of this permit available on the vessel used for the authorized transportation and disposal of dredged material.

3. You must advise this office in writing, at least two weeks before you start maintenance dredging activities under the authority of this permit.

4. You must install and maintain, at your expense, any safety lights and signals prescribed by the United States Coast Guard (USCG), through regulations or otherwise, on your authorized facilities. The USCG may be reached at the following address and telephone number:

---

5. The condition below will be used when a Corps permit authorizes an artificial reef, an aerial transmission line, a submerged cable or pipeline, or a structure on the outer continental shelf.

National Ocean Service (NOS) has been notified of this authorization. You must notify NOS and this office in writing, at least two weeks before you begin work and upon completion of the activity authorized by this permit. Your notification of completion must include a drawing which certifies the location and configuration of the completed activity (a certified permit drawing may be used). Notifications to NOS will be sent to the following address: The Director, National Ocean Service (N/CG 222), Rockville, Maryland 20852.

6. The following condition should be used for every permit where legal recordation of the permit would be reasonably practicable and recordation could put a subsequent purchaser or owner of property on notice of permit conditions.

You must take the actions required to record this permit with the Registrar of Deeds or other appropriate official charged with the responsibility for maintaining records of title to or interest in real property.

APPENDIX B TO PART 325–NEPA IMPLEMENTATION PROCEDURES FOR THE REGULATORY PROGRAM

1. Introduction
2. General
3. Development of Information and Data
4. Elimination of Duplication with State and Local Procedures

5. Public Involvement

6. Categorical Exclusions

7. EA/FONSI Document

8. Environmental Impact Statement-General

9. Organization and Content of Draft EISs

10. Notice of Intent

11. Public Hearing

12. Organization and Content of Final EIS

13. Comments Received on the Final EIS

14. EIS Supplement

15. Filing Requirements

16. Timing

17. Expedited Filing

18. Record of Decision

19. Predecision Referrals by Other Agencies

20. Review of Other Agencies' EISs

21. Monitoring

1. *Introduction.* In keeping with Executive Order 12291 and 40 CFR 1500.2, where interpretive problems arise in implementing this regulation, and consideration of all other factors do not give a clear indication of a reasonable interpretation, the interpretation (consistent with the spirit and intent of NEPA) which results in the least paperwork and delay will be used. Specific examples of ways to reduce paperwork in the NEPA process are found at 40 CFR 1500.4.Maximum advantage of these recommendations should be taken.

2. *General.* This Appendix sets forth implementing procedures for the Corps regulatory program. For additional guidance, see the Corps NEPA regulation 33 CFR part 230 and for general policy guidance, see the CEQ regulations 40 CFR 1500-1508.

3. *Development of Information and Data.* See 40 CFR 1506.5.The district engineer may require the applicant to furnish appropriate information that the district engineer considers necessary for the preparation of an Environmental Assessment (EA) or Environmental Impact Statement (EIS). See also 40 CFR 1502.22 regarding incomplete or unavailable information.

4. *Elimination of Duplication with State and Local Procedures.* See 40 CFR 1506.2.

5. *Public Involvement.* Several paragraphs of this appendix (paragraphs 7, 8, 11, 13, and 19) provide information on the requirements for district engineers to make available to the public certain environmental documents in accordance with 40 CFR 1506.6.

6. *Categorical Exclusions*–

a. *General.* Even though an EA or EIS is not legally mandated for any Federal action falling within one of the "categorical exclusions," that fact does not exempt any Federal action from procedural or substantive compliance with any other Federal law. For example, compliance with the Endangered Species Act, the Clean Water Act, etc., is always mandatory, even for actions not requiring an EA or EIS. The following activities are not considered to be major Federal actions significantly affecting the quality of the human environment and are therefore categorically excluded from NEPA documentation:

(1) Fixed or floating small private piers, small docks, boat hoists and boathouses.

(2) Minor utility distribution and collection lines including irrigation;

(3) Minor maintenance dredging using existing disposal sites;

(4) Boat launching ramps;

(5) All applications which qualify as letters of permission (as described at 33 CFR 325.5(b)(2)).

b. *Extraordinary Circumstances.* District engineers should be alert for extraordinary circumstances where normally excluded actions could have substantial environmental effects and thus require an EA or EIS. For a period of one year from the effective data of these regulations, district engineers should maintain an information list on the type and number of categorical exclusion actions which, due to extraordinary circumstances, triggered the need for an EA/FONSI or EIS. If a district engineer determines that a categorical exclusion should be modified, the information will be furnished to the division engineer who will review and analyze the actions and circumstances to determine if there is a basis for recommending a modification to the list of categorical exclusions. HQUSACE (CECW-OR) will review recommended changes for Corps-wide consistency and revise the list accordingly.

7. *EA/FONSI Document.* (See 40 CFR 1508.9 and 1508.13 for definitions)-

a. *Environmental Assessment (EA) and Findings of No Significant Impact (FONSI).* The EA should normally be combined with other required documents (EA/404(b)(1)/SOF/FONSI). "EA" as used throughout this Appendix normally refers to this combined document. The district engineer should complete an EA as soon as practicable after all relevant information is available (i.e., after the comment period for the public notice of the permit application has expired) and when the EA is a separate document it must be completed prior to completion of the statement of finding (SOF). When the EA confirms that the impact of the applicant's proposal is not significant and there are no "unresolved conflicts concerning alternative uses of available resources * * *" (section 102(2)(E) of NEPA), and the proposed activity is a "water dependent" activity as defined in 40 CFR 230.10(a)(3), the EA need not include a discussion on alternatives. In all other cases where the district engineer determines that there are unresolved conflicts concerning alternative uses of available resources, the EA shall include a discussion of the reasonable alternatives which are to be considered by the ultimate decision-maker. The decision options available to the Corps, which embrace all of the applicant's alternatives, are issue the permit, issue with modifications or deny the permit. Modifications are limited to those project modifications within the scope of established permit conditioning policy (See 33 CFR 325.4). The decision option to deny the permit results in the "no action" alternative (i.e. no activity requiring a Corps permit). The combined document normally should not exceed 15 pages and shall conclude with a FONSI (See 40 CFR 1508.13) or a determination that an EIS is required. The district engineer may delegate the signing of the NEPA document. Should the EA demonstrate that an EIS is necessary, the district engineer shall follow the procedures outlined in paragraph 8 of this Appendix. In those cases where it is obvious an EIS is required, an EA is not required. However, the district engineer should document his reasons for requiring an EIS.

b. *Scope of Analysis.*

(1) In some situations, a permit applicant may propose to conduct a specific activity requiring a Department of the Army (DA) permit (e.g., construction of a pier in a navigable water of the United States) which is merely one component of a larger project (e.g., construction of an oil refinery on an upland area). The district engineer should establish the scope of the NEPA document (e.g., the EA or EIS) to address the impacts of the specific activity requiring a DA permit and those portions of the entire project over which the district engineer has sufficient control and responsibility to warrant Federal review.

(2) The district engineer is considered to have control and responsibility for portions of the project beyond the limits of Corps jurisdiction where the Federal involvement is sufficient to turn an essentially private action into a Federal action. These are cases where the environmental consequences of the larger project are essentially products of the Corps permit action.

Typical factors to be considered in determining whether sufficient "control and responsibility" exists include:

(i) Whether or not the regulated activity comprises "merely a link" in a corridor type project (e.g., a transportation or utility transmission project).

(ii) Whether there are aspects of the upland facility in the immediate vicinity of the regulated activity which affect the location and configuration of the regulated activity.

(iii) The extent to which the entire project will be within Corps jurisdiction.

(iv) The extent of cumulative Federal control and responsibility.

A. Federal control and responsibility will include the portions of the project beyond the limits of Corps jurisdiction where the cumulative Federal involvement of the Corps and other Federal agencies is sufficient to grant legal control over such additional portions of the project. These are cases where the environmental consequences of the additional portions of the projects are essentially products of Federal financing, assistance, direction, regulation, or approval (not including funding assistance solely in the form of general revenue sharing funds, with no Federal agency control over the subsequent use of such funds, and not including judicial or administrative civil or criminal enforcement actions).

B. In determining whether sufficient cumulative Federal involvement exists to expand the scope of Federal action the district engineer should consider whether other Federal agencies are required to take Federal action under the Fish and Wildlife Coordination Act (16 U.S.C. 661 *et seq.*), the National Historic Preservation Act of 1966 (16 U.S.C. 470 *et seq.*), the Endangered Species Act of 1973 (16 U.S.C. 1531 *et seq.*), Executive Order 11990, Protection of Wetlands, (42 U.S.C. 4321 91977), and other environmental review laws and executive orders.

C. The district engineer should also refer to paragraphs 8(b) and 8(c) of this appendix for guidance on determining whether it should be the lead or a cooperating agency in these situations.

These factors will be added to or modified through guidance as additional field experience develops.

(3) *Examples:* If a non-Federal oil refinery, electric generating plant, or industrial facility is proposed to be built on an upland site and the only DA permit requirement relates to a connecting pipeline, supply loading terminal or fill road, that pipeline, terminal or fill road permit, in and of itself, normally would not constitute sufficient overall Federal involvement with the project to justify expanding the scope of a Corps NEPA document to cover upland portions of the facility beyond the structures in the immediate vicinity of the regulated activity that would effect the location and configuration of the regulated activity.

Similarly, if an applicant seeks a DA permit to fill waters or wetlands on which other construction or work is proposed, the control and responsibility of the Corps, as well as its overall Federal involvement would extend to the portions of the project to be located on the permitted fill. However, the NEPA review would be extended to the entire project, including portions outside waters of the United States, only if sufficient Federal control and responsibility over the entire project is determined to exist; that is, if the regulated activities, and those activities involving regulation, funding, etc. by other Federal agencies, comprise a substantial portion of the overall project. In any case, once the scope of analysis has been defined, the NEPA analysis for that action should include direct, indirect and cumulative impacts on all Federal interests within the purview of the NEPA statute. The district engineer should, whenever practicable, incorporate by reference and rely upon the reviews of other Federal and State agencies.

For those regulated activities that comprise merely a link in a transportation or utility transmission project, the scope of analysis should address the Federal action, i.e., the specific activity requiring a DA permit and any other portion of the project that is within the control or responsibility of the Corps of Engineers (or other Federal agencies).

For example, a 50-mile electrical transmission cable crossing a 1 1/4 mile wide river that is a navigable water of the United States requires a DA permit. Neither the origin and destination of the cable nor its route to and from the navigable water, except as the route applies to the location and configuration of the crossing, are within the control or responsibility of the Corps of Engineers. Those matters would not be included in the scope of analysis which, in this case, would address the impacts of the specific cable crossing.

Conversely, for those activities that require a DA permit for a major portion of a transportation or utility transmission project, so that the Corps permit bears upon the origin and destination as well as the route of the project outside the Corps regulatory boundaries, the scope of analysis should include those portions of the project outside the boundaries of the Corps section 10/404 regulatory jurisdiction. To use the same example, if 30 miles of the 50-mile transmission line crossed wetlands or other "waters of the United States," the scope of analysis should reflect impacts of the whole 50-mile transmission line.

For those activities that require a DA permit for a major portion of a shoreside facility, the scope of analysis should extend to upland portions of the facility. For example, a shipping terminal normally requires dredging, wharves, bulkheads, berthing areas and disposal of dredged material in order to function. Permits for such activities are normally considered sufficient Federal control and responsibility to warrant extending the scope of analysis to include the upland portions of the facility.

In all cases, the scope of analysis used for analyzing both impacts and alternatives should be the same scope of analysis used for analyzing the benefits of a proposal.

8. *Environmental Impact Statement-General-*

a. *Determination of Lead and Cooperating Agencies.* When the district engineer determines that an EIS is required, he will contact all appropriate Federal agencies to determine their respective role(s), i.e., that of lead agency or cooperating agency.

b. *Corps as Lead Agency.* When the Corps is lead agency, it will be responsible for managing the EIS process, including those portions which come under the jurisdiction of other Federal agencies. The district engineer is authorized to require the applicant

to furnish appropriate information as discussed in paragraph 3 of this appendix. It is permissible for the Corps to reimburse, under agreement, staff support from other Federal agencies beyond the immediate jurisdiction of those agencies.

c. *Corps as Cooperating Agency.* If another agency is the lead agency as set forth by the CEQ regulations (40 CFR 1501.5 and 1501.6(a) and 1508.16), the district engineer will coordinate with that agency as a cooperating agency under 40 CFR 1501.6(b) and 1508.5 to insure that agency's resulting EIS may be adopted by the Corps for purposes of exercising its regulatory authority. As a cooperating agency the Corps will be responsible to the lead agency for providing environmental information which is directly related to the regulatory matter involved and which is required for the preparation of an EIS. This in no way shall be construed as lessening the district engineer's ability to request the applicant to furnish appropriate information as discussed in paragraph 3 of this appendix.

When the Corps is a cooperating agency because of a regulatory responsibility, the district engineer should, in accordance with 40 CFR 1501.6(b)(4), "make available staff support at the lead agency's request" to enhance the latter's interdisciplinary capability provided the request pertains to the Corps regulatory action covered by the EIS, to the extent this is practicable. Beyond this, Corps staff support will generally be made available to the lead agency to the extent practicable within its own responsibility and available resources. Any assistance to a lead agency beyond this will normally be by written agreement with the lead agency providing for the Corps expenses on a cost reimbursable basis. If the district engineer believes a public hearing should be held and another agency is lead agency, the district engineer should request such a hearing and provide his reasoning for the request. The district engineer should suggest a joint hearing and offer to take an active part in the hearing and ensure coverage of the Corps concerns.

d. *Scope of Analysis.* See paragraph 7b.

e. *Scoping Process.* Refer to 40 CFR 1501.7 and 33 CFR 230.12.

f. *Contracting.* See 40 CFR 1506.5.

(1) The district engineer may prepare an EIS, or may obtain information needed to prepare an EIS, either with his own staff or by contract. In choosing a contractor who reports directly to the district engineer, the procedures of 40 CFR 1506.5(c) will be followed.

(2) Information required for an EIS also may be furnished by the applicant or a consultant employed by the applicant. Where this approach is followed, the district engineer will (i) advise the applicant and/or his consultant of the Corps information requirements, and (ii) meet with the applicant and/or his consultant from time to time and provide him with the district engineer's views

regarding adequacy of the data that are being developed (including how the district engineer will view such data in light of any possible conflicts of interest).

The applicant and/or his consultant may accept or reject the district engineer's guidance. The district engineer, however, may after specifying the information in contention, require the applicant to resubmit any previously submitted data which the district engineer considers inadequate or inaccurate. In all cases, the district engineer should document in the record the Corps independent evaluation of the information and its accuracy, as required by 40 CFR 1506.5(a).

g. *Change in EIS Determination.* If it is determined that an EIS is not required after a notice of intent has been published, the district engineer shall terminate the EIS preparation and withdraw the notice of intent. The district engineer shall notify in writing the appropriate division engineer; HQUSACE (CECW-OR); the appropriate EPA regional administrator, the Director, Office of Federal Activities (A-104), EPA, 401 M Street SW., Washington, DC 20460 and the public of the determination.

h. *Time Limits.* For regulatory actions, the district engineer will follow 33 CFR 230.17(a) unless unusual delays caused by applicant inaction or compliance with other statutes require longer time frames for EIS preparation. At the outset of the EIS effort, schedule milestones will be developed and made available to the applicant and the public. If the milestone dates are not met the district engineer will notify the applicant and explain the reason for delay.

9. *Organization and Content of Draft EISs-*

a. *General.* This section gives detailed information for preparing draft EISs. When the Corps is the lead agency, this draft EIS format and these procedures will be followed. When the Corps is one of the joint lead agencies, the joint lead agencies will mutually decide which agency's format and procedures will be followed.

b. *Format-*

(1) *Cover Sheet.*

(a) Ref. 40 CFR 1502.11.

(b) The "person at the agency who can supply further information" (40 CFR 1502.11(c) is the project manager handling that permit application.

(c) The cover sheet should identify the EIS as a Corps permit action and state the authorities (sections 9, 10, 404, 103, etc.) under which the Corps is exerting its jurisdiction.

(2) *Summary.* In addition to the requirements of 40 CFR 1502.12, this section should identify the proposed action as a Corps permit action stating the authorities (sections 9, 10, 404, 103, etc.) under which the Corps is exerting its jurisdiction. It shall also summarize the purpose and need for the proposed action and shall briefly state the beneficial/adverse impacts of the proposed action.

(3) *Table of Contents.*

(4) *Purpose and Need.* See 40 CFR 1502.13.If the scope of analysis for the NEPA document (see paragraph 7b) covers only the proposed specific activity requiring a Department of the Army permit, then the underlying purpose and need for that specific activity should be stated. (For example, "The purpose and need for the pipe is to obtain cooling water from the river for the electric generating plant.") If the scope of analysis covers a more extensive project, only part of which may require a DA permit, then the underlying purpose and need for the entire project should be stated. (For example, "The purpose and need for the electric generating plant is to provide increased supplies of electricity to the (named) geographic area.") Normally, the applicant should be encouraged to provide a statement of his proposed activity's purpose and need from his perspective (for example, "to construct an electric generating plant"). However, whenever the NEPA document's scope of analysis renders it appropriate, the Corps also should consider and express that activity's underlying purpose and need from a public interest perspective (to use that same example, "to meet the public's need for electric energy"). Also, while generally focusing on the applicant's statement, the Corps, will in all cases, exercise independent judgment in defining the purpose and need for the project from both the applicant's and the public's perspective.

(5) *Alternatives.* See 40 CFR 1502.14.The Corps is neither an opponent nor a proponent of the applicant's proposal; therefore, the applicant's final proposal will be identified as the "applicant's preferred alternative" in the final EIS. Decision options available to the district engineer, which embrace all of the applicant's alternatives, are issue the permit, issue with modifications or conditions or deny the permit.

(a) Only reasonable alternatives need be considered in detail, as specified in 40 CFR 1502.14(a). Reasonable alternatives must be those that are feasible and such feasibility must focus on the accomplishment of the underlying purpose and need (of the applicant or the public) that would be satisfied by the proposed Federal action (permit issuance). The alternatives analysis should be thorough enough to use for both the public interest review and the 404(b)(1) guidelines (40 CFR part 230) where applicable. Those alternatives that are unavailable to the applicant, whether or not they require Federal action (permits), should normally be included in the analysis of the no-Federal-action (denial) alternative. Such alternatives should be evaluated only to the extent necessary to allow a complete and objective evaluation of the public interest and a fully informed decision regarding the permit application.

(b) The "no-action" alternative is one which results in no construction requiring a Corps permit. It may be brought by (1) the applicant electing to modify his proposal to eliminate work under the jurisdiction of the Corps or (2) by the denial of the permit. District engineers, when evaluating this alternative, should discuss, when appropriate, the consequences of other likely uses of a project site, should the permit be denied.

(c) The EIS should discuss geographic alternatives, e.g., changes in location and other site specific variables, and functional alternatives, e.g., project substitutes and design modifications.

(d) The Corps shall not prepare a cost-benefit analysis for projects requiring a Corps permit. 40 CFR 1502.23 states that the weighing of the various alternatives need not be displayed in a cost-benefit analysis and "* * * should not be when there are important qualitative considerations." The EIS should, however, indicate any cost considerations that are likely to be relevant to a decision.

(e) Mitigation is defined in 40 CFR 1508.20, and Federal action agencies are directed in 40 CFR 1502.14 to include appropriate mitigation measures. Guidance on the conditioning of permits to require mitigation is in 33 CFR 320.4(r) and 325.4. The nature and extent of mitigation conditions are dependent on the results of the public interest review in 33 CFR 320.4.

(6) *Affected Environment.* See Ref. 40 CFR 1502.15.

(7) *Environmental Consequences.* See Ref. 40 CFR 1502.16.

(8) *List of Preparers.* See Ref. 40 CFR 1502.17.

(9) *Public Involvement.* This section should list the dates and nature of all public notices, scoping meetings and public hearings and include a list of all parties notified.

(10) *Appendices.* See 40 CFR 1502.18. Appendices should be used to the maximum extent practicable to minimize the length of the main text of the EIS. Appendices normally should not be circulated with every copy of the EIS, but appropriate appendices should be provided routinely to parties with special interest and expertise in the particular subject.

(11) *Index.* The Index of an EIS, at the end of the document, should be designed to provide for easy reference to items discussed in the main text of the EIS.

10. *Notice of Intent.* The district engineer shall follow the guidance in 33 CFR part 230, Appendix C in preparing a notice of intent to prepare a draft EIS for publication in the Federal Register.

11. *Public Hearing.* If a public hearing is to be held pursuant to 33 CFR part 327 for a permit application requiring an EIS, the actions analyzed by the draft EIS should be considered at the public hearing. The district engineer should make the draft EIS available to the public at least 15 days in advance of the hearing. If a hearing request is received from another agency having jurisdiction as provided in 40 CFR 1506.6(c)(2), the district engineer should coordinate a joint hearing with that agency whenever appropriate.

12. *Organization and Content of Final EIS.* The organization and content of the final EIS including the abbreviated final EIS procedures shall follow the guidance in 33 CFR 230.14(a).

13. *Comments Received on the Final EIS.* For permit cases to be decided at the district level, the district engineer should consider all incoming comments and provide responses when substantive issues are raised which have not been addressed in the final EIS. For permit cases decided at higher authority, the district engineer shall forward the final EIS comment letters together with appropriate responses to higher authority along with the case. In the case of a letter recommending a referral under 40 CFR part 1504, the district engineer will follow the guidance in paragraph 19 of this appendix.

14. *EIS Supplement.* See 33 CFR 230.13(b).

15. *Filing Requirements.* See 40 CFR 1506.9.Five (5) copies of EISs shall be sent to Director, Office of Federal Activities (A-104), Environmental Protection Agency, 401 M Street SW., Washington, DC 20460. The official review periods commence with EPA's publication of a notice of availability of the draft or final EISs in the Federal Register. Generally, this notice appears on Friday of each week. At the same time they are mailed to EPA for filing, one copy of each draft or final EIS, or EIS supplement should be mailed to HQUSACE (CECW-OR) WASH DC 20314-1000.

16. *Timing.* 40 CFR 1506.10 describes the timing of an agency action when an EIS is involved.

17. *Expedited Filing.* 40 CFR 1506.10 provides information on allowable time reductions and time extensions associated with the EIS process. The district engineer will provide the necessary information and facts to HQUSACE (CECW-RE) WASH DC 20314-1000 (with copy to CECW-OR) for consultation with EPA for a reduction in the prescribed review periods.

18. *Record of Decision.* In those cases involving an EIS, the statement of findings will be called the record of decision and shall incorporate the requirements of 40 CFR 1505.2.The record of decision is not to be included when filing a final EIS and may not be signed until 30 days after the notice of availability of the final EIS is published in the Federal Register. To avoid duplication, the record of decision may reference the EIS.

19. *Predecision Referrals by Other Agencies.* See 40 CFR part 1504. The decisionmaker should notify any potential referring Federal agency and CEQ of a final decision if it is contrary to the announced position of a potential referring agency. (This pertains to a NEPA re-

ferral, not a 404(q) referral under the Clean Water Act. The procedures for a 404(q) referral are outlined in the 404(q) Memoranda of Agreement. The potential referring agency will then have 25 calendar days to refer the case to CEQ under 40 CFR part 1504. Referrals will be transmitted through division to CECW-RE for further guidance with an information copy to CECW-OR.

20. *Review of Other Agencies' EISs.* District engineers should provide comments directly to the requesting agency specifically related to the Corps jurisdiction by law or special expertise as defined in 40 CFR 1508.15 and 1508.26 and identified in Appendix II of CEQ regulations (49 FR 49750, December 21, 1984). If the district engineer determines that another agency's draft EIS which involves a Corps permit action is inadequate with respect to the Corps permit action, the district engineer should attempt to resolve the differences concerning the Corps permit action prior to the filing of the final EIS by the other agency. If the district engineer finds that the final EIS is inadequate with respect to the Corps permit action, the district engineer should incorporate the other agency's final EIS or a portion thereof and prepare an appropriate and adequate NEPA document to address the Corps involvement with the proposed action. See 33 CFR 230.21 for guidance. The agency which prepared the original EIS should be given the opportunity to provide additional information to that contained in the EIS in order for the Corps to have all relevant information available for a sound decision on the permit.

21. *Monitoring.* Monitoring compliance with permit requirements should be carried out in accordance with 33 CFR 230.15 and with 33 CFR part 325.
[53 FR 3134, Feb. 3, 1988]

APPENDIX C TO PART 325-PROCEDURES FOR THE PROTECTION OF HISTORIC PROPERTIES

1. Definitions
2. General Policy
3. Initial Review
4. Public Notice
5. Investigations
6. Eligibility Determinations
7. Assessing Effects
8. Consultation
9. ACHP Review and Comment
10. District Engineer Decision
11. Historic Properties Discovered During Construction
12. Regional General Permits
13. Nationwide General Permits
14. Emergency Procedures
15. Criteria of Effect and Adverse Effect

1. *Definitions*

a. *Designated historic property* is a historic property listed in the National Register of Historic Places (National Register) or which has been determined eligible for listing in the National Register pursuant to 36 CFR part 63. A historic property that, in both the opinion of the SHPO and the district engineer, appears to meet the criteria for inclusion in the National Register will be treated as a "designated historic property."

b. *Historic property* is a property which has historical importance to any person or group. This term includes the types of districts, sites, buildings, structures or objects eligible for inclusion, but not necessarily listed, on the National Register.

c. *Certified local government* is a local government certified in accordance with section 101(c)(1) of the NHPA (See 36 CFR part 61).

d. The term "criteria for inclusion in the National Register" refers to the criteria published by the Department of Interior at 36 CFR 60.4.

e. An "effect" on a "designated historic property" occurs when the undertaking may alter the characteristics of the property that qualified the property for inclusion in the National Register. Consideration of effects on "designated historic properties" includes indirect effects of the undertaking. The criteria for effect and adverse effect are described in Paragraph 15 of this appendix.

f. The term "undertaking" as used in this appendix means the work, structure or discharge that requires a Department of the Army permit pursuant to the Corps regulations at 33 CFR 320-334.

g. Permit area.

(1) The term "permit area" as used in this appendix means those areas comprising the waters of the United States that will be directly affected by the proposed work or structures and uplands directly affected as a result of authorizing the work or structures. The following three tests must all be satisfied for an activity undertaken outside the waters of the United States to be included within the "permit area":

(i) Such activity would not occur but for the authorization of the work or structures within the waters of the United States;

(ii) Such activity must be integrally related to the work or structures to be authorized within waters of the United States. Or, conversely, the work or structures to be authorized must be essential to the completeness of the overall project or program; and

(iii) Such activity must be directly associated (first order impact) with the work or structures to be authorized.

(2) For example, consider an application for a permit to construct a pier and dredge an access channel so that an industry may be established and operated on an upland area.

(i) Assume that the industry requires the access channel and the pier and that without such channel and pier the project would not be feasible. Clearly then, the industrial site, even though upland, would be within the "permit area." It would not be established "but for" the access channel and pier; it also is integrally related to the work and structure to be authorized; and finally it is directly associated with the work and structure to be authorized. Similarly, all three tests are satisfied for the dredged material disposal site and it too is in the "permit area" even if located on uplands.

(ii) Consider further that the industry, if established, would cause local agencies to extend water and sewer lines to service the area of the industrial site. Assume that the extension would not itself involve the waters of the United States and is not solely the result of the industrial facility. The extensions would not be within the "permit area" because they would not be directly associated with the work or structure to be authorized.

(iii) Now consider that the industry, if established, would require increased housing for its employees, but that a private developer would develop the housing. Again, even if the housing would not be developed but for the authorized work and structure, the housing would not be within the permit area because it would not be directly associated with or integrally related to the work or structure to be authorized.

(3) Consider a different example. This time an industry will be established that requires no access to the navigable waters for its operation. The plans for the facility, however, call for a recreational pier with an access channel. The pier and channel will be used for the company-owned yacht and employee recreation. In the example, the industrial site is not included within the permit area. Only areas of dredging, dredged material disposal, and pier construction would be within the permit area.

(4) Lastly, consider a linear crossing of the waters of the United States; for example, by a transmission line, pipeline, or highway.

(i) Such projects almost always can be undertaken without Corps authorization, if they are designed to avoid affecting the waters of the United States. Corps authorization is sought because it is less expensive or more convenient for the applicant to do so than to avoid affecting the waters of the United States. Thus the "but for" test is not met by the entire project right-of-way. The "same undertaking" and "integral relationship" tests are met, but this is not sufficient to make the whole right-of-way part of the permit area. Typically, however, some portion of the right-of-way, approaching the crossing, would not occur in its given configuration "but for" the authorized activity. This portion of the right-of-way, whose location is determined by the location of the crossing, meets all three tests and hence is part of the permit area.

(ii) Accordingly, in the case of the linear crossing, the permit area shall extend in either direction from the crossing to that point at which alternative alignments leading to reasonable alternative locations for the crossing can be considered and evaluated. Such a point may often coincide with the physical feature of the waterbody to be crossed, for example, a bluff, the limit of the flood plain, a vegetational change, etc., or with a jurisdictional feature associated with the waterbody, for example, a zoning change, easement limit, etc., although such features should not be controlling in selecting the limits of the permit area.

2. General Policy

This appendix establishes the procedures to be followed by the U.S. Army Corps of Engineers (Corps) to fulfill the requirements set forth in the National Historic Preservation Act (NHPA), other applicable historic preservation laws, and Presidential directives as they relate to the regulatory program of the Corps of Engineers (33 CFR parts 320-334).

a. The district engineer will take into account the effects, if any, of proposed undertakings on historic properties both within and beyond the waters of the U.S. Pursuant to section 110(f) of the NHPA, the district engineer, where the undertaking that is the subject of a permit action may directly and adversely affect any National Historic Landmark, shall, to the maximum extent possible, condition any issued permit as may be necessary to minimize harm to such landmark.

b. In addition to the requirements of the NHPA, all historic properties are subject to consideration under the National Environmental Policy Act, (33 CFR part 325, appendix B), and the Corps' public interest review requirements contained in 33 CFR 320.4. Therefore, historic properties will be included as a factor in the district engineer's decision on a permit application.

c. In processing a permit application, the district engineer will generally accept for Federal or Federally assisted projects the Federal agency's or Federal lead agency's compliance with the requirements of the NHPA.

d. If a permit application requires the preparation of an Environmental Impact Statement (EIS) pursuant to the National Environmental Policy Act, the draft EIS will contain the information required by paragraph 9.a. below. Furthermore, the SHPO and the ACHP will be given the opportunity to participate in the scoping process and to comment on the Draft and Final EIS.

e. During pre-application consultations with a prospective applicant the district engineer will encourage the consideration of historic properties at the earliest practical time in the planning process.

f. This appendix is organized to follow the Corps standard permit process and to indicate how historic property considerations are to be addressed during the processing and evaluating of permit applications. The procedures of this Appendix are not intended to diminish the full consideration of historic properties in the Corps regulatory program. Rather, this appendix is intended to provide for the maximum consideration of historic properties within the time and jurisdictional constraints of the Corps regulatory program. The Corps will make every effort to provide information on historic properties and the effects of proposed undertakings on them to the public by the public notice within the time constraints required by the Clean Water Act. Within the time constraints of applicable laws, executive orders, and regulations, the Corps will provide the maximum coordination and comment opportunities to interested parties especially the SHPO and ACHP. The Corps will discuss with and encourage the applicant to avoid or minimize effects on historic properties. In reaching its decisions on permits, the Corps will adhere to the goals of the NHPA and other applicable laws dealing with historic properties.

3. Initial Review

a. Upon receipt of a completed permit application, the district engineer will consult district files and records, the latest published version(s) of the National Register, lists of properties determined eligible, and other appropriate sources of information to determine if there are any designated historic properties which may be affected by the proposed undertaking. The district engineer will also consult with other appropriate sources of information for knowledge of undesignated historic properties which may be affected by the proposed undertaking. The district engineer will establish procedures (e.g., telephone calls) to obtain supplemental information from the SHPO and other appropriate sources. Such procedures shall be accomplished within the time limits specified in this appendix and 33 CFR part 325.

b. In certain instances, the nature, scope, and magnitude of the work, and/or structures to be permitted may be such that there is little likelihood that a historic property exists or may be affected. Where the district engineer determines that such a situation exists, he will include a statement to this effect in the public notice. Three such situations are:

(1) Areas that have been extensively modified by previous work. In such areas, historic properties that may have at one time existed within the permit area may be presumed to have been lost unless specific information indicates the presence of such a property (e.g., a shipwreck).

(2) Areas which have been created in modern times. Some recently created areas, such as dredged material disposal islands, have had no human habitation. In such cases, it may be presumed that there is no potential for the existence of historic properties unless specific information indicates the presence of such a property.

(3) Certain types of work or structures that are of such limited nature and scope that there is little likelihood of impinging upon a historic property even if such properties were to be present within the affected area.

c. If, when using the pre-application procedures of 33 CFR 325.1(b), the district engineer believes that a designated historic property may be affected, he will inform the prospective applicant for consideration during project planning of the potential applicability of the Secretary of the Interior's Standards and Guidelines for Archeology and Historic Preservation (48 FR 44716). The district engineer will also inform the prospective applicant that the Corps will consider any effects on historic properties in accordance with this appendix.

d. At the earliest practical time the district engineer will discuss with the applicant measures or alternatives to avoid or minimize effects on historic properties.

4. Public Notice.

a. Except as specified in subparagraph 4.c., the district engineer's current knowledge of the presence or absence of historic properties and the effects of the undertaking upon these properties will be included in the public notice. The public notice will be sent to the SHPO, the regional office of the National Park Service (NPS), certified local governments (see paragraph (1.c.) and Indian tribes, and interested citizens. If there are designated historic properties which reasonably may be affected by the undertaking or if there are undesignated historic properties within the affected area which the district engineer reasonably expects to be affected by the undertaking and which he believes meet the criteria for inclusion in the National Register, the public notice will also be sent to the ACHP.

b. During permit evaluation for newly designated historic properties or undesignated historic properties which reasonably may be affected by the undertaking and which have been newly identified through the public interest review process, the district engineer will immediately inform the applicant, the SHPO, the appropriate certified local government and the ACHP of the district engineer's current knowledge of the effects of the undertaking upon these properties. Commencing from the date of the district engineer's letter, these entities will be given 30 days to submit their comments.

c. Locational and sensitive information related to archeological sites is excluded from the Freedom of Information Act (Section 304 of the NHPA and Section 9 of ARPA). If the district engineer or the Secretary of the Interior determine that the disclosure of information to the public relating to the location or character of sensitive historic resources may create a substantial risk of harm, theft, or destruction to such resources or to the area or place where such resources are located, then the district engineer will not include such information in the public notice nor otherwise make it available to the public. Therefore, the district engineer will furnish such information to the ACHP and the SHPO by separate notice.

5. Investigations

a. When initial review, addition submissions by the applicant, or response to the public notice indicates the existence of a potentially eligible property, the district engineer shall examine the pertinent evidence to determine the need for further investigation. The evidence must set forth specific reasons for the need to further investigate within the permit area and may consist of:

(1) Specific information concerning properties which may be eligible for inclusion in the National Register and which are known to exist in the vicinity of the project; and

(2) Specific information concerning known sensitive areas which are likely to yield resources eligible for inclusion in the National Register, particularly where such sensitive area determinations are based upon data collected from other, similar areas within the general vicinity.

b. Where the scope and type of work proposed by the applicant or the evidence presented leads the district engineer to conclude that the chance of disturbance by the undertaking to any potentially eligible historic property is too remote to justify further investigation, he shall so advise the reporting party and the SHPO.

c. If the district engineer's review indicates that an investigation for the presence of potentially eligible historic properties on the upland locations of the permit area (see paragraph 1.g.) is justified, the district engineer will conduct or cause to be conducted such an investigation. Additionally, if the notification indicates that a potentially eligible historic property may exist within waters of the U.S., the district engineer will conduct or cause to be conducted an investigation to determine whether this property may be eligible for inclusion in the National Register. Comments or information of a general nature will not be considered as sufficient evidence to warrant an investigation.

d. In addition to any investigations conducted in accordance with paragraph 6.a. above, the district engineer may conduct or cause to be conducted additional investigations which the district engineer determines are essential to reach the public interest decision . As part of any site visit, Corps personnel will examine the permit area for the presence of potentially eligible historic properties. The Corps will notify the SHPO, if any evidence is found which indicates the presence of potentially eligible historic properties.

e. As determined by the district engineer, investigations may consist of any of the following: further consultations with the SHPO, the State Archeologist, local governments, Indian tribes, local historical and archeological societies, university archaeologists, and others with knowledge and expertise in the identification of historical, archeological, cultural and scientific resources; field examinations; and archeological testing. In most cases, the district engineer will require, in accordance with 33 CFR 325.1(e), that the applicant conduct the investigation at his expense and usually by third party contract.

f. The Corps of Engineers' responsibilities to seek eligibility determinations for potentially eligible historic properties is limited to resources located within waters of the U.S. that are directly affected by the undertaking. The Corps responsibilities to identify potentially eligible historic properties is limited to resources located within the permit area that are directly affected by related upland activities. The Corps is not responsible for identifying or assessing potentially eligible historic properties outside the permit area, but will consider the effects of undertakings on any known historic properties that may occur outside the permit area.

6. Eligibility determinations

a. For a historic property within waters of the U.S. that will be directly affected by the undertaking the district engineer will, for the purposes of this Appendix and compliance with the NHPA:

(1) Treat the historic property as a "designated historic property," if both the SHPO and the district engineer agree that it is eligible for inclusion in the National Register; or

(2) Treat the historic property as not eligible, if both the SHPO and the district engineer agree that it is not eligible for inclusion in the National Register; or

(3) Request a determination of eligibility from the Keeper of the National Register in accordance with applicable National Park Service regulations and notify the applicant, if the SHPO and the district engineer disagree or the ACHP or the Secretary of the Interior so request. If the Keeper of the National Register determines that the resources are not eligible for listing in the National Register or fails to respond within 45 days of receipt of the request, the district engineer may proceed to conclude his action on the permit application.

b. For a historic property outside of waters of the U.S. that will be directly affected by the undertaking the district engineer will, for the purposes of this appendix and compliance with the NHPA:

(1) Treat the historic property as a "designated historic property," if both the SHPO and the district engineer agree that it is eligible for inclusion in the National Register; or

(2) Treat the historic property as not eligible, if both the SHPO and the district engineer agree that it is not eligible for inclusion in the National Register; or

(3) Treat the historic property as not eligible unless the Keeper of the National Register determines it is eligible for or lists it on the National Register. (See paragraph 6.c. below.)

c. If the district engineer and the SHPO do not agree pursuant to paragraph 6.b.(1) and the SHPO notifies the district engineer that it is nominating a potentially eligible historic property for the National Register that may be affected by the undertaking, the district engineer will wait a reasonable period of time for that determination to be made before concluding his action on the permit. Such a reasonable period of time would normally be 30 days for the SHPO to nominate the historic property plus 45 days for the Keeper of the National Register to make such determination. The district engineer will encourage the applicant to cooperate with the SHPO in obtaining the information necessary to nominate the historic property.

7. Assessing Effects

a. *Applying the Criteria of Effect and Adverse Effect.* During the public notice comment period or within 30 days after the determination or discovery of a designated history property the district engineer will coordinate with the SHPO and determine if there is an effect and if so, assess the effect. (See Paragraph 15.)

b. *No Effect.* If the SHPO concurs with the district engineer's determination of no effect or fails to respond within 15 days of the district engineer's notice to the SHPO of a no effect determination, then the district engineer may proceed with the final decision.

c. *No Adverse Effect.* If the district engineer, based on his coordination with the SHPO (see paragraph 7.a.), determines that an effect is not adverse, the district engineer will notify the ACHP and request the comments of the ACHP. The district engineer's notice will include a description of both the project and the designated historic property; both the district engineer's and the SHPO's views, as well as any views of affected local governments, Indian tribes, Federal agencies, and the public, on the no adverse effect determination; and a description of the efforts to identify historic properties and solicit the views of those above. The district engineer may conclude the permit decision if the ACHP does not object to the district engineer's determination or if the district engineer accepts any conditions requested by the ACHP for a no adverse effect determination, or the ACHP fails to respond within 30 days of the district engineer's notice to the ACHP. If the ACHP objects or the district engineer does not accept the conditions proposed by the ACHP, then the effect shall be considered as adverse.

d. *Adverse Effect.* If an adverse effect on designated historic properties is found, the district engineer will notify the ACHP and coordinate with the SHPO to seek ways to avoid or reduce effects on designated historic properties. Either the district engineer or the SHPO may request the ACHP to participate. At its discretion, the ACHP may participate without such a request. The district engineer, the SHPO or the ACHP may state that further coordination will not be productive. The district engineer shall then request the ACHP's comments in accordance with paragraph 9.

8. Consultation

At any time during permit processing, the district engineer may consult with the involved parties to discuss and consider possible alternatives or measures to avoid or minimize the adverse effects of a proposed activity. The district engineer will terminate any consultation immediately upon determining that further consultation is not productive and will immediately notify the consulting parties. If the consultation results in a mutual agreement among the SHPO, ACHP, applicant and the district engineer regarding the treatment of designated historic properties, then the district

engineer may formalize that agreement either through permit conditioning or by signing a Memorandum of Agreement (MOA) with these parties. Such MOA will constitute the comments of the ACHP and the SHPO, and the district engineer may proceed with the permit decision. Consultation shall not continue beyond the comment period provided in paragraph 9.b.

9. ACHP Review and Comment

a. If: (i) The district engineer determines that coordination with the SHPO is unproductive; or (ii) the ACHP, within the appropriate comment period, requests additional information in order to provide its comments; or (iii) the ACHP objects to any agreed resolution of impacts on designated historic properties; the district engineer, normally within 30 days, shall provide the ACHP with:

(1) A project description, including, as appropriate, photographs, maps, drawings, and specifications (such as, dimensions of structures, fills, or excavations; types of materials and quantity of material);

(2) A listing and description of the designated historic properties that will be affected, including the reports from any surveys or investigations;

(3) A description of the anticipated adverse effects of the undertaking on the designated historic properties and of the proposed mitigation measures and alternatives considered, if any; and

(4) The views of any commenting parties regarding designated historic properties.

In developing this information, the district engineer may coordinate with the applicant, the SHPO, and any appropriate Indian tribe or certified local government.

Copies of the above information also should be forwarded to the applicant, the SHPO, and any appropriate Indian tribe or certified local government. The district engineer will not delay his decision but will consider any comments these parties may wish to provide.

b. The district engineer will provide the ACHP 60 days from the date of the district engineer's letter forwarding the information in paragraph 9.a., to provide its comments. If the ACHP does not comment by the end of this comment period, the district engineer will complete processing of the permit application. When the permit decision is otherwise delayed as provided in 33 CFR 325.2(d) (3) & (4), the district engineer will provide additional time for the ACHP to comment consistent with, but not extending beyond that delay.

10. District Engineer Decision

a. In making the public interest decision on a permit application, in accordance with 33 CFR 320.4, the district engineer shall weigh all factors, including the effects of the undertaking on historic properties and any comments of the ACHP and the SHPO, and any views of other interested parties. The district engineer will add permit conditions to avoid or reduce effects on historic properties which he determines are necessary in accordance with 33 CFR 325.4. In reaching his determination, the district engineer will consider the Secretary of the Interior's Standards and Guidelines for Archeology and Historic Preservation (48 FR 44716).

b. If the district engineer concludes that permitting the activity would result in the irrevocable loss of important scientific, prehistoric, historical, or archeological data, the district engineer, in accordance with the Archeological and Historic Preservation Act of 1974, will advise the Secretary of the Interior (by notifying the National Park Service (NPS)) of the extent to which the data may be lost if the undertaking is permitted, any plans to mitigate such loss that will be implemented, and the permit conditions that will be included to ensure that any required mitigation occurs.

11. Historic Properties Discovered During Construction

After the permit has been issued, if the district engineer finds or is notified that the permit area contains a previously unknown potentially eligible historic property which he reasonably expects will be affected by the undertaking, he shall immediately inform the Department of the Interior Departmental Consulting Archeologist and the regional office of the NPS of the current knowledge of the potentially eligible historic property and the expected effects, if any, of the undertaking on that property. The district engineer will seek voluntary avoidance of construction activities that could affect the historic property pending a recommendation from the National Park Service pursuant to the Archeological and Historic Preservation Act of 1974. Based on the circumstances of the discovery, equity to all parties, and considerations of the public interest, the district engineer may modify, suspend or revoke a permit in accordance with 33 CFR 325.7.

12. Regional General Permits

Potential impacts on historic properties will be considered in development and evaluation of general permits. However, many of the specific procedures contained in this appendix are not normally applicable to general permits. In developing general permits, the district engineer will seek the views of the SHPO and, the ACHP and other organizations and/or individuals with expertise or interest in historic properties. Where designated historic properties are reasonably likely to be affected, general permits shall be conditioned to protect such properties or to limit the applicability of the permit coverage.

13. Nationwide General Permit

a. The criteria at paragraph 15 of this Appendix will be used for determining compliance with the nationwide permit condition at 33 CFR 330.5(b)(9) regarding the effect on designated historic properties. When making this determination the district engineer may consult with the SHPO, the ACHP or other interested parties.

b. If the district engineer is notified of a potentially eligible historic property in accordance with nationwide permit regulations and conditions, he will immediately notify the SHPO. If the district engineer believes that the potentially eligible historic property meets the criteria for inclusion in the National Register and that it may be affected by the proposed undertaking then he may suspend authorization of the nationwide permit until he provides the ACHP and the SHPO the opportunity to comment in accordance with the provisions of this Appendix. Once these provisions have been satisfied, the district engineer may notify the general permittee that the activity is authorized including any special activity specific conditions identified or that an individual permit is required.

14. Emergency Procedures

The procedures for processing permits in emergency situations are described at 33 CFR 325.2(e)(4). In an emergency situation the district engineer will make every reasonable effort to receive comments from the SHPO and the ACHP, when the proposed undertaking can reasonably be expected to affect a potentially eligible or designated historic property and will comply with the provisions of this Appendix to the extent time and the emergency situation allows.

15. Criteria of Effect and Adverse Effect

(a) An undertaking has an effect on a designated historic property when the undertaking may alter characteristics of the property that qualified the property for inclusion in the National Register. For the purpose of determining effect, alteration to features of a property's location, setting, or use may be relevant, and depending on a property's important characteristics, should be considered.

(b) An undertaking is considered to have an adverse effect when the effect on a designated historic property may diminish the integrity of the property's location, design, setting, materials, workmanship, feeling, or association. Adverse effects on designated historic properties include, but are not limited to:

(1) Physical destruction, damage, or alteration of all or part of the property;

(2) Isolation of the property from or alteration of the character of the property's setting when that character contributes to the property's qualification for the National Register;

(3) Introduction of visual, audible, or atmospheric elements that are out of character with the property or alter its setting;

(4) Neglect of a property resulting in its deterioration or destruction; and

(5) Transfer, lease, or sale of the property.

(c) Effects of an undertaking that would otherwise be found to be adverse may be considered as being not adverse for the purpose of this appendix:

(1) When the designated historic property is of value only for its potential contribution to archeological, historical, or architectural research, and when such value can be substantially preserved through the conduct of appropriate research, and

such research is conducted in accordance with applicable professional standards and guidelines;

(2) When the undertaking is limited to the rehabilitation of buildings and structures and is conducted in a manner that preserves the historical and architectural value of affected designated historic properties through conformance with the Secretary's "Standards for Rehabilitation and Guidelines for Rehabilitating Historic Buildings", or

(3) When the undertaking is limited to the transfer, lease, or sale of a designated historic property, and adequate restrictions or conditions are included to ensure preservation of the property's important historic features.

[55 FR 27003, June 29, 1990]

PART 326   ENFORCEMENT

Authority: 33 U.S.C. 401 et seq.; 33 U.S.C. 1344; 33 U.S.C. 1413; 33 U.S.C. 2101.

Source: 51 FR 41246, Nov. 13, 1986, unless otherwise noted.

§ 326.1   Purpose.

This part prescribes enforcement policies (§ 326.2) and procedures applicable to activities performed without required Department of the Army permits (§ 326.3) and to activities not in compliance with the terms and conditions of issued Department of the Army permits (§ 326.4). Procedures for initiating legal actions are prescribed in § 326.5. Nothing contained in this part shall establish a non-discretionary duty on the part of district engineers nor shall deviation from these procedures give rise to a private right of action against a district engineer.

§ 326.2   Policy.

Enforcement, as part of the overall regulatory program of the Corps, is based on a policy of regulating the waters of the United States by discouraging activities that have not been properly authorized and by requiring corrective measures, where appropriate, to ensure those waters are not misused and to maintain the integrity of the program. There are several methods discussed in the remainder of this part which can be used either singly or in combination to implement this policy, while making the most effective use of the enforcement resources available. As EPA has independent enforcement authority under the Clean Water Act for unauthorized discharges, the district engineer should normally coordinate with EPA to determine the most effective and efficient manner by which resolution of a section 404 violation can be achieved.

§ 326.3   Unauthorized activities.

(a) *Surveillance.* To detect unauthorized activities requiring permits, district engineers should make the best use of all available resources. Corps employees; members of the public; and representatives of state,

local, and other Federal agencies should be encouraged to report suspected violations. Additionally, district engineers should consider developing joint surveillance procedures with Federal, state, or local agencies having similar regulatory responsibilities, special expertise, or interest.

(b) *Initial investigation.* District engineers should take steps to investigate suspected violations in a timely manner. The scheduling of investigations will reflect the nature and location of the suspected violations, the anticipated impacts, and the most effective use of inspection resources available to the district engineer. These investigations should confirm whether a violation exists, and if so, will identify the extent of the violation and the parties responsible.

(c) *Formal notifications to parties responsible for violations.* Once the district engineer has determined that a violation exists, he should take appropriate steps to notify the responsible parties.

(1) If the violation involves a project that is not complete, the district engineer's notification should be in the form of a cease and desist order prohibiting any further work pending resolution of the violation in accordance with the procedures contained in this part. See paragraph (c)(4) of this section for exception to this procedure.

(2) If the violation involves a completed project, a cease and desist order should not be necessary. However, the district engineer should still notify the responsible parties of the violation.

(3) All notifications, pursuant to paragraphs (c)(1) and (2) of this section, should identify the relevant statutory authorities, indicate potential enforcement consequences, and direct the responsible parties to submit any additional information that the district engineer may need at that time to determine what course of action he should pursue in resolving the violation; further information may be requested, as needed, in the future.

(4) In situations which would, if a violation were not involved, qualify for emergency procedures pursuant to 33 CFR part 325.2(e)(4), the district engineer may decide it would not be appropriate to direct that the unauthorized work be stopped. Therefore, in such situations, the district engineer may, at his discretion, allow the work to continue, subject to appropriate limitations and conditions as he may prescribe, while the violation is being resolved in accordance with the procedures contained in this part.

(5) When an unauthorized activity requiring a permit has been undertaken by American Indians (including Alaskan natives, Eskimos, and Aleuts, but not including Native Hawaiians) on reservation lands or in pursuit of specific treaty rights, the district engineer should use appropriate means to coordinate proposed directives and orders with the Assistant Chief Counsel for Indian Affairs (DAEN-CCI).

(6) When an unauthorized activity requiring a permit has been undertaken by an official acting on behalf of a foreign government, the district engineer

should use appropriate means to coordinate proposed directives and orders with the Office, Chief of Engineers, ATTN: DAEN-CCK.

(d) *Initial corrective measures.*

(1) The district engineer should, in appropriate cases, depending upon the nature of the impacts associated with the unauthorized, completed work, solicit the views of the Environmental Protection Agency; the U.S. Fish and Wildlife Service; the National Marine Fisheries Service, and other Federal, state, and local agencies to facilitate his decision on what initial corrective measures are required. If the district engineer determines as a result of his investigation, coordination, and preliminary evaluation that initial corrective measures are required, he should issue an appropriate order to the parties responsible for the violation. In determining what initial corrective measures are required, the district engineer should consider whether serious jeopardy to life, property, or important public resources (see 33 CFR 320.4) may be reasonably anticipated to occur during the period required for the ultimate resolution of the violation. In his order, the district engineer will specify the initial corrective measures required and the time limits for completing this work. In unusual cases where initial corrective measures substantially eliminate all current and future detrimental impacts resulting from the unauthorized work, further enforcement actions should normally be unnecessary. For all other cases, the district engineer's order should normally specify that compliance with the order will not foreclose the Government's options to initiate appropriate legal action or to later require the submission of a permit application.

(2) An order requiring initial corrective measures that resolve the violation may also be issued by the district engineer in situations where the acceptance or processing of an after-the-fact permit application is prohibited or considered not appropriate pursuant to § 326.3(e)(1) (iii) through (iv) below. However, such orders will be issued only when the district engineer has reached an independent determination that such measures are necessary and appropriate.

(3) It will not be necessary to issue a Corps permit in connection with initial corrective measures undertaken at the direction of the district engineer.

(e) *After-the-fact permit applications.*

(1) Following the completion of any required initial corrective measures, the district engineer will accept an after-the-fact permit application unless he determines that one of the exceptions listed in subparagraphs i-iv below is applicable. Applications for after-the-fact permits will be processed in accordance with the applicable procedures in 33 CFR parts 320 through 325. Situations where no permit application will be processed or where the acceptance of a permit application must be deferred are as follows:

(i) No permit application will be processed when restoration of the waters of the United States has been completed that eliminates current and future detrimental impacts to the satisfaction of the district engineer.

(ii) No permit application will be accepted in connection with a violation where the district engineer determines that legal action is appropriate (§ 326.5(a)) until such legal action has been completed.

(iii) No permit application will be accepted where a Federal, state, or local authorization or certification, required by Federal law, has already been denied.

(iv) No permit application will be accepted nor will the processing of an application be continued when the district engineer is aware of enforcement litigation that has been initiated by other Federal, state, or local regulatory agencies, unless he determines that concurrent processing of an after-the-fact permit application is clearly appropriate.

(2) Upon completion of his review in accordance with 33 CFR parts 320 through 325, the district engineer will determine if a permit should be issued, with special conditions if appropriate, or denied. In reaching a decision to issue, he must determine that the work involved is not contrary to the public interest, and if section 404 is applicable, that the work also complies with the Environmental Protection Agency's section 404(b)(1) guidelines. If he determines that a denial is warranted, his notification of denial should prescribe any final corrective actions required. His notification should also establish a reasonable period of time for the applicant to complete such actions unless he determines that further information is required before the corrective measures can be specified. If further information is required, the final corrective measures may be specified at a later date. If an applicant refuses to undertake prescribed corrective actions ordered subsequent to permit denial or refuses to accept a conditioned permit, the district engineer may initiate legal action in accordance with § 326.5.

(f) Combining steps. The procedural steps in this section are in the normal sequence. However, these regulations do not prohibit the streamlining of the enforcement process through the combining of steps.

(g) Coordination with EPA. In all cases where the district engineer is aware that EPA is considering enforcement action, he should coordinate with EPA to attempt to avoid conflict or duplication. Such coordination applies to interim protective measures and after-the-fact permitting, as well as to appropriate legal enforcement actions.

§ 326.4 Supervision of authorized activities.

(a) *Inspections.* District engineers will, at their discretion, take reasonable measures to inspect permitted activities, as required, to ensure that these activities comply with specified terms and conditions. To supplement inspections by their enforcement personnel, district engineers should encourage their other personnel; members of the public; and interested state, local, and other Federal agency representatives to report suspected violations of Corps permits. To facilitate inspections, district engineers will, in appropriate cases, require that copies of ENG Form 4336 be posted conspicuously at the sites of authorized activities and will make available to all interested persons information on the terms and conditions of issued permits. The U.S. Coast Guard will inspect permitted ocean dumping activities pursuant to section 107(c) of the Marine Protection, Research and Sanctuaries Act of 1972, as amended.

(b) *Inspection limitations.* Section 326.4 does not establish a non-discretionary duty to inspect permitted activities for safety, sound engineering practices, or interference with other permitted or unpermitted structures or uses in the area. Further, the regulations implementing the Corps regulatory program do not establish a non-discretionary duty to inspect permitted activities for any other purpose.

(c) *Inspection expenses.* The expenses incurred in connection with the inspection of permitted activities will normally be paid by the Federal Government unless daily supervision or other unusual expenses are involved. In such unusual cases, the district engineer may condition permits to require permittees to pay inspection expenses pursuant to the authority contained in section 9701 of Pub L. 97-258 (33 U.S.C. 9701). The collection and disposition of inspection expense funds obtained from applicants will be administered in accordance with the relevant Corps regulations governing such funds.

(d) *Non-compliance.* If a district engineer determines that a permittee has violated the terms or conditions of the permit and that the violation is sufficiently serious to require an enforcement action, then he should, unless at his discretion he deems it inappropriate:

(1) First contact the permittee;

(2) Request corrected plans reflecting actual work, if needed; and

(3) Attempt to resolve the violation. Resolution of the violation may take the form of the permitted project being voluntarily brought into compliance or of a permit modification (33 CFR 325.7(b)). If a mutually agreeable solution cannot be reached, a written order requiring compliance should normally be issued and delivered by personal service. Issuance of an order is not, however, a prerequisite to legal action. If an order is issued, it will specify a time period of not more than 30 days for bringing the permitted project into compliance, and a copy will be sent to the appropriate state official pursuant to section 404(s)(2) of the Clean Water Act. If the permittee fails to comply with the order within the specified period of time, the district engineer may consider using the suspension/revocation procedures in 33 CFR 325.7(c) and/or he may recommend legal action in accordance with § 326.5.

§ 326.5   Legal action.

(a) *General.* For cases the district engineer determines to be appropriate, he will recommend criminal or civil actions to obtain penalties for violations, compliance with the orders and directives he has issued pursuant to §§ 326.3 and 326.4, or other relief as appropriate. Appropriate cases for criminal or civil action include, but are not limited to, violations which, in the district engineer's opinion, are willful, repeated, flagrant, or of substantial impact.

(b) *Preparation of case.* If the district engineer determines that legal action is appropriate, he will prepare a litigation report or such other documentation that he and the local U.S. Attorney have mutually agreed to, which contains an analysis of the information obtained during his investigation of the violation or during the processing of a permit application and a recommendation of appropriate legal action. The litigation report or alternative documentation will also recommend what, if any, restoration or mitigative measures are required and will provide the rationale for any such recommendation.

(c) *Referral to the local U.S. Attorney.* Except as provided in paragraph (d) of this section, district engineers are authorized to refer cases directly to the U.S. Attorney. Because of the unique legal system in the Trust Territories, all cases over which the Department of Justice has no authority will be referred to the Attorney General for the trust Territories. Information copies of all letters of referral shall be forwarded to the appropriate division counsel, the Office, Chief of Engineers, ATTN: DAEN-CCK, the Office of the Assistant Secretary of the Army (Civil Works), and the Chief of the Environmental Defense Section, Lands and Natural Resources Division, U.S. Department of Justice.

(d) *Referral to the Office, Chief of Engineers.* District engineers will forward litigation reports with recommendations through division offices to the Office, Chief of Engineers, ATTN: DAEN-CCK, for all cases that qualify under the following criteria:

(1) Significant precedential or controversial questions of law or fact;

(2) Requests for elevation to the Washington level by the Department of Justice;

(3) Violations of section 9 of the Rivers and Harbors Act of 1899;

(4) Violations of section 103 the Marine Protection, Research and Sanctuaries Act of 1972;

(5) All cases involving violations by American Indians (original of litigation report to DAEN-CCI with copy to DAEN-CCK) on reservation lands or in pursuit of specific treaty rights;

(6) All cases involving violations by officials acting on behalf of foreign governments; and

(7) Cases requiring action pursuant to paragraph (e) of this section.

(e) *Legal option not available.* In cases where the local U.S. Attorney declines to take legal action, it would be appropriate for the district engineer to close the enforcement case record unless he believes that the case warrants special attention. In that situation, he is encouraged to forward a litigation report to the Office, Chief of Engineers, ATTN: DAEN-CCK, for direct coordination through the Office of the Assistant Secretary of the Army (Civil Works) with the Department of Justice. Further, the case record should not be closed if the district engineer anticipates that further administrative enforcement actions, taken in accordance with the procedures prescribed in this part, will identify remedial measures which, if not complied with by the parties responsible for the violation, will result in appropriate legal action at a later date.

§ 326.6   Class I Administrative penalties.

(a) *Introduction.*

(1) This section sets forth procedures for initiation and administration of Class I administrative penalty orders under section 309(g) of the Clean Water Act, and section 205 of the National Fishing Enhancement Act. Section 309(g)(2)(A) specifies that Class I civil penalties may not exceed $10,000 per violation, except that the maximum amount of any Class I civil penalty shall not exceed $25,000. The National Fishing Enhancement Act, section 205(e), provides that penalties for violations of permits issued in accordance with that Act shall not exceed $10,000 for each violation.

(2) These procedures supplement the existing enforcement procedures at §§ 326.1 through 326.5. However, as a matter of Corps enforcement discretion once the Corps decides to proceed with an administrative penalty under these procedures it shall not subsequently pursue judicial action pursuant to § 326.5. Therefore, an administrative penalty should not be pursued if a subsequent judicial action for civil penalties is desired. An administrative civil penalty may be pursued in conjunction with a compliance order; request for restoration and/or request for mitigation issued under § 326.4.

(3) *Definitions.* For the purposes of this section of the regulation:

(i) *Corps* means the Secretary of the Army, acting through the U.S. Army Corps of Engineers, with respect to the matters covered by this regulation.

(ii) *Interested person outside the Corps* includes the permittee, any person who filed written comments on the proposed penalty order, and any other person not employed by the Corps with an interest in the subject of proposed penalty order, and any attorney of record for those persons.

(iii) *Interested Corps staff* means those Corps employees, whether temporary or permanent, who may investigate, litigate, or present evidence, arguments, or the position of the Corps in the hearing or who participated in the preparation, investigation or deliberations concerning the proposed penalty order, including any employee, contractor, or consultant who may be called as a witness.

(iv) *Permittee* means the person to whom the Corps issued a permit under section 404 of the Clean Water Act, (or section 10 of the Rivers and Harbors Act for an Artificial Reef) the conditions and limitations of which permit have allegedly been violated.

(v) *Presiding Officer* means a member of Corps Counsel staff or any other qualified person designated by the District Engineer (DE), to hold a hearing on a proposed administrative civil penalty order (hereinafter referred to as "proposed order") in accordance with the rules set forth in this regulation and to make such recommendations to the DE as prescribed in this regulation.

(vi) *Ex parte communication* means any communication, written or oral, relating to the merits of the proceeding, between the Presiding Officer and an interested person outside the Corps or the interested Corps staff, which was not originally filed or stated in the administrative record or in the hearing. Such communication is not an "ex parte communication" if all parties have received prior written notice of the proposed communication and have been given the opportunity to participate herein.

(b) *Initiation of action.*

(1) If the DE or a delegatee of the DE finds that a recipient of a Department of the Army permit (hereinafter referred to as "the permittee") has violated any permit condition or limitation contained in that permit, the DE is authorized to prepare and process a proposed order in accordance with these procedures. The proposed order shall specify the amount of the penalty which the permittee may be assessed and shall describe with reasonable specificity the nature of the violation.

(2) The permittee will be provided actual notice, in writing, of the DE's proposal to issue an administrative civil penalty and will be advised of the right to request a hearing and to present evidence on the alleged violation. Notice to the permittee will be provided by certified mail, return receipt requested, or other notice, at the discretion of the DE when he determines justice so requires. This notice will be accompanied by a copy of the proposed order, and will include the following information:

(i) A description of the alleged violation and copies of the applicable law and regulations;

(ii) An explanation of the authority to initiate the proceeding;

(iii) An explanation, in general terms, of the procedure for assessing civil penalties, including opportunities for public participation;

(iv) A statement of the amount of the penalty that is proposed and a statement of the maximum amount of the penalty which the DE is authorized to assess for the violations alleged;

(v) A statement that the permittee may within 30 calendar days of receipt of the notice provided under this subparagraph, request a hearing prior to issuance of any final order. Further, that the permittee must request a hearing within 30 calendar days of receipt of the notice provided under this subparagraph in order to be entitled to receive such a hearing;

(vi) The name and address of the person to whom the permittee must send a request for hearing;

(vii) Notification that the DE may issue the final order on or after 30 calendar days following receipt of the notice provided under these rules, if the permittee does not request a hearing; and

(viii) An explanation that any final order issued under this section shall become effective 30 calendar days following its issuance unless a petition to set aside the order and to hold a hearing is filed by a person who commented on the proposed order and such petition is granted or an appeal is taken under section 309(g)(8) of the Clean Water Act.

(3) At the same time that actual notice is provided to the permittee, the DE shall give public notice of the proposed order, and provide reasonable opportunity for public comment on the proposed order, prior to issuing a final order assessing an administrative civil penalty. Procedures for giving public notice and providing the opportunity for public comment are contained in § 326.6(c).

(4) At the same time that actual notice is provided to the permittee, the DE shall provide actual notice, in writing, to the appropriate state agency for the state in which the violation occurred. Procedures for providing actual notice to and consulting with the appropriate state agency are contained in § 326.6(d).

(c) *Public notice and comment.*

(1) At the same time the permittee and the appropriate state agency are provided actual notice, the DE shall provide public notice of and a reasonable opportunity to comment on the DE's proposal to issue an administrative civil penalty against the permittee.

(2) A 30 day public comment period shall be provided. Any person may submit written comments on the proposed administrative penalty order. The DE shall include all written comments in an administrative record relating to the proposed order. Any person who comments on a proposed order shall be given notice of any hearing held on the proposed order. Such persons shall have a reasonable opportunity to be heard and to present evidence in such hearings.

(3) If no hearing is requested by the permittee, any person who has submitted comments on the proposed order shall be given notice by the DE of any final order issued, and will be given 30 calendar days in which to petition the DE to set aside the order and to provide a hearing on the penalty. The DE shall set aside the order and provide a hearing

in accordance with these rules if the evidence presented by the commenter in support of the commenter's petition for a hearing is material and was not considered when the order was issued. If the DE denies a hearing, the DE shall provide notice to the commenter filing the petition for the hearing, together with the reasons for the denial. Notice of the denial and the reasons for the denial shall be published in the Federal Register by the DE.

(4) The DE shall give public notice by mailing a copy of the information listed in paragraph (c)(5), of this section to:

(i) Any person who requests notice;

(ii) Other persons on a mailing list developed to include some or all of the following sources:

(A) Persons who request in writing to be on the list;

(B) Persons on "area lists" developed from lists of participants in past similar proceedings in that area, including hearings or other actions related to section 404 permit issuance as required by § 325.3(d)(1). The DE may update the mailing list from time to time by requesting written indication of continued interest from those listed. The DE may delete from the list the name of any person who fails to respond to such a request.

(5) All public notices under this subpart shall contain at a minimum the information provided to the permittee as described in § 326.6(b)(2) and:

(i) A statement of the opportunity to submit written comments on the proposed order and the deadline for submission of such comments;

(ii) Any procedures through which the public may comment on or participate in proceedings to reach a final decision on the order;

(iii) The location of the administrative record referenced in § 326.6(e), the times at which the administrative record will be available for public inspection, and a statement that all information submitted by the permittee and persons commenting on the proposed order is available as part of the administrative record, subject to provisions of law restricting the public disclosure of confidential information.

(d) *State consultation.*

(1) At the same time that the permittee is provided actual notice, the DE shall send the appropriate state agency written notice of proposal to issue an administrative civil penalty order. This notice will include the same information required pursuant to § 326.6(c)(5).

(2) For the purposes of this regulation, the appropriate State agency will be the agency administering the 401 certification program, unless another state agency is agreed to by the District and the respective state through formal/informal agreement with the state.

(3) The appropriate state agency will be provided the same opportunity to comment on the proposed

order and participate in any hearing that is provided pursuant to § 326.6(c).

(e) *Availability of the administrative record.*

(1) At any time after the public notice of a proposed penalty order is given under §326.6(c), the DE shall make available the administrative record at reasonable times for inspection and copying by any interested person, subject to provisions of law restricting the public disclosure of confidential information. Any person requesting copies of the administrative record or portions of the administrative record may be required by the DE to pay reasonable charges for reproducing the information requested.

(2) The administrative record shall include the following:

(i) Documentation relied on by the DE to support the violations alleged in the proposed penalty order with a summary of violations, if a summary has been prepared;

(ii) Proposed penalty order or assessment notice;

(iii) Public notice of the proposed order with evidence of notice to the permittee and to the public;

(iv) Comments by the permittee and/or the public on the proposed penalty order, including any requests for a hearing;

(v) All orders or notices of the Presiding Officer;

(vi) Subpoenas issued, if any, for the attendance and testimony of witnesses and the production of relevant papers, books, or documents in connection with any hearings;

(vii) All submittals or responses of any persons or comments to the proceeding, including exhibits, if any;

(viii) A complete and accurate record or transcription of any hearing;

(ix) The recommended decision of the Presiding Officer and final decision and/or order of the Corps issued by the DE; and

(x) Any other appropriate documents related to the administrative proceeding;

(f) *Counsel.* A permittee may be represented at all stages of the proceeding by counsel. After receiving notification that a permittee or any other party or commenter is represented by counsel, the Presiding Officer and DE shall direct all further communications to that counsel.

(g) *Opportunity for hearing.*

(1) The permittee may request a hearing and may provide written comments on the proposed administrative penalty order at any time within 30 calendar days after receipt of the notice set forth in § 326.6(b)(2). The permittee must request the hearing in writing, specifying in summary form the factual and legal issues which are in dispute and the specific factual and legal grounds for the permittee's defense.

(2) The permittee waives the right to a hearing to present evidence on the alleged violation or vio-

lations if the permittee does not submit the request for the hearing to the official designated in the notice of the proposed order within 30 calendar days of receipt of the notice. The DE shall determine the date of receipt of notice by permittee's signed and dated return receipt or such other evidence that constitutes proof of actual notice on a certain date.

(3) The DE shall promptly schedule requested hearings and provide reasonable notice of the hearing schedule to all participants, except that no hearing shall be scheduled prior to the end of the thirty day public comment period provided in § 326.6(c)(2). The DE may grant any delays or continuances necessary or desirable to resolve the case fairly.

(4) The hearing shall be held at the district office or a location chosen by the DE, except the permittee may request in writing upon a showing of good cause that the hearing be held at an alternative location. Action on such request is at the discretion of the DE.

(h) *Hearing.*

(1) Hearings shall afford permittees with an opportunity to present evidence on alleged violations and shall be informal, adjudicatory hearings and shall not be subject to section 554 or 556 of the Administrative Procedure Act. Permittees may present evidence either orally or in written form in accordance with the hearing procedures specified in § 326.6(i).

(2) The DE shall give written notice of any hearing to be held under these rules to any person who commented on the proposed administrative penalty order under § 326.6(c). This notice shall specify a reasonable time prior to the hearing within which the commenter may request an opportunity to be heard and to present oral evidence or to make comments in writing in any such hearing. The notice shall require that any such request specify the facts or issues which the commenter wishes to address. Any commenter who files comments pursuant to § 326.6(c)(2) shall have a right to be heard and to present evidence at the hearing in conformance with these procedures.

(3) The DE shall select a member of the Corps counsel staff or other qualified person to serve as Presiding Officer of the hearing. The Presiding Officer shall exercise no other responsibility, direct or supervisory, for the investigation or prosecution of any case before him. The Presiding Officer shall conduct hearings as specified by these rules and make a recommended decision to the DE.

(4) The Presiding Officer shall consider each case on the basis of the evidence presented, and must have no prior connection with the case. The Presiding Officer is solely responsible for the recommended decision in each case.

(5) *Ex Parte Communications.*

(i) No interested person outside the Corps or member of the interested Corps staff shall make, or knowingly cause to be made, any ex parte communication on the merits of the proceeding.

(ii) The Presiding Officer shall not make, or knowingly cause to be made, any ex parte communication on the proceeding to any interested person outside the Corps or to any member of the interested Corps staff.

(iii) The DE may replace the Presiding Officer in any proceeding in which it is demonstrated to the DE's satisfaction that the Presiding Officer has engaged in prohibited ex parte communications to the prejudice of any participant.

(iv) Whenever an ex parte communication in violation of this section is received by the Presiding Officer or made known to the Presiding Officer, the Presiding Officer shall immediately notify all participants in the proceeding of the circumstances and substance of the communication and may require the person who made the communication or caused it to be made, or the party whose representative made the communication or caused it to be made, to the extent consistent with justice and the policies of the Clean Water Act, to show cause why that person or party's claim or interest in the proceedings should not be dismissed, denied, disregarded, or otherwise adversely affected on account of such violation.

(v) The prohibitions of this paragraph apply upon designation of the Presiding Officer and terminate on the date of final action or the final order.

(i) *Hearing Procedures.*

(1) The Presiding Officer shall conduct a fair and impartial proceeding in which the participants are given a reasonable opportunity to present evidence.

(2) The Presiding Officer may subpoena witnesses and issue subpoenas for documents pursuant to the provisions of the Clean Water Act.

(3) The Presiding Officer shall provide interested parties a reasonable opportunity to be heard and to present evidence. Interested parties include the permittee, any person who filed a request to participate under 33 CFR 326.6(c), and any other person attending the hearing. The Presiding Officer may establish reasonable time limits for oral testimony.

(4) The permittee may not challenge the permit condition or limitation which is the subject matter of the administrative penalty order.

(5) Prior to the commencement of the hearing, the DE shall provide to the Presiding Officer the complete administrative record as of that date. During the hearing, the DE, or an authorized representative of the DE may summarize the basis for the proposed administrative order. Thereafter, the administrative record shall be admitted into evidence and the Presiding Officer shall maintain the administrative record of the proceedings and shall include in that record all documentary evidence, written statements, correspondence, the record of hearing, and any other relevant matter.

(6) The Presiding Officer shall cause a tape recording, written transcript or other permanent, verbatim record of the hearing to be made, which shall be included in the administrative record, and shall, upon written request, be made available, for inspection or copying, to the permittee or any person, subject to provisions of law restricting the public disclosure of confidential information. Any person making a request may be required to pay reasonable charges for copies of the administrative record or portions thereof.

(7) In receiving evidence, the Presiding Officer is not bound by strict rules of evidence. The Presiding Officer may determine the weight to be accorded the evidence.

(8) The permittee has the right to examine, and to respond to the administrative record. The permittee may offer into evidence, in written form or through oral testimony, a response to the administrative record including, any facts, statements, explanations, documents, testimony, or other exculpatory items which bear on any appropriate issues. The Presiding Officer may question the permittee and require the authentication of any written exhibit or statement. The Presiding Officer may exclude any repetitive or irrelevant matter.

(9) At the close of the permittee's presentation of evidence, the Presiding Officer should allow the introduction of rebuttal evidence. The Presiding Officer may allow the permittee to respond to any such rebuttal evidence submitted and to cross-examine any witness.

(10) The Presiding Officer may take official notice of matters that are not reasonably in dispute and are commonly known in the community or are ascertainable from readily available sources of known accuracy. Prior to taking official notice of a matter, the Presiding Officer shall give the Corps and the permittee an opportunity to show why such notice should not be taken. In any case in which official notice is taken, the Presiding Officer shall place a written statement of the matters as to which such notice was taken in the record, including the basis for such notice and a statement that the Corps or permittee consented to such notice being taken or a summary of the objections of the Corps or the permittee.

(11) After all evidence has been presented, any participant may present argument on any relevant issue, subject to reasonable time limitations set at the discretion of the Presiding Officer.

(12) The hearing record shall remain open for a period of 10 business days from the date of the hearing so that the permittee or any person who has submitted comments on the proposed order may examine and submit responses for the record.

(13) At the close of this 10 business day period, the Presiding Officer may allow the introduction of rebuttal evidence. The Presiding Officer may hold the record open for an additional 10 business days to allow the presentation of such rebuttal evidence.

(j) *The decision.*

(1) Within a reasonable time following the close of the hearing and receipt of any statements following the hearing and after consultation with the state

pursuant to § 326.6(d), the Presiding Officer shall forward a recommended decision accompanied by a written statement of reasons to the DE. The decision shall recommend that the DE withdraw, issue, or modify and issue the proposed order as a final order. The recommended decision shall be based on a preponderance of the evidence in the administrative record. If the Presiding Officer finds that there is not a preponderance of evidence in the record to support the penalty or the amount of the penalty in a proposed order, the Presiding Officer may recommend that the order be withdrawn or modified and then issued on terms that are supported by a preponderance of evidence on the record. The Presiding Officer also shall make the complete administrative record available to the DE for review.

(2) The Presiding Officer's recommended decision to the DE shall become part of the administrative record and shall be made available to the parties to the proceeding at the time the DE's decision is released pursuant to § 326.6(j)(5). The Presiding Officer's recommended decision shall not become part of the administrative record until the DE's final decision is issued, and shall not be made available to the permittee or public prior to that time.

(3) The rules applicable to Presiding Officers under § 326.6(h)(5) regarding ex parte communications are also applicable to the DE and to any person who advises the DE on the decision or the order, except that communications between the DE and the Presiding Officer do not constitute ex parte communications, nor do communications between the DE and his staff prior to issuance of the proposed order.

(4) The DE may request additional information on specified issues from the participants, in whatever form the DE designates, giving all participants a fair opportunity to be heard on such additional matters. The DE shall include this additional information in the administrative record.

(5) Within a reasonable time following receipt of the Presiding Officer's recommended decision, the DE shall withdraw, issue, or modify and issue the proposed order as a final order. The DE's decision shall be based on a preponderance of the evidence in the administrative record, shall consider the penalty factors set out in section 309(g)(3) of the CWA, shall be in writing, shall include a clear and concise statement of reasons for the decision, and shall include any final order assessing a penalty. The DE's decision, once issued, shall constitute final Corps action for purposes of judicial review.

(6) The DE shall issue the final order by sending the order, or written notice of its withdrawal, to the permittee by certified mail. Issuance of the order under this subparagraph constitutes final Corps action for purposes of judicial review.

(7) The DE shall provide written notice of the issuance, modification and issuance, or withdrawal of the proposed order to every person who submitted written comments on the proposed order.

(8) The notice shall include a statement of the right to judicial review and of the procedures and deadlines for obtaining judicial review. The notice shall also note the right of a commenter to petition for a hearing pursuant to 33 CFR 326.6(c)(3) if no hearing was previously held.

(k) *Effective date of order.*

(1) Any final order issued under this subpart shall become effective 30 calendar days following its issuance unless an appeal is taken pursuant to section 309(g)(8) of the Clean Water Act, or in the case where no hearing was held prior to the final order, and a petition for hearing is filed by a prior commenter.

(2) If a petition for hearing is received within 30 days after the final order is issued, the DE shall:

(i) Review the evidence presented by the petitioner.

(ii) If the evidence is material and was not considered in the issuance of the order, the DE shall immediately set aside the final order and schedule a hearing. In that case, a hearing will be held, a new recommendation will be made by the Presiding Officer to the DE and a new final decision issued by the DE.

(iii) If the DE denies a hearing under this subparagraph, the DE shall provide to the petitioner, and publish in the Federal Register, notice of, and the reasons for, such denial.

(l) *Judicial review.*

(1) Any permittee against whom a final order assessing a civil penalty under these regulations or any person who provided written comments on a proposed order may obtain judicial review of the final order.

(2) In order to obtain judicial review, the permittee or commenter must file a notice of appeal in the United States District Court for either the District of Columbia, or the district in which the violation was alleged to have occurred, within 30 calendar days after the date of issuance of the final order.

(3) Simultaneously with the filing of the notice of appeal, the permittee or commenter must send a copy of such notice by certified mail to the DE and the Attorney General.

[54 FR 50709, Dec. 8, 1989]

PART 327   PUBLIC HEARINGS

Authority: 33 U.S.C. 1344; 33 U.S.C. 1413.

Source: 51 FR 41249, Nov. 13, 1986,
unless otherwise noted.

§ 327.1   Purpose.

This regulation prescribes the policy, practice and procedures to be followed by the U.S. Army Corps of Engineers in the conduct of public hearings conducted in the evaluation of a proposed DA permit action or

Federal project as defined in § 327.3 of this part including those held pursuant to section 404 of the Clean Water Act (33 U.S.C. 1344) and section 103 of the Marine Protection, Research and Sanctuaries Act (MPRSA), as amended (33 U.S.C. 1413).

§ 327.2   Applicability.

This regulation is applicable to all divisions and districts responsible for the conduct of public hearings.

§ 327.3   Definitions.

(a) *Public hearing* means a public proceeding conducted for the purpose of acquiring information or evidence which will be considered in evaluating a proposed DA permit action, or Federal project, and which affords the public an opportunity to present their views, opinions, and information on such permit actions or Federal projects.

(b) *Permit action,* as used herein means the evaluation of and decision on an application for a DA permit pursuant to sections 9 or 10 of the Rivers and Harbors Act of 1899, section 404 of the Clean Water Act, or section 103 of the MPRSA, as amended, or the modification, suspension or revocation of any DA permit (see 33 CFR 325.7).

(c) *Federal project* means a Corps of Engineers project (work or activity of any nature for any purpose which is to be performed by the Chief of Engineers pursuant to Congressional authorizations) involving the discharge of dredged or fill material into waters of the United States or the transportation of dredged material for the purpose of dumping it in ocean waters subject to section 404 of the Clean Water Act, or section 103 of the MPRSA.

§ 327.4   General policies.

(a) A public hearing will be held in connection with the consideration of a DA permit application or a Federal project whenever a public hearing is needed for making a decision on such permit application or Federal project. In addition, a public hearing may be held when it is proposed to modify or revoke a permit. (See 33 CFR 325.7).

(b) Unless the public notice specifies that a public hearing will be held, any person may request, in writing, within the comment period specified in the public notice on a DA permit application or on a Federal project, that a public hearing be held to consider the material matters at issue in the permit application or with respect to Federal project. Upon receipt of any such request, stating with particularity the reasons for holding a public hearing, the district engineer may expeditiously attempt to resolve the issues informally. Otherwise, he shall promptly set a time and place for the public hearing, and give due notice thereof, as prescribed in § 327.11 of this part. Requests for a public hearing under this paragraph shall be granted, unless the district engineer determines that the issues raised are insubstantial or there is otherwise no valid interest to be served by a hearing. The district engineer will make such a determination in writing, and communicate his reasons therefor to all requesting parties. Comments received as form letters or petitions may be acknowledged as a group to the person or organization responsible for the form letter or petition.

(c) In case of doubt, a public hearing shall be held. HQDA has the discretionary power to require hearings in any case.

(d) In fixing the time and place for a hearing, the convenience and necessity of the interested public will be duly considered.

§ 327.5   Presiding officer.

(a) The district engineer, in whose district a matter arises, shall normally serve as the presiding officer. When the district engineer is unable to serve, he may designate the deputy district engineer or other qualified person as presiding officer. In cases of unusual interest, the Chief of Engineers or the division engineer may appoint such person as he deems appropriate to serve as the presiding officer.

(b) The presiding officer shall include in the administrative record of the permit action the request or requests for the hearing and any data or material submitted in justification thereof, materials submitted in opposition to or in support of the proposed action, the hearing transcript, and such other material as may be relevant or pertinent to the subject matter of the hearing. The administrative record shall be available for public inspection with the exception of material exempt from disclosure under the Freedom of Information Act.

§ 327.6   Legal adviser.

At each public hearing, the district counsel or his designee may serve as legal advisor to the presiding officer. In appropriate circumstances, the district engineer may waive the requirement for a legal advisor to be present.

§ 327.7   Representation.

At the public hearing, any person may appear on his own behalf, or may be represented by counsel, or by other representatives.

§ 327.8   Conduct of hearings.

(a) The presiding officer shall make an opening statement outlining the purpose of the hearing and prescribing the general procedures to be followed.

(b) Hearings shall be conducted by the presiding officer in an orderly but expeditious manner. Any person shall be permitted to submit oral or written statements concerning the subject matter of the hearing, to call witnesses who may present oral or written statements, and to present recommendations as to an appropriate decision. Any person may present written statements for the hearing record prior to the time the hearing record is closed to public submissions, and may present proposed findings and recommendations. The presiding officer shall afford participants a reasonable opportunity for rebuttal.

(c) The presiding officer shall have discretion to establish reasonable limits upon the time allowed for statements of witnesses, for arguments of parties or their counsel or representatives, and upon the number of rebuttals.

(d) Cross-examination of witnesses shall not be permitted.

(e) All public hearings shall be reported verbatim. Copies of the transcripts of proceedings may be purchased by any person from the Corps of Engineers or the reporter of such hearing. A copy will be available for public inspection at the office of the appropriate district engineer.

(f) All written statements, charts, tabulations, and similar data offered in evidence at the hearing shall, subject to exclusion by the presiding officer for reasons of redundancy, be received in evidence and shall constitute a part of the record.

(g) The presiding officer shall allow a period of not less than 10 days after the close of the public hearing for submission of written comments.

(h) In appropriate cases, the district engineer may participate in joint public hearings with other Federal or state agencies, provided the procedures of those hearings meet the requirements of this regulation. In those cases in which the other Federal or state agency allows a cross-examination in its public hearing, the district engineer may still participate in the joint public hearing but shall not require cross examination as a part of his participation.

§ 327.9   Filing of the transcript of the public hearing.

Where the presiding officer is the initial action authority, the transcript of the public hearing, together with all evidence introduced at the public hearing, shall be made a part of the administrative record of the permit action or Federal project. The initial action authority shall fully consider the matters discussed at the public hearing in arriving at his initial decision or recommendation and shall address, in his decision or recommendation, all substantial and valid issues presented at the hearing. Where a person other than the initial action authority serves as presiding officer, such person shall forward the transcript of the public hearing and all evidence received in connection therewith to the initial action authority together with a report summarizing the issues covered at the hearing. The report of the presiding officer and the transcript of the public hearing and evidence submitted thereat shall in such cases be fully considered by the initial action authority in making his decision or recommendation to higher authority as to such permit action or Federal project.

§ 327.10   Authority of the presiding officer.

Presiding officers shall have the following authority:

(a) To regulate the course of the hearing including the order of all sessions and the scheduling thereof, after any initial session, and the recessing, reconvening, and adjournment thereof; and

(b) To take any other action necessary or appropriate to the discharge of the duties vested in them, consistent with the statutory or other authority under which the Chief of Engineers functions, and with the policies and directives of the Chief of Engineers and the Secretary of the Army.

§ 327.11   Public notice.

(a) Public notice shall be given of any public hearing to be held pursuant to this regulation. Such notice should normally provide for a period of not less than 30 days following the date of public notice during which time interested parties may prepare themselves for the hearing. Notice shall also be given to all Federal agencies affected by the proposed action, and to state and local agencies and other parties having an interest in the subject matter of the hearing. Notice shall be sent to all persons requesting a hearing and shall be posted in appropriate government buildings and provided to newspapers of general circulation for publication. Comments received as form letters or petitions may be acknowledged as a group to the person or organization responsible for the form letter or petition.

(b) The notice shall contain time, place, and nature of hearing; the legal authority and jurisdiction under which the hearing is held; and location of and availability of the draft environmental impact statement or environmental assessment.

PART 328   DEFINITION OF WATERS OF THE UNITED STATES

Authority: 33 U.S.C. 1344.

Source: 51 FR 41250, Nov. 13, 1986,
unless otherwise noted.

§ 328.1   Purpose.

This section defines the term "waters of the United States" as it applies to the jurisdictional limits of the authority of the Corps of Engineers under the Clean Water Act. It prescribes the policy, practice, and procedures to be used in determining the extent of jurisdiction of the Corps of Engineers concerning "waters of the United States." The terminology used by section 404 of the Clean Water Act includes "navigable waters" which is defined at section 502(7) of the Act as "waters of the United States including the territorial seas." To provide clarity and to avoid confusion with other Corps of Engineer regulatory programs, the term "waters of the United States" is used throughout 33 CFR parts 320 through 330. This section does not apply to authorities under the Rivers and Harbors Act of 1899 except that some of the same waters may be regulated under both statutes (see 33 CFR parts 322 and 329).

§ 328.2   General scope.

Waters of the United States include those waters listed in § 328.3(a). The lateral limits of jurisdiction in those waters may be divided into three categories. The categories include the territorial seas, tidal waters, and non-tidal waters (see 33 CFR 328.4 (a), (b), and (c), respectively).

§ 328.3   Definitions.

For the purpose of this regulation these terms are defined as follows:

(a) The term *waters of the United States* means

(1) All waters which are currently used, or were used in the past, or may be susceptible to use in interstate or foreign commerce, including all waters which are subject to the ebb and flow of the tide;

(2) All interstate waters including interstate wetlands;

(3) All other waters such as intrastate lakes, rivers, streams (including intermittent streams), mudflats, sandflats, wetlands, sloughs, prairie potholes, wet meadows, playa lakes, or natural ponds, the use, degradation or destruction of which could affect interstate or foreign commerce including any such waters:

(i) Which are or could be used by interstate or foreign travelers for recreational or other purposes; or

(ii) From which fish or shellfish are or could be taken and sold in interstate or foreign commerce; or

(iii) Which are used or could be used for industrial purpose by industries in interstate commerce;

(4) All impoundments of waters otherwise defined as waters of the United States under the definition;

(5) Tributaries of waters identified in paragraphs (a) (1) through (4) of this section;

(6) The territorial seas;

(7) Wetlands adjacent to waters (other than waters that are themselves wetlands) identified in paragraphs (a) (1) through (6) of this section.

Waste treatment systems, including treatment ponds or lagoons designed to meet the requirements of CWA (other than cooling ponds as defined in 40 CFR 123.11(m) which also meet the criteria of this definition) are not waters of the United States.

(8) Waters of the United States do not include prior converted cropland. Notwithstanding the determination of an area's status as prior converted cropland by any other federal agency, for the purposes of the Clean Water Act, the final authority regarding Clean Water Act jurisdiction remains with EPA.

(b) The term *wetlands* means those areas that are inundated or saturated by surface or ground water at a frequency and duration sufficient to support, and that under normal circumstances do support, a prevalence of vegetation typically adapted for life in saturated soil conditions. Wetlands generally include swamps, marshes, bogs, and similar areas.

(c) The term *adjacent* means bordering, contiguous, or neighboring. Wetlands separated from other waters of the United States by man-made dikes or barriers, natural river berms, beach dunes and the like are "adjacent wetlands."

(d) The term *high tide line* means the line of intersection of the land with the water's surface at the maximum height reached by a rising tide. The high tide line may be determined, in the absence of actual data, by a line of oil or scum along shore objects, a more or less continuous deposit of fine shell or debris on the foreshore or berm, other physical markings or characteristics, vegetation lines, tidal gages, or other suitable means that delineate the general height reached by a rising tide. The line encompasses spring high tides and other high tides that occur with periodic frequency but does not include storm surges in which there is a departure from the normal or predicted reach of the tide due to the piling up of water against a coast by strong winds such as those accompanying a hurricane or other intense storm.

(e) The term *ordinary high water mark* means that line on the shore established by the fluctuations of water and indicated by physical characteristics such as clear, natural line impressed on the bank, shelving, changes in the character of soil, destruction of terrestrial vegetation, the presence of litter and debris, or other appropriate means that consider the characteristics of the surrounding areas.

(f) The term *tidal waters* means those waters that rise and fall in a predictable and measurable rhythm or cycle due to the gravitational pulls of the moon and sun. Tidal waters end where the rise and fall of the water surface can no longer be practically measured in a predictable rhythm due to masking by hydrologic, wind, or other effects. [58 FR 45037, August 25, 1993]

§ 328.4   Limits of jurisdiction.

(a) *Territorial Seas.* The limit of jurisdiction in the territorial seas is measured from the baseline in a seaward direction a distance of three nautical miles. (See 33 CFR 329.12)

(b) *Tidal Waters of the United States.* The landward limits of jurisdiction in tidal waters:

(1) Extends to the high tide line, or

(2) When adjacent non-tidal waters of the United States are present, the jurisdiction extends to the limits identified in paragraph (c) of this section.

(c) *Non-Tidal Waters of the United States.* The limits of jurisdiction in non-tidal waters:

(1) In the absence of adjacent wetlands, the jurisdiction extends to the ordinary high water mark, or

(2) When adjacent wetlands are present, the jurisdiction extends beyond the ordinary high water mark to the limit of the adjacent wetlands.

(3) When the water of the United States consists only of wetlands the jurisdiction extends to the limit of the wetland.

§ 328.5　Changes in limits of waters of the United States.

Permanent changes of the shoreline configuration result in similar alterations of the boundaries of waters of the United States. Gradual changes which are due to natural causes and are perceptible only over some period of time constitute changes in the bed of a waterway which also change the boundaries of the waters of the United States. For example, changing sea levels or subsidence of land may cause some areas to become waters of the United States while siltation or a change in drainage may remove an area from waters of the United States. Man-made changes may affect the limits of waters of the United States; however, permanent changes should not be presumed until the particular circumstances have been examined and verified by the district engineer. Verification of changes to the lateral limits of jurisdiction may be obtained from the district engineer.

PART 329　DEFINITION OF NAVIGABLE WATERS OF THE UNITED STATES

Authority: 33 U.S.C. 401 et seq.

Source: 51 FR 41251, Nov. 13, 1986, unless otherwise noted.

§ 329.1　Purpose.

This regulation defines the term "navigable waters of the United States" as it is used to define authorities of the Corps of Engineers. It also prescribes the policy, practice and procedure to be used in determining the extent of the jurisdiction of the Corps of Engineers and in answering inquiries concerning "navigable waters of the United States." This definition does not apply to authorities under the Clean Water Act which definitions are described under 33 CFR parts 323 and 328.

§ 329.2　Applicability.

This regulation is applicable to all Corps of Engineers districts and divisions having civil works responsibilities.

§ 329.3　General policies.

Precise definitions of "navigable waters of the United States" or "navigability" are ultimately dependent on judicial interpretation and cannot be made conclusively by administrative agencies. However, the policies and criteria contained in this regulation are in close conformance with the tests used by Federal courts and determinations made under this regulation are considered binding in regard to the activities of the Corps of Engineers.

§ 329.4　General definition.

Navigable waters of the United States are those waters that are subject to the ebb and flow of the tide and/or are presently used, or have been used in the past, or may be susceptible for use to transport interstate or foreign commerce. A determination of navigability, once made, applies laterally over the entire surface of the waterbody, and is not extinguished by later actions or events which impede or destroy navigable capacity.

§ 329.5　General scope of determination.

The several factors which must be examined when making a determination whether a waterbody is a navigable water of the United States are discussed in detail below. Generally, the following conditions must be satisfied:

(a) Past, present, or potential presence of interstate or foreign commerce;

(b) Physical capabilities for use by commerce as in paragraph (a) of this section; and

(c) Defined geographic limits of the waterbody.

§ 329.6　Interstate or foreign commerce.

(a) *Nature of commerce: type, means, and extent of use.* The types of commercial use of a waterway are extremely varied and will depend on the character of the region, its products, and the difficulties or dangers of navigation. It is the waterbody's capability of use by the public for purposes of transportation of commerce which is the determinative factor, and not the time, extent or manner of that use. As discussed in § 329.9 of this part, it is sufficient to establish the potential for commercial use at any past, present, or future time. Thus, sufficient commerce may be shown by historical use of canoes, bateaux, or other frontier craft, as long as that type of boat was common or well-suited to the place and period. Similarly, the particular items of commerce may vary widely, depending again on the region and period. The goods involved might be grain, furs, or other commerce of the time. Logs are a common example; transportation of logs has been a substantial and well-recognized commercial use of many navigable waters of the United States. Note, however, that the mere presence of floating logs will not of itself make the river "navigable"; the logs must have been related to a commercial venture. Similarly, the presence of recreational craft may indicate that a waterbody is capable of bearing some forms of commerce, either presently, in the future, or at a past point in time.

(b) *Nature of commerce: interstate and intrastate.* Interstate commerce may of course be existent on an intrastate voyage which occurs only between places within the same state. It is only necessary that goods may be brought from, or eventually be destined to go to, another state. (For purposes of this regulation, the term "interstate commerce" hereinafter includes "foreign commerce" as well.)

§ 329.7　Intrastate or interstate nature of waterway.

A waterbody may be entirely within a state, yet still be capable of carrying interstate commerce. This is especially clear when it physically connects with a generally acknowledged avenue of interstate commerce, such as the ocean or one of the Great Lakes, and is yet wholly within one state. Nor is it necessary that there be a physically navigable connection across a state boundary. Where a waterbody extends through one or more states, but substantial portions, which are capable of bearing interstate commerce, are located in only one of the states, the entirety of the waterway up to the head (upper limit) of navigation is subject to Federal jurisdiction.

§ 329.8 Improved or natural conditions of the waterbody.

Determinations are not limited to the natural or original condition of the waterbody. Navigability may also be found where artificial aids have been or may be used to make the waterbody suitable for use in navigation.

(a) *Existing improvements: artificial waterbodies.*

(1) An artificial channel may often constitute a navigable water of the United States, even though it has been privately developed and maintained, or passes through private property. The test is generally as developed above, that is, whether the waterbody is capable of use to transport interstate commerce. Canals which connect two navigable waters of the United States and which are used for commerce clearly fall within the test, and themselves become navigable. A canal open to navigable waters of the United States on only one end is itself navigable where it in fact supports interstate commerce. A canal or other artificial waterbody that is subject to ebb and flow of the tide is also a navigable water of the United States.

(2) The artificial waterbody may be a major portion of a river or harbor area or merely a minor backwash, slip, or turning area (see § 329.12(b) of this part).

(3) Private ownership of the lands underlying the waterbody, or of the lands through which it runs, does not preclude a finding of navigability. Ownership does become a controlling factor if a privately constructed and operated canal is not used to transport interstate commerce nor used by the public; it is then not considered to be a navigable water of the United States. However, a private waterbody, even though not itself navigable, may so affect the navigable capacity of nearby waters as to nevertheless be subject to certain regulatory authorities.

(b) *Non-existing improvements, past or potential.* A waterbody may also be considered navigable depending on the feasibility of use to transport interstate commerce after the construction of whatever "reasonable" improvements may potentially be made. The improvement need not exist, be planned, nor even authorized; it is enough that potentially they could be made. What is a "reasonable" improvement is always a matter of degree; there must be a balance between cost and need at a time when the improvement would be (or would have been) useful. Thus, if an improvement were "reasonable" at a time of past use, the water was therefore navigable in law from that time forward. The changes in engineering practices or the coming of new industries with varying classes of freight may affect the type of the improvement; those which may be entirely reasonable in a thickly populated, highly developed industrial region may have been entirely too costly for the same region in the days of the pioneers. The determination of reasonable improvement is often similar to the cost analyses presently made in Corps of Engineers studies.

§ 329.9 Time at which commerce exists or determination is made.

(a) *Past use.* A waterbody which was navigable in its natural or improved state, or which was susceptible of reasonable improvement (as discussed in § 329.8(b) of this part) retains its character as "navigable in law" even though it is not presently used for commerce, or is presently incapable of such use because of changed conditions or the presence of obstructions. Nor does absence of use because of changed economic conditions affect the legal character of the waterbody. Once having attained the character of "navigable in law," the Federal authority remains in existence, and cannot be abandoned by administrative officers or court action. Nor is mere inattention or ambiguous action by Congress an abandonment of Federal control. However, express statutory declarations by Congress that described portions of a waterbody are non-navigable, or have been abandoned, are binding upon the Department of the Army. Each statute must be carefully examined, since Congress often reserves the power to amend the Act, or assigns special duties of supervision and control to the Secretary of the Army or Chief of Engineers.

(b) *Future or potential use.* Navigability may also be found in a waterbody's susceptibility for use in its ordinary condition or by reasonable improvement to transport interstate commerce. This may be either in its natural or improved condition, and may thus be existent although there has been no actual use to date. Non-use in the past therefore does not prevent recognition of the potential for future use.

§ 329.10 Existence of obstructions.

A stream may be navigable despite the existence of falls, rapids, sand bars, bridges, portages, shifting currents, or similar obstructions. Thus, a waterway in its original condition might have had substantial obstructions which were overcome by frontier boats and/or portages, and nevertheless be a "channel" of commerce, even though boats had to be removed from the water in some stretches, or logs be brought around an obstruction by means of artificial chutes. However, the question is ultimately a matter of degree, and it must be recognized that there is some point beyond which navigability could not be established.

§ 329.11 Geographic and jurisdictional limits of rivers and lakes.

(a) *Jurisdiction over entire bed.* Federal regulatory jurisdiction, and powers of improvement for navigation, extend laterally to the entire water surface and bed of a navigable waterbody, which includes all the land and waters below the ordinary high water mark. Jurisdiction thus extends to the edge (as determined above) of all such waterbodies, even though portions of the waterbody may be extremely shallow, or obstructed by shoals, vegetation or other barriers. Marshlands and similar areas are thus considered navigable in law, but only so far as the area is subject to inundation by the ordinary high waters.

(1) The "ordinary high water mark" on nontidal rivers is the line on the shore established by the fluctuations of water and indicated by physical characteristics such as a clear, natural line impressed on the bank; shelving; changes in the character of soil; destruction of terrestrial vegetation; the presence of litter and debris; or other appropriate means that consider the characteristics of the surrounding areas.

(2) Ownership of a river or lake bed or of the lands between high and low water marks will vary according to state law; however, private ownership of the underlying lands has no bearing on the existence or extent of the dominant Federal jurisdiction over a navigable waterbody.

(b) *Upper limit of navigability.* The character of a river will, at some point along its length, change from navigable to non-navigable. Very often that point will be at a major fall or rapids, or other place where there is a marked decrease in the navigable capacity of the river. The upper limit will therefore often be the same point traditionally recognized as the head of navigation, but may, under some of the tests described above, be at some point yet farther upstream.

§ 329.12   Geographic and jurisdictional limits of oceanic and tidal waters.

(a) *Ocean and coastal waters.* The navigable waters of the United States over which Corps of Engineers regulatory jurisdiction extends include all ocean and coastal waters within a zone three geographic (nautical) miles seaward from the baseline (The Territorial Seas). Wider zones are recognized for special regulatory powers exercised over the outer continental shelf. (See 33 CFR 322.3(b)).

(1) *Baseline defined.* Generally, where the shore directly contacts the open sea, the line on the shore reached by the ordinary low tides comprises the baseline from which the distance of three geographic miles is measured. The baseline has significance for both domestic and international law and is subject to precise definitions. Special problems arise when offshore rocks, islands, or other bodies exist, and the baseline may have to be drawn seaward of such bodies.

(2) *Shoreward limit of jurisdiction.* Regulatory jurisdiction in coastal areas extends to the line on the shore reached by the plane of the mean (average) high water. Where precise determination of the actual location of the line becomes necessary, it must be established by survey with reference to the available tidal datum, preferably averaged over a period of 18.6 years. Less precise methods, such as observation of the "apparent shoreline" which is determined by reference to physical markings, lines of vegetation, or changes in type of vegetation, may be used only where an estimate is needed of the line reached by the mean high water.

(b) *Bays and estuaries.* Regulatory jurisdiction extends to the entire surface and bed of all waterbodies subject to tidal action. Jurisdiction thus extends to the edge (as determined by paragraph (a)(2) of this section) of all such waterbodies, even though portions of the waterbody may be extremely shallow, or obstructed by shoals, vegetation, or other barriers. Marshlands and similar areas are thus considered "navigable in law," but only so far as the area is subject to inundation by the mean high waters. The relevant test is therefore the presence of the mean high tidal waters, and not the general test described above, which generally applies to inland rivers and lakes.

§ 329.13   Geographic limits: Shifting boundaries.

Permanent changes of the shoreline configuration result in similar alterations of the boundaries of the navigable waters of the United States. Thus, gradual changes which are due to natural causes and are perceptible only over some period of time constitute changes in the bed of a waterbody which also change the shoreline boundaries of the navigable waters of the United States. However, an area will remain "navigable in law," even though no longer covered with water, whenever the change has occurred suddenly, or was caused by artificial forces intended to produce that change. For example, shifting sand bars within a river or estuary remain part of the navigable water of the United States, regardless that they may be dry at a particular point in time.

§ 329.14   Determination of navigability.

(a) *Effect on determinations.* Although conclusive determinations of navigability can be made only by federal Courts, those made by federal agencies are nevertheless accorded substantial weight by the courts. It is therefore necessary that when jurisdictional questions arise, district personnel carefully investigate those waters which may be subject to Federal regulatory jurisdiction under guidelines set out above, as the resulting determination may have substantial impact upon a judicial body. Official determinations by an agency made in the past can be revised or reversed as necessary to reflect changed rules or interpretations of the law.

(b) *Procedures of determination.* A determination whether a waterbody is a navigable water of the United States will be made by the division engineer, and will be based on a report of findings prepared at the district level in accordance with the criteria set out in this regulation. Each report of findings will be prepared by the district engineer, accompanied by an opinion of the district counsel, and forwarded to the division engineer for final determination. Each report of findings will be based substantially on applicable portions of the format in paragraph (c) of this section.

(c) *Suggested format of report of findings:*

(1) Name of waterbody:

(2) Tributary to:

(3) Physical characteristics:

(i) Type: (river, bay, slough, estuary, etc.)

(ii) Length:

(iii) Approximate discharge volumes: maximum, Minimum, Mean:

(iv) Fall per mile:

(v) Extent of tidal influence:

(vi) Range between ordinary high and ordinary low water:

(vii) Description of improvements to navigation not listed in paragraph (c)(5) of this section:

(4) Nature and location of significant obstructions to navigation in portions of the waterbody used or potentially capable of use in interstate commerce:

(5) Authorized projects:

(i) Nature, condition and location of any improvements made under projects authorized by Congress:

(ii) Description of projects authorized but not constructed:

(iii) List of known survey documents or reports describing the waterbody:

(6) Past or present interstate commerce:

(i) General types, extent, and period in time:

(ii) Documentation if necessary:

(7) Potential use for interstate commerce, if applicable:

(i) If in natural condition:

(ii) If improved:

(8) Nature of jurisdiction known to have been exercised by Federal agencies if any:

(9) State or Federal court decisions relating to navigability of the waterbody, if any:

(10) Remarks:

(11) Finding of navigability (with date) and recommendation for determination:

§ 329.15   Inquiries regarding determinations.

(a) Findings and determinations should be made whenever a question arises regarding the navigability of a waterbody. Where no determination has been made, a report of findings will be prepared and forwarded to the division engineer, as described above. Inquiries may be answered by an interim reply which indicates that a final agency determination must be made by the division engineer. If a need develops for an emergency determination, district engineers may act in reliance on a finding prepared as in section 329.14 of this part. The report of findings should then be forwarded to the division engineer on an expedited basis.

(b) Where determinations have been made by the division engineer, inquiries regarding the *navigability* of specific portions of waterbodies covered by these determinations may be answered as follows:

This Department, in the administration of the laws enacted by Congress for the protection and preservation of the navigable waters of the United States, has determined that ___ (River) (Bay) (Lake, etc.) is a navigable water of the United States from ___ to ___. Actions which modify or otherwise affect those waters are subject to the jurisdiction of this Department, whether such actions occur within or outside the navigable areas.

(c) Specific inquiries regarding the *jurisdiction* of the Corps of Engineers can be answered only after a determination whether

(1) the waters are navigable waters of the United States or

(2) If not navigable, whether the proposed type of activity may nevertheless so affect the navigable waters of the United States that the assertion of regulatory jurisdiction is deemed necessary.

§ 329.16   Use and maintenance of lists of determinations.

(a) Tabulated lists of final determinations of navigability are to be maintained in each district office, and be updated as necessitated by court decisions, jurisdictional inquiries, or other changed conditions.

(b) It should be noted that the lists represent only those waterbodies for which determinations have been made; absence from that list should not be taken as an indication that the waterbody is not navigable.

(c) Deletions from the list are not authorized. If a change in status of a waterbody from navigable to non-navigable is deemed necessary, an updated finding should be forwarded to the division engineer; changes are not considered final until a determination has been made by the division engineer.

PART 330   NATIONWIDE PERMIT PROGRAM

Authority: 33 U.S.C. 401 et seq.; 33 U.S.C. 1344; 33 U.S.C. 1413.

Source: 56 FR 59134, Nov. 22, 1991, unless otherwise noted.

§ 330.1   Purpose and policy.

(a) *Purpose.* This part describes the policy and procedures used in the Department of the Army's nationwide permit program to issue, modify, suspend, or revoke nationwide permits; to identify conditions, limitations, and restrictions on the nationwide permits; and, to identify any procedures, whether required or optional, for authorization by nationwide permits.

(b) *Nationwide permits.* Nationwide permits (NWPs) are a type of general permit issued by the Chief of Engineers and are designed to regulate with little, if any, delay or paperwork certain activities having minimal impacts. The NWPs are proposed, issued, modified, reissued (extended), and revoked from time to time after an opportunity for public notice and comment. Proposed NWPs or modifications to or reissuance of existing NWPs will be adopted only after the Corps gives notice and allows the public an opportunity to comment on and request a public hearing regarding the proposals. The Corps will give full consideration to all comments received prior to reaching a final decision.

(c) *Terms and conditions.* An activity is authorized under an NWP only if that activity and the permittee satisfy all of the NWP's terms and conditions. Activities that do not qualify for authorization under an NWP still may be authorized by an individual or regional general permit. The Corps will consider unauthorized any activity requiring Corps authorization if that activity is under construction or completed and does not comply with all of the terms and conditions of an NWP, regional general permit, or an individual permit. The Corps will evaluate unauthorized activities for enforcement action under 33 CFR part 326. The district engineer (DE) may elect to suspend enforcement proceedings if the permittee modifies his project to comply with an NWP or a regional general permit. After considering whether a violation was knowing or intentional, and other indications of the need for a penalty, the DE can elect to terminate an enforcement proceeding with an after-the-fact authorization under an NWP, if all terms and conditions of the NWP have been satisfied, either before or after the activity has been accomplished.

(d) *Discretionary authority.* District and division engineers have been delegated a discretionary authority to suspend, modify, or revoke authorizations under an NWP. This discretionary authority may be used by district and division engineers only to further condition or restrict the applicability of an NWP for cases where they have concerns for the aquatic environment under the Clean Water Act section 404(b)(1) Guidelines or for any factor of the public interest. Because of the nature of most activities authorized by NWP, district and division engineers will not have to review every such activity to decide whether to exercise discretionary authority. The terms and conditions of certain NWPs require the DE to review the proposed activity before the NWP authorizes its construction. However, the DE has the discretionary authority to review any activity authorized by NWP to determine whether the activity complies with the NWP. If the DE finds that the proposed activity would have more than minimal individual or cumulative net adverse effects on the environment or otherwise may be contrary to the public interest, he shall modify the NWP authorization to reduce or eliminate those adverse effects, or he shall instruct the prospective permittee to apply for a regional general permit or an individual permit. Discretionary authority is also discussed at 33 CFR 330.4(e) and 330.5.

(e) *Notifications.*

(1) In most cases, permittees may proceed with activities authorized by NWPs without notifying the DE. However, the prospective permittee should carefully review the language of the NWP to ascertain whether he must notify the DE prior to commencing the authorized activity. For NWPs requiring advance notification, such notification must be made in writing as early as possible prior to commencing the proposed activity. The permittee may presume that his project qualifies for the NWP unless he is otherwise notified by the DE within a 30-day period. The 30-day period starts on the date of receipt of the notification in the Corps district office and ends 30 calendar days later regardless of weekends or holidays. If the DE notifies the prospective permittee that the notification is incomplete, a new 30-day period will commence upon receipt of the revised notification. The prospective permittee may not proceed with the proposed activity before expiration of the 30-day period unless otherwise notified by the DE. If the DE fails to act within the 30-day period, he must use the procedures of 33 CFR 330.5 in order to modify, suspend, or revoke the NWP authorization.

(2) The DE will review the notification and may add activity-specific conditions to ensure that the activity complies with the terms and conditions of the NWP and that the adverse impacts on the aquatic environment and other aspects of the public interest are individually and cumulatively minimal.

(3) For some NWPs involving discharges into wetlands, the notification must include a wetland delineation. The DE will review the notification and determine if the individual and cumulative adverse environmental effects are more than minimal. If the adverse effects are more than minimal the DE will notify the prospective permittee that an individual permit is required or that the prospective permittee may propose measures to mitigate the loss of special aquatic sites, including wetlands, to reduce the adverse impacts to minimal. The prospective permittee may elect to propose mitigation with the original notification. The DE will consider that proposed mitigation when deciding if the impacts are minimal. The DE shall add activity-specific conditions to ensure that the mitigation will be accomplished. If sufficient mitigation cannot be developed to reduce the adverse environmental effects to the minimal level, the DE will not allow authorization under the NWP and will instruct the prospective permittee on procedures to seek authorization under an individual permit.

(f) *Individual Applications.* DEs should review all incoming applications for individual permits for possible eligibility under regional general permits or NWPs. If the activity complies with the terms and conditions of one or more NWP, he should verify the authorization and so notify the applicant. If the DE determines that the activity could comply after reasonable project modifications and/or activity-specific conditions, he should notify the applicant of such modifications and conditions. If such modifications and conditions are accepted by the applicant, verbally or in writing, the DE will verify the authorization with the modifications and conditions in accordance with 33 CFR 330.6(a). However, the

DE will proceed with processing the application as an individual permit and take the appropriate action within 15 calendar days of receipt, in accordance with 33 CFR 325.2(a)(2), unless the applicant indicates that he will accept the modifications or conditions.

(g) *Authority.* NWPs can be issued to satisfy the permit requirements of section 10 of the Rivers and Harbors Act of 1899, section 404 of the Clean Water Act, section 103 of the Marine Protection, Research, and Sanctuaries Act, or some combination thereof. The applicable authority will be indicated at the end of each NWP. NWPs and their conditions previously published at 33 CFR 330.5 and 330.6 will remain in effect until they expire or are modified or revoked in accordance with the procedures of this part.

§ 330.2 Definitions.

(a) The definitions found in 33 CFR parts 320-329 are applicable to the terms used in this part.

(b) *Nationwide* permit refers to a type of general permit which authorizes activities on a nationwide basis unless specifically limited. (Another type of general permit is a "regional permit" which is issued by division or district engineers on a regional basis in accordance with 33 CFR part 325). (See 33 CFR 322.2(f) and 323.2(h) for the definition of a general permit.)

(c) *Authorization* means that specific activities that qualify for an NWP may proceed, provided that the terms and conditions of the NWP are met. After determining that the activity complies with all applicable terms and conditions, the prospective permittee may assume an authorization under an NWP. This assumption is subject to the DE's authority to determine if an activity complies with the terms and conditions of an NWP. If requested by the permittee in writing, the DE will verify in writing that the permittee's proposed activity complies with the terms and conditions of the NWP. A written verification may contain activity-specific conditions and regional conditions which a permittee must satisfy for the authorization to be valid.

(d) *Headwaters* means non-tidal rivers, streams, and their lakes and impoundments, including adjacent wetlands, that are part of a surface tributary system to an interstate or navigable water of the United States upstream of the point on the river or stream at which the average annual flow is less than five cubic feet per second. The DE may estimate this point from available data by using the mean annual area precipitation, area drainage basin maps, and the average runoff coefficient, or by similar means. For streams that are dry for long periods of the year, DEs may establish the point where headwaters begin as that point on the stream where a flow of five cubic feet per second is equaled or exceeded 50 percent of the time.

(e) *Isolated waters* means those non-tidal waters of the United States that are:

(1) Not part of a surface tributary system to interstate or navigable waters of the United States; and

(2) Not adjacent to such tributary waterbodies.

(f) *Filled area* means the area within jurisdictional waters which is eliminated or covered as a direct result of the discharge (i.e., the area actually covered by the discharged material). It does not include areas excavated nor areas impacted as an indirect effect of the fill.

(g) *Discretionary authority* means the authority described in §§ 330.1(d) and 330.4(e) which the Chief of Engineers delegates to division or district engineers to modify an NWP authorization by adding conditions, to suspend an NWP authorization, or to revoke an NWP authorization and thus require individual permit authorization.

(h) *Terms and conditions.* The "terms" of an NWP are the limitations and provisions included in the description of the NWP itself. The "conditions" of NWPs are additional provisions which place restrictions or limitations on all of the NWPs. These are published with the NWPs. Other conditions may be imposed by district or division engineers on a geographic, category-of-activity, or activity-specific basis (See 33 CFR 330.4(e)).

(i) *Single and complete project* means the total project proposed or accomplished by one owner/developer or partnership or other association of owners/developers. For example, if construction of a residential development affects several different areas of a headwater or isolated water, or several different headwaters or isolated waters, the cumulative total of all filled areas should be the basis for deciding whether or not the project will be covered by an NWP. For linear projects, the "single and complete project" (i.e. single and complete crossing) will apply to each crossing of a separate water of the United States (i.e. single waterbody) at that location; except that for linear projects crossing a single waterbody several times at separate and distant locations, each crossing is considered a single and complete project. However, individual channels in a braided stream or river, or individual arms of a large, irregularly-shaped wetland or lake, etc., are not separate waterbodies.

(j) *Special aquatic sites* means wetlands, mudflats, vegetated shallows, coral reefs, riffle and pool complexes, sanctuaries, and refuges as defined at 40 CFR 230.40 through 230.45.

§ 330.3 Activities occurring before certain dates.

The following activities were permitted by NWPs issued on July 19, 1977, and, unless the activities are modified, they do not require further permitting:

(a) Discharges of dredged or fill material into waters of the United States outside the limits of navigable waters of the United States that occurred before the phase-in dates which extended Section 404 jurisdiction to all waters of the United States. The phase-in dates were: After July 25, 1975, discharges into navigable waters of the United States and adjacent wetlands; after September 1, 1976, discharges into navigable waters of the United States and their primary tributaries, including adjacent wetlands, and into natural lakes, greater than 5 acres in surface area; and after July 1, 1977, discharges into all waters of the United States, including wetlands. (section 404)

(b) Structures or work completed before December 18, 1968, or in waterbodies over which the DE had not asserted jurisdiction at the time the activity occurred, provided in both instances, there is no interference with navigation. Activities completed shoreward of applicable Federal Harbor lines before May 27, 1970 do not require specific authorization. (section 10)

§ 330.4   Conditions, limitations, and restrictions.

(a) *General.* A prospective permittee must satisfy all terms and conditions of an NWP for a valid authorization to occur. Some conditions identify a "threshold" that, if met, requires additional procedures or provisions contained in other paragraphs in this section. It is important to remember that the NWPs only authorize activities from the perspective of the Corps regulatory authorities and that other Federal, state, and local permits, approvals, or authorizations may also be required.

(b) *Further information.*

(1) DEs have authority to determine if an activity complies with the terms and conditions of an NWP.

(2) NWPs do not obviate the need to obtain other Federal, state, or local permits, approvals, or authorizations required by law.

(3) NWPs do not grant any property rights or exclusive privileges.

(4) NWPs do not authorize any injury to the property or rights of others.

(5) NWPs do not authorize interference with any existing or proposed Federal project.

(c) *State 401 water quality certification.*

(1) State 401 water quality certification pursuant to section 401 of the Clean Water Act, or waiver thereof, is required prior to the issuance or reissuance of NWPs authorizing activities which may result in a discharge into waters of the United States.

(2) If, prior to the issuance or reissuance of such NWPs, a state issues a 401 water quality certification which includes special conditions, the division engineer will make these special conditions regional conditions of the NWP for activities which may result in a discharge into waters of United States in that state, unless he determines that such conditions do not comply with the provisions of 33 CFR 325.4.In the latter case, the conditioned 401 water quality certification will be considered a denial of the certification (see paragraph (c)(3) of this section).

(3) If a state denies a required 401 water quality certification for an activity otherwise meeting the terms and conditions of a particular NWP, that NWP's authorization for all such activities within that state is denied without prejudice until the state issues an individual 401 water quality certification or waives its right to do so. State denial of 401 water quality certification for any specific NWP affects only

those activities which may result in a discharge. That NWP continues to authorize activities which could not reasonably be expected to result in discharges into waters of the United States.{1}

> {FN1} NWPs numbered 1, 2, 8, 9, 10, 11, 19, 24, 28, and 35, do not require 401 water quality certification since they would authorize activities which, in the opinion of the Corps, could not reasonably be expected to result in a discharge and in the case of NWP 8 is seaward of the territorial seas. NWPs numbered 3, 4, 5, 6, 7, 13,14, 18, 20, 21, 22, 23, 27, 32, 36, 37, and 38, involve various activities, some of which may result in a discharge and require 401 water quality certification, and others of which do not. State denial of 401 water quality certification for any specific NWP in this category affects only those activities which may result in a discharge. For those activities not involving discharges, the NWP remains in effect. NWPs numbered 12, 15, 16, 17, 25, 26, and 40 involve activities which would result in discharges and therefore 401 water quality certification is required.

(4) DEs will take appropriate measures to inform the public of which activities, waterbodies, or regions require an individual 401 water quality certification before authorization by NWP.

(5) The DE will not require or process an individual permit application for an activity which may result in a discharge and otherwise qualifies for an NWP solely on the basis that the 401 water quality certification has been denied for that NWP. However, the district or division engineer may consider water quality, among other appropriate factors, in determining whether to exercise his discretionary authority and require a regional general permit or an individual permit.

(6) In instances where a state has denied the 401 water quality certification for discharges under a particular NWP, permittees must furnish the DE with an individual 401 water quality certification or a copy of the application to the state for such certification. For NWPs for which a state has denied the 401 water quality certification, the DE will determine a reasonable period of time after receipt of the request for an activity-specific 401 water quality certification (generally 60 days), upon the expiration of which the DE will presume state waiver of the certification for the individual activity covered by the NWP's. However, the DE and the state may negotiate for additional time for the 401 water quality certification, but in no event shall the period exceed one (1) year (see 33 CFR 325.2(b)(1)(ii)). Upon receipt of an individual 401 water quality certification, or if the prospective permittee demonstrates to the DE state waiver of such certification, the proposed work can be authorized under the NWP. For NWPs requiring a 30-day predischarge notification the district engineer will

immediately begin, and complete, his review prior to the state action on the individual section 401 water quality certification. If a state issues a conditioned individual 401 water quality certification for an individual activity, the DE will include those conditions as activity-specific conditions of the NWP.

(7) Where a state, after issuing a 401 water quality certification for an NWP, subsequently attempts to withdraw it for substantive reasons after the effective date of the NWP, the division engineer will review those reasons and consider whether there is substantial basis for suspension, modification, or revocation of the NWP authorization as outlined in § 330.5. Otherwise, such attempted state withdrawal is not effective and the Corps will consider the state certification to be valid for the NWP authorizations until such time as the NWP is modified or reissued.

(d) *Coastal zone management consistency determination.*

(1) Section 307(c)(1) of the Coastal Zone Management Act (CZMA) requires the Corps to provide a consistency determination and receive state agreement prior to the issuance, reissuance, or expansion of activities authorized by an NWP that authorizes activities within a state with a Federally-approved Coastal Management Program when activities that would occur within, or outside, that state's coastal zone will affect land or water uses or natural resources of the state's coastal zone.

(2) If, prior to the issuance, reissuance, or expansion of activities authorized by an NWP, a state indicates that additional conditions are necessary for the state to agree with the Corps consistency determination, the division engineer will make such conditions regional conditions for the NWP in that state, unless he determines that the conditions do not comply with the provisions of 33 CFR 325.4 or believes for some other specific reason it would be inappropriate to include the conditions. In this case, the state's failure to agree with the Corps consistency determination without the conditions will be considered to be a disagreement with the Corps consistency determination.

(3) When a state has disagreed with the Corps consistency determination, authorization for all such activities occurring within or outside the state's coastal zone that affect land or water uses or natural resources of the state's coastal zone is denied without prejudice until the prospective permittee furnishes the DE an individual consistency certification pursuant to section 307(c)(3) of the CZMA and demonstrates that the state has concurred in it (either on an individual or generic basis), or that concurrence should be presumed (see paragraph (d)(6) of this section).

(4) DEs will take appropriate measures, such as public notices, to inform the public of which activities, waterbodies, or regions require prospective permittees to make an individual consistency determination and seek concurrence from the state.

(5) DEs will not require or process an individual permit application for an activity otherwise qualifying for an NWP solely on the basis that the activity has not received CZMA consistency agreement from the state. However, the district or division engineer may consider that factor, among other appropriate factors, in determining whether to exercise his discretionary authority and require a regional general permit or an individual permit application.

(6) In instances where a state has disagreed with the Corps consistency determination for activities under a particular NWP, permittees must furnish the DE with an individual consistency concurrence or a copy of the consistency certification provided to the state for concurrence. If a state fails to act on a permittee's consistency certification within six months after receipt by the state, concurrence will be presumed. Upon receipt of an individual consistency concurrence or upon presumed consistency, the proposed work is authorized if it complies with all terms and conditions of the NWP. For NWPs requiring a 30-day predischarge notification the DE will immediately begin, and may complete, his review prior to the state action on the individual consistency certification. If a state indicates that individual conditions are necessary for consistency with the state's Federally-approved coastal management program for that individual activity, the DE will include those conditions as activity-specific conditions of the NWP unless he determines that such conditions do not comply with the provisions of 33 CFR 325.4.In the latter case the DE will consider the conditioned concurrence as a nonconcurrence unless the permittee chooses to comply voluntarily with all the conditions in the conditioned concurrence.

(7) Where a state, after agreeing with the Corps consistency determination, subsequently attempts to reverse it's agreement for substantive reasons after the effective date of the NWP, the division engineer will review those reasons and consider whether there is substantial basis for suspension, modification, or revocation as outlined in 33 CFR 330.5.Otherwise, such attempted reversal is not effective and the Corps will consider the state CZMA consistency agreement to be valid for the NWP authorization until such time as the NWP is modified or reissued.

(8) Federal activities must be consistent with a state's Federally-approved coastal management program to the maximum extent practicable. Federal agencies should follow their own procedures and the Department of Commerce regulations appearing at 15 CFR part 930 to meet the requirements of the CZMA. Therefore, the provisions of 33 CFR 330.4(d)(1)-(7) do not apply to Federal activities. Indian tribes doing work on Indian Reservation lands shall be treated in the same manner as Federal applicants.

(e) *Discretionary authority.* The Corps reserves the right (i.e., discretion) to modify, suspend, or revoke NWP authorizations. Modification means the imposition of additional or revised terms or conditions on the authorization. Suspension means the temporary cancellation of the authorization while a decision is made to either modify, revoke, or reinstate the authorization. Revocation means the cancellation of the authorization. The procedures for modifying, suspending, or revoking NWP authorizations are detailed in § 330.5.

(1) A division engineer may assert discretionary authority by modifying, suspending, or revoking NWP authorizations for a specific geographic area, class of activity, or class of waters within his division, including on a statewide basis, whenever he determines sufficient concerns for the environment under the section 404(b)(1) Guidelines or any other factor of the public interest so requires, or if he otherwise determines that the NWP would result in more than minimal adverse environmental effects either individually or cumulatively.

(2) A DE may assert discretionary authority by modifying, suspending, or revoking NWP authorization for a specific activity whenever he determines sufficient concerns for the environment or any other factor of the public interest so requires. Whenever the DE determines that a proposed specific activity covered by an NWP would have more than minimal individual or cumulative adverse effects on the environment or otherwise may be contrary to the public interest, he must either modify the NWP authorization to reduce or eliminate the adverse impacts, or notify the prospective permittee that the proposed activity is not authorized by NWP and provide instructions on how to seek authorization under a regional general or individual permit.

(3) The division or district engineer will restore authorization under the NWPs at any time he determines that his reason for asserting discretionary authority has been satisfied by a condition, project modification, or new information.

(4) When the Chief of Engineers modifies or reissues an NWP, division engineers must use the procedures of § 330.5 to reassert discretionary authority to reinstate regional conditions or revocation of NWP authorizations for specific geographic areas, class of activities, or class of waters. Division engineers will update existing documentation for each NWP. Upon modification or reissuance of NWPs, previous activity-specific conditions or revocations of NWP authorization will remain in effect unless the DE specifically removes the activity-specific conditions or revocations.

(f) *Endangered species.* No activity is authorized by any NWP if that activity is likely to jeopardize the continued existence of a threatened or endangered species as listed or proposed for listing under the Federal Endangered Species Act (ESA), or to destroy or adversely modify the critical habitat of such species.

(1) Federal agencies should follow their own procedures for complying with the requirements of the ESA.

(2) Non-federal permittees shall notify the DE if any Federally listed (or proposed for listing) endangered or threatened species or critical habitat might be affected or is in the vicinity of the project. In such cases, the prospective permittee will not begin work under authority of the NWP until notified by the district engineer that the requirements of the Endangered Species Act have been satisfied and that the activity is authorized. If the DE determines that the activity may affect any Federally listed species or critical habitat, the DE must initiate section 7 consultation in accordance with the ESA. In such cases, the DE may:

(i) Initiate section 7 consultation and then, upon completion, authorize the activity under the NWP by adding, if appropriate, activity-specific conditions; or

(ii) Prior to or concurrent with section 7 consultation, assert discretionary authority (see 33 CFR 330.4(e)) and require an individual permit (see 33 CFR 330.5(d)).

(3) Prospective permittees are encouraged to obtain information on the location of threatened or endangered species and their critical habitats from the U.S. Fish and Wildlife Service, Endangered Species Office, and the National Marine Fisheries Service.

(g) *Historic properties.* No activity which may affect properties listed or properties eligible for listing in the National Register of Historic Places, is authorized until the DE has complied with the provisions of 33 CFR part 325, appendix C.

(1) Federal permittees should follow their own procedures for compliance with the requirements of the National Historic Preservation Act and other Federal historic preservation laws.

(2) Non-federal permittees will notify the DE if the activity may affect historic properties which the National Park Service has listed, determined eligible for listing, or which the prospective permittee has reason to believe may be eligible for listing, on the National Register of Historic Places. In such cases, the prospective permittee will not begin the proposed activity until notified by the DE that the requirements of the National Historic Preservation Act have been satisfied and that the activity is authorized. If a property in the permit area of the activity is determined to be an historic property in accordance with 33 CFR part 325, appendix C, the DE will take into account the effects on such properties in accordance with 33 CFR part 325, appendix C. In such cases, the district engineer may:

(i) After complying with the requirements of 33 CFR part 325, appendix C, authorize the activity under the NWP by adding, if appropriate, activity-specific conditions; or

(ii) Prior to or concurrent with complying with the requirements of 33 CFR part 325, appendix C, he may assert discretionary authority (see 33 CFR 330.4(e)) and instruct the prospective permittee of procedures to seek authorization under a regional general permit or an individual permit. (See 33 CFR 330.5(d).)

(3) The permittee shall immediately notify the DE if, before or during prosecution of the work authorized, he encounters an historic property that has not been listed or determined eligible for listing on the National Register, but which the prospective permittee has reason to believe may be eligible for listing on the National Register.

(4) Prospective permittees are encouraged to obtain information on the location of historic properties from the State Historic Preservation Officer and the National Register of Historic Places.

§ 330.5 Issuing, modifying, suspending, or revoking nationwide permits and authorizations.

(a) *General.* This section sets forth the procedures for issuing and reissuing NWPs and for modifying, suspending, or revoking NWPs and authorizations under NWPs.

(b) *Chief of Engineers.*

(1) Anyone may, at any time, suggest to the Chief of Engineers, (ATTN: CECW-OR), any new NWPs or conditions for issuance, or changes to existing NWPs, which he believes to be appropriate for consideration. From time-to-time new NWPs and revocations of or modifications to existing NWPs will be evaluated by the Chief of Engineers following the procedures specified in this section. Within five years of issuance of the NWPs, the Chief of Engineers will review the NWPs and propose modification, revocation, or reissuance.

(2) *Public notice.*

(i) Upon proposed issuance of new NWPs or modification, suspension, revocation, or reissuance of existing NWPs, the Chief of Engineers will publish a document seeking public comments, including the opportunity to request a public hearing. This document will also state that the information supporting the Corps' provisional determination that proposed activities comply with the requirements for issuance under general permit authority is available at the Office of the Chief of Engineers and at all district offices. The Chief of Engineers will prepare this information which will be supplemented, if appropriate, by division engineers.

(ii) Concurrent with the Chief of Engineers' notification of proposed, modified, reissued, or revoked NWPs, DEs will notify the known interested public by a notice issued at the district level. The notice will include proposed regional conditions or proposed revocations of NWP authorizations for specific geographic areas, classes of activities, or classes of waters, if any, developed by the division engineer.

(3) *Documentation.* The Chief of Engineers will prepare appropriate NEPA documents and, if applicable, section 404(b)(1) Guidelines compliance analyses for proposed NWPs. Documentation for existing NWPs will be modified to reflect any changes in these permits and to reflect the Chief of Engineers' evaluation of the use of the permit since the last issuance. Copies of all comments received on the document will be included in the administrative record. The Chief of Engineers will consider these comments in making his decision on the NWPs, and will prepare a statement of findings outlining his views regarding each NWP and discussing how substantive comments were considered. The Chief of Engineers will also determine the need to hold a public hearing for the proposed NWPs.

(4) *Effective dates.* The Chief of Engineers will advise the public of the effective date of any issuance, modification, or revocation of an NWP.

(c) *Division Engineer.*

(1) A division engineer may use his discretionary authority to modify, suspend, or revoke NWP authorizations for any specific geographic area, class of activities, or class of waters within his division, including on a statewide basis, by issuing a public notice or notifying the individuals involved. The notice will state his concerns regarding the environment or the other relevant factors of the public interest. Before using his discretionary authority to modify or revoke such NWP authorizations, division engineers will:

(i) Give an opportunity for interested parties to express their views on the proposed action (the DE will publish and circulate a notice to the known interested public to solicit comments and provide the opportunity to request a public hearing);

(ii) Consider fully the views of affected parties;

(iii) Prepare supplemental documentation for any modifications or revocations that may result through assertion of discretionary authority. Such documentation will include comments received on the district public notices and a statement of findings showing how substantive comments were considered;

(iv) Provide, if appropriate, a grandfathering period as specified in § 330.6(b) for those who have commenced work or are under contract to commence in reliance on the NWP authorization; and

(v) Notify affected parties of the modification, suspension, or revocation, including the effective date (the DE will publish and circulate a notice to the known interested public and to anyone who commented on the proposed action).

(2) The modification, suspension, or revocation of authorizations under an NWP by the division engineer will become effective by issuance of public notice or a notification to the individuals involved.

(3) A copy of all regional conditions imposed by division engineers on activities authorized by NWPs will be forwarded to the Office of the Chief of Engineers, ATTN: CECW-OR.

(d) *District Engineer.*

(1) When deciding whether to exercise his discretionary authority to modify, suspend, or revoke a case specific activity's authorization under an NWP,

the DE should consider to the extent relevant and appropriate: Changes in circumstances relating to the authorized activity since the NWP itself was issued or since the DE confirmed authorization under the NWP by written verification; the continuing need for, or adequacy of, the specific conditions of the authorization; any significant objections to the authorization not previously considered; progress inspections of individual activities occurring under an NWP; cumulative adverse environmental effects resulting from activities occurring under the NWP; the extent of the permittee's compliance with the terms and conditions of the NWPs; revisions to applicable statutory or regulatory authorities; and, the extent to which asserting discretionary authority would adversely affect plans, investments, and actions the permittee has made or taken in reliance on the permit; and, other concerns for the environment, including the aquatic environment under the section 404(b)(1) Guidelines, and other relevant factors of the public interest.

(2) *Procedures.*

(i) When considering whether to modify or revoke a specific authorization under an NWP, whenever practicable, the DE will initially hold informal consultations with the permittee to determine whether special conditions to modify the authorization would be mutually agreeable or to allow the permittee to furnish information which satisfies the DE's concerns. If a mutual agreement is reached, the DE will give the permittee written verification of the authorization, including the special conditions. If the permittee furnishes information which satisfies the DE's concerns, the permittee may proceed. If appropriate, the DE may suspend the NWP authorization while holding informal consultations with the permittee.

(ii) If the DE's concerns remain after the informal consultation, the DE may suspend a specific authorization under an NWP by notifying the permittee in writing by the most expeditious means available that the authorization has been suspended, stating the reasons for the suspension, and ordering the permittee to stop any activities being done in reliance upon the authorization under the NWP. The permittee will be advised that a decision will be made either to reinstate or revoke the authorization under the NWP; or, if appropriate, that the authorization under the NWP may be modified by mutual agreement. The permittee will also be advised that within 10 days of receipt of the notice of suspension, he may request a meeting with the DE, or his designated representative, to present information in this matter. After completion of the meeting (or within a reasonable period of time after suspending the authorization if no meeting is requested), the DE will take action to reinstate, modify, or revoke the authorization.

(iii) Following completion of the suspension procedures, if the DE determines that sufficient

concerns for the environment, including the aquatic environment under the section 404(b)(1) Guidelines, or other relevant factors of the public interest so require, he will revoke authorization under the NWP. The DE will provide the permittee a written final decision and instruct him on the procedures to seek authorization under a regional general permit or an individual permit.

(3) The DE need not issue a public notice when asserting discretionary authority over a specific activity. The modification, suspension, or revocation will become effective by notification to the prospective permittee.

§ 330.6   Authorization by nationwide permit.

(a) *Nationwide permit verification.*

(1) Nationwide permittees may, and in some cases must, request from a DE confirmation that an activity complies with the terms and conditions of an NWP. DEs should respond as promptly as practicable to such requests.

(2) If the DE decides that an activity does not comply with the terms or conditions of an NWP, he will notify the person desiring to do the work and instruct him on the procedures to seek authorization under a regional general permit or individual permit.

(3) If the DE decides that an activity does comply with the terms and conditions of an NWP, he will notify the nationwide permittee.

(i) The DE may add conditions on a case-by-case basis to clarify compliance with the terms and conditions of an NWP or to ensure that the activity will have only minimal individual and cumulative adverse effects on the environment, and will not be contrary to the public interest.

(ii) The DE's response will state that the verification is valid for a specific period of time (generally but no more than two years) unless the NWP authorization is modified, suspended, or revoked. The response should also include a statement that the verification will remain valid for the specified period of time, if during that time period, the NWP authorization is reissued without modification or the activity complies with any subsequent modification of the NWP authorization. Furthermore, the response should include a statement that the provisions of § 330.6(b) will apply, if during that period of time, the NWP authorization expires, or is suspended or revoked, or is modified, such that the activity would no longer comply with the terms and conditions of an NWP. Finally, the response should include any known expiration date that would occur during the specified period of time. A period of time less than two years may be used if deemed appropriate.

(iii) For activities where a state has denied 401 water quality certification and/or did not agree with the Corps consistency determination for an NWP the DE's response will state that the proposed activity meets the terms and conditions for authorization under the NWP with the exception of a state 401 water quality certification and/or CZM consistency concurrence. The response will also indicate the activity is denied without prejudice and cannot be authorized until the requirements of §§ 330.4(c)(3), 330.4(c)(6), 330.4(d)(3), and 330.4(d)(6) are satisfied. The response will also indicate that work may only proceed subject to the terms and conditions of the state 401 water quality certification and/or CZM concurrence.

(iv) Once the DE has provided such verification, he must use the procedures of 33 CFR 330.5 in order to modify, suspend, or revoke the authorization.

(b) *Expiration of nationwide permits.* The Chief of Engineers will periodically review NWPs and their conditions and will decide to either modify, reissue, or revoke the permits. If an NWP is not modified or reissued within five years of its effective date, it automatically expires and becomes null and void. Activities which have commenced (i.e, are under construction) or are under contract to commence in reliance upon an NWP will remain authorized provided the activity is completed within twelve months of the date of an NWP's expiration, modification, or revocation, unless discretionary authority has been exercised on a case-by-case basis to modify, suspend, or revoke the authorization in accordance with 33 CFR 330.4(e) and 33 CFR 330.5 (c) or (d). Activities completed under the authorization of an NWP which was in effect at the time the activity was completed continue to be authorized by that NWP.

(c) *Multiple use of nationwide permits.* Two or more different NWPs can be combined to authorize a "single and complete project" as defined at 33 CFR 330.2(i). However, the same NWP cannot be used more than once for a single and complete project.

(d) *Combining nationwide permits with individual permits.* Subject to the following qualifications, portions of a larger project may proceed under the authority of the NWPs while the DE evaluates an individual permit application for other portions of the same project, but only if the portions of the project qualifying for NWP authorization would have independent utility and are able to function or meet their purpose independent of the total project. When the functioning or usefulness of a portion of the total project qualifying for an NWP is dependent on the remainder of the project, such that its construction and use would not be fully justified even if the Corps were to deny the individual permit, the NWP does not apply and all portions of the project must be evaluated as part of the individual permit process.

(1) When a portion of a larger project is authorized to proceed under an NWP, it is with the understanding that its construction will in no way prejudice the decision on the individual permit for the rest of the project. Furthermore, the individual permit documentation must include an analysis of the impacts of the entire project, including related activities authorized by NWP.

(2) NWPs do not apply, even if a portion of the project is not dependent on the rest of the project, when any portion of the project is subject to an enforcement action by the Corps or EPA.

(e) *After-the-fact authorizations.* These authorizations often play an important part in the resolution of violations. In appropriate cases where the activity complies with the terms and conditions of an NWP, the DE can elect to use the NWP for resolution of an after-the-fact permit situation following a consideration of whether the violation being resolved was knowing or intentional and other indications of the need for a penalty. For example, where an unauthorized fill meets the terms and conditions of NWP 13, the DE can consider the appropriateness of allowing the residual fill to remain, in situations where said fill would normally have been permitted under NWP 13. A knowing, intentional, willful violation should be the subject of an enforcement action leading to a penalty, rather than an after-the-fact authorization. Use of after-the-fact NWP authorization must be consistent with the terms of the Army/EPA Memorandum of Agreement on Enforcement. Copies are available from each district engineer.

APPENDIX A TO PART 330-NATIONWIDE PERMITS AND CONDITIONS

A. INDEX OF THE NATIONWIDE PERMITS AND CONDITIONS

Nationwide Permits
1. Aids to Navigation
2. Structures in Artificial Canals
3. Maintenance
4. Fish and Wildlife Harvesting, Enhancement, and Attraction Devices and Activities
5. Scientific Measurement Devices
6. Survey Activities
7. Outfall Structures
8. Oil and Gas Structures
9. Structures in Fleeting and Anchorage Areas
10. Mooring Buoys
11. Temporary Recreational Structures
12. Utility Line Backfill and Bedding
13. Bank Stabilization
14. Road Crossing
15. U.S. Coast Guard Approved Bridges
16. Return Water From Upland Contained Disposal Areas
17. Hydropower Projects
18. Minor Discharges
19. 25 Cubic Yard Dredging
20. Oil Spill Cleanup

21. Surface Mining Activities
22. Removal of Vessels
23. Approved Categorical Exclusions
24. State Administered Section 404 Programs
25. Structural Discharge
26. Headwaters and Isolated Waters Discharges
27. Wetland Restoration Activities
28. Modifications of Existing Marinas
29. Reserved
30. Reserved
31. Reserved
32. Completed Enforcement Actions
33. Temporary Construction and Access
34. Cranberry Production Activities
35. Maintenance Dredging of Existing Basins
36. Boat Ramps
37. Emergency Watershed Protection
38. Cleanup of Hazardous and Toxic Waste
39. Reserved
40. Farm Buildings

Nationwide Permit Conditions
General Conditions

1. Navigation
2. Proper Maintenance
3. Erosion and Siltation Controls
4. Aquatic Life Movements
5. Equipment
6. Regional and Case-By-Case Conditions
7. Wild and Scenic Rivers
8. Tribal Rights
9. Water Quality Certification
10. Coastal Zone Management
11. Endangered Species
12. Historic Properties
13. Notification

Section 404 Only Conditions

1. Water Supply Intakes
2. Shellfish Production
3. Suitable Material
4. Mitigation
5. Spawning Areas
6. Obstruction of High Flows
7. Adverse Impacts From Impoundments
8. Waterfowl Breeding Areas
9. Removal of Temporary Fills

B. NATIONWIDE PERMITS

1. *Aids to Navigation.* The placement of aids to navigation and regulatory markers which are approved by and installed in accordance with the requirements of the U.S. Coast Guard. (See 33 CFR part 66, chapter I, subchapter C). (section 10)

2. *Structures in Artificial Canals.* Structures constructed in artificial canals within principally residential developments where the connection of the canal to a navigable water of the United States has been previously authorized (see 33 CFR 322.5(g)). (section 10)

3. *Maintenance.* The repair, rehabilitation, or replacement of any previously authorized, currently serviceable, structure or fill, or of any currently serviceable structure or fill authorized by 33 CFR 330.3, provided that the structure or fill is not to be put to uses differing from those uses specified or contemplated for it in the original permit or the most recently authorized modification. Minor deviations in the structure's configuration or filled area including those due to changes in materials, construction techniques, or current construction codes or safety standards which are necessary to make repair, rehabilitation, or replacement are permitted, provided the environmental impacts resulting from such repair, rehabilitation, or replacement are minimal. Currently serviceable means useable as is or with some maintenance, but not so degraded as to essentially require reconstruction. This nationwide permit authorizes the repair, rehabilitation, or replacement of those structures destroyed by storms, floods, fire or other discrete events, provided the repair, rehabilitation, or replacement is commenced or under contract to commence within two years of the date of their destruction or damage. In cases of catastrophic events, such as hurricanes or tornadoes, this two-year limit may be waived by the District Engineer, provided the permittee can demonstrate funding, contract, or other similar delays. Maintenance dredging and beach restoration are not authorized by this nationwide permit. (sections 10 and 404)

4. *Fish and Wildlife Harvesting, Enhancement, and Attraction Devices and Activities.* Fish and wildlife harvesting devices and activities such as pound nets, crab traps, crab dredging, eel pots, lobster traps, duck blinds, clam and oyster digging; and small fish attraction devices such as open water fish concentrators (sea kites, etc). This nationwide permit authorizes shellfish seeding provided this activity does not occur in wetlands or vegetated shallows. This nationwide permit does not authorize artificial reefs or impoundments and semi-impoundments of waters of the United States for the culture or holding of motile species such as lobster. (sections 10 and 404)

5. *Scientific Measurement Devices.* Staff gages, tide gages, water recording devices, water quality testing and improvement devices and similar structures. Small weirs and flumes constructed primarily to record water quantity and velocity are also authorized provided the discharge is limited to 25 cubic yards and further for discharges of 10 to 25 cubic yards provided the permittee notifies the district engineer in accordance with "Notification" general condition. (sections 10 and 404)

6. *Survey Activities.* Survey activities including core sampling, seismic exploratory operations, and plugging of seismic shot holes and other exploratory-type bore holes. Drilling and the discharge of excavated material from test wells for oil and gas exploration is not authorized by this nationwide permit; the plugging of such wells is authorized. Fill placed for roads, pads and other similar activities is not authorized by this nationwide permit. The discharge of drilling muds and cuttings may require a permit under section 402 of the Clean Water Act. (sections 10 and 404)

7. *Outfall Structures.* Activities related to construction of outfall structures and associated intake structures where the effluent from the outfall is authorized, conditionally authorized, or specifically exempted, or are otherwise in compliance with regulations issued under the National Pollutant Discharge Elimination System program (section 402 of the Clean Water Act), provided that the nationwide permittee notifies the district engineer in accordance with the "Notification" general condition. (Also see 33 CFR 330.1(e)). Intake structures per se are not included-only those directly associated with an outfall structure. (sections 10 and 404)

8. *Oil and Gas Structures.* Structures for the exploration, production, and transportation of oil, gas, and minerals on the outer continental shelf within areas leased for such purposes by the Department of the Interior, Minerals Management Service. Such structures shall not be placed within the limits of any designated shipping safety fairway or traffic separation scheme, except temporary anchors that comply with the fairway regulations in 33 CFR 322.5(l). (Where such limits have not been designated, or where changes are anticipated, district engineers will consider asserting discretionary authority in accordance with 33 CFR 330.4(e) and will also review such proposals to ensure they comply with the provisions of the fairway regulations in 33 CFR 322.5(l)). Such structures will not be placed in established danger zones or restricted areas as designated in 33 CFR part 334: nor will such structures be permitted in EPA or Corps designated dredged material disposal areas. (section 10)

9. *Structures in Fleeting and Anchorage Areas.* Structures, buoys, floats, and other devices placed within anchorage or fleeting areas to facilitate moorage of vessels where such areas have been established for that purpose by the U.S. Coast Guard. (section 10)

10. *Mooring Buoys.* Non-commercial, single-boat, mooring buoys. (section 10)

11. *Temporary Recreational Structures.* Temporary buoys, markers, small floating docks, and similar structures placed for recreational use during specific events such as water skiing competitions and boat races or seasonal use provided that such structures are removed within 30 days after use has been discontinued. At Corps of Engineers reservoirs, the reservoir manager must approve each buoy or marker individually. (section 10)

12. *Utility Line Backfill and Bedding.* Discharges of material for backfill or bedding for utility lines, including outfall and intake structures, provided there is no change in preconstruction contours. A "utility line" is defined as any pipe or pipeline for the transportation of any gaseous, liquid, liquefiable, or slurry substance, for any purpose, and any cable, line, or wire for the transmission for any purpose of electrical energy, telephone and telegraph messages, and radio and television communication. The term "utility line" does not include activities which drain a water of the United States, such as drainage tile, however, it does apply to pipes conveying drainage from another area. Material resulting from trench excavation may be temporarily sidecast (up to three months) into waters of the United States provided that the material is not placed in such a manner that it is dispersed by currents or other forces. The DE may extend the period of temporary side-casting up to 180 days, where appropriate. The area of waters of the United States that is disturbed must be limited to the minimum necessary to construct the utility line. In wetlands, the top 6" to 12" of the trench should generally be backfilled with topsoil from the trench. Excess material must be removed to upland areas immediately upon completion of construction. Any exposed slopes and streambanks must be stabilized immediately upon completion of the utility line. The utility line itself will require a Section 10 permit if in navigable waters of the United States. (See 33 CFR part 322). (section 404)

13. *Bank Stabilization.* Bank stabilization activities necessary for erosion prevention provided:

a. No material is placed in excess of the minimum needed for erosion protection;

b. The bank stabilization activity is less than 500 feet in length;

c. The activity will not exceed an average of one cubic yard per running foot placed along the bank below the plane of the ordinary high water mark or the high tide line;

d. No material is placed in any special aquatic site, including wetlands;

e. No material is of the type or is placed in any location or in any manner so as to impair surface water flow into or out of any wetland area;

f. No material is placed in a manner that will be eroded by normal or expected high flows (properly anchored trees and treetops may be used in low energy areas); and,

g. The activity is part of a single and complete project.

Bank stabilization activities in excess of 500 feet in length or greater than an average of one cubic yard per running foot may be authorized if the permittee notifies the district engineer in accordance with the "Notification" general condition and the district engineer determines the activity complies with the other terms and conditions of the nationwide permit and the adverse environmental impacts are minimal both individually and cumulatively. (sections 10 and 404)

14. *Road Crossing.* Fills for roads crossing waters of the United States (including wetlands and other special aquatic sites) provided:

a. The width of the fill is limited to the minimum necessary for the actual crossing;

b. The fill placed in waters of the United States is limited to a filled area of no more than 1/3 acre. Furthermore, no more than a total of 200 linear feet of the fill for the roadway can occur in special aquatic sites, including wetlands;

c. The crossing is culverted, bridged or otherwise designed to prevent the restriction of, and to withstand, expected high flows and tidal flows, and to prevent the restriction of low flows and the movement of aquatic organisms;

d. The crossing, including all attendant features, both temporary and permanent, is part of a single and complete project for crossing of a water of the United States; and,

e. For fills in special aquatic sites, including wetlands, the permittee notifies the district engineer in accordance with the "Notification" general condition. The notification must also include a delineation of affected special aquatic sites, including wetlands.

Some road fills may be eligible for an exemption from the need for a Section 404 permit altogether (see 33 CFR 323.4). Also, where local circumstances indicate the need, district engineers will define the term "expected high flows" for the purpose of establishing applicability of this nationwide permit. (sections 10 and 404)

15. *U.S. Coast Guard Approved Bridges.* Discharges of dredged or fill material incidental to the construction of bridges across navigable waters of the United States, including cofferdams, abutments, foundation seals, piers, and temporary construction and access fills provided such discharges have been authorized by the U.S. Coast Guard as part of the bridge permit. Causeways and approach fills are not included in this nationwide permit and will require an individual or regional section 404 permit. (section 404)

16. *Return Water From Upland Contained Disposal Areas.* Return water from an upland, contained dredged material disposal area. The dredging itself requires a section 10 permit if located in navigable waters of the United States. The return water from a contained disposal area is administratively defined as a discharge of dredged material by 33 CFR 323.2(d) even though the disposal itself occurs on the upland and thus does not require a section 404 permit. This nationwide permit satisfies the technical requirement for a section 404 permit for the return water where the quality of the return water is controlled by the state through the section 401 certification procedures. (section 404)

17. *Hydropower Projects.* Discharges of dredged or fill material associated with (a) small hydropower projects at existing reservoirs where the project, which includes the fill, is licensed by the Federal Energy Regulatory Commission (FERC) under the Federal Power Act of 1920, as amended; and has a total generating capacity of not more than 5000 KW; and the permittee notifies the district engineer in accordance with the "Notifica-

tion" general condition; or (b) hydropower projects for which the FERC has granted an exemption from licensing pursuant to section 408 of the Energy Security Act of 1980 (16 U.S.C. 2705 and 2708) and section 30 of the Federal Power Act, as amended; provided the permittee notifies the district engineer in accordance with the "Notification" general condition. (section 404)

18. *Minor Discharges.* Minor discharges of dredged or fill material into all waters of the United States provided:

a. The discharge does not exceed 25 cubic yards;

b. The discharge will not cause the loss of more than 1/10 acre of a special aquatic site, including wetlands. For the purposes of this nationwide permit, the acreage limitation includes the filled area plus special aquatic sites that are adversely affected by flooding and special aquatic sites that are drained so that they would no longer be a water of the United States as a result of the project;

c. If the discharge exceeds 10 cubic yards or the discharge is in a special aquatic site, including wetlands, the permittee notifies the district engineer in accordance with the "Notification" general condition. For discharges in special aquatic sites, including wetlands, the notification must also include a delineation of affected special aquatic sites, including wetlands. (Also see 33 CFR 330.1(e)); and

d. The discharge, including all attendant features, both temporary and permanent, is part of a single and complete project and is not placed for the purpose of stream diversion. (sections 10 and 404)

19. *Minor Dredging.* Dredging of no more than 25 cubic yards below the plane of the ordinary high water mark or the mean high water mark from navigable waters of the United States as part of a single and complete project. This nationwide permit does not authorize the dredging or degradation through siltation of coral reefs, submerged aquatic vegetation, anadromous fish spawning areas, or wetlands or, the connection of canals or other artificial waterways to navigable waters of the United States (see 33 CFR 322.5(g)). (section 10)

20. *Oil Spill Cleanup.* Activities required for the containment and cleanup of oil and hazardous substances which are subject to the National Oil and Hazardous Substances Pollution Contingency Plan, (40 CFR part 300), provided that the work is done in accordance with the Spill Control and Countermeasure Plan required by 40 CFR 112.3 and any existing State contingency plan and provided that the Regional Response Team (if one exists in the area) concurs with the proposed containment and cleanup action. (sections 10 and 404)

21. *Surface Coal Mining Activities.* Activities associated with surface coal mining activities provided they are authorized by the Department of the Interior, Office of Surface Mining, or by states with approved programs under Title V of the Surface Mining Control and Reclamation Act of 1977 and provided the permittee notifies the district engineer in accordance with the "Notification" general condition. For discharges in spe-

cial aquatic sites, including wetlands, the notification must also include a delineation of affected special aquatic sites, including wetlands. (Also see 33 CFR 330.1(e)). (sections 10 and 404)

22. *Removal of Vessels.* Temporary structures or minor discharges of dredged or fill material required for the removal of wrecked, abandoned, or disabled vessels, or the removal of man-made obstructions to navigation. This nationwide permit does not authorize the removal of vessels listed or determined eligible for listing on the National Register of Historic Places unless the district engineer is notified and indicates that there is compliance with the "Historic Properties" general condition. This nationwide permit does not authorize maintenance dredging, shoal removal, or river bank snagging. Vessel disposal in waters of the United States may need a permit from EPA (see 40 CFR 229.3). (sections 10 and 404)

23. *Approved Categorical Exclusions.* Activities undertaken, assisted, authorized, regulated, funded, or financed, in whole or in part, by another Federal agency or department where that agency or department has determined, pursuant to the Council on Environmental Quality Regulation for Implementing the Procedural Provisions of the National Environmental Policy Act (40 CFR part 1500 *et seq.*), that the activity, work, or discharge is categorically excluded from environmental documentation because it is included within a category of actions which neither individually nor cumulatively have a significant effect on the human environment, and the Office of the Chief of Engineers (ATTN: CECW-OR) has been furnished notice of the agency's or department's application for the categorical exclusion and concurs with that determination. Prior to approval for purposes of this nationwide permit of any agency's categorical exclusions, the Chief of Engineers will solicit public comment. In addressing these comments, the Chief of Engineers may require certain conditions for authorization of an agency's categorical exclusions under this nationwide permit. (sections 10 and 404)

24. *State Administered Section 404 Program.* Any activity permitted by a state administering its own section 404 permit program pursuant to 33 U.S.C. 1344(g)-(l) is permitted pursuant to section 10 of the Rivers and Harbors Act of 1899. Those activities which do not involve a section 404 state permit are not included in this nationwide permit, but certain structures will be exempted by section 154 of Public Law 94-587, 90 Stat. 2917 (33 U.S.C. 591) (see 33 CFR 322.3(a)(2)). (section 10)

25. *Structural Discharge.* Discharges of material such as concrete, sand, rock, etc. into tightly sealed forms or cells where the material will be used as a structural member for standard pile supported structures, such as piers and docks; and for linear projects, such as bridges, transmission line footings, and walkways. The NWP does not authorize filled structural members that would support buildings, homes, parking areas, storage areas and other such structures. Housepads or other building pads are also not in-

cluded in this nationwide permit. The structure itself may require a section 10 permit if located in navigable waters of the United States. (section 404)

26. *Headwaters and Isolated Waters Discharges.* Discharges of dredged or fill material into headwaters and isolated waters provided:

a. The discharge does not cause the loss of more than 10 acres of waters of the United States;

b. The permittee notifies the district engineer if the discharge would cause the loss of waters of the United States greater than one acre in accordance with the "Notification" general condition. For discharges in special aquatic sites, including wetlands, the notification must also include a delineation of affected special aquatic sites, including wetlands. (Also see 33 CFR 330.1(e)); and

c. The discharge, including all attendant features, both temporary and permanent, is part of a single and complete project.

For the purposes of this nationwide permit, the acreage of loss of waters of the United States includes the filled area plus waters of the United States that are adversely affected by flooding, excavation or drainage as a result of the project. The ten-acre and one-acre limits of NWP 26 are absolute, and cannot be increased by any mitigation plan offered by the applicant or required by the DE.

Subdivisions: For any real estate subdivision created or subdivided after October 5, 1984, a notification pursuant to subsection b. of this nationwide permit is required for any discharge which would cause the aggregate total loss of waters of the United States for the entire subdivision to exceed one (1) acre. Any discharge in any real estate subdivision which would cause the aggregate total loss of waters of the United States in the subdivision to exceed ten (10) acres is not authorized by this nationwide permit; unless the DE exempts a particular subdivision or parcel by making a written determination that: (1) The individual and cumulative adverse environmental effects would be minimal and the property owner had, after October 5, 1984, but prior to January 21, 1992, committed substantial resources in reliance on NWP 26 with regard to a subdivision, in circumstances where it would be inequitable to frustrate his investment-backed expectations, or (2) that the individual and cumulative adverse environmental effects would be minimal, high quality wetlands would not be adversely affected, and there would be an overall benefit to the aquatic environment. Once the exemption is established for a subdivision, subsequent lot development by individual property owners may proceed using NWP 26. For purposes of NWP 26, the term "real estate subdivision" shall be interpreted to include circumstances where a landowner or developer divides a tract of land into smaller parcels for the purpose of selling, conveying, transferring, leasing, or developing said parcels. This would include the entire area of a residential, commercial or other real estate subdivision, including all parcels and parts thereof. (section 404)

27. *Wetland and Riparian Restoration and Creation Activities.* Activities in waters of the United States associated with the restoration of altered and degraded non-tidal wetlands and creation of wetlands on private lands in accordance with the terms and conditions of a binding wetland restoration or creation agreement between the landowner and the U.S. Fish and Wildlife Service (USFWS) or the Soil Conservation Service (SCS); or activities associated with the restoration of altered and degraded non-tidal wetlands, riparian areas and creation of wetlands and riparian areas on U.S. Forest Service and Bureau of Land Management lands, Federal surplus lands (e.g., military lands proposed for disposal), Farmers Home Administration inventory properties, and Resolution Trust Corporation inventory properties that are under Federal control prior to being transferred to the private sector. Such activities include, but are not limited to: Installation and maintenance of small water control structures, dikes, and berms; backfilling of existing drainage ditches; removal of existing drainage structures; construction of small nesting islands; and other related activities. This nationwide permit applies to restoration projects that serve the purpose of restoring "natural" wetland hydrology, vegetation, and function to altered and degraded non-tidal wetlands and "natural" functions of riparian areas. For agreement restoration and creation projects only, this nationwide permit also authorizes any future discharge of dredged or fill material associated with the reversion of the area to its prior condition and use (i.e., prior to restoration under the agreement) within five years after expiration of the limited term wetland restoration or creation agreement, even if the discharge occurs after this nationwide permit expires. The prior condition will be documented in the original agreement, and the determination of return to prior conditions will be made by the Federal agency executing the agreement. Once an area is reverted back to its prior physical condition, it will be subject to whatever the Corps regulatory requirements will be at that future date. This nationwide permit does not authorize the conversion of natural wetlands to another aquatic use, such as creation of waterfowl impoundments where a forested wetland previously existed. (sections 10 and 404)

28. *Modifications of Existing Marinas.* Reconfigurations of existing docking facilities within an authorized marina area. No dredging, additional slips or dock spaces, or expansion of any kind within waters of the United States are authorized by this nationwide permit. (section 10)

29. Reserved

30. Reserved

31. Reserved

32. *Completed Enforcement Actions.* Any structure, work or discharge of dredged or fill material undertaken in accordance with, or remaining in place in compliance with, the terms of a final Federal court decision, consent decree, or settlement agreement in an enforcement action brought by the United States under section 404 of the Clean Water Act and/or section 10 of the Rivers and Harbors Act of 1899. (sections 10 and 404)

33. *Temporary Construction, Access and Dewatering.* Temporary structures and discharges, including cofferdams, necessary for construction activities or access fills or dewatering of construction sites; provided the associated permanent activity was previously authorized by the Corps of Engineers or the U.S. Coast Guard, or for bridge construction activities not subject to Federal regulation. Appropriate measures must be taken to maintain near normal downstream flows and to minimize flooding. Fill must be of materials and placed in a manner that will not be eroded by expected high flows. Temporary fill must be entirely removed to upland areas following completion of the construction activity and the affected areas restored to the pre-project conditions. Cofferdams cannot be used to dewater wetlands or other aquatic areas so as to change their use. Structures left in place after cofferdams are removed require a section 10 permit if located in navigable waters of the United States. (See 33 CFR part 322). The permittee must notify the district engineer in accordance with the "Notification" general condition. The notification must also include a restoration plan of reasonable measures to avoid and minimize impacts to aquatic resources. The district engineer will add special conditions, where necessary, to ensure that adverse environmental impacts are minimal. Such conditions may include: limiting the temporary work to the minimum necessary; requiring seasonal restrictions; modifying the restoration plan; and requiring alternative construction methods (e.g. construction mats in wetlands where practicable). This nationwide permit does not authorize temporary structures or fill associated with mining activities or the construction of marina basins which have not been authorized by the Corps. (sections 10 and 404)

34. *Cranberry Production Activities:* Discharges of dredged or fill material for dikes, berms, pumps, water control structures or leveling of cranberry beds associated with expansion, enhancement, or modification activities at existing cranberry production operations provided:

a. The cumulative total acreage of disturbance per cranberry production operation, including but not limited to, filling, flooding, ditching, or clearing, does not exceed 10 acres of waters of the United States, including wetlands;

b. The permittee notifies the District Engineer in accordance with the notification procedures; and

c. The activity does not result in a net loss of wetland acreage.

This nationwide permit does not authorize any discharge of dredged or fill material related to other cranberry production activities such as warehouses, processing facilities, or parking areas. For the purposes of this nationwide permit, the cumulative total of 10 acres will be measured over the period that this nationwide permit is valid. (section 404)

35. *Maintenance Dredging of Existing Basins.* Excavation and removal of accumulated sediment for maintenance of existing marina basins, canals, and boat slips to previously authorized depths or controlling depths for ingress/egress' whichever is less provided the dredged material is disposed of at an upland site and proper siltation controls are used. (section 10)

36. *Boat Ramps.* Activities required for the construction of boat ramps provided:

a. The discharge into waters of the United States does not exceed 50 cubic yards of concrete, rock, crushed stone or gravel into forms, or placement of pre-cast concrete planks or slabs. (Unsuitable material that causes unacceptable chemical pollution or is structurally unstable is not authorized);

b. The boat ramp does not exceed 20 feet in width;

c. The base material is crushed stone, gravel or other suitable material;

d. The excavation is limited to the area necessary for site preparation and all excavated material is removed to the upland; and

e. No material is placed in special aquatic sites, including wetlands.

Dredging to provide access to the boat ramp may be authorized by another NWP, regional general permit, or individual permit pursuant to section 10 if located in navigable waters of the United States. (sections 10 and 404)

37. *Emergency Watershed Protection and Rehabilitation.* Work done by or funded by the Soil Conservation Service qualifying as an "exigency" situation (requiring immediate action) under its Emergency Watershed Protection Program (7 CFR part 624) and work done or funded by the Forest Service under its Burned-Area Emergency Rehabilitation Handbook (FSH 509.13) provided the district engineer is notified in accordance with the notification general condition. (Also see 33 CFR 330.1(e)). (sections 10 and 404)

38. *Cleanup of Hazardous and Toxic Waste.* Specific activities required to effect the containment, stabilization or removal of hazardous or toxic waste materials that are performed, ordered, or sponsored by a government agency with established legal or regulatory authority provided the permittee notifies the district engineer in accordance with the "Notification" general condition. For discharges in special aquatic sites, including wetlands, the notification must also include a delineation of affected special aquatic sites, including wetlands. Court ordered remedial action plans or related settlements are also authorized by this nationwide permit. This nationwide permit does not authorize the establishment of new disposal sites or the expansion of existing sites used for the disposal of hazardous or toxic waste. (sections 10 and 404)

39. Reserved

40. *Farm Buildings.* Discharges of dredged or fill material into jurisdictional wetlands (but not including prairie potholes, playa lakes, or vernal pools) that were in agricultural crop production prior to December 23, 1985 (i.e., farmed wetlands) for foundations and building pads for buildings or agricultural related structures necessary for farming activities. The discharge will be limited to the minimum necessary but will in no case exceed 1 acre (see the "Minimization" section 404 only condition). (section 404)

C. NATIONWIDE PERMIT CONDITIONS

General Conditions: The following general conditions must be followed in order for any authorization by a nationwide permit to be valid:

1. *Navigation.* No activity may cause more than a minimal adverse effect on navigation.

2. *Proper maintenance.* Any structure or fill authorized shall be properly maintained, including maintenance to ensure public safety.

3. *Erosion and siltation controls.* Appropriate erosion and siltation controls must be used and maintained in effective operating condition during construction, and all exposed soil and other fills must be permanently stabilized at the earliest practicable date.

4. *Aquatic life movements.* No activity may substantially disrupt the movement of those species of aquatic life indigenous to the waterbody, including those species which normally migrate through the area, unless the activity's primary purpose is to impound water.

5. *Equipment.* Heavy equipment working in wetlands must be placed on mats or other measures must be taken to minimize soil disturbance.

6. *Regional and case-by-case conditions.* The activity must comply with any regional conditions which may have been added by the division engineer (see 33 CFR 330.4(e)) and any case specific conditions added by the Corps.

7. *Wild and Scenic Rivers.* No activity may occur in a component of the National Wild and Scenic River System; or in a river officially designated by Congress as a "study river" for possible inclusion in the system, while the river is in an official study status. Information on Wild and Scenic Rivers may be obtained from the National Park Service and the U.S. Forest Service.

8. *Tribal rights.* No activity or its operation may impair reserved tribal rights, including, but not limited to, reserved water rights and treaty fishing and hunting rights.

9. *Water quality certification.* In certain states, an individual state water quality certification must be obtained or waived (see 33 CFR 330.4(c)).

10. *Coastal zone management.* In certain states, an individual state coastal zone management consistency concurrence must be obtained or waived. (see 33 CFR 330.4(d)).

11. *Endangered Species.* No activity is authorized under any NWP which is likely to jeopardize the continued existence of a threatened or endangered species or a species proposed for such designation, as identified under the Federal Endangered Species Act, or which is likely to destroy or adversely modify the crit-

ical habitat of such species. Non-federal permittees shall notify the district engineer if any listed species or critical habitat might be affected or is in the vicinity of the project and shall not begin work on the activity until notified by the district engineer that the requirements of the Endangered Species Act have been satisfied and that the activity is authorized. Information on the location of threatened and endangered species and their critical habitat can be obtained from the U.S. Fish and Wildlife Service and National Marine Fisheries Service. (see 33 CFR 330.4(f))

12. *Historic properties.* No activity which may affect Historic properties listed, or eligible for listing, in the National Register of Historic Places is authorized, until the DE has complied with the provisions of 33 CFR 325, appendix C. The prospective permittee must notify the district engineer if the authorized activity may affect any historic properties listed, determined to be eligible, or which the prospective permittee has reason to believe may be eligible for listing on the National Register of Historic Places, and shall not begin the activity until notified by the District Engineer that the requirements of the National Historic Preservation Act have been satisfied and that the activity is authorized. Information on the location and existence of historic resources can be obtained from the State Historic Preservation Office and the National Register of Historic Places (see 33 CFR 330.4(g)).

13. *Notification.*

(a) Where required by the terms of the NWP, the prospective permittee must notify the District Engineer as early as possible and shall not begin the activity:

(1) Until notified by the District Engineer that the activity may proceed under the NWP with any special conditions imposed by the district or division engineer; or

(2) If notified by the District or Division engineer that an individual permit is required; or

(3) Unless 30 days have passed from the District Engineer's receipt of the notification and the prospective permittee has not received notice from the District or Division Engineer. Subsequently, the permittee's right to proceed under the NWP may be modified, suspended, or revoked only in accordance with the procedure set forth in 33 CFR 330.5(d)(2).

(b) The notification must be in writing and include the following information and any required fees:

(1) Name, address and telephone number of the prospective permittee;

(2) Location of the proposed project;

(3) Brief description of the proposed project; the project's purpose; direct and indirect adverse environmental effects the project would cause; any other NWP(s), regional general permit(s) or individual permit(s) used or intended to be used to authorize any part of the proposed project or any related activity;

(4) Where required by the terms of the NWP, a delineation of affected special aquatic sites, including wetlands; and

(5) A statement that the prospective permittee has contacted:

(i) The USFWS/NMFS regarding the presence of any Federally listed (or proposed for listing) endangered or threatened species or critical habitat in the permit area that may be affected by the proposed project; and any available information provided by those agencies. (The prospective permittee may contact Corps District Offices for USFWS/NMFS agency contacts and lists of critical habitat.)

(ii) The SHPO regarding the presence of any historic properties in the permit area that may be affected by the proposed project; and the available information, if any, provided by that agency.

(c) The standard individual permit application form (Form ENG 4345) may be used as the notification but must clearly indicate that it is a PDN and must include all of the information required in (b) (1)-(5) of General Condition 13.

(d) In reviewing an activity under the notification procedure, the District Engineer will first determine whether the activity will result in more than minimal individual or cumulative adverse environmental effects or will be contrary to the public interest. The prospective permittee may, at his option, submit a proposed mitigation plan with the predischarge notification to expedite the process and the District Engineer will consider any optional mitigation the applicant has included in the proposal in determining whether the net adverse environmental effects of the proposed work are minimal. The District Engineer will consider any comments from Federal and State agencies concerning the proposed activity's compliance with the terms and conditions of the nationwide permits and the need for mitigation to reduce the project's adverse environmental effects to a minimal level. The district engineer will upon receipt of a notification provide immediately (e.g. facsimile transmission, overnight mail or other expeditious manner) a copy to the appropriate offices of the Fish and Wildlife Service, State natural resource or water quality agency, EPA, and, if appropriate, the National Marine Fisheries Service. With the exception of NWP 37, these agencies will then have 5 calendar days from the date the material is transmitted to telephone the District Engineer if they intend to provide substantive, site-specific comments. If so contacted by an agency, the District Engineer will wait an additional 10 calendar days before making a decision on the notification. The District Engineer will fully consider agency comments received within the specified time frame, but will provide no response to the resource agency. The District Engineer will indicate in the administrative record associated with each notification that the resource agencies' concerns were considered. Applicants are encouraged to provide the Corps multiple copies of notifications to expedite agency notification. If the District Engineer determines that the activity complies with the terms and conditions of the NWP and that the adverse effects are minimal, he will notify the permittee and include any conditions he deems necessary. If the District Engineer determines that the adverse effects of the proposed work are more than minimal, then he will notify the applicant either:

(1) That the project does not qualify for authorization under the NWP and instruct the applicant on the procedures to seek authorization under an individual permit; or (2) that the project is authorized under the nationwide permit subject to the applicant's submitting a mitigation proposal that would reduce the adverse effects to the minimal level. This mitigation proposal must be approved by the District Engineer prior to commencing work. If the prospective permittee elects to submit a mitigation plan, the DE will expeditiously review the proposed mitigation plan, but will not commence a second 30-day notification procedure. If the net adverse effects of the project (with the mitigation proposal) are determined by the District Engineer to be minimal, the District Engineer will provide a timely written response to the applicant informing him that the project can proceed under the terms and conditions of the nationwide permit.

(e) *Wetlands Delineations:* Wetland delineations must be prepared in accordance with the current method required by the Corps. The permittee may ask the Corps to delineate the special aquatic site. There may be some delay if the Corps does the delineation. Furthermore, the 30-day period will not start until the wetland delineation has been completed.

(f) *Mitigation:* Factors that the District Engineer will consider when determining the acceptability of appropriate and practicable mitigation include, but are not limited to:

(1) To be practicable the mitigation must be available and capable of being done considering costs, existing technology, and logistics in light of overall project purposes;

(2) To the extent appropriate, permittees should consider mitigation banking and other forms of mitigation including contributions to wetland trust funds, which contribute to the restoration, creation, replacement, enhancement, or preservation of wetlands.

Furthermore, examples of mitigation that may be appropriate and practicable include but are not limited to: reducing the size of the project; establishing buffer zones to protect aquatic resource values; and replacing the loss of aquatic resource values by creating, restoring, and enhancing similar functions and values. In addition, mitigation must address impacts and cannot

be used to offset the acreage of wetland losses that would occur in order to meet the acreage limits of some of the nationwide permits (e.g. 5 acres of wetlands cannot be created to change a 6 acre loss of wetlands to a 1 acre loss; however, the 5 created acres can be used to reduce the impacts of the 6 acre loss).

§ 404 Only Conditions

In addition to the General Conditions, the following conditions apply only to activities that involve the discharge of dredged or fill material and must be followed in order for authorization by the nationwide permits to be valid:

1. *Water supply intakes.* No discharge of dredged or fill material may occur in the proximity of a public water supply intake except where the discharge is for repair of the public water supply intake structures or adjacent bank stabilization.

2. *Shellfish production.* No discharge of dredged or fill material may occur in areas of concentrated shellfish production, unless the discharge is directly related to a shellfish harvesting activity authorized by nationwide permit 4.

3. *Suitable material.* No discharge of dredged or fill material may consist of unsuitable material (e.g., trash, debris, car bodies, etc.) and material discharged must be free from toxic pollutants in toxic amounts (see section 307 of the Clean Water Act).

4. *Mitigation.* Discharges of dredged or fill material into waters of the United States must be minimized or avoided to the maximum extent practicable at the project site (i.e. on-site), unless the DE has approved a compensation mitigation plan for the specific regulated activity.

5. *Spawning areas.* Discharges in spawning areas during spawning seasons must be avoided to the maximum extent practicable.

6. *Obstruction of high flows.* To the maximum extent practicable, discharges must not permanently restrict or impede the passage of normal or expected high flows or cause the relocation of the water (unless the primary purpose of the fill is to impound waters).

7. *Adverse impacts from impoundments.* If the discharge creates an impoundment of water, adverse impacts on the aquatic system caused by the accelerated passage of water and/or the restriction of its flow shall be minimized to the maximum extent practicable.

8. *Waterfowl breeding areas.* Discharges into breeding areas for migratory waterfowl must be avoided to the maximum extent practicable.

9. *Removal of temporary fills.* Any temporary fills must be removed in their entirety and the affected areas returned to their preexisting elevation.

Appendix D

U.S. Environmental Protection Agency
40 CFR 230-233

PART 230

SECTION 404(b)(1) GUIDELINES FOR SPECIFICATION
OF DISPOSAL SITES FOR DREDGED OR FILL MATERIAL

Authority: Secs. 404(b) and 501(a) of the Clean Water Act of 1977 (33 U.S.C. 1344(b) and 1361(a)).

Source: 45 FR 85344, Dec. 24, 1980, unless otherwise noted.

Subpart A—General

§ 230.1   Purpose and policy.

(a) The purpose of these Guidelines is to restore and maintain the chemical, physical, and biological integrity of waters of the United States through the control of discharges of dredged or fill material.

(b) Congress has expressed a number of policies in the Clean Water Act. These Guidelines are intended to be consistent with and to implement those policies.

(c) Fundamental to these Guidelines is the precept that dredged or fill material should not be discharged into the aquatic ecosystem, unless it can be demonstrated that such a discharge will not have an unacceptable adverse impact either individually or in combination with known and/or probable impacts of other activities affecting the ecosystems of concern.

(d) From a national perspective, the degradation or destruction of special aquatic sites, such as filling operations in wetlands, is considered to be among the most severe environmental impacts covered by these Guidelines. The guiding principle should be that degradation or destruction of special sites may represent an irreversible loss of valuable aquatic resources.

§ 230.2   Applicability.

(a) These Guidelines have been developed by the Administrator of the Environmental Protection Agency in conjunction with the Secretary of the Army acting through the Chief of Engineers under section 404(b)(1) of the Clean Water Act (33 U.S.C. 1344). The Guidelines are applicable to the specification of disposal sites for discharges of dredged or fill material into waters of the United States. Sites may be specified through:

(1) The regulatory program of the U.S. Army Corps of Engineers under sections 404(a) and (e) of the Act (see 33 CFR Parts 320, 323 and 325);

(2) The civil works program of the U.S. Army Corps of Engineers (see 33 CFR 209.145 and section 150 of Pub. L. 94-587, Water Resources Development Act of 1976);

(3) Permit programs of States approved by the Administrator of the Environmental Protection Agency in accordance with section 404(g) and (h) of the Act (see 40 CFR Parts 122, 123 and 124);

(4) Statewide dredged or fill material regulatory programs with best management practices approved under section 208(b)(4)(B) and (C) of the Act (see 40 CFR 35.1560);

(5) Federal construction projects which meet criteria specified in section 404(r) of the Act.

(b) These Guidelines will be applied in the review of proposed discharges of dredged or fill material into navigable waters which lie inside the baseline from which the territorial sea is measured, and the discharge of fill material into the territorial sea, pursuant to the procedures referred to in paragraphs (a)(1) and (2) of this section. The discharge of dredged material into the territorial sea is governed by the Marine Protection, Research, and Sanctuaries Act of 1972, Pub. L. 92-532, and regulations and criteria issued pursuant thereto (40 CFR Parts 220 through 228).

(c) Guidance on interpreting and implementing these Guidelines may be prepared jointly by EPA and the Corps at the national or regional level from time to time. No modifications to the basic application, meaning, or intent of these Guidelines will be made without rulemaking by the Administrator under the Administrative Procedure Act (5 U.S.C. 551 *et seq.*).

§ 230.3   Definitions.

For purposes of this part, the following terms shall have the meanings indicated:

(a) The term *Act* means the Clean Water Act (also known as the Federal Water Pollution Control Act or FWPCA) Pub. L. 92-500, as amended by Pub. L. 95-217, 33 U.S.C. 1251, *et seq.*

(b) The term *adjacent* means bordering, contiguous, or neighboring. Wetlands separated from other waters of the United States by man-made dikes or barriers, natural river berms, beach dunes, and the like are "adjacent wetlands."

(c) The terms *aquatic environment* and *aquatic ecosystem* mean waters of the United States, including wetlands, that serve as habitat for interrelated and interacting communities and populations of plants and animals.

(d) The term *carrier of contaminant* means dredged or fill material that contains contaminants.

(e) The term *contaminant* means a chemical or biological substance in a form that can be incorporated into, onto or be ingested by and that harms aquatic organisms, consumers of aquatic organisms, or users of the aquatic environment, and includes but is not limited to the substances on the 307(a)(1) list of toxic pollutants promulgated on January 31, 1978 (43 FR 4109).

(f)-(g) [Reserved]

(h) The term discharge point means the point within the disposal site at which the dredged or fill material is released.

(i) The term disposal site means that portion of the "waters of the United States" where specific disposal activities are permitted and consist of a bottom surface area and any overlying volume of water. In the case of wetlands on which surface water is not present, the disposal site consists of the wetland surface area.

(j) [Reserved]

(k) The term *extraction site* means the place from which the dredged or fill material proposed for discharge is to be removed.

(l) [Reserved]

(m) The term *mixing zone* means a limited volume of water serving as a zone of initial dilution in the immediate vicinity of a discharge point where receiving water quality may not meet quality standards or other requirements otherwise applicable to the receiving water. The mixing zone should be considered as a place where wastes and water mix and not as a place where effluents are treated.

(n) The term *permitting authority* means the District Engineer of the U.S. Army Corps of Engineers or such other individual as may be designated by the Secretary of the Army to issue or deny permits under section 404 of the Act; or the State Director of a permit program approved by EPA under section 404(g) and section 404(h) or his delegated representative.

(o) The term *pollutant* means dredged spoil, solid waste, incinerator residue, sewage, garbage, sewage sludge, munitions, chemical wastes, biological materials, radioactive materials not covered by the Atomic Energy Act, heat, wrecked or discarded equipment, rock, sand, cellar dirt, and industrial, municipal, and agricultural waste discharged into water. The legislative history of the Act reflects that "radioactive materials" as included within the definition of "pollutant" in section 502 of the Act means only radioactive materials which are not encompassed in the definition of source, byproduct, or special nuclear materials as defined by the Atomic Energy Act of 1954, as amended, and regulated under the Atomic Energy Act. Examples of radioactive materials not covered by the Atomic Energy Act and, therefore, included within the term "pollutant", are radium and accelerator produced isotopes. See *Train v. Colorado Public Interest Research Group, Inc.*, 426 U.S. 1 (1976).

(p) The term pollution means the man-made or man-induced alteration of the chemical, physical, biological or radiological integrity of an aquatic ecosystem.

(q) The term *practicable* means available and capable of being done after taking into consideration cost, existing technology, and logistics in light of overall project purposes.

(q-1) *Special aquatic sites* means those sites identified in Subpart E. They are geographic areas, large or small, possessing special ecological characteristics of productivity, habitat, wildlife protection, or other important and easily disrupted ecological values. These areas are generally recognized as significantly influencing or positively contributing to the general overall environmental health or vitality of the entire ecosystem of a region. (See § 230.10(a)(3))

(r) The term *territorial sea* means the belt of the sea measured from the baseline as determined in accordance with the Convention on the Territorial Sea and the Contiguous Zone and extending seaward a distance of three miles.

(s) The term *waters of the United States* means:

(1) All waters which are currently used, or were used in the past, or may be susceptible to use in interstate or foreign commerce, including all waters which are subject to the ebb and flow of the tide;

(2) All interstate waters including interstate wetlands;

(3) All other waters such as intrastate lakes, rivers, streams (including intermittent streams), mudflats, sandflats, wetlands, sloughs, prairie potholes, wet meadows, playa lakes, or natural ponds, the use, degradation or destruction of which could affect interstate or foreign commerce including any such waters:

(i) Which are or could be used by interstate or foreign travelers for recreational or other purposes; or

(ii) From which fish or shellfish are or could be taken and sold in interstate or foreign commerce; or

(iii) Which are used or could be used for industrial purposes by industries in interstate commerce;

(4) All impoundments of waters otherwise defined as waters of the United States under this definition;

(5) Tributaries of waters identified in paragraphs (s)(1) through (4) of this section;

(6) The territorial sea;

(7) Wetlands adjacent to waters (other than waters that are themselves wetlands) identified in paragraphs (s)(1) through (6) of this section; waste treatment systems, including treatment ponds or lagoons designed to meet the requirements of CWA (other than cooling ponds as defined in 40 CFR 423.11(m) which also meet the criteria of this definition) are not waters of the United States.

(t) The term wetlands means those areas that are inundated or saturated by surface or ground water at a frequency and duration sufficient to support, and that under normal circumstances do support, a prevalence of vegetation typically adapted for life in saturated soil conditions. Wetlands generally include swamps, marshes, bogs and similar areas.

§ 230.4 Organization.

The Guidelines are divided into eight subparts. Subpart A presents those provisions of general applicability, such as purpose and definitions. Subpart B establishes the four conditions which must be satisfied in order to make a finding that a proposed discharge of dredged or fill material complies with the Guidelines. Section 230.11 of Subpart B, sets forth factual determinations which are to be considered in determining whether or not a proposed discharge satisfies the Subpart B conditions of compliance. Subpart C describes the physical and chemical components of a site and provides guidance as to how proposed discharges of dredged or fill material may affect these components. Subparts D through F detail the special characteristics of particular aquatic ecosystems in terms of their values, and the possible loss of these values due to discharges of dredged or fill material. Subpart G prescribes a number of physical, chemical, and biological evaluations and testing procedures to be used in reaching the required factual determinations. Subpart H details the means to prevent or minimize adverse effects. Subpart I concerns advanced identification of disposal areas.

§ 230.5 General procedures to be followed.

In evaluating whether a particular discharge site may be specified, the permitting authority should use these Guidelines in the following sequence:

(a) In order to obtain an overview of the principal regulatory provisions of the Guidelines, review the restrictions on discharge in § 230.10(a) through (d), the measures to minimize adverse impact of Subpart H, and the required factual determinations of § 230.11.

(b) Determine if a General permit (§ 230.7) is applicable; if so, the applicant needs merely to comply with its terms, and no further action by the permitting authority is necessary. Special conditions for evaluation of proposed General permits are contained in § 230.7. If the discharge is not covered by a General permit:

(c) Examine practicable alternatives to the proposed discharge, that is, not discharging into the waters of the U.S. or discharging into an alternative aquatic site with potentially less damaging consequences (§ 230.10(a)).

(d) Delineate the candidate disposal site consistent with the criteria and evaluations of § 230.11(f).

(e) Evaluate the various physical and chemical components which characterize the non-living environment of the candidate site, the substrate and the water including its dynamic characteristics (Subpart C).

(f) Identify and evaluate any special or critical characteristics of the candidate disposal site, and surrounding areas which might be affected by use of such site, related to their living communities or human uses (Subparts D, E, and F).

(g) Review Factual Determinations in § 230.11 to determine whether the information in the project file is sufficient to provide the documentation required by § 230.11 or to perform the pre-testing evaluation described in § 230.60, or other information is necessary.

(h) Evaluate the material to be discharged to determine the possibility of chemical contamination or physical incompatibility of the material to be discharged (§ 230.60).

(i) If there is a reasonable probability of chemical contamination, conduct the appropriate tests according to the section on Evaluation and Testing (§ 230.61).

(j) Identify appropriate and practicable changes to the project plan to minimize the environmental impact of the discharge, based upon the specialized methods of minimization of impacts in Subpart H.

(k) Make and document Factual Determinations in § 230.11.

(l) Make and document Findings of Compliance (§ 230.12) by comparing Factual Determinations with the requirements for discharge of § 230.10.

This outline of the steps to follow in using the Guidelines is simplified for purposes of illustration. The actual process followed may be iterative, with the results of one step leading to a reexamination of previous steps. The permitting authority must address all of the relevant provisions of the Guidelines in reaching a Finding of Compliance in an individual case.

§ 230.6 Adaptability.

(a) The manner in which these Guidelines are used depends on the physical, biological, and chemical nature of the proposed extraction site, the material to be discharged, and the candidate disposal site, including any other important components of the ecosystem being evaluated. Documentation to demonstrate knowledge about the extraction site, materials to be extracted, and the candidate disposal site is an essential component of guideline application. These Guidelines allow evaluation and documentation for a variety of activities, ranging from those with large, complex impacts on the aquatic environment to those for which the impact is likely to be innocuous. It is unlikely that the Guidelines will apply in their entirety to any one activity, no matter how complex. It is anticipated that substantial numbers of permit applications will be for minor, routine activities that have little, if any, potential for significant degradation of the aquatic environment. It generally is not intended or expected that extensive testing, evaluation or analysis will be needed to make findings of compliance in such routine cases. Where the conditions for General permits are met, and where numerous applications for similar activities are likely, the use of General permits will eliminate repetitive evaluation and documentation for individual discharges.

(b) The Guidelines user, including the agency or agencies responsible for implementing the Guidelines, must recognize the different levels of effort that should be associated with varying degrees of impact and require or prepare commensurate documentation. The level of documentation should reflect the significance and complexity of the discharge activity.

(c) An essential part of the evaluation process involves making determinations as to the relevance of any portion(s) of the Guidelines and conducting further evaluation only as needed. However, where portions of the Guidelines review procedure are "short form" evaluations, there still must be sufficient information (including consideration of both individual and cumulative impacts) to support the decision of whether to specify the site for disposal of dredged or fill material and to support the decision to curtail or abbreviate the evaluation process. The presumption against the discharge in § 230.1 applies to this decision-making.

(d) In the case of activities covered by General permits or section 208(b)(4)(B) and (C) Best Management Practices, the analysis and documentation required by the Guidelines will be performed at the time of General permit issuance or section 208(b)(4)(B) and (C) Best Management Practices promulgation and will not be repeated when activities are conducted under a General permit or section 208(b)(4)(B) and (C) Best Management Practices control. These Guidelines do not require reporting or formal written communication at the time individual activities are initiated under a General permit or section 208(b)(4)(B) and (C) Best Management Practices. However, a particular General permit may require appropriate reporting.

§ 230.7 General permits.

(a) *Conditions for the issuance of General permits.* A General permit for a category of activities involving the discharge of dredged or fill material complies with the Guidelines if it meets the applicable restrictions on the discharge in § 230.10 and if the permitting authority determines that:

(1) The activities in such category are similar in nature and similar in their impact upon water quality and the aquatic environment;

(2) The activities in such category will have only minimal adverse effects when performed separately; and

(3) The activities in such category will have only minimal cumulative adverse effects on water quality and the aquatic environment.

(b) *Evaluation process.* To reach the determinations required in paragraph (a) of this section, the permitting authority shall set forth in writing an evaluation of the potential individual and cumulative impacts of the category of activities to be regulated under the General permit. While some of the information necessary for this evaluation can be obtained from potential permittees and others through the proposal of General permits for public review, the evaluation must be completed before any General permit is issued, and the results must be published with the final permit.

(1) This evaluation shall be based upon consideration of the prohibitions listed in § 230.10(b) and the factors listed in § 230.10(c), and shall include documented information supporting each factual determination in § 230.11 of the Guidelines (consideration of alternatives in § 230.10(a) are not directly applicable to General permits);

(2) The evaluation shall include a precise description of the activities to be permitted under the General permit, explaining why they are sufficiently similar in nature and in environmental impact to warrant regulation under a single General permit based on Subparts C through F of the Guidelines. Allowable differences between activities which will be regulated under the same General permit shall be specified. Activities otherwise similar in nature may differ in environmental impact due to their location in or near ecologically sensitive areas, areas with unique chemical or physical characteristics, areas containing concentrations of toxic substances, or areas regulated for specific human uses or by specific land or water management plans (e.g., areas regulated under an approved Coastal Zone Management Plan). If there are specific geographic areas within the purview of a proposed General permit (called a draft General permit under a State 404 program), which are more appropriately regulated by individual permit due to the considerations cited in this paragraph, they shall be clearly delineated in the evaluation and excluded from the permit. In addition, the permitting authority may require an individual permit for any proposed activity under a General permit where the nature or location of the activity makes an individual permit more appropriate.

(3) To predict cumulative effects, the evaluation shall include the number of individual discharge activities likely to be regulated under a General permit until its expiration, including repetitions of individual discharge activities at a single location.

Subpart B—Compliance With the Guidelines

§ 230.10 Restrictions on discharge.

Note: Because other laws may apply to particular discharges and because the Corps of Engineers or State 404 agency may have additional procedural and substantive requirements, a discharge complying with the requirement of these Guidelines will not automatically receive a permit.

Although all requirements in § 230.10 must be met, the compliance evaluation procedures will vary to reflect the seriousness of the potential for adverse impacts on the aquatic ecosystems posed by specific dredged or fill material discharge activities.

(a) Except as provided under section 404(b)(2), no discharge of dredged or fill material shall be permitted if there is a practicable alternative to the proposed discharge which would have less adverse impact on the aquatic ecosystem, so long as the alternative does not have other significant adverse environmental consequences.

(1) For the purpose of this requirement, practicable alternatives include, but are not limited to:

(i) Activities which do not involve a discharge of dredged or fill material into the waters of the United States or ocean waters;

(ii) Discharges of dredged or fill material at other locations in waters of the United States or ocean waters;

(2) An alternative is practicable if it is available and capable of being done after taking into consideration cost, existing technology, and logistics in light of overall project purposes. If it is otherwise a practicable alternative, an area not presently owned by the applicant which could reasonably be obtained, utilized, expanded, or managed in order to fulfill the basic purpose of the proposed activity may be considered.

(3) Where the activity associated with a discharge which is proposed for a special aquatic site (as defined in Subpart E) does not require access or proximity to or siting within the special aquatic site in question to fulfill its basic purpose (i.e., is not "water dependent"), practicable alternatives that do not involve special aquatic sites are presumed to be available, unless clearly demonstrated otherwise. In addition, where a discharge is proposed for a special aquatic site, all practicable alternatives to the proposed discharge which do not involve a discharge into a special aquatic site are presumed to have less adverse impact on the aquatic ecosystem, unless clearly demonstrated otherwise.

(4) For actions subject to NEPA, where the Corps of Engineers is the permitting agency, the analysis of alternatives required for NEPA environmental documents, including supplemental Corps NEPA documents, will in most cases provide the information for the evaluation of alternatives under these Guidelines. On occasion, these NEPA documents may address a broader range of alternatives than required to be considered under this paragraph or may not have considered the alternatives in sufficient detail to respond to the requirements of these Guidelines. In the latter case, it may be necessary to supplement these NEPA documents with this additional information.

(5) To the extent that practicable alternatives have been identified and evaluated under a Coastal Zone Management program, a section 208 program, or other planning process, such evaluation shall be considered by the permitting authority as part of the consideration of alternatives under the Guidelines. Where such evaluation is less complete than that contemplated under this subsection, it must be supplemented accordingly.

(b) No discharge of dredged or fill material shall be permitted if it:

(1) Causes or contributes, after consideration of disposal site dilution and dispersion, to violations of any applicable State water quality standard;

(2) Violates any applicable toxic effluent standard or prohibition under section 307 of the Act;

(3) Jeopardizes the continued existence of species listed as endangered or threatened under the Endangered Species Act of 1973, as amended, or results in likelihood of the destruction or adverse modification of a habitat which is determined by the Secretary of

Interior or Commerce, as appropriate, to be a critical habitat under the Endangered Species Act of 1973, as amended. If an exemption has been granted by the Endangered Species Committee, the terms of such exemption shall apply in lieu of this subparagraph;

(4) Violates any requirement imposed by the Secretary of Commerce to protect any marine sanctuary designated under Title III of the Marine Protection, Research, and Sanctuaries Act of 1972.

(c) Except as provided under section 404(b)(2), no discharge of dredged or fill material shall be permitted which will cause or contribute to significant degradation of the waters of the United States. Findings of significant degradation related to the proposed discharge shall be based upon appropriate factual determinations, evaluations, and tests required by Subparts B and G, after consideration of Subparts C through F, with special emphasis on the persistence and permanence of the effects outlined in those subparts. Under these Guidelines, effects contributing to significant degradation considered individually or collectively, include:

(1) Significantly adverse effects of the discharge of pollutants on human health or welfare, including but not limited to effects on municipal water supplies, plankton, fish, shellfish, wildlife, and special aquatic sites.

(2) Significantly adverse effects of the discharge of pollutants on life stages of aquatic life and other wildlife dependent on aquatic ecosystems, including the transfer, concentration, and spread of pollutants or their byproducts outside of the disposal site through biological, physical, and chemical processes;

(3) Significantly adverse effects of the discharge of pollutants on aquatic ecosystem diversity, productivity, and stability. Such effects may include, but are not limited to, loss of fish and wildlife habitat or loss of the capacity of a wetland to assimilate nutrients, purify water, or reduce wave energy; or

(4) Significantly adverse effects of discharge of pollutants on recreational, aesthetic, and economic values.

(d) Except as provided under section 404(b)(2), no discharge of dredged or fill material shall be permitted unless appropriate and practicable steps have been taken which will minimize potential adverse impacts of the discharge on the aquatic ecosystem. Subpart H identifies such possible steps.

§ 230.11 Factual determinations.

The permitting authority shall determine in writing the potential short-term or long-term effects of a proposed discharge of dredged or fill material on the physical, chemical, and biological components of the aquatic environment in light of Subparts C through F. Such factual determinations shall be used in § 230.12 in making findings of compliance or non-compliance with the restrictions on discharge in § 230.10. The evaluation and testing procedures described in § 230.60 and § 230.61 of Subpart G shall be used as necessary to make, and shall be described in, such determination. The determinations of effects of each proposed discharge shall include the following:

(a) *Physical substrate determinations.* Determine the nature and degree of effect that the proposed discharge will have, individually and cumulatively, on the characteristics of the substrate at the proposed disposal site. Consideration shall be given to the similarity in particle size, shape, and degree of compaction of the material proposed for discharge and the material constituting the substrate at the disposal site, and any potential changes in substrate elevation and bottom contours, including changes outside of the disposal site which may occur as a result of erosion, slumpage, or other movement of the discharged material. The duration and physical extent of substrate changes shall also be considered. The possible loss of environmental values (§ 230.20) and actions to minimize impact (Subpart H) shall also be considered in making these determinations. Potential changes in substrate elevation and bottom contours shall be predicted on the basis of the proposed method, volume, location, and rate of discharge, as well as on the individual and combined effects of current patterns, water circulation, wind and wave action, and other physical factors that may affect the movement of the discharged material.

(b) *Water circulation, fluctuation, and salinity determinations.* Determine the nature and degree of effect that the proposed discharge will have individually and cumulatively on water, current patterns, circulation including downstream flows, and normal water fluctuation. Consideration shall be given to water chemistry, salinity, clarity, color, odor, taste, dissolved gas levels, temperature, nutrients, and eutrophication plus other appropriate characteristics. Consideration shall also be given to the potential diversion or obstruction of flow, alterations of bottom contours, or other significant changes in the hydrologic regime. Additional consideration of the possible loss of environmental values (SS 230.23 through 230.25) and actions to minimize impacts (Subpart H), shall be used in making these determinations. Potential significant effects on the current patterns, water circulation, normal water fluctuation and salinity shall be evaluated on the basis of the proposed method, volume, location, and rate of discharge.

(c) *Suspended particulate/turbidity determinations.* Determine the nature and degree of effect that the proposed discharge will have, individually and cumulatively, in terms of potential changes in the kinds and concentrations of suspended particulate/turbidity in the vicinity of the disposal site. Consideration shall be given to the grain size of the material proposed for discharge, the shape and size of the plume of suspended particulates, the duration of the discharge and resulting plume and whether or not the potential changes will cause violations of applicable water quality standards. Consideration should also be given to the possible loss of environmental values (§ 230.21) and to actions for minimizing impacts (Subpart H). Consideration shall include the proposed method, volume, location, and rate of discharge, as well as the individual and combined effects of current patterns, water circulation and fluctuations, wind and wave action, and other physical factors on the movement of suspended particulates.

(d) *Contaminant determinations.* Determine the degree to which the material proposed for discharge will introduce, relocate, or increase contaminants. This determination shall consider the material to be discharged, the aquatic environment at the proposed disposal site, and the availability of contaminants.

(e) *Aquatic ecosystem and organism determinations.* Determine the nature and degree of effect that the proposed discharge will have, both individually and cumulatively, on the structure and function of the aquatic ecosystem and organisms. Consideration shall be given to the effect at the proposed disposal site of potential changes in substrate characteristics and elevation, water or substrate chemistry, nutrients, currents, circulation, fluctuation, and salinity, on the recolonization and existence of indigenous aquatic organisms or communities. Possible loss of environmental values (§ 230.31), and actions to minimize impacts (Subpart H) shall be examined. Tests as described in § 230.61 (Evaluation and Testing), may be required to provide information on the effect of the discharge material on communities or populations of organisms expected to be exposed to it.

(f) *Proposed disposal site determinations.*

(1) Each disposal site shall be specified through the application of these Guidelines. The mixing zone shall be confined to the smallest practicable zone within each specified disposal site that is consistent with the type of dispersion determined to be appropriate by the application of these Guidelines. In a few special cases under unique environmental conditions, where there is adequate justification to show that widespread dispersion by natural means will result in no significantly adverse environmental effects, the discharged material may be intended to be spread naturally in a very thin layer over a large area of the substrate rather than be contained within the disposal site.

(2) The permitting authority and the Regional Administrator shall consider the following factors in determining the acceptability of a proposed mixing zone:

(i) Depth of water at the disposal site;

(ii) Current velocity, direction, and variability at the disposal site;

(iii) Degree of turbulence;

(iv) Stratification attributable to causes such as obstructions, salinity or density profiles at the disposal site;

(v) Discharge vessel speed and direction, if appropriate;

(vi) Rate of discharge;

(vii) Ambient concentration of constituents of interest;

(viii) Dredged material characteristics, particularly concentrations of constituents, amount of material, type of material (sand, silt, clay, etc.) and settling velocities;

(ix) Number of discharge actions per unit of time;

(x) Other factors of the disposal site that affect the rates and patterns of mixing.

(g) *Determination of cumulative effects on the aquatic ecosystem.*

(1) Cumulative impacts are the changes in an aquatic ecosystem that are attributable to the collective effect of a number of individual discharges of dredged or fill material. Although the impact of a particular discharge may constitute a minor change in itself, the cumulative effect of numerous such piecemeal changes can result in a major impairment of the water resources and interfere with the productivity and water quality of existing aquatic ecosystems.

(2) Cumulative effects attributable to the discharge of dredged or fill material in waters of the United States should be predicted to the extent reasonable and practical. The permitting authority shall collect information and solicit information from other sources about the cumulative impacts on the aquatic ecosystem. This information shall be documented and considered during the decision-making process concerning the evaluation of individual permit applications, the issuance of a General permit, and monitoring and enforcement of existing permits.

(h) *Determination of secondary effects on the aquatic ecosystem.*

(1) Secondary effects are effects on an aquatic ecosystem that are associated with a discharge of dredged or fill materials, but do not result from the actual placement of the dredged or fill material. Information about secondary effects on aquatic ecosystems shall be considered prior to the time final section 404 action is taken by permitting authorities.

(2) Some examples of secondary effects on an aquatic ecosystem are fluctuating water levels in an impoundment and downstream associated with the operation of a dam, septic tank leaching and surface runoff from residential or commercial developments on fill, and leachate and runoff from a sanitary landfill located in waters of the U.S. Activities to be conducted on fast land created by the discharge of dredged or fill material in waters of the United States may have secondary impacts within those waters which should be considered in evaluating the impact of creating those fast lands.

§ 230.12 Findings of compliance or non-compliance with the restrictions on discharge.

(a) On the basis of these Guidelines (Subparts C through G) the proposed disposal sites for the discharge of dredged or fill material must be:

(1) Specified as complying with the requirements of these Guidelines; or

(2) Specified as complying with the requirements of these Guidelines with the inclusion of appropri-

ate and practicable discharge conditions (see Subpart H) to minimize pollution or adverse effects to the affected aquatic ecosystems; or

(3) Specified as failing to comply with the requirements of these Guidelines where:

(i) There is a practicable alternative to the proposed discharge that would have less adverse effect on the aquatic ecosystem, so long as such alternative does not have other significant adverse environmental consequences; or

(ii) The proposed discharge will result in significant degradation of the aquatic ecosystem under § 230.10(b) or (c); or

(iii) The proposed discharge does not include all appropriate and practicable measures to minimize potential harm to the aquatic ecosystem; or

(iv) There does not exist sufficient information to make a reasonable judgment as to whether the proposed discharge will comply with these Guidelines.

(b) Findings under this section shall be set forth in writing by the permitting authority for each proposed discharge and made available to the permit applicant. These findings shall include the factual determinations required by § 230.11, and a brief explanation of any adaptation of these Guidelines to the activity under consideration. In the case of a General permit, such findings shall be prepared at the time of issuance of that permit rather than for each subsequent discharge under the authority of that permit.

Subpart C—Potential Impacts on Physical and Chemical Characteristics of the Aquatic Ecosystem

Note: The effects described in this subpart should be considered in making the factual determinations and the findings of compliance or non-compliance in Subpart B.

§ 230.20 Substrate.

(a) The substrate of the aquatic ecosystem underlies open waters of the United States and constitutes the surface of wetlands. It consists of organic and inorganic solid materials and includes water and other liquids or gases that fill the spaces between solid particles.

(b) Possible loss of environmental characteristics and values: The discharge of dredged or fill material can result in varying degrees of change in the complex physical, chemical, and biological characteristics of the substrate. Discharges which alter substrate elevation or contours can result in changes in water circulation, depth, current pattern, water fluctuation and water temperature. Discharges may adversely affect bottom-dwelling organisms at the site by smothering immobile forms or forcing mobile forms to migrate. Benthic forms present prior to a discharge are unlikely to recolonize on the discharged material if it is very dissimilar from that of the discharge site. Erosion, slumping, or lateral displacement of surrounding bottom of such deposits can adversely affect areas of the substrate outside the perimeters of the disposal site by changing or destroying habitat. The bulk and composition of the discharged material and the location, method, and timing of discharges may all influence the degree of impact on the substrate.

§ 230.21 Suspended particulates/turbidity.

(a) Suspended particulates in the aquatic ecosystem consist of fine-grained mineral particles, usually smaller than silt, and organic particles. Suspended particulates may enter water bodies as a result of land runoff, flooding, vegetative and planktonic breakdown, resuspension of bottom sediments, and man's activities including dredging and filling. Particulates may remain suspended in the water column for variable periods of time as a result of such factors as agitation of the water mass, particulate specific gravity, particle shape, and physical and chemical properties of particle surfaces.

(b) Possible loss of environmental characteristics and values: The discharge of dredged or fill material can result in greatly elevated levels of suspended particulates in the water column for varying lengths of time. These new levels may reduce light penetration and lower the rate of photosynthesis and the primary productivity of an aquatic area if they last long enough. Sight-dependent species may suffer reduced feeding ability leading to limited growth and lowered resistance to disease if high levels of suspended particulates persist. The biological and the chemical content of the suspended material may react with the dissolved oxygen in the water, which can result in oxygen depletion. Toxic metals and organics, pathogens, and viruses absorbed or adsorbed to fine-grained particulates in the material may become biologically available to organisms either in the water column or on the substrate. Significant increases in suspended particulate levels create turbid plumes which are highly visible and aesthetically displeasing. The extent and persistence of these adverse impacts caused by discharges depend upon the relative increase in suspended particulates above the amount occurring naturally, the duration of the higher levels, the current patterns, water level, and fluctuations present when such discharges occur, the volume, rate, and duration of the discharge, particulate deposition, and the seasonal timing of the discharge.

§ 230.22 Water.

(a) Water is the part of the aquatic ecosystem in which organic and inorganic constituents are dissolved and suspended. It constitutes part of the liquid phase and is contained by the substrate. Water forms part of a dynamic aquatic life-supporting system. Water clarity, nutrients and chemical content, physical and biological content, dissolved gas levels, pH, and temperature contribute to its life-sustaining capabilities.

(b) Possible loss of environmental characteristics and values: The discharge of dredged or fill material can change the chemistry and the physical characteristics of the receiving water at a disposal site through the introduction of chemical constituents in suspended or dissolved form. Changes in the clarity, color, odor, and taste of water and the addition of contaminants can reduce or eliminate the suitability of water bodies for populations of aquatic organisms, and for human consumption, recreation, and aesthetics. The introduction of nutrients or organic material to the water column as a result of the discharge can lead to a high biochemical oxygen demand (BOD), which in turn can lead to reduced dissolved oxygen, thereby potentially affecting the survival of many aquatic organisms. Increases in nutrients can favor one group of organisms such as algae to the detriment of other more desirable types such as submerged aquatic vegetation, potentially causing adverse health effects, objectionable tastes and odors, and other problems.

§ 230.23 Current patterns and water circulation.

(a) Current patterns and water circulation are the physical movements of water in the aquatic ecosystem. Currents and circulation respond to natural forces as modified by basin shape and cover, physical and chemical characteristics of water strata and masses, and energy dissipating factors.

(b) Possible loss of environmental characteristics and values: The discharge of dredged or fill material can modify current patterns and water circulation by obstructing flow, changing the direction or velocity of water flow, changing the direction or velocity of water flow and circulation, or otherwise changing the dimensions of a water body. As a result, adverse changes can occur in: Location, structure, and dynamics of aquatic communities; shoreline and substrate erosion and deposition rates; the deposition of suspended particulates; the rate and extent of mixing of dissolved and suspended components of the water body; and water stratification.

§ 230.24 Normal water fluctuations.

(a) Normal water fluctuations in a natural aquatic system consist of daily, seasonal, and annual tidal and flood fluctuations in water level. Biological and physical components of such a system are either attuned to or characterized by these periodic water fluctuations.

(b) Possible loss of environmental characteristics and values: The discharge of dredged or fill material can alter the normal water-level fluctuation pattern of an area, resulting in prolonged periods of inundation, exaggerated extremes of high and low water, or a static, nonfluctuating water level. Such water level modifications may change salinity patterns, alter erosion or sedimentation rates, aggravate water temperature extremes, and upset the nutrient and dissolved oxygen balance of the aquatic ecosystem. In addition, these modifications can alter or destroy communities and populations of aquatic animals and vegetation, induce populations of nuisance organisms, modify habitat, reduce food supplies, restrict movement of aquatic fauna, destroy spawning areas, and change adjacent, upstream, and downstream areas.

§ 230.25 Salinity gradients.

(a) Salinity gradients form where salt water from the ocean meets and mixes with fresh water from land.

(b) Possible loss of environmental characteristics and values: Obstructions which divert or restrict flow of either fresh or salt water may change existing salinity gradients. For example, partial blocking of the entrance to an estuary or river mouth that significantly restricts the movement of the salt water into and out of that area can effectively lower the volume of salt water available for mixing within that estuary. The downstream migration of the salinity gradient can occur, displacing the maximum sedimentation zone and requiring salinity-dependent aquatic biota to adjust to the new conditions, move to new locations if possible, or perish. In the freshwater zone, discharge operations in the upstream regions can have equally adverse impacts. A significant reduction in the volume of fresh water moving into an estuary below that which is considered normal can affect the location and type of mixing thereby changing the characteristic salinity patterns. The resulting changed circulation pattern can cause the upstream migration of the salinity gradient displacing the maximum sedimentation zone. This migration may affect those organisms that are adapted to freshwater environments. It may also affect municipal water supplies.

Note: Possible actions to minimize adverse impacts regarding site characteristics can be found in Subpart H.

Subpart D—Potential Impacts on Biological Characteristics of the Aquatic Ecosystem

Note: The impacts described in this subpart should be considered in making the factual determinations and the findings of compliance or non-compliance in Subpart B.

§ 230.30 Threatened and endangered species.

(a) An endangered species is a plant or animal in danger of extinction throughout all or a significant portion of its range. A threatened species is one in danger of becoming an endangered species in the foreseeable future throughout all or a significant portion of its range. Listings of threatened and endangered species as well as critical habitats are maintained by some individual States and by the U.S. Fish and Wildlife Service of the Department of the Interior (codified annually at 50 CFR 17.11). The Department of Commerce has authority over some threatened and endangered marine mammals, fish and reptiles.

(b) Possible loss of values: The major potential impacts on threatened or endangered species from the discharge of dredged or fill material include:

(1) Covering or otherwise directly killing species;

(2) The impairment or destruction of habitat to which these species are limited. Elements of the aquatic habitat which are particularly crucial to the continued survival of some threatened or endangered species include adequate good quality water, spawning and maturation areas, nesting areas, protective cover, adequate and reliable food supply, and resting areas for migratory species. Each of these elements can be adversely affected by changes in either the normal water conditions for clarity, chemical content, nutrient balance, dissolved oxygen, pH, temperature, salinity, current patterns, circulation and fluctuation, or the physical removal of habitat; and

(3) Facilitating incompatible activities.

(c) Where consultation with the Secretary of the Interior occurs under section 7 of the Endangered Species Act, the conclusions of the Secretary concerning the impact(s) of the discharge on threatened and endangered species and their habitat shall be considered final.

§ 230.31 Fish, crustaceans, mollusks, and other aquatic organisms in the food web.

(a) Aquatic organisms in the food web include, but are not limited to, finfish, crustaceans, mollusks, insects, annelids, planktonic organisms, and the plants and animals on which they feed and depend upon for their needs. All forms and life stages of an organism, throughout its geographic range, are included in this category.

(b) Possible loss of values: The discharge of dredged or fill material can variously affect populations of fish, crustaceans, mollusks and other food web organisms through the release of contaminants which adversely affect adults, juveniles, larvae, or eggs, or result in the establishment or proliferation of an undesirable competitive species of plant or animal at the expense of the desired resident species. Suspended particulates settling on attached or buried eggs can smother the eggs by limiting or sealing off their exposure to oxygenated water. Discharge of dredged and fill material may result in the debilitation or death of sedentary organisms by smothering, exposure to chemical contaminants in dissolved or suspended form, exposure to high levels of suspended particulates, reduction in food supply, or alteration of the substrate upon which they are dependent. Mollusks are particularly sensitive to the discharge of material during periods of reproduction and growth and development due primarily to their limited mobility. They can be rendered unfit for human consumption by tainting, by production and accumulation of toxins, or by ingestion and retention of pathogenic organisms, viruses, heavy metals or persistent synthetic organic chemicals. The discharge of dredged or fill material can redirect, delay, or stop the reproductive and feeding movements of some species of fish and crustacea, thus preventing their aggregation in accustomed places such as spawning or nursery grounds and potentially leading to reduced populations. Reduction of detrital feeding species or other representatives of lower trophic levels can impair the flow of energy from primary consumers to higher trophic levels. The reduction or potential elimination of food chain organism populations decreases the overall productivity and nutrient export capability of the ecosystem.

§ 230.32 Other wildlife.

(a) Wildlife associated with aquatic ecosystems are resident and transient mammals, birds, reptiles, and amphibians.

(b) Possible loss of values: The discharge of dredged or fill material can result in the loss or change of breeding and nesting areas, escape cover, travel corridors, and preferred food sources for resident and transient wildlife species associated with the aquatic ecosystem. These adverse impacts upon wildlife habitat may result from changes in water levels, water flow and circulation, salinity, chemical content, and substrate characteristics and elevation. Increased water turbidity can adversely affect wildlife species which rely upon sight to feed, and disrupt the respiration and feeding of certain aquatic wildlife and food chain organisms. The availability of contaminants from the discharge of dredged or fill material may lead to the bioaccumulation of such contaminants in wildlife. Changes in such physical and chemical factors of the environment may favor the introduction of undesirable plant and animal species at the expense of resident species and communities. In some aquatic environments lowering plant and animal species diversity may disrupt the normal functions of the ecosystem and lead to reductions in overall biological productivity.

Note: Possible actions to minimize adverse impacts regarding characteristics of biological components of the aquatic ecosystem can be found in Subpart H.

Subpart E—Potential Impacts on Special Aquatic Sites

Note: The impacts described in this subpart should be considered in making the factual determinations and the findings of compliance or non-compliance in Subpart B. The definition of special aquatic sites is found in § 230.3(q-1).

§ 230.40 Sanctuaries and refuges.

(a) Sanctuaries and refuges consist of areas designated under State and Federal laws or local ordinances to be managed principally for the preservation and use of fish and wildlife resources.

(b) Possible loss of values: Sanctuaries and refuges may be affected by discharges of dredged or fill material which will:

(1) Disrupt the breeding, spawning, migratory movements or other critical life requirements of resident or transient fish and wildlife resources;

(2) Create unplanned, easy and incompatible human access to remote aquatic areas;

(3) Create the need for frequent maintenance activity;

(4) Result in the establishment of undesirable competitive species of plants and animals;

(5) Change the balance of water and land areas needed to provide cover, food, and other fish and wildlife habitat requirements in a way that modifies sanctuary or refuge management practices;

(6) Result in any of the other adverse impacts discussed in Subparts C and D as they relate to a particular sanctuary or refuge.

§ 230.41 Wetlands.

(a)(1) Wetlands consist of areas that are inundated or saturated by surface or ground water at a frequency and duration sufficient to support, and that under normal circumstances do support, a prevalence of vegetation typically adapted for life in saturated soil conditions.

(2) Where wetlands are adjacent to open water, they generally constitute the transition to upland. The margin between wetland and open water can best be established by specialists familiar with the local environment, particularly where emergent vegetation merges with submerged vegetation over a broad area in such places as the lateral margins of open water, headwaters, rainwater catch basins, and groundwater seeps. The landward margin of wetlands also can best be identified by specialists familiar with the local environment when vegetation from the two regions merges over a broad area.

(3) Wetland vegetation consists of plants that require saturated soils to survive (obligate wetland plants) as well as plants, including certain trees, that gain a competitive advantage over others because they can tolerate prolonged wet soil conditions and their competitors cannot. In addition to plant populations and communities, wetlands are delimited by hydrological and physical characteristics of the environment. These characteristics should be considered when information about them is needed to supplement information available about vegetation, or where wetland vegetation has been removed or is dormant.

(b) Possible loss of values: The discharge of dredged or fill material in wetlands is likely to damage or destroy habitat and adversely affect the biological productivity of wetlands ecosystems by smothering, by dewatering, by permanently flooding, or by altering substrate elevation or periodicity of water movement. The addition of dredged or fill material may destroy wetland vegetation or result in advancement of succession to dry land species. It may reduce or eliminate nutrient exchange by a reduction of the system's productivity, or by altering current patterns and velocities. Disruption or elimination of the wetland system can degrade water quality by obstructing circulation patterns that flush large expanses of wetland systems, by interfering with the filtration function of wetlands, or by changing the aquifer recharge capability of a wetland. Discharges can also change the wetland habitat value for fish and wildlife as discussed in Subpart D. When disruptions in flow and circulation patterns occur, apparently minor loss of wetland acreage may result in major losses through secondary impacts. Discharging fill material in wetlands as part of municipal, industrial or recreational development may modify the capacity of wetlands to retain and store floodwaters and to serve as a buffer zone shielding upland areas from wave actions, storm damage and erosion.

§ 230.42 Mud flats.

(a) Mud flats are broad flat areas along the sea coast and in coastal rivers to the head of tidal influence and in inland lakes, ponds, and riverine systems. When mud flats are inundated, wind and wave action may resuspend bottom sediments. Coastal mud flats are exposed at extremely low tides and inundated at high tides with the water table at or near the surface of the substrate. The substrate of mud flats contains organic material and particles smaller in size than sand. They are either unvegetated or vegetated only by algal mats.

(b) Possible loss of values: The discharge of dredged or fill material can cause changes in water circulation patterns which may permanently flood or dewater the mud flat or disrupt periodic inundation, resulting in an increase in the rate of erosion or accretion. Such changes can deplete or eliminate mud flat biota, foraging areas, and nursery areas. Changes in inundation patterns can affect the chemical and biological exchange and decomposition process occurring on the mud flat and change the deposition of suspended material affecting the productivity of the area. Changes may reduce the mud flat's capacity to dissipate storm surge runoff.

§ 230.43 Vegetated shallows.

(a) Vegetated shallows are permanently inundated areas that under normal circumstances support communities of rooted aquatic vegetation, such as turtle grass and eelgrass in estuarine or marine systems as well as a number of freshwater species in rivers and lakes.

(b) Possible loss of values: The discharge of dredged or fill material can smother vegetation and benthic organisms. It may also create unsuitable conditions for their continued vigor by: (1) Changing water circulation patterns; (2) releasing nutrients that increase undesirable algal populations; (3) releasing chemicals that adversely affect plants and animals; (4) increasing turbidity levels, thereby reducing light penetration and hence photosynthesis; and (5) changing the capacity of a vegetated shallow to stabilize bottom materials and decrease channel shoaling. The discharge of dredged or fill material may reduce the value of vegetated shallows as nesting, spawning, nursery, cover, and forage areas, as well as their value in protecting shorelines from erosion and wave actions. It may also encourage the growth of nuisance vegetation.

§ 230.44 Coral reefs.

(a) Coral reefs consist of the skeletal deposit, usually of calcareous or siliceous materials, produced by the vital activities of anthozoan polyps or other invertebrate organisms present in growing portions of the reef.

(b) Possible loss of values: The discharge of dredged or fill material can adversely affect colonies of reef building organisms by burying them, by releasing contaminants such as hydrocarbons into the water column, by reducing light penetration through the water, and by increasing the level of suspended particulates. Coral organisms are extremely sensitive to even slight reductions in light penetration or increases in suspended particulates. These adverse effects will cause a loss of productive colonies which in turn provide habitat for many species of highly specialized aquatic organisms.

§ 230.45 Riffle and pool complexes.

(a) Steep gradient sections of streams are sometimes characterized by riffle and pool complexes. Such stream sections are recognizable by their hydraulic characteristics. The rapid movement of water over a coarse substrate in riffles results in a rough flow, a turbulent surface, and high dissolved oxygen levels in the water. Pools are deeper areas associated with riffles. Pools are characterized by a slower stream velocity, a steaming flow, a smooth surface, and a finer substrate. Riffle and pool complexes are particularly valuable habitat for fish and wildlife.

(b) Possible loss of values: Discharge of dredged or fill material can eliminate riffle and pool areas by displacement, hydrologic modification, or sedimentation. Activities which affect riffle and pool areas and especially riffle/pool ratios, may reduce the aeration and filtration capabilities at the discharge site and downstream, may reduce stream habitat diversity, and may retard repopulation of the disposal site and downstream waters through sedimentation and the creation of unsuitable habitat. The discharge of dredged or fill material which alters stream hydrology may cause scouring or sedimentation of riffles and pools. Sedimentation induced through hydrological modification or as a direct result of the deposition of unconsolidated dredged or fill material may clog riffle and pool areas, destroy habitats, and create anaerobic conditions. Eliminating pools and meanders by the discharge of dredged or fill material can reduce water holding capacity of streams and cause rapid runoff from a watershed. Rapid runoff can deliver large quantities of flood water in a short time to downstream areas resulting in the destruction of natural habitat, high property loss, and the need for further hydraulic modification.

Note: Possible actions to minimize adverse impacts on site or material characteristics can be found in Subpart H.

Subpart F—Potential Effects on Human Use Characteristics

Note: The effects described in this subpart should be considered in making the factual determinations and the findings of compliance or non-compliance in Subpart B.

§ 230.50 Municipal and private water supplies.

(a) Municipal and private water supplies consist of surface water or ground water which is directed to the intake of a municipal or private water supply system.

(b) Possible loss of values: Discharges can affect the quality of water supplies with respect to color, taste, odor, chemical content and suspended particulate concentration, in such a way as to reduce the fitness of the water for consumption. Water can be rendered unpalatable or unhealthy by the addition of suspended particulates, viruses and pathogenic organisms, and dissolved materials. The expense of removing such substances before the water is delivered for consumption can be high. Discharges may also affect the quantity of water available for municipal and private water supplies. In addition, certain commonly used water treatment chemicals have the potential for combining with some suspended or dissolved substances from dredged or fill material to form other products that can have a toxic effect on consumers.

§ 230.51 Recreational and commercial fisheries.

(a) Recreational and commercial fisheries consist of harvestable fish, crustaceans, shellfish, and other aquatic organisms used by man.

(b) Possible loss of values: The discharge of dredged or fill materials can affect the suitability of recreational and commercial fishing grounds as habitat for populations of consumable aquatic organisms. Discharges can result in the chemical contamination of recreational or commercial fisheries. They may also interfere with the reproductive success of recreational and commercially important aquatic species through disruption of migration and spawning areas. The introduction of pollutants at critical times in their life cycle may directly reduce populations of commercially important aquatic organisms or indirectly reduce them by reducing organisms upon which they depend for food. Any of these impacts can be of short duration or prolonged, depending upon the physical and chemical impacts of the discharge and the biological availability of contaminants to aquatic organisms.

§ 230.52 Water-related recreation.

(a) Water-related recreation encompasses activities undertaken for amusement and relaxation. Activities encompass two broad categories of use: consumptive, e.g., harvesting resources by hunting and fishing; and non-comsumptive, e.g. canoeing and sight-seeing.

(b) Possible loss of values: One of the more important direct impacts of dredged or fill disposal is to impair or destroy the resources which support recreation activities. The disposal of dredged or fill material may adversely modify or destroy water use for recreation by changing turbidity, suspended particulates, temperature, dissolved oxygen, dissolved materials, toxic materials, pathogenic organisms, quality of habitat, and the aesthetic qualities of sight, taste, odor, and color.

§ 230.53 Aesthetics.

(a) Aesthetics associated with the aquatic ecosystem consist of the perception of beauty by one or a combination of the senses of sight, hearing, touch, and smell. Aesthetics of aquatic ecosystems apply to the quality of life enjoyed by the general public and property owners.

(b) Possible loss of values: The discharge of dredged or fill material can mar the beauty of natural aquatic ecosystems by degrading water quality, creating distracting disposal sites, inducing inappropriate development, encouraging unplanned and incompatible human access, and by destroying vital elements that contribute to the compositional harmony or unity, visual distinctiveness, or diversity of an area. The discharge of dredged or fill material can adversely affect the particular features, traits, or characteristics of an aquatic area which make it valuable to property owners. Activities which degrade water quality, disrupt natural substrate and vegetational characteristics, deny access to or visibility of the resource, or result in changes in odor, air quality, or noise levels may reduce the value of an aquatic area to private property owners.

§ 230.54 Parks, national and historical monuments, national seashores, wilderness areas, research sites, and similar preserves.

(a) These preserves consist of areas designated under Federal and State laws or local ordinances to be managed for their aesthetic, educational, historical, recreational, or scientific value.

(b) Possible loss of values: The discharge of dredged or fill material into such areas may modify the aesthetic, educational, historical, recreational and/or scientific qualities thereby reducing or eliminating the uses for which such sites are set aside and managed.

Note: Possible actions to minimize adverse impacts regarding site or material characteristics can be found in Subpart H.

Subpart G—Evaluation and Testing

§ 230.60 General evaluation of dredged or fill material.

The purpose of these evaluation procedures and the chemical and biological testing sequence outlined in § 230.61 is to provide information to reach the determinations required by § 230.11. Where the results of prior evaluations, chemical and biological tests, scientific research, and experience can provide information helpful in making a determination, these should be used. Such prior results may make new testing unnecessary. The information used shall be documented. Where the same information applies to more than one determination, it may be documented once and referenced in later determinations.

(a) If the evaluation under paragraph (b) indicates the dredged or fill material is not a carrier of contaminants, then the required determinations pertaining to the presence and effects of contaminants can be made without testing. Dredged or fill material is most likely to be free from chemical, biological, or other pollutants where it is composed primarily of sand, gravel, or other naturally occurring inert material. Dredged material so composed is generally found in areas of high current or wave energy such as streams with large bed loads or coastal areas with shifting bars and channels. However, when such material is discolored or contains other indications that contaminants may be present, further inquiry should be made.

(b) The extraction site shall be examined in order to assess whether it is sufficiently removed from sources of pollution to provide reasonable assurance that the proposed discharge material is not a carrier of contaminants. Factors to be considered include but are not limited to:

(1) Potential routes of contaminants or contaminated sediments to the extraction site, based on hydrographic or other maps, aerial photography, or other materials that show watercourses, surface relief, proximity to tidal movement, private and public roads, location of buildings, municipal and industrial areas, and agricultural or forest lands.

(2) Pertinent results from tests previously carried out on the material at the extraction site, or carried out on similar material for other permitted projects in the vicinity. Materials shall be considered similar if the sources of contamination, the physical configuration of the sites and the sediment composition of the materials are comparable, in light of water circulation and stratification, sediment accumulation and general sediment characteristics. Tests from other sites may be relied on only if no changes have occurred at the extraction sites to render the results irrelevant.

(3) Any potential for significant introduction of persistent pesticides from land runoff or percolation;

(4) Any records of spills or disposal of petroleum products or substances designated as hazardous under section 311 of the Clean Water Act (See 40 CFR Part 116);

(5) Information in Federal, State and local records indicating significant introduction of pollutants from industries, municipalities, or other sources, including types and amounts of waste materials discharged along the potential routes of contaminants to the extraction site; and

(6) Any possibility of the presence of substantial natural deposits of minerals or other substances which could be released to the aquatic environment in harmful quantities by man-induced discharge activities.

(c) To reach the determinations in § 230.11 involving potential effects of the discharge on the characteristics of the disposal site, the narrative guidance in Subparts C through F shall be used along with the general evaluation procedure in § 230.60 and, if necessary, the chemical and biological testing sequence in § 230.61. Where the discharge site is adjacent to the ex-

traction site and subject to the same sources of contaminants, and materials at the two sites are substantially similar, the fact that the material to be discharged may be a carrier of contaminants is not likely to result in degradation of the disposal site. In such circumstances, when dissolved material and suspended particulates can be controlled to prevent carrying pollutants to less contaminated areas, testing will not be required.

(d) Even if the § 230.60(b) evaluation (previous tests, the presence of polluting industries and information about their discharge or runoff into waters of the U.S., bioinventories, etc.) leads to the conclusion that there is a high probability that the material proposed for discharge is a carrier of contaminants, testing may not be necessary if constraints are available to reduce contamination to acceptable levels within the disposal site and to prevent contaminants from being transported beyond the boundaries of the disposal site, if such constraints are acceptable to the permitting authority and the Regional Administrator, and if the potential discharger is willing and able to implement such constraints. However, even if tests are not performed, the permitting authority must still determine the probable impact of the operation on the receiving aquatic ecosystem. Any decision not to test must be explained in the determinations made under § 230.11.

§ 230.61 Chemical, biological, and physical evaluation and testing.

Note: The Agency is today proposing revised testing guidelines. The evaluation and testing procedures in this section are based on the 1975 section 404(b)(1) interim final Guidelines and shall remain in effect until the revised testing guidelines are published as final regulations.

(a) No single test or approach can be applied in all cases to evaluate the effects of proposed discharges of dredged or fill materials. This section provides some guidance in determining which test and/or evaluation procedures are appropriate in a given case. Interim guidance to applicants concerning the applicability of specific approaches or procedures will be furnished by the permitting authority.

(b) Chemical-biological interactive effects. The principal concerns of discharge of dredged or fill material that contain contaminants are the potential effects on the water column and on communities of aquatic organisms.

(1) Evaluation of chemical-biological interactive effects. Dredged or fill material may be excluded from the evaluation procedures specified in paragraphs (b) (2) and (3) of this section if it is determined, on the basis of the evaluation in § 230.60, that the likelihood of contamination by contaminants is acceptably low, unless the permitting authority, after evaluating and considering any comments received from the Regional Administrator, determines that these procedures are necessary. The Regional Administrator may require, on a case-by-case basis, testing approaches and procedures by stating what additional information is

needed through further analyses and how the results of the analyses will be of value in evaluating potential environmental effects.

If the General Evaluation indicates the presence of a sufficiently large number of chemicals to render impractical the identification of all contaminants by chemical testing, information may be obtained from bioassays in lieu of chemical tests.

(2) Water column effects.

(i) Sediments normally contain constituents that exist in various chemical forms and in various concentrations in several locations within the sediment. An elutriate test may be used to predict the effect on water quality due to release of contaminants from the sediment to the water column. However, in the case of fill material originating on land which may be a carrier of contaminants, a water leachate test is appropriate.

(ii) Major constituents to be analyzed in the elutriate are those deemed critical by the permitting authority, after evaluating and considering any comments received from the Regional Administrator, and considering results of the evaluation in § 230.60. Elutriate concentrations should be compared to concentrations of the same constituents in water from the disposal site. Results should be evaluated in light of the volume and rate of the intended discharge, the type of discharge, the hydrodynamic regime at the disposal site, and other information relevant to the impact on water quality. The permitting authority should consider the mixing zone in evaluating water column effects. The permitting authority may specify bioassays when such procedures will be of value.

(3) Effects on benthos. The permitting authority may use an appropriate benthic bioassay (including bioaccumulation tests) when such procedures will be of value in assessing ecological effects and in establishing discharge conditions.

(c) Procedure for comparison of sites.

(1) When an inventory of the total concentration of contaminants would be of value in comparing sediment at the dredging site with sediment at the disposal site, the permitting authority may require a sediment chemical analysis. Markedly different concentrations of contaminants between the excavation and disposal sites may aid in making an environmental assessment of the proposed disposal operation. Such differences should be interpreted in terms of the potential for harm as supported by any pertinent scientific literature.

(2) When an analysis of biological community structure will be of value to assess the potential for adverse environmental impact at the proposed disposal site, a comparison of the biological characteristics between the excavation and disposal sites may be required by the permitting authority. Biological indicator species may be useful in evaluating the existing degree of stress at both sites. Sensitive species representing community components colonizing various substrate types within the sites should be identified as possible bioassay organisms if tests for toxicity are required. Community structure studies should be performed only when they will be of value in determining discharge conditions. This is particularly applicable to large quantities of dredged material known to contain adverse quantities of toxic materials. Community studies should include benthic organisms such as microbiota and harvestable shellfish and finfish. Abundance, diversity, and distribution should be documented and correlated with substrate type and other appropriate physical and chemical environmental characteristics.

(d) Physical tests and evaluation. The effect of a discharge of dredged or fill material on physical substrate characteristics at the disposal site, as well as on the water circulation, fluctuation, salinity, and suspended particulates content there, is important in making factual determinations in § 230.11. Where information on such effects is not otherwise available to make these factual determinations, the permitting authority shall require appropriate physical tests and evaluations as are justified and deemed necessary. Such tests may include sieve tests, settleability tests, compaction tests, mixing zone and suspended particulate plume determinations, and site assessments of water flow, circulation, and salinity characteristics.

Subpart H—Actions To Minimize Adverse Effects

Note: There are many actions which can be undertaken in response to § 203.10(d) to minimize the adverse effects of discharges of dredged or fill material. Some of these, grouped by type of activity, are listed in this subpart.

§ 230.70 Actions concerning the location of the discharge.

The effects of the discharge can be minimized by the choice of the disposal site. Some of the ways to accomplish this are by:

(a) Locating and confining the discharge to minimize smothering of organisms;

(b) Designing the discharge to avoid a disruption of periodic water inundation patterns;

(c) Selecting a disposal site that has been used previously for dredged material discharge;

(d) Selecting a disposal site at which the substrate is composed of material similar to that being discharged, such as discharging sand on sand or mud on mud;

(e) Selecting the disposal site, the discharge point, and the method of discharge to minimize the extent of any plume;

(f) Designing the discharge of dredged or fill material to minimize or prevent the creation of standing bodies of water in areas of normally fluctuating water levels, and minimize or prevent the drainage of areas subject to such fluctuations.

§ 230.71 Actions concerning the material to be discharged.

The effects of a discharge can be minimized by treatment of, or limitations on the material itself, such as:

(a) Disposal of dredged material in such a manner that physiochemical conditions are maintained and the potency and availability of pollutants are reduced.

(b) Limiting the solid, liquid, and gaseous components of material to be discharged at a particular site;

(c) Adding treatment substances to the discharge material;

(d) Utilizing chemical flocculants to enhance the deposition of suspended particulates in diked disposal areas.

§ 230.72 Actions controlling the material after discharge.

The effects of the dredged or fill material after discharge may be controlled by:

(a) Selecting discharge methods and disposal sites where the potential for erosion, slumping or leaching of materials into the surrounding aquatic ecosystem will be reduced. These sites or methods include, but are not limited to:

(1) Using containment levees, sediment basins, and cover crops to reduce erosion;

(2) Using lined containment areas to reduce leaching where leaching of chemical constituents from the discharged material is expected to be a problem;

(b) Capping in-place contaminated material with clean material or selectively discharging the most contaminated material first to be capped with the remaining material;

(c) Maintaining and containing discharged material properly to prevent point and nonpoint sources of pollution;

(d) Timing the discharge to minimize impact, for instance during periods of unusual high water flows, wind, wave, and tidal actions.

§ 230.73 Actions affecting the method of dispersion.

The effects of a discharge can be minimized by the manner in which it is dispersed, such as:

(a) Where environmentally desirable, distributing the dredged material widely in a thin layer at the disposal site to maintain natural substrate contours and elevation;

(b) Orienting a dredged or fill material mound to minimize undesirable obstruction to the water current or circulation pattern, and utilizing natural bottom contours to minimize the size of the mound;

(c) Using silt screens or other appropriate methods to confine suspended particulate/turbidity to a small area where settling or removal can occur;

(d) Making use of currents and circulation patterns to mix, disperse and dilute the discharge;

(e) Minimizing water column turbidity by using a submerged diffuser system. A similar effect can be accomplished by submerging pipeline discharges or otherwise releasing materials near the bottom;

(f) Selecting sites or managing discharges to confine and minimize the release of suspended particulates to give decreased turbidity levels and to maintain light penetration for organisms;

(g) Setting limitations on the amount of material to be discharged per unit of time or volume of receiving water.

§ 230.74 Actions related to technology.

Discharge technology should be adapted to the needs of each site. In determining whether the discharge operation sufficiently minimizes adverse environmental impacts, the applicant should consider:

(a) Using appropriate equipment or machinery, including protective devices, and the use of such equipment or machinery in activities related to the discharge of dredged or fill material;

(b) Employing appropriate maintenance and operation on equipment or machinery, including adequate training, staffing, and working procedures;

(c) Using machinery and techniques that are especially designed to reduce damage to wetlands. This may include machines equipped with devices that scatter rather than mound excavated materials, machines with specially designed wheels or tracks, and the use of mats under heavy machines to reduce wetland surface compaction and rutting;

(d) Designing access roads and channel spanning structures using culverts, open channels, and diversions that will pass both low and high water flows, accommodate fluctuating water levels, and maintain circulation and faunal movement;

(e) Employing appropriate machinery and methods of transport of the material for discharge.

§ 230.75 Actions affecting plant and animal populations.

Minimization of adverse effects on populations of plants and animals can be achieved by:

(a) Avoiding changes in water current and circulation patterns which would interfere with the movement of animals;

(b) Selecting sites or managing discharges to prevent or avoid creating habitat conducive to the development of undesirable predators or species which have a competitive edge ecologically over indigenous plants or animals;

(c) Avoiding sites having unique habitat or other value, including habitat of threatened or endangered species;

(d) Using planning and construction practices to institute habitat development and restoration to produce a new or modified environmental state of higher ecological value by displacement of some or all of the existing environmental characteristics. Habitat development and restoration techniques can be used to minimize adverse impacts and to compensate for destroyed habitat. Use techniques that have been demonstrated to be effective in circumstances similar to those under consideration wherever possible. Where proposed development and restoration techniques have not yet advanced to the pilot demonstration stage, initiate their use on a small scale to allow corrective action if unanticipated adverse impacts occur;

(e) Timing discharge to avoid spawning or migration seasons and other biologically critical time periods;

(f) Avoiding the destruction of remnant natural sites within areas already affected by development.

§ 230.76 Actions affecting human use.

Minimization of adverse effects on human use potential may be achieved by:

(a) Selecting discharge sites and following discharge procedures to prevent or minimize any potential damage to the aesthetically pleasing features of the aquatic site (e.g. viewscapes), particularly with respect to water quality;

(b) Selecting disposal sites which are not valuable as natural aquatic areas;

(c) Timing the discharge to avoid the seasons or periods when human recreational activity associated with the aquatic site is most important;

(d) Following discharge procedures which avoid or minimize the disturbance of aesthetic features of an aquatic site or ecosystem;

(e) Selecting sites that will not be detrimental or increase incompatible human activity, or require the need for frequent dredge or fill maintenance activity in remote fish and wildlife areas;

(f) Locating the disposal site outside of the vicinity of a public water supply intake.

§ 230.77 Other actions.

(a) In the case of fills, controlling runoff and other discharges from activities to be conducted on the fill;

(b) In the case of dams, designing water releases to accommodate the needs of fish and wildlife;

(c) In dredging projects funded by Federal agencies other than the Corps of Engineers, maintain desired water quality of the return discharge through agreement with the Federal funding authority on scientifically defensible pollutant concentration levels in addition to any applicable water quality standards;

(d) When a significant ecological change in the aquatic environment is proposed by the discharge of dredged or fill material, the permitting authority should consider the ecosystem that will be lost as well as the environmental benefits of the new system.

Subpart I—Planning To Shorten Permit Processing Time

§ 230.80 Advanced identification of disposal areas.

(a) Consistent with these Guidelines, EPA and the permitting authority, on their own initiative or at the request of any other party and after consultation with any affected State that is not the permitting authority, may identify sites which will be considered as:

(1) Possible future disposal sites, including existing disposal sites and non-sensitive areas; or

(2) Areas generally unsuitable for disposal site specification;

(b) The identification of any area as a possible future disposal site should not be deemed to constitute a permit for the discharge of dredged or fill material within such area or a specification of a disposal site. The identification of areas that generally will not be available for disposal site specification should not be deemed as prohibiting applications for permits to discharge dredged or fill material in such areas. Either type of identification constitutes information to facilitate individual or General permit application and processing.

(c) An appropriate public notice of the proposed identification of such areas shall be issued;

(d) To provide the basis for advanced identification of disposal areas, and areas unsuitable for disposal, EPA and the permitting authority shall consider the likelihood that use of the area in question for dredged or fill material disposal will comply with these Guidelines. To facilitate this analysis, EPA and the permitting authority should review available water resources management data including data available from the public, other Federal and State agencies, and information from approved Coastal Zone Management programs and River Basin Plans;

(e) The permitting authority should maintain a public record of the identified areas and a written statement of the basis for identification.

PART 231
SECTION 404(C) PROCEDURES

§ 231.1 Purpose and scope.

(a) The Regulations of this part include the procedures to be followed by the Environmental Protection agency in prohibiting or withdrawing the specification, or denying, restricting, or withdrawing the use for specification, of any defined area as a disposal site for dredged or fill material pursuant to section 404(c) of the Clean Water Act ("CWA"), 33 U.S.C. 1344(c). The U.S. Army Corps of Engineers or a state with a 404 program which has been approved under section 404(h) may grant permits specifying disposal sites for dredged or fill material by determining that the section 404(b)(1) Guidelines (40 CFR Part 230) allow specification of a particular site to receive dredged or fill material. The Corps may also grant permits by determining that the discharge of dredged or fill material is necessary under the economic impact provision of section 404(b)(2). Under section 404(c), the Administrator may exercise a veto over the specification by the U.S. Army Corps of Engineers or by a state of a site for the discharge of dredged or fill material. The Administrator may also prohibit the specification of a site under section 404(c) with regard to any existing or potential disposal site before a permit application has been submitted to or approved by the Corps or a state. The Administrator is authorized to prohibit or otherwise restrict a site whenever he determines that the discharge of dredged or fill material is having or will have an "unacceptable adverse effect" on municipal water supplies, shellfish beds and fishery areas (including spawning and breeding areas), wildlife, or recreational areas. In making this determination, the Administrator will take into account all information available to him, including any written determination of compliance with the section 404(b)(1) Guidelines made in 40 CFR Part 230, and will consult with the Chief of Engineers or with the state.

(b) These regulations establish procedures for the following steps:

(1) The Regional Administrator's proposed determinations to prohibit or withdraw the specification of a defined area as a disposal site, or to deny, restrict or withdraw the use of any defined area for the discharge of any particular dredged or fill material;

(2) The Regional Administrator's recommendation to the Administrator for determination as to the specification of a defined area as a disposal site.

(3) The Administrator's final determination to affirm, modify or rescind the recommended determination after consultation with the Chief of Engineers or with the state.

(c) Applicability: The regulations set forth in this part are applicable whenever the Administrator is considering whether the specification of any defined area as a disposal site should be prohibited, denied, restricted, or withdrawn. These regulations apply to all existing, proposed or potential disposal sites for discharges of dredged or fill material into waters of the United States, as defined in 40 CFR 230.2.

§ 231.2   Definitions

For the purposes of this part, the definitions of terms in 40 CFR 230.2 shall apply. In addition, the term:

(a) "Withdraw specification" means to remove from designation any area already specified as a disposal site by the U.S. Army Corps of Engineers or by a state which has assumed the section 404 program, or any portion of such area.

(b) "Prohibit specification" means to prevent the designation of an area as a present or future disposal site.

(c) "Deny or restrict the use of any defined area for specification" is to deny or restrict the use of any area for the present or future discharge of any dredged or fill material.

(d) "Person" means an individual, corporation, partnership, association, Federal agency, state, municipality, or commission, or political subdivision of a state, or any interstate body.

(e) "Unacceptable adverse effect" means impact on an aquatic or wetland ecosystem which is likely to re-

sult in significant degradation of municipal water supplies (including surface or ground water) or significant loss of or damage to fisheries, shellfishing, or wildlife habitat or recreation areas. In evaluating the unacceptability of such impacts, consideration should be given to the relevant portions of the section 404(b)(1) guidelines (40 CFR Part 230).

(f) "State" means any state agency administering a 404 program which has been approved under section 404(h).

§ 231.3   Procedures for proposed determinations.

(a) If the Regional Administrator has reason to believe after evaluating the information available to him, including any record developed under the section 404 referral process specified in 33 CFR 323.5(b), that an "unacceptable adverse effect" could result from the specification or use for specification of a defined area for the disposal of dredged or fill material, he may initiate the following actions:

(1) The Regional Administrator will notify the District Engineer or the state, if the site is covered by an approved state program, the owner of record of the site, and the applicant, if any, in writing that the Regional Administrator intends to issue a public notice of a proposed determination to prohibit or withdraw the specification, or to deny, restrict or withdraw the use for specification, whichever the case may be, of any defined area as a disposal site.

(2) If within 15 days of receipt of the Regional Administrator's notice under paragraph (a)(1) of this section, it has not been demonstrated to the satisfaction of the Regional Administrator that no unacceptable adverse effect(s) will occur or the District Engineer or state does not notify the Regional Administrator of his intent to take corrective action to prevent an unacceptable adverse effect satisfactory to the Regional Administrator, the Regional Administrator shall publish notice of a proposed determination in accordance with the procedures of this section. Where the Regional Administrator has notified the District Engineer under paragraph (a)(1) of this section that he is considering exercising section 404(c) authority with respect to a particular disposal site for which a permit application is pending but for which no permit has been issued, the District Engineer, in accordance with 33 CFR 325.8, shall not issue the permit until final action is taken under this Part.

Comment. In cases involving a proposed disposal site for which a permit application is pending, it is anticipated that the procedures of the section 404 referral process will normally be exhausted prior to any final decision of whether to initiate a 404(c) proceeding.

(b) Public notice of every proposed determination and notice of all public hearings shall be given by the Regional Administrator. Every public notice shall contain, at a minimum:

(1) An announcement that the Regional Administrator has proposed a determination to prohibit or withdraw specification, or to deny, restrict, or with-

draw the use for specification, of an area as a disposal site, including a summary of the facts on which the proposed determination is based;

(2) The location of the existing, proposed or potential disposal site, and a summary of its characteristics;

(3) A summary of information concerning the nature of the proposed discharge, where applicable;

(4) The identity of the permit applicant, if any;

(5) A brief description of the right to, and procedures for requesting, a public hearing; and

(6) The address and telephone number of the office where interested persons may obtain additional information, including copies of the proposed determination; and

(7) Such additional statements, representations, or information as the Regional Administrator considers necessary or proper.

(c) In addition to the information required under paragraph (b) of this section, public notice of a public hearing held under § 231.4 shall contain the following information:

(1) Reference to the date of public notice of the proposed determination;

(2) Date, time and place of the hearing; and

(3) A brief description of the nature and purpose of the hearing including the applicable rules and procedures.

(d) The following procedures for giving public notice of the proposed determination or of a public hearing shall be followed:

(1) Publication at least once in a daily or weekly newspaper of general circulation in the area in which the defined area is located. In addition the Regional Administrator may (i) post a copy of the notice at the principal office of the municipality in which the defined area is located, or if the defined area is not located near a sizeable community, at the principal office of the political subdivision (State, county or local, whichever is appropriate) with general jurisdiction over the area in which the disposal site is located, and (ii) post a copy of the notice at the United States Post Office serving that area.

(2) A copy of the notice shall be mailed to the owner of record of the site, to the permit applicant or permit holder, if any, to the U.S. Fish and Wildlife Service, National Marine Fisheries Service and any other interested Federal and State water pollution control and resource agencies, and to any person who has filed a written request with the Regional Administrator to receive copies of notices relating to section 404(c) determinations;

(3) A copy of the notice shall be mailed to the appropriate District and Division Engineer(s) and state;

(4) The notice will also be published in the Federal Register.

§ 231.4   Public comments and hearings.

(a) The Regional Administrator shall provide a comment period of not less than 30 or more than 60 days following the date of public notice of the proposed determination. During this period any interested persons may submit written comments on the proposed determination. Comments should be directed to whether the proposed determination should become the final determination and corrective action that could be taken to reduce the adverse impact of the discharge. All such comments shall be considered by the Regional Administrator or his designee in preparing his recommended determination in § 231.5.

(b) Where the Regional Administrator finds a significant degree of public interest in a proposed determination or that it would be otherwise in the public interest to hold a hearing, or if an affected landowner or permit applicant or holder requests a hearing, he or his designee shall hold a public hearing. Public notice of that hearing shall be given as specified in § 231.3(c). No hearing may be held prior to 21 days after the date of the public notice. The hearing may be scheduled either by the Regional Administrator at his own initiative, or in response to a request received during the comment period provided for in paragraph (a) of this section. If no public hearing is held the Regional Administrator shall notify any persons who requested a hearing of the reasons for that decision. Where practicable, hearings shall be conducted in the vicinity of the affected site.

(c) Hearings held under this section shall be conducted by the Regional Administrator, or his designee, in an orderly and expeditious manner. A record of the proceeding shall be made by either tape recording or verbatim transcript.

(d) Any person may appear at the hearing and submit oral or written statements and data and may be represented by counsel or other authorized representative. Any person may present written statements for the hearing file prior to the time the hearing file is closed to public submissions, and may present proposed findings and recommendations. The Regional Administrator or his designee shall afford the participants an opportunity for rebuttal.

(e) The Regional Administrator, or his designee, shall have discretion to establish reasonable limits on the nature, amount or form of presentation of documentary material and oral presentations. No cross examination of any hearing participant shall be permitted, although the Regional Administrator, or his designee, may make appropriate inquiries of any such participant.

(f) The Regional Administrator or his designee shall allow a reasonable time not to exceed 15 days after the close of the public hearing for submission of written comments. After such time has expired, unless such period is extended by the Regional Administrator or his designee for good cause, the hearing file shall be closed to additional public written comments.

(g) No later than the time a public notice of proposed determination is issued, a Record Clerk shall be designated with responsibility for maintaining the administrative record identified in § 231.5(e). Copying of any documents in the record shall be permitted under appropriate arrangements to prevent their loss. The charge for such copies shall be in accordance with the written schedule contained in Part 2 of this chapter.

§ 231.5   Recommended determination.

(a) The Regional Administrator or his designee shall, within 30 days after the conclusion of the public hearing (but not before the end of the comment period), or, if no hearing is held, within 15 days after the expiration of the comment period on the public notice of the proposed determination, either withdraw the proposed determination or prepare a recommended determination to prohibit or withdraw specification, or to deny, restrict, or withdraw the use for specification, of the disposal site because the discharge of dredged or fill material at such site would be likely to have an unacceptable adverse effect.

(b) Where a recommended determination is prepared, the Regional Administrator or his designee shall promptly forward the recommended determination and administrative record to the Administrator for review, with a copy of the recommended determination to the Assistant Administrator for Water and Waste Management.

(c) Where the Regional Administrator, or his designee, decides to withdraw the proposed determination, he shall promptly notify the Administrator by mail, with a copy to the Assistant Administrator for Water and Waste Management, who shall have 10 days from receipt of such notice to notify the Regional Administrator of his intent to review such withdrawal. Copies of the notification shall be sent to all persons who commented on the proposed determination or participated at the hearing. Such persons may submit timely written recommendations concerning review.

(1) If the Administrator does not notify him, the Regional Administrator shall give notice at the withdrawal of the proposed determination as provided in § 231.3(d). Such notice shall constitute final agency action.

(2) If the Administrator does decide to review, the Regional Administrator or his designee shall forward the administrative record to the Administrator for a final determination under § 231.6. Where there is review of a withdrawal of proposed determination or review of a recommended determination under § 231.6, final agency action does not occur until the Administrator makes a final determination.

(d) Any recommended determination under paragraph (b) of this section shall include the following:

(1) A summary of the unacceptable adverse effects that could occur from use of the disposal site for the proposed discharge;

(2) Recommendations regarding a final determination to prohibit, deny, restrict, or withdraw, which shall confirm or modify the proposed determination, with a statement of reasons.

(e) The administrative record shall consist of the following:

(1) A copy of the proposed determination, public notice, written comments on the public notice and written submissions in the hearing file;

(2) A transcript or recording of the public hearing, where a hearing was held;

(3) The recommended determination;

(4) Where possible a copy of the record of the Corps or the state pertaining to the site in question;

(5) Any other information considered by the Regional Administrator or his designee.

§ 231.6   Administrator's final determinations

After reviewing the recommendations of the Regional Administrator or his designee, the Administrator shall within 30 days of receipt of the recommendations and administrative record initiate consultation with the Chief of Engineers, the owner of record, and, where applicable, the State and the applicant, if any. They shall have 15 days to notify the Administrator of their intent to take corrective action to prevent an unacceptable adverse effect(s), satisfactory to the Administrator. Within 60 days of receipt of the recommendations and record, the Administrator shall make a final determination affirming, modifying, or rescinding the recommended determination. The final determination shall describe the satisfactory corrective action, if any, make findings, and state the reasons for the final determination. Notice of such final determination shall be published as provided in § 231.3, and shall be given to all persons who participated in the public hearing. Notice of the Administrator's final determination shall also be published in the Federal Register. For purposes of judicial review, a final determination constitutes final agency action under section 404(c) of the Act.

§ 231.7   Emergency procedure

Where a permit has already been issued, and the Administrator has reason to believe that a discharge under the permit presents an imminent danger of irreparable harm to municipal water supplies, shellfish beds and fishery areas (including spawning and breeding areas) wildlife, or recreational areas, and that the public health, interest, or safety requires, the Administrator may ask the Chief of Engineers to suspend the permit under 33 CFR 325.7, or the state, pending completion of proceedings under Part 231. The Administrator may also take appropriate action as authorized under section 504 of the Clean Water Act. If a permit is suspended, the Administrator and Regional Administrator (or his designee) may, where appropriate, shorten the times allowed by these regulations to take particular actions.

§ 231.8   Extension of time

The Administrator or the Regional Administrator may, upon a showing of good cause, extend the time requirements in these regulations. Notice of any such extension shall be published in the Federal Register and, as appropriate, through other forms of notice.

PART 232
404 PROGRAM DEFINITIONS;
EXEMPT ACTIVITIES NOT REQUIRING 404 PERMITS

§ 232.1 Purpose and scope of this part.

Part 232 contains definitions applicable to the Section 404 program for discharges of dredged or fill material. These definitions apply to both the Federally operated program and State administered programs after program approval. This part also describes those activities which are exempted from regulation. Regulations prescribing the substantive environmental criteria for issuance of Section 404 permits appear at 40 CFR Part 230. Regulations establishing procedures to be followed by the EPA in denying or restricting a disposal site appear at 40 CFR Part 231. Regulations containing the procedures and policies used by the Corps in administering the 404 program appear at 33 CFR Parts 320-330. Regulations specifying the procedures EPA will follow, and the criteria EPA will apply in approving, monitoring, and withdrawing approval of Section 404 State programs appear at 40 CFR Part 233.

§ 232.2 Definitions.

Administrator means the Administrator of the Environmental Protection Agency or an authorized representative.

Application means a form for applying for a permit to discharge dredged or fill material into waters of the United States.

Approved program means a State program which has been approved by the Regional Administrator under Part 233 of this chapter or which is deemed approved under Section 404(h)(3), 33 U.S.C. 1344(h)(3).

Best management practices (BMPs) means schedules of activities, prohibitions of practices, maintenance procedures, and other management practices to prevent or reduce the pollution of waters of the United States from discharges of dredged or fill material. BMPs include methods, measures, practices, or design and performance standards which facilitate compliance with the Section 404(b)(1) Guidelines (40 CFR Part 230), effluent limitations or prohibitions under Section 307(a), and applicable water quality standards.

Discharge of dredged material.

(1) Except as provided below in paragraph (2), the term discharge of dredged material means any addition of dredged material into, including any redeposit of dredged material within, the waters of the United States. The term includes, but is not limited to, the following:

(i) The addition of dredged material to a specified discharge site located in waters of the Untied States;

(ii) The runoff or overflow, associated with a dredging operation, from a contained land or water disposal area; and

(iii) Any addition, including any redeposit, of dredged material, including excavated material, into waters of the United States which is incidental to any activity, including mechanized landclearing, ditching, channelization, or other excavation.

(2) The term discharge of dredged material does not include the following:

(i) Discharges of pollutants into waters of the United States resulting from the onshore subsequent processing of dredged material that is extracted for any commercial use (other than fill). These discharges are subject to section 402 of the Clean Water Act even though the extraction and deposit of such material may require a permit from the Corps or applicable state.

(ii) Activities that involve only the cutting or removing of vegetation above the ground (e.g., mowing, rotary cutting, and chainsawing) where the activity neither substantially disturbs the root system nor involves mechanized pushing, dragging, or other similar activities that redeposit excavated soil material.

(3) Section 404 authorization is not required for the following:

(i) Any incidental addition, including redeposit, of dredged material associated with any activity that does not have or would not have the effect of destroying or degrading an area of waters of the U.S. as defined in paragraphs (4) and (5) of this definition; however, this exception does not apply to any person preparing to undertake mechanized landclearing, ditching, channelization and other excavation activity in a water of the United States, which would result in a redeposit of dredged material, unless the person demonstrates to the satisfaction of the Corps, or EPA as appropriate, prior to commencing the activity involving the discharge, that the activity would not have the effect of destroying or degrading any area of waters of the United States, as defined in paragraphs (4) and (5) of this definition. The person proposing to undertake mechanized landclearing, ditching, channelization or other excavation activity bears the burden of demonstrating that such activity would not destroy or degrade any area of waters of the United States.

(ii) Incidental movement of dredged material occurring during normal dredging operations, defined as dredging for navigation in navigable waters of the United States, as that term is defined in 33 CFR part 329, with proper authorization from the Congress or the Corps pursuant to 33 CFR part 322; however, this exception is not applicable to dredging activities in wetlands, as that term is defined at § 232.2(r) of this Chapter.

(iii) Those discharges of dredged material associated with ditching, channelization or other excavation activities in waters of the United States, including wetlands, for which Section 404 authorization was not previously required, as determined by the Corps district in which the activity occurs or would occur, provided that prior to August 25, 1993, the excavation activity commenced or was under contract to commence work and that the activity will be completed no later that August 25, 1994. This provision does not apply to discharges associated with mechanized landclearing. For those excavation activities that occur on an ongoing basis (either continuously or periodically), e.g., mining operations, the Corps retains the authority to grant, on a case-by-case basis, an extension of this 12-month grandfather provision provided that the discharger has submitted to the Corps within the 12-month period an individual permit application seeking Section 404 authorization for such excavation activity. In no event can the grandfather period under this paragraph extend beyond August 25, 1996.

(iv) Certain discharges, such as those associated with normal farming, silviculture, and ranching activities, are not prohibited by or otherwise subject to regulation under Section 404. See 40 CFR 232.3 for discharges that do not require permits.

(4) For purposes of this section, an activity associated with a discharge of dredged material destroys an area of waters of the United States if it alters the area in such a way that it would no longer be a water of the United States.

Note: Unauthorized discharges into waters of the United States do not eliminate Clean Water Act jurisdiction, even where such unauthorized discharges have the effect of destroying waters of the United States.

(5) For purposes of this section, an activity associated with a discharge of dredged material degrades an area of waters of the United States if it has more than a de minimis (i.e., inconsequential) effect on the area by causing an identifiable individual or cumulative adverse effect on any aquatic function.

Discharge of fill material.

(1) The term discharge of fill material means the addition of fill material into waters of the United States. The term generally includes, without limitation, the following activities: Placement of fill that is necessary for the construction of any structure in a water of the United States; the building of any structure or impoundment requiring rock, sand, dirt, or other material for its construction; site-development fills for recreational, industrial, commercial, residential, and other uses; causeways or road fills; dams and dikes; artificial islands; property protection and/or reclamation devices such as riprap, groins, seawalls, breakwaters, and revetments; beach nourishment; levees; fill for structures such as sewage treatment facilities, intake and outfall pipes associated with power plants and subaqueous utility lines; and artificial reefs.

(2) In addition, placement of pilings in waters of the United States constitutes a discharge of fill material and requires a Section 404 permit when such placement has or would have the effect of a discharge of fill material. Examples of such activities that have the effect of a discharge of fill material include, but are not limited to, the following: Projects where the pilings are so closely spaced that sedimentation rates would be increased; projects in which the pilings themselves effectively would replace the bottom of a waterbody; projects involving the placement of pilings that would reduce the reach or impair the flow or circulation of waters of the United States; and projects involving the placement of pilings which would result in the adverse alteration or elimination of aquatic functions.

(i) Placement of pilings in waters of the United States that does not have or would not have the effect of a discharge of fill material shall not require a Section 404 permit. Placement of pilings for linear projects, such as bridges, elevated walkways, and powerline structures, generally does not have the effect of a discharge of fill material. Furthermore, placement of pilings in waters of the United States for piers, wharves, and an individual house on stilts generally does not have the effect of a discharge of fill material. All pilings, however, placed in the navigable waters of the United States, as that term is defined in 33 CFR part 329, require authorization under section 10 of the Rivers and Harbors Act of 1899 (see 33 CFR part 322).

(ii) [Reserved]

Dredged material means material that is excavated or dredged from waters of the United States.

Effluent means dredged material or fill material, including return flow from confined sites.

Federal Indian reservation means all land within the limits of any Indian reservation under the jurisdiction of the United States Government, notwithstanding the issuance of any patent, and including rights-of-way running through the reservation.

Fill material means any "pollutant" which replaces portions of the "waters of the United States" with dry land or which changes the bottom elevation of a water body for any purpose.

General permit means a permit authorizing a category of discharges of dredged or fill material under the Act. General permits are permits for categories of discharge which are similar in nature, will cause only minimal adverse environmental effects when performed separately, and will have only minimal cumulative adverse effect on the environment.

Indian Tribe means any Indian Tribe, band, group, or community recognized by the Secretary of the Interior and exercising governmental authority over a Federal Indian reservation.

Owner or operator means the owner or operator of any activity subject to regulation under the 404 program.

Permit means a written authorization issued by an approved State to implement the requirements of Part 233, or by the Corps under 33 CFR Parts 320-330. When used in these regulations, "permit" includes "general permit" as well as individual permit.

Person means an individual, association, partnership, corporation, municipality, State or Federal agency, or an agent or employee thereof.

Regional Administrator means the Regional Administrator of the appropriate Regional Office of the Environmental Protection Agency or the authorized representative of the Regional Administrator.

Secretary means the Secretary of the Army acting through the Chief of Engineers.

State means any of the 50 States, the District of Columbia, Guam, the Commonwealth of Puerto Rico, the Virgin Islands, American Samoa, the Commonwealth of the Northern Mariana Islands, the Trust Territory of the Pacific Islands, or an Indian Tribe as defined in this part, which meet the requirements of § 233.60.

State regulated waters means those waters of the United States in which the Corps suspends the issuance of Section 404 permits upon approval of a State's Section 404 permit program by the Administrator under Section 404(h). The program cannot be transferred for those waters which are presently used, or are susceptible to use in their natural condition or by reasonable improvement as a means to transport interstate or foreign commerce shoreward to their ordinary high water mark, including all waters which are subject to the ebb and flow of the tide shoreward to the high tide line, including wetlands adjacent thereto. All other waters of the United States in a State with an approved program shall be under jurisdiction of the State program, and shall be identified in the program description as required by Part 233.

Waters of the United States means:

All waters which are currently used, were used in the past, or may be susceptible to us in interstate or foreign commerce, including all waters which are subject to the ebb and flow of the tide.

All interstate waters including interstate wetlands.

All other waters, such as intrastate lakes, rivers, streams (including intermittent streams), mudflats, sandflats, wetlands, sloughs, prairie potholes, wet meadows, playa lakes, or natural ponds, the use, degradation, or destruction of which would or could affect interstate or foreign commerce including any such waters:

Which are or could be used by interstate or foreign travelers for recreational or other purposes; or

From which fish or shellfish are or could be taken and sold in interstate or foreign commerce; or

Which are used or could be used for industrial purposes by industries in interstate commerce.

All impoundments of waters otherwise defined as waters of the United States under this definition;

Tributaries of waters identified in paragraphs (g)(1)-(4) of this section;

The territorial sea; and

Wetlands adjacent to waters (other than waters that are themselves wetlands) identified in paragraphs (q)(1)-(6) of this section.

Waste treatment systems, including treatment ponds or lagoons designed to meet the requirements of the Act (other than cooling ponds as defined in 40 CFR 123.11(m) which also meet the criteria of this definition) are not waters of the United States.

Waters of the United States do not include prior converted cropland. Notwithstanding the determination of an area's status as prior converted cropland by any other federal agency, for the purposes of the Clean Water Act, the final authority regarding Clean Water Act jurisdiction remains with EPA.

Wetlands means those areas that are inundated or saturated by surface or ground water at a frequency and duration sufficient to support, and that under normal circumstances do support, a prevalence of vegetation typically adapted for life in saturated soil conditions. Wetlands generally include swamps, marshes, bogs, and similar areas.

[58 FR 8182, Feb. 11, 1993; 58 FR 45037, Aug. 25, 1993]

§ 232.3 Activities not requiring permits.

Except as specified in paragraphs (a) and (b) of this section, any discharge of dredged or fill material that may result from any of the activities described in paragraph (c) of this section is not prohibited by or otherwise subject to regulation under this Part.

(a) If any discharge of dredged or fill material resulting from the activities listed in paragraph (c) of this section contains any toxic pollutant listed under Section 307 of the Act, such discharge shall be subject to any applicable toxic effluent standard or prohibition, and shall require a Section 404 permit.

(b) Any discharge of dredged or fill material into waters of the United States incidental to any of the activities identified in paragraph (c) of this section must have a permit if it is part of an activity whose purpose is to convert an area of the waters of the United States into a use to which it was not previously subject, where the flow or circulation of waters of the United States may be impaired or the reach of such waters reduced. Where the proposed discharge will result in significant discernable alterations to flow or circulation, the presumption is that flow or circulation may be impaired by such alteration.

[Note. For example, a permit will be required for the conversion of a cypress swamp to some other use or the conversion of a wetland from silvicultural to agricultural use when there is a discharge of dredged or fill material into waters of the United States in conjunction with construction of dikes, drainage ditches or other works or structures used to effect such conversion. A conversion of Section 404 wetland to a non-wetland is a change in use of an area of waters of the U.S. A discharge which elevates the bottom of waters of the United States without converting it to dry land does not thereby reduce the reach of, but may alter the flow or circulation of, waters of the United States.]

(c) The following activities are exempt from Section 404 permit requirements, except as specified in paragraphs (a) and (b) of this section:

(1)(i) Normal farming, silviculture and ranching activities such as plowing, seeding, cultivating, minor drainage, and harvesting for the production of food, fiber, and forest products, or upland soil and water conservation practices, as defined in paragraph (d) of this section.

(ii)(A) To fall under this exemption, the activities specified in paragraph (c)(1) of this section must be part of an established (i.e., ongoing) farming, silviculture, or ranching operation, and must be in accordance with definitions in paragraph (d) of this section. Activities on areas lying fallow as part of a conventional rotational cycle are part of an established operation.

(B) Activities which bring an area into farming, silviculture or ranching use are not part of an established operation. An operation ceases to be established when the area in which it was conducted has been converted to another use or has lain idle so long that modifications to the hydrological regime are necessary to resume operation. If an activity takes place outside the waters of the United States, or if it does not involve a discharge, it does not need a Section 404 permit whether or not it was part of an established farming, silviculture or ranching operation.

(2) Maintenance, including emergency reconstruction of recently damaged parts, of currently serviceable structures such as dikes, dams, levees, groins, riprap, breakwaters, causeways, bridge abutments or approaches, and transportation structures. Maintenance does not include any modification that changes the character, scope, or size of the original fill design. Emergency reconstruction must occur within a reasonable period of time after damage occurs in order to qualify for this exemption.

(3) Construction or maintenance of farm or stock ponds or irrigation ditches or the maintenance (but not construction) of drainage ditches. Discharge associated with siphons, pumps, headgates, wingwalls, wiers, diversion structures, and such other facilities as are appurtenant and functionally related to irrigation ditches are included in this exemption.

(4) Construction of temporary sedimentation basins on a construction site which does not include placement of fill material into waters of the United States. The term "construction site" refers to any site involving the erection of buildings, roads, and other discrete structures and the installation of support facilities necessary for construction and utilization of such structures. The term also includes any other land areas which involve land- disturbing excavation activities, including quarrying or other mining activities, where an increase in the runoff of sediment is controlled through the use of temporary sedimentation basins.

(5) Any activity with respect to which a State has an approved program under Section 208(b)(4) of the Act which meets the requirements of Section 208(b)(4)(B) and (C).

(6) Construction or maintenance of farm roads, forest roads, or temporary roads for moving mining equipment, where such roads are constructed and maintained in accordance with best management practices (BMPs) to assure that flow and circulation patterns and chemical and biological characteristics of waters of the United States are not impaired, that the reach of the waters of the United States is not reduced, and that any adverse effect on the aquatic environment will be otherwise minimized. The BMPs which must be applied to satisfy this provision include the following baseline provisions:

(i) Permanent roads (for farming or forestry activities), temporary access roads (for mining, forestry, or farm purposes) and skid trails (for logging) in waters of the United States shall be held to the minimum feasible number, width, and total length consistent with the purpose of specific farming, silvicultural or mining operations, and local topographic and climatic conditions;

(ii) All roads, temporary or permanent, shall be located sufficiently far from streams or other water bodies (except for portions of such roads which must cross water bodies) to minimize discharges of dredged or fill material into waters of the United States;

(iii) The road fill shall be bridged, culverted, or otherwise designed to prevent the restriction of expected flood flows;

(iv) The fill shall be properly stabilized and maintained to prevent erosion during and following construction;

(v) Discharges of dredged or fill material into waters of the United States to construct a road fill shall be made in a manner that minimizes the encroachment of trucks, tractors, bulldozers, or other heavy equipment within the waters of the United States (including adjacent wetlands) that lie outside the lateral boundaries of the fill itself;

(vi) In designing, constructing, and maintaining roads, vegetative disturbance in the waters of the United States shall be kept to a minimum;

(vii) The design, construction and maintenance of the road crossing shall not disrupt the migration or other movement of those species of aquatic life inhabiting the water body;

(viii) Borrow material shall be taken from upland sources whenever feasible;

(ix) The discharge shall not take, or jeopardize the continued existence of, a threatened or endangered species as defined under the Endangered Species Act, or adversely modify or destroy the critical habitat of such species;

(x) Discharges into breeding and nesting areas for migratory waterfowl, spawning areas, and wetlands shall be avoided if practical alternatives exist;

(xi) The discharge shall not be located in the proximity of a public water supply intake;

(xii) The discharge shall not occur in areas of concentrated shellfish production;

(xiii) The discharge shall not occur in a component of the National Wild and Scenic River System;

(xiv) The discharge of material shall consist of suitable material free from toxic pollutants in toxic amounts; and

(xv) All temporary fills shall be removed in their entirety and the area restored to its original elevation.

(d) For purpose of paragraph (c)(1) of this section, cultivating, harvesting, minor drainage, plowing, and seeding are defined as follows:

(1) Cultivating means physical methods of soil treatment employed within established farming, ranching and silviculture lands on farm, ranch, or forest crops to aid and improve their growth, quality, or yield.

(2) Harvesting means physical measures employed directly upon farm, forest, or ranch crops within established agricultural and silvicultural lands to bring about their removal from farm, forest, or ranch land, but does not include the construction of farm, forest, or ranch roads.

(3)(i) Minor drainage means:

(A) The discharge of dredged or fill material incidental to connecting upland drainage facilities to waters of the United States, adequate to effect the removal of excess soil moisture from upland croplands. Construction and maintenance of upland (dryland) facilities, such as ditching and tiling, incidental to the planting, cultivating, protecting, or harvesting of crops, involve no discharge of dredged or fill material into waters of the United States, and as such never require a Section 404 permit;

(B) The discharge of dredged or fill material for the purpose of installing ditching or other water control facilities incidental to planting, cultivating, protecting, or harvesting of rice, cranberries or other wetland crop species, where these activities and the discharge occur in waters of the United States which are in established use for such agricultural and silvicultural wetland crop production;

(C) The discharge of dredged or fill material for the purpose of manipulating the water levels of, or regulating the flow or distribution of water within, existing impoundments which have been constructed in accordance with applicable requirements of the Act, and which are in established use for the production or rice, cranberries, or other wetland crop species.

[Note.–The provisions of paragraphs (d)(3)(i) (B) and (C) of this section apply to areas that are in established use exclusively for wetland crop production as well as areas in established use for conventional wetland/non- wetland crop rotation (e.g., the rotations of rice and soybeans) where such rotation results in the cyclical or intermittent temporary dewatering of such areas.]

(D) The discharge of dredged or fill material incidental to the emergency removal of sandbars, gravel bars, or other similar blockages which are formed during flood flows or other events, where such blockages close or constrict previously existing drainageways and, if not promptly removed, would result in damage to or loss of existing crops or would impair or prevent the plowing, seeding, harvesting or cultivating of crops on land in established use for crop production. Such removal does not include enlarging or extending the dimensions of, or changing the bottom elevations of, the affected drainageway as it existed prior to the formation of the blockage. Removal must be accomplished within one year after such blockages are discovered in order to be eligible for exemption.

(ii) Minor drainage in waters of the United States is limited to drainage within areas that are part of an established farming or silviculture operation. It does not include drainage associated with the immediate or gradual conversion of a wetland to a non-wetland (e.g., wetland species to upland species not typically adequate to life in saturated soil conditions), or conversion from one wetland use to another (for example, silviculture to farming). In addition, minor drainage does not include the construction of any canal, ditch, dike or other waterway or structure which drains or otherwise significantly modifies a stream, lake, swamp, bog or any other wetland or aquatic area constituting waters of the United States. Any discharge of dredged or fill material into the waters of the United States incidental to the construction of any such structure or waterway requires a permit.

(4) Plowing means all forms of primary tillage, including moldboard, chisel, or wide-blade plowing, discing, harrowing, and similar physical means used on farm, forest or ranch land for the breaking up, cutting, turning over, or stirring of soil to prepare it for the planting of crops. Plowing does not include the redistribution of soil, rock, sand, or other surficial materials in a manner which changes any area of the waters of the United States to dryland. For example, the redistribution of surface materials by blading, grading, or other means to fill in wetland areas is not plowing. Rock crushing activities which result in the loss of natural drainage characteristics, the reduction of water storage and recharge capabilities, or the overburden of natural water filtration capacities do not constitute plowing. Plowing, as described above, will never involve a discharge of dredged or fill material.

(5) Seeding means the sowing of seed and placement of seedlings to produce farm, ranch, or forest crops and includes the placement of soil beds for seeds or seedlings on established farm and forest lands.

(e) Federal projects which qualify under the criteria contained in Section 404(r) of the Act are exempt from Section 404 permit requirements, but may be subject to other State or Federal requirements.

PART 233
404 STATE PROGRAM REGULATIONS

SUBPART A—GENERAL

§ 233.1   Purpose and scope.

(a) This Part specifies the procedures EPA will follow, and the criteria EPA will apply, in approving, reviewing, and withdrawing approval of State programs under Section 404 of the Act.

(b) Except as provided in § 232.3, a State program must regulate all discharges of dredged or fill material into waters regulated by the State under section 404(g)-(1). Partial State programs are not approvable under section 404. A State's decision not to assume existing Corps' general permits does not constitute a partial program. The discharges previously authorized by general permit will be regulated by State individual permits. However, in many cases, States other than Indian Tribes will lack authority to regulate activities on Indian lands. This lack of authority does not impair that State's ability to obtain full program approval in accordance with this part, i.e., inability of a State which is not an Indian Tribe to regulate activities on Indian lands does not constitute a partial program. The Secretary of the Army acting through the Corps of Engineers will continue to administer the program on Indian lands if a State which is not an Indian Tribe does not seek and have authority to regulate activities on Indian lands.

(c) Nothing in this Part precludes a State from adopting or enforcing requirements which are more stringent or from operating a program with greater scope, than required under this Part. Where an approved State program has a greater scope than required by Federal law, the additional coverage is not part of the Federally approved program and is not subject to Federal oversight or enforcement.

Note: State assumption of the Section 404 program is limited to certain waters, as provided in section 404(g)(1). The Federal program operated by the Corps of Engineers continues to apply to the remaining waters in the State even after program approval. However, this does not restrict States from regulating discharges of dredged or fill material into those waters over which the Secretary retains Section 404 jurisdiction.

(d) Any approved State Program shall, at all times, be conducted in accordance with the requirements of the Act and of this Part. While States may impose more stringent requirements, they may not impose any less stringent requirements for any purpose.

[58 FR 8183, Feb. 11, 1993]

§ 233.2   Definitions.

The definitions in Parts 230 and 232 as well as the following definitions apply to this Part.

Act means the Clean Water Act (33 U.S.C. 1251 *et seq.*).

Corps means the U.S. Army Corps of Engineers.

Federal Indian reservation means all land within the limits of any Indian reservation under the jurisdiction of the United States Government, notwithstanding the issuance of any patent, and including rights-of-way running through the reservation.

FWS means the U.S. Fish and Wildlife Service.

Indian Tribe means any Indian Tribe, band, group, or community recognized by the Secretary of the Interior and exercising governmental authority over a Federal Indian reservation.

Interstate agency means an agency of two or more States established by or under an agreement or compact approved by the Congress, or any other agency of two or more States having substantial powers or duties pertaining to the control of pollution.

NMFS means the National Marine Fisheries Service.

State means any of the 50 States, the District of Columbia, Guam, the Commonwealth of Puerto Rico, the Virgin Islands, American Samoa, the Commonwealth of the Northern Mariana Islands, the Trust Territory of the Pacific Islands, or an Indian Tribe, as defined in this part, which meet the requirements of § 233.60. For purposes of this part, the word State also includes any interstate agency requesting program approval or administering an approved program.

State Director (Director) means the chief administrative officer of any State or interstate agency operating an approved program, or the delegated representative of the Director. If responsibility is divided among two or more State or interstate agencies, Director means the chief administrative officer of the State or interstate agency authorized to perform the particular procedure or function to which reference is made.

State 404 program or State program means a State program which has been approved by EPA under Section 404 of the Act to regulate the discharge of dredged or fill material into certain waters as defined in § 232.2(p).

[58 FR 8183, Feb. 11, 1993]

§ 233.3   Confidentiality of information.

(a) Any information submitted to EPA pursuant to these regulations may be claimed as confidential by the submitter at the time of submittal and a final determination as to that claim will be made in accordance with the procedures of 40 CFR Part 2 and paragraph (c) of this section.

(b) Any information submitted to the Director may be claimed as confidential in accordance with State law, subject to paragraphs (a) and (c) of this section.

(c) Claims of confidentiality for the following information will be denied:

(1) The name and address of any permit applicant or permittee,

(2) Effluent data,

(3) Permit application, and

(4) Issued permit.

§ 233.4 Conflict of interest.

Any public officer or employee who has a direct personal or pecuniary interest in any matter that is subject to decision by the agency shall make known such interest in the official records of the agency and shall refrain from participating in any manner in such decision.

SUBPART B—PROGRAM APPROVAL

§ 233.10 Elements of a program submission.

Any State that seeks to administer a 404 program under this Part shall submit to the Regional Administrator at least three copies of the following:

(a) A letter from the Governor of the State requesting program approval.

(b) A complete program description, as set forth in § 233.11.

(c) An Attorney General's statement, as set forth in § 233.12.

(d) A Memorandum of Agreement with the Regional Administrator, as set forth in § 233.13.

(e) A Memorandum of Agreement with the Secretary, as set forth in § 233.14.

(f) Copies of all applicable State statutes and regulations, including those governing applicable State administrative procedures.

§ 233.11 Program description.

The program description as required under § 233.10 shall include:

(a) A description of the scope and structure of the State's program. The description should include extent of State's jurisdiction, scope of activities regulated, anticipated coordination, scope of permit exemptions if any, and permit review criteria;

(b) A description of the State's permitting, administrative, judicial review, and other applicable procedures;

(c) A description of the basic organization and structure of the State agency (agencies) which will have responsibility for administering the program. If more than one State agency is responsible for the administration of the program, the description shall address the responsibilities of each agency and how the agencies intend to coordinate administration and evaluation of the program;

(d) A description of the funding and manpower which will be available for program administration;

(e) An estimate of the anticipated workload, e.g., number of discharges.

(f) Copies of permit application forms, permit forms, and reporting forms;

(g) A description of the State's compliance evaluation and enforcement programs, including a descrip-

tion of how the State will coordinate its enforcement strategy with that of the Corps and EPA;

(h) A description of the waters of the United States within a State over which the State assumes jurisdiction under the approved program; a description of the waters of the United States within a State over which the Secretary retains jurisdiction subsequent to program approval; and a comparison of the State and Federal definitions of wetlands.

Note.–States should obtain from the Secretary an identification of those waters of the U.S. within the State over which the Corps retains authority under Section 404(g) of the Act.

(i) A description of the specific best management practices proposed to be used to satisfy the exemption provisions of Section 404(f)(1)(E) of the Act for construction or maintenance of farm roads, forest roads, or temporary roads for moving mining equipment.

§ 233.12 Attorney General's statement.

(a) Any State that seeks to administer a program under this Part shall submit a statement from the State Attorney General (or the attorney for those State or interstate agencies which have independence legal counsel), that the laws and regulations of the State, or an interstate compact, provide adequate authority to carry out the program and meet the applicable requirements of this Part. This statement shall cite specific statutes and administrative regulations which are lawfully adopted at the time the statement is signed and which shall be fully effective by the time the program is approved, and, where appropriate, judicial decisions which demonstrate adequate authority. The attorney signing the statement required by this section must have authority to represent the State agency in court on all matters pertaining to the State program.

(b) If a State seeks approval of a program covering activities on Indian lands, the statement shall contain an analysis of the State's authority over such activities.

(c) The State Attorney General's statement shall contain a legal analysis of the effect of State law regarding the prohibition on taking private property without just compensation on the successful implementation of the State's program.

(d) In those States where more than one agency has responsibility for administering the State program, the statement must include certification that each agency has full authority to administer the program within its category of jurisdiction and that the State, as a whole, has full authority to administer a complete State Section 404 program.

§ 233.13 Memorandum of Agreement with Regional Administrator.

(a) Any State that seeks to administer a program under this Part shall submit a Memorandum of Agreement executed by the Director and the Regional Administrator. The Memorandum of Agreement shall become effective upon approval of the State program. When more than one agency within a State has responsibility for administering the State program, Directors of each of the responsible State agencies shall be parties to the Memorandum of Agreement.

(b) The Memorandum of Agreement shall set out the State and Federal responsibilities for program administration and enforcement. These shall include, but not be limited to:

(1) Provisions specifying classes and categories of permit applications for which EPA will waive Federal review (as specified in § 233.51).

(2) Provisions specifying the frequency and content of reports, documents and other information which the State may be required to submit to EPA in addition to the annual report, as well as a provision establishing the submission date for the annual report. The State shall also allow EPA routinely to review State records, reports and files relevant to the administration and enforcement of the approved program.

(3) Provisions addressing EPA and State roles and coordination with respect to compliance monitoring and enforcement activities.

(4) Provisions addressing modification of the Memorandum of Agreement.

§ 233.14 Memorandum of Agreement with the Secretary.

(a) Before a State program is approved under this Part, the Director shall enter into a Memorandum of Agreement with the Secretary. When more than one agency within a State has responsibility for administering the State program, Directors of each of the responsible agencies shall be parties of the Memorandum of Agreement.

(b) The Memorandum of Agreement shall include:

(1) A description of waters of the United States within the State over which the Secretary retains jurisdiction, as identified by the Secretary.

(2) Procedures whereby the Secretary will, upon program approval, transfer to the State pending 404 permit applications for discharges in State regulated waters and other relevant information not already in the possession of the Director.

Note. Where a State permit program includes coverage of those traditionally navigable waters in which only the Secretary may issue Section 404 permits, the State is encouraged to establish in this MOA procedures for joint processing of Federal and State permits, including joint public notices and public hearings.

(3) An identification of all general permits issued by the Secretary the terms and conditions of which the State intends to administer and enforce upon receiving approval of its program, and a plan for transferring responsibility for these general permits to the State, including procedures for the prompt transmission from the Secretary to the Director of relevant information not already in the possession of the Director, including support files for permit issuance, compliance reports and records of enforcement actions.

§ 233.15 Procedures for approving State programs.

(a) The 120 day statutory review period shall commence on the date of receipt of a complete State program submission as set out in § 233.10 of this Part. EPA shall determine whether the submission is complete within 30 days of receipt of the submission and shall notify the State of its determination. If EPA finds that a State's submission is incomplete, the statutory review period shall not begin until all the necessary information is received by EPA.

(b) If EPA determines the State significantly changes its submission during the review period, the statutory review period shall begin again upon the receipt of a revised submission.

(c) The State and EPA may extend the statutory review period by agreement.

(d) Within 10 days of receipt of a complete State Section 404 program submission, the Regional Administrator shall provide copies of the State's submission to the Corps, FWS, and NMFS (both Headquarters and appropriate Regional organizations.)

(e) After determining that a State program submission is complete, the Regional Administrator shall publish notice of the State's application in the Federal Register and in enough of the largest newspapers in the State to attract statewide attention. The Regional Administrator shall also mail notice to persons known to be interested in such matters. Existing State, EPA, Corps, FWS, and NMFS mailing lists shall be used as a basis for this mailing. However, failure to mail all such notices shall not be grounds for invalidating approval (or disapproval) of an otherwise acceptable (or unacceptable) program. This notice shall:

(1) Provide for a comment period of not less than 45 days during which interested members of the public may express their views on the State program.

(2) Provide for a public hearing within the State to be held not less than 30 days after notice of hearing is published in the Federal Register;

(3) Indicate where and when the State's submission may be reviewed by the public;

(4) Indicate whom an interested member of the public with questions should contact; and

(5) Briefly outline the fundamental aspects of the State's proposed program and the process for EPA review and decision.

(f) Within 90 days of EPA's receipt of a complete program submission, the Corps, FWS, and NMFS shall submit to EPA any comments on the State's program.

(g) Within 120 days of receipt of a complete program submission (unless an extension is agreed to by the State), the Regional Administrator shall approve or disapprove the program based on whether the State's program fulfills the requirements of this Part and the Act, taking into consideration all comments received. The Regional Administrator shall prepare a responsiveness summary of significant comments received and his response to these comments. The Regional Administrator shall respond individually to comments received from the Corps, FWS, and NMFS.

(h) If the Regional Administrator approves the State's Section 404 program, he shall notify the State and the Secretary of the decision and publish notice in the Federal Register. Transfer of the program to the State shall not be considered effective until such notice appears in the Federal Register. The Secretary shall suspend the issuance by the Corps of Section 404 permits in State regulated waters on such effective date.

(i) If the Regional Administrator disapproves the State's program based on the State not meeting the requirements of the Act and this Part, the Regional Administrator shall notify the State of the reasons for the disapproval and of any revisions or modifications to the State's program which are necessary to obtain approval. If the State resubmits a program submission remedying the identified problem areas, the approval procedure and statutory review period shall begin upon receipt of the revised submission.

§ 233.16 Procedures for revision of State programs.

(a) The State shall keep the Regional Administrator fully informed of any proposed or actual changes to the State's statutory or regulatory authority or any other modifications which are significant to administration of the program.

(b) Any approved program which requires revision because of a modification to this Part or to any other applicable Federal statute or regulation shall be revised within one year of the date of promulgation of such regulation, except that if a State must amend or enact a statute in order to make the required revision, the revision shall take place within two years.

(c) States with approved programs shall notify the Regional Administrator whenever they propose to transfer all or part of any program from the approved State agency to any other State agency. The new agency is not authorized to administer the program until approved by the Regional Administrator under paragraph (d) of this section.

(d) Approval of revision of a State program shall be accomplished as follows:

(1) The Director shall submit a modified program description or other documents which the Regional Administrator determines to be necessary to evaluate whether the program complies with the requirements of the Act and this Part.

(2) Notice of approval of program changes which are not substantial revisions may be given by letter from the Regional Administrator to the Governor or his designee.

(3) Whenever the Regional Administrator determines that the proposed revision is substantial, he shall publish and circulate notice to those persons known to be interested in such matters, provide opportunity for a public hearing, and consult with the Corps, FWS, and NMFS. The Regional Administrator shall approve or disapprove program revisions based on whether the program fulfills the requirements of the Act and this Part, and shall publish notice of his

decision in the Federal Register. For purposes of this paragraph, substantial revisions include, but are not limited to, revisions that affect the area of jurisdiction, scope of activities regulated, criteria for review of permits, public participation, or enforcement capability.

(4) Substantial program changes shall become effective upon approval by the Regional Administrator and publication of notice in the Federal Register.

(e) Whenever the Regional Administrator has reason to believe that circumstances have changed with respect to a State's program, he may request and the State shall provide a supplemental Attorney General's statement, program description, or such other documents or information as are necessary to evaluate the program's compliance with the requirements of the Act and this Part.

SUBPART C—PERMIT REQUIREMENTS

§ 233.20 Prohibitions.

No permit shall be issued by the Director in the following circumstances:

(a) When permit does not comply with the requirements of the Act or regulations thereunder, including the Section 404(b)(1) Guidelines (Part 230 of this Chapter).

(b) When the Regional Administrator has objected to issuance of the permit under § 233.50 and the objection has not been resolved.

(c) When the proposed discharges would be in an area which has been prohibited, withdrawn, or denied as a disposal site by the Administrator under Section 404(c) of the Act, or when the discharge would fail to comply with a restriction imposed thereunder.

(d) If the Secretary determines, after consultation with the Secretary of the Department in which the Coast Guard is operating, that anchorage and navigation of any of the navigable waters would be substantially impaired.

§ 233.21 General permits.

(a) Under Section 404(h)(5) of the Act, States may, after program approval, administer and enforce general permits previously issued by the Secretary in State regulated waters.

Note: If States intend to assume existing general permits, they must be able to ensure compliance with existing permit conditions an any reporting monitoring, or prenotification requirements.

(b) The Director may issue a general permit for categories of similar activities if he determines that the regulated activities will cause only minimal adverse environmental effects when performed separately and will have only minimal cumulative adverse effects on the environment. Any general permit issued shall be in compliance with the Section 404(b)(1) Guidelines.

(c) In addition to the conditions specified in § 233.23, each general permit shall contain:

(1) A specific description of the type(s) of activities which are authorized, including limitations for any single operation. The description shall be detailed enough to ensure that the requirements of paragraph (b) of this section are met. (This paragraph supercedes § 233.23(c)(1) for general permits.)

(2) A precise description of the geographic area to which the general permit applies, including limitations on the type(s) of water where operations may be conducted sufficient to ensure that the requirements of paragraph (b) of this section are met.

(d) Predischarge notification or other reporting requirements may be required by the Director on a permit-by-permit basis as appropriate to ensure that the general permit will comply with the requirement (section 404(e) of the Act) that the regulated activities will cause only minimal adverse environmental effects when performed separately and will have only minimal cumulative adverse effects on the environment.

(e) The Director may, without revoking the general permit, require any person authorized under a general permit to apply for an individual permit. This discretionary authority will be based on concerns for the aquatic environment including compliance with paragraph (b) of this section and the 404(b)(1) Guidelines (40 CFR Part 230.)

(1) This provision in no way affects the legality of activities undertaken pursuant to the general permit prior to notification by the Director of such requirement.

(2) Once the Director notifies the discharger of his decision to exercise discretionary authority to require an individual permit, the discharger's activity is no longer authorized by the general permit.

§ 233.22 Emergency permits.

(a) Notwithstanding any other provision of this Part, the Director may issue a temporary emergency permit for a discharge of dredged or fill material if unacceptable harm to life or severe loss of physical property is likely to occur before a permit could be issued or modified under procedures normally required.

(b) Emergency permits shall incorporate, to the extent possible and not inconsistent with the emergency situation, all applicable requirements of § 233.23.

(1) Any emergency permit shall be limited to the duration of time (typically no more than 90 days) required to complete the authorized emergency action.

(2) The emergency permit shall have a condition requiring appropriate restoration of the site.

(c) The emergency permit may be terminated at any time without process (§ 233.36) if the Director determines that termination is necessary to protect human health or the environment.

(d) The Director shall consult in an expeditious manner, such as by telephone, with the Regional Administrator, the Corps, FWS, and NMFS about issuance of an emergency permit.

(e) The emergency permit may be oral or written. If oral, it must be followed within 5 days by a written emergency permit. A copy of the written permit shall be sent to the Regional Administrator.

(f) Notice of the emergency permit shall be published and public comments solicited in accordance with § 233.32 as soon as possible but no later than 10 days after the issuance date.

§ 233.23 Permit conditions.

(a) For each permit the Director shall establish conditions which assure compliance with all applicable statutory and regulatory requirements, including the 404(b)(1) Guidelines, applicable Section 303 water quality standards, and applicable Section 307 effluent standards and prohibitions.

(b) Section 404 permits shall be effective for a fixed term not to exceed 5 years.

(c) Each 404 permit shall include conditions meeting or implementing the following requirements:

(1) A specific identification and complete description of the authorized activity including name and address of permittee, location and purpose of discharge, type and quantity of material to be discharged. (This subsection is not applicable to general permits).

(2) Only the activities specifically described in the permit are authorized.

(3) The permittee shall comply with all conditions of the permit even if that requires halting or reducing the permitted activity to maintain compliance. Any permit violation constitutes a violation of the Act as well as of State statute and/or regulation.

(4) The permittee shall take all reasonable steps to minimize or prevent any discharge in violation of this permit.

(5) The permittee shall inform the Director of any expected or known actual noncompliance.

(6) The permittee shall provide such information to the Director, as the Director requests, to determine compliance status, or whether cause exists for permit modification, revocation or termination.

(7) Monitoring, reporting and recordkeeping requirements as needed to safeguard the aquatic environment. (Such requirements will be determined on a case-by-case basis, but at a minimum shall include monitoring and reporting of any expected leachates, reporting of noncompliance, planned changes or transfer of the permit.)

(8) Inspection and entry. The permittee shall allow the Director, or his authorized representative, upon presentation of proper identification, at reasonable times to:

(i) Enter upon the permittee's premises where a regulated activity is located or where records must be kept under the conditions of the permit,

(ii) Have access to and copy any records that must be kept under the conditions of the permit,

(iii) Inspect operations regulated or required under the permit, and

(iv) Sample or monitor, for the purposes of assuring permit compliance or as otherwise authorized by the Act, any substances or parameters at any location.

(9) Conditions assuring that the discharge will be conducted in a manner which minimizes adverse impacts upon the physical, chemical and biological integrity of the waters of the United States, such as requirements for restoration or mitigation.

SUBPART D—PROGRAM OPERATION

§ 233.30 Application for a permit.

(a) Except when an activity is authorized by a general permit issued pursuant to § 233.21 or is exempt from the requirements to obtain a permit under § 232.3, any person who proposes to discharge dredged or fill material into State regulated waters shall complete, sign and submit a permit application to the Director. Persons proposing to discharge dredged or fill material under the authorization of a general permit must comply with any reporting requirements of the general permit.

(b) A complete application shall include:

(1) Name, address, telephone number of the applicant and name(s) and address(es) of adjoining property owners.

(2) A complete description of the proposed activity including necessary drawings, sketches or plans sufficient for public notice (the applicant is not generally expected to submit detailed engineering plans and specifications); the location, purpose and intended use of the proposed activity; scheduling of the activity; the location and dimensions of adjacent structures; and a list of authorizations required by other Federal, interstate, State or local agencies for the work, including all approvals received or denials already made.

(3) The application must include a description of the type, composition, source and quantity of the material to be discharged, the method of discharge, and the site and plans for disposal of the dredged or fill material.

(4) A certification that all information contained in the application is true and accurate and acknowledging awareness of penalties for submitting false information.

(5) All activities which the applicant plans to undertake which are reasonably related to the same project should be included in the same permit application.

(c) In addition to the information indicated in § 233.30(b), the applicant will be required to furnish such additional information as the Director deems appropriate to assist in the evaluation of the application. Such additional information may include environmental data and information on alternate methods and sites as may be necessary for the preparation of the required environmental documentation.

(d) The level of detail shall be reasonably commensurate with the type and size of discharge, proximity to critical areas, likelihood of long-lived toxic chemical substances, and potential level of environmental degradation.

Note: EPA encourages States to provide permit applicants guidance regarding the level of detail of information and documentation required under this subsection. This guidance can be provided either through the application form or on an individual basis. EPA also encourages the State to maintain a program to inform potential applicants for permits of the requirements of the State program and of the steps required to obtain permits for activities in State regulated waters.

§ 233.31 Coordination requirements.

(a) If a proposed discharge may affect the biological, chemical, or physical integrity of the waters of any State(s) other than the State in which the discharge occurs, the Director shall provide an opportunity for such State(s) to submit written comments within the public comment period and to suggest permit conditions. If these recommendations are not accepted by the Director, he shall notify the affected State and the Regional Administrator prior to permit issuance in writing of his failure to accept these recommendations, together with his reasons for so doing. The Regional Administrator shall then have the time provided for in § 233.50(d) to comment upon, object to, or make recommendations.

(b) State Section 404 permits shall be coordinated with Federal and Federal- State water related planning and review processes.

§ 233.32 Public notice.

(a) Applicability.

(1) The Director shall give public notice of the following actions:

(i) Receipt of a permit application.

(ii) Preparation of a draft general permit.

(iii) Consideration of a major modification to an issued permit.

(iv) Scheduling of a public hearing.

(v) Issuance of an emergency permit.

(2) Public notices may describe more than one permit or action.

(b) Timing.

(1) The public notice shall provide a reasonable period of time, normally at least 30 days, within which interested parties may express their views concerning the permit application.

(2) Public notice of a public hearing shall be given at least 30 days before the hearing.

(3) The Regional Administrator may approve a program with shorter public notice timing if the Regional Administrator determines that sufficient public notice is provided for.

(c) The Director shall give public notice by each of the following methods:

(1) By mailing a copy of the notice to the following persons (any person otherwise entitled to re-

ceive notice under this paragraph may waive his rights to receive notice for any classes or categories of permits):

(i) The applicant.

(ii) Any agency with jurisdiction over the activity or the disposal site, whether or not the agency issues a permit.

(iii) Owners of property adjoining the property where the regulated activity will occur.

(iv) All persons who have specifically requested copies of public notices. (The Director may update the mailing list from time to time by requesting written indication of continued interest from those listed. The Director may delete from the list the name of any person who fails to respond to such a request.)

(v) Any State whose waters may be affected by the proposed discharge.

(2) In addition, by providing notice in at least one other way (such as advertisement in a newspaper of sufficient circulation) reasonably calculated to cover the area affected by the activity.

(d) All public notices shall contain at least the following information:

(1) The name and address of the applicant and, if different, the address or location of the activity(ies) regulated by the permit.

(2) The name, address, and telephone number of a person to contact for further information.

(3) A brief description of the comment procedures and procedures to request a public hearing, including deadlines.

(4) A brief description of the proposed activity, its purpose and intended use, so as to provide sufficient information concerning the nature of the activity to generate meaningful comments, including a description of the type of structures, if any, to be erected on fills, and a description of the type, composition and quantity of materials to be discharged.

(5) A plan and elevation drawing showing the general and specific site location and character of all proposed activities, including the size relationship of the proposed structures to the size of the impacted waterway and depth of water in the area.

(6) A paragraph describing the various evaluation factors, including the 404(b)(1) Guidelines or State-equivalent criteria, on which decisions are based.

(7) Any other information which would significantly assist interested parties in evaluating the likely impact of the proposed activity.

(e) Notice of public hearing shall also contain the following information:

(1) Time, date, and place of hearing.

(2) Reference to the date of any previous public notices relating to the permit.

(3) Brief description of the nature and purpose of the hearing.

§ 233.33 Public hearing.

(a) Any interested person may request a public hearing during the public comment period as specified in § 233.32. Requests shall be in writing and shall state the nature of the issues proposed to be raised at the hearing.

(b) The Director shall hold a public hearing whenever he determines there is a significant degree of public interest in a permit application or a draft general permit. He may also hold a hearing, at his discretion, whenever he determines a hearing may be useful to a decision on the permit application.

(c) At a hearing, any person may submit oral or written statements or data concerning the permit application or draft general permit. The public comment period shall automatically be extended to the close of any public hearing under this section. The presiding officer may also extend the comment period at the hearing.

(d) All public hearings shall be reported verbatim. Copies of the record of proceedings may be purchased by any person from the Director or the reporter of such hearing. A copy of the transcript (or if none is prepared, a tape of the proceedings) shall be made available for public inspection at an appropriate State office.

§ 233.34 Making a decision on the permit application.

(a) The Director will review all applications for compliance with the 404(b)(1) Guidelines and/or equivalent State environmental criteria as well as any other applicable State laws or regulations.

(b) The Director shall consider all comments received in response to the public notice, and public hearing if a hearing is held. All comments, as well as the record of any public hearing, shall be made part of the official record on the application.

(c) After the Director has completed his review of the application and consideration of comments, the Director will determine, in accordance with the record and all applicable regulations, whether or not the permit should be issued. No permit shall be issued by the Director under the circumstances described in § 233.20. The Director shall prepare a written determination on each application outlining his decision and rationale for his decision. The determination shall be dated, signed and included in the official record prior to final action on the application. The official record shall be open to the public.

§ 233.35 Issuance and effective date of permit.

(a) If the Regional Administrator comments on a permit application or draft general permit under § 233.50, the Director shall follow the procedures specified in that section in issuing the permit.

(b) If the Regional Administrator does not comment on a permit application or draft general permit, the Director shall make a final permit decision after the close of the public comment period and shall notify the applicant.

(1) If the decision is to issue a permit, the permit becomes effective when it is signed by the Director and the applicant.

(2) If the decision is to deny the permit, the Director will notify the applicant in writing of the reason(s) for denial.

§ 233.36 Modification, suspension or revocation of permits.

(a) General. The Director may reevaluate the circumstances and conditions of a permit either on his own motion or at the request of the permittee or of a third party and initiate action to modify, suspend, or revoke a permit if he determines that sufficient cause exists. Among the factors to be considered are:

(1) Permittee's noncompliance with any of the terms or conditions of the permit;

(2) Permittee's failure in the application or during the permit issuance process to disclose fully all relevant facts or the permittee's misrepresentation of any relevant facts at the time;

(3) Information that activities authorized by a general permit are having more than minimal individual or cumulative adverse effect on the environment, or that the permitted activities are more appropriately regulated by individual permits;

(4) Circumstances relating to the authorized activity have changed since the permit was issued and justify changed permit conditions or temporary or permanent cessation of any discharge controlled by the permit;

(5) Any significant information relating to the activity authorized by the permit if such information was not available at the time the permit was issued and would have justified the imposition of different permit conditions or denial at the time of issuance;

(6) Revisions to applicable statutory or regulatory authority, including toxic effluent standards or prohibitions or water quality standards.

(b) Limitations. Permit modifications shall be in compliance with § 233.20.

(c) Procedures.

(1) The Director shall develop procedures to modify, suspend or revoke permits if he determines cause exists for such action (§ 233.36(a)). Such procedures shall provide opportunity for public comment (§ 233.32), coordination with the Federal review agencies (§ 233.50), and opportunity for public hearing (§ 233.33) following notification of the permittee. When permit modification is proposed, only the conditions subject to modification need be reopened.

(2) Minor modification of permits. The Director may, upon the consent of the permittee, use abbreviated procedures to modify a permit to make the following corrections or allowance for changes in the permitted activity:

(i) Correct typographical errors;

(ii) Require more frequent monitoring or reporting by permittee;

(iii) Allow for a change in ownership or operational control of a project or activity where the Director determines that no other change in the permit is necessary, provided that a written agreement containing a specific date for transfer of permit responsibility, coverage, and liability between the current and new permittees has been submitted to the Director;

(iv) Provide for minor modification of project plans that do not significantly change the character, scope, and/or purpose of the project or result in significant change in environmental impact;

(v) Extend the term of a permit, so long as the modification does not extend the term of the permit beyond 5 years from its original effective date and does not result in any increase in the amount of dredged or fill material allowed to be discharged.

§ 233.37 Signatures on permit applications and reports.

The application and any required reports must be signed by the person who desires to undertake the proposed activity or by that person's duly authorized agent if accompanied by a statement by that person designating the agent. In either case, the signature of the applicant or the agent will be understood to be an affirmation that he possesses or represents the person who possesses the requisite property interest to undertake the activity proposed in the application.

§ 233.38 Continuation of expiring permits.

A Corps 404 permit does not continue in force beyond its expiration date under Federal law if, at that time, a State is the permitting authority. States authorized to administer the 404 Program may continue Corps or State-issued permits until the effective date of the new permits, if State law allows. Otherwise, the discharge is being conducted without a permit from the time of expiration of the old permit to the effective date of a new State-issued permit, if any.

SUBPART E—COMPLIANCE EVALUATION AND ENFORCEMENT

§ 233.40 Requirements for compliance evaluation programs.

(a) In order to abate violations of the permit program, the State shall maintain a program designed to identify persons subject to regulation who have failed to obtain a permit or to comply with permit conditions.

(b) The Director and State officers engaged in compliance evaluation, upon presentation of proper identification, shall have authority to enter any site or premises subject to regulation or in which records relevant to program operation are kept in order to copy any records, inspect, monitor or otherwise investigate compliance with the State program.

(c) The State program shall provide for inspections to be conducted, samples to be taken and other information to be gathered in a manner that will produce evidence admissible in an enforcement proceeding.

(d) The State shall maintain a program for receiving and ensuring proper consideration of information submitted by the public about violations.

§ 233.41 Requirements for enforcement authority.

(a) Any State agency administering a program shall have authority:

(1) To restrain immediately and effectively any person from engaging in any unauthorized activity;

(2) To sue to enjoin any threatened or continuing violation of any program requirement;

(3) To assess or sue to recover civil penalties and to seek criminal remedies, as follows:

(i) The agency shall have the authority to assess or recover civil penalties for discharges of dredged or fill material without a required permit or in violation of any Section 404 permit condition in an amount of at least $5,000 per day of such violation.

(ii) The agency shall have the authority to seek criminal fines against any person who willfully or with criminal negligence discharges dredged or fill material without a required permit or violates any permit condition issued under Section 404 in the amount of at least $10,000 per day of such violation.

(iii) The agency shall have the authority to seek criminal fines against any person who knowingly makes false statements, representation, or certification in any application, record, report, plan, or other document filed or required to be maintained under the Act, these regulations or the approved State program, or who falsifies, tampers with, or knowingly renders inaccurate any monitoring device or method required to be maintained under the permit, in an amount of at least $5,000 for each instance of violation.

(b)(1) The approved maximum civil penalty or criminal fine shall be assessable for each violation and, if the violation is continuous, shall be assessable in that maximum amount for each day of violation.

(2) The burden of proof and degree of knowledge or intent required under State law for establishing violations under paragraph (a)(3) of this section, shall be no greater than the burden of proof or degree of knowledge or intent EPA must bear when it brings an action under the Act.

(c) The civil penalty assessed, sought, or agreed upon by the Director under paragraph (a)(3) of this section shall be appropriate to the violation.

Note: To the extent that State judgments or settlements provide penalties in amounts which EPA believes to be substantially inadequate in comparison to the amounts which EPA would require under similar facts, EPA may, when authorized by Section 309 of the Act, commence separate action for penalties.

(d)(1) The Regional Administrator may approve a State program where the State lacks authority to recover penalties of the levels required under paragraphs (a)(3)(i)-(iii) of this section only if the Regional Administrator determines, after evaluating a record of at least one year for an alternative enforcement program, that the State has an alternate, demonstrably effective method of ensuring compliance which has both punitive and deterrence effects.

(2) States whose programs were approved via waiver of monetary penalties shall keep the Regional Administrator informed of all enforcement actions taken under any alternative method approved pursuant to paragraph (d)(1) of this section. The manner of reporting will be established in the Memorandum of Agreement with the Regional Administrator (§ 233.13).

(e) Any State administering a program shall provide for public participation in the State enforcement process by providing either:

(1) Authority which allows intervention of right in any civil or administrative action to obtain remedies specified in paragraph (a)(3) of this section by any citizen having an interest which is or may be adversely affected, or

(2) Assurance that the State agency or enforcement authority will:

(i) Investigate and provide written responses to all citizen complaints submitted pursuant to State procedures;

(ii) Not oppose intervention by any citizen when permissive intervention may be authorized by statute, rule, or regulation; and

(iii) Publish notice of and provide at least 30 days for public comment on any proposed settlement of a State enforcement action.

(f) Provision for Tribal criminal enforcement authority. To the extent that an Indian Tribe does not assert or is precluded from asserting criminal enforcement authority (§ 233.41(a)(3) (ii) and (iii)), the Federal government will continue to exercise primary criminal enforcement responsibility. The Tribe, with the EPA Region and Corps District(s) with jurisdiction, shall develop a system where the Tribal agency will refer such a violation to the Regional Administrator or the District Engineer(s), as agreed to by the parties, in an appropriate and timely manner. This agreement shall be incorporated into joint or separate Memorandum of Agreement with the EPA Region and the Corps District(s), as appropriate.

[58 FR 8183, Feb. 11, 1993]

SUBPART F—FEDERAL OVERSIGHT

§ 233.50 Review of and objection to State permits.

(a) The Director shall promptly transmit to the Regional Administrator:

(1) A copy of the public notice for any complete permit applications received by the Director, except those for which permit review has been waived

under § 233.51. The State shall supply the Regional Administrator with copies of public notices for permit applications for which permit review has been waived whenever requested by EPA.

(2) A copy of a draft general permit whenever the State intends to issue a general permit.

(3) Notice of every significant action taken by the State agency related to the consideration of any permit application except those for which Federal review has been waived or draft general permit.

(4) A copy of every issued permit.

(5) A copy of the Director's response to another State's comments/recommendations, if the Director does not accept these recommendations (§ 233.32(a)).

(b) Unless review has been waived under § 233.51, the Regional Administrator shall provide a copy of each public notice, each draft general permit, and other information needed for review of the application to the Corps, FWS, and NMFS, within 10 days of receipt. These agencies shall notify the Regional Administrator within 15 days of their receipt if they wish to comment on the public notice or draft general permit. Such agencies should submit their evaluation and comments to the Regional Administrator within 50 days of such receipt. The final decision to comment, object or to require permit conditions shall be made by the Regional Administrator. (These times may be shortened by mutual agreement of the affected Federal agencies and the State.)

(c) If the information provided is inadequate to determine whether the permit application or draft general permit meets the requirements of the Act, these regulations, and the 404(b)(1) Guidelines, the Regional Administrator may, within 30 days of receipt, request the Director to transmit to the Regional Administrator the complete record of the permit proceedings before the State, or any portions of the record, or other information, including a supplemental application, that the Regional Administrator determines necessary for review.

(d) If the Regional Administrator intends to comment upon, object to, or make recommendations with respect to a permit application, draft general permit, or the Director's failure to accept the recommendations of an affected State submitted pursuant to § 233.31(a), he shall notify the Director of his intent within 30 days of receipt. If the Director has been so notified, the permit shall not be issued until after the receipt of such comments or 90 days of the Regional Administrator's receipt of the public notice, draft general permit or Director's response (§ 233.31(a)), whichever comes first. The Regional Administrator may notify the Director within 30 days of receipt that there is no comment but that he reserves the right to object within 90 days of receipt, based on any new information brought out by the public during the comment period or at a hearing.

(e) If the Regional Administrator has given notice to the Director under paragraph (d) of this section, he shall submit to the Director, within 90 days of receipt of the public notice, draft general permit, or Director's response (§ 233.31(a)), a written statement of his comments, objections, or recommendations; the reasons for the comments, objections, or recommendations; and the actions that must be taken by the Director in order to eliminate any objections. Any such objection shall be based on the Regional Administrator's determination that the proposed permit is (1) the subject of an interstate dispute under § 233.31(a) and/or (2) outside requirements of the Act, these regulations, or the 404(b)(1) Guidelines. The Regional Administrator shall make available upon request a copy of any comment, objection, or recommendation on a permit application or draft general permit to the permit applicant or to the public.

(f) When the Director has received an EPA objection or requirement for a permit condition to a permit application or draft general permit under this section, he shall not issue the permit unless he has taken the steps required by the Regional Administrator to eliminate the objection.

(g) Within 90 days of receipt by the Director of an objection or requirement for a permit condition by the Regional Administrator, the State or any interested person may request that the Regional Administrator hold a public hearing on the objection or requirement. The Regional Administrator shall conduct a public hearing whenever requested by the State proposing to issue the permit, or if warranted by significant public interest based on requests received.

(h) If a public hearing is held under paragraph (g) of this section, the Regional Administrator shall, following that hearing, reaffirm, modify or withdraw the objection or requirement for a permit condition, and notify the Director of this decision.

(1) If the Regional Administrator withdraws his objection or requirement for a permit condition, the Director may issue the permit.

(2) If the Regional Administrator does not withdraw the objection or requirement for a permit condition, the Director must issue a permit revised to satisfy the Regional Administrator's objection or requirement for a permit condition or notify EPA of its intent to deny the permit within 30 days of receipt of the Regional Administrator's notification.

(i) If no public hearing is held under paragraph (g) of this section, the Director within 90 days of receipt of the objection or requirement for a permit condition shall either issue the permit revised to satisfy EPA's objections or notify EPA of its intent to deny the permit.

(j) In the event that the Director neither satisfies EPA's objections or requirement for a permit condition nor denies the permit application, the Secretary shall process the permit application.

[53 FR 41649, Oct. 24, 1988]

§ 233.51 Waiver of review.

(a) The MOA with the Regional Administrator shall specify the categories of discharge for which EPA will waive Federal review of State permit applications. After program approval, the MOA may be modified to reflect any additions or deletions of categories of discharge for which EPA will waive review. The Regional Administrator shall consult with the Corps, FWS, and NMFS prior to specifying or modifying such categories.

(b) With the following exceptions, any category of discharge is eligible for consideration for waiver:

(1) Draft general permits;

(2) Discharges with reasonable potential for affecting endangered or threatened species as determined by FWS;

(3) Discharges with reasonable potential for adverse impacts on waters of another State;

(4) Discharges known or suspected to contain toxic pollutants in toxic amounts (Section 101(a)(3) of the Act) or hazardous substances in reportable quantities (Section 311 of the Act);

(5) Discharges located in proximity of a public water supply intake;

(6) Discharges within critical areas established under State or Federal law, including but not limited to National and State parks, fish and wildlife sanctuaries and refuges, National and historical monuments, wilderness areas and preserves, sites identified or proposed under the National Historic Preservation Act, and components of the National Wild and Scenic Rivers System.

(c) The Regional Administrator retains the right to terminate a waiver as to future permit actions at any time by sending the Director written notice of termination.

§ 233.52 Program reporting

(a) The starting date for the annual period to be covered by reports shall be established in the Memorandum of Agreement with the Regional Administrator (§ 233.13.)

(b) The Director shall submit to the Regional Administrator within 90 days after completion of the annual period, a draft annual report evaluating the State's administration of its program identifying problems the State has encountered in the administration of its program and recommendations for resolving these problems. Items that shall be addressed in the annual report include an assessment of the cumulative impacts of the State's permit program on the integrity of the State regulated waters; identification of areas of particular concern and/or interest within the State; the number and nature of individual and general permits issued, modified, and denied; number of violations identified and number and nature of enforcement actions taken; number of suspected unauthorized activities reported and nature of action taken; an estimate of extent of activities regulated by general permits; and the number of permit applications received but not yet processed.

(c) The State shall make the draft annual report available for public inspection.

(d) Within 60 days of receipt of the draft annual report, the Regional Administrator will complete review of the draft report and transmit comments, questions, and/or requests for additional evaluation and/or information to the Director.

(e) Within 30 days of receipt of the Regional Administrator's comments, the Director will finalize the annual report, incorporating and/or responding to the Regional Administrator's comments, and transmit the final report to the Regional Administrator.

(f) Upon acceptance of the annual report, the Regional Administrator shall publish notice of availability of the final annual report.

§ 233.53 Withdrawal of program approval.

(a) A State with a program approved under this Part may voluntarily transfer program responsibilities required by Federal law to the Secretary by taking the following actions, or in such other manner as may be agreed upon with the Administrator.

(1) The State shall give the Administrator and the Secretary 180 days notice of the proposed transfer. The State shall also submit a plan for the orderly transfer of all relevant program information not in the possession of the Secretary (such as permits, permit files, reports, permit applications) which are necessary for the Secretary to administer the program.

(2) Within 60 days of receiving the notice and transfer plan, the Administrator and the Secretary shall evaluate the State's transfer plan and shall identify for the State any additional information needed by the Federal government for program administration.

(3) At least 30 days before the transfer is to occur the Administrator shall publish notice of transfer in the Federal Register and in a sufficient number of the largest newspapers in the State to provide statewide coverage, and shall mail notice to all permit holders, permit applicants, other regulated persons and other interested persons on appropriate EPA, Corps and State mailing lists.

(b) The Administrator may withdraw program approval when a State program no longer complies with the requirements of this Part, and the State fails to take corrective action. Such circumstances include the following:

(1) When the State's legal authority no longer meets the requirements of this Part, including:

(i) Failure of the State to promulgate or enact new authorities when necessary; or

(ii) Action by a State legislature or court striking down or limiting State authorities.

(2) When the operation of the State program fails to comply with the requirements of this Part, including:

(i) Failure to exercise control over activities required to be regulated under this Part, including failure to issue permits;

(ii) Issuance of permits which do not conform to the requirements of this Part; or

(iii) Failure to comply with the public participation requirements of this Part.

(3) When the State's enforcement program fails to comply with the requirements of this Part, including:

(i) Failure to act on violations of permits or other program requirements;

(ii) Failure to seek adequate enforcement penalties or to collect administrative fines when imposed, or to implement alternative enforcement methods approved by the Administrator; or

(iii) Failure to inspect and monitor activities subject to regulation.

(4) When the State program fails to comply with the terms of the Memorandum of Agreement required under § 233.13.

(c) The following procedures apply when the Administrator orders the commencement of proceedings to determine whether to withdraw approval of a State program:

(1) Order. The Administrator may order the commencement of withdrawal proceedings on the Administrator's initiative or in response to a petition from an interested person alleging failure of the State to comply with the requirements of this Part as set forth in subsection (b) of this section. The Administrator shall respond in writing to any petition to commence withdrawal proceedings. He may conduct an informal review of the allegations in the petition to determine whether cause exists to commence proceedings under this paragraph. The Administrator's order commencing proceedings under this paragraph shall fix a time and place for the commencement of the hearing, shall specify the allegations against the State which are to be considered at the hearing, and shall be published in the Federal Register. Within 30 days after publication of the Administrator's order in the Federal Register, the State shall admit or deny these allegations in a written answer. The party seeking withdrawal of the State's program shall have the burden of coming forward with the evidence in a hearing under this paragraph.

(2) Definitions. For purposes of this paragraph the definition of "Administrative Law Judge," "Hearing Clerk," and "Presiding Officer" in 40 CFR 22.03 apply in addition to the following:

(i) "Party" means the petitioner, the State, the Agency, and any other person whose request to participate as a party is granted.

(ii) "Person" means the Agency, the State and any individual or organization having an interest in the subject matter of the proceedings.

(iii) "Petitioner" means any person whose petition for commencement of withdrawal proceedings has been granted by the Administrator.

(3) Procedures.

(i) The following provisions of 40 CFR Part 22 [Consolidated Rules of Practice] are applicable to proceedings under this paragraph:

(A) Section 22.02–(use of number/gender);

(B) Section 22.04–(authorities of Presiding Officer);

(C) Section 22.06–(filing/service of rulings and orders);

(D) Section 22.09–(examination of filed documents);

(E) Section 22.19 (a), (b) and (c)–(prehearing conference);

(F) Section 22.22–(evidence);

(G) Section 22.23–(objections/offers of proof);

(H) Section 22.25–(filing the transcript; and

(I) Section 22.26–(findings/conclusions).

(ii) The following provisions are also applicable:

(A) Computation and extension of time.

(1) Computation. In computing any period of time prescribed or allowed in these rules of practice, except as otherwise provided, the day of the event from which the designated period begins to run shall not be included. Saturdays, Sundays, and Federal legal holidays shall be included. When a stated time expires on a Saturday, Sunday or Federal legal holiday, the stated time period shall be extended to include the next business day.

(2) Extensions of time. The Administrator, Regional Administrator, or Presiding Officer, as appropriate, may grant an extension of time for the filing of any pleading, document, or motion (i) upon timely motion of a party to the proceeding, for good cause shown and after consideration of prejudice to other parties, or (ii) upon his own motion. Such a motion by a party may only be made after notice to all other parties, unless the movant can show good cause why serving notice is impracticable. The motion shall be filed in advance of the date on which the pleading, document or motion is due to be filed, unless the failure of a party to make timely motion for extension of time was the result of excusable neglect.

(3) The time for commencement of the hearing shall not be extended beyond the date set in the Administrator's order without approval of the Administrator.

(B) Ex parte discussion of proceeding. At no time after the issuance of the order commencing proceedings shall the Administrator, the Regional Administrator, the Regional Judicial Officer, the Presiding Officer, or any other person who is likely to advise these officials in the decisions on the case, discuss ex parte the merits of the proceeding with any interested person outside the Agency, with any Agency staff member who performs a prosecutorial or investigative function in such proceeding or a factually related proceeding, or with any representative of such person. Any ex parte memorandum or other communication addressed to the Administrator, the Regional Administrator, the Regional Judicial Officer, or the Presiding Officer during the pendency of the proceeding and relating to the merits thereof, by or on behalf of any party shall be regarded as argument made in the proceeding and shall be served upon all other parties. The other parties shall be given an opportunity to reply to such memorandum or communication.

(C) Intervention.

(1) Motion. A motion for leave to intervene in any proceeding conducted under these rules of practice must set forth the grounds for the proposed intervention, the position and interest of the movant and the likely impact that intervention will have on the expeditious progress of the proceeding. Any person already a party to the proceeding may file an answer to a motion to intervene, making specific reference to the factors set forth in the foregoing sentence and paragraph (b)(3)(ii)(C)(3) of this section, within ten (10) days after service of the motion for leave to intervene.

(2) However, motions to intervene must be filed within 15 days from the date the notice of the Administrator's order is published in the Federal Register.

(3) Disposition. Leave to intervene may be granted only if the movant demonstrates that (i) his presence in the proceeding would not unduly prolong or otherwise prejudice the adjudication of the rights of the original parties; (ii) the movant will be adversely affected by a final order; and (iii) the interests of the movant are not being adequately represented by the original parties. The intervenor shall become a full party to the proceeding upon the granting of leave to intervene.

(4) Amicus curiae. Persons not parties to the proceeding who wish to file briefs may so move. The motion shall identify the interest of the applicant and shall state the reasons why the proposed amicus brief is desirable. If the motion is granted, the Presiding Officer or Administrator shall issue an order setting the time for filing such brief. An amicus curiae is eligible to participate in any briefing after his motion is granted, and shall be served with all briefs, reply briefs, motions, and orders relating to issues to be briefed.

(D) Motions.

(1) General. All motions, except those made orally on the record during a hearing, shall (i) be in writing; (ii) state the grounds therefore with particularity; (iii) set forth the relief or order sought; and (iv) be accompanied by any affidavit, certificate, other evidence, or legal memorandum relied upon. Such motions shall be served as provided by paragraph (b)(4) of this section.

(2) Response to motions. A party's response to any written motion must be filed within ten (10) days after service of such motion, unless additional time is allowed for such response. The response shall be accompanied by any affidavit, certificate, other evidence, or legal memorandum relied upon. If no response is filed within the designated period, the parties may be deemed to have waived any objection to the granting of the motion. The Presiding Officer, Regional Administrator, or Administrator, as appropriate, may set a shorter time for response, or make such other orders concerning the disposition of motions as they deem appropriate.

(3) Decision. The Administrator shall rule on all motions filed or made after service of the recommended decision upon the parties. The Presiding Officer shall rule on all other motions. Oral argument on motions will be permitted where the Presiding Officer, Regional Administrator, or the Administrator considers it necessary or desirable.

(4) Record of proceedings.

(i) The hearing shall be either stenographically reported verbatim or tape recorded, and thereupon transcribed by an official reporter designated by the Presiding Officer;

(ii) All orders issued by the Presiding Officer, transcripts of testimony, written statements of position, stipulations, exhibits, motions, briefs, and other written material of any kind submitted in the hearing shall be a part of the record and shall be available for inspection or copying in the Office of the Hearing Clerk, upon payment of costs. Inquiries may be made at the Office of the Administrative Law Judges, Hearing Clerk, 401 M Street SW., Washington, DC 20460;

(iii) Upon notice to all parties the Presiding Officer may authorize corrections to the transcript which involve matters of substance;

(iv) An original and two (2) copies of all written submissions to the hearing shall be filed with the Hearing Clerk;

(v) A copy of each such submission shall be served by the person making the submission upon the Presiding Officer and each party of record. Service under this paragraph shall take place by mail or personal delivery;

(vi) Every submission shall be accompanied by acknowledgement of service by the person served or proof of service in the form of a statement of the date, time, and manner of service and the names of the persons served, certified by the person who made service; and

(vii) The Hearing Clerk shall maintain and furnish to any person upon request, a list containing the name, service address, and telephone number of all parties and their attorneys or duly authorized representatives.

(5) Participation by a person not a party. A person who is not a party may, in the discretion of the Presiding Officer, be permitted to make a limited appearance by making an oral or written statement of his/her position on the issues within such limits and on such conditions as may be fixed by the Presiding Officer, but he/she may not otherwise participate in the proceeding.

(6) Rights of parties.

(i) All parties to the proceeding may:

(A) Appear by counsel or other representative in all hearing and prehearing proceedings;

(B) Agree to stipulations of facts which shall be made a part of the record.

(7) Recommended decision.

(i) Within 30 days after the filing of proposed findings and conclusions and reply briefs, the Presiding Officer shall evaluate the record before him/her, the proposed findings and conclusions and any briefs filed by the parties, and shall prepare a recommended decision, and shall certify the entire record, including the recommended decision, to the Administrator.

(ii) Copies of the recommended decision shall be served upon all parties.

(iii) Within 20 days after the certification and filing of the record and recommended decision, all parties may file with the Administrator exceptions to the recommended decision and a supporting brief.

(8) Decision by Administrator.

(i) Within 60 days after certification of the record and filing of the Presiding Officer's recommended decision, the Administrator shall review the record before him and issue his own decision.

(ii) If the Administrator concludes that the State has administered the program in conformity with the Act and this Part, his decision shall constitute "final agency action" within the meaning of 5 U.S.C. 704.

(iii) If the Administrator concludes that the State has not administered the program in conformity with the Act and regulations, he shall list the deficiencies in the program and provide the State a reasonable time, not to exceed 90 days, to take such appropriate corrective action as the Administrator determines necessary.

(iv) Within the time prescribed by the Administrator the State shall take such appropriate corrective action as required by the Administrator and shall file with the Administrator and all parties a statement certified by the State Director that appropriate corrective action has been taken.

(v) The Administrator may require a further showing in addition to the certified statement that corrective action has been taken.

(vi) If the state fails to take appropriate corrective action and file a certified statement thereof within the time prescribed by the Administrator, the Administrator shall issue a supplementary order withdrawing approval of the State program. If the State takes appropriate corrective action, the Administrator shall issue a supplementary order stating that approval of authority is not withdrawn.

(vii) The Administrator's supplementary order shall constitute final Agency action within the meaning of 5 U.S. 704.

(d) Withdrawal of authorization under this section and the Act does not relieve any person from complying with the requirements of State law, nor does it affect the validity of actions taken by the State prior to withdrawal.

[57 FR 5346, Feb. 13, 1992]

SUBPART G—TREATMENT OF INDIAN TRIBES AS STATES

Source: 58 FR 8183, Feb. 11, 1993, unless otherwise noted.

§ 233.60 Requirements for treatment as a State.

Section 518(e) of the CWA, 33 U.S.C. 1378(e), authorizes the Administrator to treat an Indian Tribe as a State for purposes of making the Tribe eligible to apply for the 404 permit program under section 404(g)(1) if it meets the following criteria:

(a) The Indian Tribe is recognized by the Secretary of the Interior.

(b) The Indian Tribe has a governing body carrying out substantial governmental duties and powers.

(c) The functions to be exercised by the Indian Tribe pertain to the management and protection of water resources which are held by an Indian Tribe, held by the Untied States in trust for the Indians, held by a member of an Indian Tribe if such property interest is subject to a trust restriction an alienation, or otherwise within the borders of the Indian reservation.

(d) The Indian Tribe is reasonably expected to be capable, in the Administrator's judgment, of carrying out the functions to be exercised, in a manner consistent with the terms and purposes of the Act and applicable regulations, of an effective section 404 dredge and fill permit program.

§ 233.61 Request by an Indian Tribe for a determination of treatment as a State.

An Indian Tribe may apply to the Regional Administrator for a determination that it qualifies for treatment as a State pursuant to section 518 of the Act, for purposes of the section 404 program. The application shall be concise and describe how the Indian Tribe will meet each of the requirements of § 233.60. The application shall include the following information:

(a) A statement that the Tribe is recognized by the Secretary of the Interior.

(b) A descriptive statement demonstrating that the Tribal governing body is currently carrying out substantial governmental duties and powers over a defined area. This Statement shall:

(1) Describe the form of the Tribal government.

(2) Describe the types of governmental functions currently performed by the Tribal governing body, such as, but not limited to, the exercise of police powers affecting (or relating to) the health, safety, and welfare of the affected population; taxation; and the exercise of the power of eminent domain; and

(3) Identify the source of the Tribal government's authority to carry out the governmental functions currently being performed.

(c)(1) A map or legal description of the area over which the Indian Tribe asserts regulatory authority pursuant to section 518(e)(2) of the CWA and § 233.60(c);

(2) A statement by the Tribal Attorney General (or equivalent official) which describes the basis for the Tribe's assertion under section 518(e)(2) (including the nature or subject matter of the asserted regulatory authority);

(3) A copy of all documents such as Tribal constitutions, laws, charters, executive orders, codes, ordinances, and/or resolutions which support the Tribe's assertion of regulatory authority;

(d) A narrative statement describing the capability of the Indian Tribe to administer an effective 404 permit program. The Statement shall include:

(1) A description of the Indian Tribe's previous management experience including, but not limited to, the administration of programs and services authorized by the Indian Self Determination & Education Act (25 U.S.C. 450 *et seq.*), The Indian Mineral Development Act (25 U.S.C. 2101 *et seq.*), or the Indian Sanitation Facility Construction Activity Act (42 U.S.C. 2004a).

(2) A list of existing environmental or public health programs administered by the Tribal governing body, and a copy of related Tribal laws, regulations, and policies;

(3) A description of the entity (or entities) which exercise the executive, legislative, and judicial functions of the Tribal government.

(4) A description of the existing, or proposed, agency of the Indian Tribe which will assume primary responsibility for establishing and administering a section 404 dredge and fill permit program or plan which proposes how the Tribe will acquire additional administrative and technical expertise. The plan must address how the Tribe will obtain the funds to acquire the administrative and technical expertise.

(5) A description of the technical and administrative abilities of the staff to administer and manage an effective, environmentally sound 404 dredge and fill permit program.

(e) The Administrator may, at his discretion, request further documentation necessary to support a Tribal request for treatment as a State.

(f) If the Administrator has previously determined that a Tribe has met the requirements for "treatment as a State" for programs authorized under the Safe Drinking Water Act or the Clean Water Act, then that Tribe need only provide additional information unique to the particular statute or program for which the Tribe is seeking additional authorization.

(Approved by the Office of Management and Budget under control number 2040- 0140)

§ 233.62 Procedures for processing an Indian Tribe's application for treatment as a State.

(a) The Regional Administrator shall process an application of an Indian Tribe for treatment as a State submitted pursuant to § 233.61 in a timely manner. He shall promptly notify the Indian Tribe of receipt of the application.

(b) Within 30 days after receipt of the Indian Tribe's complete application for treatment as a State, the Regional Administrator shall notify all appropriate governmental entities. Notice shall include information on the substance and basis for the Tribe's assertion that it meets the requirements of § 233.60(c).

(c) Each governmental entity so notified by the Regional Administrator shall have 30 days to comment upon the Tribe's assertion under § 233.60(c). Comments by governmental entities shall be limited to the Tribe's assertion under § 233.60(c).

(d) If a Tribe's assertion under § 233.60(c) is subject to a competing or conflicting claim, the Regional Administrator, after consultation with the Secretary of the Interior, or his designee, and in consideration of other comments received, shall determine whether the Tribe has adequately demonstrated that it meets the requirements of § 233.60(c) for the dredge and fill permit program.

(e) If the Regional Administrator determines that a Tribe meets the requirements of § 233.61, the Indian Tribe is then eligible to apply for 404 program assumption.

(f) The Regional Administrator shall follow the procedures described in § 233.15 in processing a Tribe's request to assume the 404 dredge and fill permit program.

SUBPART H—APPROVED STATE PROGRAMS

§ 233.70 Michigan.

The applicable regulatory program for discharges of dredged or fill material into waters of the United States in Michigan that are not presently used, or susceptible for use in their natural condition or by reasonable improvement as a means to transport interstate or foreign commerce shoreward to the ordinary high water mark, including wetlands adjacent thereto, except those on Indian lands, is the program administered by the Michigan Department of Natural Resources, approved by EPA, pursuant to Section 404 of the CWA. Notice of this approval was published in the Federal Register on October 2, 1984; the effective date of this program is October 16, 1984. This program consists of the following elements, as submitted to EPA in the State's program application.

(a) Incorporation by reference. The requirements set forth in the State statutes and regulations cited in this paragraph are hereby incorporated by reference and made a part of the applicable 404 Program under the CWA for the State of Michigan. This incorporation by reference was approved by the Director of the Federal Register on October 16, 1984.

(1) The Great Lakes Submerged Lands Act, MCL 322.701 *et seq.*, reprinted in Michigan 1983 Natural Resources Law.

(2) The Water Resources Commission Act, MCL 323.1 *et seq.*, reprinted in Michigan 1983 Natural Resources Law.

(3) The Goemaere-Anderson Wetland Protection Act, MCL 281.701 *et seq.*, reprinted in Michigan 1983 Natural Resources Law.

(4) The Inland Lakes and Stream Act, MCL 281.951 *et seq.*, reprinted in Michigan 1983 Natural Resources Law.

(5) The Michigan Administrative Procedures Act of 1969, MCL 24-201 *et seq.*

(6) An act concerning the Erection of Dams, MCL 281.131 *et seq.*, reprinted in Michigan 1983 Natural Resources Law.

(7) R 281.811 through R 281.819 inclusive, R 281.821, R 281.823, R 281.824, R 281.832 through R 281.839 inclusive, and R 281.841 through R 281.845 inclusive of the Michigan Administrative Code (1979 ed., 1982 supp.).

(b) Other Laws. The following statutes and regulations, although not incorporated by reference, also are part of the approved State-administered program:

(1) Administrative Procedures Act, MCLA 24.201 *et seq.*

(2) Freedom of Information Act, MCLA 15.231 *et seq.*

(3) Open Meetings Act, MCLA 15.261 *et seq.*

(4) Michigan Environmental Protection Act, MCLA 691.1201 *et seq.*

(c) Memoranda of Agreement.

(1) The Memorandum of Agreement between EPA Region V and the Michigan Department of Natural resources, signed by the EPA Region V Administrator on December 9, 1983.

(2) The Memorandum of Agreement between the U.S. Army Corps of Engineers and the Michigan Department of Natural Resources, signed by the Commander, North Central Division, on March 27, 1984.

(d) Statement of Legal Authority.

(1) "Attorney General Certification Section 404/ State of Michigan", signed by Attorney General of Michigan, as submitted with the request for approval of "The State of Michigan 404 Program", October 26, 1983.

(e) The Program description and any other materials submitted as part of the original application or supplements thereto.

(33 U.S.C. 13344, CWA 404)

Appendix E

Memorandum of Understanding
Jurisdiction of Dredged and Fill Program
U.S. Army Corps of Engineers/
U.S. Environmental Protection Agency

Vol. 45, No. 45018
Wednesday, July 2, 1980

NOTICE.

Notice is hereby given that pursuant to their authorities under the Clean Water Act (33 U.S.C. 1125 *et seq.*), the Administrator of the Environmental Protection Agency (EPA) and the Chief, U.S. Army of Corps of Engineers (COE), have entered into a Memorandum of Understanding (MOU) which establishes policies and procedures which EPA and the Corps of Engineers will follow in resolving geographic jurisdictional problems arising in connection with the section 404 program regulating the discharge of dredged or fill materials.

On September 5, 1979, Attorney General Civiletti issued an opinion that the Administrator of the Environmental Protection Agency has the ultimate administrative responsibility of determining the jurisdictional scope of waters of the United States for purposes of Section 404 of the Clean Water Act. In order to administer the section 404 program efficiently and effectively under this opinion, EPA and the COE have adopted the procedures in the following Memorandum of Understanding. These procedures are intended to ensure that the public receives prompt, definitive answers to inquiries about jurisdiction.

The Corps of Engineers has significantly greater resources at the field level than EPA's 404 Program. Thus, the MOU recognizes that the District Engineer will continue to make the great majority of jurisdictional decisions. In most cases, the methods and standards for making jurisdictional determinations are well-established. However, the MOU recognized that certain cases may present scientific, technical, or policy complexities. Accordingly, the EPA Regional Administrators may, subject to headquarters review, identify special categories or types of cases that will be referred to EPA for jurisdictional determinations. The first list of such special cases will be published with complete descriptions in the Federal Register by October 24, 1980.

When a pre-permit inquiry or permit application is presented to the District Engineer, he will first determine if a special case is involved. If he decides that the inquiry does not involve a special case, he will make the jurisdictional determination. If the District Engineer doubts the status of a case, he shall treat it as a special case or consult with EPA as to its status. he may, if he wishes, consult with EPA even when no special case is involved. Of course all determinations, whether made by the COE or EPA, will be based on the applicable law and regulations defining waters of the United States.

We anticipate that the precedents established under the special case procedure, together with joint scientific research and consultation, will eventually reduce the number of special cases. Both agencies pledge to administer their joint section 404 responsibilities fairly, fully, efficiently and expeditiously.

The effective date of this Memorandum of Understanding is April 23, 1980.

Within twelve months of the effective date, the Environmental Protection Agency and the Corps of Engineers will begin a review of the Memorandum of Understanding and will consider all comments received.

Written comments on this Memorandum of Understanding should be submitted to either of the following addresses before January 20, 1981. Joseph A. Krivak, Criteria and Standards Division (WH-585), Office of Water and Waste Management, Environmental Protection Agency, 401 M street SW., Washington, D.C. 20460. Curtis Clark, Office of the Chief of Engineers, Attn: (DAEN-CWO-N), Washington, D.C. 20314.

This Memorandum of Understanding will expire eighteen months from the effective date unless it has been revised, or extended unrevised, by mutual consent.

For further information, contact Joseph A. Krivak, (202) 755-0100 or Curtis Clark, (202) 272-0199.

Dated: June 4, 1980.
Eckardt C. Beck,
Assistant Administrator for Water and Waste Management.

U.S. Army Corps of Engineers/
U.S. Environmental Protection Agency
Memorandum of Understanding
Geographical Jurisdiction of the
Section 404 Program

1.   This Memorandum of Understanding is essential to ensure the continued orderly administration of Section 404 of the Clean Water Act as a result of the Attorney General's Opinion of September 5, 1979, wherein the Attorney General of the United States opined that the Administrator of the Environmental Protection Agency (Administrator) has the ultimate authority to determine the jurisdictional scope of Section 404 waters of the United States. For the purpose of the Memorandum of Understanding, 'jurisdictional questions' are limited to those relating to the extent of the waters of the United States.

2.   In recognition of the responsibilities of the Secretary of the Army (Secretary), acting through the Chief of Engineers, in administering the Federal permit program under Section 404 of the Clean Water Act, in recognition of the responsibilities of the Administrator in administering the Clean Water Act, in recognition of the resources of our agencies, in recognition of the enforcement responsibilities of our agencies, and in recognition of the need for an understanding on how jurisdictional matters may best be handled in light of those responsibilities and resources, we the Secretary and the Administrator adopt the following policies and procedures.

3.   Our policy is to ensure that Section 404 is administered fully, fairly, efficiently, and expeditiously. It is our policy to cooperate in research and in development of joint technical guidance on jurisdictional matters. It is also our policy to resolve jurisdictional questions within the framework of existing procedures to the extent practical, consistent with the above policies.

4.   *Pre-application Inquiry.* When pre-application inquiries are made regarding the geographic jurisdiction of the 404 permit program the District Engineer (DE) shall, to the maximum extent practical, establish the boundaries of waters of the United States, as they apply to the inquiry, at the earliest possible date. However, delineation of these waters in areas involving special cases as defined in paragraph 7 shall follow the procedures set forth in paragraph 8. The DE shall first determine if the inquiry involves a special case. If the circumstances do not involve a special case as defined in paragraph 7 below, the DE shall inform the inquirer in writing of his decision on the extent of jurisdiction and provide a copy of his decision to the Regional Administrator (RA). The DE may, prior to making this decision, consult with the RA if the DE deems it appropriate. [FN1]

> FN1 Paragraphs 4 and 5 provide for consultation in non-special cases 'if the DE deems it appropriate.' These provisions recognize the DE's discretion to consult even if the case involved is not a special case. Factors which might lead the DE to consider consultation include the presence of novel issues, complicated evidence, prior to EPA experience with the site, likelihood that a segment of the public will challenge the determination, etc. However, it should be stressed that under this MOU, except in special cases previously agreed to, the DE is authorized to make a final determination and to communicate if to the public without prior consultation with EPA and such determination shall be binding.

If the circumstances involve a special case as defined in paragraph 7 below, the provisions set forth in paragraph 8 shall apply. In all other circumstances where special cases are not involved, the ultimate findings of the DE, subject to discretionary review by the Chief of Engineers or his delegate, shall be binding.

5. *Permit situation.* The DE shall first determine if the permit application involves a special case. In reviewing a permit application for completeness, where the circumstances do not involve a special case as set forth in paragraph 7 below, the DE shall make a determination of the extent of jurisdiction over the proposed area. The DE may consult with the RA if the DE deems it appropriate. If the circumstances involve a special case as defined in paragraph 7 below, the provisions set forth in paragraph 8 shall apply. In all other cases, the ultimate findings of the DE, subject to discretionary review by the Chief of Engineers or his delegate, shall be binding.

When the DE issues a public notice of the permit application, such notice shall include, in addition to any other requirements, a map or other appropriate description of the extent of jurisdiction over the proposed area, as determined under the above procedures. If comments are received from the public (including other government agencies) which raise new matters which the DE believes establish the situation as a special case as defined in paragraph 7 below, the DE shall furnish to the RA all relevant comments and any rebuttal submitted by the applicant, for handling under the provisions of paragraph 8.

6. *Enforcement situations.* The Corps of Engineers (Corps) has sole authority under Section 404 of the Act to issue Federal permits for the discharge of dredged or fill material into waters of the United States. The Corps has authority under Section 404(s)(1) either to issue an order requiring persons in violation of a permit condition issued under Section 404 to comply with such Section or to bring a judicial action to compel compliance. The Environmental Protection Agency (EPA) has authority under Section 309(a)(3) to issue an order requiring persons discharging any pollutants (including dredged or fill materials) into waters of the United States (established consistent with this MOU) to comply with Sections 404 or 402 or to bring a judicial action. The Corps and EPA shall consult with one another when either agency discovers an unpermitted activity which may represent a violation of the Act. Such activities include those occurring in areas designated 'special cases' as defined in paragraph 7 of this memorandum. Until it is updated or otherwise changed, the June 1, 1976 EPA/Corps/Justice enforcement memorandum sets out procedures which are to be used in instances were there may be a difference of opinion between our agencies on the jurisdiction of Section 404 over particular unpermitted activities. Any jurisdictional determination made by EPA as a result of an enforcement action will be used by the DE as the jurisdiction for all subsequent 404 actions on that case.

7. *Special cases.*

a. Special cases are those situations where significant issues or technical difficulties exist concerning the jurisdictional scope of Section 404 waters, the environmental consequences of jurisdiction are significant, and EPA has declared a special interest. Each RA shall consult with the Division Engineers in his/her region in order to delineate those types of areas to be defined routinely as special cases. Delineation will include types of ecosystems, size limitations, and other appropriate factors to insure clarity. Such detailed special cases shall be developed by the Regional Administrator, in consultation with the Division Engineer, within 120 days after the date of this agreement and be forwarded to both EPA and Corps Headquarters for review and consultation. After consultation with the Chief of Engineers, the Administration shall approve and consolidate the list of special cases and shall publish it, with descriptions, in the Federal Register within 180 days after the date of this agreement. Prior to publication of this list, the procedures of paragraph 7(c) may be used to establish interim special cases.

b. Each DE will use this published list to assist in identifying special cases involved in pre-application inquiries or in permit applications. The DE, when reviewing an inquiry or application where the evidence is unclear as to whether a special case is involved or where particular difficulties or issues may be involved in determining jurisdiction, should resolve any doubts in favor of declaring the situation to be a special case unless he deems it appropriate to consult with the RA. If, upon consultation, the RA concludes that the situation should be treated as a special case, it shall be treated as such on an interim basis pending notification of Corps Headquarters and concurrence by EPA Headquarters. When a special case is designated under paragraphs 7(a) or (c), it shall apply to all future cases and to all inquiries for which a written determination has not been made and permit applications for which no public notice has been issued.

c. Changes to the published list of special cases may be initiated by either the Division Engineer or the RA and may include additions to, deletions from, or amendments to, the list. Additions or amendments to such cases shall be treated as special cases on an interim basis, pending joint EPA/Corps Headquarters consultation and EPA approval. Such changes shall be published in the Federal Register as soon as practical after approval. Once published, a given special case may not be removed from the special case category for 90 days.

8. *Procedure for handling special cases.*

a. In determining jurisdiction of waters of the United States when presented with a pre-application inquiry or a permit application, the DE shall determine initially if the situation involves a special case. This decision shall be made in accordance with the special cases designated pursuant to paragraph 7 above. Where the DE reasonably questions the status of a given case, he shall treat it as special case or consult with the EPA prior to designating the status. If the DE elects to consult with EPA, prior to designating the status, EPA's opinion will be deciding. The District Engineer's determination as to the status of a case shall be completed as expeditiously as possible, but not to exceed ten working days from the time of inquiry or receipt of a complete application.

b. For those inquiries or applications designated as special cases pursuant to this MOU, the RA, subject to discretionary review by EPA Headquarters, shall determine the jurisdiction of the waters of the United States. The determination and any subsequent review shall be completed as expeditiously as possible, within thirty (30) working days of referral by the DE, except when additional time is required by applicant delay or as a result of unusually large or complicated cases. Upon completion, the results of that determination shall be {45020} forwarded to the DE, who is turn shall forward the results to the pre-application inquirer or process a permit as appropriate.

c. For those areas designated as special cases pursuant to this MOU, the RA may request the DE to determine the scope of jurisdiction. [FN2] In those cases, the DE's jurisdictional determination shall be binding. The DE shall send the RA a copy of such determination.

> FN2 Each case will differ and must be considered individually, even if it has been designated in advance as a special case. Options to be considered include deciding not to treat the case as a special case, having the RA make the determination, or seeking advice from the Corps before deciding how to proceed. Where practical and consistent with the MOU and EPA's responsibilities, it is preferable to have the DE make the jurisdictional determinations.

9. *Joint review and guidance.*

a. In order to avoid technical disagreement and to forecast significant issues, the RA and the Division Engineer may mutually agree to initiate a joint technical review by a board whose composition and responsibilities will be determined by the two parties. The board shall consist of an equal number of selections by EPA an the Corps and any other members mutually acceptable to EPA and the Corps. The board will be used only in significant cases when both the RA and the Division Engineer believe that the views of the board would be helpful. This review board will, after consideration of relevant information and appropriate inquiry, make a recommended determination by majority vote of extent of jurisdiction as quickly as possible but no later than 60 days after being convened. This recommended determination will identify the issues involved and explain the basis for the extent of jurisdiction. These findings will be accepted by the RA unless he/she provides to the Division Engineer a written explanation of his/her basis for non-acceptance.

b. Members should have a broad understanding of issues involved in wetlands determinations, familiarity with wetlands flora and the Section 404 program, freedom from real or perceived conflicts of interest, and be available on relatively short notice. The review board shall have the authority and resources to employ consultants and perform appropriate field investigations.

c. The agencies shall cooperate in technical research and preparation of joint guidance on technical issues. Where such joint guidance exists, it shall be used in resolving differences in specific cases.

10. *Public comment.* This agreement shall be effective immediately and shall be published in the Federal Register. Public comment on the agreement will be received. Within twelve (12) months after the effective date, EPA and the Corps will institute review of this agreement, consider any comments received and make such revisions as we deem appropriate. Such revisions shall be published in the Federal Register within eighteen (18) months of the effective date. This agreement may be extended beyond a period of 18 months only by mutual consent.

11. *Applicability.* This agreement will apply to all inquiries or permit applications received after the effective date of this MOU. Written determinations, including permits, issued prior to September 5, 1979, in response to specific inquiries or permit applications shall not be reconsidered with respect to any discharge activities subject to the 404 permit program where the inquirer or applicant has undertaken such activities in substantial reliance upon such determination and where such activities are completed within three years of such written determination (or such longer period, if any, specified in the permit). Substantial reliance must have occurred after receipt of such determination and prior to the effective date of this MOU, and may include commencement of construction, incurrence of substantial contractual obligations for construction, purchase of land at a price substantially dependent on such determination, or the like.

Dated: April 14, 1980.
J. W. Morris,
Lieutenant General, USA, Chief of Engineers.
Dated: April 23, 1980.
Douglas M. Costle,
Administrator, Environmental Protection Agency.

Appendix F

Memorandum Concerning Federal Enforcement
for the Section 404 Program of the Clean Water Act
U.S. Army Corps of Engineers/
U.S. Environmental Protection Agency

I. PURPOSE AND SCOPE

The United States Department of the Army (Army) and the United States Environmental Protection Agency (EPA) hereby establish policy and procedures pursuant to which they will undertake federal enforcement of the dredged and fill material permit requirements ("Section 404 program") of the Clean Water Act (CWA). The U.S. Army Corps of Engineers (Corps) and EPA have enforcement authorities for the Section 404 program, as specified in Sections 301(a), 308, 309, 404(n), and 404(s) of the CWA. In addition, the 1987 Amendments to the CWA (the Water Quality Act of 1987) provide new administrative penalty authority under Section 309(g) for violations of the Section 404 program. For purposes of effective administration of theses statutory authorities, this Memorandum of Agreement (MOA) sets forth an appropriate allocation of enforcement responsibilities between EPA and the Corps. The Prime goal of the MOA is to strengthen the Section 404 enforcement program by using the expertise, resources and initiative of both agencies in a manner which is effective and efficient in achieving the goals of the CWA.

II. POLICY

A. *General.* It shall be the policy of the Army and EPA to maintain the integrity of the program through federal enforcement of Section 404 requirements. The basic premise of this effort is to establish a framework for effective Section 404 enforcement with very little overlap. EPA will conduct initial on-site investigations when it is efficient with respect to available time, resources and/or expenditures, and use its authorities as provided in this agreement. In the majority of enforcement cases the Corps, because it has more field resources, will conduct initial investigations and use its authorities as provided in this agreement. This will allow each agency to play a role in enforcement which concentrates its resources in those areas for which its authorities and expertise are best suited. The Corps and EPA are encouraged to consult with each other on cases involving novel or important legal issues and/or technical situations. Assistance from the U.S. Fish and Wildlife Service (FWS), the National Marine Fisheries Service (NMFS) and other federal, state, tribal and local agencies will be sought and accepted when appropriate.

B. *Geographic Jurisdictional Determinations.* Geographic jurisdictional determinations for a specific case will be made by the investigating agency. If asked for an oral decision, the investigator will caution that oral statements regarding jurisdiction are not an official agency determination. Each agency will advise the other of any problem trends that they become aware of through case by case determinations and initiate interagency discussions or other action to address the issue. (Note: Geographic jurisdictional determinations for "special case" situations and interpretation of Section 404(f) exemptions for "special

Section 404(f) matters" will be handled in accordance with the Memorandum of Agreement Between the Department of the Army and the Environmental Protection Agency Concerning the Determination of the Geographic Jurisdiction of the Section 404 Program and the Application of the Exemptions Under Section 404(f) of the Clean Water Act.)

C. *Violation Determinations.* The investigating agency shall be responsible for violation determinations, for example, the need for a permit. Each agency will advise the other of any problem trends that they become aware of through case by case determinations and initiate interagency discussions or other action to address the issue.

D. *Lead Enforcement Agency.* The Corps will act as the lead enforcement agency for all violations of Corps-issued permits. The Corps will also act as the lead enforcement agency for unpermitted discharge violations which do not meet the criteria for forwarding to EPA, as listed in Section III.D. of this MOA. EPA will act as the lead enforcement agency on all unpermitted discharge violations which meet those criteria. The lead enforcement agency will complete the enforcement action once an investigation has established that a violation exists. A lead enforcement agency decision with regard to any issue in a particular case, including a decision that no enforcement action be taken, is final for that case. This provision does not preclude the lead enforcement agency from referring the matter to the other agency under Sections III.D.2 and III.D.4 of this MOA.

E. *Environmental Protection Measures.* It is the policy of both agencies to avoid permanent environmental harm caused by the violator's activities by requiring remedial actions or ordering removal and restoration. In those cases where a complete remedy/removal is not appropriate, the violator may be required, in addition to other legal remedies which are appropriate (e.g., payment of administrative penalties) to provide compensatory mitigation to compensate for the harm caused by such illegal actions. Such compensatory mitigation activities shall be placed as an enforceable requirement upon a violator as authorized by law.

III. PROCEDURES

A. *Flow chart.* The attached flow chart provides an outline of the procedures EPA and Corps will follow in enforcement cases involving unpermitted discharges. The procedures in (B.), (C.), (D.), (E.) and (F.) below are in a sequence in which they could occur. However, these procedures may be combined in an effort to expedite the enforcement process.

B. *Investigation.* EPA, if it so requests and upon prior notification to the Corps, will be the investigating agency for unpermitted activities occurring in specially defined geographic areas (e.g., a particular wetland type, areas declared a "special case" within the meaning of the Memorandum of Agreement Between the Department of the Army and the Environmental Protection Agency Concerning the Determination of the Geographic Jurisdiction of the Section 404 Program and the Application of the Exemptions Under Section 404(f) of the Clean Water Act). Timing of investigations will be commensurate with agency resources and potential environmental damage. To reduce the potential for duplicative federal effort, each agency should verify prior to initiating an investigation that the other agency does not intend or has not already begun an investigation of the same reported violation. If a violation exists, a field investigation report will be prepared which at a minimum provides a detailed description of the illegal activity, the existing environmental setting, initial view on potential impacts and a recommendation on the need for initial corrective measures. Both agencies agree that investigations must be conducted in a professional, legal manner that will not prejudice future enforcement action on the case. Investigation reports will be provided to the agency selected as the lead on the case.

C. *Immediate Enforcement Action.* The investigating of lead enforcement agency should inform the responsible parties of the violation and inform them that all illegal activity should cease pending further federal action. A notification letter or administrative order to that effect will be sent in the most expeditious manner. If time allows, an order for initial corrective measures may be included with the notification letter or administrative order. Also, if time allows, input from other federal, state, tribal and local agencies will be considered when determining the need for such initial corrective measures. In all cases the Corps will provide EPA a copy of its violation letters and EPA will provide the Corps copies of its § 308 letters and/or §309 administrative orders. These communications will include language requesting the other agency's views and recommendations on the case. The violator will also be notified that the other agency has been contacted.

D. *Lead Enforcement Agency Selection.* Using the following criteria, the investigating agency will determine which agency will complete action on the enforcement case:

1. EPA will act as the lead enforcement agency when an unpermitted activity involves the following:
   a. Repeat Violator(s);
   b. Flagrant Violation(s);
   c. Where EPA requests a class of cases or a particular case; or
   d. The Corps recommends that an EPA administrative penalty action may be warranted.

2. The Corps will act as the lead enforcement agency in all other unpermitted cases not identified in Part III D.1. above. Where EPA notifies the Corps that, because of limited staff resources or other reasons, it will not take action on a specific case, the Corps may take action commensurate with resource availability.

3. The Corps will act as the lead enforcement agency for Corps-issued permit condition violations.

4. Where EPA requests the Corps to take action on a permit condition violation, this MOA establishes a "right of first refusal" for the Corps. Where the Corps notifies EPA that, because of limited staff resources or other reasons, it will not take an action on a permit condition violation case, the EPA may take action commensurate with resource availability. However, a determination by the Corps that the activity is in compliance with the permit will represent a final enforcement decision for that case.

E. *Enforcement Response.* The lead enforcement agency shall determine, based on its authority, the appropriate enforcement response taking into consideration any views provided by the other agency. An appropriate enforcement response may include an administrative order, administrative penalty complaint, a civil or criminal judicial referral or other appropriate formal enforcement response.

F. *Resolution.* The lead enforcement agency shall make a final determination that a violation is resolved and notify interested parties so that concurrent enforcement files within another agency can be closed. In addition, the lead enforcement agency shall make arrangements for proper monitoring when required for any remedy/removal, compensatory mitigation or other corrective measures.

G. *After-the-Fact Permits.* No after-the-fact (ATF) permit application shall be accepted until resolution has been reached through an appropriate enforcement response as determined by the lead enforcement agency (e.g., until all administrative, legal and/or corrective action has been completed, or a decision has been made that no enforcement action is to be taken).

IV. RELATED MATTERS

A. *Interagency Agreements.* The Army and EPA are encouraged to enter into interagency agreements with other federal, state, tribal and local agencies which will provide assistance to the Corps and EPA in pursuit of Section 404 enforcement activities. For example, the preliminary enforcement site investigations or post-case monitoring activities required to ensure compliance with any enforcement order can be delegated to third parties (e.g., FWS) who agree to assist Corps/EPA in compliance efforts. However, only the Corps or EPA may make a violation determination and/or pursue an appropriate enforcement response based upon information received from a third party.

B. *Corps/EPA Field Agreements.* Corps Division or District offices and their respective EPA Regional offices are encouraged to enter into field level agreements to more specifically implement the provisions of this MOA.

C. *Data Information Exchange.* Data which would enhance either agency's enforcement efforts should be exchanged between the Corps and EPA where available. At a minimum, each agency shall begin to develop a computerized data list of persons receiving ATF permits or that have been subject to a Section 404 enforcement action subsequent to February 4, 1987 (enactment date of the 1987 Clean Water Act Amendments) in order to provide historical compliance data on persons found to have illegally discharged. Such information will help in an administrative penalty action to evaluate the statutory factor concerning history of a violator and will help to determine whether pursuit of a criminal action is appropriate.

V. GENERAL

A. The procedures and responsibilities of each agency specified in this MOA may be delegated to subordinates consistent with established agency procedures.

B. The policy and procedures contained within this MOA do not create any rights, either substantive or procedural, enforceable by any party regarding an enforcement action brought by either agency or by the U. S. Deviation or variance from these MOA procedures will not constitute a defense for violators or others concerned with any Section 404 enforcement action.

C. Nothing in this document is intended to diminish, modify or otherwise affect the statutory or regulatory authorities of either agency. All formal guidance interpreting this MOA shall be issued jointly.

D. This agreement Shall take effect 60 days after the date of the last signature below and will continue in effect for five years unless extended, modified or revoked by agreement of both parties, or revoked by either party alone upon six months written notice, prior to that time.

(signed)
Robert W. Page Jan. 19, 1989
Assistant Secretary of the Army
(Civil Works)

(signed)
Rebecca W. Hanmer Jan. 19, 1989
Acting Assistant Administrator for Water
U.S. Environmental Protection Agency

Appendix G

Memorandum of Agreement Concerning the Determination of Mitigation Under the Clean Water Act Section 404(b)(1) Guidelines U.S. Army Corps of Engineers/ U.S. Environmental Protection Agency

Vol. 54, No. 239
Thursday, December 14, 1989

NOTICE.

Notice is hereby given that pursuant to their authorities under the Clean Water Act (33 U.S.C. 1251 et seq.), the Assistant Administrator for Water of the Environmental Protection Agency and the Assistant Secretary of the Army (Civil Works) have entered into a Memorandum of Agreement which articulates the policy and procedures to be used in the determination of the type and level of mitigation necessary to demonstrate compliance with the Clean Water Act section 404(b)(1) Guidelines.

TEXT:

The Memorandum of Agreement (MOA) between the Environmental Protection Agency and the Department of the Army Concerning the Determination of Mitigation Under the Clean Water Act section 404(b)(1) Guidelines articulates the policy and procedures to be used in the determination of the type and level of mitigation necessary to demonstrate compliance with the Clean Water Act section 404(b)(1) Guidelines. The MOA published today provides general guidance to Corps and EPA personnel on implementing the Guidelines published at 40 CFR 230.10 pursuant to section 404(b)(1) of the Clean Water Act. It does not impose requirements on or otherwise affect the rights of public parties, which continue to be determined by reference to applicable statutory and regulatory provisions. Consequently, the MOA qualifies as an "interpretative rule" and a "general statement of policy," which are exempted from the notice-and-comment requirements of the Administrative Procedure Act. Therefore the MOA has been made effective 30 days after its date of signature. (See also 5 U.S.C. 553(b)(3)(B), discussing the waiver of prior notice and comment when such process is found by the agency for good cause to be impracticable, unnecessary or contrary to the public interest.)

LaJuana S. Wilcher,
Assistant Administrator for Water.
Robert W. Page,
Assistant Secretary of the Army (Civil Works).

Memorandum of Agreement Between the Environmental Protection Agency and the Department of the Army Concerning the Determination of Mitigation Under the Clean Water Act Section 404(b)(1) Guidelines

I. PURPOSE

The United States Environmental Protection Agency (EPA) and the United States Department of the Army (Army) hereby articulate the policy and procedures to be used in the determination of the type and level of mitigation necessary to demonstrate compliance with the Clean Water Act (CWA) section 404(b)(1) Guidelines ("Guidelines"). This Memorandum of Agreement (MOA) expresses the explicit intent of the Army and EPA to implement the objective of the CWA to restore and maintain the chemical, physical, and biological integrity of the Nation's waters, including wetlands. This MOA is specifically limited to the section 404 Regulatory Program and is written to provide clarification for agency field personnel on the type and level of mitigation required to demonstrate compliance with requirements in the Guidelines. The policies and procedures discussed herein are consistent with current section 404 regulatory practices and are provided in response to questions that have been raised about how the Guidelines are implemented.

Although the Guidelines are clearly applicable to all discharges ofdredged or fill material, including general permits and Corps of Engineers(Corps) civil works projects, this MOA focuses on standard permits (33 CFR325.5(b)(1)). fn 1 This focus is intended solely to reflect the uniqueprocedural aspects associated with the review of standard permits, and doesnot obviate the need for other regulated activities to comply fully withthe Guidelines. EPA and Army will seek to develop supplemental guidance for other regulated activities consistent with the policies and principles established in this document.

> fn 1 Standard permits are those individual permits which have been processed through application of the Corps public interest review procedures (33 CFR 325) and EPA's section 404(b)(1) Guidelines, including public notice and receipt of comments. Standard permits do not include letters of permission, regional permits, nationwide permits, or programmatic permits.

This MOA is a directive for Corps and EPA personnel and must be adhered to when considering mitigation requirements for standard permit applications. The Corps will use this MOA when making its determination of compliance with the Guidelines with respect to mitigation for standard permit applications. EPA will use this MOA in developing its positions on compliance with the Guidelines for proposed discharges and will reflect this MOA when commenting on standard permit applications.

II. POLICY

A. The Council on Environmental Quality (CEQ) has defined mitigation in its regulations at 40 CFR 1508.20 to include: avoiding impacts, minimizing impacts, rectifying impacts, reducing impacts over time, and compensating for impacts. The Guidelines establish environmental criteria which must be met for activities to be permitted under section 404. fn 2 The types of mitigation enumerated by CEQ are compatible with the requirements of the Guidelines; however, as a practical matter, they can be combined to form three general types: Avoidance, minimization and compensatory mitigation. The remainder of this MOA will speak in terms of these more general types of mitigation.

> fn 2 (except where section 404(b)(2) applies).

B. The Clean Water Act and the Guidelines set forth a goal of restoring and maintaining existing aquatic resources. The Corps will strive to avoid adverse impacts and offset unavoidable adverse impacts to existing aquatic resources, and for wetlands, will strive to achieve a goal of no overall net loss of values and functions. In focusing the goal of no overall net loss to wetlands only, EPA and Army have explicitly recognized the special significance of the nation's wetlands resources. This special recognition of wetlands resources does not in any manner diminish the value of other waters of the United States, which are often of high value. All waters of the United States, such as streams, rivers, lakes, etc., will be accorded the full measure of protection under the Guidelines, including the requirements for appropriate and practicable mitigation. The determination of what level of mitigation constitutes "appropriate" mitigation shall be based on the values and functions of the aquatic resource that will be impacted. This determination shall not be based upon characteristics of the proposed project such as need, societal value, or the nature or investment objectives of the project's sponsor. "Practicable" shall be defined as in Sec. 230.10(a)(2) of the Guidelines. However, the level of mitigation determined to be appropriate and practicable under Sec. 230.10(d) may lead to individual permit decisions which do not fully meet this goal because the mitigation measures necessary to meet this goal are not feasible, not practicable, or would accomplish only inconsequential reductions in impacts. Consequently, it is recognized that no net loss of wetlands functions and values may not be achieved in each and every permit action. However, it remains a goal of the Section 404 regulatory program to contribute to the national goal of no overall net loss of the nation's remaining wetlands base. EPA and Army are committed to working with others through the Administration's interagency task force and other avenues to help achieve this national goal.

C. In evaluating standard section 404 permit applications, as a practical matter, information on all facets of a project, including potential mitigation, is typically gathered and reviewed at the same time. Notwithstanding this procedural approach, the Corps will, except as indicated below, first make a determination that potential impacts have been avoided to the maximum extent practicable; remaining unavoidable impacts will then be mitigated to the extent appropriate and practicable by requiring steps to minimize impacts and, only as a last resort, compensate for aquatic resource values. This sequence will be considered satisfied where the proposed mitigation is in accordance with specific provisions of a Corps and EPA approved comprehensive plan that ensures compliance with the compensation requirements of this MOA, as set forth at section II.B (examples of such comprehensive plans may include Special Area Management Plans, Advance Identification areas (section 230.80), and State Coastal Zone Management Plans). In some circumstances, it may be appropriate to deviate from the sequence when EPA and the Corps agree the proposed discharge is necessary to avoid environmental harm (e.g., to protect a natural aquatic community from saltwater intrusion, chemical contamination, or other deleterious physical or chemical impacts), or EPA and the Corps agree that the proposed discharge can reasonably be expected to result in environmental gain. This environmental gain must be solely attributable to the project itself, exclusive of benefits which may accrue from proposed compensatory mitigation.

In determining "appropriate and practicable" measures to offset unavoidable impacts, such measures should be appropriate to the scope and degree of those impacts and practicable in terms of cost, existing technology, and logistics in light of overall project purposes. The Corps will give full consideration to the views of the resource agencies when making this determination.

1. *Avoidance.* fn 3 Section 230.10(a) allows permit issuance for only the least environmentally damaging practicable alternative. fn 4 The thrust of this section on alternatives is avoidance of impacts.

Section 230.10(a)(1) requires that, to be permittable, an alternative must be the least environmentally damaging practicable alternative. In addition, Sec. 230.10(a)(3) sets forth rebuttable presumptions that (1) alternatives for non-water dependent activities that do not involve special aquatic sites fn 5 are available and (2) alternatives that do not involve special aquatic sites have less adverse impact on the aquatic environment. Compensatory mitigation may not be used as a method to reduce environmental impacts on the selection of the least environmentally damaging practicable alternatives for the purposes of requirements under Sec. 230.10(a).

fn 3 Avoidance as used in this MOA does not include compensatory mitigation.

fn 4 It is important to recognize that there are circumstances where the impacts of the project are so significant that even if alternatives are not available, the discharge may not be permitted regardless of the compensatory mitigation proposed (40 CFR 230.10(c)).

fn 5 Special aquatic sites include sanctuaries and refuges, wetlands, mud flats, vegetated shallows, coral reefs and riffle pool complexes.

2. *Minimization.* Section 230.10(d) states that appropriate and practicable steps to minimize the adverse impacts will be required through project modifications and permit conditions. Subpart H of the Guidelines describes several (but not all) means for minimizing impacts of an activity.

3. *Compensatory Mitigation.* Appropriate and practicable compensatory mitigation will be required for unavoidable adverse impacts which remain after all appropriate and practicable minimization has been required. Compensatory actions (e.g., restoration of existing degraded wetlands or creation of man-made wetlands) should be undertaken, when practicable, in areas adjacent or contiguous to the discharge site (on-site compensatory mitigation). If on-site compensatory mitigation is not practicable, off-site compensatory mitigation should be undertaken in the same geographic area (i.e., in close physical proximity and, to the extent possible, the same watershed). In determining compensatory mitigation, the functional values lost by the resource to be impacted must be considered. In most cases, in-kind compensatory mitigation is preferable to out-of-kind. There is continued uncertainty regarding the success of wetland creation or other habitat development. Therefore, in determining the nature and extent of habitat development of this type, careful consideration should be given to its likelihood of success. Because the likelihood of success is greater and the impacts to potentially valuable uplands are reduced, restoration should be the first option considered. In the situation where the Corps is evaluating a project where a permit issued by another agency requires compensatory mitigation, the Corps may consider that mitigation as part of the overall application for purposes of public notice, but avoidance and minimization shall still be sought.

Mitigation banking may be an acceptable form of compensatory mitigation under specific criteria designed to ensure an environmentally successful bank. Where a mitigation bank has been approved by EPA and the Corps for purposes of providing compensatory mitigation for specific identified projects, use of that mitigation bank for those particular projects will be considered as meeting the requirements of section II.C.3 of this MOA, regardless of the practicability of other forms of compensatory mitigation. Additional guidance on mitigation banking will be provided. Simple purchase or "preservation" of existing wetlands resources may in only exceptional circumstances be accepted as compensatory mitigation. EPA and Army will develop specific guidance for preservation in the context of compensatory mitigation at a later date.

III. OTHER PROCEDURES

A. Potential applicants for major projects should be encouraged to arrange preapplication meetings with the Corps and appropriate federal, state or Indian tribal, and local authorities to determine requirements and documentation required for proposed permit evaluations. As a result of such meetings, the applicant often revises a proposal to avoid or minimize adverse impacts after developing an understanding of the Guidelines requirements by which a future section 404 permit decision will be made, in addition to gaining an understanding of other state or tribal, or local requirements.

B. In achieving the goals of the CWA, the Corps will strive to avoid adverse impacts and offset unavoidable adverse impacts to existing aquatic resources. Measures which can accomplish this can be identified only through resource assessments tailored to the site performed by qualified professionals because ecological characteristics of each aquatic site are unique. Functional values should be assessed by applying aquatic site assessment techniques generally recognized by experts in the field and/or the best professional judgment of federal and state agency representatives, provided such assessments fully consider ecological functions included in the Guidelines. The objective of mitigation for unavoidable impacts is to offset environmental losses. Additionally for wetlands, such mitigation will provide, at a minimum, one for one functional replacement (i.e., no net loss of values), fn 6 with an adequate margin of safety to reflect the expected degree of success associated with the mitigation plan, recognizing that this minimum requirement may not be relevant in some cases, as discussed in section II.B of this MOA.

> fn 6 In most cases a minimum of 1 to 1 acreage replacement of wetlands will be required to achieve no net loss of values. However, this ratio may be greater where the functional values of the area being impacted are demonstrably high. Conversely, the ratio may be less than 1 to 1 for areas where the functional values associated with the area being impacted are demonstrably low and the likelihood of success associated with the mitigation proposal is high.

C. The Guidelines are established as the environmental standard for section 404 permit issuance under the CWA. Aspects of a proposed project may be affected through a determination of requirements needed to comply with the Guidelines to achieve these CWA environmental goals. Other reviews, such as NEPA and the Corps public interest review, cannot be used to nullify any Guidelines requirements or to justify less rigorous Guidelines evaluations.

D. Monitoring is an important aspect of mitigation, especially in areas of scientific uncertainty. Monitoring should be directed toward determining whether permit conditions are complied with and whether the purpose intended to be served by the condition is actually achieved.

Any time it is determined that a permittee is in non-compliance with mitigation requirements of the permit, the Corps will take action in accordance with 33 CFR part 326. Monitoring should not be required for purposes other than these, although information for other uses may accrue from the monitoring requirements. For projects to be permitted involving mitigation with higher levels of scientific uncertainty, such as some forms of compensatory mitigation, long term monitoring, reporting and potential remedial action should be required. This can be required of the applicant through permit conditions.

E. Mitigation requirements shall be conditions of standard section 404 permits. Army regulations authorize mitigation requirements to be added as special conditions to an Army permit to satisfy legal requirements (e.g., conditions necessary to satisfy the Guidelines) (33 CFR 325.4(a)). This ensures legal enforceability of the mitigation conditions and enhances the level of compliance. If the mitigation plan necessary to ensure compliance with the Guidelines is not reasonably implementable or enforceable, the permit shall be denied.

F. Nothing in this document is intended to diminish, modify or otherwise affect the statutory or regulatory authorities of the agencies involved. Furthermore, formal policy guidance on or interpretation of this document shall be issued jointly.

G. This MOA shall take effect thirty (30) days after the date of the last signature below, and will apply to those completed standard permit applications which are received on or after the effective date. This MOA may be modified or revoked by agreement of both parties, or revoked by either party alone upon six (6) months written notice.

Dated: November 14, 1989.
Robert W. Page,
Assistant Secretary of the Army (Civil Works).

Dated: November 15, 1989.
LaJuana S. Wilcher,
Assistant Administrator for Water Environmental Protection Agency.

Appendix H

Interagency Statement of Principles Concerning Federal Wetlands Programs on Agriculture Lands

August 23, 1993

The Departments of the Army, Agriculture, Interior, and the Environmental Protection Agency recognize fully that the protection of the Nation's remaining wetlands is an important objective that will be supported through the implementation of the Swampbuster provisions of the Food Security Act and Section 404 of the Clean Water Act. Our agencies recognize and value the important contribution of agricultural producers to society, our economy, and our environment. We are committed to ensuring that the Federal wetlands programs are administered in a manner that minimizes the impacts on affected landowners to the extent possible consistent with the goals of protecting wetlands. Specifically, we are concerned that previous practices have led to confusion and inconsistent application of Federal wetlands policies on agricultural lands.

To minimize duplication and inconsistencies between Swampbuster and the Clean Water Act wetlands programs we agree to undertake the following within 120 days from the date of this agreement:

(1) The Soil Conservation Service (SCS), Army Corps of Engineers (Corps), the Environmental Protection Agency (EPA) and the Fish and Wildlife Service (FWS) will enter into a Memorandum of Agreement (MOA) which will ensure that the Nation's farmers can rely on SCS wetlands jurisdictional determinations for purposes of the Clean Water Act and Swampbuster. In accordance with the MOA, the Corps and EPA will accept written SCS wetland determinations as the final government position on the extent of Clean Water Act jurisdiction. The MOA will include provisions to ensure that agency personnel are properly trained, that standard, agreed upon methods are utilized in making such determinations, and that the Corps and EPA have the ability to monitor SCS determinations, made in consultation with FWS, on a programmatic basis consistent with EPA's authority to determine the geographic scope of Clean Water Act jurisdiction. The MOA will also address enforcement responsibilities on agriculture lands to ensure that the Federal government's activities are coordinated and consistent.

(2) The SCS, Corps, EPA, and FWS will complete technical guidance for agency field staff on conducting wetlands jurisdictional determinations and for the development of mitigation on lands managed for agriculture. This guidance will provide uniform interagency procedures and ensure greater consistency between the Clean Water Act and Swampbuster programs.

(3) The Corps, in coordination with the EPA, SCS, FWS and the National Marine Fisheries Service, will propose a Nationwide General Permit for discharges associated with "minimal effects" and "frequently cropped with mitigation" conversions determined by SCS and FWS to qualify for exemption from the provisions of Swampbuster. This will provide greater certainty to the Nation's farmers that they can

rely on SCS/FWS mitigation determinations. While the nationwide permit will contain appropriate conditions to ensure wetlands are properly protected, an individual review by the Corps and EPA will generally not be required.

Completion of the above initiatives within the next 120 days will ensure consistency among Federal wetlands protection programs and provide farmers with a single point of contact, the SCS, for wetlands jurisdiction and mitigation determinations. These initiatives should be viewed as a strengthening of our commitment to protect the Nation's wetlands. Effective and consistent administration of wetlands programs will help meet this commitment as well as reduce impacts on the agriculture community.

(signed)

Jim Lyons

Assistant Secretary for Natural Resources

and Environment

Department of Agriculture

(signed)

G. Edward Dickey

Acting Assistant Secretary of the Army

for Civil Works

Department of the Army

(signed)

Martha G. Prothro

Acting Assistant Administrator for Water

Environmental Protection Agency

(signed)

George Frampton, Jr.

Assistant Secretary for Fish, Wildlife and Parks

Department of the Interior

Appendix I

U.S. Army Corps of Engineers/ U.S. Environmental Protection Agency Memorandum on Section 404 Regulation of Agricultural Activities

3 May 1990
MEMORANDUM FOR THE FIELD

SUBJECT: Clean Water Act Section 404 Regulatory Program and Agricultural Activities

A number of questions have recently been raised about the applicability of the Clean Water Act Section 404 Regulatory Program to agriculture. This memorandum is intended to assist Section 404 field personnel in responding to those questions and to assure that the program is implemented in a consistent manner. At the outset, we should emphasize that we respect and support the underlying purposes of the Clean Water Act regarding the exemption from Section 404 permitting requirements for "normal farming" activities. The exemptions (at Section 404(f) of the Act) recognize that American agriculture fulfills the vitally important public need for supplying abundant and affordable food and fiber and it is our intent to assure that the exemptions are appropriately implemented.

What are normal farming activities? Who makes that determination? Can agricultural producers plant crops in wetlands areas that have been farmed for many years? These are questions that have generated significant confusion and concern in the agricultural community. This memorandum will explain the extent of the Section 404 program and clarify some misunderstandings that may exist in the field. Therefore we encourage you to widely distribute this memorandum.

WHAT IS SECTION 404?

The Federal Water Pollution Control Act Amendments of 1972 established the Section 404 Regulatory Program. Under this Act, it is unlawful to discharge dredged or fill material into waters of the United States without first receiving authorization (usually a permit) from the Corps, unless the discharge is covered under an exemption. The term "waters of the United States" defines the extent of geographic jurisdiction of the Section 404 program. The term includes such waters as rivers, lakes, streams, tidal waters, and most wetlands. A discharge of dredged or fill material involves the physical placement of soil, sand, gravel, dredged material or other such materials into the waters of the United States. Section 404(f) exemptions, which were added in 1977, provide that discharges that are part of normal farming, ranching, and forestry activities associated with an active and continuous ("ongoing") farming or forestry operation generally do not require a Section 404 permit.

With this background in mind, we can now turn to the issues that are the focus of concern. As previously noted, Section 404(f) exempts discharges of dredged or fill material into waters of the United States associated with certain normal agricultural activities. Of course, activities that do not involve a discharge of dredged or fill material into waters of the United States never require a Section 404 permit. Further, as provided in the Interagency Federal Manual for Identifying and Delineating Jurisdictional Wetlands, while a site is effectively and legally drained to the extent that it no longer meets the regulatory wetlands hydrology criteria (as interpreted by the Interagency Manual), it is not a wetland subject to jurisdiction under Section 404 of the Clean Water Act.

WHAT IS THE "NORMAL FARMING" ACTIVITIES EXEMPTION?

The Clean Water Act exempts from the Section 404 program discharges associated with normal farming, ranching and forestry activities such as plowing, cultivating, minor drainage, and harvesting for the production of food, fiber, and forest products, or upland soil and water conservation practices (Section 404(f)(1)(A)). To be exempt, these activities must be part of an established, ongoing operation. For example, if a farmer has been plowing, planting and harvesting in wetlands, he can continue to do so without the need for a Section 404 permit, so long as he does not convert the wetlands to dry land. Activities which convert a wetland which has not been used for farming or forestry into such uses are not considered part of an established operation, and are not exempt. For example, the conversion of a bottomland hardwood wetland to crop production is not exempt.

In determining whether an activity is part of an established operation, several points need to be considered. First, the specific farming activity need not itself have been ongoing as long as it is introduced as part of an ongoing farming operation. For example, if crops have been grown and harvested on a regular basis, the mere addition or change of a cultivation technique (e.g. discing between crop rows to control weeds rather than using herbicides) is considered to be part of the established farming operation. Second, the planting of different agricultural crops as part of an established rotation (e.g., soybeans to rice) is exempt. Similarly, the rotation of rice and crawfish production is also exempt (construction of fish ponds is not an exempt activity and is addressed on page 5 of this memorandum). Third, the resumption of agricultural production in areas laying fallow as part of a normal rotational cycle are considered to be part of an established operation and would be exempted under Section 404(f). However, if a wetland area has not been used for farming for so long that it would require hydrological modifications (modifications to the surface or groundwater flow) that would result in a discharge of dredged or fill material, the farming operation would no longer be established or ongoing.

As explained earlier, normal farming operation include cultivating, harvesting, minor drainage, plowing, and seeding. While these terms all have common, everyday definitions, it is important to recognize that these terms have specific, regulatory meanings in relation to the Section 404(f) exemptions. For example, plowing that is exempt under Section 404(f) means all mechanical means of manipulating soil, including land levelling, to prepare it for the planting of crops. However, grading activities that would change any area of waters of the United States, including wetland, into dry land are not exempt. Minor drainage that is exempt under Section 404(f) is limited to discharges associated with the continuation of established wetland crop production (e.g., building rice levees) or the connection of upland crop drainage facilities to waters of the United States. In addition, minor drainage also refers to the emergency removal of blockages that close or constrict existing drainageways used as part of an established crop production. Minor drainage is defined such that it does not include discharges associated with the construction of ditches which drain or significantly modify any wetlands or aquatic areas considered as waters of the United States. Seeding that is exempt under Section 404(f) includes not only the placement of seeds themselves, but also the placement of soil beds for seeds or seedlings on established farm or forest lands. Cultivating under Section 404(f) includes physical methods of soil treatment to aid and improve the growth, quality, or yield of established crops. Except as provided under Section 404(f)(2) as explained below, construction or maintenance of irrigation ditches or maintenance of drainage ditches is also exempt.

Recognizing area and regional differences in normal farming practices, EPA and the Corps agree to develop additional definitions of normal farming practices in consultation with the designated Land Grant Colleges and the Cooperative Extension Services. We also further encourage our field staffs to utilize the expertise in the colleges and agricultural services in the ongoing implementation of the Section 404 program.

WHEN THE NORMAL FARMING ACTIVITY EXEMPTIONS DO NOT APPLY

Section 404(f)(2) provides that discharges related to activities that change the use of the waters of the United States, including wetlands, and reduce the reach, or impair the flow or circulation of waters of the United States are not exempted. This "recapture" provision involves a two-part test that results in an activity being considered not exempt when both parts are met: 1) does the activity represent a "new use" of the wetland and, 2) would the activity result in a "reduction in reach/impairment of flow or circulation" of waters of the United States? Consequently, any discharge of dredged or fill material that results in the destruction of the wetland character of an area (e.g., its conversion to uplands due to new or expanded drainage) is considered a change in use of the waters of the United States, and by definition, a reduction of their reach, and is not exempt under Section 404(f). In addition, Section 404(f)(1) of the Act provides that discharges that contain toxic pollutants listed under Section 307 are not exempted and must be permitted.

However, discharges that are not exempt are not necessarily prohibited. Nonexempt discharges must first be authorized either through a general or individual Section 404 permit before they are initiated.

WHAT ARE GENERAL PERMITS?

Even if a farming activity is one that does not fall under an exemption and a permit is required, some farming activities are eligible for General Permits. Section 404(e) of the Act authorizes the Corps, after notice and opportunity for public hearing, to issue General Permits on a State, regional or nationwide basis for certain categories of activities involving a discharge of dredged or fill material in waters of the United States. Such activities must be similar in nature and cause only minimal adverse environmental effects. Discharges authorized under a General Permit may proceed without applying to the Corps for an individual permit. However, in some circumstances, conditions associated with a General Permit may require that persons wishing to discharge under that permit must notify the Corps or other designated State or local agency before the discharge takes place. A list of current General Permits is available from each Corps District Office, as well as information regarding notification requirements or other relevant conditions.

RICE FARMING

Questions have arisen regarding the relationship of the Section 404 program to rice farming. We understand these concerns, and recently have initiated actions that will allow farmers to understand better the regulatory program and provide more efficient and equitable mechanisms for implementing provisions of the Section 404 program.

In an April 19, 1990 letter responding to a request from Senator Patrick J. Leahy, Chairman and 11 members of the Senate Committee on Agriculture, Nutrition, and Forestry, we stated our position that discharges of dredged material associated with the construction of rice levees for rice farming in wetlands which are in established agricultural crop production are "normal farming activities" within the meaning of Section 404(f)(1)(A) and are therefore exempt from Section 404 regulation under the following conditions:

1) the purpose of these levees is limited to the maintenance and manipulation of shallow water levels for the production of rice crops; and

2) consistent with current agricultural practices associated with rice cultivation,
    –the height of the rice levees should generally not exceed 24 inches above their base; and
    –the material to be discharged for levee construction should generally be derived exclusively
      from the distribution of soil immediately adjacent to the constructed levee.

Land levelling for rice farming in wetlands which are in established crop production also is a "normal farming activity" within the meaning of Section 404(f)(1)(A) and is therefore exempt from Section 404 regulation.

FISH PONDS

We are developing a General Permit authorizing discharges of dredged or fill material associated with the construction of levees and ditches for the construction of fish ponds in wetlands that were in agricultural crop production prior to December 23, 1985. A draft General Permit has been developed by the Vicksburg District, Army Corps of Engineers and should be issued by June 1, 1990. This General Permit should serve as a model permit for other areas of the country and this activity will be considered for a nationwide General Permit.

It should be made clear, however, that the Section 404(f) exemption for "normal farming activities" and the General Permit being developed for fish ponds apply only to the use of wetlands which are already in use for agricultural crop production. These provisions do not apply to 1) wetlands that were once in use for agricultural crop production but have lain idle so long that modifications to the hydrologic regime are necessary to resume crop production or, 2) the conversion of naturally vegetated wetlands to agriculture, such as the conversion of bottomland hardwood wetlands to agriculture.

LIMITATIONS OF THE SECTION 404(F) EXEMPTIONS

It should be emphasized that the use of Section 404(f) exemptions does not affect Section 404 jurisdiction. For example, the fact that an activity in wetlands is exempted as normal farming practices does not authorize the filling of the wetland for the construction of building without a Section 404 permit. Similarly, a Section 404 permit would be required for the discharge of dredged or fill material associated with draining a wetland area and converting it to dry land.

ENFORCEMENT

Given that the normal farming practices as described above are exempt from regulation under Section 404, neither EPA nor the Corps will initiate enforcement actions against farmers or other persons for engaging in such normal farming activities. Further, there will be no enforcement against actions that meet the description of activities covered by, and any conditions contained in, general permits issued by the Corps.

CONCLUSION

Proper implementation of the Section 404 program is an issue of extreme importance to the nation. We encourage you to distribute this memorandum not only to your staffs but to the public at large so that there will be a better understanding of the program and how it operates. If you have any questions regarding this memorandum, please contact us or have your staff contact Suzanne Schwartz in EPA's office of Wetlands Protection at 202-475-7799, or John Studt in the Headquarters' Office of the U.S. Army Corps of Engineers at 202-272-1785 (temporary number 202-272-1294).

LaJuana S. Wilcher
Assistant Administrator for Water
U.S. Environmental Protection Agency

Robert W. Page
Assistant Secretary of the Army
(Civil Works)

Appendix J

Regulatory Guidance Letters Issued by the U.S. Army Corps of Engineers

Vol. 59, No. 023, 59 FR 5182
Thursday, February 3, 1994

ACTION: Notice.

SUMMARY: The purpose of this notice is to provide current Regulatory Guidance Letters (RGL's) to all interested parties. RGL's are used by the U.S. Army Corps of Engineers Headquarters as a means to transmit guidance on the permit program (33 CFR 320-330) to its division and district engineers (DE's). Each future RGL will be published in the Notice section of the Federal Register as a means to insure the widest dissemination of this information while reducing costs to the Federal Government. The Corps no longer maintains a mailing list to furnish copies of the RGL's to the public.

TEXT:

SUPPLEMENTARY INFORMATION: RGL's were developed by the Corps as a system to organize and track written guidance issued to its field agencies. RGL's are normally issued as a result of evolving policy; judicial decisions and changes to the Corps regulations or another agency's regulations which affect the permit program. RGL's are used only to interpret or clarify existing regulatory program policy, but do provide mandatory guidance to Corps district offices. RGL's are sequentially numbered and expire on a specified date. After a RGL's expiration date has passed, it no longer constitutes mandatory guidance for Corps district and division offices. Nevertheless, many expired RGL's still provide useful, non-mandatory guidance which Corps field offices have the discretion to follow. On the other hand, some RGL's have been superseded by specific provisions of subsequently issued regulations or RGL's. In addition, other expired RGL's, in whole or in part, may not be consistent with current Corps policy. The Corps incorporates most of the guidance provided by RGL's whenever it revises its permit regulations.

There were three RGL's issued by the Corps during 1993, and all were published in the Notices section of the Federal Register upon issuance. We are hereby publishing all current RGL's, beginning with RGL 91-1 and ending with RGL 93-3. We will continue to publish each RGL in the Notice Section of the Federal Register upon issuance and in early 1995, we will again publish the complete list of all current RGL's.

Dated: January 19, 1994.

Approved:
John R. Brown, Colonel, Corps of Engineers, Executive Director of Civil Works.

REGULATORY GUIDANCE LETTER (RGL 91-1)

RGL 91-1

Date: Dec 31, 1991, Expires: Dec 31, 1996

Subject: Extensions of Time for Individual Permit Authorizations

1. The purpose of this guidance is to provide clarification for district and division offices relating to extensions of time for Department of Army permits (See 33 CFR 325.6).

2. General: A permittee is informed of the time limit for completing an authorized activity by General Condition 1 of the standard permit form (ENG Form 1721). This condition states that a request for an extension of time should be submitted to the authorizing official at least one month prior to the expiration date. This request should be in writing and should explain the basis of the request. The DE may consider an oral request from the permittee provided it is followed up with a written request prior to the expiration date. A request for an extension of time will usually be granted unless the DE determines that the time extension would be contrary to the public interest. The one month submittal requirement is a workload management time limit designed to prevent permittees from filing last minute time extension requests. Obviously, the one month period is not sufficient to make a final decision on all time extension requests that are processed in accordance with 33 CFR 325.2. It should be noted that a permittee may choose to request a time extension sooner than this (e.g., six months prior to the expiration date). While there is no formal time limit of this nature, a request for an extension of time should generally not be considered by the DE more than one year prior to the expiration date. A permit will automatically expire if an extension is not requested and granted prior to the applicable expiration date (See 33 CFR 325.6(d)).

3. Requests for Time Extensions Prior to Expiration: For requests of time extensions received prior to the expiration date, the DE should consider the following procedures if a decision on the request cannot be completed prior to the permit expiration date:

   (a) The DE may grant an interim time extension while a final decision is being made; or

   (b) The DE may, when appropriate, suspend the

permit at the same time that an interim time extension is granted, while a final decision is being made.

4. Requests for Time Extensions After Expiration: At time extension cannot be granted if a time extension request is received after the applicable time limit. In such cases, a new permit application must be processed, if the permittee wishes to pursue the work. However, the DE may consider expedited processing procedures when: (1) The request is received shortly (generally 30 days) after the expiration date, (2) the DE determines that there have been no substantial changes in the attendant circumstances since the original authorization was issued, and (3) the DE believes that the time extension would likely have been granted. Expedited processing procedures may include, but are not limited to, not requiring that a new application form be submitted or issuing a 15 day public notice.

5. This guidance expires 31 December 1996 unless sooner revised or rescinded.

For the Director of Civil Works:

John P. Elmore, Chief, Operations, Construction and Readiness Division Directorate of Civil Works.

REGULATORY GUIDANCE LETTER (RGL 92-1

RGL 92-1

Date: 13 May 1992, Expires: 31 December 1997

Subject: Federal Agencies Roles and Responsibilities

1. Purpose: The purpose of this guidance is to clarify the Army Corps of Engineers leadership and decision-making role as "project manager" for the evaluation of permit applications pursuant to section 404 of the Clean Water Act (CWA) and section 10 of the Rivers and Harbors Act. This guidance is also intended to encourage effective and efficient coordination among prospective permittees, the Corps, and the Federal resource agencies (i.e., Environmental Protection Agency (EPA), Fish and Wildlife Service (FWS), and National Marine Fisheries Service (NMFS)). Implementation of this guidance will help to streamline the permit process by minimizing delays and ensuring more timely decisions, while providing a meaningful opportunity for substantive input from all Federal agencies.

2. Background:

(a) The Department of the Army Regulatory Program must operate in an efficient manner in order to protect the aquatic environment and provide fair, equitable, and timely decisions to the regulated public. Clear leadership and a predictable decision-making framework will enhance the public acceptance of the program and allow the program to meet the important objective of effectively protecting the Nation's valuable aquatic resources.

(b) On August 9, 1991, the President announced a comprehensive plan for improving the protection of the Nation's wetlands. The plan seeks to balance two important objectives-the protection, restoration, and creation of wetlands and the need for sustained economic growth and development. The plan, which is designed to slow and eventually stop the net loss of wetlands, includes measures that will improve and streamline the current wetlands regulatory system. This Regulatory Guidance Letter is issued in accordance with the President's plan for protecting wetlands.

(c) The intent of this guidance is to express clearly that the Corps is the decision-maker and project manager for the Department of Army's Regulatory Program. The Corps will consider, to the maximum extent possible, all timely, project- related comments from other Federal agencies when making regulatory decisions. Furthermore, the Corps and relevant Federal agencies will maintain and improve as necessary their working relationships.

(d) The Federal resource agencies have reviewed and concurred with this guidance and have agreed to act in accordance with these provisions. While this guidance does not restrict or impair the exercise of legal authorities vested in the Federal resource agencies or States under the CWA or other statutes and regulations (e.g., EPA's authority under section 404(c), section 404(f), and CWA geographic jurisdiction and FWS/NMFS authorities under the Fish and Wildlife Coordination Act and the Endangered Species Act (ESA)), agency comments on Department of the Army permit applications must be consistent with the provisions contained in this regulatory guidance letter.

3. The Corps Project Management/Decision Making Role:

(a) The Corps is solely responsible for making final permit decisions pursuant to section 10 and section 404(a), including final determinations of compliance with the Corps permit regulations, the section 404(b)(1) Guidelines, and section 7(a)(2) of the ESA. As such, the Corps will act as the project manager for the evaluation of all permit applications. The Corps will advise potential applicants of its role as the project manager and decision-maker. This guidance does not restrict EPA's authority to make determinations of compliance with the Guidelines in carrying out its responsibilities under sections 309 and 404(c) of the Clean Water Act.

(b) As the project manager, the Corps is responsible for requesting and evaluating information concerning all permit applications. The Corps will obtain and utilize this information in a manner that moves, as rapidly as practical, the regulatory process towards a final permit decision. The Corps will not evaluate applications as a project opponent or advocate--but instead will maintain an objective evaluation, fully considering all relevant factors.

(c) The Corps will fully consider other Federal agencies' project-related comments when determining compliance with the National Environmental Policy Act (NEPA), the section 404(b)(1) Guidelines, the ESA, the National Historic Preservation Act, and other relevant statutes, regulations, and policies. The Corps will also fully consider the agencies' views when determining whether to issue the permit, to issue the permit with conditions and/or mitigation, or to deny the permit.

4. The Federal Resource Agencies' Role:

(a) It is recognized that the Federal resource agencies have an important role in the Department of the Army Regulatory Program under the CWA, NEPA, ESA, Magnuson Fisheries Conservation and Management Act, and other relevant statutes.

(b) When providing comments, Federal resource agencies will submit to the Corps only substantive, project-related information on the impacts of activities being evaluated by the Corps and appropriate and practicable measures to mitigate adverse impacts. The comments will be submitted within the time frames established in interagency agreements and regulations. Federal resource agencies will limit their comments to their respective areas of expertise and authority to avoid duplication with the Corps and other agencies and to provide the Corps with a sound basis for making permit decisions. The Federal resource agencies should not submit comments that attempt to interpret the Corps regulations or for the purposes of section 404(a) make determinations concerning compliance with the section 404(b)(1) Guidelines. Pursuant to its authority under section 404(b)(1) of the CWA, the EPA may provide comments to the Corps identifying its views regarding compliance with the Guidelines. While the Corps will fully consider and utilize agency comments, the final decision regarding the permit application, including a determination of compliance with the Guidelines, rests solely with the Corps.

5. Pre-application Consultation:

(a) To provide potential applicants with the maximum degree of relevant information at an early phase of project planning, the Corps will increase its efforts to encourage pre-application consultations in accordance with regulations at 33 CFR 325.1(b). Furthermore, while encouraging pre-application consultation, the Corps will emphasize the need for early consultation concerning mitigation requirements, if impacts to aquatic resources may occur. The Corps is responsible for initiating, coordinating, and conducting pre-application consultations and other discussions and meetings with applicants regarding Department of the Army permits. This may not apply in instances where the consultation is associated with the review of a separate permit or license required from another Federal agency (e.g., the Federal Energy Regulatory Commission or the Nuclear Regulatory Commission) or in situations

where resource agencies perform work for others outside the context of a specific Department of the Army permit application (e.g., the conservation Reserve Program and technical assistance to applicants of Federal grants).

(b) For those pre-application consultations involving activities that may result in impacts to aquatic resources, the Corps will provide EPA, FWS, NMFS (as appropriate), and other appropriate Federal and State agencies, a reasonable opportunity to participate in the pre-application process. The invited agencies will participate to the maximum extent possible in the pre- application consultation, since this is generally the best time to consider alternatives for avoiding or reducing adverse impacts. To the extent practical, the Corps and the Federal resource agencies will develop local procedures (e.g., teleconferencing) to promote reasonable and effective pre-application consultations within the logistical constraints of all affected parties.

6. Applications for Individual Permits:

(a) The Corps is responsible for determining the need for, and the coordination of, interagency meetings, requests for information, and other interactions between permit applicants and the Federal Government. In this regard, Federal resource agencies will contact the Corps to discuss and coordinate any additional need for information for the applicant. The Corps will cooperate with the Federal resource agencies to ensure, to the extent practical, that information necessary for the agencies to carry out their responsibilities is obtained. If it is determined by the Corps that an applicant meeting is necessary for the exchange of information with a Federal resource agency and the Corps chooses not to participate in such a meeting, the Federal resource agency will apprise the Corps, generally in writing, of that agency's discussions with the applicant. Notwithstanding such meetings, the Corps is solely responsible for permit requirements, including mitigation and other conditions-the Federal resource agencies must not represent their views as regulatory requirements. In circumstances where the Corps meets with the applicant and develops information that will affect the permit decision, the Corps will apprise the Federal resource agencies of such information.

(b) Consistent with 33 CFR part 325, the Corps will ensure that public notices contain sufficient information to facilitate the timely submittal of project-specific comments from the Federal resource agencies. The resource agencies comments will provide specific information and/or data related to the proposed project site. The Corps will fully consider comments regarding the site from a watershed or landscape scale, including an evaluation of potential cumulative and secondary impacts.

(c) The Corps must consider cumulative impacts in reaching permit decisions. In addition to the Corps own expertise and experience, the Corps will fully consider comments from the Federal resource agencies, which can provide valuable information on cumulative impacts. Interested Federal agencies are encouraged to provide periodically to the Corps generic comments and assessments of impacts (outside the context of a specific permit application) on issues within the agencies' area of expertise.

7. General Permits:

(a) The Corps is responsible for proposing potential general permits, assessing impacts of and comments on proposed general permits, and deciding whether to issue general permits. The Corps will consider proposals for general permits from other sources, including the Federal resource agencies, although the final decision regarding the need to propose a general permit rests with the Corps. Other interested Federal agencies should provide comments to the Corps on proposed general permits. These Federal agency comments will be submitted consistent with established agreements and regulations and will focus on the Federal agencies' area(s) of expertise. The Corps will fully consider such agencies' comments in deciding whether to issue general permits, including programmatic general permits.

(b) The Corps is responsible for initiating and conducting meetings that may be necessary in developing and evaluating potential general permits. Any discussions with a State or local Government regarding proposed programmatic general permits will be coordinated through and conducted by the Corps. Prior to issuing a programmatic general permit, the Corps will ensure that the State or local program, by itself or with appropriate conditions, will protect the aquatic environment, including wetlands, to the level required by the section 404 program.

8.   This guidance expires 31 December 1997 unless sooner revised or rescinded.

For the Commander.

Arthur R. Williams,
Major General, USA, Director of Civil Works.

RGL 92-2

Date: 26 June 92, Expires: 31 December 95
CECW-OR
Subject: Water Dependency and Cranberry Production

1. Enclosed for implementation is a joint Army Corps of Engineers/Environmental Protection Agency Memorandum to the Field on water dependency with cranberry production. This guidance was developed jointly by the Army Corps of Engineers and the U.S. Environmental Protection Agency.

2. This guidance will expire 31 December 1995 unless sooner revised or rescinded.

For the Director of Civil Works.

John P. Elmore, Chief, Operations, Construction and Readiness Division, Directorate of Civil Works.

Memorandum to the Field
Subject: Water Dependency and Cranberry Production

1. The purpose of this memorandum is to clarify the applicability of the section 404(b)(1) Guidelines water dependency provisions (40 CFR 230.10(a)) to the cultivation of cranberries, in light of Army Corps of Engineers (Corps) regulations at 33 CFR 323.4(a)(1) (iii)(C)(1) (ii) and (iii), and Environmental Protection Agency (EPA) regulations at 40 CFR 232.3(d)(3)(i) (B) and (C). These sections of the Corps and EPA regulations state, among other things, that cranberries are a wetland crop, and that some discharges associated with cranberry production are considered exempt from regulation under the provisions of section 404(f) of the Clean Water Act. The characterization of cranberries as a wetland crop has led to inconsistency in determining if cranberry production is a water dependent activity as defined in the section 404(b)(1) Guidelines (Guidelines).

2. The intent of Corps regulations at 33 CFR 320.4(b) and of the Guidelines is to avoid the unnecessary destruction or alteration of waters of the U.S., including wetlands, and to compensate for the unavoidable loss of such waters. The Guidelines specifically required that "no discharge of dredged or fill material shall be permitted if there is a practicable alternative to the proposed discharge which would have less adverse impact on the aquatic ecosystem, so long as the alternative does not have other significant adverse environmental consequences" (see 40 CFR 230.10(a)). Based on this provision, an evaluation is required in every case for use of non-aquatic areas and other aquatic sites that would result in less adverse impact to the aquatic ecosystem, irrespective of whther the discharge site is a special aquatic site or whether the activity associated with the discharge is water depen-

dent. A permit cannot be issued, therefore, in circumstances where an environmentally preferable practicable alternative for the proposed discharge exists (except as provided for under section 404(b)(2)).

3. For proposed discharges into wetlands and other "special aquatic sites," the Guidelines alternatives analysis requirement further considers whether the activity associated with the proposed discharge is "water dependent". The Guidelines define water dependency in terms of an activity requiring access or proximity to or siting within a special aquatic site to fulfill its basic project purpose. Special aquatic sites (as defined in 40 CFR 230.40-230.45) are: (1) Sanctuaries and refuges; (2) wetlands; (3) mud flats; (4) vegetated shallows; (5) coral reefs; and (6) riffle and pool complexes. If an activity is determined not to be water dependent, the Guidelines establish the follow two presumptions (40 CFR 230.10(a)(3)) that the applicant is required to rebut before satisfying the alternatives analysis requirements:

a. That practicable alternatives that do not involve special aquatic sites are presumed to be available; and,

b. That all practicable alternatives to the proposed discharge which do not involve a discharge into a special aquatic site are presumed to have less adverse impact on the aquatic ecosystem. It is the responsibility of the applicant to clearly rebut these presumptions in order to demonstrate compliance with the Guidelines alternatives test.

4. If an activity is determined to be water dependent, the rebuttable presumptions stated in paragraph 3 of this memorandum do not apply. However, the proposed discharge, whether or not it is associated with a water dependent activity, must represent the least environmentally damaging practicable alternative in order to comply with the alternatives analysis requirement of the Guidelines as described in paragraph 2 of this memorandum.

5. As previously indicated, Corps and EPA regulations consider cranberries as a wetland crop species. This characterization of cranberries as a wetland crop species is based primarily on the listing of cranberries as an obligate hydrophyte in the National List of Plant Species That Occur in Wetlands (U.S. Fish and Wildlife Service Biological Report 88 (26.1-26.13)) and the fact that cranberries must be grown in wetlands or areas altered to create a wetland environment. Therefore, the Corps and EPA consider the construction of cranberry beds, including associated dikes and water control structures associated with dikes (i.e., headgates, weirs, drop inlet structures), to be a water dependent activity. Consequently, discharges directly associated with cranberry bed construction are not subject to the presumptions applicable to non-water dependent activities discussed in paragraph 3 of this memorandum. However, consistent with the requirements of Sec. 230.10(a), the proposed discharge must represent the least environmentally damaging practicable alterna-

tive, after considering aquatic and non-aquatic alternatives as appropriate. To be considered practicable, an alternative must be available and capable of being done after taking into consideration cost, existing technology, and logistics in light of overall project purposes. For commercial cranberry cultivation, practicable alternatives may include upland sites with proper characteristics for creating the necessary conditions to grow cranberries. Factors that must be considered in making a determination of whether or not upland alternatives are practicable include soil pH, topography, soil permeability, depth to bedrock, depth to seasonal high water table, adjacent land uses, water supply, and, for expansion of existing cranberry operations, proximity to existing cranberry farms. EPA Regions and Corps Districts are encouraged to work together with local cranberry growers to refine these factors to reflect their regional conditions.

6. In contrast, the following activities often associated with the cultivation and harvesting of cranberries are not considered water dependent: construction of roads, ditches, reservoirs, and pump houses that are used during the cultivation of cranberries, and construction of secondary support facilities for shipping, storage, packaging, parking, etc. Therefore, the rebuttable practicable alternatives presumptions discussed in paragraph 3 of this memorandum apply to the discharges associated with these non-water dependent activities. However, since determinations of practicability under the Guidelines includes consideration of cost, technical, and logistics factors, determining the availability of practicable alternatives to discharges associated with these non-water dependent activities must involve consideration of the need of an alternative to be proximate to the cranberry bed in order to achieve the basic project purpose of cranberry cultivation. Once it has been determined that the location of the cranberry bed, including associated dikes, and water control structures, represents the least environmentally damaging practicable alternative, practicable alternatives for maintenance roads, ditches, reservoirs and pump houses will generally be limited to the bed itself and the area in the vicinity of the actual bed. For example, the bed dikes may be the only practicable alternative for location of maintenance roads. When practicable alternatives cannot be identified within such geographic constraints, the applicant must minimize the impacts of the roads, reservoirs, etc., to the maximum extent practicable.

7. During review of applications for discharges associated with cranberry cultivation, it is important to reiterate that proposed discharges must also comply with the other requirements of the Guidelines (i.e., 40 CFR 230.10 (b) (c) and (d)). In addition, evaluations of all discharges, whether or not the proposed discharge is associated with a water dependent activity, must comply with the provisions of the National Environmental Policy Act, including an investigation of alternatives to the proposed discharge. Further, applications for discharges associated with cranberry cultivation

will continue to be evaluated in accordance with current Corps and EPA policy and practice concerning mitigation, cumulative impact analysis, and public interest review factors.

8. This guidance expires 31 December 1995 unless sooner revised orrescinded.

For the Director of Civil Works.

Robert H. Wayland, III, Director, Office of Wetlands, Oceans, and Watersheds, U.S. Environmental Protection.

John P. Elmore, Chief, Operations, Construction and Readiness Division, Directorate of Civil Works.

REGULATORY GUIDANCE LETTER (RGL 92-3)

RGL 92-3

Date: 19 Aug 92, Expires: 31 Dec 97

Subject: Extension of Regulatory Guidance Letter (RGL) 86-10 RGL 86-10, subject: "Special Area Management Plans (SAMP's)" is extended until 31 December 1997 unless sooner revised or rescinded.

For the Director of Civil Works

John P. Elmore, Chief, Operations, Construction and Readiness Division, Directorate of Civil Works.

RGL 86-10

Special Area Management Plans (SAMP's)
Issued 10/2/86, Expired 12/31/88

1. The 1980 Amendments to the Coastal Zone Management Act define the SAMP process as "a comprehensive plan providing for natural resource protection and reasonable coastal-dependent economic growth containing a detailed and comprehensive statement of policies, standards and criteria to guide public and private uses of lands and waters; and mechanisms for timely implementation in specific geographic areas within the coastal zone." This process of collaborative interagency planning within a geographic area of special sensitivity is just as applicable in non-coastal areas.

2. A good SAMP reduces the problems associated with the traditional case-by-case review. Developmental interests can plan with predictability and environmental interests are assured that individual and cumulative impacts are analyzed in the context of broad ecosystem needs.

3. Because SAMP's are very labor intensive, the following ingredients should usually exist before a district engineer becomes involved in a SAMP:

a. The area should be environmentally sensitive and under strong developmental pressure.

b. There should be a sponsoring local agency to ensure that the plan fully reflects local needs and interests.

c. Ideally there should be full public involvement in the planning and development process.

d. All parties must express a willingness at the outset to conclude the SAMP process with a definitive regulatory product (see next paragraph).

4. An ideal SAMP would conclude with two products: (1) Appropriate local/State approvals and a Corps general permit (GP) or abbreviated processing procedure (APP) for activities in specifically defined situations; and (2) a local/State restriction and/or an Environmental Protection Agency (EPA) 404(c) restriction (preferably both) for undesirable activities. An individual permit review may be conducted for activities that do not fall into either category above. However, it should represent a small number of the total cases addressed by the SAMP. We recognize that an ideal SAMP is difficult to achieve, and, therefore, it is intended to represent an upper limit rather than an absolute requirement.

5. Do not assume that an environmental impact statement is automatically required to develop a SAMP.

6. EPA's program for advance identification of disposal areas found at 40 CFR 230.80 can be integrated into a SAMP process.

7. In accordance with this guidance, district engineers are encouraged to participate in development of SAMP's. However, since development of a SAMP can require a considerable investment of time, resources, and money, the SAMP process should be entered only if it is likely to result in a definitive regulatory product as defined in paragraph 4. above.

8. This guidance expires 31 December 1988 unless sooner revised or rescinded.

For the Chief of Engineers.

Peter J. Offringa, Brigadier General, USA, Deputy Director of Civil Works.

REGULATORY GUIDANCE LETTER (RGL 92-4)

RGL 92-4

Date: 14 Sep 1992, Expires: 21 January 1997

Subject: Section 401 Water Quality Certification and Coastal Zone Management Act Conditions for Nationwide Permits

1. The purpose of this Regulatory Guidance Letter (RGL) is to provide additional guidance and clarification for divisions and districts involved in developing acceptable conditions under the section 401 Water Quality Certifications and Coastal Zone Management Act (CZM) concurrences for the Nationwide Permit (NWP) Program. This RGL represents a clarification if 330.4(c) (2) and (3) and 330.4(d) (2) and (3), concerning when NWP Section 401 and CZM conditions should not be accepted and thus treated as a denial without prejudice. The principles contained in this RGL also apply to 401 certification and CZM concurrence conditions associated with individual permits and regional general permits.

2. Corps divisions and districts should work closely and cooperatively with the States to develop reasonable 401 and CZM conditions. All involved parties should participate in achieving the purpose of the NWP program, which is to provide the public with an expeditious permitting process while, at the same time, safeguarding the environment by only authorizing activities which result in no more than minimal individual and cumulative adverse effects. When a State certifying agency or CZM agency proposes conditions, the division engineer is responsible for determining whether 401 Water Quality Certification or CZM concurrence conditions are acceptable and comply with the provisions of 33 CFR 325.4. In most cases it is expected that the conditions will be acceptable and the division engineer shall recognize these conditions as regional conditions of the NWP's.

3. Unacceptable Conditions: There will be cases when certain conditions will clearly be unacceptable and those conditioned 401 certifications or CZM concurrences shall be considered administratively denied. Consequently, authorization for an activity which meets the terms and conditions of such NWP(s) is denied without prejudice.

    a. Illegal conditions are clearly unacceptable. Illegal conditions would result in violation of a law or regulation, or would require an illegal action. For example, a condition which would require an applicant to obtain a 401 certification or CZM concurrence, where the State as previously denied certification or concurrence, prior to submitting a predischarge notification (PDN) to the Corps in accordance with PDN procedures, would violate the Corps regulation at 33 CFR 330.4(c)(6). Another example would be a case where an applicant would be required, through a condition, to apply for an individual Department of the Army permit. Another example is a requirement by the State agency to utilize the 1989 Federal Wetland Delineation Manual to establish jurisdiction.

    b. As a general rule, a condition that would require the Corps or another Federal agency to take an action which we would not otherwise take and do not choose to take, would be clearly unacceptable. For example, where the certification or concurrence is conditioned to require a PDN, where the proposed activity did not previously require a PDN, the Corps should not accept that condition, since implicitly the Corps would have to accept and utilize the PDN. Another example would be a situation where the U.S. Fish and Wildlife Service is required, through a condition, to provide any type of formal review or approval.

    c. Section 401 or CZM conditions which provide for limits (quantities, dimensions, etc.) different from those imposed by the NWP do not change the NWP limits.

        1. Higher limits are clearly not acceptable. For example, increasing NWP 18 for minor discharges from 10 to 50 cubic yards would not be acceptable. Such conditions would confuse the regulated public and could contribute to violations.

        2. Lower limits are acceptable but have the effect of denial without prejudice of those activities that are higher than the Section 401 or CZM condition limit but within the NWP limit. Thus, if an applicant obtains an individual 401 water quality certification and/or CZM concurrence for work within the limits of an NWP where the State had denied certification and/or CZM concurrence, then the activity could be authorized by the NWP. d. A condition which would delete, modify, or reduce NWP conditions would be clearly unacceptable.

4. Discretionary Enforcement: The initiation of enforcement actions by the Corps, whether directed at unauthorized activities or to ensure compliance with permit conditions, is discretionary. The district engineer will consider the following situations when determining whether to enforce 401 and/or CZM conditions.

    a. Unenforceable Conditions-Some conditions that a State may propose will not be reasonably enforceable by the Corps (e.g., a condition requiring compliance with the specific terms of another State permit). Provided such conditions do not violate paragraph 3 above, the conditions will be accepted by the Corps as regional conditions. However, limited Corps resources should not be utilized in an attempt to enforce compliance with 401 or CZM conditions which the district engineer believes to be essentially unenforceable, or of low enforcement priority for limited Corps resources.

    b. Enforceable Conditions-Some other conditions proposed by a State may be considered enforceable, (e.g., a condition requiring the applicant to obtain another State permit), but of low priority for Federal enforcement, since the Federal Government would not have required those conditions but for the State's requirement. Furthermore, the Corps will generally not enforce such State-imposed conditions except in very unusual cases, due to our limited personnel and financial resources.

5. NWP Verification and PDN Responses: In response to NWP verification requests and PDN's, district engineers should utilize the sample paragraphs presented below. This language should be used where conditional 401 certification or CZM concurrence has been issued. This specifically addresses situations when the conditions included with the certification or concurrence are such that the district engineer determines they are unforceable or the district engineer cannot clearly determine compliance with the 401/CZM conditions (see 4.a.). "Based on our review of your proposal to describe proposal, we have determined that the activity qualifies for the nationwide permit authorizations insert NWP No(s.), subject to the terms and conditions of the permit.

Insert paragraph on any Corps required activity-specific conditions.

Enclosed you will find a copy of the Section 401 Water Quality Certification and/or Coastal Zone Management special conditions, which are conditions of your authorization under Nationwide Permit insert NWP No(s.). If you have questions concerning compliance with the conditions of the 401 certification or Coastal Zone Management concurrence, you should contact the insert appropriate State agency. If you do not or cannot comply with these State Section 401 certification conditions and/or CZM conditions, then in order to be authorized by this Nationwide Permit, you must furnish this office with an individual 401 certification or Coastal Zone Management concurrence from insert appropriate State agency, or a copy of the application to the State for such certification or concurrence, insert "60 days" for Section 401 water quality certification, unless another reasonable period of time has been determined pursuant to 33 CFR 330.4(c)(6), or insert "six months" for CZM concurrence after you submit it to the State agency."

6. This guidance expires 21 January 1997 unless sooner revised or rescinded.

For the Director of Civil Works.

John P. Elmore, Chief, Operations, Construction Readiness Division, Directorate of Civil Works.

REGULATORY GUIDANCE LETTER (RGL 92-5)

RGL 92-5

Date: 29 October 1992, Expires: 31 December 1997

Subject: Alternatives Analysis Under the section 404(b)(1) Guidelines for Projects Subject to Modification Under the Clean Air Act.

1. Enclosed for implementation is a joint Army Corps of Engineers/Environmental Protection Agency Memorandum to the Field on alternatives analysis for existing power plants that must be modified to meet requirements of the 1990 Clean Air Act. This guidance was developed jointly by the Corps and EPA.

2. This guidance expires 31 December 1997 unless sooner revised or rescinded.

For the Director of Civil Works.
John P. Elmore, Chief, Operations, Construction and Readiness Division, Directorate of Civil Works.

EPA/Corps Joint Memorandum for the Field

Subject: Alternatives Analysis under the section 404(b)(1) Guidelines for Projects Subject to Modification Under the Clean Air Act.

1. The 1990 Clean Air Act (CAA) amendments require most electric generating plants to reduce emissions of sulfur dioxide in phases beginning in 1995 and requiring full compliance by 2010. The congressional endorsement of the industry's ability to select the most effective compliance method (e.g., sulfur dioxide scrubbers, low sulfur coal, or other methods) recognizes the expertise of the industry in these cases and is a fundamental element in the CAA market-based pollution control program. Given the need for cooling water, a substantial number of electric power generating plants are located adjacent, or in close proximity, to waters of the United States, including wetlands. Depending on the method chosen by the plants to reduce emissions, we expect that these facilities will be applying for Clean Water Act section 404 permits for certain proposed activities.

2. The analysis and regulation under section 404 of the Clean Water Act of activities in waters of the United States conducted by specific power plants to comply with the 1990 Clean Air Act amendments must ensure protection of the aquatic environment consistent with the requirements of the Clean Water Act. The review of applications for such projects will fully consider, consistent with requirements under the section 404(b)(1) Guidelines, all practicable alternatives including non-aquatic alternatives, for proposed discharges associated with the method selected by the utility to comply with the 1990 Clean Air Act amendments. For the purposes of the section 404(b)(1) Guidelines analysis, the project

purpose will be that pollutant reduction method selected by the permit applicant.

3. For example, a utility may have decided to install sulfur dioxide scrubbers on an existing power plant in order to meet the new 1990 Clean Air Act standards. The proposed construction of the scrubbers, treatment ponds and a barge unloading facility could impact wetlands. In this case, the section 404 review would evaluate practicable alternative locations and configurations for the scrubbers, ponds and of the docking facilities. The analysis will also consider practicable alternatives which satisfy the project purpose (i.e., installing scrubbers) but which have a less adverse impact on the aquatic environment or do not involve discharges into waters of the United States. However, in order to best effectuate Congressional intent reflected in the CAA that electric utilities retain flexibility to reduce sulfur dioxide emissions in the most cost effective manner, the section 404 review should not evaluate alternative methods of complying with the Clean Air Act standards not selected by the applicant (e.g., in this example use of low sulfur coal).

4. In evaluating the scope of practicable alternatives which satisfy the project purpose (e.g., constructing additional scrubber capacity), the alternatives analysis should not be influenced by the possibility that, based on a conclusion that practicable upland alternatives are available to the applicant, the project proponent may decide to pursue other options for meeting Clean Air Act requirements. Continuing the above example, a Corps determination that practicable upland alternatives are available for scrubber waste disposal should not be affected by the possibility that an applicant may subsequently decide to select a different method for meeting the Clean Air Act standards (e.g., use of low sulfur coal that reduces waste generated by scrubbers).

5. The Corps and EPA will also recognize the tight time-frames under which the industry must meet these new air quality standards.

Robert H. Wayland,
Director, Office of Wetlands, Oceans and Watersheds.

John P. Elmore, Chief, Operations, Construction and Readiness Division, Directorate of Civil Works.

REGULATORY GUIDANCE LETTER (RGL 93-1)

RGL 93-1

Issued: April 20, 1993, Expires: December 31, 1998
CECW-OR
Subject: Provisional Permits

1. Purpose: The purpose of this guidance is to establish a process that clarifies for applicants when the U.S. Army Corps of Engineers has completed its evaluation and at what point the applicant should contact the State concerning the status of the Section 401 Water Quality Certification and/or Coastal Zone Management (CZM) consistency concurrence. This process also allows for more accurate measurement of the total length of time spent by the Corps in evaluating permit applications (i.e., from receipt of a complete application until the Corps reaches a permit decision). For verification of authorization of activities under regional general permits, the Corps will use the appropriate nationwide permit procedures at 33 CFR 330.6.

2. Background:

a. A Department of the Army permit involving a discharge of dredged or fill material cannot be issued until a State Section 401 Water Quality Certification has been issued or waived. Also, a Department of the Army permit cannot be issued for a activity within a State with a federally-approved Coastal Management Program when that activity that would occur within, or outside, a State's coastal zone will affect land or water uses or natural resources of the State's coastal zone, until the State concurs with the applicant's consistency determination, or concurrence is presumed. In many cases, the Corps completes its review before the State Section 401 Water Quality Certification or CZM concurrence requirements have been satisfied. In such cases, applicants and the public are often confused regarding who to deal with regarding resolution of any State issues.

b. The "provisional permit" procedures described below will facilitate a formal communication between the Corps and the applicant to clearly indicate that the applicant should be in contact with the appropriate State agencies to satisfy the State 401 Water Quality Certification or CZM concurrence requirements. In addition, the procedures will allow for a more accurate measurement of the Corps permit evaluation time.

3. Provisional Permit Procedures: The provisional permit procedures are optional and may only be used in those cases where: (i) The District Engineer (DE) has made a provisional individual permit decision that an individual permit should be issued, and (ii) the only action(s) preventing the issuance of that permit is that the State has not issued a required Section 401 Water Quality Certification (or waiver has not occurred) or the State has not concurred in the applicant's CZM

consistency determination (or there is not a presumed concurrence). In such cases, the DE may, using these optional procedures, send a provisional permit to the applicant.

a. First, the DE will prepare and sign the provisional permit decision document. Then the provisional permit will be sent to the applicant by transmittal letter. (The sample transmittal letter at enclosure 1 contains the minimum information that must be provided.)

b. Next, the applicant would obtain the Section 401 Water Quality Certification (or waiver) and/or CZM consistency concurrence (or presumed concurrence). Then the applicant would sign the provisional permit and return it to the DE along with the appropriate fee and the Section 401 Water Quality Certification (or proof of wavier) and/or the CZM consistency concurrence (or proof of presumed concurrence).

c. Finally, the Corps would attach any Section 401 Water Quality Certification and/or CZM consistency concurrence to the provisional permit, then sign the provisional permit (which then becomes the issued final permit), and forward the permit to the applicant.

d. This is the same basic process as the normal standard permit transmittal process except that the applicant is sent an unsigned permit (i.e., a provisional permit) prior to obtaining the Section 401 Water Quality Certification (or waiver) and/or CZM consistency concurrence (or presumed concurrence). (See enclosure 2.) A permit cannot be issued (i.e., signed by the Corps) until the Section 401 and CZM requirements are satisfied.

4. Provisional Permit: A provisional permit is a standard permit document with a cover sheet. The cover sheet must clearly indicate the following: that a provisional permit is enclosed, that the applicant must obtain the section 401 Water Quality Certification or CZM concurrence from the State, that these documents must be sent to the Corps along with the provisional permit signed by the applicant, and that the Corps will issue the permit upon receipt of these materials. The issued permit is the provisional permit signed by the applicant and the Corps. The provisional permit must contain a statement indicating that the applicant is required to comply with the Section 401 Water Quality Certification, including any conditions, and/or the CZM consistency concurrence, including any conditions. At enclosure 3 is a sample cover sheet for the provisional permit.

5. Provisional Permit Decision: The DE may reach a final decision that a permit should be issued provided that the State issues a Section 401 Water Quality Certification and/or a CZM concurrence. In order to reach such a decision the DE must complete the normal standard permit evaluation process, prepare and sign a decision document, and prepare a standard permit, including any conditions or mitigation (i.e., a provisional permit). The decision document must include

a statement that the DE has determined that the permit will be issued if the State issues a Section 401 Water Quality Certification or waiver and/or a CZM concurrence, or presumed concurrence. The standard permit will not contain a condition that requires or provides for the applicant to obtain a Section 401 Water Quality Certification and/or CZM concurrence. Once the decision document is signed, the applicant has the right to a DA permit if the State issues a Section 401 Water Quality Certification or waiver and/or a CZM concurrence, or if concurrence is presumed. Once the decision document is signed, the permittee's right to proceed can only be changed by using the modification, suspension and revocation procedures of 33 CFR 325.7, unless the State denies the Section 401 Water Quality Certification or nonconcurs with the applicant's CZM consistency determination.

6. Enforcement: In some cases, applicants might proceed with the project upon receipt of the provisional permit. The provisional permit is not a valid permit. In such cases, the Corps has a discretionary enforcement action to consider and should proceed as the DE determines to be appropriate. This occurs on occasion during the standard permit transmittal process. Since the Corps is not changing the normal process of sending unsigned permits to the applicant for signature, there should not be an increase in occurrence of such unauthorized activities.

7. Modification:

a. In most cases the Section 401 Water Quality Certification, including conditions, and/or CZM consistency concurrence, including conditions, will be consistent with the provisional permit. In such cases, the DE will simply sign the final permit enclose the 401 water quality certification and/or CZM consistency concurrence with the final permit (i.e., the signed provisional permit).

b. In a few cases such State approval may necessitate modifications to the Corps preliminary permit decision. Such modifications will be processed in accordance with 33 CFR 325.7.

(1) When the modifications are minor and the DE agrees to such modifications, then a supplement to the provisional decision document may be prepared, as appropriate, and the permit issued with such modifications. (This should usually be done by enclosing the State 401 Water Quality Certification and/or CZM consistency concurrence to the permit, but in a few cases may require a revision to the permit document itself.)

(2) When the modification results in substantial change or measurable increase in adverse impacts or the Corps does not initially agree with the change, then the modification will be processed and counted as a separate permit action for reporting purposes. This may require a new public notice or additional coordination with appropriate Federal and/or state agencies. The provisional decision document will be sup-

plemented or may be completely rewritten, as necessary.

8. Denial: If the State denies the Section 401 Water Quality Certification and/or the State nonconcurs with the applicant's CZM consistency determination, then the Corps permit is denied without prejudice.

9. This guidance expires 31 December 1998 unless sooner revised or rescinded.

For the Director of Civil Works.

3 Encls

John P. Elmore, Chief, Operations, Construction and Readiness Division, Directorate of Civil Works.

Sample

Provisional Permit Transmittal Letter

Dear :

We have completed our review of your permit application identified as File No., appl. name, etc. for the following proposed work:

near/in/at X.

Enclosed is a "PROVISIONAL PERMIT." The provisional permit is NOT VALID and does not authorize you to do your work. The provisional permit describes the work that will be authorized, and the General and Special Conditions if any which will be placed on your final Department of the Army (DA) permit, if the State of Water Quality Certification and/or Coastal Zone Management (CZM) consistency requirements are satisfied as described below. No work is to be performed in the waterway or adjacent wetlands until you have received a validated copy of the DA permit.

By Federal law no DA permit can be issued until a State Section 401 Water Quality Certification has been issued or has been waived and/or the State has concurred with a permit applicant's CZM consistency determination or concurrence has been presumed. As of this date the State 401 certification agency has not issued a Section 401 Water Quality Certification for your proposed work. If the State 401 certification agency fails or refuses to act by date 401 certification must be issued the Section 401 Water Quality Certification requirement will be automatically waived. Also, as of this date the State CZM agency has not concurred with your CZM consistency determination. If the State does not act by six months from receipt by the State of the applicant's CZM consistency determination then concurrence with your CZM consistency determination will automatically be presumed.

Conditions of the State Section 401 Water Quality Certification and/or the State CZM concurrence will become conditions to the final DA permit.

Should the State's action on the required certification or concurrence preclude validation of the provisional permit in its current form, a modification to the provisional permit will be evaluated and you will be notified as appropriate. Substantial changes may require a new permit evaluation process, including issuing a new public notice.

Enclosure 1

Final Permit Actions

Normal Permit Process

1. Corps Completes permit decision, and state 401/CZM issued/waived
2. Corps sends unsigned permit to applicant
3. Applicant signs permit and returns with fee
4. Corps signs permit

Draft Permit Process

1. Corps Completes permit decision, but state 401/CZM not complete
2. Corps sends draft permit to applicant
3. State 401/CZM issued waived
4. Applicant signs permit and returns with fee and 401/CZM action
5. Corps reviews 401/CZM action and signs permit
   1. The signed draft permit with the attached 401/CZM action is to be treated as the applicant's request for a permit subject to any 401/CZM certification/concurrence including any conditions.
   2. If the 401/CZM action results in a modification to the draft permit, then step 4. would be treated as a request for such modification and if we agree with the modification, then the permit would be issued with the modification and the decision document supplemented, as appropriate. If the Corps does not initially agree with the modification, or it involves a substantial change or measurable increase in adverse impacts, then the modification would be processed as a separate permit action for reporting purposes.

Enclosure 2

Once the State has issued the required Section 401 Water Quality Certification and/or concurred with your CZM consistency determination or the dates above have passed without the State acting, and you agree to the terms and conditions of the provisional permit, you should sign and date both copies and return them to us along with your $100.00/$10.00 permit fee. Your DA permit will not be valid until we have returned a copy to you bearing both your signature and the signature of the appropriate Corps official.

If the State denies the required Section 401 Water Quality Certification and/or nonconcurs with your CZM consistency determination, then the DA permit is denied without prejudice. If you should subsequently obtain a Section 401 Water Quality Certification and/or a CZM consistency determination concurrence, you should contact this office to determine how to proceed with your permit application.

If you have any questions concerning your State Section 401 Water Quality Certification, please contact (State 401 certification contact).

If you have any questions concerning your CZM consistency determination, please contact (State CZM contact).

If you have any other questions concerning your application for a DA permit, please contact Corps contact at Corps contact telephone number.

Provisional Permit Not Valid; Do Not Begin Work

This PROVISIONAL PERMIT is NOT VALID until:
  (1) You obtain:
      a Section 401 Water Quality Certification from State Agency)
      a Coastal Zone Consistency determination concurrence from (State Agency)
  (2) You sign and return the enclosed provisional permit with the State Section 401 Water Quality Certification and/or CZM concurrence and the appropriate permit fee as indicated below:
      $10.00
      $100.00
      No fee required
  (3) The Corps signs the permit and returns it to you. Your permit is denied without prejudice, if the State denies your Section 401 Water Quality Certification and/or nonconcurs with your Coastal Zone Management consistency determination.

(Do Not Begin Work)

REGULATORY GUIDANCE LETTER (RGL 93-2)

RGL 93-2

Date: 23 August 1993, Expires: 31 December 1998

Subject: Guidance on Flexibility of the 404(b)(1) Guidelines and Mitigation Banking.

1. Enclosed are two guidance documents signed by the Office of the Assistant Secretary of the Army (Civil Works) and the Environmental Protection Agency. The first document provides guidance on the flexibility that the U.S. Army Corps of Engineers should be utilizing when making determinations of compliance with the Section 404(b)(1) Guidelines, particularly with regard to the alternatives analysis. The second Document provides guidance on the use of mitigation banks as a means of providing compensatory mitigation for Corps regulatory Decisions.

2. Both enclosed guidance documents should be implemented immediately. These guidance documents constitute an important aspect of the President's plan for protecting the Nation's wetlands, "Protecting America's Wetlands: A Fair, Flexible and Effective Approach" (published on 24 August 1993).

3. This guidance expires 31 December 1998 unless sooner revised or rescinded.

For the Director of Civil Works.

John P. Elmore, Chief, Operations, Construction and Readiness Division, Directorate of Civil Works.

Memorandum to the Field

Subject: Appropriate Level of Analysis Required for Evaluating Compliance with the Section 404(b)(1) Guidelines Alternatives Requirements

1. Purpose: The purpose of this memorandum is to clarify the appropriate level of analysis required for evaluating compliance with the Clean Water Act Section 404(b)(1) Guidelines' (Guidelines) requirements for consideration of alternatives. 40 CFR 230.10(a). Specifically, this memorandum describes the flexibility afforded by the Guidelines to make regulatory decisions based on the relative severity of the environmental impact of proposed discharges of dredged or fill material into waters of the United States.

2. Background: The Guidelines are the substantive environmental standards by which all Section 404 permit applications are evaluated. The Guidelines, which are binding regulations, were published by the Environmental Protection Agency at 40 CFR part 230 on December 24, 1980. The fundamental precept of the Guidelines is that discharges of dredged or fill material into waters of the United States, including wetlands, should not occur unless it can be demonstrated that such discharges, either individually or cumulatively, will not result in unacceptable adverse effects on the aquatic ecosystem. The Guidelines specifically require that "no discharge of dredged or fill material shall be permitted if there is a practicable alternative to the proposed discharge which would have less adverse impact on the aquatic ecosystem, so long as the alternative does not have other significant adverse environmental consequences." 40 CFR 230.10(a). Based on this provision, the applicant is required in every case (irrespective of whether the discharge site is a special aquatic site or whether the activity associated with the discharge is water dependent) to evaluate opportunities for use of non-aquatic areas and other

aquatic sites that would result in less adverse impact on the aquatic ecosystem. A permit cannot be issued, therefore, in circumstances where a less environmentally damaging practicable alternative for the proposed discharge exists (except as provided for under Section 404(b)(2)).

3. Discussion: The Guidelines are, as noted above, binding regulations. It is important to recognize, however, that this regulatory status does not limit the inherent flexibility provided in the Guidelines for implementing these provisions. The preamble to the Guidelines is very clear in this regard:

Of course, as the regulation itself makes clear, a certain amount of flexibility is still intended. For example, while the ultimate conditions of compliance are "regulatory", the Guidelines allow some room for judgment in determining what must be done to arrive at a conclusion that those conditions have or have not been met.

Guidelines Preamble, "Regulation versus Guidelines", 45 FR 85336 (December 24, 1980).

Notwithstanding this flexibility, the record must contain sufficient information to demonstrate that the proposed discharge complies with the requirements of Section 230.10(a) of the Guidelines. The amount of information needed to make a determination and the level of scrutiny required by the Guidelines is commensurate with the severity of the environmental impact (as determined by the functions of the aquatic resource and the nature of the proposed activity) and the scope/cost of the project.

a. Analysis Associated With Minor Impacts

The Guidelines do not contemplate that the same intensity of analysis will be required for all types of projects but instead envision a correlation between the scope of the evaluation and the potential extent of adverse impacts on the aquatic environment. The introduction to Sec. 230.10(a) recognizes that the level of analysis required may vary with the nature and complexity of each individual case:

Although all requirements in Sec. 230.10 must be met, the compliance evaluation procedures will vary to reflect the seriousness of the potential for adverse impacts on the aquatic ecosystems posed by specific dredged or fill material discharge activities.

40 CFR 230.10

Similarly, Sec. 230.6 ("Adaptability") makes clear that the Guidelines:

Allow evaluation and documentation for a variety of activities, ranging from those large, complex impacts on the aquatic environment to those for which the impact is likely to be innocuous. It is unlikely that the Guidelines will apply in their entirety to any one activity, no matter how complex. It is anticipated that substantial numbers of permit applications will be for minor, routine activities that have little, if any, potential for significant degradation of the aquatic environment. It generally is not intended or expected that extensive testing, evaluation or analysis will be needed to make findings of compliance in such routine cases.

40 CFR 230.6(9) (emphasis added)

Section 230.6 also emphasizes that when making determinations of compliance with the Guidelines, users:

Must recognize the different levels of effort that should be associated with varying degrees of impact and require or prepare commensurate documentation. The level of documentation should reflect the significance and complexity of the discharge activity.

40 CFR 230.6(b) (emphasis added)

Consequently, the Guidelines clearly afford flexibility to adjust the stringency of the alternatives review for projects that would have only minor impacts. Minor impacts are associated with activities that generally would have little potential to degrade the aquatic environment and include one, and frequently more, of the following characteristics: Are located in aquatic resources of limited natural function; are small in size and cause little direct impact; have little potential for secondary or cumulative impacts; or cause only temporary impacts. It is important to recognize, however, that in some circumstances even small or temporary fills result in substantial impacts, and that in such cases a more detailed evaluation is necessary. The Corps Districts and EPA Regions will, through the standard permit evaluation process, coordinate with the U.S. Fish and Wildlife Service, National Marine Fisheries Service and other appropriate state and Federal agencies in evaluating the likelihood that adverse impacts would result from a particular proposal. It is not appropriate to consider compensatory mitigation in determining whether a proposed discharge will cause only minor impacts for purposes of the alternatives analysis required by Sec. 230.10(a).

In reviewing projects that have the potential for only minor impacts on the aquatic environment, Corps and EPA field offices are directed to consider, in coordination with state and Federal resource agencies, the following factors:

(i) Such projects by their nature should not cause or contribute to significant degradation individually or cumulatively. Therefore, it generally should not be necessary to conduct or require detailed analyses to determine compliance with Sec. 230.10(c).

(ii) Although sufficient information must be developed to determine whether the proposed activity is in fact the least damaging practicable alternative, the Guidelines do not require an elaborate search for practicable alternatives if it is reasonably anticipated that there are only minor differences between the environmental impacts of the proposed activity and potentially practicable alternatives. This decision will be made after consideration of resource agency comments on the proposed project. It often makes sense to examine first whether potential alternatives would result in no identifiable or discernible difference in impact on the aquatic ecosystem. Those alternatives that do not may be eliminated from the analysis since Sec. 230.10(a) of the Guidelines only prohibits discharges when a practicable alternative exists which would have less adverse impact on the aquatic ecosystem. Because evaluating practicability is generally the more difficult aspect of the alternatives analysis, this approach should save time and effort for both the applicant and the regulatory agencies. fn 1 By initially focusing the alternatives analysis on the question of impacts on the aquatic ecosystem, it may be possible to limit (or in some instances eliminate altogether) the number of alternatives that have to be evaluated for practicability.

fn 1 In certain instances, however, it may be easier to examine practicability first. Some projects may be so site-specific (e.g., erosion control, bridge replacement) that no offsite alternative could be practicable. In such cases the alternatives analysis may appropriately be limited to onsite options only.

(iii) When it is determined that there is no identifiable or discernible difference in adverse impact on the environment between the applicant's proposed alternative and all other practicable alternatives, then the applicant's alternative is considered as satisfying the requirements of Section 230.10(a).

(iv) Even where a practicable alternative exists that would have less adverse impact on the aquatic ecosystem, the Guidelines allow it to be rejected if it would have "other significant adverse environmental consequences." 40 CFR 230.10(a). As explained in the preamble, this allows for consideration of "evidence of damages to other ecosystems in deciding whether there is a "better" alternative." Hence, in applying the alternatives analysis required by the Guidelines, it is not appropriate to select an alternative where minor impacts on the aquatic environment are avoided at the cost of substantial impacts to other natural environmental values.

(v) In cases of negligible or trivial impacts (e.g., small discharges to construct individual driveways), it may be possible to conclude that no alternative location could result in less adverse impact on the aquatic environment within the meaning of the Guidelines. In such cases, it may not be necessary to conduct an offsite alternatives analysis but instead require only any practicable onsite minimization.

This guidance concerns application of the Section 404(b)(1) Guidelines to projects with minor impacts. Projects which may cause more than minor impacts on the aquatic environment, either individually or cumulatively, should be subjected to a proportionately more detailed level of analysis to determine compliance or noncompliance with the Guidelines. Projects which cause substantial impacts, in particular, must be thoroughly evaluated through the standard permit evaluation process to determine compliance with all provisions of the Guidelines.

b. Relationship Between the Scope of Analysis and the Scope/Cost of the Proposed Project

The Guidelines provide the Corps and EPA with discretion for determining the necessary level of analysis to support a conclusion as to whether or not an alternative is practicable. Practicable alternatives are those alternatives that are "available and capable of being done after taking into consideration cost, existing technology, and logistics in light of overall project purposes." 40 CFR 230.10(a)(2). The preamble to the Guidelines provides clarification on how cost is to be considered in the determination of practicability:

Our intent is to consider those alternatives which are reasonable in terms of the overall scope/cost of the proposed project. The term economic for which the term "cost" was substituted in the final rule might be construed to include consideration of the applicant's financial standing, or investment, or market share, a cumbersome inquiry which is not necessarily material to the objectives of the Guidelines.

Guidelines Preamble, "Alternatives", 45 FR 85339 (December 24, 1980) (emphasis added).

Therefore, the level of analysis required for determining which alternatives are practicable will vary depending on the type of project proposed. The determination of what constitutes an unreasonable expense should generally consider whether the projected cost is substantially greater than the costs normally associated with the particular type of project. Generally, as the scope/cost of the project increases, the level of analysis should also increase. To the extent the Corps obtains information on the costs associated with the project, such information may be considered when making a determination of what constitutes an unreasonable expense.

The preamble to the Guidelines also states that " if an alleged alternative is unreasonably expensive to the applicant, the alternative is not "practicable."" Guidelines Preamble, "Economic Factors", 45 FR 85343 (December 24, 1980). Therefore, to the extent that individual homeowners and small businesses may typically be associated with small projects with minor impacts, the nature of the applicant may also be a relevant consideration in determining what constitutes a practicable alternative. It is important to emphasize, however, that it is not a particular applicant's financial standing that is the primary consideration for determining practicability, but rather characteristics of the project and what constitutes a reasonable expense for these projects that are most relevant to practicability determinations.

4. The burden of proof to demonstrate compliance with the Guidelines rests with the applicant; where insufficient information is provided to determine compliance, the Guidelines require that no permit be issued. 40 CFR 230.12(a)(3)(iv).

5. A reasonable, common sense approach in applying the requirements of the Guidelines' alternatives analysis is fully consistent with sound environmental protection. The Guidelines clearly contemplate that reasonable discretion should be applied based on the nature of the aquatic resource and potential impacts of a proposed activity in determining compliance with the alternatives test. Such an approach encourages effective decisionmaking and fosters a better understanding and enhanced confidence in the Section 404 program.

6. This guidance is consistent with the February 6, 1990 "Memorandum of Agreement Between the Environmental Protection Agency and the Department of the Army Concerning the Determination of Mitigation under the Clean Water Act Section 404(b)(1) Guidelines."

Signed: August 23, 1993.

Robert H. Wayland, III, Director, Office of Wetlands, Oceans, and Watersheds, U.S. Environmental Protection Agency.

Michael L. Davis, Office of the Assistant Secretary of the Army (Civil Works), Department of the Army.

Memorandum to the Field

Subject: Establishment and Use of Wetland Mitigation Banks in the Clean Water Act Section 404 (Regulatory Program

1. This memorandum provides general guidelines for the establishment and use of wetland mitigation banks in the Clean Water Act Section 404 regulatory program. This memorandum serves as interim guidance pending completion of Phase I by the Corps of Engineer's Institute for Water Resources study on wetland mitigation banking, fn 2 at which time this guidance will be reviewed and any appropriate revisions will be incorporated into final guidelines.

fn 2 The Corps of Engineers Institute for Water Resources, under the authority of Section 307(d) of the Water Resources Development Act of 1990, is undertaking a comprehensive two-year review and evaluation of wetland mitigation banking to assist in the development of a national policy on this issue. The interim summary report documenting the results of the first phase of the study is scheduled for completion in the fall of 1993.

2. For purposes of this guidance, wetland mitigation banking refers to the restoration, creation, enhancement, and, in exceptional circumstances, preservation of wetlands or other aquatic habitats expressly for the purpose of providing compensatory mitigation in advance of discharges into wetlands permitted under the Section 404 regulatory program. Wetland mitigation banks can have several advantages over individual mitigation projects, some of which are listed below:

(a) Compensatory mitigation can be implemented and functioning in advance of project impacts, thereby reducing temporal losses of wetland functions and uncertainty over whether the mitigation will be successful in offsetting wetland losses.

(b) It may be more ecologically advantageous for maintaining the integrity of the aquatic ecosystem to consolidate compensatory mitigation for impacts to many smaller, isolated or fragmented habitats into a single large parcel or contiguous parcels.

(c) Development of a wetland mitigation bank can bring together financial resources and planning and scientific expertise not practicable to many individual mitigation proposals. This consolidation of resources can increase the potential for the establishment and long-term management of successful mitigation.

(d) Wetland mitigation banking proposals may reduce regulatory uncertainty and Provide more cost-effective compensatory mitigation opportunities.

3. The Section 404(b)(1) Guidelines (Guidelines), as clarified by the "Memorandum of Agreement Concerning the Determination of Mitigation under the section 404(b)(1) Guidelines" (Mitigation (MOA) signed February 6, 1990, by the Environmental Protection Agency and the Department of the Army, establish a mitigation sequence that is used in the evaluation of individual permit applications. Under this sequence, all appropriate and practicable steps must be undertaken by the applicant to first avoid and then minimize adverse impacts to the aquatic ecosystem. Remaining unavoidable impacts must then be offset through compensatory mitigation to the extent appropriate and practicable. Requirements for compensatory mitigation may be satisfied through the use of wetland mitigation banks, so long as their use is consistent with standard practices for evaluating compensatory mitigation proposals outlined in the Mitigation MOA. It is important to emphasize that, given the mitigation sequence requirements described above, permit applicants should not anticipate that the establishment of, or participation in, a wetland mitigation bank will ultimately lead to a determination of compliance with the section 404(b)(1) Guidelines without adequate demonstration that impacts associated with the proposed discharge have been avoided and minimized to the extent practicable.

4. The agencies' preference for on-site, in-kind compensatory mitigation does not preclude the use of wetland mitigation banks where it has been determined by the Corps, or other appropriate permitting agency, in coordination with the Federal resource agencies through the standard permit evaluation process, that the use of a particular mitigation bank as compensation for proposed wetland impacts would be appropriate for offsetting impacts to the aquatic ecosystem. In making such a determination, careful consideration must be given to wetland functions, landscape position, and affected species populations at both the impact and mitigation bank sites. In addition, compensation for wetland impacts should occur, where appropriate and practicable, within the same watershed as the impact site. Where a mitigation bank is being developed in conjunction with a wetland resource planning initiative (e.g., Special Area Management Plan, State Wetland Conservation Plan) to satisfy particular wetland restoration objectives, the permitting agency will determine, in coordination with the Federal resource agencies, whether use of the bank should be considered an appropriate form of compensatory mitigation for impacts occurring within the same watershed.

5. Wetland mitigation banks should generally be in place and functional before credits may be used to offset permitted wetland losses. However, it may be appropriate to allow incremental distribution of credits corresponding to the appropriate stage of successful establishment of wetland functions. Moreover, variable mitigation ratios (credit acreage to impacted wetland acreage) may be used in such circumstances to reflect the wetland functions attained at a bank site at a particular point in time. For example, higher ratios would be required when a bank is not yet fully functional at the time credits are to be withdrawn.

6. Establishment of each mitigation bank should be accompanied by the development of a formal written agreement (e.g., memorandum of agreement) among the Corps, EPA, other relevant resource agencies, and those parties who will own, develop, operate or otherwise participate in the bank. The purpose of the agreement is to establish clear guidelines for establishment and use of the mitigation bank. A wetlands mitigation bank may also be established through issuance of a Section 404 permit where establishing the proposed bank involves a discharge of dredged or fill material into waters of the United States. The banking agreement or, where applicable, special conditions of the permit establishing the bank should address the following considerations, where appropriate:

(a) Location of the mitigation bank;

(b) Goals and objectives for the mitigation bank project;

(c) Identification of bank sponsors and participants;

(d) Development and maintenance plan;

(e) Evaluation methodology acceptable to all signatories to establish bank credits and assess bank success in meeting the project goals and objectives;

(f) Specific accounting procedures for tracking crediting and debiting;

(g) Geographic area of applicability;

(h) Monitoring requirements and responsibilities;

(i) Remedial action responsibilities including funding; and

(j) Provisions for protecting the mitigation bank in perpetuity.

Agency participation in a wetlands mitigation banking agreement may not, in any way, restrict or limit the authorities and responsibilities of the agencies.

7. An appropriate methodology, acceptable to all signatories, should be identified and used to evaluate the success of wetland restoration and creation efforts within the mitigation bank and to identify the appropriate stage of development for issuing mitigation credits. A full range of wetland functions should be assessed. Functional evaluations of the mitigation bank should generally be conducted by a multi-disciplinary team representing involved resource and regulatory agencies and other appropriate parties. The same methodology should be used to determine the functions and values of both credits and debits. As an alternative, credits and debits can be based on acres of various types of wetlands (e.g., National Wetland Inventory classes). Final determinations regarding debits and credits will be made by the Corps, or other appropriate permitting agency, in consultation with Federal resource agencies.

8. Permit applicants may draw upon the available credits of a third party mitigation bank (i.e., a bank developed and operated by an entity other than the permit applicant). The section 404 permit, however, must state explicitly that the permittee remains responsible for ensuring that the mitigation requirements are satisfied.

9. To ensure legal enforceability of the mitigation conditions, use of mitigation bank credits must be conditioned in the section 404 permit by referencing the banking agreement or section 404 permit establishing the bank; however, such a provision should not limit the responsibility of the section 404 permittee for satisfying all legal requirements of the permit.

Signed: August 23, 1993.

Robert H. Wayland, III, Director, Office of Wetlands, Oceans, and Watersheds, U.S. Environmental Protection Agency.

Michael L. Davis, Office of the Assistant Secretary of the Army (Civil Works), Department of the Army.

REGULATORY GUIDANCE LETTER (RGL 93-3)

RGL 93-3

Issued: September 13, 1993, Expires: not applicable

Subject: Rescission of Regulatory Guidance Letters (RGL) 90-5, 90-7, and 90-8

1. On 25 August 1993 the final "Excavation Rule" was published in the Federal Register (58 FR 45008) and becomes effective on 24 September 1993. This regulation modifies the definition of "Discharge of Dredged Material" to address landclearing activities (see 33 CFR 323.2(d)); modifies the definitions of "Fill Material" and "Discharge of Fill Material" to address the placement of pilings (see 33 CFR 323.2(e) and (f) and 323.3(c)); and modifies the definition of "waters of the United States" to address prior converted cropland (see 33 CFR 328.(a)(8)).

2. Therefore, RGL 90-5, Subject: "Landclearing Activities Subject to Section 404 Jurisdiction"; RGL 90-7, Subject: "Clarification of the Phrase "Normal Circumstances" as it pertains to Cropped Wetlands"; and RGL 90-8, Subject: "Applicability of section 404 to Pilings"; are hereby rescinded effective 24 September 1993. Furthermore, although RGL 90-5, Subject: "Landclearing Activities Subject to section 404 Jurisdiction" expired on 31 December 1992 it should continue to be applied until 24 September 1993.

3. In addition, RGL's 90-5, 90-7, and 90-8 as of 24 September 1993 will no longer be used for guidance since the guidance contained in those RGL's has been superseded by the regulation.

For the Director of Civil Works.

John P. Elmore, P.E., Chief, Operations, Construction and Readiness Division, Directorate of Civil Works.

Appendix K

U.S. Army Corps of Engineers
Instructions for Preparing
a Permit Application

The instructions given below, together with the sample application and drawings, should help in completing the required application form. If you have additional questions, do not hesitate to contact the district regulatory office.

Block 1. Application Number.

Leave this block blank. When you completed application is received, it will be assigned a number for identification. You will be notified of the number in an acknowledgement letter. Please refer to this number in any correspondence or inquiry concerning your application.

Block 2. Name and Address of Applicant(s).

Fill in name, mailing address, and telephone number(s) for all applicants. The telephone number(s) should be a number where you can be reached during business hours. If space is needed for additional names, attach a sheet of white 8½ x 11 inch paper labeled, "Block 2 Continued".

Block 3. Name, Address, and
          Title of Authorized Agent.

It is not necessary to have an agent represent you; however, if you do, fill in the agent's name, address, title, and telephone number(s). If your agent is submitting and signing the application, you must fill out and sign the Statement of Authorization in Block 3.

Block 4. Detailed Description of Proposed Activity.

The written description and the drawings are the most important parts of the application. If there is not enough space in Block 4, (a), (b), or (c), attach additional sheet(s) of white, 8½ x 11 inch paper labeled, "Block 4 Continued".

- a. Activity. Describe the overall activity. Give the approximate dimensions of structures, fills, and/or excavations (lengths, widths, heights, or depths).
- b. Purpose. Describe the purpose, need, and intended use (public, private, commercial, or other use) of the proposed activity. Include a description of related facilities, if any, to be constructed on adjacent land. Give the date you plan to begin work on the activity and the date work is expected to be completed.

- c. Discharge of Dredged or Fill Material. If the activity will involve the discharge of dredged or fill material, describe the type (rock, sand, dirt, rubble, etc.), quantity (in cubic yards), and mode of transportation to the discharge site.

Block 5. Names and Addresses of Adjoining
          Property Owners, Lessees, etc., Whose
          Property Adjoins the Waterbody.

List complete names, addresses, and zip codes of adjacent property owners (both public and private), lessee, etc., whose property also adjoins the waterbody or wetland, in order that they may be notified of the proposed activity. This information is usually available at the local tax assessor's office. If more space is needed, attach a sheet of white 8½ x 11 inch paper labeled, "Block 5 Continued".

Block 6. Water Body and Location
          on Waterbody Where Activity
          Exists or is Proposed.

Fill in the name of the waterbody and the river mile (if known) at the location of the activity. Include easily recognizable landmarks on the shore of the waterbody to aid in locating the site of the activity.

Block 7. Location and Land Where
          Activity Exists or Is Proposed.

This information is used to locate the site. Give the street address of the property where the proposed activity will take place. If the site does not have a street address, give the best descriptive location (name or waterbody), names and/or numbers of roads or highways, name of nearest community or town, name of county and state, and directions, such as 2 miles east of Brown's Store on Route 105. Do not use your home address unless that is the location of the proposed activity. Do not use a post office box number.

Block 8. Information about
          Completed Activity.

Provide information about parts of the activity which may be complete. An activity may have been authorized by a previously issued permit, may exist from a time before a Corps permit was required, or may be constructed on adjacent upland.

Block 9. Information about Approvals or Denials by Other Government Agencies.

You may need approval or certification from other federal, interstate, state, or local government agencies for the activity described in your application. Applications you have submitted, and approvals, certifications, or disapprovals that you have received, should be recorded in Block 9. It is not necessary to obtain other federal, state, and local permits before applying for a Corps of Engineers permit.

Block 10. Signature of Applicant or Agent.

The application must be signed in Block 10 by the owner, lessee, or a duly authorized agent. The person named in Block 3 will be accepted as the officially designated agent of the applicant. The signature will be understood to be affirmation that the applicant possesses the requisite property interest to undertake the proposed activity.

GENERAL INFORMATION

Three types of drawings–vicinity, plan, and elevation are required to accurately depict activities (see sample drawings on pages 16 and 17).

Submit one original, or good quality copy, of all drawings on 8½ x 11 inch white paper (tracing cloth or film may be used). Submit the fewest number of sheets necessary to adequately show the proposed activity. Drawings should be prepared in accordance with the general format of the samples, using block style lettering. Each page should have a title block. See check list below. Drawings do not have to be prepared by an engineer, but professional assistance may become necessary if the project is large or complex.

Leave a 1-inch margin at the top edge of each sheet for purposes of reproduction and binding.

In the title block of each sheet of drawings, identify the proposed activity and include the name of the body of water, river mile (if applicable), name of county and state, name of applicant, number of the sheet and total number of sheets in the set, and date the drawing was prepared.

Since drawings must be reproduced, use heavy dark lines. Color shading cannot be used; however, dot shading, hatching, or similar graphic symbols may be used to clarify line drawings.

VICINITY MAP

The vicinity map you provide will be printed in any public notice that is issued and used by the Corps of Engineers and other reviewing agencies to locate the site of the proposed activity. You may use an existing road map or U.S. Geological Survey topographic map (scale 1:24,000) as the vicinity map. Please include sufficient details to simplify locating the site from both the waterbody and from land. Identify the source of the map or chart from which the vicinity map was taken and, if not already shown, add the following:

- location of activity site (draw an arrow showing the exact location of the site on the map).
- latitude, longitude, river mile, if known, and/or other information that coincides with Block 6 on the application form.
- name of waterbody and the name of the larger creek, river, bay, etc., to which the waterbody is immediately tributary.
- names, descriptions, and location of landmarks.
- name of all applicable political (county, parish, borough, town, city, etc.) jurisdictions.
- name of and distance to nearest town, community, or other identifying locations.
- names or numbers of all roads in the vicinity of the site.
- north arrow.
- scale.

PLAN VIEW

The plan view shows the proposed activity as if you were looking straight down on it from above. Your plan view should clearly show the following:

- Name of waterbody (river, creek, lake, wetland, etc.) and river mile (if known) at location of activity.
- Existing shorelines.
- Mean high and mean low water lines and maximum (spring) high tide line in tidal areas.
- Ordinary high water line and ordinary low water line if the proposed activity is located on a non-tidal waterbody.
- Average water depths around the activity.
- Dimensions of the activity and distance it extends from the high water line into the water.
- Distances to nearby federal projects, if applicable.
- Distance between proposed activity and navigation channel, where applicable.
- Location of structures, if any, in navigable waters immediately adjacent to the proposed activity.
- Location of any wetlands (marshes, swamps, tidal flats, etc.).
- North arrow.
- Scale.
- If dredged material is involved, you must describe the type of material, number of cubic yards, method of handling, and the location of fill and spoil disposal area. The drawings should show proposed retention levees, weirs, and/or other means for retaining hydraulically placed materials.
- Mark the drawing to indicate previously completed portions of the activity.

ELEVATION AND/OR CROSS SECTION VIEW

The elevation and/or cross section view is a scale drawing that shows the side, front, or rear of the proposed activity. If a section view is shown, it represents the proposed structure as it would appear if cut internally for display. Your elevation should clearly show the following:

- Water elevations as shown in the plan view.
- Water depth at waterward face of proposed activity or, if dredging is proposed, dredging and estimated disposal grades.
- Dimensions from mean high water line (in tidal waters) for proposed fill or float, or high tide line for pile supported platform. Describe any structures to be built on the platform.
- Cross section of excavation or fill, including approximate side slopes.
- Graphic or numerical scale.
- Principal dimensions of the activity.

Notes on Drawings*

- Names of adjacent property owners who may be affected. Complete names and addresses should be shown in Block 5 on ENG Form 4345.
- Legal property description: Number, name of subdivision, block, and lot number. Section, township, and range (if applicable) from plot, deed, or tax assessment.
- Photographs of the site of the proposed activity are not required; however, pictures are helpful and may be submitted as part of any application.

---

* Drawings should be as clear and simple as possible (i.e., not too "busy").

Appendix L

Permit Evaluation and Decision Document

Applicant:

Applicant No:

This document constitutes my Environmental Assessment, Statement of Findings and review and compliance determination according to the Section 404 (b)(1) guidelines for the proposed work (applicant's preferred alternative) described in the attached public notice.

I. Proposed Project: The location and description of work are described in the attached public notice. (Any modifications since the public notice are listed below).

II. Environmental and Public Interest Factors Considered:

A. Purpose and need:

B. Alternatives [33 CFR 320.4 (b), 40 CFR 230.10]
   1. No action
   2. Other project designs (smaller, larger, different, etc.)
   3. Other sites available to the applicant (40 CFR 230.10)
   4. Other sites not available to the applicant.
   5. Corps' selected alternative.

C. Physical/chemical characteristics and anticipated changes (check applicable blocks and provide concise description of impacts).

( ) substrate
( ) currents, circulation or drainage patterns
( ) suspended particulates; turbidity
( ) water quality (temperature, salinity patterns parameters)
( ) flood control functions
( ) storm, wave, and erosion buffers
( ) erosion and accretion patterns
( ) aquifer recharge
( ) baseflow

Additionally, for projects involving the discharge of dredged material;

( ) Mixing zone, in light of the depth of water at the disposal site; current velocity, direction and variability at the disposal site; degree of turbulence; water column stratification; discharge vessel speed and direction; rate of discharges per unit of time; and any other relevant factors affecting rates and patterns of mixing

D. Biological characteristics and anticipated changes (check applicable blocks and provide concise description of impacts)

( ) special aquatic sites (wetlands, mudflats, coral reefs, pool and riffle areas, vegetated shallows, sanctuaries and refuges, as defined in 40 CFR 230.40-45)
( ) habitat for fish and other aquatic organisms
( ) wildlife habitat (breeding, cover, food, travel, general)
( ) endangered or threatened species
( ) biological availability of possible contaminants in dredged or fill material, considering hydrography in relation to known or anticipated sources of contaminants; results of previous testing of material from the vicinity of the project; known significant sources or persistent pesticides from land runoff or percolation; spill records for petroleum products or designated (Section 311 of the CWA) hazardous substances; other public records of significant introduction of contaminants from industries, municipalities or other sources

E. Human use characteristics and impact (check applicable blocks and provide concise description of impacts):

( ) existing and potential water supplies; water conservation
( ) recreational or commercial fisheries
( ) other water related recreation
( ) aesthetics of the aquatic ecosystem
( ) parks, national and historic monuments, national seashores, wild and scenic rivers, wilderness area, research sites, etc.
( ) traffic/transportation patterns
( ) energy consumption or generation
( ) navigation
( ) safety
( ) air quality
( ) noise
( ) historic properties (Section 106 National Historic Preservation Act)
( ) land use classification
( ) economics
( ) prime and unique farmland (7 CFR Part 658)
( ) food and fiber production
( ) general water quality
( ) mineral needs
( ) consideration of private property
( ) other

F. Summary of secondary and cumulative effects:

III. Findings:
    A. Other authorizations:
        1. Water quality certification:
           Date: ___issued ___denied ___waived
           Special Conditions ___Yes ___No
           (If yes see attached)
        2. State and/or local authorizations
           (if issued):
    B. A complete application was received on
      _____. A public notice describing the project was issued on _____, and sent to all interested parties (mailing list) including appropriate state and Federal agencies. All comments received on this action have been reviewed and are summarized below.
        1. Summary of comments received.
           a. Federal agencies:
               1) U.S. Environmental Protection Agency (EPA)
               2) U.S. Fish and Wildlife Service (USFWS)
               3) National Marine Fisheries Service (NMFS)
               4) Other
           b. State and local agencies:
           c. Organizations:
           d. Individuals:
        2. Evaluation:

I have reviewed and evaluated, in light of the overall public interest, the documents and factors concerning this permit application as well as the stated views of other interested agencies and the concerned public. In doing so, I have considered the possible consequences of this proposed work in accordance with regulations published in 33 CFR Parts 320 to 330 and 40 CFR Part 230. The following paragraphs include my evaluation of comments received and how the project complies with the above cited regulations.

           a. Consideration of comments:
           b. Evaluation of Compliance with Section 404 (b)(1) guidelines (restrictions on discharge, 40 CFR 230.10). (A check in a block denoted by an asterisk indicates that the project does not comply with the guidelines.):
               1) Alternatives test:

Yes No i) Based on the discussion in II B, are there available, less adverse impact on the aquatic ecosystem and without other significant adverse environmental consequences that do not involve discharges into "waters of the United States" or at other locations within these waters?

Yes No ii) Based on II B, if the project is in a special aquatic site and is not water-dependent, has the applicant clearly demonstrated that there are no practicable alternative sites available?

    2) Special restrictions. Will the discharge:

Yes No i) violate state water quality standards?

Yes No ii) violate toxic effluent standards (under Section 307 of the Act)?

Yes No iii) jeopardize endangered or threatened species or their critical habitat?

Yes No iv) violate standards set by the Department of Commerce to protect marine sanctuaries?

    v) Evaluation of the information in II C and D above indicates that the proposed discharge material meets testing exclusion criteria for the following reason(s).

    ( ) based on the above information, the material is not a carrier of contaminants.

    ( ) the levels of contaminants are substantially similar at the extraction and disposal sites and the discharge is not likely to result in degradation of the disposal site and pollutants will not be transported to less contaminated areas.

    ( ) acceptable constraints are available and will be implemented to reduce contamination to acceptable levels within the disposal site and prevent contaminants from being transported beyond the boundaries of the disposal site.

    3) Other restrictions. Will the discharge contribute to significant degradation of "waters of the United States" through adverse impacts to:

Yes No i) human health or welfare, through pollution of municipal water supplies, fish, shellfish, wildlife and special aquatic sites?

Yes No ii) life states of aquatic life and other wildlife?

Yes No iii) diversity, productivity and stability of the aquatic ecosystem, such as loss of fish or wildlife habitat, or loss of the capacity of wetlands to assimilate nutrients, purify water or reduce wave energy?

Yes No iv) recreational, aesthetic and economic values?

Yes No 4) Actions to minimize potential adverse impacts (mitigation). Will all appropriate and practicable steps (40 CFR 230.70-77) be taken to minimize the potential adverse impacts of the discharge on the aquatic ecosystem?

c. General Evaluation [33 CFR 320.4 (a)]:

1) The relative extent of the public and private need for the proposed work.

2) The practicability of using reasonable alternative locations and methods to accomplish the objective of the proposed structure or work.

3) The extent and permanence of the beneficial and/or detrimental effects that the proposed structures or work may have on the public and private uses to which the area is suited.

3. Determinations:

a. Finding of No Significant Impact (FONSI) (33 CFR Part 325).
Having reviewed the information provided by the applicant, all interested parties and the assessment of environmental impacts contained in Part II of this document, I find that this permit action will not have a significant impact on the quality of the human environment. Therefore, an Environmental Impact Statement will not be required.

b. Section 404(b)(1) Compliance/Non-compliance Review (40 CFR 230-12).

( ) The discharge complies with the guidelines.

( ) The discharge complies with the guidelines, with the inclusion of the appropriate and practicable conditions listed above (in III.B.2.b.4) to minimize pollution or adverse effects to the affected ecosystem.

( ) The discharge fails to comply with the requirements of these guidelines because:

( ) There is a practicable alternative to the proposed discharge that would have less adverse effect on the aquatic ecosystem and that alternative does not have other significant adverse environmental consequences.

( ) The proposed discharge will result in significant degradation of the aquatic ecosystem under 40 CFR 230.10(b) or (c).

( ) The discharge does not include all appropriate and practicable measures to minimize potential harm to the aquatic ecosystem, namely.

( ) There is not sufficient information to make a reasonable judgement as to whether the proposed discharge will comply with the guidelines.

c. Public interest determination: I find that issuance of a Department of the Army permit (with special conditions), as prescribed by regulations published in 33 CFR Parts 320 to 330, and 40 CFR Part 230 is (not) contrary to the public interest:

PREPARED BY: _____ DATE:_____
Biologist, Regulatory Unit 1

REVIEWED BY: _____ DATE:
Chief, Regulatory Unit 1

FOR THE DISTRICT ENGINEER:

APPROVED BY: _____ DATE: _____
Chief, Regulatory Section

Appendix M

United States Map of U.S. Army Corps of Engineers Boundaries for Regulatory Activities

Western United States

NORTH CENTRAL DIVISION

MN
St. Paul ▲
WI
MI
IA
Chicago ■ Detroit ▲
Rock Island ▲
Buffalo ▲ NY

NEW ENGLAND DIVISION

ME
VT
NH
MA ● Waltham
CT
RI

OHIO RIVER DIVISION

IN
Cincinnati
OH
Pittsburgh ▲
Louisville ▲
WV
Huntington ▲
KY
TN
Nashville ▲

NY
PA
Philadelphia ▲
New York ■
NJ
Baltimore
DE
VA
MD
Norfolk ▲

NORTH ATLANTIC DIVISION

IL
St. Louis ▲
AR
Vicksburg ■
MS
LA
New Orleans ▲
Memphis ▲

Eastern United States

NC
SC
Wilmington ▲
Atlanta ●
AL
GA
Charleston ▲
Mobile ▲
Savannah ▲
Jacksonville ▲
FL

SOUTH ATLANTIC DIVISION

LOWER MISSISSIPPI VALLEY DIVISION

■ Division and District Headquarters
● Division Headquarters
▲ District Headquarters
— State Boundary
━ District Boundary

Appendix N

**California Map of U.S. Army
Corps of Engineers District Offices**

Appendix O

U.S. Army Corps of Engineers
Locations of Regulatory Offices

Address correspondence to:

The District Engineer
U.S. Army Engineer District

Please include attention
line in address.

Alaska
P.O. Box 898
Anchorage, AK
99506-0898
Attention: NPACO-RF
907/753-2712

Albuquerque
P.O. Box 1580
Albuquerque, NM
87103-1580
Attention: SWACO-OR
505/766-2776

Baltimore
P.O. Box 1715
Baltimore, MD 21203-1715
Attention: NABOP-R
301/962-3670
*Joint application with
New York, Maryland*

Buffalo
1776 Niagara Street
Buffalo, NY 14207-3199
Attention: NCBCO-S
716/876-5454 x2313
Joint application with New York

Charleston
P.O. Box 919
Charleston, SC
29402-0919
Attention: SACCO-P
803/724-4330

Chicago
219 S. Dearborn Street
Chicago, IL 60604-1797
Attention: NCCCO-R
312/353-6428
Joint application with Illinois

Detroit
P.O. Box 1027
Detroit, MI
48231-1027
Attention: NCECO-L
313/226-2218
*Joint application
with Michigan*

Fort Worth
P.O. Box 17300
Ft. Worth, TX
76102-0300
Attention: SWFOD-O
817/334-2681

Galveston
P.O. Box 1229
Galveston, TX
77553-1229
Attention: SWGCO-R
409/766-3925

Huntington
502 8th Street
Huntington, WV
25702-2070
Attention: ORHOP-F
304/529-5487
*Joint application with
West Virginia*

Honolulu
Building 230, Fort Shafter
Honolulu, HI
96858-5440
Attention: PODCO-O
808/438-9258

Jacksonville
P.O. Box 4970
Jacksonville, FL
32232-0019
Attention: SAJRD
904/791-1659
*Joint application with
Florida, Virgin Islands*

Kansas City
700 Federal Building
601 E. 12th Street
Kansas City, MO
64106-2896
Attention: MRKOD-P
816/374-3645

Little Rock
P.O. Box 867
Little Rock, AR
72203-0867
Attention: SWLCO-P
501/378-5295

Los Angeles
P.O. Box 2711
Los Angeles, CA
90053-2325
Attention: CESPLCO-R
213/894-5606

Louisville
P.O. Box 59
Louisville, KY
40201-0059
Attention: ORLOP-F
502/582-5452
*Joint application
with Illinois*

Memphis
Clifford Davis Federal
Building, Room B-202
Memphis, TN
38103-1894
Attention: LMMCO-G
901/521-3471
*Joint application with
Missouri, Tennessee, Kentucky*

Mobile
P.O. Box 2288
Mobile, AL
36628-0001
Attention: SAMOP-S
205/690-2658
Joint application with Mississippi

Nashville
P.O. Box 1070
Nashville, TN
37202-1070
Attention: ORNOR-F
615/251-5181
*Joint application with
TVA, Tennessee, Alabama*

New Orleans
P.O. Box 60267
New Orleans, LA
70160-0267
Attention: LMNOD-S
504/838-2255

New York
26 Federal Plaza
New York, NY
10278-0090
Attention: NANOP-R
212/264-3996

Norfolk
803 Front Street
Norfolk, VA
23510-1096
Attention: NAOOP-P
804/446-3652
*Joint application
with Virginia*

Omaha
P.O. Box 5
Omaha, NE
68101-0005
Attention: MROOP-N
402/221-4133

Philadelphia
U.S. Custom House
2nd and Chestnut Street
Philadelphia, PA
19106-2991
Attention: NAPOP-R
215/597-2812

Pittsburgh
Federal Building
1000 Liberty Avenue
Pittsburgh, PA
15222-4186
Attention: ORPOP-F
412/644-4204
*Joint application
with New York*

Portland
P.O. Box 2946
Portland, OR
97208-2946
Attention: NPPND-RF
503/221-6995
*Joint application
with Oregon*

Rock Island
Clock Tower Building
Rock Island, IL
61201-2004
Attention: NCROD-S
309/788-6361 x6370
*Joint application
with Illinois*

Sacramento
1325 J Street
Sacramento, CA
95814-2922
Attention: SPKCO-O
916/557-5250

St. Louis
210 Tucker Boulevard
N St. Louis, MO
63101-1986
314/263-5703
*Joint application
with Illinois, Missouri*

St. Paul
1135 USPO & Custom House
St. Paul, MN
55101-1479
Attention: NCSCO-RF
612/725-5819

San Francisco
211 Main Street
San Francisco, CA
94105-1905
Attention: CESPNCO-R
415/744-3036

Savannah
P.O. Box 889
Savannah, GA
31402-0889
Attention: SASOP-F
912/944-5347
*Joint application
with Georgia*

Seatt;e
P.O. Box C-3755
Seattle, WA
98124-2255
Attention: NPSOP-RF
206/764-3495
*Joint application
with Idaho*

Tulsa
P.O. Box 61
Tulsa, OK
74121-0061
Attention: SWTOD-RF
918/581-7261

Vicksburg
P.O. Box 60
Vicksburg, MS
39180-0060
Attention: LMKOD-F
601/634-5276
*Joint application
with Mississippi*

Walla Walla
Building 602
City-County Airport
Walla Walla, WA
99362-9265
Attention: NPWOP-RF
509/522-6718
*Joint application
with Idaho*

Wilmington
P.O. Box 1890
Wilmington, NC
28402-1890
Attention: SAWCO-E
919/343-4511
*Joint application with
North Carolina*

**The Division Engineer
U.S. Army Engineer Division
New England**
424 Trapelo Road
Waltham, MA
02254-9149
Attention: NEDOD-R
617/647-8338
*Joint application with
Massachusetts, Maine*

California Materials

Appendix P

California Fish and Game Code
Division 2. Department of Fish and Game

Title 33. Navigation and Navigable Waters

CHAPTER 6. FISH AND WILDLIFE
PROTECTION AND CONSERVATION

§ 1600. Declaration of public interest

The protection and conservation of the fish and wildlife resources of this state are hereby declared to be of utmost public interest. Fish and wildlife are the property of the people and provide a major contribution to the economy of the state as well as providing a significant part of the people's food supply and therefore their conservation is a proper responsibility of the state. This chapter is enacted to provide such conservation for these resources.

§ 1601. Public construction projects impacting rivers, streams or lakes; approval; arbitration panel

(a) Except as provided in this section, general plans sufficient to indicate the nature of a project for construction by, or on behalf of, any state or local governmental agency or any public utility shall be submitted to the department if the project will (1) divert, obstruct, or change the natural flow or the bed, channel, or bank of any river, stream, or lake designated by the department in which there is at any time an existing fish or wildlife resource or from which these resources derive benefit, (2) use material from the streambeds designated by the department, or (3) result in the disposal or deposition of debris, waste, or other material containing crumbled, flaked, or ground pavement where it can pass into any river, stream, or lake designated by the department. If an existing fish or wildlife resource may be substantially adversely affected by that construction, the department shall notify the governmental agency or public utility of the existence of the fish or wildlife resource together with a description thereof and shall propose reasonable modifications in the proposed construction that will allow for the protection and continuance of the fish or wildlife resource, including procedures to review the operation of those protective measures. The proposals shall be submitted within 30 days of receipt of the plans, with the provision that this time may be extended by mutual agreement. Upon a determination by the department and after notice to the affected parties of the necessity for an onsite investigation or upon the request for an onsite investigation by the affected parties, the department shall make an onsite investigation of the proposed construction and shall make the investigation before it proposes any modifications.

(b) Within 14 days of receipt of the department's proposals, the affected agency or public utility shall notify the department in writing whether the proposals are acceptable, except that this time may be extended by mutual agreement. If the proposals are not acceptable to the affected agency or public utility, the agency or public utility shall so notify the department. Upon request, the department shall meet with the affected agency or public utility within seven days of receipt of the notification, or at a time mutually agreed upon, for the purpose of developing proposals that are acceptable to the department and the affected agency or public utility. If mutual agreement is not reached at the meeting, a panel of arbitrators shall be established . The panel of arbitrators shall be established within seven days of the meeting, or at a time mutually agreed upon, and shall be composed of one representative of the department, one representative of the affected agency or public utility, and a third person mutually agreed upon, or if no agreement can be reached, the third person shall be appointed in the manner provided by Section 1281.6 of the Code of Civil Procedure. The third person shall act as chair of the panel . The panel may settle disagreements and make binding decisions regarding the fish and wildlife modifications. The arbitration shall be completed within 14 days from the day that the composition of the panel is established, unless the time is extended by mutual agreement. The expenses of the department representative shall be paid by the department; the expenses of the representative of the governmental agency or the public utility shall be paid by the governmental agency or the public utility; and the expenses of the chair of the panel shall be paid one-half by each party.

(c) A governmental agency or public utility proposing a project subject to this section shall not commence operations on that project until the department has found that the project will not substantially adversely affect an existing fish or wildlife resource or until the department's proposals, or the decisions of a panel of arbitrators, have been incorporated into the project.

(d) The department shall determine and specify types of work, methods of performance, or remedial measures that are exempt from the operation of this section.

(e) With regard to any project that involves routine maintenance and operation of water supply, drainage, flood control, or waste treatment and disposal facilities, notice to, and agreement with, the department is not required subsequent to the initial notification and agreement, unless the work as described in the agreement is substantially changed or conditions affecting fish and wildlife resources substantially change, and the resources are adversely affected by the activity conducted under the agreement. This subdivision is applicable in any instance where notice to, and agreement with, the department has been attained prior to January 1, 1977.

(f) This section is not applicable to emergency work necessary to protect life or property; however, notification by the agency or public utility performing that emergency work shall be made to the department within 14 days of the commencement of the emergency work.

§ 1601.5.　　Repealed by Stats.1976, c. 603, p. 1446, § 1

Repealed

§ 1602.　Review of modifications prior to submission to arbitration panel

In addition to the provisions of Section 1601, the department, following submission of the modifications referred to in Section 1601, shall by mutual agreement with any state agency proposing such project, establish such procedures that the parties deem necessary to provide adequate review of the proposed modifications and consideration of alternative conditions designed to protect existing fish and wildlife resources. If no agreement can be reached between the department and the state agency proposing the project, the procedures for arbitration specified in Section 1601 shall then apply.

§ 1602.5.　Repealed by Stats.1976, c. 603, p. 1446, § 1

Repealed

§ 1603.　Substantial diversion or obstruction of natural flow; notice of existence of resource; onsite investigation; mutual agreement; arbitration; violations

It is unlawful for any person to substantially divert or obstruct the natural flow or substantially change the bed, channel, or bank of any river, stream or lake designated by the department, or use any material from the streambeds, without first notifying the department of such activity, except when the department has been notified pursuant to Section 1601. The department within 30 days of receipt of such notice, or within the time determined by mutual written agreement, shall, when an existing fish or wildlife resource may be substantially adversely affected by such activity, notify the person of the existence of such fish and wildlife resource together with a description thereof, and shall submit to the person its proposals as to measures necessary to protect fish and wildlife. Upon a determination by the department of the necessity for onsite investigation or upon the request for an onsite inves-

tigation by the affected parties, the department shall notify the affected parties that it shall make onsite investigation of the activity and shall make such investigation before it shall propose any measure necessary to protect the fish and wildlife.

Within 14 days of receipt of the department's proposals, the affected person shall notify the department in writing as to the acceptability of the proposals, except that this time may be extended by mutual agreement. If such proposals are not acceptable to the affected person, then that person shall so notify the department. Upon request the department shall meet with the affected person within seven days of receipt of such notification or such time as may be mutually agreed upon for the purpose of developing proposals which are acceptable to the department and the affected person. If mutual agreement is not reached at such meeting a panel of arbitrators shall be established; provided, however, that the appointment of such panel may be deferred by mutual consent of the parties. The panel shall be established within seven days of such meeting and shall be composed of one representative of the department, one representative of the affected person, and a third person mutually agreed upon, or if no agreement can be reached, the third person shall be appointed in the manner provided by Section 1281.6 of the Code of Civil Procedure. The third person shall act as panel chairman. The panel shall have power to settle disagreements and make binding decisions regarding fish and wildlife modifications. Such arbitration shall be completed within 14 days from the day that the composition of the panel is established, unless the time is extended by mutual agreement. Expenses of the department representative are to be borne by the department, expenses of the representative of the person who diverts or obstructs the natural flow or changes the bed of any river, stream or lake, or uses any material from the streambeds shall be borne by such person; expenses of the chairman are to be paid one-half by each party.

It is unlawful for any person to commence any activity affected by this section until the department has found it will not substantially adversely affect an existing fish or wildlife resource or until the department's proposals, or the decisions of a panel of arbitrators, have been incorporated into such projects. If the department fails to act within 30 days of the receipt of the notice, the person may commence such activity.

It is unlawful for any person to engage in a project or activity affected by this section, unless such project or activity is conducted in accordance with the department's proposals or the decisions of the panel of arbitrators.

With regard to any project which involves routine maintenance and operation of water supply, drainage, flood control, or waste treatment and disposal facilities, notice to and agreement with the department shall not be required subsequent to the initial notification and agreement unless the work as described in the agreement is substantially changed, or conditions affecting fish and wildlife resources substantially change, and such resources are adversely affected by the activity conducted under the agreement. This provision shall be applicable in any instance where notice to and agreement with the department have been attained prior to the effective date of this chapter.

The provisions of this section shall not be applicable to emergency work necessary to protect life or property. Notification by the person performing such emergency work shall be made to the department within 14 days of commencement of such emergency work.

§ 1603.1. Violation of § 1603; civil penalty; enforcement

(a) Every person who violates Section 1603 is subject to a civil penalty of not more than twenty-five thousand dollars ($25,000) for each violation.

(b) The civil penalty imposed for each separate violation pursuant to this section is separate, and in addition to, any other civil penalty imposed for a separate violation pursuant to this section or any other provision of law.

(c) In determining the amount of any civil penalty imposed pursuant to this section, the court shall take into consideration the nature, circumstance, extent, and gravity of the violation. In making this determination, the court may consider the degree of toxicity and volume of the discharge, whether the effects of the violation may be reversed or mitigated, and with respect to the defendant, the ability to pay, the effect of any civil penalty on the ability to continue in business, any voluntary cleanup efforts undertaken, any prior history of violations, the gravity of the behavior, the economic benefit, if any, resulting from the violation, and any other matters the court determines justice may require.

(d) Every civil action brought under this section shall be brought by the Attorney General upon complaint by the department, or by the district attorney or city attorney in the name of the people of the State of California, and any actions relating to the same violation may be joined or consolidated.

(e) In any civil action brought pursuant to this chapter in which a temporary restraining order, preliminary injunction, or permanent injunction is sought, it is not necessary to allege or prove at any stage of the proceeding any of the following:

(1) That irreparable damage will occur if the temporary restraining order, preliminary injunction, or permanent injunction is not issued.

(2) The remedy at law is inadequate. The court shall issue a temporary restraining order, preliminary injunction, or permanent injunction in a civil action brought pursuant to this chapter without the allegations and without the proof specified in this paragraph or paragraph (1).

(f) All civil penalties collected pursuant to this section shall not be considered fines or forfeitures as defined in Section 13003 and shall be apportioned in the following manner:

(1) Fifty percent shall be distributed to the county treasurer of the county in which the action is prosecuted. Amounts paid to the county treasurer shall be deposited in the county fish and wildlife propagation fund established pursuant to Section 13100.

(2) Fifty percent shall be distributed to the department for deposit in the Fish and Game Preservation Fund. These funds may be expended to cover the costs of any legal actions or for any other law enforcement purpose consistent with Section 9 of Article XVI of the California Constitution.

§ 1604. Review by court

Any party affected by a decision made by an arbitration panel pursuant to Section 1601 or 1603 may petition a court of competent jurisdiction for confirmation, correction, or vacation of the decision in accordance with the provisions of Chapter 4 (commencing with Section 1285) of Title 9 of Part 3 of the Code of Civil Procedure.

§ 1605. Location of construction material specified by public agency; notice of modification in bid invitations

Any governmental agency, state or local, or public utility which intends to specify any location of possible construction material such as borrow pits or gravel beds, for the use in any construction project undertaken on its behalf which would be subject to this chapter, shall include in any notice inviting bids, any modifications or conditions established pursuant to Section 1601 of this code.

§ 1606. Timber harvesting plans; contents

Persons submitting timber harvesting plans under provisions of Section 4581 of the Public Resources Code may consider that notification to the department as required in Section 1603 has been given, provided, however, the following information is provided in the contents of such plan:

(a) The volume, type, and equipment to be used in removing or displacing any one or combination of soil, sand, gravel or boulders.

(b) The volume of water, intended use, and equipment to be used in any water diversion or impoundment, if applicable.

(c) The equipment to be used in road or bridge construction.

(d) The type and density of vegetation to be affected and an estimate of the area involved.

(e) A diagram or sketch of the location of the operation which clearly indicates the stream or other water and access from a named public road. Locked gates shall be indicated. The compass direction must be shown.

(f) A description of the period of time in which operations will be carried out.

§ 1607. Fees

(a) The director may establish a schedule of fees to be charged to any entity or person subject to this chapter. The fees charged shall be established in an amount necessary to pay the total costs incurred by the department in preparing and submitting proposals and conducting investigations pursuant to this chapter and administering and enforcing this chapter. Fees received pursuant to this section shall be deposited in the Fish and Game Preservation Fund as a reimbursement.

(b) Pursuant to subdivision (a), the department shall establish the fees in an amount not less than fifty dollars ($50) or more than two thousand four hundred dollars ($2,400), as adjusted pursuant to Section 713.

Appendix Q

California Fish and Game Code
Division 2. Department of Fish and Game

Chapter 7.8. Sacramento–San Joaquin Valley Wetlands Mitigation Bank of 1993

ARTICLE 1. GENERAL PROVISIONS

§ 1775.   Short title

This chapter shall be known and may be cited as the Sacramento-San Joaquin Valley Wetlands Mitigation Bank Act of 1993.

§ 1776.   Legislative findings and declaration

The Legislature finds and declares the following:

(a) Wetlands are an important natural resource of the Sacramento-San Joaquin Valley because they provide significant habitat for migratory waterfowl of the Pacific flyway, for endangered species, and for many other resident wildlife and fish populations. Wetlands provide additional public benefits, including water quality improvement, flood protection, stream bank stabilization, recreation, and scientific research.

(b) Active and voluntary involvement by private landowners is necessary for the long-term availability and productivity of wetlands in the Sacramento-San Joaquin Valley.

(c) Large wetland preserves in the Sacramento-San Joaquin Valley, under certain circumstances, can provide an environmentally preferable alternative to a number of small, isolated wetland preserves of the same type surrounded by urban development.

(d) It is the policy of the state with respect to the Sacramento-San Joaquin Valley:

(1) To provide for the protection, preservation, restoration, enhancement, and expansion of the wetland habitat in the Sacramento-San Joaquin Valley.

(2) To promote the protection, preservation, restoration, enhancement, and expansion of the Sacramento-San Joaquin Valley wetlands in concert with other federal, state, and local programs, and interested parties.

(3) To improve cooperative efforts among private, nonprofit, and public entities for the management and protection of wetlands.

(4) To assure that no net loss of either wetland acreage or habitat values results from activities pursuant to this chapter in the Sacramento-San Joaquin Valley that otherwise comply with state and federal law.

(5) To encourage and maintain a predictable, efficient, and timely regulatory framework for environmentally acceptable development.

(6) To assure that the construction or maintenance of wetland mitigation banks in the Sacramento-San Joaquin Valley does not reduce any local tax base, does not create any uncompensated increased requirement for local services, and does not create conditions that have the potential to adversely affect the public health.

(7) To provide an alternative for accomplishing offsite mitigation in the Sacramento-San Joaquin Valley when offsite mitigation is required under a fill permit issued pursuant to Section 404 of the federal Clean Water Act (33 U.S.C. Sec. 1344 *et seq.*).

(e) This chapter constitutes a nonexclusive alternative to other lawful methods of mitigating project impacts upon wetlands and maintaining and increasing wetlands acreage and habitat values generally. Specifically, this chapter is not intended to, and shall not be interpreted to:

(1) Condone or encourage the removal, loss, or degradation of wetlands.

(2) Condone or encourage the removal, loss, or degradation of habitat for any rare, threatened, or endangered species.

(3) Abrogate any other local, state, or federal law or policy relating to wetlands, nor prohibit any city or county from prohibiting the removal, filling, or other destruction of particular wetlands.

(4) Establish maximum or minimum standards or any other requirements for wetland fill or mitigation, except for mitigation banks established pursuant to this chapter.

(5) Have legal or necessary precedential application to any other area of the state, or to other lands, resources, situations, or circumstances.

(6) Preclude other forms of mitigation banking, including private or for-profit programs, within the Sacramento-San Joaquin Valley.

(7) Be the exclusive method of providing compensation by permittees for the loss of wetlands within the Sacramento-San Joaquin Valley.

§ 1776.5.   Administration of chapter; source of funding

It is the intent of the Legislature that the funds necessary to cover the costs of administering this chapter be provided by the purchase of credits in mitigation bank sites.

§ 1777.   Chapter definitions

Unless the context otherwise requires, the definitions in this article govern the construction of this chapter.

§ 1777.2.   Bank site or mitigation bank site defined

"Bank site" or "mitigation bank site" means a publicly or privately owned and operated site on which wetlands have been or will be created in accordance with this chapter to compensate for adverse impacts caused by removal or fill permit activities authorized pursuant to Section 404 of the federal Clean Water Act (33 U.S.C. Sec. 1344 *et seq.*).

§ 1777.5.   Credit defined

"Credit" means a numerical value that represents the wetland acreage and habitat values of a mitigation bank site.

§ 1778.   Operator defined

"Operator" means the department, or a public or private person or entity approved by the department, to administer a wetlands mitigation bank site.

§ 1778.5.   Permittee defined

"Permittee" means a public or private person or entity that meets all of the following conditions:

(a) Has received a permit pursuant to Section 404 of the federal Clean Water Act (33 U.S.C. Sec. 1344 *et seq.*) for the removal or filling of wetlands, subject to a condition that allows the permittee to compensate for the wetland loss through participation in a wetland mitigation bank pursuant to this chapter.

(b) Proposes to compensate for the loss of the wetlands through participation in a wetlands mitigation bank pursuant to this chapter.

(c) Proposes the discharge at a site within a qualifying urban area and not more than 40 miles from a bank site with sufficient acreage of the same types of wetlands that will provide suitable replacement habitat for the values that may be lost from the conversion of the existing wetlands.

§ 1779.   Qualifying urban area defined

"Qualifying urban area" means any of the following when they occur within the Sacramento-San Joaquin Valley:

(a) A geographical area having a population of 50,000 or more inhabitants within the jurisdiction of a city, or a town, as defined by Sections 20 and 21 of the Government Code.

(b) A portion of any geographical area within a town, as defined in Section 21 of the Government Code, which has a population density equal to, or exceeding, 1,500 persons per square mile and which has a population of 50,000 or more inhabitants.

(c) A geographical area having a population density equal to, or exceeding, 1,500 persons per square mile, and an adjacent city, as defined in Section 20 of the Government Code, where the combined population of the geographical area and the city equals 50,000 or more inhabitants.

(d) A geographical area within the sphere of influence of a city or community services district for which the projected population of the adopted general plan equals 10,000 or more inhabitants.

§ 1779.5.   Sacramento-San Joaquin Valley defined

"Sacramento-San Joaquin Valley" means the central valley region, as defined in subdivision (g) of Section 13200 of the Water Code.

ARTICLE 2.   LEGISLATIVE GOALS

§ 1780.   Purpose of chapter

The purpose of this chapter is to ensure that no net loss of wetland acreage or habitat values within the Sacramento-San Joaquin Valley occurs as a result of fill permit activities pursuant to Section 404 of the federal Clean Water Act (33 U.S.C. Sec. 1344 *et seq.*).

§ 1781.   Increase of wetland acreage and values

It is the state's goal to increase the total wetlands acreage and values within the Sacramento-San Joaquin Valley.

ARTICLE 3.   WETLANDS MITIGATION BANKS

§ 1784.   Standards and criteria; implementation of bank sites.

(a) The department, in cooperation with those agencies specified in Section 1786, shall adopt regulations that establish standards and criteria for the bank site qualification process, for the evaluation of wetland acreage and habitat values created at the bank sites, and for the operation and evaluation of bank sites, and any other regulations that are necessary to implement this chapter.

These criteria shall require, at a minimum, that the newly created wetland provide the hydrologic, vegetative, and wildlife characteristics, including the food web components, of a naturally occurring wetland system.

(b) With respect to bank site standards and operator qualifications, the department shall consider, at a minimum, all of the following criteria:

(1) A requirement that the bank site have a reliable, adequate, and available water supply necessary to provide wetland values. For wetlands dependent only on rainfall, rainfall satisfies this requirement.

(2) The relative ease or difficulty of converting uplands into wetlands at the bank site.

(3) The anticipated maintenance necessary to sustain the recreated and created wetlands at the bank site.

(4) The proximity of the bank site to other established preserves or natural features historically associated with abundant wildlife values.

(5) The proximity of the bank site to urban or populated areas that could reduce the bank site's long-term biological values.

(6) The demonstrated ability of the bank site operator to create, administer, maintain, and protect the bank site in perpetuity, including financial, technical, and management ability.

(7) The relative abundance or scarcity of the wetland type to be created at the bank site.

§ 1785. Application for determination that bank site and operator qualify

If any person desires to establish a wetlands mitigation bank site under this chapter, the person shall apply to the department for a determination that the bank site and the operator qualify under the criteria established by the department pursuant to this chapter. The determination that a bank site qualifies under this chapter is a project for purposes of Section 21065 of the Public Resources Code.

§ 1786. Memorandum of understanding

(a) Before any wetlands are created on the bank site qualified pursuant to Section 1785, the department shall coordinate and shall be a signatory to a memorandum of understanding with the operator. The United States Environmental Protection Agency, the United States Army Corps of Engineers, the Fish and Wildlife Service of the United States Department of the Interior, the Central Valley Regional Water Quality Control Board, and the State Department of Health Services or its designee, or any of them, may be signatories by indicating to the department their interest in participating within 90 days of being notified by the department of the department's intent to initiate the procedures described in this section. Any county located in whole or in part in the Sacramento-San Joaquin Valley may, by ordinance, require that it be a signatory to any memorandum of understanding for a bank site to be established within its boundary.

(b) The memorandum of understanding shall include, but is not limited to, all of the following items:

(1) Identification of the mitigation bank site, including the legal property description, acreage, types, and location of existing wetlands within the boundaries of the bank site.

(2) An agreement, by each of the governmental agencies in subdivision (a), that all new, successfully created wetland acreage shall qualify to be credited against the approved removal or fill of wetlands located in the qualifying urban area and within 40 miles of the bank site and is consistent with the procedures set out in this chapter.

(3) An agreement by the operator to do both of the following:

(A) Maintain all wetland habitat within the bank in optimum condition in perpetuity, barring an unforeseen natural catastrophe that precludes the viability of wetlands.

(B) Establish a trust or bond in favor of the department that provides sufficient funds to ensure administration, protection, operation, and maintenance in perpetuity of the wetland habitat acreage and values at the mitigation bank site if the operator defaults in performing the duties required pursuant to subparagraph (A).

(4) In the case of privately owned bank sites, identification of the circumstances that would constitute a major breach of the agreement and that would result in either the replacement of the operator, or the passing of title from the owner to the state, or both, including identification of procedures for adequate notice and opportunity for the operator to be heard and to correct any breach.

§ 1787. Public entity bank site owner; payment of amount equal to taxes on property transferred to entity

(a) If the bank site owner is a public entity, that entity shall pay annually to the county in which the property is located an amount equal to the county taxes levied on the property at the time title to the bank site is transferred to that entity. The public entity shall also pay the assessments levied upon the property by any irrigation, drainage, or reclamation district.

(b) Payments under this section shall be made on or before December 10 of each year, except for newly acquired bank sites, for which payments shall be made pursuant to subdivision (c).

(c) Payments for newly acquired bank sites shall be made within one year of the date title to the property was transferred to the state, prorated for the balance of the year from the date title was transferred to the 30th day of June following the date title was transferred, and, thereafter, payments shall be made on or before December 10 of each year.

ARTICLE 4. WETLANDS

§ 1790. Request for determination of mitigation bank credits

Upon the successful creation of any wetlands of at least 20 acres, or in the case of vernal pools, upon successful creation of vernal pools on a site at least 20 acres in size, the operator may request a determination by the department of the number of acres in the mitigation bank site, and the relative habitat value thereof, that qualify for credit against prospective wetland loss in the qualifying urban area. In determining the amount of mitigation bank credit, no credit shall be provided for habitat values or acreage that was in existence prior to the establishment of the bank.

§ 1791. Determination of number of wetland acres; wetland types

(a) Upon receipt of a request pursuant to Section 1790, the department shall determine the number of acres which are wetlands in the bank site based on the criteria established pursuant to Section 1784, and the department shall classify those wetlands according to established biological criteria.

(b) The classifications shall include, but are not limited to, the following wetland types:

(1) Perennial freshwater marsh.
(2) Perennial brackish marsh.
(3) Seasonal freshwater marsh.
(4) Wet meadow.
(5) Vernal pool.

(6) Riparian woodland.

(7) Riparian scrub.

§ 1792. Determination of minimum price for wetland credit; factors in accounting for costs of wetland acres

In the interest of assuring that the minimum price for wetland credit is sufficient to ensure the financial integrity of the bank, the department may establish a minimum price for each bank established pursuant to this chapter. The operator may set a higher price to the extent that price is consistent with the terms of the memorandum of understanding executed pursuant to Section 1785. After the department determines the number of wetland acres in the bank site that qualify for credit against wetland loss in a qualifying urban area, the operator shall provide to the department, and the department shall verify, an accounting of the average cost for each wetland acre created, by wetland type for the purpose of determining credits, using the following factors:

(a) Land costs, including the reasonable interest cost of holding the land.

(b) Wetland creation costs.

(c) Wetland administration, maintenance, and protection costs.

(d) Annual taxes, including all tax increases allowed under applicable state law, and in-lieu payments pursuant to Section 1787, if applicable.

(e) Costs incurred by the department in establishing the bank site, and the direct cost of necessary ongoing monitoring and oversight.

(f) Any other information relevant to a determination of the cost of preserving the wetlands in perpetuity.

§ 1792.5. Department reimbursements; agreements

The department shall be reimbursed for those expenses of the department identified in Section 1792 according to a schedule contained in an agreement with the person establishing a wetland mitigation bank. The agreement shall be approved by all parties prior to the commencement of planning activities.

ARTICLE 5. DISCHARGE INTO WETLANDS

§ 1793. Permittee compensation under federal Clean Water Act; classification of wetlands permittee to remove

A permittee shall provide compensation pursuant to Section 404 of the federal Clean Water Act (33 U.S.C. Sec. 1344 *et seq.*). The department shall classify the wetlands that the permittee will remove according to wetland type, consistent with Article 4 (commencing with Section 1790).

§ 1794. Conditions for compensation under § 1793

Compensation pursuant to Section 1793 is subject to the condition that the operator establish the trust or bond required by subparagraph (B) of paragraph (3) of subdivision (b) of Section 1786 and, in addition, is subject to the following conditions:

(a) The full payment shall be used to purchase credits in the mitigation bank site.

(b) The payment shall provide for purchase of bank site wetland acreage required by Section 1793 that has the same hydrologic, vegetative, and other characteristics as the system for which it will serve as mitigation.

(c) A permittee shall not participate in a wetlands mitigation bank if a net loss of wetland habitat values or acreage occurs.

§ 1795. Permittee obligations following payment to operator under article

After payment to the operator pursuant to this article, the permittee has no further obligations with respect to the operation of the bank site to which payment was made, unless the permittee has an equity involvement in the bank.

§ 1796. Time for bank site qualification; reports to legislature

No bank site shall be qualified under Section 1785 on or after January 1, 2010. Notwithstanding Section 7550.5 of the Government Code, the department shall report to the Legislature on or before February 1, 1996, and once annually thereafter, with a description and evaluation of each mitigation bank site approved pursuant to this chapter, including, but not limited to, the number of wetland acres and habitat values created, the number of credits issued, an assessment of the biological productivity of the created wetlands, a comparison of the wetlands acreage and values that were created in the mitigation bank and those that were lost by the various projects for which credits were obtained, and any recommendations for improving the program.

Appendix R

**California Code of Regulations
Title 14, Natural Resources
Section 699.5**

§ 699.5. Fees for Lake/Streambed Alteration Agreements.

(a) 1601 Applications (from Public Agencies)–$132.00 non-refundable application fee, plus:

(1) No additional fee for projects costing less than $25,000.

(2) $530.00 additional processing fee for projects costing from $25,000 to $500,000.

(3) $1059.00 additional processing fee for projects costing over $500,000.

(b) 1601 Routine Maintenance Activities (public agencies) if performed under a Memorandum of Understanding with the Department of Fish and Game:

(1) $111.00 each for the first 20 maintenance projects.

(2) $88.00 each for the second 20 maintenance projects.

(3) $67.00 each for maintenance projects in excess of 40.

(4) Projects under this subsection pertain to those waterways under prior 1601 agreement upon which public agencies propose to perform routine maintenance; to be submitted at least 30 days prior to commencement of work.

(c) 1603 Applications (private) excluding commercial gravel operations and timber harvest–$132.00 non-refundable application fee, plus:

(1) No additional fee for private individuals who do the work themselves or projects costing less than $25,000.

(2) $530.00 additional processing fee for projects costing $25,000 to $500,000.

(3) $1059.00 additional processing fee for projects costing over $500,000.

(d) 1603 Applications–Commercial Gravel Operations.

(1) $530.00 fee per application.

(e) 1603/1606 Applications–Timber Harvest.

(1) $530.00 fee per application with 1 or 2 stream encroachments.

(2) $662.00 fee per application with 3 or 4 stream encroachments.

(3) $794.00 fee per application with 5 to 9 stream encroachments.

(4) $883.00 fee per application with 10 or more stream encroachments.

(f) One year time extensions for 1601/1603 agreements, excluding gravel operations, if the project has not changed.

(1) $109.00 fee per application for a one year extension.

(2) For the purpose of this subsection, extensions include those agreements which expire before completion of the project and which have no changes in the work described in the original agreement. If the agreement expires prior to a request for an extension, a new notification will be required and all appropriate fees will be charged.

(g) Amendments to 1601/1603 existing agreements.

(1) 50% of the fee of the existing agreement.

(h) Unusual Project Applications. Public or private projects which are unusually extensive and/or protracted, including but not limited to projects that (1) involve more than one departmental administrative region, or (2) involve more than 15 streams (excluding timber harvest applications), shall be charged fees under the following provisions:

(1) The project sponsor shall submit the appropriate application fee required in the above fee schedule. Should this application fee be insufficient to defer the department's costs, then the department and the project sponsor shall arrange for a billing schedule to recover the department's additional project-related costs.

Note: Authority cited: Section 1607, Fish and Game Code. Reference: Section 1607, Fish and Game Code.

Appendix S

California Department of Fish and Game
Application for Streambed Alteration

The department has 30 days from date of receipt of a completed application in which to make its recommendations. This time period does not begin until the department receives the appropriate fee (see attached fee schedule).

T.H.P. No. _____

Notification No. _____ Received _____

STATE OF CALIFORNIA

THE RESOURCES AGENCY

DEPARTMENT OF FISH AND GAME

NOTIFICATION OF REMOVAL OF MATERIALS AND/OR ALTERATION
OF LAKE, RIVER, OR STREAMBED BOTTOM, OR MARGIN

A. APPLICANT Pursuant to Sections 1601-1607 of the California Fish and Game Code

I, _____ of _____ ,
$\qquad$ Name of Applicant $\qquad$ Mailing Address

Representing_____
$\qquad$ Name and address of Individual, Agency, Company, etc. owning property or doing work.

Hereby notify the California Department of Fish and Game of operations to be carried out by or for me

from _____ to _____ on or affecting
$\qquad$ Starting Date $\qquad$ Ending Date

_____ of _____ County, tributary to _____
$\qquad$ Name of Stream, River, or Lake $\qquad$ Major Water Body

Located _____
$\qquad$ Distance and Direction to Landmarks

Section _____ Township _____ Range _____

USGS Map _____ Co. Assessor's Parcel No. _____

Property owner's name and address (if different from applicant) _____

_____ is responsible for operations at the site.
$\qquad$ Name of Person to Be Contacted at Site During Operations

He/she can be reached at _____
$\qquad$ Mailing Address $\qquad$ Telephone

B. Description of operation. 1. The nature of said operations will be as follows:
Check all squares which apply.

❏ Soil, sand, gravel, and/or boulder removal or displacement
❏ Water diversion or impoundment
❏ Mining–other than aggregate removal
❏ Road or bridge construction
❏ Levee or channel construction

❏ Timber harvesting or any related activity required for harvesting timber
❏ Temporary, recreational or irrigation dam
❏ Fill or spoil in bed, bank, or channel
❏ Other–Describe below

2. Type of material removed, displaced or added   ❏ Soil   ❏ Sand   ❏ Gravel   ❏ Boulders
   Volume _____

3. Equipment to be used in the described site _____

4. Use of water (i.e., domestic, irrigation, gravel, washing, etc.) _____ Quantity _____

5. Describe type and density of vegetation to be affected, and estimate area involved.

_____

6. What actions are proposed to protect fish and wildlife resources and/or mitigate for project impacts? _____

_____

7a. Does project have a local or state lead agency or require other permits?   ❏ Yes   ❏ No

7b. If answer is yes, please attach or identify any available environmental document.

7c. For state-designated wild and scenic rivers, a determination of the project's consistency with the California Wild and Scenic Rivers Act must be made by the Secretary for Resources. Until the Secretary determines the project is consistent with the Act, the Department cannot issue a valid agreement. A tentative agreement will be issued, conditioned upon a finding of consistency by the Resources Secretary.

7d. THIS AGREEMENT IS NOT INTENDED AS AN APPROVAL OF A PROJECT OR OF SPECIFIC PROJECT FEATURES BY THE DEPARTMENT OF FISH AND GAME. INDEPENDENT REVIEW AND RECOMMENDATIONS WILL BE PROVIDED BY THE DEPARTMENT AS APPROPRIATE ON THOSE PROJECTS WHERE LOCAL, STATE, OR FEDERAL PERMITS OR OTHER ENVIRONMENTAL REPORTS ARE REQUIRED.

8. Briefly describe proposed construction methods. Attach diagram or sketch of the location of your operation to clearly indicate the stream or other water and access and distance from named public road. Indicate locked gates with an "X". Show existing features with a solid line (——————) and proposed features with a broken line (- - - - - - - - -). Show compass direction. Attach larger scale map if necessary.

9. Project Cost $ _____

_____
Signature of Applicant   Date

NO CARBON NEEDED

FG2023 (Rev. 11/87)   87 83409

Appendix T

California Department of Fish and Game
Regional Offices

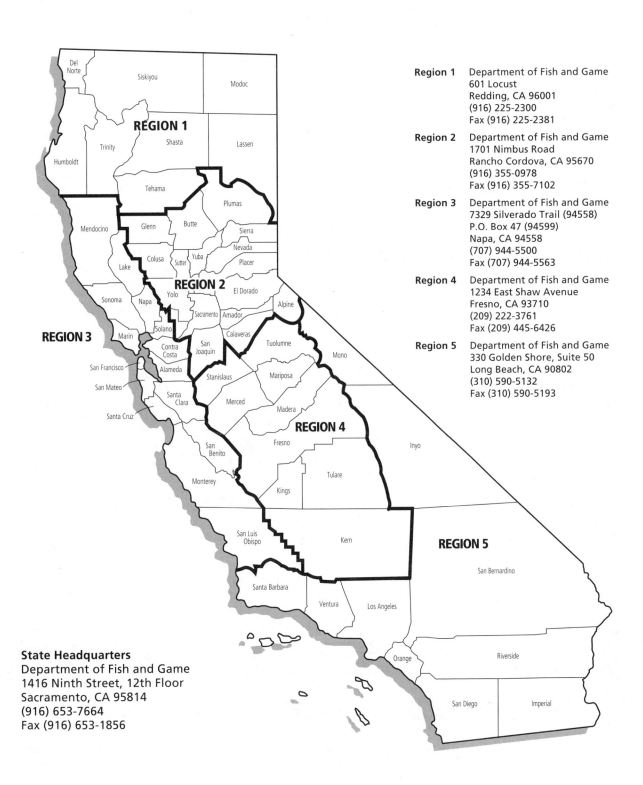

Region 1 Department of Fish and Game
601 Locust
Redding, CA 96001
(916) 225-2300
Fax (916) 225-2381

Region 2 Department of Fish and Game
1701 Nimbus Road
Rancho Cordova, CA 95670
(916) 355-0978
Fax (916) 355-7102

Region 3 Department of Fish and Game
7329 Silverado Trail (94558)
P.O. Box 47 (94599)
Napa, CA 94558
(707) 944-5500
Fax (707) 944-5563

Region 4 Department of Fish and Game
1234 East Shaw Avenue
Fresno, CA 93710
(209) 222-3761
Fax (209) 445-6426

Region 5 Department of Fish and Game
330 Golden Shore, Suite 50
Long Beach, CA 90802
(310) 590-5132
Fax (310) 590-5193

State Headquarters
Department of Fish and Game
1416 Ninth Street, 12th Floor
Sacramento, CA 95814
(916) 653-7664
Fax (916) 653-1856

Appendix U

California Regional Water Quality Control Boards

1 North Coast Region
5550 Skylane Blvd., Suite A
Santa Rosa, CA 95403
(707) 576-2220

2 San Francisco Bay Region
2101 Webster Street, Suite 500
Oakland, CA 94612
(510) 286-1255

3 Central Coast Region
81 Higuera Street, Suite 200
San Luis Obispo, CA 93401-5414
(805) 549-3147

4 Los Angeles Region
101 Centre Plaza Drive
Monterey Park, CA 91754-2156
(213) 266-7500

5 Central Valley Region
3443 Routier Road, Suite A
Sacramento, CA 95827-3098
(916) 255-3000

Fresno Branch Office
3614 East Ashlan Avenue
Fresno, CA 93726
(209) 445-5116

Redding Branch Office
415 Knollcrest Drive
Redding, CA 96002
(916) 224-4845

6 Lahonton Region
2092 Lake Tahoe Blvd.
South Lake Tahoe, CA 96150
(916) 544-3481

Victorville Branch Office
Civic Plaza
15428 Civic Drive, Suite 100
Victorville, CA 92392-2359
(619) 241-6583

7 Colorado River Basin
73-720 Fred Waring, Suite 100
Palm Desert, CA 92260
(619) 346-74911

8 Santa Ana Region
2010 Iowa Avenue
Suite 100
Riverside, CA 92507-2409
(714) 782-4130

9 San Diego Region
9771 Clairemont
Mesa Blvd., Suite B
San Diego, CA 92124
(619) 467-2952

Glossary

Anaerobic conditions
Lack of oxygen in either a gaseous or dissolved form.

Buffer (area, zone, or habitat)
An intervening upland area or other form of barrier that separates wetlands from developed or disturbed areas and reduces the impacts on the wetlands that may result from human activities.

Creation
Artificial establishment of wetlands at an upland site.

Department of the Army (DA) Permit
Same as a Section 404 permit.

Discharge
The placement of dredged or fill material into waters of the United States, including wetlands, that results in more than a minimal effect on the aquatic system, including redeposition of material during excavation, mechanized land clearing, and ditching.

Dredged material
Material removed from waters of the United States.

Enhancement
Increasing the functions and values of a low-quality or degraded wetland.

EPA Section 404(b)(1) Guidelines
Regulations put forth by EPA that provide the standards for unacceptable adverse impacts on and preferred mitigation procedures for waters of the United States, including wetlands, used to determine whether a Section 404 permit should be issued.

Facultative hydrophyte
Plants that can tolerate wetland conditions, but can also survive in upland habitats.

Fill material
Material taken from an upland site and used to change the bottom features of waters of the United States (includes soil, rock, vegetative material, debris, pilings).

Functions
Conditions and natural processes that occur in wetlands.

General permit
A permit for a specific class of activities within a specified area issued by the Corps, authorizing the discharge of dredged or fill material into waters of the United States, including wetlands.

Habitat evaluation procedure (HEP)
A method used by USFWS to assess and score the quality of habitat for wildlife.

Hydric soil
Soils that are saturated or inundated for a long enough period to develop anaerobic conditions in the upper part.

Hydrology
The distribution and movement of surface water and groundwater in an ecosystem.

Hydrophyte
Plants that can grow and reproduce in wetland conditions (hydric soils and wetland hydrology); literally 'water plants'.

Individual permit
A Section 404 permit issued by the Corps for an individual project for which a specific review was conducted.

In-kind mitigation
Mitigation that results in wetlands that are the same

habitat type and provide similar functions and values of the wetlands removed.

Mitigation
Actions or project design features that reduce impacts on wetlands by avoiding adverse effects, minimizing adverse effects, or compensating for adverse effects.

Mitigation banking
Use of a single site, suitable for wetlands enhancement, restoration, and/or creation, for the mitigation of impacts on wetlands that result from more than one project at other sites.

Monitoring
Collecting data over time to document the success or failure of wetland mitigation measures.

Nationwide permit (NWP)
A general permit issued by the Corp for the entire United States.

Navigable waters
Waterways that are, could, or were used to transport interstate or foreign commerce.

Obligate hydrophyte
Plants dependent on wetland conditions for growth and reproduction.

Off-site mitigation
Mitigation that occurs on a site distant from the site of wetland impacts.

On-site mitigation
Mitigation that occurs contiguous with or near the site of wetland impacts, typically on the same project site.

Ordinary high water mark
The point on the shore of a water body where sustained high water levels typically occur; *see* chapter 3 for legal definition.

Out-of-kind mitigation
Mitigation that results in wetlands that are not the same habitat type or do not replace the functions and values of the wetlands removed.

Performance standards
Specified goals of a mitigation plan that must be met for wetland mitigation to be determined successful.

Preapplication meeting
A meeting between the project proponent and Corps conducted prior to application for a Section 404 permit and often attended by EPA, USFWS, and DFG.

Public interest review
Corps evaluation under the Clean Water Act of the probable impacts of a proposed project and its intended use on the public interest; *see* chapter 4.

Restoration
Establishing wetland habitat at an upland site that previously had supported wetlands.

Riparian habitat
Vegetation associated with river, stream, or lake banks and floodplains.

Saturated soil
Soil that contains as much water as it can physically hold; all pore spaces are filled.

Section 404(b)(1) Guidelines
See EPA Section 404(b)(1) Guidelines.

Section 404 permit
The permit issued by the Corps under Section 404 of the Clean Water Act for authorizing the discharge of dredged or fill material into waters of the United States, including wetlands; also known as Corps permit, fill permit, Department of the Army permit, DA permit, individual permit, 404 permit.

Special aquatic sites
Specific types of waters of the United States for which mitigation requirements are more stringent under Section 404(b)(1) Guidelines; *see* chapter 3 for list of regulatory special aquatic sites and definitions.

Streambed alteration agreement
Agreement between a public or private entity and the California Department of Fish and Game for actions that would affect stream or lake beds or banks.

Takings
The appropriation, including excessive regulation that amounts to an appropriation of private property by the federal government.

Upland
Sites that are not saturated or inundated frequently enough or long enough to be considered wetlands.

Values
Recognized benefits that wetlands provide people.

Waters of the United States
Water bodies that are regulated under Section 404 of the Clean Water Act; *see* chapter 3 for regulatory definition.

Wetland evaluation technique (WET)
A method used by the Corps to assess the functions and values of wetlands.

Wetland hydrology
Hydrologic conditions in which a site is inundated or saturated frequently and for long duration. Under Corps criteria, 'frequently' means more than 50 out of 100 years and 'long duration' means more than 5% of the growing season.

Wetlands
Habitats that are frequently inundated or saturated for long duration and support characteristic plant life; vegetated waters of the United States; *see* chapter 3 for detailed definitions.

Acronyms

ACHP	Advisory Council on Historic Preservation
ADID	Advanced Identification
APA	Administrative Procedures Act
ARNI	Aquatic resource of national importance
BCDC	Bay Conservation and Development Commission
Cal-EPA	California Environmental Protection Agency
CCC	California Coastal Commission
CCR	California Code of Regulations
CEQA	California Environmental Quality Act
Corps	U.S. Army Corps of Engineers
CWA	Clean Water Act
CZMA	Coastal Zone Management Act
DA	Department of the Army
DFG	California Department of Fish and Game
EA	Environmental assessment
EIS	Environmental impact statement
EPA	U.S. Environmental Protection Agency
FONSI	Finding of no significant impact
GAO	Government Accounting Office
HEP	Habitat evaluation procedure
LCP	Local coastal program
MOA	Memorandum of agreement
MOU	Memorandum of Understanding
NEPA	National Environmental Policy Act
NMFS	National Marine Fisheries Service
NPDES	National Pollution Discharge Elimination System
NRCS	Natural Resources Conservation Service
NRDC	National Resources Defense Council
NWP	Nationwide permit
PDN	Predischarge notification
ROD	Record of decision
RWQCB	Regional Water Quality Control Board
SAMP	Special area management plan
SHPO	State Historic Preservation Officer
SWRCB	California State Water Resources Control Board
TRPA	Tahoe Regional Planning Agency
USFWS	U.S. Fish and Wildlife Service
USGS	U.S. Geological Survey
WET	Wetland evaluation technique

Printed References

California. Department of Fish and Game. 1992. *A field guide to lake and streambed alteration agreements: Section 1600-1607 California Fish and Game Code.* (Administrative report 92-1.) Sacramento, CA.

_____. Office of Planning and Research. 1992. *CEQA: California Environmental Quality Act statutes and guidelines 1992.* Sacramento, CA.

California Coastal Commission. 1981. *Statewide interpretive guidelines as of December 16, 1981.* San Francisco, CA.

Central Valley Habitat Joint Venture. 1990. *Central Valley habitat joint venture implementation plan: a component of the North American waterfowl management plan.* Sacramento, CA.

Cohen, A. N. 1991. *An introduction to the ecology of the San Francisco estuary.* Save San Francisco Bay Association. 2nd edition. Oakland, CA. Prepared for San Francisco Estuary Project, Oakland, CA.

Cowardin, L. M., V. Carter, F. C. Golet, and E. T. LaRoe. 1979. *Classification of wetlands and deepwater habitats of the United States.* (FWS/OBS-79/31.) U.S. Fish and Wildlife Service. Washington, DC.

Dahl, T. E. 1990. *Wetland losses in the United States: 1780's to 1980's.* U.S. Fish and Wildlife Service. Washington, DC.

Environmental Law Institute. 1993. *Wetland mitigation banking: an Environmental Law Institute report.* Washington, DC.

Ferren, W. R. 1990. *Recent research on and new management issues for southern California estuarine wetlands.* Pages 55-79 in A. A. Schoenherr (ed.), *Endangered plant communities of southern California.* (Special Publication No. 3.) Southern California Botanists. Claremont, CA.

Frayer, W. E., D. D. Peters, and H. R. Pywell. 1989. *Wetlands of the California Central Valley: status and trends–1939 to mid-1980s.* U.S. Fish and Wildlife Service. Portland, OR.

Holland, R. F. 1986. *Preliminary descriptions of the terrestrial natural communities of California.* California Department of Fish and Game. Sacramento, CA.

Jones & Stokes Associates, Inc. 1987. *Sliding toward extinction: the state of California's natural heritage.* (JSA 87-010.) Sacramento, CA. Prepared for The California Nature Conservancy, San Francisco, CA.

MacDonald, R. B. 1988. *Coastal salt marsh.* Pages 263-294 in M. G. Barbour and J. Major (eds.), *Terrestrial vegetation of California.* New expanded edition. California Native Plant Society. Sacramento, CA.

McCullough, D. R. 1971. *The tule elk: its history, behavior, and ecology.* University of California Press. Berkeley, CA.

Mitsch, W., and J. G. Gosselink. 1993. *Wetlands.* Second edition. Van Nostrand Reinhold. New York, NY.

Preston, W. L. 1981. *Vanishing landscapes: land and life in the Tulare Lake basin.* University of California Press. Berkeley, CA.

Reed, P. B., Jr. 1988. *National list of plant species that occur in wetlands: California (Region 0).* (Biological Report 88 [26.10].) U.S. Fish and Wildlife Service. Washington, DC.

Salvesen, D. 1990. *Wetlands: Mitigating and regulating development impacts.* The Urban Land Institute. Washington, DC.

San Francisco Estuary Project. 1991. *Status and trends report on wetlands and related habitats in the San Francisco estuary.* December. Oakland, CA.

Shabman, L., D. King, and P. Scodari. 1993. *Wetland mitigation success through credit market systems.* Environmental Concern Wetland Journal 5(2):9-12.

Smith, F. E. 1977. *A short review of the status of riparian forests in California.* Pages 1-2 in A. Sands (ed.), *Riparian forests in California: their ecology and conservation.* (Publication No. 15.) University of California, Institute of Ecology. Davis, CA.

Sullivan, M.E. and M.E. Richardson. 1993. *Functions and values of the Verde River riparian ecosystem and an assessment of adverse impacts to resources: A supporting document for the initiation of the Verde River advanced identification.* U.S. Fish and Wildlife Service. Phoenix, AZ. Prepared for U.S. Environmental Protection Agency, Region 9, San Francisco, CA.

U.S. Army Corps of Engineers. 1987. *Corps of Engineers wetlands delineation manual.* (Technical report Y-87-1.) Vicksburg, MI. Prepared for the Department of the Army, Washington, DC.

_____. 1991. *Habitat mitigation and monitoring proposal guidelines.* San Francisco District. San Francisco, CA.

_____. 1993. Habitat mitigation and monitoring proposal guidelines. Los Angeles District Regulatory Branch. Los Angeles, CA.

U.S. Environmental Protection Agency. 1991. *Mitigation banking guidance: U.S. Environmental Protection Agency Region 9, San Francisco, California.* Region 9. San Francisco, CA.

U.S. Fish and Wildlife Service. 1988. *Mitigation banking.* By Cathleen Short. July 1988. (USFWS Biological Report 88[41].) National Ecology Research Center, Research and Development. Washington, DC.

Vepraskas, M. J. 1992. *Redoximorphic features for identifying aquic conditions (Technical Bulletin 301.)* North Carolina State University. Raleigh, NC.

Index

NOTE: Bold page numbers indicate photographs, tables, illustrations and sidebar material.

comments *(continued)*
    interagency, in Corps permit review process, 71
    NEPA consideration of, 82
    See also Department of Army permit process; public notice
conservation of wetland
    federal-local partnerships for, 124-128
    regulatory tools for, 124
    special area management plans (SAMP) for, 126-128
    See also creation of wetland; mitigation; planning; restoration of wetland
Conservation Reserve Program, for reducing erosion, 83
construction equipment
    impact of on vernal pools, **1**
    See also development
consultants. *See* experts
contamination of water. *See* pollution; toxics; water quality
Contra Costa county, exclusion of from Corps-SCS agreements, 24-25
coral reef
    as special aquatic site, 28
    See also oceans; special aquatic sites
cord grass
    as tidal salt marsh plant, 11
    See also tidal salt marsh; vegetation
corn lily
    in wet montane meadow, **55**
    See also wet meadows
Corps. *See* U.S. Army Corps of Engineers
costs
    consideration of in alternatives assessment, 57, 58
    of wetland mitigation, 122
cottonwood
    naturally establishing, **105**
    planting detail, **117**
    in riparian forest, 11
    See also riparian habitat; vegetation
Cowardin system of wetland classification, 12
creation of wetland
    as compensatory mitigation, 106, 112, 135
    with mitigation banking, 129, 130
    of vernal pools, **131**
    See also conservation of wetland; mitigation; wetland
creeping wildrye, as wetland facultative species, 10
creosote bush
    as upland species, 10
    See also upland habitat
critical habitat
    activities affecting require individual permit, 69
    maintaining for endangered species, 73
    See also Endangered Species Act; wetland ecosystem
cumulative effects
    consideration of required, 81, 108
    See also adverse impacts; environmental review
CWA. *See* Clean Water Act
CZMA. *See* Coastal Zone Management Act

D

dams
    Corps permit required for, 36, **69**
    Dept. of Fish and Game regulation of, 93
    EPA veto of Corps permit for, 66
    impact of on wetland, 18

dams *(continued)*
    See also impoundment of water; reservoirs; water supplies
deep water habitat
    classifications for, 12
    open water habitat boundaries determination, 23
    in relation to wetland ecosystem, 7-**8**
    See also ocean; tidal waters
Delta. *See* Sacramento-San Joaquin Delta
Delta Protection Commission, 98
    See also state wetland regulation
deltas
    as tidal areas, 27
    See also bays; estuaries; tidal waters
Department of Army (DA) permit process, 49-65
    'after-the-fact' permits, 53-54
    challenges to, 75-76
    'discharge activity area' definition, 52-53
    elevation process for 'aquatic resources of national importance', 61, **62-63**
    EPA, USFWS, NMFS review of proposed permit, 60-61
    federal laws related to permit issuance, 72-75
        Clean Water Act, Section 401, 74-75
        Coastal Zone Management Act, 31-32, 49, 75
        Endangered Species Act, 73-74, 82
        executive orders, 84
        Fish and Wildlife Coordination Act, **3**, 37, 82-83
        Food Security Act of 1985, 83
        National Environmental Policy Act, 59-60, 72-73, 81-82
        National Historic Preservation Act, 49, 70, 74
    general permit process, 49-50, 53, 66-72, 124-126
        compared to advanced identification and special area management plan, 129
        state and regional general permits, 71, 125-126
    individual permit process, 49-**50**, 52, 53-66, 124-125
        application requirements, 53-55
        compared to nationwide permit process, 67, 69, 126
        NEPA compliance required for, 72-73
        public notice requirements, 55-56
    judicial review of, 75-76
    jurisdictional determination, 51
    nationwide permit (NWP) process, 49, **51**, 52, 66-72, **93**
        activities covered under, 67
        compared to individual permit process, 67, 69, 126
        permit types and numbers, **68**
        predischarge notification (PDN) requirements, 67, 69-71
        specific conditions allowed for, 67-68
    NEPA compliance requirements, 59-60
        environmental assessment (EA) preparation, 59
        environmental impact statement (EIS) preparation, 59
        finding of no significant impact (FONSI) preparation, 59
    permit application fees, 54
    permit denial is taking of private property, **86-87**
    pre-application meeting, 52

Department of Army permit process *(continued)*
    public interest review, 60
    Section 404(b)(1) guidelines compliance requirements, 56-59
    substantive standards for Corps decision, 56
    takings consideration, 35, 84-88
    See also permit process; U.S. Army Corps of Engineers
Department of Fish and Game (DFG)
    authority of for wetland regulation, 2, **3**, 19, 92-95, 108
    Corps inter-agency consultation with, 59, 83
    jurisdiction of, compared to Corps, 92-93
    pre-application consultation with, 52
    relation of to CEQA, 97
    role of in mitigation banking, 134
    role of in Sacramento-San Joaquin wetlands mitigation banking, 134-135
    stream and lake regulation by, 29-31, 71
    See also California Fish and Game Code; U.S. Fish and Wildlife Service
desert arroyos
    Clean Water Act protection for, 21
    Corps jurisdiction for, 42
desert ephemeral drainage, as waters of the United States, **73**
desert playa wetland, 11
    Clean Water Act protection for, 21
design approach for mitigation, 113-116, **114**
    See also mitigation
development
    coastal, **3**, **121**
        Coastal Commission regulation of, **3**
    infeasibility of on wetland project site, **102**
    local agency regulation of, **99**
    nationwide permit importance for, 67
    special area management plan for, 128
    urban,
        affecting wetland credit, 134, 135
        contributing to wetland loss, 16, 17, 18, **96**, 127, 130
        EPA veto of Corps permit for, 66
    of wetland, with cross-section, 7-**8**
    See also project proponent; projects
DFG. *See* Department of Fish and Game
dikes
    in CAD-based Wetland Delineation, 25
    Corps permit required for, 36
    effect of on navigable waters, 29
    See also impoundment of water
discharge activity area, defined, 52-53
discharge of any material
    Clean Water Act definition for, 45-46
    as 'continuing violation', 77
    Corps permit required for, 45-48
    examples of regulated activities as, 47
    liability for, 77
    permit application requirements for, 54
    'possible future disposal sites' for, 125
    Section 404(b)(1) guidelines regulation of, 58
    See also Department of Army permit process; fill material
discharge of 'any refuse matter of any kind' into navigable waters
    Corps permit required for, 36, 39
    See also Department of Army permit process; dredged material; pollution
disposal sites
    EPA identification of, 124-125
    See also dredged material

ditches
    artificial, connecting wetlands to U.S.
        waters, 42
    drainage ditches, 21, 48
    excluded from Clean Water Act
        regulation, 21
    impact of on wetland, 18
    irrigation ditches, 21, 30, 48
    as streams, 30
    See also specific ditch types
docks, Corps permit required for, 36
dolphins, Corps permit required for, **43**
downingias
    as vernal pool plant, 12
    See also vegetation; vernal pools
downstream resources
    findings required for effect of fill on, 58
    See also filling; streams
drainage ditches
    excluded from Clean Water Act regula-
        tion, 21
    exempt from Section 404 requirements, 48
    See also ditches
drainage of wetland soils, 7
    See also ditches; soil saturation
dredged material
    in CAD-based Wetland Delineation, **25**
    Clean Water Act definition of, 46
    Clean Water Act regulation of, 19-20, 105
    Corps permit required for, 35, 36, 38, 39,
        43, 44-45, 49-65
    Corps regulation of, **3**, 21-22, **27**
    EPA authority for veto of Corps permit
        for, 39
    EPA determination of sites for, 124-125
    permit requirements for, 54
    suction dredging, 71
    See also discharge of any material; fill
        material
drinking water. *See* water supplies

E

EA. *See* environmental assessment
educational values, as mitigation goal, 110
endangered species
    activities affecting require CEQA
        review, 97
    activities affecting require individual
        permit, 69
    See also migratory birds; wildlife
Endangered Species Act
    authority of for wetland regulation, **3**, 49,
        58, 62-63, 70, 73-74, 82
    biological opinion's reasonable and
        prudent alternatives (RPAs), 73-74
    See also animals; plants
enforcement. *See* Department of Army permit
        process; violations of Clean Water Act
enhancement of wetland
    as compensatory mitigation, 106, 112
    with mitigation banking, 129, 130
    See also mitigation; wetland
environmental assessment (EA)
    preparation of in Corps permit process,
        59, 72, 101
    See also biological assessment
environmental impact report (EIR)
    concurrent preparation of with EIS, 59, 73
    See also California Environmental
        Quality Act
environmental impact statement (EIS)
    identifying wetland boundaries for, **26**

environmental impact statement *(continued)*
    issuance of in Corps permit process, 59,
        72, 73, 101
    See also National Environmental Policy
        Act
Environmental Protection Agency (EPA)
    assistance of to other public agencies, 124
    authority of for wetland regulation, **3**
    enforcement authority, 75, 76-80
        civil and criminal actions, 77-80
        liability under, 77
    isolated wetland authority of, **45**
    memorandum of agreement (MOA) with
        other federal agencies, 52-53, 60-61, 77
    1993 Comprehensive Conservation and
        Management Plan for San Francisco
        Bay and Delta, 123
    permit review and veto authority of, 61-66
    pre-application consultation with, 52
    Region 9 guidance of, on mitigation
        banking, 132-133
    relation of with Corps permit process, 38,
        39, 52-53, 60-61, 70-71
    role of in mitigation banking, 132-133
    role of in special aquatic sites determina-
        tion, 28
    role of in wetland regulation, 35-37, 38,
        48, 49
    Section 404 authority transferred to states
        by, 49, **91**
    Section 404(b)(1) guidelines, 39, 56-59,
        74-75, 124
    Section 404(c) veto authority over Corps
        permits, 39, 61-66, **64-65**
    See also California Environmental
        Protection Agency
environmental review
    lead agency determination for, 72-73
    See also California Environmental Quality
        Act; Environmental Protection Agency
EPA. *See* Environmental Protection Agency
erosion, 2, 18, 116
    activities contributing to require
        individual permit, 69
    Conservation Reserve Program for
        reducing, 83
    See also discharge of any material
estuaries
    California Coastal Commission regulation
        of, 33
    deltas, 27
    identification of in coastal zone, 34
    National Estuaries Program, 123
    300 foot buffer required for, 33
    See also bays; rivers
evaporation
    affecting vernal pools, 12
    affecting wetland water loss, 8
    See also percolation
excavation
    impact of on wetland, 18
    See also discharge of any material;
        dredged material; land clearing
'excavation rule'
    for clarifying dredged and fill material,
        46-47
    See also dredged material; fill material
executive orders
    for protecting wetland, 84, 90, 123
    See also federal wetland regulation;
        state wetland regulation
experts
    for mitigation, 112, 113, 116

experts *(continued)*
    for mitigation banks, 131
    in restoration project process, **107**
    retention of by project proponents, 100

F

fairy shrimp
    in vernal pools, 62-63
    See also endangered species
farming activities
    nonestablished, as 'discharge of
        material', 47
    normal, exempt from Section 404
        requirements, 48
    pollution reduction assistance for, 83
    See also agricultural land; grazing;
        ranching
farm ponds
    Clean Water Act regulation of, 21
    exempt from Section 404 requirements, 48
    See also agricultural land; ponds
farm roads
    construction of exempt from Section 404
        requirements, 48
    See also bridges; road crossings
Federal Water Pollution Control Act, 35
    See also Clean Water Act; federal wetland
        regulation
federal wetland regulation, 1, 4, 19, 35-88
    advance planning and cooperative
        programs policies, 123-124
    history of, 36-37, 39-40
    mitigation banking for, 131-134
    other federal regulatory authority for, 80-84
    in partnership with state, 124-129
    related to Corps permit issuance, 72-75
    See also Clean Water Act; state wetland
        regulation
fens, California Coastal Act regulation of, 32
fertilizers
    wetland contamination by, 18
    See also agricultural land; pollution
filling of wetland
    findings required for impact of, 58
    impact of, 18, **27**
    imprisonment of property owner for, **78-79**
    See also discharge of any material; fill
        material
fill material
    Clean Water Act definition of, 46
    Clean Water Act regulation of, 19-20, 105
    Corps permit required for, 35, 36, 38, 39,
        43, 44-45, 49-65
    Corps regulation of, **3**, 22
    EPA determination of sites for, 124-125
    EPA veto authority of permits for, **64-65**
    permit requirements for, 54
    removal of required without permit, 53-54,
        78-79
    See also discharge of any material;
        dredged material; filling of wetland
finding of no significant impact (FONSI),
    preparation of in Corps permit
    process, 59, 72
findings
    permit process requirements for, 56, 58,
        65
    See also Department of Army permit
        process
fish
    CEQA protections for, 97
    Clean Water Act protections for, 20

integrated approach (continued)
    See also Department of Army permit
        process; planning
integrated method
    for identifying wetland resources, 33-34
    See also identification methods
interstate or foreign commerce
    Corps relation to, 41-43, 44
    upon navigable waters, 29, 37
    See also navigable waters
interstate or foreign commerce clause
    as derivation of federal regulatory
        authority, 39-41
    relation of with 'navigable waters', 40-41
    See also Rivers and Harbors Act
iron, presence of in hydric soils, 9
irrigation ditches
    excluded from Clean Water Act regula-
        tion, 21
    exempt from Section 404 requirements, 48
    as streams, 30
    See also ditches
'isolated waters'
    defined, 71
    See also wetland, isolated
Italian ryegrass
    as wetland facultative species, 9
    See also vegetation

J

jetties, Corps permit required for, **43**
judicial review, of Corps and EPA
    administrative actions, 75-76
jurisdictional boundaries, of Clean Water Act
    Section 404, 39-44
jurisdictional limits determination
    challenges to, 75
    Corps and CCC differences for, 32-33
    in Corps permit process, 51
    for DFG stream and lake regulation, 30-31
    and takings consideration, 84-88
    between wetland and 'other waters of the
        United States', 24
    for wetlands and other waters, 19-34, **121**
    See also boundaries
jurisdictional wetland, expert help required
    for determination of, 24

L

lakes
    Clean Water Act protections for, 19-20,
        21
    compared to wetland ecosystem, 7-**8**
    Dept. of Fish and Game regulation of, **3**,
        29-31, 92
    federal authority for regulating, 39
    isolated, Corps regulation of, 42
    as navigable waters, 29
    playa lakes, 20
    recreational, Corps regulation of wetland
        adjoining, 42
    tule lakes, 16
    See also rivers; streams
Lake Tahoe basin, 89, 126
    See also Tahoe Regional Planning Agency
land clearing
    consideration of as 'discharge' activity,
        46-47
    consideration of in restoration and mitiga-
        tion, 113, 116
    See also dredged material; excavation

land leveling, as 'discharge of material', 47
landowner. See property owner
land use issues
    consideration for when jurisdictions
        overlap, **121**
    consideration of in mitigation site
        analysis, 113
    See also mitigation
lead agency
    determining for federal multi-agency
        permit review, 72-73
    determining for state and federal
        multi-agency review, 75
    See also state wetland regulation
levees
    effect of on navigable waters, 29
    effect of on wetland, 18, **27**
    See also impoundment of water
liability
    test for under Clean Water Act, 77
    See also Department of Army permit
        process
local agencies
    Dept. of Fish and Game regulation of, 92
    grants to for coastal restoration projects, 96
    request for advanced identification by,
        125
    wetland regulation by, 2-4, **99**-100, 102,
        112, 124
    See also regional agencies; state wetland
        regulation
local coastal programs (LCPs)
    preparation requirements, 75, 95
    See also California Coastal Act
local government
    regulation of wetland by, 1
    See also regional agencies; state wetland
        regulation

M

McAteer-Petris Act of 1965, **3**, 98
maintenance or reconstruction of structures
    exempt from Section 404 requirements, 48
    See also specific structures
manganese, presence of in hydric soils, 9
mangrove forest
    Corps regulation of, 42, **86-87**
    See also riparian forest; tidal waters
manzanita
    as upland species, 10
    See also upland habitat; vegetation
maps
    constraints map for mitigation, 114
    for delineation of wetland, **26**, 33-34,
        100-101
    for determination of historically navigable
        waters, 29
    geological survey and other topographic
        maps, 29
    in restoration project process, **107**
    See also boundaries of wetland
Marin county, exclusion of from Corps-SCS
    agreements, 24-25
marine sanctuaries
    protections for under Section 404(b)(1)
        guidelines, 58
    as special aquatic sites, 28-29
    See also aquatic resources of national
        importance; special aquatic sites
'market entry test', 64
marketing appeal, as basis for 'no practical
    alternatives', 57

marshes
    as adjacent wetland, 41-42
    bogs, 12, 21
    brackish, 17, 32
    California Coastal Act regulation of, 32
    cattail, 16, **19**
    salt marsh, 16-17, **24**, 32
        coastal, **12**, 29, **33**
        tidal, **11**, **12**, 29
    seasonal freshwater, **4**, 11, 12
    tidal freshwater, 11
    tule marsh, 11, 16
    wet meadows, 20, **25**, 39, **55**
    See also specific marsh types
Maryland Nontidal Wetlands Protection Act, **91**
meadowfoam
    as vernal pool plant, 12
    See also vegetation; vernal pools
mean high tide line
    for determining navigable waters limits, 29
    See also high water mark; tidal waters
Mediterranean barley
    as wetland facultative species, 10
    See also vegetation
memorandum of agreement (MOA), between
    Corps, EPA, NMFS, USFWS, 52-53,
    60-61
memorandum of understanding (MOU),
    between Dept. of Fish and Game, and
    public agencies, 95
metals
    heavy metals contamination of wetland, 18
    presence of in hydric soils, 9
    See also pollution; toxics
microbial activity, reduction of in hydric
    soils, 8-9
migratory birds
    CEQA protections for, 97
    Corps protection of habitat for, 43
    EPA and USFWS protection of wetland
        for, 62-63
    test for, in relation to isolated wetland,
        44-45
    use of wetlands by, 16-17, **20**
    Wetlands Reserve Program for habitat
        restoration of, 83
    See also animals; Pacific Flyway; wildlife
minerals
    in wetland waters, 9
    See also metals
mining operations
    contamination of wetland by, 18
    Dept. of Fish and Game regulation of, 93
    exclusion of from Clean Water Act
        regulation, 21
    gravel mining, 93
    See also discharge of any material
mining roads
    construction of exempt from Section 404
        requirements, 48
    See also bridges; road crossings
mitigation
    boundary determination for, **26**
    compensatory, 106, 108, 130, 132-133,
        134
    goals for, 110, 113, 114, 117, 119
    Habitat Mitigation and Monitoring
        Proposal Guidelines, San Francisco
        District Corps of Engineers, **109**
    insufficient to prevent permit denial if
        'significant degradation' exists, 58,
        64-65
    for losses of wetland, 4-5

mitigation (continued)
for mining operations, 21
onsite v. offsite, 108, 132-133, 134
permit conditions may be required for, 59
planning and implementation, 105-137
compensatory wetland mitigation
methods, 106
construction for, **116-117**
design approach for, 113-116, **114**
failure of, 121-122
key concepts for, 106
maintenance of mitigated areas,
117-118
monitoring and performance
standards, **118**-121
multipurpose objectives, 110-112
opportunities and constraints
evaluation, 113
regulatory objectives, 107-110
remediation for, 120-121
site analysis, 112-113
priority assessment for, 53, 72, 81, 112, 122
proposing in permit application, 54-55,
101
proposing in pre-application meeting, 52
replacement ratio determination, 108-110,
129-130
required for riparian habitats, 97
required under special area management
plan, 128
See also adverse impacts; alternatives;
mitigation plan
mitigation banking
benefits of, 130-131
credit systems for, 135-137
described, 129-130
federal policies for, 131-134
financial assurances and contingency
plans for, 137
regional and planning concerns recognized
by, 92, 100, 105
for regulating wetland impacts outside
project area, 5
role of Corps in, 131-132
role of DFG in, 134-136
role of EPA in, 132-133
role of USFWS in, 133-134
use of in Central Valley project, 90
wetland credit system, 135-137
See also mitigation; mitigation plan
mitigation plan
key concepts for, 106
required by Dept. of Fish and Game, **93**
requirements for, 58-59, 117
See also mitigation; planning
Modoc Plateau, wetland remaining in, 17
monitoring program, 106
ecological parameters for evaluation of,
120
Habitat Mitigation and Monitoring
Proposal Guidelines, San Francisco
District Corps of Engineers, **109**
and mitigation performance standards,
118-121
project proponent responsibility for,
117-118
in restoration project process, **107**
See also mitigation; mitigation banking;
restoration of wetland
Mono County, special area management plans
for, 128
Monterey County, vernal pools in, **7**
mosquito and vector control, 112, 116

MOU. *See* memorandum of understanding
Moyle and Ellison system of wetland
classification, 12
muck
organic material in, 8-9
See also biological component; peat; soil
mudflats
California Coastal Act regulation of, 32
Clean Water Act regulation of, 20
Corps regulation of, 32
federal authority for regulating, 39
as 'special aquatic sites', 28, **53**, 56-57
tidal, **53**
See also special aquatic sites; tidal waters
municipal water supplies
EPA authority for protecting, 39
See also groundwater; water quality;
water supplies

N

Napa county, exclusion of from Corps-SCS
agreements, 24-25
National Environmental Policy Act (NEPA)
authority of for wetland regulation, **3**, 48,
49, 53, 56, 101, 104, 108, 110
Corps authority expansion under, 37
Corps permit process compliance with
required, 59-60, 72-73, 81
National Estuaries Program, 123
See also estuaries
National Historic Preservation Act
authority of for wetland regulation, 49,
70, 74
See also National Register of Historic
Places
National Marine Fisheries Service (NMFS)
authority of for wetland regulation, **3**
endangered species protection by, 73-74
pre-application consultation with, 52
relation of with Corps permit process,
60-61, 70-71, 73, 82-83
National Pollution Discharge Elimination
System (NPDES)
permit authority under, 38, 81
See also pollution
National Register of Historic Places
activities affecting listed properties
require individual permit, 69, 74
See also National Historic Preservation Act
National Resources Defense Council
(NRDC), challenges of to Section 404
limitations, 40, 43
nationwide permits (NWP). *See* Department
of Army permit process, nationwide
permits
Natural Resources Conservation Service
(NRCS)
responsibility of for agricultural lands, 24
'Swampbuster' program of, 43, 83
See also agricultural land
navigable waters
Corps authority for regulation of, **3**, 36-37,
38, 40, 41
defined, 29, 37
historically navigable waters, 29
integrated method for identifying, 33-34
relation of with interstate or foreign
commerce clause, 40-44
wetlands adjoining considered as 'waters
of the United States', 41
See also Rivers and Harbors Act; 'waters
of the United States'

navigation
activities affecting require individual
permit, 69
consideration of on public trust lands, 96
navigational aids, NWP allowed for
placement of, 67, **68**
NEPA. *See* National Environmental Policy
Act
1993 Comprehensive Conservation and
Management Plan for San Francisco
Bay and Delta, 123
nitrogen, presence of in hydric soils, 9
NPDES. *See* National Pollution Discharge
Elimination System
NRDC. *See* National Resources Defense
Council
nutrients
in wetland substrates, 11
in wetland waters, 11
NWP. *See* Department of Army permit
process, nationwide permits

O

oak
coast live oak, 10
planting detail, **117**
See also upland habitat; vegetation
oceans
Clean Water Act protections for, 19-20, 21
as navigable waters, 29
territorial seas, 20, 26
oil drilling
contamination of wetland from, 18
See also pollution; toxics
open space
provided by wetland, 2
See also recreational values
open water habitat. *See* deep water habitat
'other waters of the United States', 24
boundaries determination for, 26-28, **27**
inclusion of in 'waters of the United
States', 39
See also 'waters of the United States'
outfall structures, NWP allowed for, 67, **68**
overhead wire crossings
Corps permit may not be required for, 47
Corps permit required for, **43**
overland flow of water, 7, 96
oxygen
absence of in wetland soils, 8-9
adaptations for by wetland plants, 9-10

P

Pacific Flyway, over Central Valley
wetlands, 16
peat
organic material in, 8-9
See also hydric soils; muck
people. *See* citizens; property owner; project
proponent
percolation
affecting wetland maintenance, 10, 113
affecting wetland water loss, 8
See also hydrology of wetland; soil
saturation
performance standards
establishing for mitigation, **118**-121
See also mitigation; monitoring program
permit applicants. *See* project proponent
permit process
Corps authority for, 35-37, 38-39

permit process (continued)
  Department of Army (DA) permit require-
    ments, 49-65
  diagram of example activities requiring, **43**
  exemptions under, 47-48
  integrated approach to, in California,
    100-104
  mitigation banking for expedition of, 130
  permit strategy plan recommended for
    project proponent, 102-104
  for regulation of wetland activities, 3-4
  of San Francisco Bay Conservation and
    Development Commission, 98
  Section 404 individual permit process
    flow chart, **50**
  streamlining for, 5
  See also Clean Water Act; Department
    of Army permit process
permits
  general, activities covered under, 49-**50**
  individual, activities covered under, 49-**50**
  nationwide, 49, **51**
  See also Department of Army permit
    process
'person'
  defined by Clean Water Act, 77
  See also Department of Army permit
    process
pesticides
  wetland contamination by, 18
  See also agricultural land; pollution;
    toxics
photographic documentation
  for mitigation monitoring, **118**, 120
  See also mitigation
pickleweed
  as tidal salt marsh plant, 11
  See also hydrophytes; vegetation
piers
  Corps permit may not be required for, 47
  Corps permit required for, 36, **43**
pilings
  construction of requiring Corps permit, 47
  effect of on wetland, **72**
Placer County Draft 1994 General Plan
  Wetlands Goals and Policies, **103**
planning
  advanced wetland and watershed plan-
    ning, 122-124
  for minimal disturbance to wetland,
    100-101
  for monitoring program, 119-120
  regional, 5, 90
  special area management plan (SAMP),
    124, 126-128
  for wetland mitigation, 105-137
  for wetland regulation, 5, 90, 95, 99
  See also development; mitigation plan;
    projects
plants
  actions of in saturated soils, 8
  decomposition of in hydric soils, 8-9
  non-native, impact of on wetland, 18
  in tidal salt marsh, 11
  in vernal pools, 12
  as wetland indicator, 10
  wetland plants (hydrophytes), **9-10**
  See also Endangered Species Act;
    hydrophytes; vegetation
playa lakes, federal authority for regulating, 39
plowing
  impact of on wetland, 18
  See also agricultural land; farming

politics, impact of on wetland protection, 1
polluters
  Corps and EPA authority for prosecuting, 38
  See also violations of Clean Water Act
pollution
  Clean Water Act definition for, 45-46
  Corps permit required for discharge of,
    45-48, 81
  Corps regulation of discharges of, 37
  EPA regulation of discharges of, 38
  federal assistance to farmers who mini-
    mize, 83
  findings required for creation of, 58
  impacts of on wetland, 18
  removal of by wetland, 2
  See also discharge of any material;
    National Pollution Discharge
    Elimination System; toxics
ponderosa pine, as upland species, 10
ponding, effect of on soil saturation, 7-8
ponds
  Clean Water Act protections for, 19-20, 21
  compared to wetland ecosystem, 7-**8**
  farm ponds, 21
  natural, federal authority for regulating, 39
  treatment ponds for wastewater systems, 21
  See also impoundment of water
pondweed
  as wetland obligate species, 9
  See also hydrophytes
popcorn flowers, as vernal pool indicator, 12
Porter-Cologne Act, 99
'possible future disposal sites'
  identification of, 125
  See also discharge of any material;
    dredged material
power line towers
  Corps permit may not be required for, 47
  Corps permit required for, **43**
  See also bridges; hydroelectric power
    project; road crossings
prairie potholes
  Clean Water Act regulation of, 20
  federal authority for regulating, 39
  See also seeps; vernal pools
precipitation
  regulation of farm ponds fed by, 21
  role of in vernal pools, 12
  role of in wetland maintenance, 7, 10, 119
prickly lettuce
  as wetland facultative species, 9-10
  See also plants
private property
  adjoining project site, notification required
    for, 55
  consideration of for project alternatives, 57
  considered as open to public, 85
  Corps regulation of federal dam release
    flooding on, 42
  federal authority over, 39
  permit denial as taking of, **86-87**
  respect for in California Wetlands
    Conservation Policy, 90
  takings claims for regulation of, 35, 84-88
  See also property owner; takings
project proponent
  alternatives assessment required from,
    52-53
  benefits to of mitigation banking, 130-131
  integrated permitting approach for, 100-104
  inventory of regulatory requirements
    recommended for, 101-102
  NEPA review obligations for, 73

project proponent (continued)
  'no practical alternatives' requirements
    for, 57
  objectives of considered in alternatives
    assessment, 57, 101, **121**
  other agency obligations for, 74, 75,
    80-81, 89
  permit strategy plan recommended for,
    102-104
  pre-application meetings encouraged
    for, 52
  public comments transmitted to, 56
  required to provide project information,
    56, 70-71, 72
  responsibility of for mitigation
    maintenance, 117-118
  streambed alteration notification required
    by, 93-94
  See also property owner
projects
  Corps permits required for, 35-37
  description of required for permit
    application, 54
  federal, exempt from Clean Water Act
    regulation, 48
  'joined', permit process for, 60
  methods for increasing effectiveness of, 5
  mitigation planning and implementation
    for, 105-137
  presumption of alternatives for, 56-57, **65**
  proper sequence of mitigation priority
    for, 53
  restoration project process, **107**
  water-dependent, 57, 95-96
  See also Department of Army permit
    requirements; development; permit
    process
property owner
  benefits to of mitigation banking, 131
  cooperation with for wetland restoration,
    92, 122-123, 128
  imprisonment of for filling wetland, **78-79**
  integrated permitting approach for,
    100-104
  liability of for unpermitted discharge, 77
  See also private property; project proponent
Proposal on Protection of U.S. Wetlands, 131
public
  involvement of in wetland protection, 4
  See also citizens
public access, California Coastal Act
    requirements for, 96
public agencies, memorandum of
    understanding with Department
    of Fish and Game, 95
public hearings, Corps determination for
    following public notice, 55-56
public interest review standards
  of Corps permit process, 37, 53, 56
  factors considered within, 60
  of National Environmental Policy Act, 82
  presumption of, against discharge into
    'important' wetlands, 60
  See also citizens; comments
public notice
  allowance for in permit process, 38, 53
  for impacts covered under National
    Historic Preservation Act, 74
  individual Corps permit requirements for,
    55-56
  See also comments; public hearings
Public Trust Doctrine, as authority for wet-
    land protection, **3**

vernal pools
    activities affecting, 18
    as 'aquatic resources of national
        importance', **62-63**
    in CAD-based Wetland Delineation, **25**
    in Central Valley grasslands, 16
    Clean Water Act protection for, 21
    creation of, **131**, 135
    disturbance to by construction equipment, **1**
    duration of water retention in, 11
    in early spring, **7**
    as herbaceous wetland habitat, 12
    local agency protection for, **99**
    out-of-kind mitigation considered for, 108
    plants and soils of, 12
    as seasonal wetland, 12
    See also aquatic resources of national
        importance; prairie potholes
violations of Clean Water Act, 75-80
    civil and criminal actions for, 77-80
    Class I and Class II administrative
        penalties, 77-78
    Corps and EPA authority for enforcing,
        76-77
    judicial review for, 75-76
    liability for, 77
    See also Clean Water Act; Department
        of Army permit process

W

waste discharge
    agency regulation of, **3**
    See also discharge of any material;
        pollution
wastewater discharge
    design of to minimize wetland impacts, **101**
    as violation of Clean Water Act, 81
    See also discharge of any material;
        pollution
wastewater systems, excluded from Clean
    Water Act regulation, 21
water
    characteristics of in wetland, 11
    derivation of in wetland, 7-8
    loss of in wetland, 8
    overland flow of, 7, 96
    permanent or seasonal, in wetland
        definition, 1, 7
    in saturated soils, 8-9
water-associated habitat, extending beyond
    wetland, 2
water bodies
    artificial or disturbed,
        Clean Water Act regulation of, 21, 23
        compensatory mitigation for, 106
    changes to bottom elevation of as
        'discharge of material', 47
    extending beyond wetland, 2
water bottom. *See* bottom contours; bottom
    elevations
water circulation, findings required for effect
    of fill to, 58
water-dependent projects
    as basis for 'no practical alternative', 57
    California Coastal Act regulation
        of, 95-96
    See also development; projects
water diversions, contributing to wetland loss,
    17-18
water flow, findings required for effect of fill
    on, 58
waterfowl. *See* migratory birds

water levels, in wetland, compared to deep
    water, 7
water plantain, as wetland obligate species, 9
water plants. *See* hydrophytes; vegetation
water quality, 10-11
    certification of under nationwide permit,
        70
    consideration of in restoration and
        mitigation, **107**, 113, 115, 123
    improvement of by wetland, 2
    protection of as mitigation goal, 110
    restrictions on discharges affecting, 58,
        74-75
    Section 401 water quality certification, 102
    See also groundwater; water supplies
waters, jurisdictional limits determination for,
    19-34
watershed
    nationwide permit allowed for protection
        of, **68**
    reductions in size of impacting wetland, 18
watershed planning
    advanced, 122-124
    for wetland regulation, 5, 105
    See also mitigation plan; planning
'waters of the United States'
    adjacent wetland included within, 41-42
    Clean Water Act regulation of, 19-**20**, 40
    Corps regulation of, **3**, 36-37
    definition development of through courts,
        40-41
    impairment to flow, circulation, or reach
        of requiring Corps permit, 48
    including 'other waters', 39
    jurisdictional limits of, 39-44
    navigable waters within boundaries of, 29
    special aquatic sites determination within,
        28-29
    tidelands inclusion within, 41
    wetland included in definition of, 41
    See also Clean Water Act; U.S. Army
        Corps of Engineers
water sources
    affecting wetland type, 11
    for wetland maintenance, 7-8
water supplies
    EPA veto authority for Corps permits
        affecting, 61-66
    EPA veto authority of Corps permits
        for, **65**
    municipal water supply protection by
        EPA, 39
    recharge of by wetland, 2
    See also groundwater; reservoirs; water
        quality
water table
    identification of in CCC wetland
        definition, 32
    in riparian forest, 11
    in wetland, 7, 10
    See also groundwater; hydric soils; soil
        saturation
weed control, consideration of in mitigation
    monitoring, 120
weed mat
    typical installation for, **119**
    See also restoration of wetland
wetland
    activities affecting, 17-18
    and adjacent marshes, 41-42
    'adjacent wetland' and isolated
        wetland, 43
    adjacent to riparian areas, 31

wetland *(continued)*
    artificial,
        Clean Water Act regulation of, 21
        Corps jurisdiction over, 42
        not allowed as mitigation, **64-65**
        with water control structure, **89**
    avoiding disturbance to, **48**, **101**, 105, 115
    biological components of, 2, **4**, 8-9, 30,
        58, 114
    in California,
        losses of, 1, 7, 12-17
        varieties of, 10-12
    characteristic plants of, 9-10
    classification systems for, **10**, 12
    Clean Water Act definition for, 21-22
    Clean Water Act protection for, 19-21
    coastal/freshwater, **27**
    connected to United States waters by
        artificial ditches, Corps jurisdiction
        over, 42
    creation of as compensatory mitigation,
        106
    defined, 1-2, 21-22
        under California Coastal Act, 32
        under California Code of
        Regulations, 32
        when 'above the headwaters', 71
    development and cross-section of, 7-**8**
    enhancement of as compensatory
        mitigation, 106
    farmed,
        Clean Water Act regulation of, 21
        not subject to Clean Water Act, 43-44
    federal authority for regulating, 39
    function and value assessment, 110, 125
    high and low value, 128, 133
    'important' wetland, 60
    isolated,
        consolidation of with mitigation
        banking, 130-131
        Corps regulation of, 42, 43
        migratory bird test for, **43-44**
        nationwide permits allowed for filling
        of, 67, **68**
    jurisdictional limits determination for,
        19-34
    mitigation for loss of, 4-5
    regulation of, 2-4, **3**, 5
    relation of to interstate commerce and
        foreign commerce, 41-43
    restoration of as compensatory
        mitigation, 106
    seasonal, 16, **62-63**, **72**
        in CAD-based Wetland Delineation, **25**
        compared to perennial (permanent), 12
    as special aquatic sites, 28-29
    specific indicators for, 1
    value of, 2
    in 'waters of the United States'
        definition, 41
    within navigable waters, 29
    See also hydrology of wetland; mitigation;
        wetland ecosystem
wetland credits. *See* mitigation banking
wetland ecology, 7-18
wetland ecosystem
    activities affecting, 18
    CEQA protections for, 97
    classification systems for, 12
    defined, 106
    Endangered Species Act protection for, 82
    findings required for effect of fill on, 58
    as model for mitigation, 112, 119

Photography Credits

Cover: Louisa Squires
Pages 1, 4, 12, 35, 37, 39, 48, 55, 72, 139, 140: Paul Cylinder
Pages 7, 19, 31, 41, 61, 82, 96: David Magney
Pages 15, 46, 53: Louisa Squires
Page 29: Lise McNaughton
Page 33: Debra Percy
Page 73: Stephanie Myers
Pages 89, 105, 113, 115, 123, 131: Greg Sutter

California Water

By Arthur L. Littleworth and Eric L. Garner

This is the first handbook since Wells Hutchins' 1956 'bible', *California Law of Water Rights*, to serve as a comprehensive reference guide to the historical, legal, and policy issues affecting the use of water in California. This book serves as a major resource for elected officials, water district managers, board members, engineers, and planners, as well as lawyers, judges, developers, and environmentalists.

The authors have prepared in an easy-to-read style thorough and interesting responses to such questions as: Where does our water come from? How much water does California have? Are we really a water-short state? How is our water used? How much water do we need? What are the dramatic changes in federal and state water laws that have occurred in the last decade? What are the critical issues that environmental, urban, and agricultural interests must address to reconcile their competing demands for water?

This book not only reviews the historic and traditional principles of conferring water rights through age-old court decisions, but also considers the effects on decision-making processes posed by the Endangered Species Act, the Clean Water Act, the public trust doctrine, the Bay-Delta proceedings, litigation, water transfers, water conservation, and newly developing water management programs.

The authors address the evolution of law and policy affecting the state's great aqueduct systems, including San Francisco's Hetch Hetchy, Los Angeles' Owens Valley, the Mokelumne River aqueduct of the East Bay Municipal Utility District, the Colorado River aqueduct of The Metropolitan Water District of Southern California, the federal government's Central Valley Project, and the State Water Project.

California Water • Paperback, 384 pages, $47.50
plus California sales tax and $3 for shipping
• ISBN 0-923956-25-5

Guide to CEQA and California Land Use and Planning Law on CD-ROM disk

Indispensable research tools for any lawyer, land use planner, or environmental planner

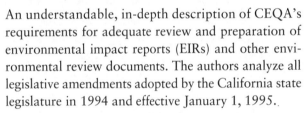

NOW ON CD-ROM—

Guide to the California Environmental Quality Act (CEQA), 1994 Edition and the 1995 Supplement, fully integrated, by Michael H. Remy, Tina A. Thomas, and James G. Moose

An understandable, in-depth description of CEQA's requirements for adequate review and preparation of environmental impact reports (EIRs) and other environmental review documents. The authors analyze all legislative amendments adopted by the California state legislature in 1994 and effective January 1, 1995.

Included in one complete package are—

■ The entire text of the 1994 Edition of the book and the 1995 Supplement

■ Expert commentary on statutory and case law

■ A complete set of case summaries

■ The entire text of the 1995 CEQA Statutes

■ The entire text of the CEQA Guidelines, including 1994 amendments

NOW ON CD-ROM—

Curtin's *California Land Use and Planning Law*, 1995 Edition—by Daniel J. Curtin, Jr. (includes extensive commentary on the Subdivision Map Act)

Featuring selected case summaries of important judicial decisions from *California Planning & Development Report (CP&DR)*, William Fulton, publisher

This well known, definitive summary of the major provisions of land use and planning law that apply to California cities and counties has been cited by the California courts as an authoritative source. In this edition the author sets forth the basic code sections and summarizes relevant opinions of the courts in clear language useful to planners, attorneys, developers, local legislators, environmental activists, and students. Included in one complete package are—

- Expert commentary on statutory and case law, including a thorough analysis of the *Dolan* case and other 1994 case opinions and statutory amendments

- The entire text of the 1995 Planning and Zoning Law, including the Subdivision Map Act

- The entire text of relevant U.S. Code and California Fish and Game Code sections

- Selected case summaries from *CP&DR*

BOTH CD-ROM EDITIONS INCLUDE THE FOLLOWING FEATURES—

- Hypertext 'jump links' providing instantaneous access to, and electronic cross-references between, the authors' commentary, case summaries, the statutes, and footnotes; *Guide to CEQA* version also links commentary and statutes to CEQA Guidelines

- Super indexing functions offering immediate access to the entire book via electronic search and query capabilities, allowing the user to either key in words, phrases, or specific citations or 'browse' the Table of Contents, Table of Authorities, or any one of several indexes for selective categories

- 'Bookmarking' placeholders permitting the user to mark points of interest throughout the text, which can then be referred back to with the click of a button

- 'User Notes' for adding personalized comments in the margins adjacent to relevant text—clicking on 'notes' icon retrieves comments instantly for editing or copying

- Export functions allowing the user to copy words, sentences, paragraphs, and whole sections from the CD-ROM file and 'paste' them into briefs, reports, or analyses

- Cross-platform functionality providing access to this entire information database on DOS, Windows, and Macintosh systems

- Network or multi-user options

Guide to CEQA CD-ROM disk, 1995 • $224 • ISBN 0-923956-40-9

California Land Use and Planning Law CD-ROM disk, 1995 • $190 • ISBN 0-923956-41-7

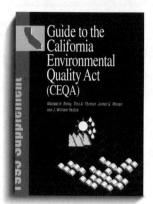

1995 Supplement to 1994 Edition of Guide to CEQA

By Michael H. Remy, Tina A. Thomas, and James G. Moose

In this NEW SUPPLEMENT, the authors analyze all statutory amendments approved in 1994 by the California state legislature and all revisions to the CEQA Guidelines approved in 1994 by the California Resources Agency. These new provisions—

- Clarify the rules governing the preparation of alternatives analyses within environmental impact reports

- Revise the definition of 'projects' subject to CEQA

- Modify the rules governing the use of subsequent EIRs, supplemental EIRs, and addenda

- Allow agencies, in some circumstances, to modify mitigation measures for negative declarations after the completion of public review

- Revise the form of the standard initial study and clarify the rules governing the use of initial studies both to support the use of negative declarations and to justify reliance on previously prepared environmental documents

- Strengthen mitigation monitoring requirements

- Identify new classes of projects for which 'Master EIRs' can be prepared

- Exempt from CEQA review certain kinds of low-income housing projects

- Create special rules governing environmental review for the closure and 'reuse' of federal military bases

- Create new procedural rules governing CEQA litigation

- Specify the materials that must go into the 'record of proceedings' in CEQA litigation

This supplement also contains the full text of the CEQA Statutes, as amended by the legislature in 1994, and the newest version of the CEQA Guidelines, incorporating amendments adopted in 1994.

For a complete catalog of Solano Press Books, call (707) 884-4508 or Fax (707) 884-4109.

To be effective, this supplement should be used only in connection with the 1994 edition of *Guide to CEQA*.

Guide to the California Environmental Quality Act (CEQA)

1994 [Eighth] Edition

By Michael H. Remy, Tina A. Thomas, James G. Moose, and J. William Yeates

Guide to the California Environmental Quality Act offers the reader an understandable, in-depth description of CEQA's requirements for adequate review and preparation of environmental impact reports (EIRs) and other environmental review documents. In this edition, the authors analyze actions taken by the California legislature to change the CEQA process by—

■ Authorizing the preparation and use of Master Environmental Impact Reports for some projects

■ Specifying what qualifies as 'substantial evidence' to support a 'fair argument' that a project may cause significant environmental effects which require an EIR

■ Requiring certain regulatory agencies to conduct environmental analysis of the impacts resulting from industry compliance with regulations which mandate the installation of pollution control equipment

■ Creating statutory exemptions for air quality decisions involving automotive paint coatings within an existing manufacturing plant

■ Allowing agencies to consider the legal and technological feasibility of mitigation measures and alternatives as part of the 'findings' required by CEQA

■ Establishing a time limit whereby the cumulative impact analysis for a Project EIR need not consider newly proposed related projects

■ Requiring contracts for EIR preparation to be in force within a specified time period from the date a permit application is deemed complete

■ Providing for an optional 'expanded notice of preparation'

■ Authorizing applicants to request that a responsible agency begin processing an application prior to a lead agency's final action on another aspect of the overall project

This edition includes an appendix with summaries of important cases as of December 1993 and a comprehensive subject index with more than 1600 entries.

Guide to CEQA serves as—

■ The definitive and only available document containing in one place the Act, the Guidelines, and 'Discussions', with expert summaries and commentary

■ A resource for the most significant judicial decisions interpreting the Act

■ The principal reference commonly used by planners, environmental specialists, authors of EIRs, attorneys, environmental activists, and others who deal regularly with CEQA issues and environmental review

1995 Supplement to the 1994 Edition of Guide to CEQA
● Paperback, 334 pages, $30 ● ISBN 0-923956-36-0

Guide to CEQA, 1994 [Eighth] Edition ● Paperback, 880 pages, $45
● ISBN 0-923956-31-X

Guide to CEQA CD-ROM disk, 1995 ● $224 ● ISBN 0-923956-40-9

1995 Supplement to 1994 Edition of Successful CEQA Compliance

By Ronald E. Bass and Albert I. Herson

In this NEW SUPPLEMENT, the authors analyze legislative and administrative changes to CEQA that occurred in 1994 and the most recent case law. Their analysis includes—

■ A review of all legislative amendments adopted by the California state legislature in 1994

■ An overview of the 1994 amendments to the state CEQA Guidelines

■ Summaries of recent California appellate court decisions

■ CEQA technical advice memoranda issued by the Governor's Office of Planning and Research

■ Revisions to the flow charts and diagrams in the 1993 Edition of the book to reflect 1994 changes

To be effective, this supplement should be used only in connection with the 1994 Edition of *Successful CEQA Compliance.*

Successful CEQA Compliance: A Step-by-Step Approach

1994 [Third] Edition

By Ronald E. Bass and Albert I. Herson

Our 1992 Edition was recognized by the California Association of Environmental Professionals with an Award of Excellence in the category of 'Outstanding Public Involvement and Education Programs'.

Successful CEQA Compliance: A Step-by-Step Approach offers a practitioner's perspective on how to successfully implement the procedural and substantive requirements of the California Environmental Quality Act. Summarizing both the Act and the CEQA Guidelines, the book explains in unambiguous, straightforward language how to proceed from the beginning to the end of the environmental review process. Step-by-step procedures for preparing Negative Declarations and Environmental Impact Reports are presented in a clear, understandable fashion, using easy-to-follow text, diagrams, and other graphics.

In this edition, the authors have expanded the book's content and reference materials to assist the user with new, more detailed information on CEQA. With the addition of redesigned graphics and illustrations, more than 90 figures summarize and highlight key points and important checklists.

Appendices feature numerous sample documents—including a Negative Declaration, Notice of Preparation, Notice of Public Hearing, a sample 'findings of fact', and a sample mitigation monitoring program. A subject index with more than 780 entries and numerous cross-references is included to make it easier to find important information.

1995 Supplement to the 1994 Edition of Successful CEQA Compliance: A Step-by-Step Approach • Paperback, 92 pages, $18.50 • ISBN 0-923956-39-5

Successful CEQA Compliance: A Step-by-Step Approach, 1994 [Third] Edition • Paperback, 696 pages, $35 • ISBN 0-923956-32-8

Mastering NEPA: A Step-by-Step Approach

by Ronald E. Bass and Albert I. Herson

Mastering NEPA: A Step-by-Step Approach is the first book to present the critical steps, basic requirements, and most important decision points of the National Environmental Policy Act in a user-friendly format. It takes you step-by-step through the provisions of the Act and the environmental review process. Intended as a user's handbook, the book includes the authors' recommendations for successful compliance, with charts and illustrations clarifying key points.

The book is written in concise, straightforward language, and includes sections on—

- Determining whether an action is subject to NEPA, and when an Environmental Assessment (EA) or a Finding of No Significant Impact (FONSI) is appropriate

- Deciding whether an Environmental Impact Statement must be prepared, and step-by-step procedures for preparing a legally adequate EIS

- Writing effective mitigation measures

- How to effectively review and evaluate an EIS

- Understanding the environmental review process and determining the role and requirements of federal agencies

This book is especially useful for—

- Federal agencies subject to NEPA and state and local government agencies using federal funds for the construction of capital projects

- Private organizations, public interest groups, and citizens concerned about the environment and environmental protection

- Students in the fields of public policy, political science, and environmental studies

- Attorneys specializing in land use, environmental, and real estate law

Mastering NEPA: A Step-by-Step Approach, 1993 • Paperback, 250 pages, $35 • ISBN 0-923956-14-X

For a complete catalog of Solano Press Books, call (707) 884-4508 or Fax (707) 884-4109.